Evolutionary Creation

About the Cover

THE OUTLINE OF the evolutionary tree of life comes from Ernst Haeckel's *The Evolution of Man* (1874). Viciously critical of Christianity, Haeckel was a materialist and rejected the existence of a personal God. He developed a philosophy of monism and claimed that mind and matter are aspects of the same universal substance. Haeckel's Monist League is often viewed as a foundation of Nazi ideology. The depiction of the Creator's arm is from Michelangelo's famed painting "The Creation of Adam" (1510) in the Sistine Chapel. Evolutionary creation frees the science of evolution from the chains of secular and liberal worldviews. This conservative Christian approach to origins asserts that the personal God of the Bible created life, including humans, through an ordained, sustained, and design-reflecting evolutionary process. The capitalization and bolding of the word "Man" indicates that we are the only living organisms who have been created in the Image of God.

Evolutionary Creation

A Christian Approach to Evolution

DENIS O. LAMOUREUX

WIPF & STOCK · Eugene, Oregon

EVOLUTIONARY CREATION
A Christian Approach to Evolution

Wipf & Stock
A Division of Wipf and Stock Publishers
199 W. 8th Ave., Suite 3
Eugene, OR 97401

www.wipfandstock.com

ISBN 13: 978-1-55635-581-3

Manufactured in the U.S.A.

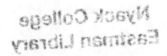

To the students of CHRTC 350
Science and Religion: Christian Perspectives
1997–2007
St. Joseph's College, University of Alberta

They taught me the meaning of
loving God faithfully and fearlessly
with our mind

Authors of the highest eminence seem to be fully satisfied with the view that each species has been independently created. To my mind it accords better with what we know of the laws impressed on matter by the Creator, that the production and extinction of the past and present inhabitants of the world should have been due to secondary causes, like those determining the birth and death of the individual.

—Charles Darwin *On the Origin of Species* (1859)

I don't think that there's any conflict at all between science today and the Scriptures. I think we have misinterpreted the Scriptures many times and we've tried to make the Scriptures say things that they weren't meant to say, and I think we have made a mistake by thinking the Bible is a scientific book. The Bible is not a book of science. The Bible is a book of Redemption, and of course, I accept the Creation story. I believe that God created man, and whether it came by an evolutionary process and at a certain point He took this person or being and made him a living soul or not, does not change the fact that God did create man . . . . whichever way God did it makes no difference as to what man is and man's relationship to God.

—Billy Graham "Doubts and Certainties" (1964)

The Bible itself speaks to us of the origin of the universe and its makeup, not in order to provide us with a scientific treatise, but in order to state the correct relationships of man with God and with the universe. Sacred scripture wishes simply to declare that the world was created by God, and in order to teach this truth it expresses itself in the terms of the cosmology in use at the time of the writer. The sacred book likewise wishes to tell men that the world was not created as the seat of the gods, as was taught by other cosmogonies and cosmologies, but was rather created for the service of man and the glory of God. Any other teaching about the origin and makeup of the universe is alien to the intentions of the Bible, which does not wish to teach how heaven was made but how one goes to heaven . . . . Today, new knowledge leads to the recognition of the theory of evolution as more than a hypothesis.

—Pope John Paul II "Scripture and Science" (1981)
                        "Message on Evolution" (1996)

Contents

Contents

Illustrations

Illustrations

List of Illustrations in the Appendices

Preface

I am a thoroughly committed and unapologetic born-again Christian who holds a PhD in theology. And I am a thoroughly committed and unapologetic evolutionist who also has a PhD in biology.

I OFTEN BEGIN PUBLIC lectures by stating these facts, and as most can appreciate, it certainly captures the attention of my audience! The common perception both inside and outside of the Church is that Christianity and evolution are forever irreconcilable. Their relationship is viewed as the main conflict in the so-called war between science and religion. Nearly everyone would suspect that a person claiming to be both an evangelical theologian and an evolutionary biologist either fails to appreciate the logical incompatibility between this religious tradition and scientific theory, or compromises the foundational principles of one or both. So, can a Christian be an evolutionist? Most people today say, "No."

My answer to this question is a resounding, "Yes." This book explains how a Christian can be an evolutionist, and even argues why it is important for those who love Jesus to accept evolution. The view of origins I will present is evolutionary creation. It asserts that evolution is purpose driven and not the result of blind chance. Stated more precisely, this position claims that *the Father, Son, and Holy Spirit created the universe and life through an ordained, sustained, and design-reflecting evolutionary process.* To be sure, mentioning the Trinity and evolution in the same sentence is rarely heard in church, if ever. To some this might be offensive. But no insult is intended, and I will ask my brothers and sisters in Christ for their patience as they read this book.

Arriving at the belief that the Lord employed evolution as His creative method is not only challenging, but also takes time. Christians who accept this origins position often use the phrase "coming to terms with evolution" to describe the intellectual and spiritual process they experienced over an extended period. On this journey a wide range of issues are considered. To mention a few, God's miraculous activity in the world, His existence reflected by intelligent design throughout nature, the interpretation of the biblical creation accounts, and the theological implications of humans descending from primitive forms of life. Consequently, anyone engaging the ideas in this book will find that it is not a quick read. Coming to terms with evolution is a gradual process that involves numerous struggles. At times it is not comfortable. And most importantly, it is done on our knees in prayerful reflection.

Evolutionary Creation: A Christian Approach to Evolution rests upon the time-honored belief that divine revelation flows from two major sources—the Book of God's Words and the Book of God's Works. Together the Bible and the physical world complement each other in revealing the glory and character of the Creator. In particular, I will explore Christian faith and evolutionary science through a Two Books model and propose an intimate and fruitful relationship between Scripture and science. A summary of the book is as follows:

The first two chapters introduce basic terminology and outline five primary positions on the origin of the universe and life. Regrettably, many Christians and non-Christians see origins as a simple black-and-white issue, and this forces them into choosing between two options—either evolution or creation. However, the opening chapters reveal that there is a spectrum of possibilities; namely, young earth (six-day) creation, progressive (old earth or day-age) creation, evolutionary creation, deistic (impersonal god) evolution, and dysteleological (atheistic) evolution. A description of the strengths and weaknesses of these positions allows readers to begin the process of making informed decisions with regard to their own views. Most will come to the conclusion that it is time for everyone to move beyond the so-called "evolution" vs. "creation" debate.

Chapter 3 explores God's activity in the world and the notion of intelligent design from an evolutionary creationist perspective. I want to make my position clear at this point: I believe in miracles and I have experienced them personally on many occasions. I see design and intelligence reflected every day in the beauty, complexity, and functionality of the physical world. As Scripture states, "The heavens declare the glory of God" (Ps 19:1–4) and the creation discloses His "eternal power and divine nature" (Rom 1:18–23). And I believe that every person is accountable before the Creator with regard to this revelation in nature. To the surprise of many, the third chapter argues that instead of undermining Christian faith, the evolutionary sciences strengthen and expand the argument from design by including the divinely ordained and sustained natural processes that created the universe and life over eons of time.

A central issue in the origins debate involves the interpretation of the opening chapters of the Bible. Today there are a lot of questions being asked by Christians. Are the six days of creation in Gen 1 literal 24-hour days or do they represent long periods of millions of years? Was Noah's flood a global event or was it limited to a local region? Was Adam the first person in history and have all human beings descended from him? Chapters 4 to 7 are the core of this book and they focus upon the interpretation of Scripture. I will present a counterintuitive approach to reading passages that deal with origins. But this proposal is rooted deeply in biblical evidence. Once more, I want to make my beliefs clear at this time: Scripture is the Holy Spirit inspired Word of God. As the apostle Paul states, it is "God-breathed" (2 Tim 3:16) and contains "the very words of God" (Rom 3:2). I came to Christ through reading the gospel of John, so I know personally the soul and mind-impacting power of the Bible. And I continue to drink deeply from it in daily morning devotions for my spiritual nourishment. Despite the innumerable ways that men and women throughout history have interpreted Scripture, those sincerely searching for God have always met the Lord Jesus while on their knees before The Word.

An assumption embraced by many Christians is that God revealed scientific facts in the Bible hundreds of generations before their discovery by modern science. This view of biblical inspiration asserts that the Holy Spirit dictated information about the natural world to secretary-like writers. As a result, there is purportedly a correspondence or alignment between Scripture and science. This is known as "concordism." Christians often claim that it is a feature of biblical inerrancy and infallibility. However, chapters 4 and 5 review the astronomy, geology, and biology in Scripture and conclude that the science in the Bible is an ancient understanding of nature—the science-of-the-day a few thousand years ago. According to this perspective, the Holy Spirit descended to the knowledge level of the inspired authors by using their conceptualization of the physical world in order to communicate as effectively as possible inerrant and infallible Messages of Faith. This approach to biblical revelation is modeled on the greatest act of revelation—the Incarnation. God revealed

Himself by descending into human flesh through Jesus, and in a similar way, the Bible uses a human understanding of the structure, operation, and origin of the world.

Chapters 6 and 7 examine Gen 1–11 in order to determine whether concordism characterizes the relationship between the biblical origins accounts and the facts of history. Like the ancient science in Scripture, it will be shown that these opening chapters include an ancient understanding of the origin of the cosmos and humanity. This ancient history is a vessel that transports inerrant and infallible foundations of the Christian faith: the universe and life were made by the God of the Bible, the creation is very good, only men and women are created in the Image of God, the Lord intended us to be in relationships with one another and in particular with Him, everyone has fallen into sin, God judges humans for their sinfulness, and He has chosen a special people through which to bless the entire world. Together, the four chapters on scriptural interpretation conclude that concordism is not a feature of Gen 1–11, and as a result there is no conflict with the modern understanding of origins offered by academic disciplines of science and history.

This conclusion opens the way for a Christian approach to human evolution. An instructive parallel assists believers to conceptualize this challenging idea. As the Lord created each of us in our mother's womb through embryological natural processes, He also made humankind using His ordained and sustained evolutionary laws of nature. In both embryology and evolution, the Image of God is mysteriously manifested. Similarly, in a way that cannot be fully understood, during these creative processes people become morally responsible and then all fall into sin. Chapter 8 also investigates the issue of justifying how the God of Love could have created humans through a method that includes suffering and death. In fact, the question that *always* arises in my public lectures on evolutionary creation is the relationship between the beginning of physical death and the original sin of Adam. Genesis 3, Rom 5–8, and 1 Cor 15 clearly state that death entered the world because Adam sinned in the garden of Eden. However, biological evolution asserts that death appeared hundreds of millions of years before human beings. The arguments in this book are set up to deal with the sin-death problem. The successful defense of evolutionary creation will depend on offering a solution that satisfies Christians.

Our generation has become particularly sensitive to the importance of personal stories. The topic of origins has consumed me throughout most of my adult life. It has shaped my beliefs, and consequently, the way I have lived. By the time I finished a course on biological evolution in my first year of college, I had lost my Christian faith. In coming to the Lord seven years later, anti-evolutionary arguments were foundational in my developing worldview. They influenced me so much that I left a rewarding professional career and followed a calling to become a six-day creation scientist in order to attack universities and the teaching of evolution. In preparation for battle, I pursued graduate school training both in theology and biology with a focus on origins. Chapter 9 presents in more detail my spiritual and intellectual adventure in opening the Book of God's Words and the Book of God's Works.

The last chapter offers some reflections on the origins debate. As much as I find this topic fascinating, my central motivation for having an academic career centered on it is pastoral. So much damage has resulted from the evolution vs. creation mindset that grips most people. Let us for a moment assume that the Lord created the universe and life through an evolutionary process. Can anyone imagine how much of a *stumbling block* (2 Cor 6:2–3) Christian anti-evolutionists have been to non-Christian scientists who see the physical evidence supporting evolution every day in their laboratories? Or what happens to the child who was taught anti-evolutionary views in a Christian school or a Sunday school, and then he or she discovers the scientific data for evolution first hand in the biology department of a college? I have personally lived that disastrous result, and I have seen it too many times at my university. Today, origins are an important discussion both inside and outside of the Church. If we are going to be credible witnesses of Jesus to an unbelieving world, then what are we to say regarding this issue?

Finally, a couple of qualifying comments are in order. I must underline that this book focuses on theology and not science. Occasionally I will appeal to scientific evidence, but only to facts held by most people (e.g., the structure of the solar system). Four short appendices offer some basic evidence and arguments for biological evolution. Of course, those familiar with the complex and overwhelming data that supports this scientific theory know that such an introduction hardly scratches the surface. Yet in drawing a modest sketch, my hope is that Christians who are skeptical of evolution will be encouraged to open the Book of God's Works to see this amazing evidence.

I strongly advise that the chapters in this book be read in sequence. The conclusions in later chapters are dependent on the terms and arguments presented in earlier ones. A short glossary is found at the end of the book to assist readers with the terminology. I suggest that they introduce themselves to these concepts before starting.

No doubt about it, *Evolutionary Creation: A Christian Approach to Evolution* is provocative. Readers must be warned that I will make a number of pointed and even disturbing statements, especially with regard to the meaning of several biblical passages. Yet as the epigraphs of this book reveal, Christian leaders in our generation are coming to terms with evolution. The Reverend Billy Graham tersely states, "The Bible is not a book of science." He acknowledges that Christians "have misinterpreted the Scriptures many times" and implies that concordism is a "mistake."[1] Pope John Paul II recognizes that the inspired authors of the Word of God held an ancient understanding of nature. He also affirms the credibility of evolution as "more than a hypothesis."[2] But most importantly, these two historic Christian figures focus on a primary intention of Holy Scripture—revelation of our relationship with the Lord.

In many ways, the debate over origins today is a recycling of the Galileo affair. As the seventeenth-century Church wrestled with the scientific fact that the earth is not stationary nor at the center of the universe, so too we will come to terms with the reality that we evolved from earlier forms of life. Hopefully, this book will offer a few suggestions in making that process somewhat more comfortable.

Acknowledgements

T**HE WRITING OF THIS** book began an embarrassingly long time ago and it evolved through numerous transitional stages. During the process, the Lord blessed me with many wonderful colleagues and students who have shared their insights on the origins debate. I will always be grateful to St. Joseph's College at the University of Alberta for establishing the first Canadian tenure-track position in Science and Religion. It is indeed a privilege to focus my career on attempting to understand the relationship between the modern science and Christian faith. I am also indebted to Michael Caldwell, Brian Glubish, Don Lewis, and Paul Seely. For many years they have been confidants and mentors in overseeing my spiritual and academic voyage. Terry Morrison and Jim Ruark provided support and encouragement during difficult periods. They also opened my eyes to the dynamics of the Christian publishing industry. And special thanks to Anna-Lisa Ptolemy for her incisive work on early drafts of the manuscript. I could not ask for a more dedicated colleague and royal friend.

It is not possible to list everyone who has played a role in shaping my views outlined in this book. In many ways, my coming to terms with evolution has been a process that has lasted throughout most of my adult life. Yet I am particularly grateful to those who have freely shared their expertise over the years: Angela Anderson-Konrad, Kristen Bareman, Braden Barr, Chris Barrigar, Rae Beaumont, Darryl Berezuik, John Bergen, Jeff Brassard, Joe Buijs, Michael Buttery, Joel Cannon, Stew Carson, David Cass, Harold Climenhaga, Harry Cook, Ron Croaker, Carrie Davidge, Andrew Demoline, Michael Denton, Andrea Dmytrash, Bill Dumbrell, Merril Edmonds, Graeme Finlay, Paul Flaman, Trevor Froehlich, Paul Fuellbrandt, Warren Gallin, Murray Gingras, Nate Glubish, Wendell Grout, Nancy Halliday, Pliny Hayes, Margolee Horn, Burl Horniachek, Brianne Hudson, Brian Irwin, Kenneth Kully, Jeremy Lafreniere,

Acknowledgements

Bob Lamoureux, Larry and Susan Martin, Jack Maze, Vivian and Mike Miketon, Bev Mitchell, George Murphy, Larissa Newell, Don Page, Jeff Quon, Karen Ridgway, Bert Robinson, Don Robinson, Jason Rohrick, Scarlettah Schaeffer, Shelly Schneider, Jerry Sheppard, Nancy Shoptaw, Andrew Snook, Bethany Sollereder, Callee Soltys, Glen Taylor, Sherry Travers, Martin Unsworth, Pam Van der Werff, John Walton, Don Wiebe, Loren Wilkinson, Tyler Williams, Mark Witwer, Carrie Wolcott, Denise Young, and Ted and Sue Zukiwsky. Their numerous suggestions have made this a much better book.

I am most grateful to the Sir John Templeton Foundation and leadership this organization has taken during the last decade to advance the modern dialogue between science and religion. I have benefited from the science-religion course initiatives, many workshops, and funding to invite leading scholars to my university. I am also indebted to the Christian Scholars Foundation for a grant.

This book would not have been completed had it not been for my eye surgeons Drs. Brad Hinz, Mark Grieve, and Harold Climenhaga. I will forever be thankful to them and their amazing clinical skills. Life's greatest lessons are those that we live through, and the potential of a career-ending eye condition made me realize once again that it is because of the Lord's grace that I enjoy every day I am given. As well, I reaffirmed that "all things," including the trials and tribulations, "work together for good for those who love God" (Rom 8:28) so that "the work of God might be displayed" in our lives (John 9:3).

Finally, I want to thank Ozzie and Bernice Lamoureux, better known as Mom and Dad, who provided a loving home and a healthy respect for education. Not every child is blessed with parents whom he not only loves, but also enjoys as friends. Our family meal every Sunday evening is the most excellent of traditions. As usual they have agreed to accept responsibility for any errors or bad points in this book, while allowing me to take credit for anything good that may come of it!

Glory be to the Father, Son, and Holy Spirit,
DOL
Christmas Day 2007

1

Introductory Categories

CATEGORIES ARE THE FOUNDATIONAL concepts that direct the way we look at the world and think about it. They function like our ability to see the many glorious colors in nature. Instead of perceiving the world only in black and white, we have in our brain a genetically constructed capacity to discern a dazzling spectrum of light. The world of ideas is similar to the world of color. We appreciate that many topics are not simple black-and-white issues and that many shades of opinion and understanding exist. Yet in contrast to the world of color, the ability to discern the spectrum of ideas is based more on our education and life experiences than on genetic predispositions. Categories are for the most part learned, and once they become part of our mindset, they act like glasses through which we "see" the world.

Today the origin of the universe and life is often seen in black-and-white categories. For many people, the cosmos and its living organisms came about through one of two ways—either evolution or creation. In other words, the subject of origins is cast as a dichotomy (in Greek *dicha* means "in two" and *temnō* "to cut"). It is an issue that is divided into only two simple positions. Regrettably, this either/or type of thinking fuels the popular perception that modern science and Christian faith are entrenched in an endless war. On one battle line, science is seen not only as a secular and godless enemy, but the theory of evolution is thought to have dealt a fatal blow to the existence of a Creator. On the other, Christianity and the biblical creation accounts are perceived as a hostile force against every new scientific discovery dealing with origins. This categorization has led numerous individuals into believing that they are forced to choose between two opposing sides: evolution or creation, science or religion, a

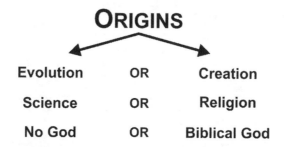

Fig 1-1. The Origins Dichotomy

world without God or one in which He reveals Himself through Scripture. Fig 1-1 presents the origins dichotomy.

The simple either/or approach to origins appears widely both inside and outside of the Church. Henry Morris, the leading Christian anti-evolutionist during the last half-century, asserts:

> After all, there are only *two* basic worldviews—the God-centered worldview and the man-centered worldview, creation *or* evolution. . . . There is no evidence whatever—past, present, or possible—that evolution of one kind of organism into a more complex organism has ever occurred, or even can occur. . . . There are no proven scientific evidences that the earth is old, and scores of circumstantial evidences that the earth is young. . . . Divine revelation from the Creator of the world [states] that He did it all in six days several thousand years ago (Genesis 1:1—2:3; Exodus 20:8–11). . . . The Bible does contain all the basic principles upon which *true* science is built. . . . The Bible is a book of science![1]

Morris argues, "If there is really a great personal Creator behind the origin and meaning of all things, then we urgently need to know Him and to order our lives according to His will, as revealed in His inspired Word."[2] And disclosing his views fully, Morris concludes, "Satan himself is the originator of the concept of evolution."[3]

Evolutionist and secular humanist Julian Huxley also upholds the popular origins dichotomy. At the centennial celebration for Charles Darwin's famed book introducing the scientific theory of evolution, *On the Origin of Species* (1859), he states:

> The earth was not created, it evolved. So did all the animals and plants that inhabit it, including our human selves, mind and soul as well as brain and body. So did religion. . . . Evolutionary man can

no longer take refuge from his loneliness in the arms of a divinized
father figure whom he has himself created, nor escape from the responsibility of making decisions by sheltering under the umbrella
of Divine Authority . . . Evolutionary truth frees us from subservi-
ent fear of the unknown and supernatural and exhorts us to face
this new freedom with courage tempered with wisdom and hope
tempered with knowledge. It shows us our destiny and our duty.[4]

Huxley concludes that with the discovery of evolution "there is no longer
either need or room for the supernatural."[5] He then proposes that a secular religion, which he calls "a religion without revelation," will arise in the
future to serve humanity.[6]

Despite the fact that Morris and Huxley embrace completely opposing positions on origins, they recognize the fundamental role that this
subject plays in shaping our worldview. Both acknowledge that religion
and ethics are connected closely to our beliefs about the origin of the
universe and life. How we conceive God, how we view ourselves, and how
we live together are intimately related to how the world came into being.
Indeed, the topic of origins is undeniably relevant.

A critical factor that fuels the origins dichotomy is the popular use
of the terms evolution and creation. These words are often merged inad-
vertently with concepts that narrow their range of meaning. This problem
is known as the conflation of ideas. Defined specifically, conflation is the
careless collapsing of distinct categories into one single poorly conceived
notion. For many people today, evolution is blended with a godless worldview, and creation is dissolved into a strict six-day literal interpretation of
Gen 1. Consequently, the common use of these terms limits thinking and
traps the discussion in a never-ending evolution vs. creation debate. In
addition, the words evolution and creation are emotionally charged and
frequently lead to less than charitable arguments. Thus, a first step toward
fruitful dialogue on origins requires moving beyond popular conflations
of the terms employed in this discussion.

Another powerful factor contributing to the origins dichotomy is the
belief embraced by many Christians that statements in the Bible about the
natural world are consistent with the findings of *true* science. This interpretive approach is known as concordism. It is a reasonable assumption
since God is both the Author of His Words and the Creator of His Works.
For that matter, most throughout Church history have been concordists.[7] Yet with the emergence of modern sciences dealing with origins,

Christians have perceived a problem. The theory of evolution does not align with the creation accounts in Scripture. For this reason, many reject the age of the earth in billions of years and the gradual appearance of life evolving through innumerable stages. In fact, some believers harshly criticize modern scientists, claiming they are intellectually incompetent and even spiritually deceived.[8] But such beliefs only entrench the origins dichotomy. Therefore, a second step toward a better understanding of the creation of the world is to reconsider the notion of concordism.

In this chapter, and the one that follows, I hope to develop one main point: the popular origins dichotomy is a *false dichotomy*. If we look at the origin of the universe and life through the popular black-and-white categories of evolution and creation, then it is a lot like being color blind, and we miss many of the colors in the spectrum of positions. To be sure, this either/or perception of origins is common throughout the Church and the general public. But this categorization is insufficient. It imprisons the mind and restricts our freedom to make informed decisions. This misleading dichotomy also blinds us from envisioning a healthy relationship between our faith and modern science.

To begin the move beyond the origins dichotomy, this chapter suggests that the professional definitions of evolution and creation be employed. Those who use them routinely, scientists and theologians, respectively, best define these terms. Next, the notion of concordism is examined. A decision on whether the science in Scripture aligns with the physical world will have to wait until relevant passages are examined in chapter 4. However, the possibility is introduced that the Holy Spirit did not intend the Bible to be scientifically concordant. The categories introduced in this chapter offer a set of glasses through which we can start to see the wide range of views on origins. In this way, the prospect emerges of an approach that envisions the God of the Bible creating the world through an evolutionary process.

EVOLUTION

For most people the term evolution refers to a biological theory of molecules-to-people that is driven only by blind chance. This word is conflated with an atheistic worldview—the belief that God does not exist and that our existence has no ultimate meaning or purpose. Understandably, this popular use of evolution produces strong negative reactions within the Church. But for some Christians, evolution is simply the method through

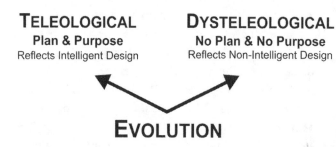

TELEOLOGICAL
Plan & Purpose
Reflects Intelligent Design

DYSTELEOLOGICAL
No Plan & No Purpose
Reflects Non-Intelligent Design

EVOLUTION

Fig 1-2. Re-Categorization of the Term 'Evolution'

which the Lord created life, including humans who bear His Image. These believers argue that God employed a set of natural mechanisms for the creation of every living organism that has existed on earth in the same way that He uses physical processes to create each individual creature.

Therefore, there are roughly two basic and radically different meanings of the word evolution, and in order to avoid confusion, qualification is necessary.[9] On the one hand, "teleological evolution" is a planned and purposeful natural process that heads toward a final outcome—the intended creation of life. The Greek word *telos* means end, goal, or destiny. On the other hand, "dysteleological evolution" is an unplanned and purposeless series of physical mechanisms driven by blind chance only. Quite unintentionally, this process generated living organisms, including humans. The term *dysteleologie* was first coined in German and refers to a worldview without any ultimate plan or significance. This belief asserts that existence is marked by nothing but pointless indifference.

Teleological evolution is also connected to the notion of intelligent design in nature.[10] History reveals that the beauty, complexity, and functionality of the world have powerfully impacted men and women throughout time. For most, this experience has led them to the conclusion that the universe and living organisms reflect the work of a rational mind, thus arguing for the existence of a Creator. Teleological evolutionists contend that the natural processes of evolution also mirror intelligent design. In contrast, dysteleological evolutionists believe that the idea of design in nature is nothing but an illusion concocted by the human mind. Of course, they acknowledge the striking elegance, intricacy, and efficiency in the cosmos, but argue that this is only an *appearance* of design that humans misinterpret and impose upon the world. For dysteleological evolutionists, design in the world is ultimately non-intelligent. Fig 1-2 re-categorizes the term evolution.

Regrettably, there is a categorical blind spot in the mind of many Christians. They find it difficult, if not impossible, to envision evolution as a planned and purposeful process that was ordained and sustained by the Lord. Even more problematic for believers is the notion that evolution reflects intelligent design and declares God's glory. But it is necessary to underline that the Father, Son, and Holy Spirit are not bound to any method of creation, or to the expectations and assumptions of any Christians. God could have created through a teleological evolutionary process—beginning from simple molecules and leading up to incredibly complex humans bearing His Image. In failing to appreciate this categorical distinction, many believers are trapped into seeing evolution only in a sinister light associated with disbelief. They often label Christians accepting biological evolution as "liberal," and even question their commitment to Jesus. Moreover, they cast suspicion on the scientific community because to them the term evolution is essentially dysteleological. However, this popular myth misrepresents the religious beliefs of modern scientists.

Landmark papers that were published in two of the most prestigious scientific journals today reveal that scientists are not all atheists embracing a dysteleological worldview. In a 1997 report entitled "Scientists Are Still Keeping the Faith" in *Nature*, Edward Larson and Larry Witham outline some basic beliefs of scientists cited in the Who's Who of American Science.[11] Respondents were asked to evaluate the following statement:

> I believe in a God in intellectual and affective [emotional] communication with humankind, i.e., a God to whom one may pray in expectation of receiving an answer. By 'answer' I mean more than the subjective, psychological effect of prayer.

In all, 40% of the scientists accept the statement, 45% "do not believe in a God as defined above," and 15% "have no definite belief regarding this question." In other words, nearly half of leading US scientists believe in a personal God who intervenes in their lives in a way that could be termed miraculous. This study also found that 40% of the respondents believe in an afterlife. Therefore, *at least* 4 out of 10 scientists surveyed have a teleological worldview.

It is important to emphasize that the Larson and Witham study employs a very narrow definition of God, that of a personal God, known as "theism." A reasonable speculation based on this research suggests that the percentage of leading American scientists holding a teleological worldview is much higher than 40%. More specifically, this study does not account for those who believe in a Creator who does not intervene personally in the world. This view of God, termed "deism," is popular among intellectuals, and it would not be surprising that a significant number in the scientific community embrace this belief. This report also places pantheists (those who believe that everything in the universe is God; e.g., Buddhism) and pagans (believers in a divine force or entity controlling the universe; e.g., new age religions) in the so-called "disbeliever" group featuring 45% of the scientists surveyed. Though deists, pantheists, and pagans are not Christians, they nevertheless accept teleology and believe the world features a plan and purpose, including the reflection of intelligent design. Finally, 15% of respondents were agnostic (those who have no belief), which means they are not dysteleologists.[12] Therefore, since evolution is the only theory of origins in science, it is reasonable to argue that a majority of leading scientists accept that the world was created through a teleological evolutionary process.

A second landmark paper in another distinguished scientific journal also argues that the modern scientific community does not unanimously accept an atheistic and dysteleological understanding of the world. In a 1997 review entitled "Science and God: A Warming Trend?" in *Science*, Gregg Easterbrook reports on new research being done in prominent universities and the world's two most powerful scientific organizations:

> Both the National Academy of Sciences and the American Association for the Advancement of Science have launched projects to promote a dialogue between science and religion. New institutions aimed at bridging the gap have been formed, including the Chicago Center for Religion and Science, and the Center for Theology and Natural Sciences in Berkeley, California. Universities such as Cambridge and Princeton also have established professorships or lectureships on the reconciliation of the two camps.[13]

This paper also interviews world-class scientists who are Christians and points out that they see no conflict between their religious beliefs and modern science. Easterbrook concludes that "rather than being driven ever farther apart, tomorrow's scientist and theologian may seek each other's solace."[14]

Clearly, these two papers in leading scientific journals burst the popular myth that most scientists are atheists defending dysteleological evolution. The gloomy spiritual picture with conspiratorial tones often painted of the scientific community must be revised. Christians need to consider seriously the possibility that teleological evolution is God's creative method and that the evolutionary sciences provide a description of the work of His hands.

Modern science is unified by the theory that the universe and life evolved through natural processes. Three basic sciences integrate the evolutionary evidence into a coherent origins model. Cosmological evolution examines the development of the inanimate world with its galaxies, stars, and planets. Physicists postulate that an explosive event 10–15 billion years ago, termed "the Big Bang," led to the emergence of space, time, and matter. Geological evolution investigates the formation of the earth. Geologists reconstruct the 4.5 billion-year history of our planet in light of the physical processes ongoing today, such as erosion, volcanic activity, and continental drift. Biological evolution describes the origin of life as revealed in the fossil record. Biologists explore the natural mechanisms that organized inanimate molecules into the first living forms about 4 billion years ago, and that later led to the evolution of all plants and animals, including humans. Modern science concludes that the origin of the world only makes sense in light of evolutionary theory.

Notably, the professional definition of evolution that scientists use in their day-to-day research rarely mentions whether this natural process is planned and designed or purposeless and driven only by blind chance. Science deals only with the laws and mechanisms of the physical world. Scientific methods and instruments cannot detect teleology or dysteleology. Consequently, science is dead silent on the ultimate religious and philosophical character of evolution. Of course, like everyone else, scientists ponder the meaning of life and reflect upon nature in their quest to understand existence. But such intellectual and spiritual contemplation extends beyond science and into the disciplines of philosophy and religion.[15]

Finally, a comment is needed with regard to the term "Darwinism." For most people it refers to dysteleological evolution. This popular definition conflates Darwin's understanding of evolution with an atheistic worldview. However, the historical evidence demonstrates that this is a mistake. In his famed *On the Origin of Species* (1859), Darwin presents a teleological interpretation of evolution and makes seven unapologetic references to the Creator. For example, he argues:

> Authors of the highest eminence seem to be fully satisfied that each species has been independently created. To my mind it accords better with what we know of the laws impressed on matter by the Creator, that the production and extinction of the past and present inhabitants of the world should have been due to secondary causes like those determining the birth and death of the individual.[16]

Notably, Darwin appeals to a parallel in divine creative activity between embryology and evolution. He contended that God ordained the laws of nature. His position in 1859 is proof that the origins dichotomy is a false dichotomy. Darwin believed both in the evolution of life and in the existence of a Creator. Only a few years before his death in 1882, he openly admitted, "I have never been an atheist in the sense of denying the existence of God."[17] Though Darwin's religious views changed over the course of his life, the historical record reveals that he never embraced dysteleological evolution.[18]

History is helpful in understanding the meaning of Darwinism, but a more relevant study for the origins debate examines the use of this word in the scientific community. A computer search of the professional litera- ture reviewing titles, abstracts, and keywords over a ten-year period start- ing in 1997 demonstrates that Darwinism seldom appears as compared to the word evolution.[19] A survey of all important scientific journals shows the incidence is 349 to 284,904 (0.12%). Limiting the investigation to literature in the biological sciences provides a similar result of 151 to 114,989 (0.13%). Narrowing the search even further to leading publica- tions focused on biological evolution—*Evolution, Journal of Evolutionary Biology, Journal of Paleontology, Journal of Vertebrate Paleontology*— reveals there are 4414 entries for evolution whereas Darwinism appears a paltry 1 time (0.02%). It is clear that modern scientists use the term evolution in their professional work, and rarely Darwinism. Thus, for the sake of historical accuracy and the respect of scientific practice, the word Darwinism should be limited to studies on the beliefs held by Charles Darwin during his career. Its use in the origins debate introduces un- necessary confusion.

In sum, caution is required when reading or employing the word evolution because it carries many meanings and nuances. The popular use of this term often refers to biological evolution and it is usually conflated with a dysteleological worldview. However, the professional definition of evolution employed by scientists refers *only* to the scientific theories describing and explaining the origin of the cosmos and living organisms through natural mechanisms with no mention whatsoever of the ultimate religious or philosophical character of these physical processes. If the term evolution is to be employed without a qualifier, then its definition by modern science should be used. In the origins debate, evolution often needs specification with the adjectives teleological or dysteleological.

CREATION

The popular understanding of the term "creation" also contributes to the entrenchment of the origins dichotomy. Most people consider a "creationist" to be an individual who believes that God created the universe and life in six 24-hour days as described by a strict literal reading of Gen 1. In other words, the concept of creation is conflated with *one* interpretation of this biblical chapter. Regrettably, this leads to the common perception both inside and outside the Church that six-day creation is the *official* Christian view of origins. However, during the last quarter of the twentieth century there has been a relatively quiet shift in the thinking of a number of believers. Some are more comfortable with the sciences of cosmology and geology, and they now accept the age of the universe to be in the billions of years. As a result, the categories "young earth creation" and "old earth creation" are appearing in churches.

God's creative method is not a central topic among professional theologians today, even though many Christians believe that it is fundamental to faith. History reveals that the subject of how the Creator made the world was not included in the great creeds that unite the three main Christian traditions: Roman Catholic, Orthodox, and Protestant. The earliest formulations of faith simply affirm God's Makership or Creatorship. For example, the Apostles' Creed (about 150 AD) proclaims, "I believe in God the Father Almighty; Maker/Creator of heaven and earth."[20] Similarly, the Creed of Nicaea (325 AD) declares, "We believe in one God, the Father Almighty, Maker of all things visible and invisible."[21] At no time in the history of the Church was a creedal council called to determine the structure of the cosmos, the age of the earth, or how life arose.

According to professional theologians, the basic meaning of creation refers only to that which God has made. Similarly, a creationist is simply someone who believes in a Creator. Today Christian scholars uphold the historic doctrine of creation and assert that it is a religious belief and not a scientific theory. This doctrine features the basic tenets:

- The creation is radically distinct and different from the Creator (Gen 1:1; John 1:1–3; Heb 1:10–12; Rev 1:8). The entire universe is not God as suggested by pantheism; nor is a part of the world divine as proposed by paganism. The Creator transcends the creation. Yet He is also imminent to His works (omnipresent) and knows their every detail (omniscient). God also enters the world to interact with His creatures at any time and in any way He so chooses (omnipotent).

- The creation is utterly dependent on the Creator (Job 34:14–15; Ps 65:9–13, 104:1–35; Acts 17:24–28; Col 1:16–17; Heb 1:2–3; Rev 4:11). God *ordained* the universe and life into being and He continues to *sustain* their existence during every single instant. The ultimate meaning of the cosmos depends on the Creator. He has ordered a plan and purpose for the world. More precisely, the teleological character of the creation is rooted in the Father, Son, and Holy Spirit.

- The creation was made out of nothing (Latin: *creatio ex nihilo*. Rom 4:17; 1 Cor 8:6; Col 1:15–17; Heb 2:10, 11:3).[22] God did not fashion the universe from eternal pre-existent material. Nor was there any timeless being or force to challenge His Lordship. The Creator existed before all things and powers, both visible and invisible.

- The creation is temporal (Gen 1:1; John 1:1–3; Matt 24:35; 2 Pet 3:7, 12–13). God not only created physical matter and empty space, but also time. The universe is not eternal. It is bound in time and has both a beginning and an end.

- The creation declares God's glory (Job 38–41; Ps 19:1–4; Rom 1:19–20). Known as "natural revelation," the Creator has written a transcendent message within the physical world. Similar to the universal language of music, this revelation is non-verbal. That is, it does not use actual words. But it clearly communicates that the universe and life are the work of God, and it even reveals some of His attributes such as His divine nature and eternal power. In particular, the beauty, complexity, and functionality of the creation reflect intelligent design, pointing to the mind of the Maker.

• The creation is very good (Gen 1:31; 1 Tim 4:4; Rom 8:28). The world offers the perfect stage for God's will to unfold. It includes a myriad of amazing features—joys and hardships, frustrations and freedoms, thrills and dangers, beauty and ugliness, love and hate, sin and grace—all intended by God to work for good. This is a cosmos made ideally for experiencing love and developing relationships between ourselves and between us and our Creator.

The historic doctrine of creation focuses upon the character of the creation and not on God's creative method. The advantages of defining the term creation in the light of traditional understanding are two-fold. First, it frees this theological doctrine from any scientific theory. The history of science shows that hypotheses about the physical world have changed dramatically over time. If God's method of creation as understood by one generation is raised to doctrinal status, then it leaves Christianity vulnerable to new discoveries by later generations of scientists. For example, had geocentricity, the theory that the earth is at the center of the universe, become an article of faith in the fifteenth century, Copernicus would have rejected it in the next century with his sun-centered, heliocentric model of the cosmos. However, the biblical revelation that God created the world is an inerrant Truth that transcends the limitations and fallibilities of human scientific research.

Second, defining creation by its historical understanding protects the Church from discord and potential divisions over the issue of origins. Christians throughout history have held countless views on how God created the universe and life. Despite these differences, the Church has remained united by the belief that God is the Creator. Moreover, the historical fact that no Christian creed or doctrine focuses on God's exact creative method underlines that this issue should never become central in modern theological formulations and statements of faith. To be sure, differences exist today between Christians in their understanding of how God created, and undoubtedly these will continue in the future. But discord and division should never arise in the Body of Christ over origins. Adopting the historic doctrine of creation provides a unifying factor within the Church to avoid this problem.

To summarize, care is needed with the word creation since it carries many meanings today. The popular use of this term usually refers to six-day creation, giving the impression that this is *the* Christian position on origins. However, such an approach conflates a strict literal interpretation of Gen 1 with the word creation. The definition of this term employed by theologians refers only to that which the Creator has created, and not to His creative method. If creation is to be used without any qualification, then it should be defined in light of the professional and historic doctrinal meaning. The next chapter will elaborate on specified uses of this term such as "young earth creation," "progressive earth creation," and "evolutionary creation."

CONCORDISM

Christians throughout the ages have firmly believed that God reveals both Himself and His will in the Bible. As the apostle Paul states, "All Scripture is God-breathed" (2 Tim 3:16) and contains "the very words of God" (Rom 3:2). The transforming power of Scripture is seen in the lives of Christians today. By reading the Bible daily, they are nourished spiritually and enter into the presence of God the Father through the Holy Spirit. In this way, believers enrich their personal relationship with the Lord and Savior Jesus Christ.

Conservative Christian theology is distinguished by the principle of biblical inerrancy and infallibility. This notion asserts that Scripture is inspired by God and consequently free from any error whatsoever. To be sure, this high view of the Bible is foundational to the best theology. However, many people conflate the concept of inerrancy and infallibility with a strict literal interpretation of Scripture. In particular, they often read the creation accounts in Genesis literally as scientific and historical records of actual events in origins. But this interpretive method is problematic if the Holy Spirit, in offering an eternal revelation about creation, inspired a type of writing style that is not a straightforward as-it-happened account. It is reasonable to suggest that God, as a loving Father, came down to the level of the ancient Hebrews and spoke using the concepts of science and history that they understood. Again, the importance of defining categories is evident.

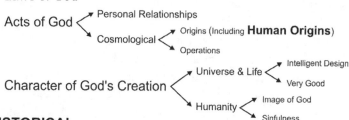

THEOLOGICAL

Character of God

Laws of God

Acts of God

Personal Relationships

Cosmological

Origins (Including **Human Origins**)

Operations

Character of God's Creation

Universe & Life

Intelligent Design

Very Good

Humanity

Image of God

Sinfulness

HISTORICAL

Jesus of Nazareth

Israel, Church & Nations

Human Origins

SCIENTIFIC

Structure

Operations

Origins (Including **Human Origins**)

Fig 1-3. **Categories of Biblical Statements.** Note that the topic of human origins appears with theological, scientific and historical statements in Scripture.

As noted previously, concordism commonly refers to a method of biblical interpretation that seeks to find a correspondence between science and Scripture. A consistency between God's Words and Works is a rational and legitimate expectation, since both come from the Creator. Moreover, an accord between beliefs and reality is necessary for psychological well-being. No one can live comfortably in a world where our deepest convictions and life experiences are in conflict. It is inevitable, then, that a generation of Christians raised in a scientific age would want to correlate science and their faith, especially with regard to the creation of the universe and life.

The rational and psychological requirement that the Scriptures align with reality extends beyond concordism in the origins debate. The Word of God makes a variety of truth claims. Fig 1-3 outlines three main categories of biblical statements: theological, historical, and scientific. As a result, it could be argued that there are three basic types of biblical concordism, and distinguishing these is necessary since they deal with different and distinct realms—spiritual reality, human history, and the physical world, respectively.

Theological concordism is the most important type of concordism.[23] It claims that there is an indispensable and non-negotiable correspondence between the theological truths in the Bible and spiritual reality. The central purpose of Scripture is to reveal God, including His character, laws, and acts. Divine revelation also discloses the spiritual nature of the physical world. It declares that the cosmos and living organisms are creations of God and that they are "very good" (Gen 1:1, 31). Scripture affirms that the universe reflects the Creator's glory, workmanship, and divine nature (Ps 19:1; Rom 1:20). And most significantly, the Bible reveals the two defining spiritual characteristics of humanity—we bear God's Image and we are sinful (Gen 1:26–27; Gen 3; Rom 3:23). Despite the many ways Christians interpret the Bible and understand God's creative method, these foundational theological truths always transcend the origins debate. Grasping the deepest truths in Scripture is not only an intellectual activity, but involves conviction and submission at a spiritual level. It takes "ears to hear" (Matt 11:15) the inerrant and infallible Messages of Faith, and it demands that we read the Bible on our knees. The primary purpose of the Book of God's Words is to deliver spiritual Truth.

Historical concordism asserts that Scripture is a reliable record of a period in human history.[24] First and foremost, the Bible offers a trustworthy account of the ministry of Jesus of Nazareth. It is also a history of the nation of Israel and her interaction with neighboring countries, and it documents the activities of the early Church. For many Christians, historical concordism extends to the first chapters of the book of Genesis and the origin of humanity beginning from a single pair of individuals—Adam and Eve. To be sure, the academic discipline of biblical archaeology confirms the historical dependability of many events recorded in Scripture. For example, there exists a remarkable correspondence between the Old Testament and the archaeological record of nations, kings, battles, etc. in the ancient Near East. Archaeology is also in accord with the New Testament. Notably, the historical reality of a man named Jesus in first-century Palestine stands firmly established, as does the existence of the fledgling early Church that He inspired.

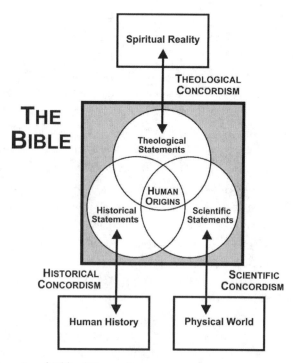

Fig 1-4. Categories of Biblical Concordism

Scientific concordism states that there is a correspondence between the Bible and the physical world. The most common form of this type of concordism aligns the Genesis creation accounts with modern science. It concedes that Scripture offers a simple account of origins, but nevertheless a reliable record of actual creative events. Debate exists among scientific concordists regarding how closely the Bible corresponds to the physical data. Strict scientific concordism accepts creation in six 24-hour days (young earth creation). General scientific concordism views creative events across six vast periods of time hundreds of millions of years long (old earth creation).[25] A less common form of scientific concordism insists that Scripture also provides accurate information regarding the present structure and operation of the world. That is, it speaks accurately about astronomy, geology, meteorology, etc. All scientific concordists agree that since the Bible predates the birth of modern science, any correspondence between the scientific statements in Scripture and science today is *proof* for divine inspiration. Only an all-knowing Creator who transcends time could reveal future scientific discoveries to ancient biblical writers.

Fig 1-4 presents diagrammatically the categories of biblical concordism. A number of questions and relationships arise regarding the different types of statements in Scripture. In particular, Christians face two basic challenges in their reading of the Book of God's Words and the Book of God's Works.

First, do the theological, historical, and scientific statements in the Bible correspond to spiritual reality, human history and the physical world, respectively? Is there actually an accord between Scripture and these three realms of existence? Of course, our rational and psychological inclinations press upon us to expect some sort of agreement if we believe the Bible to be true and relevant to our lives. However, if modern scientific discoveries do not align with statements about nature in Scripture, are Christians forced to choose between science and the Bible? Stated another way, does such a situation drive individuals into either embracing blind faith or rejecting Christianity? Moreover, does biblical inerrancy and infallibility extend to all three categories of concordism? Are theological, historical, and scientific concordism necessary for Scripture to be truly a Holy Spirit inspired revelation? Or can inerrancy and infallibility be limited to only one or two types of concordism?

Second, how do the theological, historical, and scientific statements in the Bible relate to one another? It is clear from Figs 1-3 and 1-4 why human origins is such an important and volatile issue for Christians. The origin of humanity deals with all three categories of biblical statements. But is this overlap essential and indispensable? Or is it incidental and only reflective of the ancient period when these statements were written down? Asked more precisely, are the theological, historical, and scientific claims regarding human origins necessarily connected? Or are these three categories of statements, in principle, independent of each other, having been put together at a certain time in the past by an inspired writer under the guidance of the Holy Spirit? In addition, do the theological assertions in Scripture about the origin of men and women require proof from modern research in science and history for them to be true and relevant for our lives? Is it possible to develop a biblically based theology about humanity without Scripture's historical and scientific statements on human origins?

To appreciate further these two challenges regarding biblical concordism, consider Gen 2:7: "And the Lord God formed man from the dust of the ground and breathed into his nostrils the breath of life, and man became a living being." Is this verse a theological revelation about

God's actual creative action? Does it offer a historical truth concerning the beginning of human history? Is Gen 2:7 revealing a scientific fact that men and women did not evolve from lower forms of life? The overlapping relationships between the three types of biblical statements and the correspondence of these statements to reality lead to other probing questions. If scientific and historical investigations reveal that humans arose through an evolutionary process and not from a single individual, does this invalidate the theological truths that God created us in His Image and that we are sinners? Are biblical inerrancy and infallibility dependent on the first man being fashioned quickly from the dust of the ground into a completely developed person? Asked more incisively, is Christianity built on Adam? Or Jesus?

In this book, I deal directly with these important and challenging questions. I contend that two powerful factors fuel the origins debate. First, many Christians cling firmly to scientific and historical concordism in the opening chapters of Genesis, specifically, Gen 1–11. Second, they conflate these two types of concordism with the notion of biblical inerrancy and infallibility. This conflation has led to a categorical blind spot in the mind of Christians that inhibits them from envisioning how God could create the world, including humanity, through evolution. It must be noted that many non-Christians assume that biblical faith depends on scientific and historical concordism at the beginning of Genesis, and they too stoke the origins controversy and deepen the dichotomy. However, using the Word of God itself, I will show that scientific concordism fails. The science in the Bible is an ancient science. It is the science-of-the-day a few thousand years ago in the ancient Near East. Therefore, any attempt to align science with biblical statements about the origin of the world is doomed. In addition, I will argue that the ancient science in Scripture directly informs the account of human origins. In this way, the history in Gen 1–11 is an ancient understanding of history.[26] It is an ancient history, the history-of-the-day when these chapters were conceived.* Consequently, historical concordism with regard to the beginning of humanity also fails.

---

* Note that the term "ancient history" might cause confusion. In many contexts today it refers to *actual* historical events in the past. But in this book, ancient history means the *understanding* of history that ancient peoples formulated from their perspective. In the same way that they held an ancient view of the physical world (an ancient science), they also had an ancient conception of the origins and first activities of humans.

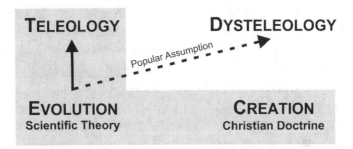

Fig 1-5. Evolutionary Creation: A Christian Approach to Evolution. The popular assumption both inside and outside the Church is that evolution is dysteleological and driven only by blind chance. In contrast, evolutionary creationists assert that the universe and life evolved through a teleological process that was ordained and sustained by the Father, Son and Holy Spirit.

As a corrective, I tenaciously defend that theological concordism is the essential feature of Gen 1–11. The intention of these chapters is to start the process of revealing God and His unconditional love for all of us. Biblical inerrancy and infallibility reside in the theological statements disclosed by the Holy Spirit. I also propose that the ancient science and ancient history in Gen 1–11 are incidental vessels that deliver eternal spiritual truths. When revealing to the early Hebrews that God created the world and their community, the Holy Spirit descended to their level of understanding and employed their scientific and historical categories in order to communicate as effectively as possible. Our challenge as modern readers of the Bible is to identify these ancient vessels and to separate them from the life-changing Messages of Faith.

CHAPTER SUMMARY

Defining categories is critical in recognizing that the origins dichotomy is a false dichotomy. The popular definitions of "evolution" and "creation" entrench into the mind of many Christians and non-Christians a so-called conflict between science and religion. As a result, the prospect of a healthy relationship that integrates our experience of spiritual reality with our knowledge of the physical world is cancelled instantly by the categories directing the way we think about life. Moreover, the origins dichotomy raises a serious pastoral concern. It conflates Christianity with a literalist six-day view of creation, and evolution with an atheistic worldview. Should God have created the cosmos and living organisms through teleological evolution, then this false dichotomy sets stumbling blocks between believers and modern science, and between non-believers familiar with the evolutionary evidence and a relationship with Jesus.

Thankfully, intellectual categories are learned and they can be improved and expanded. Professional definitions and concepts open our eyes to a spectrum of possibilities on how God could have created the world. We are beginning to see that there are a variety of evolutionist and creationist positions. In particular, evolution is not necessarily bound to dysteleology as popularly understood. This natural process might be teleological. Widening our categories also reveals that it is reasonable to hold both the scientific theory of evolution and the Christian doctrine of creation. From this perspective, the God of the Bible created the world through an ordained and sustained process of evolution. Fig 1-5 introduces such an approach to origins, termed "evolutionary creation."

Professional categories also allow Christians to reconsider how God revealed Himself in Scripture. The popular belief that the Holy Spirit disclosed scientific facts in the Bible many generations prior to their discovery by modern science must be re-evaluated in light of God's Word. It is possible that scientific concordism is not a characteristic of biblical inerrancy and infallibility. Similarly, the record of human origins in Scripture may reflect an ancient understanding of history. Stated precisely, Adam and Eve might be ancient vessels that transport divinely inspired Messages of Faith: humans are created in the Image of God, they have fallen into sin, and God judges them for their rebellion.

The introductory categories presented in this chapter open the way for viewing the colorful spectrum of positions on the origin of the universe and life in the next chapter. These foundational concepts allow Christians and non-Christians alike to make informed decisions concerning origins, and ultimately to develop their worldview.

2

Beyond the "Evolution" vs. "Creation" Debate

M ANY PEOPLE TODAY SEE origins as an "evolution" vs. "creation" debate. In this way, one is either an "evolutionist" rejecting God or a
"creationist" believing the world was made in six 24-hour days. Yet some
have a dim awareness that this topic is more complex than a simple either/
or issue. In a number of churches the categories "young earth creation"
and "old earth creation" are emerging. The concept of "theistic evolution"
also appears, though most Christians still view this position as un-biblical
and theologically liberal. The introductory categories presented in the last
chapter make it clear that the origins dichotomy is a false dichotomy. The
spectrum of possibilities for the origin of the universe and life is much
more colorful than the black-and-white positions of atheistic evolution
and six-day creation.

This chapter outlines five basic categories on origins: (1) young earth
creation, (2) progressive creation, (3) evolutionary creation, (4) deistic
evolution, and (5) dysteleological evolution. Every section begins with a
brief description, followed by the view on human origins, and then the
relationship between Scripture and science. Also included are the strongest argument and greatest problem of the position. The presentation of
these categories is not intended to be exhaustive because variations exist
within each. For example, most progressive creationists assert that Adam
was created from the dust of the ground, but a few under this categorization suggest that God modified a pre-human creature into a man. Thus,
each section focuses on the classic features of a position as understood
by the majority of its advocates. To assist readers, I would suggest that
they examine the table summarizing the origins categories in Fig 2-1 on
pages 44–45.

Origins are not limited to only five positions. Readers may find that they embrace characteristics from a number of different views. This is perfectly acceptable, and it widens the scope of possibilities. The purpose in presenting these categories is for similarities and differences between them to emerge, assisting readers to make informed choices as they develop their understanding of origins. This chapter explains further the category of evolutionary creation and begins to open a way for Christians hoping to move beyond the evolution vs. creation debate.

YOUNG EARTH CREATION

Young earth creation claims that God created the universe and life in six 24-hour days about 6000 years ago. The general public and the Christian community commonly perceive this view of origins to be *the* creationist position. Also known as "creation science" and "scientific creationism," it gained wide popularity in the United States during the second half of the twentieth century. A recent survey reveals that about 60% of American adults believe the world was created in six days and Gen 1 is "literally true, meaning that it happened that way word-for-word."[1] Young earth creationists assert that the early chapters of the Bible offer a reliable scientific and historical record upon which to base research on origins.[2]

According to creation science, God created the world quickly and completely through direct miraculous interventions. This position adamantly rejects cosmological, geological, and biological evolution, insisting that there is no genuine evidence to support these theories. It argues that viewing the physical data in light of a strict literal reading of the biblical creation accounts leads to the *true* scientific interpretation. For example, young earth creationists claim that fossils and rock layers in the crust of the earth are best explained by Noah's flood. They contend that plants and animals were trapped as these strata were being laid down during this year-long global deluge. Consequently, creation scientists reject the standard date of geological stratification in the hundreds of millions of years. Instead, they calculate the world to be around 6000 years old by adding the ages of individuals in the biblical genealogies. These anti-evolutionists conclude that the presence of scientific facts in the early chapters of Genesis is proof of the supernatural character of Scripture. Only a God who transcends time could have revealed this information many generations before its discovery by science.

Young earth creation fiercely defends the notion that humanity originates from a single man and woman—literally Adam and Eve as described in Gen 2. This position rejects any connection between this original pair of humans and lower primates because every living species is a separate and special creation. It also contends that pain, decay, and mortality did not exist in the world before Adam and Eve fell into sin. Their transgression in the garden of Eden led to God's judgment upon humanity and the unleashing of suffering and death throughout the entire creation. More precisely, creation science embraces the traditional belief known as "the cosmic fall."

In order to understand origins, young earth creationists employ a one-way relationship between Scripture and science. The Bible dictates how God created the universe and life, especially how He made humans. At best, scientific discoveries only confirm the events recorded in Gen 1–11. In other words, creation science accepts strict scientific concordism and strict historical concordism.

The strongest argument for six-day creation is that a literal interpretation is the natural and traditional way to read the opening chapter of Scripture. Undoubtedly, this view of origins is closest to that held by the inspired author of Gen 1. Other biblical writers understood this creation account literally. For example, Moses in recording the Fourth Commandment orders Israel:

> Remember the Sabbath day by keeping it holy. Six days you shall labor and do all your work, but the seventh day is a Sabbath to the Lord your God. On it you shall not do any work, neither you, nor your son or daughter, nor your manservant or maidservant, nor your animals, nor the alien within your gates. *For in six days the Lord made the heavens and the earth, the sea, and all that is in them,* but He rested on the seventh day. Therefore the Lord blessed the Sabbath day and made it holy. (Exodus 20:8–11; italics added)

Christians throughout history have also upheld the strict literal interpretation of Gen 1. Protestant reformer Martin Luther argued, "Moses spoke in the literal sense, not allegorically or figuratively, that the world with all its creatures was created within six days, as the words read. . . . We know from Moses that the world was not in existence before 6000 years ago."[3]

Powerful evidence for the strict literal interpretation of the first chapters of the Bible comes from Jesus Himself. The Lord referred to people and events in Gen 1–11 to argue a point:

Haven't you read that at the beginning the Creator 'made them male and female,' and said, 'For this reason a man will leave his father and mother and be united to his wife, and the two will become one flesh.' So they are no longer two, but one. Therefore what God has joined together, let man not separate. (Matthew 19:4–6)

And so upon you will come all the righteous blood that has been shed on the earth, from the blood of righteous Abel to the blood of Zechariah son of Berakiah, whom you murdered between the temple and the altar. (Matthew 23:35)

As it was in the days of Noah, so it will be at the coming of the Son of Man. For in the days before the flood, people were eating and drinking, marrying and giving in marriage, up until the day Noah entered the ark; and they knew nothing about what would happen until the flood took them all away. (Matthew 24:37–39)

Clearly, Jesus employed a literal reading of the first chapters of Genesis.[4] Like young earth creationists, He appealed to the creation of the first humans (Gen 1:27), the marriage of Adam and Eve (Gen 2:24), the murder of Abel (Gen 4:8) and Noah's flood (Gen 6–9). And Scripture features many similar passages.[5] Therefore, serious consideration needs to be given to this strict literal interpretation. Any Christian accepting a view of origins other than creation science must provide convincing arguments for why Gen 1–11 should not be read literally.

The greatest problem with young earth creation is that it completely contradicts every modern scientific discipline that investigates the origin of the universe and life. There are very few scientists working in disciplines like cosmology, geology, and biology who accept this anti-evolutionary position. Today, these sciences are practiced in literally tens of thousands of universities and colleges throughout the world, and according to the scientific community, the evidence for evolution is simply overwhelming.

In order to explain the unwavering acceptance of evolution by modern science, six-day creationists claim that there is a demonic delusion of incredible proportions that blinds the mind of hundreds of thousands of scientists.[6] Of course, this controversial opinion certainly raises serious pastoral concerns. Claiming that Satan blinds evolutionists also includes many Christians who accept this scientific theory as God's method of creation. Such an attitude sets the stage for uncharitable exchanges, and even potential divisions in the Church. The spiritual deception theory also alienates non-Christian evolutionists. If God created the world through an evolutionary process, and unbelieving scientists see the evidence for this theory in their laboratories every day, then is there any doubt that a stumbling block has been placed between them and Jesus by scientific creationists?

Many today see the situation with young earth creation as a recycling of the Galileo affair with only the science in question being different—evolution instead of astronomy. A part of this seventeenth-century controversy involved the challenge that astronomical discoveries posed to the traditional and literal interpretation of Scripture held for nearly 1600 years. Entrenched in scientific concordism, Church leaders assumed that the Bible reveals the earth as stationary (1 Chr 16:30; Ps 93:1, 96:10) and the sun moves across the sky each day (Eccl 1:5; Ps 19:4–6). However, Galileo disagreed. He was charged with heresy and put under house arrest for the rest of his life. Sadly, he became the symbol popularizing the perception that science and religion are at war. Yet Galileo insightfully recognized that it is a mistake to conflate science and Christianity. He argued that "the motion or rest of the earth or the sun are not articles of faith" because "the primary purpose of the Holy Writ is for the worship of God and the salvation of souls."[7] Or, tersely stated in the aphorism popularized by this famed astronomer, "The intention of the Holy Spirit is to teach us how one goes to heaven and not how heaven goes."[8]

Young earth creationists approach passages dealing with the immobility of the earth and the mobility of the sun in a fashion similar to Galileo. That is, in light of modern science, they too reject the Church's traditional literal interpretation of the astronomy in Scripture. Thus, an interpretive precedent exists among these anti-evolutionists, and interesting questions arise. Are the passages in the Bible referring to the origin of the universe and life like those dealing with the daily operation of the sun and the earth? Is it possible to apply the interpretive principles that creation scientists use for the astronomy in Scripture to the creation accounts and reconsider the traditional literal interpretation? In the future, will Christians look back on young earth creationists and their judgment that evolutionists are demonically deceived in the same way that we today are troubled by the seventeenth-century Church's treatment of Galileo?

PROGRESSIVE CREATION

Progressive creation asserts that God created life in sequential stages across the 4.5 billion-year history of earth. Often referred to as "old earth creation" and the "day-age theory," it maintains that the creation days in Gen 1 are periods of hundreds of millions of years. This position also claims that there is a general correspondence between the order of creation events in the Bible and the appearance of the inanimate universe and living organisms discovered by modern science.[9]

According to old earth creationists, the Creator made the galaxies, stars, and planets indirectly through cosmological and geological evolution. More precisely, He ordained and sustained natural processes beginning with the Big Bang to create the non-living world. However, progressive creationists emphatically reject biological evolution. They argue that God directly intervened and miraculously fashioned basic groups of plants and animals, termed "created kinds," at different points in the distant past.[10] This position concedes that these fundamental types have modified somewhat over time, yet this biological variability remains within limits because organisms cannot evolve into entirely different forms of life. Thus, day-age creation accepts "micro-evolution" (e.g., a dog modifying into another variety), but rejects the "macro-evolution" of fish into amphibians, reptiles into mammals, or primitive primates into humans.

Using general or non-strict literalism to read Gen 1, progressive creationists assert that the appearance of living organisms in the Bible corresponds to the fossil record. Scripture and geology both reveal that life on earth begins with simple forms and sequentially more complex creatures appear until finally humans arrive. These anti-evolutionists also claim that the gaps between fossil groups reflect intermittent divine creative action and the origin of distinct clusters of organisms "according to its/their kind/s" as recorded in Gen 1. Progressive creationists contend that this alignment of the Bible and science testifies to the supernatural character of Scripture because only a Creator who transcends time could have revealed such information. Lastly, modern geology and general literalism shape the interpretation of Noah's flood for old earth creationists. They maintain that the flood was historical, but a local event limited to a region in the Middle East, because the crust of the earth offers no evidence for a global deluge.

Progressive creation firmly defends that humanity arose from a single couple—Adam and Eve as stated in Gen 2. Humans are a "created kind" or basic life group that God made through direct and miraculous intervention. This view of origins fiercely opposes human evolution. However, it acknowledges that the fossil record reveals the physical suffering, decay, and death of living organisms for hundreds of millions of years prior to the appearance of humans on earth. Consequently, old earth creation asserts that the sins committed by Adam and Eve in the garden of Eden introduced only *spiritual* death into the world. In other words, this position rejects the traditional belief in a cosmic fall.

Progressive creationists embrace a two-way relationship between Scripture and science to understand the creation of the universe and life. The events in Gen 1–11 shape the explanation of biological data, in particular human origins; and discoveries in cosmology and geology direct the interpretation of these opening biblical chapters. More precisely, old earth creationists accept a general scientific concordism and hold a firm historical concordism with regard to the beginning of humanity.

The strongest argument for day-age creation is that it provides an approach to the origin of the world that employs both the Bible and modern science. Christians are nourished spiritually every day in their reading of Scripture, and at the same time they enjoy daily the fruits of scientific discovery. Most believers demand that these experiences be neither in conflict nor placed in isolated compartments. After all, God is the Author of His Words and the Creator of His Works. Moreover, the Lord has given humanity the ability to investigate Scripture and nature. It is quite reasonable, then, for Christians to assume the existence of a harmony and correspondence between these two divine books. Featuring both a belief in the Bible as the Word of God and an acceptance of the modern sciences of geology and cosmology, old earth creation meets the yearning for an integration of Christian faith and scientific investigation.

The greatest problem with progressive creation is that it is a God-of-the-gaps model of origins. This position envisions divine creative activity in "gaps" or "discontinuities" throughout the history of life. Old earth creationists claim that natural processes are insufficient and cannot produce living organisms. Therefore, the Creator's direct intervention is needed to complete a world that at first was created deficient. Many progressive creationists suggest that entirely new species were introduced during different geological periods, while others contend that genetic material was added to and/or manipulated in pre-existing species to produce new ones, and some uphold a combination of these methods. The difficulty with this understanding of divine action is that when physical processes are discovered to explain a gap once claimed to be where God acted, His purported intervention vanishes in the advancing light of science. Such a situation raises serious pastoral concerns. As these gaps fill and close through increasing scientific knowledge, many have assumed that there is less reason to believe in God. He then appears to be forced further and further back into the dark recesses of human ignorance. And yes, the frightening thought arises that the Creator might only be a resident of uninformed minds.

Another difficulty with progressive creation is that it introduces an unnecessary distinction between the physical and life sciences. On one hand, it accepts cosmology and geology, including the theory that unites these sciences—the evolution of the inanimate universe. On the other, it rejects the unifying principle of biological science—the evolution of all living organisms. This position asserts that galaxies, stars, and planets emerged through natural processes ordained and sustained by God, yet He did not equip the creation sufficiently for life to arise in a similar manner. But research reveals that there is nothing inherently different in biology that must distinguish it from cosmology and geology. All these sciences are built upon the principle that natural processes are dependable, predictable, and even extendable into the past. Medicine, agriculture, and crime scene investigations are based on the regularity of nature's biological laws in the same way that this notion is used in cosmological and geological studies.

In addition, the Hebrew terms employed in Gen 1 to describe God's creative action do not distinguish between the origin of the inanimate and living worlds. The two most important and frequent verbs, *bārā'* (to create; appears 6 times) and *'āśâ* (to make; 8 times), are used interchangeably. God created (*bārā'*) the heavens and the earth (v. 1), the creatures of the sea and air (vs. 21–22) and humanity (v. 27). Similarly, He made (*'āśâ*) the sun, moon, and stars (v. 16), the animals on the land (v. 25) and the first man (v. 26).[11] Genesis 1 does not discriminate between the creation of the inanimate objects and living organisms, including humanity. Therefore, the distinction between the life and physical sciences as proposed by old earth creation is artificial and unnecessary. It is another false dichotomy.

Today, progressive creation is often seen as the latest in the long history of God-of-the-gaps theories that Christians have defended with brimming confidence. The problem with this approach is exemplified by the astronomy of Martin Luther. In attempting to explain the brief east-to-west movement of the planets (known as "retrograde motion") from their regular west-to-east journey across the night sky, Luther appealed to direct divine intervention. He claimed, "The retrograde motion of the planets is a work of God . . . This work belongs to God Himself and is too great to be assigned to the angels."[12] Of course, everyone now realizes that the movement of the earth causes the apparent irregular motion or wandering of the planets. It was a gap in astronomical knowledge that led Luther to the mistaken belief that God directly intervened in retrograde motion.

Luther's God-of-the-gaps astronomy raises a number of relevant questions. Is progressive creation simply a recycling of this sixteenth-century understanding of divine action applied to the origin of life? Currently, many Christians claim that living cells feature "irreducible complexity" and that this characteristic could not have arisen through biological evolution.[13] To be sure, the cellular components are incredibly intricate, and modern science has yet to determine their biochemical evolution. However, do these complex features point to *a gap in nature* where God at some point in the past intervened to introduce them? Or is this only a *gap in knowledge* that reflects shortcomings in information, education, and/or conceptualization? Finally, should science discover the processes of bio-molecular evolution, will future generations of Christians look back at today's progressive creationists in the same way that we look at Luther and his explanation of retrograde motion?

EVOLUTIONARY CREATION

Evolutionary creation asserts that the Father, Son, and Holy Spirit created the universe and life through an ordained, sustained, and design-reflecting evolutionary process. This position fully embraces both the religious beliefs of Christianity and the scientific theories of cosmological, geological, and biological evolution. It contends that God established and maintains the laws of nature, including the mechanisms of a teleological evolution. Notably, this view of origins argues that humanity evolved from pre-human ancestors and through this process the Image of God and human sin were mysteriously and gradually manifested. Evolutionary creationists experience God's presence and love in their lives. In particular, these Christians have a personal relationship with the Lord that includes miraculous signs and wonders.[14]

The category "evolutionary creation" seems like a contradiction in terms. This would be the case if the words "evolution" and "creation" were restricted to their popular meanings; that is, if the former is conflated with a dysteleological worldview, and if the latter refers exclusively to young earth creation. But this understanding of origins employs professional definitions and moves beyond the simple evolution vs. creation dichotomy. The most important word in this category is the noun creation. Evolutionary creationists are first and foremost thoroughly committed and unapologetic creationists. They believe that the universe is a creation that is absolutely dependent for its every instant of existence on the will and grace of the Creator. The qualifying word in this category is the adjective evolutionary, indicating the method through which God created the world. This view of origins is often referred to as "theistic evolution." However, that word arrangement places the process of evolution as the primary term and makes the Creator secondary as only a qualifying adjective. Such an inversion in priority is unacceptable to evolutionary creationists.

In order to explain their origins position, Christian evolutionists begin by pointing out the remarkable parallels between evolution and human embryological development. They argue that God's action in the creation of each person individually is similar to His activity in the origin of every part of the world collectively.

First, embryological and evolutionary processes are both teleological and ordained by God. At conception, the DNA in a fertilized human egg is fully equipped with the necessary information for a person to develop during the nine months of pregnancy. Similarly, the Creator loaded into the Big Bang the plan and capacity for the universe and life, including humans, to evolve over 10–15 billion years.

Second, divine creative action in the origin of individual humans and the entire world is through sustained and continuous natural processes. No Christian believes that while in his or her mother's womb the Lord came out of heaven and dramatically intervened to attach a nose, set an eye, or bore an ear canal. Rather, everyone understands embryological development to be an uninterrupted natural process that

God subtly maintains during pregnancy. In the same way, evolutionary creationists assert that dramatic divine interventions were not employed in the creation of the cosmos and living organisms, including people. Instead, evolution is an unbroken natural process that the Lord sustained throughout eons of time.

Third, human embryological development in the microcosm of the womb and evolution in the macrocosm of the world reflect intelligent design. That is, each is a natural revelation authored by the Creator. As the psalmist praises his Maker, "For You created my inmost being; You knit me together in my mother's womb. I praise You because I am fearfully and wonderfully made" (Ps 139:13–14); so too, evolutionary creationists view evolution as a "knitting" process that results in a world that is "fearfully and wonderfully made." Indeed, the Big Bang "declares the Glory of God," and biological evolution "proclaims the work of His hands" (Ps 19:1).

Finally, spiritual mysteries are associated with both the embryological and evolutionary processes that created humans. Men and women are unique and distinguished from the rest of creation because they bear the Image of God and have fallen into sin. Christians throughout the ages have debated where, when, and how these spiritual realities become manifested in the development of each individual. Yet church history reveals that believers have not come to a consensus on these questions, suggesting that these issues are beyond human understanding. In other words, they are mysteries. Similarly, evolutionary creationists believe that the manifestation of God's Image and the entrance of sin during human evolution are also a mystery. Christian evolutionists firmly accept these spiritual realities, but recognize that understanding fully their origin is beyond our creaturely capacity to know.

According to evolutionary creation, God reveals Himself both through Scripture and science. In the former, He discloses specifically His character and purpose for the world. The Bible is the revelation of Jesus Christ and His love for humanity. It leads men and women into a genuine relationship with the Lord through the confession of sins and the acceptance of forgiveness through His sacrifice on the Cross. The Word also offers the principles for a holy life. As the apostle Paul states, "All Scripture is God-breathed and is useful for teaching, rebuking, correcting, and training in righteousness so that the man and woman of God may be thoroughly equipped for every good work" (2 Tim 3:16–17).

Regarding the opening chapters of the Bible, evolutionary creation asserts that Gen 1–11 is an ancient origins account inspired by the Holy Spirit. First and foremost, it reveals a Divine Theology that includes foundations of the Christian faith: (1) God created the world, (2) the creation is very good, (3) only humans are created in the Image of God, (4) we were made to be in relationships with one another and especially with the Lord, (5) every man and woman has fallen into sin, (6) God judges humanity for their sins, and (7) He has created a chosen people through which to bless all the nations.[15]

In order to reveal these spiritual truths as effectively as possible to ancient peoples, evolutionary creationists contend that the Holy Spirit employed the science-of-the-day. In this way, the ancient science of the biblical authors is a vehicle that transports this divine revelation. For example, Scripture features a 3-tiered universe with heaven above, the earth in the middle, and the underworld below (Fig 4-1). Similarly, Gen 1–11 features ancient history.[16] More precisely, it is the history-of-the-day a few thousand years ago, and it includes an ancient understanding of human origins. Finally, ancient poetry shapes the opening chapters of Genesis. Of course, the term "poetry" carries a number of meanings. Using the most basic definition, it refers simply to a structured writing style in contrast to a free-flowing narrative. To illustrate, the Gen 1 creation account features parallel panels (Fig 6-3) and Noah's flood in Gen 6–9 reflects a chiasm (Fig 6-6). Most would agree that actual historical events do not unfold in such a structured fashion. Evolutionary creationists conclude that the purpose of Gen 1–11 is to reveal the Creator's character and His will, not the details of modern science ahead of time or the history of human events at the beginning of time.

Evolutionary creation also asserts that the Lord reveals Himself through science. He gifted humanity with the ability to investigate the natural world. As a result, we can "think God's thoughts after Him" and discover His method in creating the universe and life.[17] According to this origins position, the physical evidence for cosmological, geological, and biological evolution is simply *overwhelming*. Science also contributes in identifying the non-verbal (i.e., not using words) natural revelation of the Creator's glory, power, and divine nature. History testifies that the deeper scientists have probed nature with telescopes or microscopes, greater and more magnificent pictures of His majesty have emerged. Evolutionary creationists are quick to point out that they have an expanded and more robust understanding of intelligent design than the anti-evolutionists. They not only affirm design in the present structures and operations in the universe, but these Christian evolutionists also recognize reflections of intelligence in the mechanisms of evolution.

Therefore, evolutionary creation embraces a complementary relationship between Scripture and science in understanding origins.[18] Together they fulfill each other; alone they are incomplete. Scientific discoveries reveal *how* the Creator made this design-reflecting world, while the Bible declares precisely *who* created it—the Father, Son, and Holy Spirit. More specifically, evolutionary creation accepts theological concordism, but rejects all forms of scientific concordism, and dismisses historical concordism in Gen 1–11, especially with regard to human origins.

The most compelling argument for evolutionary creation is that it embraces without any reservations modern science and biblical faith. Like a breath of fresh air, this position moves beyond the stagnant origins dichotomy and the science-religion warfare myth, both of which have characterized thinking throughout most of the twentieth century. It meets the yearning of a scientific generation in search of spiritual meaning. In particular, evolutionary creation offers an intellectually satisfying worldview for those who experience God in a personal relationship and know His creation scientifically. Though this position recognizes that science and religion operate within their respective domains, it does not suffer from the intellectual schizophrenia of placing them in isolated compartments. Rather, many areas of common interest exist, including bioethics, mind-brain neuroscience, and intelligent design in nature. With such issues, evolutionary creationists enjoy a respectful and fruitful dialogue between the best modern science and the foundations of historic Christianity.

Evolutionary creation is the only Christian view of origins that offers a unified vision of science. This position does not postulate that certain scientific disciplines are logically flawed or spiritually deceived. There is no discrimination between sciences dealing with the daily operation of the world and those investigating its past origins. And it does not segregate cosmology and geology from evolutionary biology. For example, young earth creation has a disjointed understanding of science. On the one hand, it rejects the evolutionary sciences. Yet on the other hand, these anti-evolutionists support and even practice modern engineering and medical sciences, accepting research built on the assumption of the robust regularity in nature's processes. Similarly, progressive creation has a split vision of science. It affirms the evolution of the inanimate universe as offered by cosmological and geological sciences, but it dismisses the central tenet of biological science that life evolved. Evolutionary creationists reject these false dichotomies and uphold the unity and coherence of all the natural sciences.

The greatest problem with evolutionary creation is that it does not embrace the traditional literal interpretation of the opening chapters of the Bible. Church history reveals that nearly all Christians have understood Gen 1–11 to be a record of actual events in the past. In particular, most have believed that Gen 2 reveals the history of human origins beginning with Adam and Eve. More troubling for this evolutionary position is the fact that Jesus and the biblical authors often refer to the early chapters of Genesis as a literal historical account. And the most acute issue is explaining the relationship between human sin and the origin of physical death. Genesis 3, Rom 5–8, and 1 Cor 15 clearly state that death came into the world after the creation of Adam and his original sin. Yet this Christian view of evolution asserts that the fossil record conclusively demonstrates that death existed for hundreds of millions of years prior to the appearance of humans (Appendix 7 Fig 4).

Consequently, evolutionary creationists contend that Gen 1–11 is to be read in a very unnatural and utterly counterintuitive way. They suggest that Christians must move beyond the scientific and historical concordism that has marked the interpretation of these chapters for generations. However, before any believer considers accepting evolutionary creation, the problems just cited regarding Gen 1–11 need to be addressed directly. Hopefully, I can offer some convincing solutions in the chapters that follow.

To summarize, evolutionary creation recognizes that the relationship between Scripture and science is a key to developing a Christian view of origins. This position notes that the seventeenth-century Church's struggle with the astronomy of Galileo offers valuable insights into understanding the creation accounts and the evolutionary sciences. This historical episode has led many believers to realize that the Bible is not a book of science, but a book of salvation. Christians who accept evolution as God's method of creation are especially inspired by the famed aphorism that Galileo popularized: "The intention of the Holy Spirit is to teach us how one goes to heaven and not how heaven goes." Rewritten for the Church today, evolutionary creationists encourage their brothers and sisters in Christ to understand:

> The intention of the Bible is to teach us that God is the Creator, and not how the Father, Son, and Holy Spirit created.

DEISTIC EVOLUTION

Deistic evolution asserts that god initiated the evolutionary process and then retreated from the universe, never to return. This position depicts the creator as one who winds the cosmos like a clock and lets it run down without any interference. In contrast to conservative Christianity, the supreme being of deism is impersonal. Often called the "god-of-the-philosophers," the deistic creator is not involved in the lives of men and women. This god never reveals himself personally through Scripture, prayer, or miracles. He simply does not seem to care. Regrettably, many miscategorize this view as theistic evolution, but the term "theism" refers to a personal God. In many ways, deistic evolution characterizes liberal Christianity by spurning belief in divine action and biblical revelation.

According to deistic evolutionists, god ordained natural laws through which the universe and life evolved, but he did not remain in the world to sustain these physical processes through time. Deists claim that his only act was to initiate the Big Bang 10–15 billion years ago. This origins position asserts that the creator is known only from a distance through logical analysis and scientific investigation. It claims that modern cosmology offers evidence for intelligent design, pointing to the mind of the divine being. However, these evolutionists contend that science offers no evidence for god acting in the world. Nature is a closed continuum of mechanical processes. By pushing the creator outside the universe, they deem notions such as the Holy Spirit inspiring prophets or god becoming a man in the person of Jesus to be ancient superstitions. Thus, this position firmly rejects biblical revelation. Since Scripture contains the beliefs of ignorant ancient peoples, it has little to no value for our scientific generation.

Deistic evolution asserts that humanity evolved from primitive primates. There is debate as to whether the creator specifically intended the present human species to evolve or whether the evolutionary process was loosely ordained to produce some form of intelligent life. In other words, there is no consensus on the status of humans, whether special or not. But this position definitely rejects the creation of a literal Adam and Eve as described in Gen 2. And it dismisses the foundational biblical principles that men and women bear the Image of God and have fallen into sin.

In order to understand origins, deistic evolutionists claim that there is no relationship between Scripture and science. They contend that modern scientific investigation not only reveals how the creator made the world, but it is also the sole source of information concerning his character. Stated another way, this view embraces the general revelation in God's Works and spurns the special revelation in God's Word.[19] Consequently, deistic evolutionists believe that Gen 1–11 is an irrelevant origins myth, and they reject theological, scientific, and historical concordism.

The most compelling argument for deistic evolution is that it offers a more objective approach to faith than conventional religions. Throughout history, religious individuals have produced an incredibly wide variety of contradictory beliefs, including those among the Christian traditions. But simple logic dictates that all religions cannot be true. For that matter, considering the exclusive truth claims made by each indicates that most offer false beliefs. Deistic evolution attempts to avoid this problem by restricting the primary source of religious truth to logical analysis and modern science. As a result, subjective elements and personal biases are set aside, leaving religion to be as objective as possible. Divine truth is then open to investigation by everyone, and it is not confined to any particular time, culture, or people. This approach unites humanity by the most basic religious truths. In particular, deistic evolution employs modern scientific evidence to defend the belief that the cosmos reflects intelligent design, and thus provides a firm rational basis for the existence of a creator and a world with religious significance.

The greatest problem with deistic evolution is that a god who winds the clock of the universe and then leaves it to run down on its own rarely meets the spiritual needs of people. An impersonal designer may titillate the intellectual curiosity of some for a brief period, but such a distant being is, for all practical purposes, non-existent and irrelevant. As history reveals, deism was popular in eighteenth-century Europe during the Enlightenment, but most eventually realized that an absentee designer is superfluous and dispensable. Only a century after his birth, the god of deism died from public view and was buried in the grave of private thoughts and personal beliefs where he remains today. In contrast to Christianity, deism never inspired an enduring body of believers, an educational institution, or an outreach facility like a hospital or food bank. Religious beliefs restricted to logical arguments for the existence of god, like the argument from design, seldom inspire anyone to personal commitment and involvement. The gospel of deism rarely if ever transforms lives in the way that the gospel of Jesus Christ throughout history has led men and women to be born-again.

Another difficulty with deistic evolution is that it fails to appreciate the limits of human thinking. Deism emerged following the birth of modern science in the seventeenth century. The dramatic success of the scientific method led to a flagrant optimism in human rationality. In effect, deists made an idol of reason, and this blind faith led many to assume that the principles of morality, the mysteries of life, and the knowledge of god could be worked out within their minds. However, history testifies to the failure of deism—ethical consensus does not exist, mysteries remain unanswered, and theological agreement has never emerged. This position fails to understand that human reason is a creaturely rationality with boundaries defined by God. As the apostle Paul states, "For we know in part" and "now we see but a poor reflection" of reality (1 Cor 13:9, 12). In addition, deists do not recognize the reality of sin and its impact on human rationality. According to Paul, idolatry causes thinking to become "futile" and even "depraved" (Rom 1:21, 28).[20] In a subtle way, deism points to the need for an authoritative divine revelation like the Bible, which transcends the intellectual limits and sinful tendencies of human reason.

To conclude, deistic evolution makes a valuable contribution in moving the relationship between science and religion beyond the popular warfare model. This position affirms the existence of a creator and recognizes intelligent design in nature. However, God never intended natural revelation and human rationality to replace the Bible. The creator of deism is an impersonal being that leaves most people cold. The ethics deists espouse are essentially those of humanism. That is, humanity becomes the judge of moral standards. But this self-determination puts men and women in a position that only God can occupy. In practice, this is the ethical approach of atheism. By rejecting the Bible, deistic evolutionists bar the entrance to a personal relationship with the Triune Creator. No Christian can espouse this view of origins.

The biblical picture of Jesus knocking on the door is a depiction of deistic evolution. The Lord calls out, "Here I am! I stand at the door and knock. If anyone hears my voice and opens the door, I will come in and eat with him, and he with me" (Rev 3:20). Beauty, complexity, and functionality in the world are some of the sounds of God knocking on the entrance of human hearts and minds. Deistic evolutionists hear the pounding, but claim that the door cannot be opened. As a result, the Creator is kept outside their world, leaving deists alone to lead a self-sufficient life of their own choosing. But with Creatorship comes Lordship. Sadly, history records that many deists come to recognize that an impersonal creator is redundant and expendable, and eventually they open the door to a dysteleological worldview.

DYSTELEOLOGICAL EVOLUTION

Dysteleological evolution asserts that the universe and life evolved by blind chance and without any plan or purpose whatsoever. In such a world, there is no God and no ultimate right or wrong. It is marked by meaninglessness and pointless indifference. This position is also referred to as "scientism," "atheistic evolution," and "scientific materialism."[21] Regrettably, it is also called "Darwinism," even though Charles Darwin near the end of his life explicitly stated that he never was an atheist. Dysteleological evolutionists also embrace humanism. That is, they place themselves in the position of God and then determine right and wrong. Under the powerful influence of the media and secular education, this view of origins spread throughout popular culture during the second half of the twentieth century. As a consequence, the general public and the Church commonly perceive dysteleological evolution to be *the* evolutionist position and that held by the scientific community.

Atheists reject the existence of God. They believe that matter and energy are the only realities in the universe. Dysteleologists arrive at this conclusion through a *personal commitment* to the belief that science is the only method for determining truth. In this way, all non-scientific forms of knowledge, like religion, are judged as insignificant and irrelevant. Atheists contend that religious behavior is an evolutionary by-product that arose by chance and contributed to the survival of the human herd. In particular, this position rejects natural revelation. Moral intuition, the reflection of intelligent design, and the sense that the world has purpose are "nothing but" illusions that have evolved in the human mind.[22] Dysteleological evolution also dismisses biblical revelation. It contends that the authors of Scripture wrote under the influence of a pre-scientific mindset, which led to the belief that the universe is filled with supernatural activity. From this perspective, the miracles in the Bible, including the Incarnation and the bodily resurrection of Jesus, are merely fantasies concocted by human imagination and wishful thinking.

Dysteleological evolution claims that humanity evolved entirely through blind chance and natural processes from lower primates. That is, humans are nothing but an unintended spin-off of biological evolution without any significance or ultimate purpose. This position vehemently rejects the creation of a literal Adam and Eve as described in Gen 2. In addition, it fiercely dismisses the biblical notions that men and women bear the Image of God and have fallen into sin. Instead, atheistic evolutionists assert that "sin" is only a relative cultural artifact and that humanity has in fact created God in its image.

In order to understand origins, dysteleological evolutionists defend a one-way relationship between Scripture and science. They claim that scientific evidence not only determines *how* the world originated, but it even explains *why* there is no ultimate purpose in the cosmos. Dysteleological evolutionary science reduces religion into mere biological and sociological phenomena. Genesis 1–11 is only a pre-scientific myth of the beginning of the world and it has no relevance whatsoever today. Atheistic evolutionists adamantly reject theological, scientific, and historical concordism.

The greatest support for dysteleological evolution comes from the astonishing success of science.[23] Modern society enjoys its fruits daily, and understandably atheists assume that the scientific method can be used to explain every aspect of life, including religion and morality. Science accounts for an overwhelming amount of observable and experimental data, and it organizes this information into a coherent body of knowledge. Moreover, history reveals that as science has advanced, purported supernatural activity in the world has decreased. Gods, angels, and spirits were once believed to intervene in the operation of nature, and now they have all but disappeared in light of scientific investigation.[24] According to dysteleological evolutionists, if this trend is taken to its logical conclusion, science will explain and reduce every aspect of human nature, including religion, into nothing but energy and matter.

In addition, atheistic evolution offers a reasonable explanation for an issue that has challenged men and women throughout the ages—the problem of evil. In a dysteleological world, this is not a dilemma because morality does not ultimately exist. Good and evil are only illusions fabricated by the human mind that have been projected upon reality. The problem of evil is particularly acute for Christians because God is believed to have both perfect love and unlimited power. But the existence of natural disasters, debilitating diseases, and human atrocities call into question the Creator's concern for humanity and His ability to deal with these harsh realities. Atheistic evolutionists argue that if God were like a caring father, then surely He would intervene to protect his children from evil. They also contend that the character of biological evolution reflects a mindless and indifferent process rather than a creative and beneficent plan expected of the biblical God. The wastage of living organisms through mass extinctions, the uncaring mechanism of natural selection, and the vicious competitiveness of the survival of the fittest all paint a picture of nature that is consistent with a dysteleological universe. Though Christians may not accept these arguments, it must be admitted that atheism offers a rational explanation for the existence of evil.

The greatest problem with dysteleological evolution is that it stands directly in the face of God and the First Commandment: "You shall have no other gods before Me" (Exod 20:3; Deut 5:7). This position commits the greatest of all sins. Atheists place themselves before God. They fashion a worldview that relegates the Maker to the realm of illusion. The creature in essence takes the place of the Creator. But if God and the spiritual realm exist, then dysteleological evolution is not only the most nauseating act of arrogance in intellectual history, but it is an understanding of the world that hopelessly lacks the Foundation of reality and knowledge. Scripture calls those who do not acknowledge the Creator "fools." Twice in the Psalms it states, "The fool says in his heart, 'There is no God'" (14:1, 53:1). The Proverbs also claim that "fools hate knowledge" (1:22, 29) and that "fools mock at making amends for sin" (14:9). Atheistic evolutionists reject the existence of God, construct knowledge without reference to Him, and dismiss sin as only a cultural artifact. In light of God's Word, dysteleological evolution is the origins position of fools.[25]

Another serious difficulty with dysteleological evolution is that it is a *personal commitment* to the belief that truth only comes through logical analysis and scientific investigation. This view of knowledge is known as "positivism." It asserts that all phenomena, including religious experience, can be reduced by logic and science into nothing but simple physical laws.

However, atheists fail to realize that there is no scientific test or experiment to prove this claim. As a result, they put their *faith* in the methods of science in a way similar to religious people embracing their beliefs. But even more troubling is the fact that this view of origins *trusts* the human brain, an organ that supposedly evolved merely by blind chance and was never intended to discover truth. In a dysteleological world, the brain arose for the sole *purposes* of fighting, fleeing, feeding, and "fertilizing." How can an organ fashioned by irrational processes make true statements about ultimate reality? Why should atheists *believe* in such claims arising in their brain? Clearly, dysteleological belief is self-referentially incoherent.

Finally, atheistic evolution fails to meet the spiritual and psychological needs of men and women. Few throughout history have espoused this bleak worldview marked by ultimate purposelessness, meaninglessness, and hopelessness. Today 96% of Americans believe in the existence of God or a universal spirit.[26] That is, only 4% of the general population hold dysteleological beliefs. Moreover, atheistic evolution renders human experience psychologically empty. For example, the reductionist method concludes that love is *nothing but* a manifestation of biochemical activity in the brain. In other words, this emotion is ultimately an illusion imposed on human relationships for the survival of the species. But does anyone who is in love believe that? Is a good marriage merely a herd response? No. Love is *something more* than just hormones in our head. It is a spiritual reality ordained by the God of love that is beyond scientific detection, and it is known only through the "instrument" of the human heart.

In summary, dysteleological evolution is utterly opposed to God's Creatorship and Lordship. This position is the popular understanding of evolution both inside and outside of the Church. Along with the young earth creationists, atheistic evolutionists entrench the evolution vs. creation dichotomy deeply into the mind of most people. This both fuels the science-religion warfare model and blinds anyone from seeing the possibility that God might have created the world through an ordained and sustained evolutionary process. Too often, leaders in the media and public education promote dysteleological evolution. It is not acceptable to leave the control of society's central information sources to a skewed and very small minority of individuals. They are not representative of the majority of Americans, and their spread of dysteleological propaganda is an attack against the nation's founding document, the *Declaration of Independence*, which affirms belief in the Creator.[27] The indoctrination of the United States by preachers of the gospel of atheism must be challenged.

Dysteleological evolution is reminiscent of the scene at the foot of the Cross. Soldiers divided Jesus' clothes while He was suffering and dying for them (John 19:23–24). Blind to the spiritual meaning of the crucifixion, they were only interested in their physical well being and clothing themselves. But unknowingly, the Lord's crucifiers fulfilled prophecy: "They divided my garments among them" (Ps 22:18). So too today. Atheistic evolutionists are interested only in dividing the world into its basic physical components, and they are oblivious of the spiritual message woven deeply into its fabric. Unwittingly, their scientific discoveries of the beauty, complexity, and functionality in nature provide greater revelations declaring God's glory, power, and divine nature. Like the soldiers so near to the Savior but so distant from salvation, dysteleological evolutionists are so close to the creation yet so far from its Creator.

RELATIONSHIPS BETWEEN ORIGINS CATEGORIES

Fig 2-1 outlines five basic categories on the origin of the universe and life. This table reveals that the evolution vs. creation debate is a false dichotomy. Four of the positions believe that the world is the creation of God (young earth creation, progressive creation, evolutionary creation, deistic evolution), and three accept that living organisms arose through evolution (evolutionary creation, deistic evolution, dysteleological evolution). In other words, there are four types of creationists and three types of evolutionists. The time has come to move beyond the popular either/or understanding of origins.

It is important to emphasize that Fig 2-1 is an instructional framework with limits. This table assists in organizing the wide spectrum of origins positions. In the same way that basic categories of color (red, orange, yellow, green, blue, violet) can be used to describe a rainbow, everyone knows that it is impossible to account for all shades and hues that are seen. In addition, two other categories could have been included in Fig 2-1: (1) Evolutionary Religious Agnostics (Greek: *a*: prefix for negation, *gnōsis*: knowledge)—individuals who accept evolution but are agnostic with regard to the existence of God and theological beliefs, and (2) Christian Scientific Agnostics—believers who do not know if the scientific evidence supports evolution because they are not educated in biology (e.g., lawyers, engineers, philosophers, etc). With these limits and qualifications in mind, a number of relationships between the five origin categories are evident.

Groupings appear in Fig 2-1. Sometimes science is the uniting factor and variation arises over theological and philosophical beliefs. At other times, theology and philosophy connect categories and a range of scientific views emerges. To point out a few of these:

- Young earth creation and progressive creation reject biological evolution. It is significant to note that these anti-evolutionary positions are the only two positions that accept scientific and historical concordism in Gen 1–11.

- Evolutionary creation and deistic evolution believe that God created life through evolution.[28] However, critical theological differences exist. In the former, a personal Creator ordained and sustained biological evolution. In the latter, an impersonal god only initiated the process and then had nothing to do with the creatures that evolved.

- Evolutionary creation, deistic evolution, and dysteleological evolution accept the modern scientific view of origins. But these positions have radically different religious and philosophical beliefs. The first defends conservative Christianity, the second deism, and the third atheism.

- Young earth creation and progressive creation reject human evolution. Both categories tenaciously argue for historical concordism in Gen 1–11 and claim that all humans descend from Adam and Eve.

- Evolutionary creation, deistic evolution and dysteleological evolution accept human evolution. Again, these three categories agree on the science, but they have drastic theological and philosophical differences. Only evolutionary creation affirms that humanity has been created in God's Image and that everyone has fallen into sin.

- The three evolutionary positions reject scientific and historical concordism in Gen 1–11. However, evolutionary creation stands distinctly apart from the other two. It asserts that the Holy Spirit employed both the science and history-of-the-day in order to communicate as effectively as possible a Divine Theology regarding the Creator and the creation to ancient peoples.

	YOUNG EARTH CREATION "Creationist" Position Creation Science	PROGRESSIVE CREATION Old Earth Creation Day-Age Theory
Teleology	Yes	Yes
Intelligent Design	Yes Points to a Designer	Yes Points to a Designer
Age of the Universe	Young 6000 years	Old 10-15 billion years
Evolution of Life	Rejects macro-evolution Accepts micro-evolution	Rejects macro-evolution Accepts micro-evolution
God's Activity in the Origin of the Universe & Life	Yes Direct Interventions over 6 days	Yes 1. Direct for basic "kinds" of life Interventions over billions of yrs 2. Indirect for inanimate universe *Ordained & sustained natural processes*
God's Activity in the Lives of Men & Women	Yes Personal God Dramatic & subtle	Yes Personal God Dramatic & subtle
Nature of the Bible	Word of God Inspired by Holy Spirit	Word of God Inspired by Holy Spirit
Interpretation of Genesis 1-11	Strict literalism Creation days = 24 hrs Global flood	General literalism Creation days = geologic ages Local flood
Concordism in Genesis 1-11 Theological Scientific Historical	 Yes Yes Yes	 Yes Yes Yes
Origin of Humanity	Adam & Eve Accepts Image of God Accepts sin	Adam & Eve Accepts Image of God Accepts sin
Theology/Philosophy	Conservative Christianity Accepts Trinity	Conservative Christianity Accepts Trinity
Ethics	Biblical	Biblical

Fig 2-1. Categories on the Origin of the Universe and Life. Lines and box indicate categorical features that are critical to understanding evolutionary creation.

Evolutionary Creation Theistic Evolution	Deistic Evolution God-of-the-Philosophers "Theistic" Evolution	Dysteleological Evolution "Evolutionist" Position Atheistic Evolution
Yes	Yes	No Plan & purpose an illusion
Yes Points to a Designer	Yes Points to a Designer	No Design an illusion
Old 10-15 billion years	Old 10-15 billion years	Old 10-15 billion years
Accepts macro-evolution Accepts micro-evolution	Accepts macro-evolution Accepts micro-evolution	Accepts macro-evolution Accepts micro-evolution
Yes Indirect *Ordained & sustained* *natural processes*	Yes Indirect Ordained natural processes God never enters the world	No Blind chance natural processes God an illusion
Yes Personal God Dramatic & subtle	No Impersonal God God never enters the world	No No God God an illusion
Word of God Inspired by Holy Spirit	Human beliefs about God Rejects divine revelation God never enters the world	Human superstitions Rejects divine revelation God an illusion
1. Divine Theology 2. Ancient science 3. Ancient history 4. Ancient poetry	Irrelevant origins myth	Irrelevant origins myth
Yes No No	No No No	No No No
Humanity evolved Accepts Image of God Accepts sin	Humanity evolved Rejects Image of God Rejects sin	Humanity evolved Rejects Image of God Rejects sin
Conservative Christianity Accepts Trinity	Deism & Liberal Christianity Rejects Trinity	Atheism Rejects Trinity
Biblical	Humanism	Humanism

- Deistic evolution and dysteleological evolution reject conservative Christianity. They do not believe in the Holy Trinity, personal miracles, the Holy Spirit's inspiration of Scripture, or the creation of humans in God's Image and the sinfulness of every man and woman. These non-Christian positions also dismiss biblical ethics and instead embrace humanism.

- Young earth creation, progressive creation, and evolutionary creation are distinctly conservative Christian positions. However, they feature a wide range of views on how God created the world and how to interpret the opening chapters of Scripture.

It is evident from a number of these groupings that the acceptance or rejection of scientific and historical concordism in Gen 1–11 is a central factor that shapes the five origins positions. Chapters 4 to 7 will focus on the issue of concordism.

Fig 2-1 features trends across the origins categories. In general, moving from left-to-right through this table sees an increasing acceptance of the modern scientific view of origins, but also a decrease in traditional Christian beliefs.

- Acceptance of the evolutionary sciences increases across the chart. The history of science reveals a similar pattern. Scientists came to terms first with the physical sciences (astronomy followed by geology), and then the life sciences (evolutionary biology).

- God's creative action changes and decreases from left-to-right. On the far left it involves direct interventions, in the middle categories indirect divine activity through natural laws steadily increases, until finally it disappears completely on the far right.

- God's personal activity in human lives divides sharply in the table. The conservative Christian categories accept dramatic and subtle divine action, while deists, atheists, and many liberal Christians argue it does not exist.

- The physical origins of humans and their spiritual characteristics shift through the chart. Acceptance of Adam and Eve gives way to human evolution from left-to-right, as does a loss in the belief that humanity bears God's Image and is sinful.

- The divine nature of Scripture, literalist interpretations of Gen 1–11, and biblical concordism in these chapters decreases toward the right.

The far left asserts that the Holy Spirit inspired the Bible and that it must be read verbatim. The chart shifts to general literalism and then to the view that the opening chapters of Genesis feature ancient understandings of science and the origin of human history. On the right side of the chart, biblical inspiration and all types of concordism are rejected.

- A trend in theology and philosophy emerges across the table. It begins with conservative Christianity, passes through deism and Christian liberalism, and ends in atheism.

- Finally, a pattern in ethics appears. The conservative Christian categories uphold biblical ethics; deism and liberal Christianity are essentially humanistic; and atheism completely embraces secular humanism. Clearly, a relationship exists between our beliefs on origins and the way we live our lives.

The left-to-right trends in Fig 2-1 raise concern regarding the impact of science upon theology and philosophy. Christians have long been aware of the liberalization of faith in the advancing light of scientific discovery. God's action is diminished in the world, biblical authority reduced, and human nature demeaned. However, a right-to-left trend also raises concern. Biblical literalism increases and modern science is rejected. Today, many conservative Christians trained in both Scripture and science consider this second trend to be every bit as problematic as the first. Intuitively, these believers recognize that there must exist a balanced approach to biblical faith and scientific discovery.

Fig 2-1 presents important similarities within the conservative Christian origins categories. Young earth creation, progressive creation, and evolutionary creation are ultimately united by the redeeming Blood of Jesus Christ and the hope of eternal life. The chart reveals that these positions also share the following foundational Christian beliefs: the Holy Trinity, creation of the world, personal divine action, inspiration of Scripture, intelligent design, Image of God, human sin, and biblical ethics. Anyone who knows the Lord personally will agree that these are basic tenets of faith. Church history also reveals that they have formed the core of creeds and doctrines throughout the ages. Christians in the origins debate today are united in affirming the Creatorship and Lordship of the God of the Bible.

Significant differences also appear in Fig 2-1 between the conservative Christian positions on origins. Young earth creation, progressive creation, and evolutionary creation disagree with regard to:

Evolutionary Sciences. Believers differ sharply over the modern scientific disciplines that deal with origins. Young earth creationists reject cosmological, geological, and biological evolution, claiming a lack of evidence and even suggesting demonic deception for their existence. Progressive creationists accept the first two sciences but dismiss the last. Evolutionary creationists embrace fully these three modern sciences. *However, logic dictates that the scientific views of two of these three Christian origins categories are wrong.* Undoubtedly, the popular assumption that the Scriptures feature scientific concordism is the central factor controlling young earth creation and progressive creation. In contrast, evolutionary creation rejects the presupposition that there are modern scientific facts in the Bible, and it approaches the physical evidence from a purely scientific perspective.

Divine Activity in Origins. Wide differences on how God created the world exist between the conservative Christian origins categories. Young earth creationists claim that dramatic interventions were used. Progressive creationists assert that life appeared by direct miraculous acts, while the inanimate world arose indirectly through natural processes. Evolutionary creationists reject dramatic miracles in origins. They argue that God created everything by ordaining and sustaining a teleological evolutionary process. *Again, reason indicates that two of the three Christian views on origins are mistaken.* Clearly, the literal reading of God's creative action in Gen 1 and 2 is justification for the divine interventionism assumed by young earth creation and progressive creation. Stepping away from literalism, evolutionary creation claims that this dramatic creative activity in the biblical creation accounts is the origins science-of-the-day held by the inspired Hebrew writers. Christian evolutionists conclude that quick creative action producing completely formed inanimate structures and living organisms is an ancient understanding of the assembly of the world, and not God's actual creative method.

Interpretation of Genesis 1–11. Christians strongly disagree on how to interpret the opening chapters of the Bible. Young earth creationists use strict literalism. Progressive creationists employ general literalism. Evolutionary creationists assert that Genesis 1–11 offers a Divine Theology cast in an ancient conceptualization of the origin of the universe and life, including humanity. *Once more the problem emerges, two of the three Christian origins categories are in error.* Undoubtedly, the belief that Gen 1–11 features scientific and historical concordism dictates young earth creation and progressive creation. In contrast, evolutionary creation does not read these chapters with such an assumption. Instead it argues that evidence within Scripture itself points away from these two types of concordism.[29]

Human Origins. This is the most explosive origins issue between conservative Christians, and fierce disagreements arise. Together, young earth creation and progressive creation vehemently oppose human evolution. In fact, they contend that how God actually created humanity is foundational to Christian faith. Both employ a strict literal interpretation of Gen 2 and claim that human history begins with the creation of Adam and Eve. In other words, scientific and historical concordism are the controlling factors that dictate this anti-evolutionary view of human origins. Evolutionary creation rejects these concordist assumptions and accepts the evolution of humanity. It contends that the rapid creation of Adam and Eve into fully developed human beings is an ancient science of biological origins. Evolutionary creationists argue that this ancient understanding is a vessel that transports the divine revelation that men and women bear the Image of God and are sinful. This view of Scripture contends that Gen 1–11 sets the foundations for salvation, not the principles for scientific or historical discovery. In particular, the Bible opens by dealing directly with humanity's greatest problem—our sinfulness—and anticipates the hope of redemption.

Clearly, there are differences between conservative Christians over the issue of origins, and the potential exists for divisions to arise. The apostle Paul offers an insight that is applicable to this situation today. He admonishes that divisions should never appear in the Church and that our focus should always be on Christ (1 Cor 1:10–13). Details about how the Lord made the world or how He revealed Messages of Faith in Gen 1–11 must not tear believers apart. Instead, through respectful dialogue Christians with different views on origins have an opportunity to learn from one another in order to understand more fully the Books of God's Words and Works.

Finally, Fig 2-1 dispels common misconceptions held within the Church regarding born-again Christians who believe that God employed evolution to create the world. According to evolutionary creationists, it is essential in the origins debate to define categories and move beyond conflated ideas and false dichotomies. Failure to do so has led many Christians to assume:

Evolutionary creation rejects intelligent design in nature. Not true. By being trapped in the origins dichotomy, most Christians can only view evolution as a dysteleological process. Consequently, an evolved world by definition cannot reflect design. In addition, many believers conflate intelligent design with divine interventions. That is, they assume that design in nature can only be produced through God's dramatic action. However, evolutionary creationists point out that intelligent design is imparted through natural processes as seen in the embryological development of a child in the womb. Similarly, they contend that God's ordained and sustained evolutionary processes offer a natural revelation declaring His glory.

Evolutionary creation rejects personal miracles, signs, and wonders. Not true. Another popular conflation fuels this misconception. It assumes that because God intervenes dramatically in personal lives, then He must also have created the world with similar spectacular activity. Or inverting this argument, since evolutionary creationists do not believe the Creator intervenes miraculously in evolution, then He does not do so with people. Evolutionary creation underlines that a categorical distinction is vital between "God's activity in the origin of the universe and life" and "God's activity in the lives of men and women." The box outlined at the center of Fig 2-1 is the key to understanding divine action. Evolutionary creationists assert that God created the world indirectly through ordained and sustained evolutionary processes, and that the Creator acts both dramatically and subtly in the lives of people through miracles, signs, and wonders.

Evolutionary creation rejects Genesis 1–11. Not true. Conservative Christians often conflate a literal reading of the opening chapters of the Bible with obedience to God. This leads to a regrettable false dichotomy between "faithful Christians who believe in the literal Word of God" and the "unfaithful liberals who do not take God's Word seriously." Again, evolutionary creation emphasizes that the identification of categories is essential. Genesis 1–11 features Divine Theology, ancient science, ancient history, and ancient poetry. Christian evolutionists firmly uphold that the spiritual truths in these chapters are inerrant and infallible. That is, these believers defend tenaciously theological concordism. But they reject scientific and historical concordism because these biblical chapters have an ancient understanding of origins. The lines in the lower middle column of Fig 2-1 through "Interpretation of Genesis 1–11" and "Concordism in Genesis 1–11" are the keys to understanding these early chapters of Scripture. Evolutionary creationists conclude that the purpose of the Bible is to reveal God and spiritual truths, and not how He actually created the world and humanity.

Evolutionary creation rejects human spirituality. Not true. Most Christians believe that evolution reduces men and women to animals driven only by their physical instincts. This belief is again a product of the origins false dichotomy. Evolutionary creation staunchly defends that humans bear the Image of God and that everyone throughout history has sinned and fallen short of the glory of God. That is, humanity is unique, special, and radically different from every other created entity or being, including animals. Only men and women are sinners in need of redemption through the Cross of Christ.

To conclude, many misconceptions exist within conservative Christianity regarding the beliefs of born-again men and women who accept evolution. But these misrepresentations are rooted in crude dichotomies and regrettable conflations. Consequently, the definition of categories is absolutely vital in dispelling the popular misunderstandings of evolutionary creation in our churches.

CHAPTER SUMMARY

A variety of views exist today on the origin of the universe and life. People are no longer restricted to a choice between only two positions—*either* evolution driven by blind chance *or* creation in six literal days. This false dichotomy blinds the vision and entrenches the mind, leading many to understand the relationship between science and religion in terms of conflict and warfare. Instead, there are at least five basic categories on origins, providing a colorful spectrum of views with many shades—young earth creation, progressive creation, evolutionary creation, deistic evolution, and dysteleological evolution. The time has come for those both inside and outside the Church to move beyond the simplistic and misguided evolution vs. creation debate.

A number of origins positions appear within conservative Christianity. Most importantly, these believers are united by the transforming power of the Blood of the Lamb. They also firmly uphold the Creatorship,

Lordship, and worship of the Father, Son, and Holy Spirit. In other words, all Christians embrace theological concordism throughout Scripture. However, significant differences exist between young earth creation, progressive creation, and evolutionary creation regarding how God created the world and how to read Gen 1–11. It is obvious that two of these three Christian origins positions are wrong. In other words, error is being preached and taught within our churches and Christian schools. With this being the case, most will agree that it is time we examine thoroughly our beliefs about origins, and the assumptions that shape these views. In particular, our children deserve to be informed and equipped with the best scholarship built on the Book of God's Words and the Book of God's Works.

The relationship between Scripture and science is foundational in the development of a Christian view on origins. Two basic approaches exist. The anti-evolutionary positions of young earth creation and progressive creation maintain that the Holy Spirit revealed scientific facts in the Bible many generations prior to their discovery. That is, these positions uphold scientific concordism and the popular assumption within churches that "the Bible is a book of science." In contrast, evolutionary creation recognizes that Scripture has an ancient knowledge of the structure, operation, and origin of the world. Consequently, this Christian approach to origins asserts that scientific concordism is not possible because the Bible presents the science-of-the-day a few thousand years ago.

Of course, whether or not the Holy Spirit revealed modern science in Scripture can only be determined by a thorough review of God's Word. Chapter 4 presents extensive biblical evidence from passages referring to the physical world, and readers will be able to arrive at their own conclusion regarding scientific concordism. But before entering that important discussion, it is necessary to examine further the notion of divine action and the reflection of intelligent design in an evolving creation.

3

The Creator in a Designed and Evolving Creation

POPULAR MISCONCEPTIONS ABOUND BOTH inside and outside the Church regarding evolution, divine action, and intelligent design. Many assume that if life evolved, then God is not active in the world. Of course, such a belief exhibits categorical entrapment in the origins false dichotomy. It is logically possible for the God of the Bible to employ natural processes in the creation of living organisms, and also for Him to be personally involved in the lives of men and women. Another common misunderstanding is that evolution not only rejects intelligent design in nature, but even explains it away. The misguided evolution vs. creation dichotomy is again the culprit. It is well within the Creator's power to make a design-reflecting world using the mechanisms of a teleological evolution.

Evolutionary creation offers an integrated approach to understanding divine activity and intelligent design. It presents insights into the many ways through which the Creator has acted, and continues to act, in both the natural world and the daily lives of people. This view of origins also promotes a richer and more powerful conception of divine design in the structures, operations, and origins of the universe and life. By including evolutionary processes, it magnifies the argument from design for God's existence to levels never before seen in the history of the Church. Stated more precisely, evolutionary creation argues that there is an intimate relationship between divine creative action and the reflection of intelligent design in the teleological mechanisms of evolution. To the surprise of many, such a view of nature leads to a greater appreciation of the ordained and sustained character of the creation.

This chapter opens with an examination of divine action in the world. By introducing categories, it moves beyond popular views on how

God acts in origins, operations, and personal lives. The first section also deals with the charge that evolutionary creation is a form of deism, and it explains further the problem of the God-of-the-gaps. Next, an approach to understanding intelligent design is proposed. In particular, this model is built upon the biblical notion of design as revealed in Psalm 19 and Rom 1. The chapter closes by exploring the anthropic principle. This is the notion that the evolution of the universe appears to be intended for the emergence of human life. In the last fifty years, science has shown that the laws of nature are delicately balanced, giving the impression of having been finely tuned. Some anthropic evidence is offered and considered from an evolutionary creationist perspective.

DIVINE ACTION

Christians throughout history have maintained that God acts in the world. By walking with the Lord daily, we experience personally His constant presence and specific answer to prayers.* However, most believers (as well as non-believers) conflate divine action into the single and poorly defined category of "miracles." This term usually means God's direct and dramatic activity. But this popular view fails to appreciate the variety of ways through which He acts. As a result, in the origins debate most Christians can only envision creative action through spectacular and interruptive events, overlooking the possibility that the Lord could have created the world subtly through natural processes. The importance of defining categories is again clear.

Categories of Divine Action

There are two basic *contexts* in which divine action is manifested. That is, it is found in different settings or circumstances. Personal divine activity deals with God's involvement in the lives of men and women. As noted previously 40% of leading American scientists hold this belief. Cosmological divine action is the Creator's activity in both the origin of the world and its daily operations (Greek *cosmos* means "the entire universe").[1] There are also two fundamental *modes* of divine activity. In other words, it manifests in distinct ways. Interventionism involves direct and dramatic acts that break into routine events. In contrast, providentialism

---

* Readers will note the use of the personal pronoun "we." I am a charismatic Christian who has experienced numerous signs and wonders.

refers to God's activity that is indirect and subtle, and often not perceived by everyone. This method works through regular events. Combining the differing contexts and modes leads to various categories of divine action.

Personal interventionism is the Lord's action manifested dramatically in relationships with people. The Bible abounds with this type of divine activity. To mention a few well-known examples: Jesus changing water into wine (John 2:1–11), His healing of an epileptic boy (Matt 17:14–18), and His raising Lazarus from the dead (Luke 11:38–44). The spectacular and charismatic world of "signs and wonders" that include visions, prophecies, and dramatic healings, are instances of interventionism in the lives of individuals today.

Personal providentialism involves God's subtle and indirect activity in relationships with men and women. To illustrate from Scripture, His use of the Babylonians to punish the nation of Judah for her sins was not openly evident to everyone (Jer 20:4–6). Outside observers could easily interpret the fall of Jerusalem and the deportation to Babylon as just another conquest of a small country by a more powerful kingdom. Similarly, the Lord acts through believers even though He is not seen directly. As Phil 2:13 states, "It is God who works in you to will and to act according to His good purpose." Examples of this subtle divine activity today include the sense of being nudged by God, His healing of a person by medical procedures, the Holy Spirit's conviction through reading Scripture, and the common experience of coincidences that most people contend cannot be attributed to mere chance.

Cosmological interventionism refers to direct and dramatic divine action both in the past origins and the present operations of the world. This type of activity characterizes the creation of the universe and life in six literal days (young earth creation) and the introduction of living organisms at different points through the hundreds of millions of years of earth history (progressive creation).[2] It also consists of divine interventions in the daily function of the cosmos. As noted, many scientists once argued that God was responsible for retrograde motion. They believed He directly moved planets off their normal west-to-east path and made them travel brief east-to-west loops. Of course, such a view is not accepted today.

Cosmological providentialism is God's subtle and indirect activity in the origin and operation of the universe and life. It is His working through routine and uninterrupted natural processes that He ordains and sustains. Evolutionary creation exemplifies this type of divine cosmological

PERSONAL

Interventionism

God raising a dead person to life

Providentialism

God "nudging" & working through "coincidences"

COSMOLOGICAL

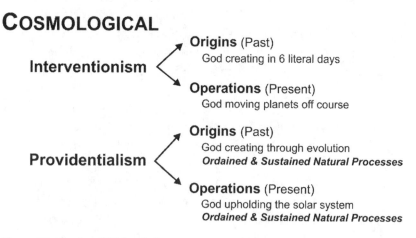

Interventionism

Origins (Past)
God creating in 6 literal days

Operations (Present)
God moving planets off course

Providentialism

Origins (Past)
God creating through evolution
Ordained & Sustained Natural Processes

Operations (Present)
God upholding the solar system
Ordained & Sustained Natural Processes

Fig 3-1. Categories of Divine Action

activity in origins. Similarly, the Lord's upholding of the solar system through astronomical mechanisms is providentialistic action in operations. The Bible affirms subtle divine action in the cosmos. As the apostle Paul stated to a crowd of non-Christians in Lystra, "The living God . . . has shown you kindness by giving you rain from heaven and crops in their seasons" (Acts 14:15, 17). Outside observers might limit the interpretation of these phenomena only to meteorological and botanical mechanisms in nature. But Christians believe that the Creator acts providentially through the natural processes that He both established and maintains in the heavens and on the earth.

Fig 3-1 outlines categories of divine action with an example for each. Clearly, there are many different ways in which to view God's activity both in the lives of people and in the origin and operation of the cosmos.[3] Similar to the views on origins presented in the last chapter, readers can combine these categories in a wide variety of ways. Like all category sets, it is an instructional framework that attempts to organize a spectrum of

	YOUNG EARTH CREATION	PROGRESSIVE CREATION	EVOLUTIONARY CREATION	DEISTIC EVOLUTION	DYSTELEOLOGICAL EVOLUTION
PERSONAL					
Interventionism	Yes	Yes	Yes	No	No
Providentialism	Yes	Yes	Yes	No	No
COSMOLOGICAL					
Interventionism					
Origins (Past)	Yes	Yes & No*	No	No	No
Operations (Present)	No	No	No	No	No
Providentialism					
Origins (Past)	No	Yes & No*	Yes	Yes**	No
Operations (Present)	Yes	Yes	Yes	No**	No

Fig 3-2. Categories of Divine Action and Origins Positions. *Progressive creation accepts interventionism in origin of living organisms and providentialism in origin of inanimate universe. **Deistic evolution only accepts ordained natural processes and rejects their sustenance.

positions, and it has limits. For example, disagreement might arise concerning when a providentialistic coincidence in someone's life becomes classified as a direct intervention by God. Nevertheless, Fig 3-1 moves away from the popular categorizing of God's activity as simply a "miracle."*

The categories of divine action shed new light on the origins debate. Fig 3-2 presents God's activity or lack thereof with the five basic origins positions outlined in chapter 2. A number of significant features and relationships emerge.

Fig 3-2 is structured on the distinction between the personal and cosmological contexts in which God acts. As noted in the previous chapter, this is the key to understanding divine activity in the origins debate. The Lord's action in personal relationships is unique to the situation and not regulated by anyone. In contrast, His daily operation in sustaining the cosmos is routine, repeatable, and predictable. Consequently, the latter is accessible to scientific investigation, while the former is not. With this being the case, the question arises: Is the Creator's activity in origins detectable by science or it is unique and beyond such analysis? More is said on this issue later.

---

* At a personal level, the type of divine action that I experience most often, nearly every day, is providentialistic. On very rare occasions, I have encountered interventionism in my life. I have yet to find evidence for cosmological interventions in origins and operations. Instead, I perceive God's activity in nature as providentialistic through His ordaining and sustaining of the creation.

Similarities and differences in divine action emerge between the origins positions. All positions reject cosmological intervention in operations. That is, none accept disruptive supernatural events as part of the daily workings in nature. Differing sharply from both deistic and atheistic evolution, the conservative Christian views on origins are united in that they embrace personal divine action. The only disagreement between believers is their understanding of divine creative action. Young earth creationists and progressive creationists believe that God intervened dramatically to create life, reflecting ultimately their acceptance of scientific concordism. But evolutionary creationists are not tied to this interpretive assumption of Scripture, and thus they are not forced to embrace cosmological interventionism in origins.

Fig 3-2 also reveals important precedents. The three Christian views of origins affirm cosmological providentialism in the present operations of the world. In other words, they believe that God acts through routine natural laws that He ordains and sustains. Consequently, young earth creationists and progressive creationists, in principle, could accept the Creator employing natural processes in the evolution of life. Moreover, all Christian positions reject divine interventionism in the daily operations of the cosmos. But in doing so, none of these believers see themselves as theologically liberal and dishonoring God, nor do they consider themselves deists. Therefore, a second precedent exists that allows anti-evolutionists to consider divine creative action without dramatic interventions, as held by evolutionary creationists.

The categories on divine action also assist in clarifying two issues often raised in the origins debate: the charge that evolutionary creation is a form of deism and the problem of the God-of-the-gaps.

Is Evolutionary Creation Deism?

The most common criticism that anti-evolutionists launch against evolutionary creation is that this view of origins is deistic. They argue that the creation of the world only through natural processes and without any direct divine intervention typifies belief in the impersonal god-of-the-philosophers. Moreover, these critics claim that if the Creator fails to act dramatically in origins, then there is no reason to believe that He intervenes personally in the lives of men and women today. Indeed, these are reasonable concerns. However, evolutionary creationists emphatically reject the distant divine being of deism.

Fig 3-2 reveals crucial differences between deism and evolutionary creation. First, evolutionary creationists embrace both personal interventionism and personal providentialism. In contrast, deists do not believe that the creator ever enters the world to be involved with people. Second, the god-of-the-philosophers only ordains the evolution of the cosmos at the beginning of time and then has nothing to do with its sustenance in the past or present. According to evolutionary creation, the Lord upholds the creation during every moment of its existence, from its evolutionary origins throughout the eons of time, right up until today in all of its operations. Clearly, a God who is intimately involved both in personal relationships and in sustaining the physical world is not the distant creator of deism.

Furthermore, evolutionary creationists are quick to point out that this so-called "deism argument" can be redirected against the anti-evolutionists. For example, no young earth creationist or progressive creationist believes that God uses dramatic interventions to create babies in the womb. Instead, they assert that the Lord fashions a child indirectly and only through natural embryological processes. But does this mean that any Christian who accepts this understanding of human development is a deist? Does the fact that science never observes a nose, ear, or arm being attached to a child *in utero* force individuals to embrace the god-of-the-philosophers? Is a Christian medical doctor who cares for pregnant women outside of God's will if he or she practices medicine with the belief that the Creator does not intervene dramatically in the normal course of embryological development? Is such a physician a deist? No, absolutely not. In the same way, Christians who believe that God created life only through the natural processes of evolution without any direct interventions are not deists either.

Of course, there is a significant difference between the creation of the world and the creation of babies. It deals with the Bible and the assumption of scientific concordism. Nowhere does Scripture state, "And God said, 'Let there be a nose attached to the face of a child in the womb.'" In contrast, Gen 1 and 2 present the Creator intervening directly and dramatically in origins. As a result, anti-evolutionists insist that spectacular events occurred in the creation of the world. However, belief in these dramatic creative events evaporates if scientific concordism is not a feature of Scripture. More specifically, if the Holy Spirit used an ancient understanding of origins as a vehicle to reveal a Divine Theology in the creation accounts, then the Bible does not disclose how God actually created the universe and life.

The accusation that evolutionary creation is a form of deism is mistaken. The God presented in Scripture is a personal God. Those holding this Christian approach to evolution defend His ordaining and sustaining activity throughout nature, both past and present. In particular, evolutionary creationists enjoy an intimate relationship with the Lord, involving His personal interventionistic and providentialistic action. The charge of deism launched by anti-evolutionists is rooted ultimately in the assumption of scientific concordism.

The God-of-the-Gaps Problem

The phrase "God-of-the-gaps" carries a negative nuance. According to this view of divine activity, the Creator is often depicted as a meddler who tinkers about at irregular times in the making and functioning of the world. As a result, gaps purportedly exist at different points in the continuum of natural processes, and these discontinuities are indicative of where God intervened directly in the cosmos. Though this approach has received much criticism, it must be underlined that the Creator can act in any way He chooses, including through cosmological interventions in origins and operations.

The God-of-the-gaps understanding of divine action is logical and reasonable. If gaps really exist in nature, then science will identify them, and they will "widen" with further research. That is, as scientists probe a "true gap" over time, physical evidence will increase and point away from natural processes accounting for the origin or operation of a physical structure. Consequently, such a gap in nature would provide scientific evidence for a supernatural intervention by God. Today, anti-evolutionists often use the God-of-the-gaps approach in biological origins. For example, they claim that natural mechanisms cannot account for the evolution of molecules into the first cell, indicating the need for direct divine action. Similarly, progressive creationists assert that the rapid appearance of nearly 100 phyla (groups of organisms with the same general body plan; e.g., chordates, which have a nerve cord in their back) in the Cambrian Explosion 550 million years ago is evidence of God's intervening hand. Notably, those leading the Intelligent Design Movement often present these two examples.[4] To be sure, modern science openly acknowledges that it does not understand all of the natural processes that led to the origin of the first cell or the abrupt appearance of the Cambrian phyla. Therefore, it is plausible that the anti-evolutionists have identified two sites of divine intervention. But the critical question arises: Does this situation indicate a *gap in nature* or a *gap in knowledge*? In other words, are the gaps actually places where God intervened in the past or are they created by a lack of information yet to be discovered by science? History offers the answer.

The God-of-the-gaps position has repeatedly fallen short. Instead of the gaps in nature getting wider with the advance of science, they have always been closed or filled by the growing body of scientific knowledge. As noted earlier, scientists once believed that God was responsible for the retrograde motion of planets. Even Isaac Newton appealed to divine intervention in order to correct "wobbles" in the orbits of Saturn and Mercury.[5] He contended that over time these irregularities would lead to the collapse of the solar system. But this was before the discovery of Uranus and its gravitational pull on the former planet, and prior to the theory of relativity to explain the latter. As well, it is now known that these wobbles are self-correcting. Similarly, only 200 years ago some of the best scientists claimed that numerous catastrophic floods caused features on the surface of the earth, with Noah's deluge being the last. Yet again, this was before the principles of geology were fully known. For example, it was once thought that massive floods scattered large boulders, termed "erratic rocks," across certain plains. But now it is known that these were carried there by glaciers, which had flattened the surface of the region and then melted.[6] In light of this historical trend, it seems clear that gaps in scientific knowledge undergird the anti-evolutionary claims that God intervened dramatically in the origin of the first cell and the Cambrian phyla.

A dangerous practical problem emerges with the God-of-the-gaps approach to nature. It disrupts and even destroys science. Imagine the implications for medical research. If one asserts that direct divine intervention causes AIDS, Asian bird flu, or mad cow disease, then there is no reason in trying to understand the natural processes through which these diseases arose. The respective viruses would run rampant through society and health authorities would not have any justification to do research on monkeys from Africa, destroy chicken farms in Asia, or block the entrance of cattle into the United States. This is also the problem with the God-of-the-gaps models of anti-evolutionists today. Making bold claims that the Creator intervened to form the first cell or Cambrian phyla arrest immediately any research into the natural processes that led to their origin. Stated another way, if God created through an uninterrupted evolutionary process, then human ignorance closes the Book of Nature and barricades scientists from discovering His creative method.

Of course, the central factor supporting the God-of-the-gaps is the assumption of scientific concordism. Genesis 1 states ten times that living organisms were created "according to their/its kinds." Consequently, anti-evolutionists need to find discontinuities in the continuum of life in order to define these basic groupings, sometimes called "created kinds" or "baramins" (Hebrew *bārā'* means "to create" and *min* "kind"). But once more, if the Holy Spirit did not reveal modern science in Scripture many generations prior to its discovery, then the God-of-the-gaps belief vaporizes. This misuse of the Bible can be illustrated in another way. The New Testament often states that demons cause epilepsy, blindness, deafness, muteness, and crippled backs.* If this is the case, does it mean that Christian medical researchers are wasting their time in attempting to understand the natural mechanisms behind these afflictions? Of course, hardly anyone believes this. But it shows the problem of assuming that the Bible is scientifically concordant and of using Scripture in medical science today. So too in origins. If Gen 1 employs an ancient origins science, then God-of-the-gaps models based on scientific concordism are unfounded.

To summarize, evolutionary creationists claim that God acts in the world in a variety of ways. As a loving Father, He reserves direct and dramatic interventions for personal relationships in order to admonish, call, and encourage us. The Lord also acts in subtle providentialistic ways with men and women. As the Ordainer and Sustainer of the cosmos, the Creator did not intervene in origins nor does He act dramatically in operations. This is not to assert that it is outside His power, but rather to state that this is His will. Thus, evolutionary creation is not deism. In addition, this Christian view of origins rejects the God-of-the-gaps. Liberated from the assumption of scientific concordism and the cosmological interventionism in origins that this interpretive approach dictates, evolutionary creationists read the Book of Nature unencumbered in its God-glorifying splendor and purity.

---

* This is not to dismiss the reality of demonic activity. It is only to point out the problem with scientific concordism. The topic of demons and ancient medicine is further discussed on pages 142–46; see also footnote on page 145.

INTELLIGENT DESIGN

The belief that nature reflects intelligent design appears widely throughout history. The beauty, complexity, and functionality of the cosmos have deeply impacted most people and led them to conclude that these features mirror a rational mind and point to a Creator. This idea is not uniquely Christian. It transcends religions and philosophies, times and cultures, even intellectual abilities and educational backgrounds. Design in nature has been proclaimed in the past by inspired Hebrew psalmists and ancient Greek philosophers, and in the present by leading physicists and anyone who enjoys looking up at the starry heavens. The argument from design is one of the most powerful defenses for the existence of God. In order to appreciate the notion of intelligent design, it is necessary to define categories on how the Lord reveals Himself to the world.

Categories of Divine Revelation

Traditional Christian doctrine asserts that God manifests Himself through design in nature. Often referred to as "natural revelation" (or natural theology), this is a category of "general revelation" because everyone experiences it and it offers a broad outline of the Creator's character. Notably, this type of divine disclosure is *non-verbal*. That is, no actual words are used. Instead, it employs the beauty, complexity, and functionality of the world to reveal general attributes of an Intelligent Designer (Ps 19:1–4; Rom 1:18–23). General revelation also includes "moral revelation." Frequently referred to as our conscience, this is a revelation that has been "written on the human heart" (Rom 2:14–15) to guide men and women in their daily lives.

In contrast, "special revelation" is more specific, and it is directed at individuals and God's chosen people. The greatest divine revelatory act is the Incarnation. God became a man in the person of Jesus to reveal Himself both through words and actions. As the gospel of John proclaims, "The Word was God . . . The Word became flesh and lived for a while among us" (John 1:1, 14). Special revelation also includes "biblical revelation." In particular, it is *verbal*. Scripture features "the very words of God" (Rom 3:2) and is "God-breathed" (1 Tim 3:16) because its authors "were carried along by the Holy Spirit" (1 Pet 1:21). It reveals precise information regarding the Creator's personal attributes and His will. As well, Christians assert that the Bible is the authority on all matters of faith

GENERAL
Natural Revelation (Natural Theology)
Nature reflects the Creator
Moral Revelation
Conscience & law written on the human heart

SPECIAL
Incarnation
The Word was God & became Flesh
Biblical Revelation
Very words of God breathed by the Holy Spirit
Personal Revelation
Prayer, providential incidents, signs & wonders

Fig 3-3. Categories of Divine Revelation

and morality. Personal revelation is also a form of special revelation in which the Lord discloses Himself and His will specifically to individuals through prayer, providential incidents, and signs and wonders (Acts 18:9; Gal 2:2; Heb 2:4). Fig 3-3 outlines the categories of divine revelation.

In recognizing that God is revealed both through the creation and the Bible, Christians have often depicted these disclosures as Two Divine Books.[7] The Book of God's Works offers a non-verbal, but discernible, general outline of His character as reflected by intelligent design in the cosmos. Through scientific investigation, greater and more amazing manifestations of the Creator's glory, power, and divinity have been discovered in the things He has made (Ps 19:1–4; Rom 1:18–23). In other words, the argument from design for God's existence is strengthened as scientists probe deeper into nature through microscopes and telescopes.

The Book of God's Words provides a verbal and specific revelation of the Intelligent Designer's personal attributes not offered through nature. In particular, the inspired writings of the Bible disclose that God is Holy (Rev 4:8, 15:4) and that He is Love (1 John 4:8, 16). He is also a just (Isa 30:18; 2 Thess 1:6) and merciful God (Deut 4:31; Dan 9:9). Through theological study, Scripture further presents the mystery that the Creator of the world and the Author of the Bible is a Trinity of the Father, the Son, and the Holy Spirit. Thus, in a complementary fashion, God's Works and Words reveal to men and women their Maker. Fig 3-4 presents the Two Divine Books Model.

BOOK OF GOD'S WORKS

Non-Verbal Revelation
Does not use words

Intelligent Design in Nature
Beauty, complexity & functionality

General Attributes of God
Glory, eternal power & divine nature

Studied by Science
Argument from design for God's existence

BOOK OF GOD'S WORDS

Verbal Revelation
Uses words

Inspired Writings of the Bible
Very words of God breathed by the Holy Spirit

Specific Attributes of God
Holy, love, just & merciful

Studied by Theology
God is a Trinity of Father, Son & Holy Spirit

Fig 3-4. Two Divine Books Model

In light of these categories on divine revelation, this chapter now turns to present a view of intelligent design that is consistent with the biblical and traditional notion of design held throughout Church history. It opens by examining the main scriptural passages affirming design in nature, then proposes a model to understand the character and limits of this non-verbal revelation, and closes with an evolutionary creationist approach to intelligent design.

Biblical Support for Intelligent Design: Psalm 19 and Romans 1

Scripture affirms that intelligent design is real and that humans have the ability to understand this revelation inscribed deeply into the Book of Nature. The classic biblical evidence supporting the notion of design appears in Ps 19:1–4 and Rom 1:18–23.[8] Together, these passages assert that an intelligible, non-verbal, and divine revelation exists in the creation; that this disclosure points to God, revealing some of His general attributes; and that humanity is accountable to the Creator with regard to the implications of this natural revelation.

In Ps 19:1–4, the psalmist records:

1 The heavens declare the glory of God;
the skies proclaim the work of His hands.
2 Day after day they pour forth speech;
night after night they display knowledge.
3 There is no speech or language
where their voice is not heard.
4 Their voice goes out into all the earth,
their words to the ends of the world.

This passage identifies five features of natural revelation: (1) The creation is *active*. The repeated use of active verbs in the psalm underlines this aspect of the world. The heavens "declare," the skies "proclaim," both "pour forth" and "display," and their voice "goes out." (2) This activity flowing from nature is *intelligible*. Employing many metaphors, the revelation is characterized by terms associated with intelligent communication: "speech," "language," "knowledge," "voice," and "words." (3) The creation's message is *incessant*. It is heard constantly "day after day" and "night after night" throughout time. (4) This cosmic revelation is *universal*. Like music, "there is no speech or language where their voice is not heard," and it travels "into all the earth" and "to the ends of the world." By being non-verbal, everyone understands this disclosure in the creation. (5) The message engraved into the cosmos is *divine* or *transcendent* in character. It "declares the glory of God" and "proclaims the work of his hands."

Romans 1:18–23 affirms the five features of natural revelation presented in Ps 19:1–4. The apostle Paul records:

18 The wrath of God is being revealed from heaven against all the godlessness and wickedness of men who suppress the truth by their wickedness, 19 since what may be known about God is plain to them, because God has made it plain to them. 20 For since the creation of the world God's invisible qualities—his eternal power and divine nature—have been clearly seen, being understood from what has been made, so that men are without excuse. 21 For although they knew God, they neither glorified him as God nor gave thanks to him, but their thinking became futile and their foolish hearts were darkened. 22 Although they claimed to be wise, they became fools and 23 exchanged the glory of the immortal God for images made to look like mortal man and birds and animals and reptiles.

The parallels to Ps 19 in this passage are evident: (1) The creation is *active*. The revelatory impact of "what has been made" is such that men and women are accountable before God. (2) This activity arising from nature is *intelligible*. It is described using verbs associated with intelligent communication, such as "known," "seen," and "understood." (3) The creation's message is *incessant*. It has flowed out ever "since the creation of the world." (4) This cosmic revelation is *universal*. Non-verbal knowledge has been "made plain" in order to be "clearly seen" by everyone "so that men are without excuse." (5) The message written deeply into the cosmos is *divine* or *transcendent* in character. In particular, the creation reveals "God's invisible qualities—His eternal power and divine nature."

However, Paul in Rom 1 goes further than the psalmist and introduces a sixth feature of natural revelation—the creation *judges*. The clear and intelligible message in nature makes humanity accountable and "without excuse" regarding its profound consequence. Accordingly, there is no justification for "godlessness and wickedness" since the creation is a constant witness declaring the existence of an eternal, powerful, and divine Creator. Yet, this inexcusability implies that people are free to ignore the message in nature. Like the gospel of Jesus in the Book of God's Words, the natural revelation in the Book of God's Works is not forced upon men and women. They can reject it if they so choose.

Romans 1:21–23 presents humanity's fundamental sin—transgression of the First Commandment ("You shall have no other gods before me," Exod 20:3; Deut 5:7). This divine decree assumes the existence of God, meaning that men and women have a knowledge of Him, but amazingly they rebel. The breaking of the First Commandment leads to idolatry and violation of the Second Commandment ("You shall not make yourself an idol in the form of anything in the heaven above or on the earth beneath or in the waters below," Exod 20:5; Deut 5:8). The apostle Paul recognizes this spiritual situation in Rom 1. He notes that even godless and wicked individuals "knew God," but "they neither glorified him as God nor gave thanks to him." For that matter, "they did not think it worthwhile to retain the knowledge of God" (Rom 1:28). As a result, these people fell into idolatry and "worshipped and served created things" (v. 25).

Paul also underlines a critical intellectual-spiritual relationship in Rom 1. The pursuit of ultimate Truth is intimately connected to the spiritual state of an individual. Violation of the First and Second Commandments impacts the human ability to think. By "exchanging the glory of the immortal God for images made to look like mortal man and birds and animals and reptiles," people "became fools" even though "they claimed to be wise." Consequently, "their thinking became futile and their foolish hearts were darkened."[9] Paul bluntly concludes, "they exchanged the truth of God for a lie" (Rom 1:25). When God is not glorified or thanked, the clear and plain knowledge about Him revealed in nature can be substituted for a falsehood. In other words, sin impacts our ability to think.

Wisdom of Solomon 13:1–9 in the apocrypha complements the features presented on natural revelation in Ps 19 and Rom 1. Throughout most of Church history, the apocryphal books of the Bible have edified believers by offering insights into the Old and New Testament.[10] The author writes:

> 1 For all people who were ignorant of God were foolish by nature; and they were unable from the good things that are seen to know the one who exists, nor did they recognize the Artisan while paying heed to His works;

> 2 but they supposed that either fire or wind or swift air, or the circle of stars, or turbulent water, or the luminaries of heaven were the gods that rule the world.

> 3 If through delight in the beauty of these things people assumed them to be gods, let them know how much better than these is their Lord, for the Author of beauty created them.

> 4 And if people were amazed at their power and working, let them perceive from them how much more powerful is the One who formed them.

> 5 For from the greatness and beauty of created things comes a corresponding perception of their Creator.

> 6 Yet these people are little to be blamed, for perhaps they go astray while seeking God and desiring to find him.

> 7 For while they live among His works, they keep searching, and they trust in what they see, because the things that are seen are beautiful.

> 8 Yet again, not even they are to be excused.

> 9 For if they had the power to know so much that they could investigate the world, how did they fail to find sooner the Lord of these things?

Wisdom 13 not only aligns with Ps 19 and Rom 1, but it sharpens and heightens our understanding of natural revelation. This passage includes four specific references to beauty in nature as a revelatory characteristic (v. 3 twice, 4 and 7). The problem with idolatry again appears, as does human inexcusability with regard to grasping the implications of the non-verbal disclosure in the world. And verse 9 offers a pointed indictment that is applicable to twenty-first century scientists who embrace a dysteleological worldview. If they have the power to open and investigate the cell, why have they not all found the Lord who created proteins and DNA?

In sum, Ps 19 and Rom 1 testify to the reality that the universe reflects intelligent design to everyone, everywhere, and in every generation. These passages also reveal that humanity has the ability to know this non-verbal message inscribed in nature and to understand its spiritual implications. In other words, natural revelation is sufficient and humans are proficient in discerning its meaning. The scriptural view of intelligent design does not indicate how this non-verbal revelation arises in the world. In particular, Ps 19 and Rom 1 do not reveal the *origin* of design by stating that it was imparted through acts of divine intervention.[11] Rather, the biblical understanding of intelligent design emphasizes only the *reality* of divine design in nature and its powerful *impact* on men and women.

Toward an Intelligent Design Model

Proposing a model for intelligent design begins with a complementary vision of the relationship between science and religion. It moves beyond the so-called warfare perceived by many people and recognizes the fundamental differences between these two methods of understanding reality. In this way, scientific discovery and religious faith fulfill each other and contribute to a model of design that respects the intentions and limits of God's Two Divine Books.

Science deals with the physical world. It investigates the structure, operation, and origin of the universe and life. Through observations and experiments, scientists advance theories and establish laws to describe *what* nature is made of and *how* it works. Science focuses on natural causes. In contrast, religion and philosophy examine the ultimate meaning of the world. These disciplines deal with the deepest questions humans have ever asked: *Why* does the world exist? *Who* or *what* is behind the universe, if anyone or anything? Is the cosmos teleological or

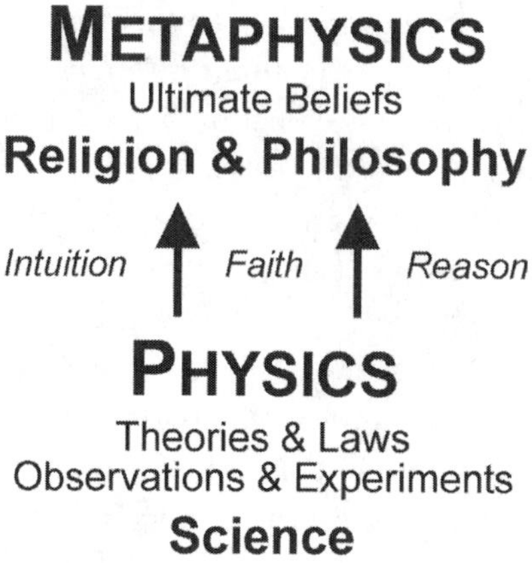

METAPHYSICS
Ultimate Beliefs
Religion & Philosophy

Intuition ↑ *Faith* ↑ *Reason*

PHYSICS
Theories & Laws
Observations & Experiments
Science

Fig 3-5. Metaphysics-Physics Principle

dysteleological? Religion and philosophy concentrate on ultimate or final causes. Employing terms derived from Greek, science investigates *phusis*, which translated literally means "nature," and from which are derived the English words "physics" and "physical." Religion and philosophy explore *metaphusis* or metaphysics. The Greek preposition *meta* means "behind," "beyond," and "after." Thus, metaphysics investigates the reality behind or beyond the physical world after it has been studied.

Fig 3-5 presents the Metaphysics-Physics Principle and depicts the intimate relationship between science and religion/philosophy. In the lower compartment, science offers vast and wonderful knowledge about the physical world. But it is dead silent with regard to the ultimate meaning of nature. For example, there is no scientific instrument that can detect whether the cosmos is teleological or dysteleological. Such a topic is metaphysical and dealt with only in religion and philosophy as depicted in the upper compartment of the diagram. However, theologians and philosophers depend on science in coming to their beliefs. They need facts about the world before they can decide on its utmost meaning. Stated concisely, metaphysics requires physics.

To arrive at an ultimate understanding of the world involves a *metaphysical jump* upward from the scientific data.[12] This is not a strict logical process like mathematics. In fact, there is no mathematical formula to move from physics to metaphysics. Of course, the jump does involve reason, a logically thought-out process that is objective in character. But it also includes intuition, an immediate impression that is more subjective.

Together, reason and intuition contribute to faith, and together these intellectual-spiritual processes lead to an ultimate belief regarding the findings of science. Indeed, this jump may legitimately be called a *leap of faith* because that is exactly what it is. To use the biblical definition, "Faith is being sure of what we hope for and certain of what we do not see" (Heb 11:1). No one today can prove the metaphysical status of the physical world with absolute and total certainty. It is a belief. And everyone makes this metaphysical jump, whether they are aware of it or not, and whether they are religious or not. In other words, we are all believers in some sort of ultimate reality.

The living cell provides an example with which to explore the Metaphysics-Physics Principle and to begin outlining an intelligent design model. Science reveals that the diameter of an average cell is about 1/1000th of an inch. If placed on the tip of a pin, the naked eye cannot see it. In the cell, about 1 yard of DNA is tightly coiled into a number of chromosomes. The information encoded in this genetic material of just one cell is approximately equivalent to that of a 30-volume encyclopedia. This is standard scientific data and no scientist, whether religious or not, denies these physical facts of biology. In fact, all professional biologists acknowledge the incredible beauty, complexity, and functionality of this basic unit of living organisms. Such information characterizes knowledge in the lower compartment of Fig 3-5.

However, when religious and non-religious scientists consider the ultimate meaning of this biological data, they come to completely opposing metaphysical beliefs. In jumping from the physical evidence to the upper compartment of religion and philosophy, religious believers argue that the cell's elegance, intricacy, and efficiency reflect intelligent design. That is, their reason and intuition lead them to the belief that the cell ultimately features teleology and points to an Intelligent Designer. In contrast, non-religious scientists assessing the identical biological facts acknowledge these physical features of the cell, but they jump to the belief that this data only offers *apparent* or *non-intelligent* design, giving nothing but an illusion of teleology. In other words, these individuals have faith that this scientific data is ultimately dysteleological.

Of course, the question immediately arises: How is this radical difference in assessing the metaphysical character of a cell accounted for between religious and non-religious scientists? Clearly, a powerful and determinative factor beyond simple logic is operating because both groups agree on the use of logic. After all, it led them to the identical physical facts about the cell. *The defining factor operative in the "metaphysical jump" from the scientific data to the assessment of this data's ultimate meaning is spiritual—it deals directly with the impact of sin on the human mind.* As the apostle Paul states in Rom 1, the knowledge of natural revelation is intimately connected to an individual's relationship with God. Violation of the First Commandment and falling into the sin of idolatry results in intellectual dysfunction. Therefore, it is not surprising that the reflection of intelligent design revealed by science would be disregarded, perverted, or rationalized away by those not wanting to acknowledge the Creator's existence and their accountability to Him.

In order to appreciate further this intellectual-spiritual dynamic, it is necessary to introduce some basic categories of knowledge. Scientific knowledge is limited to the physical world and characterized by principles of logic such as: *Correspondence*—ideas have to match external physical reality, *Coherence*—knowledge needs to be internally consistent without contradictions, and *Consilience*—concepts must interconnect into an integrated theory. Scientific knowledge is mathematical and impersonal. Consequently, the spiritual state of an individual has little to no impact on science. Competent application of the categories of correspondence, coherence, and consilience in the investigation of the natural world will invariably lead to the same physical conclusions about the world. As noted, religious and non-religious scientists discover the identical scientific facts about the cell.

In contrast, religious knowledge is metaphysical and beyond the detection of scientific instruments. It is also deeply personal and dependent on the spiritual state of individuals and their relationship with God. Categories of religious knowledge include: *Divine Foundation*—knowledge is ultimately rooted in God. As Prov 1:7 states, "The fear of the Lord is the beginning of knowledge." *Mystery*—some ideas and concepts are beyond the grasp of the human mind. In 1 Cor 13:9–12, Paul recognizes the creaturely limits of our thinking, because in this present existence "we see but a poor reflection . . . and we know in part." *Impact of Sin*—ingratitude, rebelliousness, and self-sufficiency in hardened human hearts are determinative in coming to spiritual falsehoods and unbelief. As Rom 1:21–23 reveals, the sin of idolatry and failure to be thankful to the Creator leads to futile thinking. Therefore, those scientists not wanting to acknowledge God will certainly disregard the non-verbal revelation engraved in the cell and the notion of intelligent design. But ignoring the Lord results in intellectual dysfunction and insufficient knowledge. Instead, a complete worldview requires the complementary use of both scientific and religious knowledge categories.

In light of these categories and the Metaphysics-Physics Principle, it is possible to propose a model of intelligent design. It features two interacting parameters. The first involves the nature of design, while the second deals with the human ability to know this non-verbal revelation. Using philosophical terms, the former is the *ontological parameter of intelligent design*. The term "ontology" derives from the Greek participle of the verb "to be" (*ontos*), and it refers to the ultimate essence of being. That is, what something is at its deepest and final level. The latter is the *epistemological parameter of intelligent design*. The word "epistemology" comes from the Greek noun for "knowledge" (*epistēmē*), and it deals with human knowledge and the level of certainty.

The ontological design parameter focuses on the ultimate nature of intelligent design. First, it examines the integrity of design—whether it is real or only an illusion. Nearly everyone throughout history has affirmed its reality. Second, this parameter describes the characteristics of design that are manifested across a range. At one end, it recognizes the engineered features in the universe. That is, nature is constructed like an intricate and finely tuned instrument, displaying complexity and functionality. An appreciation of this aspect of design has been dramatically magnified with the advance of science. As scientists probe deeper into nature, an internal mechanical rationality becomes more and more obvious. In particular, the mathematical essence of the cosmos is most evident, and points ultimately toward an amazingly logical Mind. At the other end of the ontological design parameter, the universe features an artistic character. Like a splendid sculpture or a moving musical piece, nature's beauty and harmony impacts humanity intuitively in an impressionistic manner. Encountering the world daily through five physical senses displays an ingrained aesthetic rationality. Fig 3-6 presents the ontological parameter of design.[13]

The epistemological parameter of design deals with the ability to know intelligent design in nature. First, it considers the integrity of human knowledge with regard to design—whether it is trustworthy or not. Most people in every generation have believed that the mind is dependable and can truly know this non-verbal revelation. Second, this parameter deals

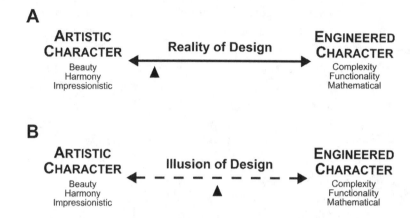

Fig 3-6. **Ontological Parameter of Intelligent Design.** The solid line in A indicates that design is real and reflects intelligence and a creative Mind. The triangle below the line exemplifies a view of design that is more aesthetic in character. The dash line in B signifies that design is only an illusion. The position of the triangle in the middle between the artistic and engineered poles indicates that the illusory experience of design is a balance between these characteristics.

with the level of certitude in recognizing design and in understanding its implications. It also exhibits a range. At one extreme, the engineered and artistic character of the world are claimed to be *proof* for design and a Designer with a level of certainty similar to that of a mathematical formula. At the other extreme, these characteristics in nature are deemed *inert* and to have no impact whatsoever. Between these epistemological boundaries, varying levels of certitude exist. Some suggest that beauty, complexity, and functionality provide a legitimate *argument* for intelligent design. Others maintain these features are only *suggestive* of its existence. A few assert that the universe's artistic and engineered characteristics are simply *consistent* with design, but no more. Fig 3-7 depicts the epistemological parameter of design.

Most importantly, the model of intelligent design that I am proposing recognizes the impact of sin on human thinking.[14] To be sure, this is a controversial notion. But as noted previously, it is rooted deeply in Scripture. The epistemological impact of sin is also a central concept in Christian tradition.[15] At worst it leads to "a depraved mind" that is completely opposed to ultimate Truth (Rom 1:28; 2 Tim 3:8–9). In refusing to acknowledge God, religious skeptics need to concoct "reasons" to explain away the powerful impact of intelligent design in order to maintain their

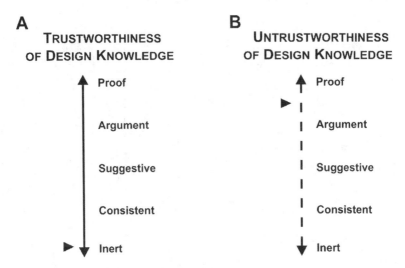

Fig 3-7. **Epistemological Parameter of Intelligent Design.** The solid line in **A** indicates that the human mind is capable of recognizing intelligent design in nature should it exist. The position of the triangle presents a rare example of an individual who claims the physical world has no impact whatsoever. The dash line in **B** signifies that the mind is not trustworthy and that it fools most people into believing that beauty, complexity and functionality are powerful evidence for intelligent design as depicted by the position of the triangle.

own psychological stability and comfort. However, the Bible affirms the sufficiency of the non-verbal revelation in nature, and the proficiency of the human mind to understand it fully, if used judiciously. I contend that a fair and honest assessment of the character of the physical world leads to the truths that design is real and that it reflects general characteristics of an Intelligent Designer.

Changing the intersection between the two design parameters produces a spectrum of intelligent design interpretations. This variability reflects differences in natural abilities, education, and spirituality. For example, believers in design who are trained and gifted in science and engineering tend to shift the ontological design parameter toward complexity and functionality (e.g., emphasis on machine-like features in the cell). As well, they often raise the epistemological certitude of design and claim it to be a proof for God's existence (Fig 3-8 A).[16] The spiritual state of an individual also shapes his or her view of design. Most skeptics acknowledge the powerful experience of nature's *apparent* artistic and engineered characteristics. But wanting nothing to do with God, they are quick to dismiss both

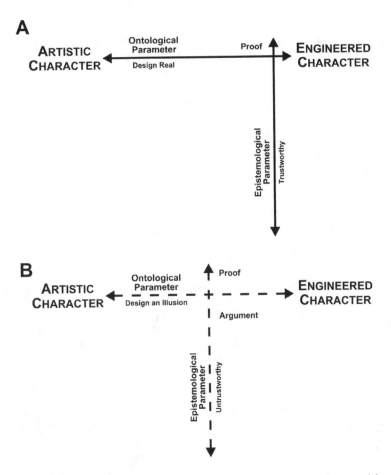

Fig 3-8. **Intelligent Design Interpretations.** Example A focuses on complexity and functionality in nature and asserts that these characteristics prove the reality of intelligent design. Skeptics claim design is only an illusion. They acknowledge the powerful impact of the apparent artistic and engineered features in the world, but assert that the mind fools most people into believing this experience is indicative of design and a Designer, as presented in example **B**.

the ontological reality of design and the epistemological trustworthiness of the human mind to assess the metaphysical implications of the amazing beauty, complexity, and functionality in the world (Fig 3-8 B).[17] In other words, non-believers state that design is "nothing but" an illusion concocted in the mind.

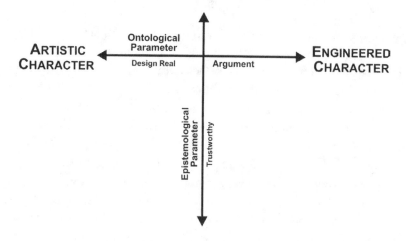

Fig 3-9. Evolutionary Creationist Approach to Intelligent Design. This interpretation affirms both the reality of intelligent design and the balance between artistic and engineered characteristics in nature. It also asserts that these features in the world provide a powerful argument for the existence of a Designer and that humans are accountable for understanding the implications of this evidence.

An Evolutionary Creationist Approach to Intelligent Design

Fig 3-9 presents intelligent design from the perspective of evolutionary creation. This approach argues for the reality of design in nature and recognizes a balanced ontological parameter. For example, beauty and harmony frequently appear in engineered structures, and complexity and mathematical symmetry are seen in art. Physicists often refer to the elegance of a mathematical formula describing the cosmos. For that matter, some of these scientists even consider the aesthetic aspect of a theory as a criterion in determining its truth value.[18] Similarly, the delightful harmonies and rhythms of a musical piece have an underlying logic that is quantifiable. Even visually pleasing bodies feature a proportionality that is identifiable through mathematics. As a result, the engineered and artistic characteristics of intelligent design are complementary reflections of the mind of God.

Evolutionary creation also affirms the trustworthiness of human ability to know intelligent design in nature and to understand its implications. This position contends that the epistemological design parameter operates at the certitude level of an *argument*. Four reasons support this assertion:

First, the notion that nature's artistic and engineered features are proof for intelligent design fails to recognize the Metaphysics-Physics Principle. It overlooks the fact that there is an intellectual-spiritual jump from the physical evidence to its metaphysical assessment. In fact, there is no formula to prove with mathematical certainty the existence of design from the characteristics of the cosmos. The belief in the proof of design overstates the epistemological certitude of the non-verbal revelation written into the creation.

Second, the idea that design in the world is only suggestive of, consistent with, or inert disregards the biblical evidence. Psalm 19 and Rom 1 state that the creation actively and incessantly reveals an intelligible and universally understandable message that points to a divine reality. Moreover, these epistemological positions fail to recognize human experience throughout history. Every generation has been powerfully impacted by nature, and almost everyone has accepted that it affirms the existence of an Intelligent Designer.[19] Of course, whether an individual develops a personal relationship with this Being is another issue. Claims that the cosmos reflects little to no design understate the epistemological certainty of natural revelation.

Third, the Bible asserts that the designed character of the world is evident to every person, and that this non-verbal revelation in nature is a powerful argument against a godless worldview. As Rom 1:20 states, "For since the creation of the world God's invisible qualities—His eternal power and divine nature—have been clearly seen, being understood from what has been made, so that men are without excuse." The judgmental tone of this verse is obvious. It is also reflected in the Greek term *anapologētos*, which appears in ancient legal documents and means without a defense.[20] Thus, natural revelation is within the intellectual grasp of humans in such a way that we are all accountable for its identification and implications. To use a modern legal category, the manifestation of intelligent design in the universe is beyond a reasonable doubt.

Finally, Scripture affirms the impact of sin on human thinking, and this spiritual factor is operative only if intelligent design functions at the certitude level of an argument. On the one hand, should recognizing design in nature be provable like a mathematical formula, then sin could not be a determinative factor. For that matter, such an approach eliminates the need for faith, and it degrades human freedom in the development of a personal relationship with God. In other words, belief in design and a Creator is not simply an intellectual exercise. On the other hand, if intelligent design were only suggestive, consistent, or inert, then humanity could hardly be held accountable for rejecting it, and ultimately God. Again, Rom 1:20 clearly states that everyone is "without excuse" if they spurn natural revelation. Evolutionary creation concludes that intelligent design in nature is knowable by all men and women to the certainty level of an argument. This knowledge is neither absolutely certain nor merely arbitrary. Rather, everyone is responsible for dealing with design and its consequences.

In light of the ontological and epistemological design parameters, evolutionary creation underlines the intellectual-spiritual dynamic of intelligent design. It recognizes the metaphysical jump from the physical features in nature to their philosophical and religious assessment. However, this is not a blind leap of faith because science and logic are factors informing this decision. Yet this dynamic also acknowledges the impact of sin on the jump to assess the artistic and engineered characteristics of the world. In particular, the human inclination to break the First and Second Commandments are determinative factors in rejecting design and its implications. It must be emphasized that idolatry is not limited to only "images made to look like mortal man and birds and animals and reptiles" (Rom 1:23). Idols are anything or anyone that are worshipped in place of God—money, careers, lifestyles, and even oneself. But according to the Bible, there is no excuse for rejecting the argument from design and falling into idolatry.

The notion that nature reflects intelligent design is indeed controversial, and some say problematic. Its implications are deeply personal. Whether consciously or subconsciously, everyone knows where it logically leads: if design is real, it points to a Designer and affirms Creatorship, and then it invites a relationship that recognizes Lordship and requires worship. The problem with design in nature is that it has a convicting message. It thrusts men and women at the feet of their Creator and calls them to accountability. It forces humans into their proper place in the cosmos—that of creatures before God. The reality of intelligent design brings us face-to-face with the First and Second Commandments. In so doing, the Book of God's Works demands profound changes in how men and women lead their lives.

It must be pointed out that evolutionary creation offers an expanded and more robust approach to intelligent design than that of the anti-evolutionary positions. Of course, this view of origins acknowledges design in the present structures and operations of the cosmos as do young earth creation and progressive creation. For example, consider the most complex structure known—our brain with its neurons (brain cells) and synapses (connections between these cells):

> [T]he human brain, with a volume of roughly a quart, encompasses a space of conceptual and cognitive possibilities that is larger, by one measure at least, than the entire astronomical universe. It has this striking feature because it exploits the combinatorics of its 100 billion neurons and their 100 trillion synaptic connections with each other. . . . If we assume, conservatively, that each synaptic connection might have any one of ten different strengths, then the total number of distinct possible configurations of synaptic weights that the brain might assume is, very roughly, ten raised to the 100 trillionth power, or $10^{100,000,000,000,000}$. Compare this with the measure of only 10^{87} cubic meters standardly estimated for the volume of the entire astronomical universe.[21]

The brain is an electrical circuitry marvel, and incredibly it arises from only one fertilized egg! The structure, function, and embryological development of this organ offer a breathtaking level of elegant complexity that few deny reflects the work of an Intelligent Designer. In other words, all the Christian origins positions embrace the *structural-operational intelligent design argument.*

But evolutionary creationists argue that design is also expressed in the natural processes and mechanisms of evolution. This component of the design argument appeals to more physical evidence than the anti-evolutionists. Moreover, it firmly rejects the notion that the introduction of design in nature necessitates acts of divine intervention in origins. Accordingly, biological complexity does not need to be imparted in "one fell swoop" as claimed by young earth creationists and progressive creationists.[22] Instead, the *evolutionary intelligent design argument* underlines the foresight, majesty, and rationality mirrored in the natural processes that created the universe and life through eons of time. In this way, the declaration of God's glory extends to the self-assembling character of the physical world. Design is evident in the finely tuned physical laws reflected in the processes necessary for life to evolve, including humans. In particular, intelligent design is obvious in the evolution of incredibly complex brains that allow men and women to relate to one another and to their Creator.

In sum, evolutionary creation presents an ontologically balanced model of intelligent design that is epistemologically rooted in human accountability before God. It affirms both the *sufficiency* of natural revelation and the *proficiency* of men and women to understand the non-verbal Message written into nature. This approach to design is consistent with Christian tradition and is based firmly upon the Bible. Evolutionary creationists view modern science as a gift from God and contend that as scientists probe deeper into the physical world, greater and more magnificent revelations of the Creator's glory, power, and divinity will emerge. This origins position asserts that the evolutionary sciences are also a divine blessing. Evolutionary creation predicts that as these disciplines advance, discoveries will reveal a design-reflecting world that features unimaginably more planning and splendor than previously believed in earlier generations.

THE ANTHROPIC PRINCIPLE

The anthropic principle asserts that evolutionary processes seem to be fashioned in such a way that they inevitably led to the origin of humanity (Greek *anthrōpos* means "man, human being"). Physicists studying the Big Bang in the 1950s first coined the term. They discovered that the fundamental laws of nature are so delicately balanced that any minor changes would not have allowed the universe and life to evolve. For some scientists, this evidence of a finely tuned cosmos points to the existence of an Intelligent Designer. The fact that data supportive of this concept comes from scientific disciplines in institutions with no religious affiliations speaks powerfully for its reality. As science probes deeper into nature, greater manifestations of exquisitely designed evolutionary processes are revealed. From its very first moments, the physical world appears to be set up in order to produce an environment that is suitable for human beings.

In their classic work, *The Anthropic Cosmological Principle* (1986), John Barrow and Frank Tippler comment on the significant implication of this scientific research:

> Over many years there had grown up a collection of largely unpublished results revealing a series of *mysterious coincidences* between the numerical values of the fundamental constants of Nature. The

possibility of our existence seems to hinge precariously upon these *coincidences*. These relationships and many other peculiar aspects of the Universe's make-up appear to be necessary to allow the evolution of carbon-based organisms like ourselves. Furthermore, the twentieth-century dogma that human observers occupy a position in the Universe that must not be privileged in any way is strongly challenged by such a line of thinking. Observers will reside only in places where conditions are conducive to their evolution and existence: such sites may well turn out to be special.[23]

Employing a divine action category, nature's "series of mysterious coincidences" is consistent with the notion of cosmological providentialism in origins.[24] Barrow and Tippler also recognize the metaphysical significance of this scientific evidence. It challenges secular "dogma" by suggesting that humans do occupy a "privileged" and "special" place in the universe. In other words, science is pointing to the world's teleological foundation and the unicity of men and women.

This section asserts that divine action and intelligent design converge in the anthropic principle, resulting in a powerful argument for the existence of God. It opens with a brief review of some scientific evidence indicative of fine-tuning in nature. Responses are then offered to arguments against the belief that this data points to the reality of intelligent design. Next, an evolutionary creationist approach to the anthropic principle is presented using a number of explanatory analogies. By identifying the strengths and limits of this Christian interpretation, the section closes with a few theological and philosophical insights.

Some Anthropic Evidence

The scientific data supporting the anthropic principle is voluminous and far-reaching. Originally arising out of Big Bang physics, it now extends to astronomy and planetary geology, and is beginning to appear in biology. The purpose of this subsection is only to introduce some anthropic evidence in hope of stimulating interest in this vast and growing body of scientific literature.[25]

The famed physicist Stephen Hawking recognizes the finely tuned character of the origin of the universe. In his popular *A Brief History of Time* (1988), he notes that "if the rate of expansion one second after the Big Bang had been smaller by even one part in a hundred thousand million million, the universe would have recollapsed before it ever reached its present size."[26] Physicist and science-religion scholar Paul Davies further explains the exquisite balance at this creative event:

> The universe is thus the product of a competition between the explosive vigour of the Big Bang, and the force of gravity which tries to pull the pieces back together again. In recent years, astrophysicists have come to realize just how delicately this competition has been balanced. Had the Big Bang been weaker, the cosmos would have soon fallen back on itself in a Big Crunch. On the other hand, had it been stronger, the cosmic material would have dispersed so rapidly that galaxies would not have formed. Either way, the observed structure of the universe seems to depend very sensitively on the precise matching of explosive vigour to gravitating power. Just how sensitively is revealed by calculation. At the so-called Planck time (10^{-43} seconds, which is the earliest moment at which the concept of space and time has meaning) the matching was accurate to a staggering one part in 10^{60}. That is to say, had the explosion differed in strength at the outset by only one part in 10^{60}, the universe we now perceive would not exist. To give meaning to these numbers, suppose you wanted to fire a bullet at a one-inch target on the other side of the universe, twenty billion light years away.* Your aim would have to be accurate to that same part in 10^{60}.[27]

Clearly, the mathematics describing this delicate balance at the Big Bang boggles the mind. But this is only one factor—the fine-tuning between explosive and gravitational forces. The statistical complexity magnifies beyond comprehension when other physical forces are taken into consideration.

According to Big Bang theory, the universe did not exist prior to this explosive event. As counterintuitive as it is to imagine, there was no space, no time, and no physical matter. Within infinitesimal fractions of a second after this explosive event, the four fundamental forces in nature emerged—strong nuclear, weak nuclear, electromagnetic, and gravitational. Fig 3-10 illustrates the evolution of these forces from the indistinguishable original force of the Big Bang. Fine-tuning exists between the constants of these forces. As scientist-theologian Alister McGrath explains, the present universe would not have evolved if their values had been slightly different:

---

* A light year is the distance light travels (186,000 miles per second) in one year. This calculates to about 6,000,000,000,000 miles. Thus, the target Davies refers to is about 1,200,000,000,000,000,000,000,000 miles away.

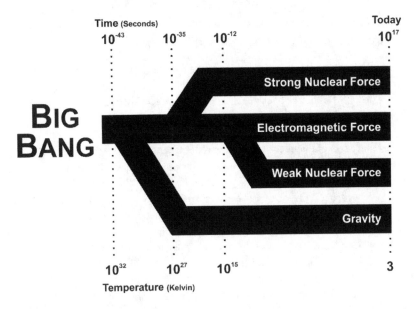

Fig 3-10. Cosmological Evolution of the Four Basic Forces in Nature. Temperature is in the Kelvin scale. Zero degrees Kevin is -273 Centigrade or -460 Fahrenheit.

If the strong coupling constant were slightly smaller, hydrogen would be the only element in the universe. Since the evolution of life as we know it is fundamentally dependent on the chemical properties of carbon, that life could not have come into being without some hydrogen being converted to carbon by fusion. On the other hand, if the strong coupling constant were slightly larger (even by as much as 2 percent), the hydrogen would have been converted to helium, with the result that no long-lived stars would have been formed. In that such stars are regarded as essential to the emergence of life, such a conversion would have led to life as we know it failing to emerge.

If the weak fine constant were slightly smaller, no hydrogen would have formed during the early history of the universe. Consequently, no stars would have been formed. On the other hand, if it were slightly larger, supernovae would have been unable to eject the heavier elements necessary for life. In either case, life as we know it could not have emerged.

84

If the electromagnetic fine structure constant were slightly larger, the stars would not be hot enough to warm planets to a temperature sufficient to maintain life in the form in which we know it. If smaller, the stars would have burned out too quickly to allow life to evolve on these planets.

If the gravitational fine structure constant were slightly smaller, stars, and planets would not have been able to form, on account of the gravitational constraints necessary for coalescence of their constituent material. If stronger, the stars thus formed would have burned out too quickly to allow the evolution of life (as with the electromagnetic fine structure constant).[28]

McGrath concludes that "these coincidences are immensely interesting and thought-provoking, leading at least some natural scientists to posit a possible religious explanation for these observations." But he correctly cautions that this evidence is not a *proof* for the existence of God.[29]

Physicists have also attempted to calculate the overall fine-tuning in the entire universe. Of course, anyone who proposes such estimations admits their speculative nature. Nevertheless, these are instructive. Eminent physicist Roger Penrose offers one of the best known and respected calculations. In arguing that the Big Bang was "so precisely organized," he reckons:

> In order to produce a universe resembling the one in which we live, the Creator would have to aim for an absurdly tiny volume of the phase space of possible universes—about $1/10$ of 10 to 10^{123} of the entire volume. . . . This is an extraordinary figure. One could not possibly even *write down the number in full*, ordinary denary [base-10] notation: it would be '1' followed by 10^{123} successive '0's! Even if we were to write a '0' on each separate proton and on each separate neutron in the entire universe—and we could throw in all the other particles for good measure—we should fall far short of writing down the figure needed.[30]

To put the number 10^{123} in perspective, it is estimated that the total number of elementary particles (protons, neutrons, etc.) in the universe is 10^{80}. Though Penrose's calculation of the fine-tuning in the Big Bang is not scientific *proof* for the existence of God, it certainly strikes forcefully. As another physicist Freeman Dyson comments, "The more I examine the universe and the details of its architecture, the more evidence I find that the universe in some sense must have known we were coming."[31]

Anthropic evidence is also found with astronomy and planetary geology. In *Rare Earth: Why Complex Life Is Uncommon in the Universe* (2000), geologist Peter Ward and astronomer Donald Brownlee challenge the common assumption, known as the "Principle of Mediocrity," that the earth is just one of a myriad of planets with advanced life. By outlining the physical requirements of a habitable environment for organisms, they counter with the "Rare Earth Hypothesis" and contend that complex life is "almost nowhere" in the universe.[32]

Ward and Brownlee argue that most of the cosmos features "dead zones" that are not hospitable for advanced living organisms. To cite a few characteristics supporting their contention, they note:

> The most distant known galaxies are too young to have enough metals for the formation of Earth-size inner planets. Hazards include energetic quasar-like activity and frequent supernova explosions. . . . Although [globular clusters] contain up to a million stars they are too metal-poor to have inner planets as large as Earth. Solar-mass stars have evolved to giants that are too hot for life on inner planets. . . . [Elliptical galaxies and small galaxies] are too metal-poor. . . . Energetic processes [at the centres of galaxies] impede complex life. . . . Many stars [at the edges of galaxies] are too metal-poor.[33]

In other words, most of the stars in the universe do not have planets suitable for life. The importance of the earth's abundant metal content cannot be over emphasized. In the core of the planet, it produces magnetic fields necessary to deflect damaging radiation from outer space. Radioactive metals also provided an internal source of heat that caused volcanoes to spew out water and gases, forming the oceans and atmosphere. And iron, zinc, copper, and other metals are essential elements in the biological pathways of living organisms.

In contrast to most of the universe, Ward and Brownlee assert that the earth is "extraordinarily rare" since it is a "habitable zone."[34] To mention but a few "Rare Earth Factors" for a life-sustaining planet, they recognize: The earth is in the "right kind of galaxy," producing enough heavy elements for life. It is also at the "right position in the galaxy," providing a stable environment without great energy fluctuations in heat, cold, gamma rays, X-rays, etc. Similarly, the sun is the "right mass," not emitting too much life-damaging ultraviolet radiation. The earth is the "right distance" from the sun, allowing for liquid water, which is absolutely necessary for living organisms. The earth is the "right planetary mass" to retain an atmosphere, but allow harmful gases to escape. The moon is the "right distance" from the earth and stabilizes the "right tilt" of the planet, resulting in seasons that are not too severe. The earth also has the "right amount" of carbon, not too much to cause excessive heating through a runaway greenhouse effect, but not too little, which would inhibit the development of life. Indeed, these "just right" scientific features from astronomy and planetary geology offer many reasons to believe that the earth is intended for humanity.[35]

Only a few biologists have extended the anthropic principle to the evolution of life. Michael Denton's *Nature's Destiny: How the Laws of Biology Reveal Purpose in the Universe* (1998) is one of the first and best attempts to recognize that nature is uniquely fitted for the evolution of the life found on earth, and in particular, intelligent life as manifested by human beings.[36] He challenges biological "orthodoxy" and the notion that evolution is *only* the result of random mutations and natural selection.[37] His book begins with coincidental characteristics in nature that are necessary for life, and then it presents features in evolutionary trends and mechanisms pointing toward intelligent design.

Denton argues that the physical and chemical characteristics of the molecules making up living organisms reflect fine-tuning. To summarize some features of water, carbon, and oxygen, he observes:

> If the properties of water were not almost precisely what they are, carbon-based life would in all probability be impossible. Even the viscosity of ice is fit. If it were any greater, then all the water on earth might be trapped in vast immobile ice sheets in the poles. ... The fitness of carbon compounds for life is maximal in the same temperature range that water is a fluid. Both the strong covalent and the weak bond are of maximal utility in this same temperature range. Such coincidences are precisely what one might expect to see in a cosmos specially adapted for carbon-based life. ... Oxygen is a very reactive atom and it can only be utilized by biochemical systems because of a number of adaptions, including: the attenuation of its reactivity below about 50° C; its low solubility; the fact that the transitional atoms such as iron and copper have just the right chemical characteristics to manipulate the oxygen atom; that the end product of oxidation of carbon is carbon dioxide, an in-

nocuous gas. Moreover, the reaction of carbon dioxide with water provides living things with a buffer—the bicarbonate buffer which has just the right characteristics to buffer organisms, especially air-breathing organisms, against increases in acidity. The chain of coincidences in the nature of things which permit higher forms of life to utilize oxygen provides further evidence of the unique fitness of nature for carbon-based life.[38]

This evidence only scratches the surface. Denton also presents comprehensive data for the fitness of solar radiation, the elements of the periodic table (in particular, the chemical properties of metals), the structure of DNA and RNA, and the self-assembling and functional characteristics of proteins. Denton even proposes that human physical features such as size, muscle strength, upright stance, and the opposable thumb of the hand are particularly suited for the exploration and comprehension of the universe.

In *Nature's Destiny*, Denton offers scientific evidence to suggest that biological evolution is "the result of an immense built-in generative program."[39] He quickly dismisses the simplistic notion that life evolved *only* by random mutations and natural selection, though he recognizes the importance of these mechanisms as contributing factors. Some genetic and morphological features pointing to designed and law-like evolutionary mechanisms include:

Synchronous Genetic Change in Populations of Species. A number of genetic processes are known that keep multiple copies of a gene the same, in both an individual and the species. That is, "gene families" do not drift off and mutate in any and every direction. In this way, synchronous genetic change in all members of a species is feasible. Denton contends that such a coordinated mechanism fits well within a "grand instructional program to bring about cohesive directional mutational change during evolution."[40]

Genetic and Developmental Constraints. Biologists recognize that the expression of genes and the pathways of embryological development are within limits. These constraints are consistent with the notion that life evolves inside preordained channels. Denton notes that these biological ranges do not need to be excessively narrow. Instead, environmental factors undoubtedly play a role in leading organisms down optional pathways on the evolutionary road to life.

Parallel Evolution. Parallel evolution refers to the evolution of similar or identical features in separate and unrelated evolutionary lines. One of the most striking examples is the eye. It has evolved independently over 40 times across a wide range of different animals such as insects, molluscs, and vertebrates. Similarly, parallel evolution is seen between placental and marsupial mammals. The isolation of Australia from other continents 60 million years ago resulted in early mammals splitting into two distinct and separate evolutionary lineages. Yet almost every marsupial has a counterpart placental, including a lion, cat, wolf, mole, anteater, and flying squirrel, to mention a few.[41] Denton notes that this evidence points away from an undirected process and toward a potentiality built into evolution for these parallel features to emerge in different creatures. Stated more precisely, nature appears to be loaded or destined for these biological traits to evolve.

Long-Term Evolutionary Trends and Modes. Biologists recognize patterns in the evolution of life. For example, with vertebrates there is a trend for the vertebral column to ossify gradually, the skull bones to reduce in number, and the heart chambers to increase from 2 to 3 to 4. More significantly, Darwin's notion of gradual change has given way to the theory of "punctuated equilibrium." The fossil record shows long periods in which species undergo little anatomical variation, and then suddenly new species evolve in a short duration of time. The classic case is the Cambrian Explosion 550 million years ago when the basic body plans of animals arose in only a 5–10 million year period.[42] Such a pattern strikes hard against a dysteleological view of evolution since an overarching evolutionary mode is not expected. As Denton asks, "If stability is the rule, and if selection tends to freeze organisms against change, then this raises the question of how selection ever transformed organisms so dramatically?"[43] The answer, he contends, lies in "the very natural but heretical idea" that this pattern was written into the laws of evolution from the beginning.

It is important to recognize that though Denton presents scientifically credible data, its organization into a comprehensive theory of evolution, which features directionality and teleology, is in the first stages of development. Nevertheless, *Nature's Destiny* challenges the secular belief that evolution is driven only by blind chance, and Denton's identification of law-like evolutionary mechanisms certainly points toward intelligent design.

As noted at the beginning of this subsection, the purpose of presenting some anthropic evidence is only to introduce it and stimulate further interest. The terms employed to describe this scientific data are striking: coincidences, fine-tuning, delicately balanced, precisely organized, just right, uniquely fit, and chain of coincidences. Significantly, many of the authors cited are not Christians. In other words, their appeal to anthropic data cannot be attributed merely to religious bias. This evidence stands on its own in providing a rational argument, and I contend a rather obvious conclusion.

Responses to Skeptics of the Anthropic Principle

The evidence presented from physics, astronomy, planetary geology, and biology is used to defend the "strong anthropic principle" (SAP). For many Christians, this is an updated and more robust version of the argument from design for the existence of God. As noted earlier, evolutionary creationists term it the evolutionary intelligent design argument. However, as can be expected, there are skeptics of this interpretation of the physical data.

The "weak anthropic principle" (WAP) does not challenge the fact that the laws of nature are exquisite and finely tuned. It simply accounts for this scientific evidence by stating the obvious: if the physical conditions of the universe were different, then humanity would not be here to discover and discuss them. Thus, there is nothing special or privileged about human existence. It just "happens to be" that intelligent beings evolved. In addition, critics of SAP propose the "multiple worlds hypothesis." This belief asserts that the present universe is only one in an infinite number of worlds, whether parallel to this one or sequential to it in time, and that given an infinite number of attempts to produce intelligent life, it was bound to happen by pure chance. However, defenders of SAP offer three responses to the skeptics.

First, affirming the obvious—if the universe was not finely tuned, then no one would be here to talk about it—fails to explain why the universe features this characteristic. Richard Swinburne offers an analogy to depict the problem with this belief:

> Suppose that a madman kidnaps a victim and shuts him in a room with a card-shuffling machine. The machine shuffles ten packs of cards simultaneously and then draws a card from each pack and

exhibits simultaneously the ten cards. The kidnapper tells the victim that he will shortly set the machine to work and it will exhibit its first draw, but that unless the draw consists of an ace of hearts from each pack, the machine will simultaneously set off an explosion which will kill the victim, in consequence of which he will not see which cards the machine drew. The machine is then set to work, and to the amazement and relief of the victim the machine exhibits an ace of hearts drawn from each pack. The victim thinks that this extraordinary fact needs an explanation in terms of the machine having been rigged in some way. But the kidnapper, who now reappears, casts doubt on this suggestion. "It is hardly surprising," he says, "that the machine draws only aces of hearts. You could not possibly see anything else. For you would not be here to see anything at all, if any other cards had been drawn."[44]

Swinburne notes that since an extraordinary combination of cards is necessary for the victim to be alive, the situation cries out for an explanation on why these exact cards were drawn. The chance of this being a random event is 1 in 10^{17}. So too with nature. Fine-tuning may be necessary for human existence, but questions remain: Why does it even exist? And Who or what is its cause?

Second, skeptics of SAP attempt to answer these questions by appealing to the multiple worlds hypothesis. Yet, such an approach is not a scientific argument, as Paul Davies points out:

The numerical coincidences could be regarded as evidence of design. The delicate fine-tuning in the values of the constants, necessary so that the various different branches of physics can dovetail so felicitously, might be attributed to God. It is hard to resist the impression that the present structure of the universe, apparently so sensitive to minor variations in the numbers, has been rather carefully thought out. Such a conclusion can, of course, only be subjective. In the end it boils down to a question of belief. Is it easier to believe in a Cosmic Designer than the multiplicity of universes necessary for the Weak Anthropic Principle to work? It is hard to see how either hypothesis could ever be tested in the strict scientific sense. If we cannot visit the other universes or experience them directly, their possible existence must remain just as much a matter of faith as belief in God. Perhaps future developments in science will lead to more direct evidence for other universes, but until then, the seemingly miraculous concurrence of numerical values that nature has assigned to her fundamental constants must remain the most compelling evidence for an element of cosmic design.[45]

Davies correctly recognizes that SAP, WAP, and the multiple worlds hypothesis are not purely scientific concepts and that they feature a component that is a "matter of faith." Employing the design model presented early in this chapter, belief in either a Cosmic Designer or many universes involves a metaphysical jump from the scientific data revealing the exquisitely balanced laws of nature.

More specifically, the multiple worlds hypothesis is ultimately a religious argument. There is no physical evidence that parallel or sequential universes exist. Ironically, this purportedly scientific hypothesis is an *out-of-this-world* argument, which is no different than belief in a heavenly realm with God and angels. It depicts perfectly the *faith* embraced by skeptics of intelligent design. As the Bible states, "Faith is being sure of what we hope for and certain of what we do not see" (Heb 11:1). Advocates of the multiple worlds hypothesis are "sure" and "certain" these other worlds exist even though they "do not see" them through any scientific instrument. Obviously, their belief is based on pure "hope," and not the facts of science. Of course, the question arises: Why do normally logical and scientific individuals cling so passionately to this hope in unseen physical realms?

Theologian John Haught offers an answer by identifying a spiritual factor that undergirds WAP and the multiple worlds hypothesis. He argues that ingratitude toward God is behind these arguments against intelligent design.

> We cannot help suspecting, therefore, that the speculation about numerous, and perhaps an infinite number of, 'worlds' often has nothing whatsoever to do with science. Rather it is a desperate conflationist attempt by a materialist belief system to ally itself with science in such a way as to diminish the plausibility of any non-materialist, religious interpretation of the cosmos. Beneath the multiple worlds hypothesis there is an implicit, though very telling, confession that if our present big bang universe is in fact the only world-phase that has ever existed, materialist and reductionist explanations would be in serious trouble. For the existence of only this one fine-tuned universe would not provide a statistically broad enough base to allow for the purely random origin of life and mind that skepticism requires. . . . In brief, the multiple-worlds hypothesis provides skeptics with a convenient way to

avoid an interpretation of the universe that would call forth the religious response of gratitude for its truly gracious existence.[46]

Haught echoes the apostle Paul who argues that despite skeptics seeing a reflection of the Creator's "eternal power and Divine nature" in the world, "they neither glorified Him as God nor gave thanks to Him" (Rom 1:20–21). If Paul were alive today, he would undoubtedly judge those embracing WAP and the multiple worlds hypothesis to be intellectually "futile" and "without excuse."

In final analysis, sin is at the root of arguments against the strong anthropic principle. The problem skeptics have with this concept is a problem with the First Commandment. They simply do not want to acknowledge their Creator and say, "Thank you." Ironically, elegant intricacy in the cosmos has driven science forward by inspiring awe and wonder in scientists, even those embracing a dysteleological worldview. But by spurning the religious implications of the fine-tuning in nature, skeptics offer evidence for the reality of a powerful force in the universe that operates beyond logical analysis and the scientific method, and that is hell-bent on not recognizing the existence of an Intelligent Designer. Unwittingly, supporters of the weak anthropic principle and the multiple worlds hypothesis testify to the reality of sin and affirm the biblical notion of natural revelation.

An Evolutionary Creationist Approach to the Anthropic Principle

Evolutionary creation asserts that divine action and intelligent design converge in the anthropic principle. This position contends that the fine-tuning evident in the natural processes that created the world reflects cosmological providentialism. In other words, God ordained and sustained cosmological, geological, and biological evolution in order that a universe would emerge that is ideally suited for human beings.[47] But it must be emphasized that the anthropic principle is based on an evolutionary view of the heavens, earth, and living organisms. Consequently, young earth creationists cannot appeal to it, and progressive creationists are restricted to using it only with cosmology and geology. In contrast, evolutionary creation is not bound by anti-evolutionary assumptions. This view of origins embraces the unity and powerful consilience seen in all the modern sciences investigating the history of the universe and life.

The word "coincidence" permeates the scientific literature on the anthropic principle.[48] Implicit in this term, in a paradoxical way, are nuances of noticeability and hiddenness. On the one hand, the many coincidences in the laws of nature offer subtle evidence of fine-tuning. Evolutionary creation asserts that God has designed these natural processes. On the other hand, cosmological providentialism in origins cannot be proven with absolute logical and scientific certainty. In this way, an evolutionary creationist approach to the anthropic principle is characterised by *divine noticeability* and *divine hiddenness*. Seeing or not seeing the Creator's action and design in nature requires an element of faith. In other words, a metaphysical jump is necessary from the fine tuning in nature that science reveals to the belief held by religion that this is the providentialistic action and intelligent design of a Fine Tuner. Thus, anthropic arguments and their vast array of coincidences are both scientific and religious, reflecting the intellectual-spiritual dynamic of the Metaphysics-Physics Principle.

Evolutionary creation recognizes that though the anthropic principle offers powerful support for the existence of an Intelligent Designer, it has limitations. First, the revelation offered by fine-tuning is non-verbal. It only points to a Designer, Designers, a Designing Force, or Designing Forces. The need for a verbal revelation, like the Bible, is obvious in order to disclose fully who or what fine-tuned the world. Second, anthropic data offers only an argument for the existence of Someone/s or Something/s, not a proof. The Metaphysic-Physics Principle is again operative. An intellectual-spiritual jump is necessary from the finely tuned data to the belief in design. Finally, anthropic arguments are limited because of their impersonal character. Though they are rational support for a Designer, alone they leave most people cold. Evidence for this is that these arguments never led to a spiritual renaissance in scientific circles after they were first put forward in the 1950s. Again, the necessity for another revelation is evident. In particular, a divine disclosure that is not confined to our minds, but one that through love also talks to our hearts.

A few analogies assist to explain further the anthropic principle from an evolutionary creationist perspective. Consider divine action in the origin of the world to be like the strokes of a cue stick in a game of billiards. Label the balls into three groups using the words "heavens," "earth," and "living organisms," and let the 8-ball represent humans. The young earth creationist depicts the Creator making single shot after single shot with no miscues until all the balls are off the table. No doubt, that is remarkable. A progressive creationist sees the opening stroke that breaks the balls as the Big Bang. All of the balls labeled "heavens" and "earth" are sunk by this initial shot. Then God sinks those that signify living organisms and humans individually. That is even more impressive.

Evolutionary creationists claim that the God-of-the-individual-shots (or "gaps") fails to reveal fully the power and foresight of the Creator. According to their view of origins, the breaking stroke is so finely tuned that not only are all the balls sunk, but they drop in order, beginning with those labeled "heavens," then "earth," followed by "living organisms," and finally the 8-ball, the most important ball in billiards, representing humans. And to complete the analogy, the Lord pulls this last ball out of the pocket and holds it in His hands to depict His personal involvement with men and women. Is not such a God infinitely more talented than that of the anti-evolutionists? Is His eternal power and divine nature not best illustrated in the last example? Of course, the evolutionary creationist view of God is challenged if there exists a billiards game "Bible" that reveals He uses individual strokes in sinking balls.

Divine action and intelligent design in the origin of life can also be compared to a game of dice. Imagine God rolling a 7 to be the creation of living organisms. According to young earth creationists, the dice are made in such a way that 7 cannot be thrown. That is, the dice are either shaved or weighted so that other numbers always appear. In playing the game, the Creator institutes a rule that players must turn their back on the dice table for a few moments before a throw. Instead of rolling the dice, God sets them down with a 7 showing. After repeating this scenario a number of times, the participants complain that the game has been rigged for them to lose. Progressive creationists also assert that the dice have been tampered with so that the 7 of life cannot be thrown. In their game, the Creator initially rolls the dice (representing the Big Bang) in front of the players. But before the pieces settle on the table, the rules call for the participants to look away. God then quickly intervenes and adjusts the dice to show the 7 of living organisms. Again, complaints of a rigged game arise.

In contrast to the interventionistic depictions of the Creator held by the anti-evolutionists, the evolutionary creationist views the origin of life like a set of dice loaded by God. In full view of everyone, He rolls the game pieces and the winning 7 appears. This Creator designed the dice to interact with gravity, material elasticity, air resistance, etc. in order to achieve

His purpose of throwing the number for the creation of life. Yet again, the evolutionary creationist picture of God is problematic should there exist a dice game "Bible" that discloses His hand tinkers interventionistically with the dice during the game. But if the purpose of such a "Scripture" is only to reveal that the Creator set up the dice of life without stating how this was done, then dice ordained and sustained by Him to roll the winning number for living organisms is a reasonable possibility. The parallel to the issue of scientific concordism in the origins debate is obvious.

More qualification is necessary to explain the dice analogy from an evolutionary creationist perspective. The best-loaded dice are those that in the end win the game, but are not recognized by the other players as having been tampered with. Poorly rigged dice are those that roll 7s every time and are easily identified. Evolutionary creationist dice of life are designed between these extremes. On the one hand, anthropic coincidences feature a non-verbal divine noticeability that reveals evolution to be a loaded process intended for humans to appear. On the other hand, fine-tuning in nature also displays an aspect of divine hiddenness. Players using these dice will eventually realize during the game that the number of 7s rolled is statistically more than expected by random chance. Most will claim that the "coincidental 7s declare" the handiwork of someone who intentionally loaded the dice. But there is no way of proving this design with absolute certainty. The possibility exists that accidental manufacturing errors at a factory produced dice that "appear" to be designed. Of course, belief in whether such factories exist or whether someone intentionally tampered with dice will be determinative in the explanation of why so many 7s were rolled. Therefore, the dice of evolutionary creation feature an intellectual tension between a noticeability pointing to a designer and a hiddenness of their maker.

Embryological development provides a final analogy to explain an evolutionary creationist perspective of the anthropic principle. This origins position contends that mechanisms of evolution are similar to the incalculable number of finely tuned developmental processes in the womb.[49] Both of these creative methods feature divine providentialistic activity that manifests intelligent design. Interestingly, the anti-evolutionary positions also hold this view of embryology. Young earth creationists do not believe that God intervenes dramatically to assemble a fully developed baby in only a few days. Nor do progressive creationists claim the insufficiency of embryological processes, forcing the Creator to enter the womb at different times during pregnancy to attach anatomical structures on a developing fetus. Significantly, there are two reasons why anti-evolutionists reject interventionism in the creation of a child: Scripture and science. No biblical passage reveals such creative events exist, and medicine has never demonstrated that these occur in pregnant women. Thus, if it can be shown that the Bible was not intended to reveal how God actually created the world, and that science finds no evidence for dramatic interventions in origins, then it is possible that divine action in the creation of the world is like providentialistic activity in the womb.

Natural processes in embryology and evolution also feature the emergence of properties and relationships. Incredibly, from one undifferentiated fertilized egg three basic tissue types emerge—endoderm, mesoderm, and ectoderm. Out of these develop the lungs and gastrointestinal tract; the bones, muscles, and heart; and the nerves and brain, respectively. Eventually, the organs come together to function in an incredibly well balanced physiological concert. It is important to note that not all the information to create a child is directly inscribed in the genes. Developmental interactions between emerging tissues above the level of gene activity provide many critical instructions (these are termed "epigenetic" interactions; Greek *epi* means "on, above, in addition to"). In other words, out of the embryological process new information appears which existed only as a potentiality in the fertilized egg. Development in the womb also features the emergence of a precious personal relationship between the mother and child. Starting modestly with kicks and hiccups, and then with responses to different voices, a new person gradually comes into existence.

In an amazing fashion similar to embryology, from the undifferentiated explosive force of the Big Bang, four finely tuned basic forces emerged in nature (Fig 3-10). As the universe expanded and cooled, the fundamental particles of matter arose. Eventually stars and galaxies formed, producing the building blocks for living organisms and a planet extraordinarily well suited for the evolution of life. In particular, humans gradually evolved from modest beginnings. The emergence of our unique intelligence is evident in the archaeological record with the sequential appearance of stone tools, fire pits, rudimentary shelters, and gear for hunting and fishing. Abstract thought is later reflected in jewelry, figurines, and cave paintings. And lastly, evidence of an incipient spirituality appears with intentional burials and placement of items near the dead that are assumed to be necessary in the next life (See Appendix 9). Through the evolutionary process, unique beings emerged to have personal relationships between themselves and with their Creator. As with embryological developmental, it must be underlined that the information to create the world is not all packed into the Big Bang. Rather, the potentiality for properties and relationships to arise exist in this initial explosive event. The evolution of a cosmos featuring the emergence of intelligent spiritual beings cries out for the reality of astonishing foresight, detailed planning, and incredible power.

Finally, divine noticeability in embryological development is tempered by the fact that developmental defects exist. The parents of a baby with a cleft palate and lip naturally wonder why God would allow their child to suffer from this awful malformation. Their experience of divine hiddenness is evident in the blunt question often asked in this situation: "Where was the Creator when the palate and lip were forming?" Similarly, the evolution of life seems at times utterly void of divine action and design. For example, the fossil record reveals that there have been five major mass extinctions on earth. The most famous of these is the wiping out of the dinosaurs and two-thirds of all plants and animals 65 million years ago when an asteroid hit the earth in a region near Mexico.[50] However, evolutionary creation does not assert that providentialistic action or intelligent design are optimal, as assumed or hoped by many Christians. God's noticeability and hiddenness are manifested in paradoxical fashion, just as He intended. But as most acknowledge, our experience of the former overwhelms by far that of the latter.

Insights of a Designed and Evolving Creation

In light of these analogies explaining an evolutionary creationist approach to the anthropic principle, a number of theological and philosophical insights arise. These include an appreciation of the traditional Christian notion of *Deus Absconditus*, the role of randomness in origins, sub-optimal design in nature, natural revelation and the structure of the brain, and a significant pastoral implication of intelligent design.

Deus Absconditus: Tempering Intelligent Design

Christians throughout the ages have wrestled with the experience that God seems to be absent from the world. Theologians have termed this divine characteristic as *Deus Absconditus* (Latin for "God who hides").[51] They assert that the Creator intentionally veils Himself so that humans are in a world with enough room and ample opportunity to develop their freedom and faith. In other words, this is a cosmos in which God does not blatantly crush people into submission with His presence. It was made in such a way that humans are given true liberty to conceive His non-existence, or to live as if He has nothing to do with them. Yet God leaves many signposts pointing to Him. From this perspective, the world is seen as ideally suited for men and women to nurture a genuine relationship with their Maker.

Evolutionary creation tempers the divine noticeability of anthropic features in evolution by acknowledging aspects of divine hiddenness in this natural process. The violent and viciously competitive character of biological evolution certainly raises questions as to whether or not there is a God, especially an all-powerful and all-loving God. In this way, divine noticeability apparent in the fine-tuning of natural processes does not force or coerce anyone into accepting a Fine Tuner, since divine hiddenness is also reflected in the ruthless and merciless characteristics of evolution. Christian evolutionists contend that an evolving universe is the perfect environment for humans to develop a true and loving relationship with the Creator. Indeed, this is a very good soul-developing world.

Randomness As Part of Divine Creative Action

Regrettably, many Christians have demonized the notion of randomness in nature. This is another distorted perception arising from the origins false dichotomy. These believers assume that since evolution is driven by blind chance and irrational necessity, then God would never use such features in creating the world. Of course, these terms are loaded with dys-teleological nuances that are unacceptable to Christian belief. However, science offers evidence that indeterminate and chaotic processes occur in nature, such as in quantum mechanics and weather patterns. According to evolutionary creation, these characteristics are a part, *and only a part*, of God's very good creation. Randomness is an ordained and sustained component in the overarching plan of the evolution of the universe and life.

More specifically, randomness in anthropic creative action contributes to divine hiddenness. Instead of an evolving creation in which the dice of life roll 7 each time, indeterminate and chaotic processes provide a

distancing from God and a non-coercive environment for humans to develop spiritually. An interesting question arises with regard to how much freedom the Creator allowed in evolution. For example, was it ordained that humans were to have exactly five fingers? Or did God load flexibility into the Big Bang so that true randomness in nature would be allowed to evolve different numbers of fingers? Similarly, do the 46 human chromosomes define humanity? Or could the Image of God and sinfulness have been manifested in a creature with a different genetic makeup? Whatever the answers to these questions, evolutionary creation underlines that creative processes met God's exact and perfect plan in making the world.

Sub-Optimal Design in Nature

A criticism commonly launched against the belief in intelligent design is that nature has many examples of sub-optimal structures and processes. Skeptics often introduce this objection with the rhetorical question, "Would a perfect God make such an imperfect feature?" To be sure, design in nature is not optimal. The creation has ugly and dysfunctional features.[52] To cite some examples: the eye has a blind spot, most people suffer back pain in their lifetime because the spine is structurally unstable, developmental processes can result in disfiguring and debilitating defects, and genetic fragility leads to cancer.

However, this criticism by skeptics conflates intelligent design with optimal or perfect design. Ironically, this is a theological argument. Like beating a straw man, unbelievers fashion in their mind a god who would only create a perfectly optimal world, and once they see any sub-optimal detail in nature, they then reject him. Of course, this is a form of idolatry. Sadly, Christians have also confused God's proclamation that the creation is "very good" (Gen 1:31) with this notion of physical perfection. But divine design in nature does not necessarily require optimization. It only needs to reflect intelligence, and in particular to fulfill the intended purposes of the Creator. The eye functions proficiently in allowing humans to see that "the heavens declare the glory of God." Civilizations have been built on the backs of humans. As well, imperfections contribute in the unfolding of the Lord's will. Suffering often finds men and women being drawn closer to Him. And in a paradoxical way, the genetic mutations that produce deadly cancers are also the evolutionary mechanisms that created living organisms. Sub-optimal design is perfect for a world intended to manifest both the noticeability and hiddenness of the Creator, and ultimately to provide an environment for us to develop a genuine relationship with Him.

Natural Revelation and the 'God Center' in the Brain

Recent studies on the structure of the brain reveal that distinct groups of cells are stimulated during prayer and religious meditation. Skeptics of religion are quick to interpret this scientific evidence as proof that God only exists in the mind of the believer. They contend that during evolution the brain was "hardwired for God" and that religious behavior contributed to the survival of the human species.[53] Of course, this interpretation of the science is often fueled by the evolution vs. creation false dichotomy.

Evolutionary creation contends that the Lord created a "God center" in our brain through an ordained and sustained evolutionary process. As visual cells evolved in the brain for seeing the physical world, groups of cells emerged during human evolution with the intention to "see" the spiritual world. In particular, this center is powerfully stimulated by intelligent design in nature. In other words, during evolution God wired our brain for natural revelation. Men and women are free to close their physical eyes and not enjoy the gift of vision to see the physical world around them. Similarly, the Lord has given us the freedom whether or not to use our "spiritual eyes" and view the spiritual realities reflected throughout the creation.

Intelligent Design and the Problem of Suffering

The book of Job is well known for its insights into human suffering. Yet few Christians appreciate fully the pastoral role that intelligent design plays in coming to terms with this problem. The account begins with God allowing Satan to torment Job in order to test his faith. At first Job's flocks are stolen, his servants murdered, and his ten children killed in a storm. A crippling and painful disease then strikes him down. Throughout most of this book, Job's friends attempt to justify his horrendous situation. The popular idea that sin is the cause of suffering is presented relentlessly. But in the final chapters, God addresses Job using primarily an intelligent design argument. He simply points to the creation and questions Job about its origin and operation: Who established the boundaries of the sea and earth (Job 38:4–8)? Who set up constellations and laws in the heavens (38:33)? Who feeds the ravens and their young, and who hunts prey for the lions (38:39–41)? Who supervises the labor pains of goats and bears giving birth (39:1–3)?

Humbled by the creation, Job confesses, "Surely I spoke of things I did not understand, things too wonderful for me to know" (42:3). No direct reason or justification for the existence of suffering is given in this biblical book. But it does affirm that intelligent design offers comfort and perspective to those who suffer. Without the use of words, the creation reveals that God is sovereign over the entire world, and that His dominion also extends over human pain and affliction. Evolutionary creation contends that this is also the case with design seen in the fine-tuning of the natural processes in origins and operations. It not only points to the existence of God, but it also, in a mysterious and non-verbal way, consoles us in our times of despair.

To conclude, the anthropic principle offers reflections of intelligent design and divine providentialistic action. It is no coincidence that the cosmos reveals countless "coincidences" in the finely tuned laws of nature. Evolutionary creation asserts that the physical world manifests, in a paradoxical manner, both divine noticeability and divine hiddenness. On the one hand, the Creator's foresight and power are seen in the evolution of the universe and life. Incredibly, out of the undifferentiated explosive force of the Big Bang, this world emerged in God-glorifying splendor with creatures capable of a personal relationship with their Maker. On the other hand, the evolutionary cosmos at times seems cold, cruel, and meaningless. It is a possibility that humanity arose in a universe that just happened to have the right physical conditions. Yet for most of us, even this fleeting darkness points toward the Light and the belief that the cosmos is indeed a very good creation.

CHAPTER SUMMARY

Evolutionary creationists affirm the Creator's involvement in a designed and evolving creation. God acted and continues to act providentialistically in ordaining and sustaining the origin and operation of the physical world, and He interacts both dramatically and subtly in the personal lives of men and women. The Lord has also inscribed in nature intelligent design, offering a non-verbal revelation of His glory, power, and divinity. Evolutionary creation embraces a healthy and complementary relationship between science and religion. It views the modern evolutionary sciences as gifts from God. In this way, these conservative Christians assert that cosmology, geology, and biology reveal an anthropic world—one intended primarily for the evolution of human beings.

Defining categories is essential in discerning divine action. Evolutionary creation claims that God's activity in the world is not restricted to the popular notion of dramatic "miracles." It is necessary first to distinguish between personal and cosmological contexts of His involvement, and then to determine whether the mode of action is either interventionism or providentialism. In recognizing these categories, it is obvious that evolutionary creationists are not deists. They assert that God is omnipresent in the world, sustaining it at every instant, and that He is involved with people in a myriad of interventionistic and providentialistic ways. These Christian evolutionists also reject the God-of-the-gaps. The creation is complete and does not need a tinkering hand to adjust it back on course or to add missing parts. Instead of fearing the discovery of transitional fossils or evolutionary mechanisms that fill gaps in knowledge, evolutionary creationists look forward to new scientific discoveries dealing with evolution, since these offer greater reflections of the Creator's omniscience and omnipotence.

The Metaphysics-Physics Principle is foundational to understanding the concept of intelligent design. Arriving at the religious/metaphysical belief that the world reflects design involves an intellectual-spiritual *jump* from the scientific/physical evidence. Natural revelation is ontologically sufficient and humans are epistemologically proficient to recognize it. Yet, this divine noticeability is tempered by a divine hiddenness. As well, sin is a determinative factor in accessing the implications of the beauty, complexity, and functionality in the cosmos. Consequently, intelligent design is not a *proof* for the existence of God, but rather an *argument* that is beyond a reasonable doubt. On the day of judgment, men and women will be accountable before God regarding their response to the revelation in nature. Psalm 19 and Romans 1 along with Wisdom 13 undergird this Christian approach to intelligent design.

It must be underlined that the impact of nature's design upon humans is only one part of their spiritual journey. As in romance, physical attraction is an initial aspect of a relationship, but it is not the foundation of a healthy and loving marriage. Similarly, the marvelous structures in the creation and the exquisite processes in their origins and operations open a door to men and women, allowing them to take a first step toward their Creator. Yet relating to God merely on the basis of intelligent design and anthropic coincidences is cold and shallow. Design arguments alone do not offer the intimate relationship that the Lord intended for humans to experience with Him. In being non-verbal, the revelation in the Book of God's Works is limited. Yet it anticipates a verbal divine disclosure—the Book of God's Words and the identification of the Intelligent Designer and His unconditional love for each of us.

The previous and present chapters note that the anti-evolutionism embraced by many Christians arises from the assumption of scientific concordism. In particular, interventionism in origins is rooted in the divine creative acts stated in the biblical creation accounts. But the question must be asked: Is the purpose of Scripture to reveal how God actually created the universe and life? Interestingly, the answer is revealed subtly in the pages of the Bible itself as the next chapter begins to point out.

4

The Ancient Science in the Bible

THE BIBLE IS A precious gift that has been given to us in order to reveal God and His will. Contained within its pages are the foundations of the Christian Faith—the creation of the world, the fall of humanity into sin, the offer of redemption through the Blood shed on the Cross, and the promise of eternal life. The Scriptures are also an everlasting source of spiritual nourishment for our soul. Through the power of the Holy Spirit, the Bible assures and encourages, challenges and admonishes, and equips men and women for a faithful life of good works. In particular, the primary purpose of God's Word is to reveal Jesus and the Father's unconditional love for all of us.

History shows that Christians have not only consulted the Bible for spiritual matters, but they have also used it in order to understand the structure, operation, and origin of the world. Scientific concordism has been a noticeable feature in theological discussions throughout the ages.[1] The belief that there is an accord or correspondence between the Bible and science is a reasonable expectation, since God is both the Author of His Words and the Creator of His Works. Today, scientific concordism remains popular within conservative Christianity. Many believers claim that the Holy Spirit revealed scientific facts in Scripture thousands of years before modern scientists discovered this knowledge. Consequently, they argue that the science in the Bible is powerful evidence that proves the supernatural character of God's Word, because only a Creator who transcends time could have given such a revelation. In this way, many Christians contend that the statements about the natural world in the Bible are inerrant and infallible. However, the question must be asked: Does the science in Scripture actually correspond to modern science?

This chapter presents evidence that an ancient science of the structure and operation of the physical world appears throughout the Bible. The first section introduces categories for interpreting statements about nature in Scripture. The core of the chapter then examines numerous passages referring to the earth, heavens, and living organisms. The presence of ancient science certainly has significant implications, especially for the origins debate. If the Word of God features an ancient understanding of nature, then the popular Christian belief in scientific concordism must be re-evaluated. Stated more precisely, if there is an ancient science regarding the structure and operation of the world, then consistency argues that this is also the case for its origin. The use of Scripture to determine how God created the universe and life would then need to be reconsidered.

INTRODUCTORY CATEGORIES

A simple thought experiment introduces the challenge of interpreting biblical passages that deal with nature. Consider the first two verses of Scripture, and then envision the scene described. Genesis 1:1–2 states, "In the beginning God created the heavens and the earth. Now the earth was formless and empty, darkness was over the surface of the deep, and the Spirit of God was hovering over the waters." Most people picture a dark, watery, and chaotic setting that features a *spherical* earth. That is, by reading the word "earth," they instantly interpreted it as a globe. But is this the biblical understanding of the earth's structure? Or are people reading their twenty-first century science *into* the Bible rather than allowing God's Word to speak for itself? A few facts from Scripture answer these questions.

First, use of the word "earth" in the Bible indicates that the Holy Spirit did not intend to reveal scientific information about the structure of the world. It appears about 2500 times in the Old Testament (*'ereṣ*) and 250 times in the New Testament (*gē*).[2] Never once is earth referred to as spherical. Nor is a globular shape implied by the context of any passage.[3] Indeed, if it was God's purpose to reveal in Scripture the scientific fact that the earth is a sphere, then there were nearly 3000 opportunities to do so. He could easily have done this by comparing the earth to something round like a ball or an orange. Surely, if it were the Lord's intention to reveal science in the Bible, then we would expect Him to tell us something about the structure of the home He made for us. But this lack of evidence argues powerfully that scientific concordism was never the goal of the Holy Spirit in biblical revelation.

Second, Scripture presents a 3-tiered universe, indicating that the inspired ancient authors believed the earth was flat. One of the most important passages in the New Testament is the Kenotic Hymn, and it employs this view of the structure of the cosmos.[4] Highlighting the fact that God emptied Himself and came down to the level of humans in the person of Jesus, the apostle Paul writes:

> Your attitude should be the same as that of Christ Jesus: Who, being in very nature God, did not consider equality with God something to be grasped, but made Himself nothing, taking the very nature of a servant, being made in human likeness. And being found in appearance as a man, He humbled Himself and became obedient to death—even death on a cross! Therefore God exalted Him to the highest place and gave Him the name that is above every name, that at the name of Jesus every knee should bow, *in heaven* and *on earth* and *under the earth*, and every tongue confess that Jesus Christ is Lord, to the glory of God the Father. (Phil 2:5–11; italics added)

Ancient peoples understood the universe to be made up of three *physical* levels: (1) the heavenly realm, (2) the earthly world, and (3) the underworld. Fig 4-1 introduces this conceptualization of the structure of the cosmos, and it will be explained in detail in this chapter. Today, Christians rarely recognize the ancient science in Phil 2.[5] Yet they correctly focus upon the central Messages of Faith—the mystery of the Incarnation and the Lordship of Jesus over the entire creation.

Of course, many Christians are quick to offer two common arguments against this 3-tier universe interpretation of Phil 2. First, they point out that this passage is in a poetic form and contend that the world is not being described in actual or concrete terms. That is, figurative expressions are being employed, and consequently these do not describe physical reality. Certainly, caution is necessary when interpreting the many poetic passages in Scripture. However, this is not to say that poetry never refers to actual physical realities. For example, the psalmist writes, "Praise the Lord, sun and moon, praise Him, all you shining stars" (Ps 148:3). No one today doubts the existence of the sun, moon, and stars. And no one in the ancient world questioned the reality of these astronomical bodies. Therefore, the "poetic language argument" must be applied carefully.

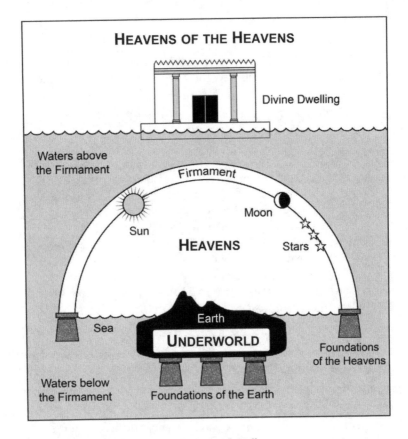

Fig 4-1. The 3-Tier Universe. Drawn by Kenneth Kully

Modern readers of Scripture need to determine what a biblical writer believed regarding the physical world before they can write-off any passage as simply "poetic" and not corresponding to concrete reality.

The second popular response to the interpretation that Phil 2 refers to a 3-tiered universe is the "phenomenological language argument." It asserts that Paul is describing the cosmos from his viewpoint, or phenomenological perspective (Greek verb *phainō* means "to appear," noun *phainōmenon* "appearance"). That is, the world looks or appears to have three tiers. So in the same way that we now speak of the "rising" or "setting" of the sun, the apostle is using phenomenological language. Therefore, Phil 2 does not affirm the reality of a 3-tiered world. But there is a subtle error in this argument. Did Paul use phenomenological language in the manner that we do today? Would he agree with us if we

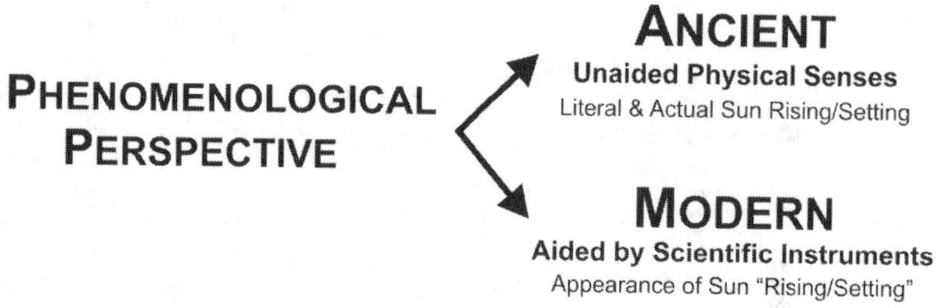

PHENOMENOLOGICAL PERSPECTIVE

ANCIENT
Unaided Physical Senses
Literal & Actual Sun Rising/Setting

MODERN
Aided by Scientific Instruments
Appearance of Sun "Rising/Setting"

Fig 4-2. Categories of Phenomenological Perspective

asked him, "The 'rising' and 'setting' of the sun are only visual effects caused by the rotation of our spherical planet, right?" History reveals that Paul would disagree. The notion that the earth rotates daily on its axis causing the phenomenon of the sun to "rise" and "set" became accepted only in the seventeenth century.

To be sure, Scripture employs phenomenological language in describing the natural world. But there is a critical and subtle difference between what the biblical writers saw and believed to be real in the universe, and what we see and assert as a scientific fact. Observation in the ancient world was limited to unaided physical senses, but scientific instruments, like telescopes, have broadened our view of the universe. As a result, it is essential to understand that statements in Scripture about nature are from an *ancient phenomenological perspective*. What the biblical writers and other ancient peoples saw with their eyes, they believed to be real, like the literal rising and setting of the sun. In contrast, we view the world from a *modern phenomenological perspective*. When we see the sun "rising" and "setting," we know that it is only an appearance or visual effect caused by the rotation of the earth. Consequently, it is crucial that these two different viewpoints of nature not be confused and conflated.[6] Failure to do so is the problem with the popular phenomenological language argument. Fig 4-2 distinguishes between the ancient and modern conceptualizations of the physical world.

The Kenotic Hymn in Phil 2 can therefore be seen in a new light. When Paul wrote this passage he understood the structure of the universe from an ancient phenomenological perspective. Viewing the natural world with unaided physical senses, most people at that time accepted that the cosmos was literally made up of three tiers. In other words, this apostle, under the inspiration of the Holy Spirit, employed the science of his

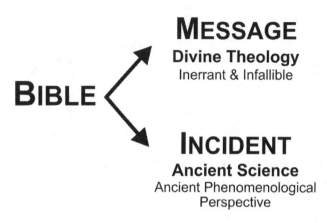

Fig 4-3. The Message-Incident Principle

generation in order to declare that God took on human flesh in the person of Jesus to become a servant, and that the Father made Him Lord over the entire creation. Paul's intention in this passage is not to inform Christians of the structure of the cosmos. It just happens to be that when he wrote this letter to the Philippian Church, the 3-tier universe was his understanding of nature and that of his readers. In this way, ancient science assists in delivering the Divine Theology in Scripture.

Fig 4-3 presents the Message-Incident Principle for the interpretation of biblical passages that refer to the physical world. This approach contends that in order to reveal spiritual truths as effectively as possible to the ancient peoples, the Holy Spirit used their ancient phenomenological perspective of nature. That is, instead of confusing or distracting the biblical writers and their readers with modern scientific concepts, God descended to their level and employed the science-of-the-day. Similar to the central message in the Kenotic Hymn, the Creator humbled Himself through the use of ancient human ideas about nature in the revelatory process. Therefore, passages in the Bible referring to the physical world feature both a *Message of Faith* and an *incidental ancient science*. According to this interpretive principle, biblical inerrancy and infallibility rest in the Divine Theology, and not in statements referring to nature. Qualifying ancient science as "incidental" does not imply that it is unimportant. The science in Scripture is vital for transporting spiritual truths. It acts as a vessel similar to a cup that delivers "living waters" (John 4:10). However, the word "incidental" carries meanings of "that which happens to be alongside" and "happening in connection with something more important." In other words, the ancient science in Scripture is "alongside" the "more important" Message of Faith.

The challenge twenty-first century Christians face in reading the Bible is demonstrated by the way most envision the shape of the earth in Gen 1:1–2. We are immersed in a scientific culture with images of a spherical planet. The moment we see the word "earth" in this verse, a picture of a globe suspended in outer space immediately comes to mind because we instinctively filter information through our intellectual categories. More precisely, we unconsciously read our modern science *into* the Bible. This interpretive error is termed "eisegesis" (Greek *eis* means "in, into" and *ēgeomai* "to guide"). But everyone agrees that the goal of reading any text is to practice "exegesis" (Greek *ek* translates "out, out of") and to draw *out* the writer's intended meaning. Therefore, in order to understand biblical statements dealing with nature correctly, we need to suspend our scientific categories and attempt to think about the physical world like ancient people thousands of years ago. No doubt about it, this is a very counterintuitive way to read.

This chapter now turns to passages in Scripture that refer to the earth, heavens, and living organisms. It will become clear that the Bible has an ancient phenomenological perspective of the physical world and features ancient geology, ancient astronomy, and ancient biology. Each section underlines the very logical process behind the conceptualization of these ancient sciences. The passages presented are also interpreted in light of the Message-Incident Principle. In this way, it will be obvious that ancient science plays an essential role in delivering the inerrant and infallible Word of God.

ANCIENT GEOLOGY

The Bible contains many references to the earth. As noted previously, this word appears nearly 3000 times. Because of their ancient phenomenological viewpoint, the inspired authors of Scripture believed that the earth was: (1) immovable, (2) set on foundations, (3) surrounded by water, (4) circular, (5) had ends, (6) an underside and underworld, and (7) was flat. In other words, the Bible presents an ancient geology.[7]

The Immobility of the Earth

Ancient peoples believed that the earth did not move. This is a reasonable idea from their perspective. Does anyone today sense that we are rotating on the earth's axis at 1000 miles per hour and traveling around the sun at 65,000 mph? The experience of this phenomenon is so powerful that belief in a stationary earth was widely upheld until the time of Galileo in the early seventeenth century. For that matter, scientific evidence that the earth moved did not appear until 1838, when telescopes were made that could confirm this fact.

The Old Testament clearly presents the immovability of the earth. In three verses it repeats word-for-word, "The world is firmly established; it cannot move" (1 Chr 16:30; Ps 93:1; Ps 96:10). The ancient Hebrews saw that mountains, hills, and plains remained constant throughout their lifetime, and they logically reasoned within their ancient category set that the earth was stationary. However, the purpose of these three verses is not to reveal a fact about nature. Rather, they are found in passages that praise God's Lordship over the creation. In other words, this ancient geological understanding is an incidental vessel used to reveal the message that the Lord is the Ordainer and Sustainer of the world.

It must be noted that these three biblical verses played a part that eventually led to Galileo's heresy trial. Church authorities forced the famed scientist to confess:

> I, Galileo, son of the late Vincenzio Galilei of Florence, seventy years of age . . . have been judged vehemently suspected of heresy, namely of having held and believed the sun is the center of the world and motionless and that the earth is not the center and moves . . . with a sincere heart and unfeigned faith I abjure, curse, and detest the above said errors and heresies.[8]

This confession certainly casts a dark shadow on the Church that continues to embarrass believers today. But it should serve as a warning to those entrenched in defending scientific concordism, not unlike Galileo's accusers. No Christian today believes the earth is stationary, and no one interprets 1 Chr 16:30, Ps 93:1, or Ps 96:10 literally. For that matter, the Galileo affair teaches us that science contributes to biblical interpretation, and this may also be the case with the evolutionary sciences.

The Foundations of the Earth

The ancients conceived the immobility of the earth to be like the stability offered by the foundations of a building. At that point in history the notion of gravity had yet to be understood. In fact, it was only in the late seventeenth century that this scientific concept was first formulated by Isaac Newton. Consequently, ancient people used familiar objects to explain the immovability of the world. This practice continues today in the development of scientific models such as the magnetic "field" theory.

The biblical writers employed engineering categories like "foundations" and "pillars" to conceptualize the world's stability. For example, 1 Sam 2:8 states, "The foundations of the earth are the Lord's, upon them He has set the world." Similarly, the psalmist writes, "When the earth and all its people quake, it is I [God] who hold its pillars firm" (Ps 75:3) and "God set the earth on its foundations; it can never be moved" (Ps 104:5). In Job 38:4–6, the Creator asks, "Where were you when I laid the foundation of the earth? . . . On what were its footings set? Or who laid its cornerstone?" Passages like these occur over 25 times in Scripture, and in most of them the earth's stability is the result of God's creative and sustaining activity. In other words, this ancient geology is employed to reveal a theological message about the creation and its Creator.

Interestingly, two other biblical passages attribute the earth's stability to a foundation of water instead of pillars. Psalm 24:2 states, "The earth is the Lord's, and everything in it, the world, and all who live in it. For He has founded it upon the seas, and established it upon the waters." Psalm 136:6 also asserts, "The Lord spreads out the earth upon the waters." Without doubt, there is a serious inconsistency between these verses and those referring to the pillars of the earth. And regrettably, some people reject the Bible because of contradictions such as these.

However, the Message-Incident Principle resolves this situation quickly. The purpose of passages referring to the foundations of the earth is to reveal the inerrant message that God is the Creator and Sustainer of the world. For the majority of inspired authors, it made sense that the phenomenon of immobility was due to engineered pillars. But the writers of Ps 24 and 136 conceived the cause of this stability differently (the reason for this is explained by the next ancient geological feature presented). In other words, the Holy Spirit revealed the identical divine message using two different incidental ancient geologies. In a subtle way, the Bible

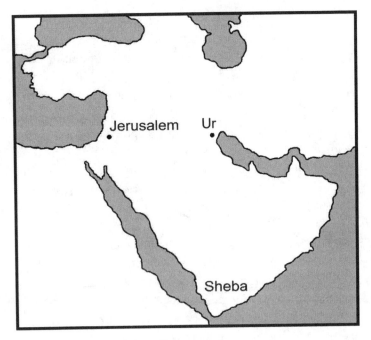

Fig 4-4. Geography of Ancient Near East.

itself through this contradiction offers evidence that its purpose is not to reveal scientific facts about the earth.[9]

The Circumferential Sea Surrounding the Earth

Ancient Near Eastern peoples thought that the earth was like an island surrounded by a circumferential sea. Two phenomenological factors led to this logical notion. First, the constant visual impact of the horizon gives the impression that the world is enclosed within a circular boundary. Second, it was common knowledge during this time that journeys in any direction eventually led to a body of water. An appreciation of the regional geography makes such a conclusion reasonable: the Mediterranean Sea is west, the Black and Caspian Seas are north, the Persian Gulf is east, and the Arabian and Red Seas are south (Fig 4-4). A sixth-century BC Babylonian map of the world confirms this notion of a sea encircling the earth (Fig 4-5). In this light, it makes perfect sense that some biblical authors conceived the earth to be founded upon water as seen in Psalm 24 and 136.

Intimations of the circumferential sea appear in Scripture. Proverbs 8:22–31 and Job 26:7–14 describe the creation of the world. The former states, "God inscribed a circle on the face of the deep" (v. 27), and the latter asserts, "God has inscribed a circle on the surface of the waters" (v. 10). The Hebrew word translated as "circle" (*ḥûg*) refers to a two-dimensional geometric figure. It is sometimes rendered in English Bibles as "horizon" or "compass," indicating its association with a flat surface. Undoubtedly, Prov 8:27 and Job 26:10 depict the opening scene in the Bible when "darkness was over the surface of the deep, and the Spirit of God was hovering over the waters" (Gen 1:2). Therefore, instead of beginning with a sphere of water enveloping a global earth, as eisegetically pictured by most twenty-first century readers, God starts with a flat surface of water upon which He draws a circle to create the horizon. The purpose of these verses is not to reveal the structure of the universe, but to deliver the Message of Faith that the Creator established the boundaries of the creation.

The Circularity of the Earth

Ancient geology asserts that the earth is circular. Undoubtedly, this notion was shaped by the concept that a circumferential sea bordered the world at the horizon. The prophet Isaiah reflects this ancient phenomenological perspective by writing, "God sits enthroned above the circle of the earth, and its people are like grasshoppers. He stretches out the heavens like a canopy, and spreads them out like a tent to live in" (Isa 40:22). Again, the Hebrew word translated "circle" (*ḥûg*) refers to a two-dimensional flat surface. The context of the verse complements this interpretation. Isaiah compares the universe to a tent that features a domed canopy over a flat floor. Other biblical passages employ the tent model in describing the structure of the world (Pss 19:4, 104:2). Thus, when God looks down from heaven, He sees the entire earth and its circular border meeting the circumferential sea. The purpose of Isa 40:22 is not to reveal the shape of the earth. Instead, the Messages of Faith in this verse are that God is the Creator and King of the entire universe and that He sees the activities of every person.

The circular earth is featured in the sixth-century BC Babylonian map of the world (Fig 4-5).[10] The Babylonians thought that the city of Babylon was literally at the center of the earth, and they termed this region the "navel" of the world. This ancient geology is also found in Scripture

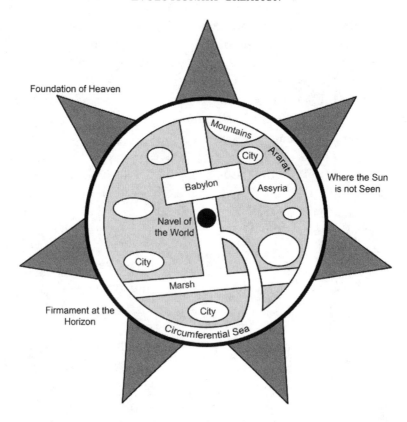

Fig 4-5. Babylonian World Map. This 6th century BC map presents a flat circular earth bordered by a circumferential sea. The solid dome of heaven ends at the horizon and is supported by seven foundations/pillars. Redrawn by Kenneth Kully.

when King Nebuchadnezzar of Babylon asks the prophet Daniel to interpret his dream. He states, "Upon my bed this is what I saw: There was a tree at the center of the earth" (Dan 4:10). Obviously, there is no "center" on the surface of a sphere. Only in the context of a two-dimensional circular earth does this verse make sense. Moreover, a tree at the center of the earth would be destroyed in an instant by the iron core, which is about 10,000°F! But again, the purpose of the Bible is not to disclose science and the shape of the earth. In this case, the Holy Spirit descended to Nebuchadnezzar's level and used the geology-of-the-day. Comparing this king to a great tree growing in the center of a circular world, God revealed that he would cut him down if he did not repent of sin.

In most English Bibles, four verses refer to the earth having "corners," conflicting possibly with the ancient notion that the earth was circular. For example, Rev 7:1 states, "I saw four angels standing at the four corners of the earth, holding back the four winds of the earth" (cf., Rev 20:8; Isa 11:12; Ezek 7:2). But the Greek term *gōnia* and the Hebrew word *kānāp* also mean "edge, extremity, or hidden place." In addition, note that this verse also refers to "four winds." The categorization of the wind (and the earth) into north, south, east, and west is phenomenological and reflects human sensory experience. We see in front of us, we hear to the left and right of us, and we have no such sensory perception behind us. Thus, there is no conflict between references to the earth being circular and having four extremities. This reflects the interaction of two phenomenological factors—the horizon and the anatomical position of human senses. But more importantly, these four verses referring to the "edges" of the earth reveal a similar Message of Faith: God is sovereign over the entire earth, even at its farthest "extremities" and "hidden places."

The Ends of the Earth

People in the ancient Near East claimed that the earth literally had ends like a table. This is reasonable because in their journeys they eventually came to the end of dry land and the shore of what they perceived to be a great circumferential sea. The Bible reflects this ancient geology in the phrase "the ends of the earth," which appears nearly 50 times. A number of these passages illustrate the relationship between this ancient science and the Message-Incident Principle.

In Dan 4:12, the tree at the center of the earth "grew great and strong, its top reached to heaven and it was visible to the ends of the whole earth."[11] Only in the context of a flat earth with ends does this passage make sense. On a spherical planet, it is not possible to see the "whole" earth from any tree, no matter how tall it might be. Ancient geology also appears with the call of Abraham from the city of Ur, which was near the Persian Gulf (Gen 11:31; Heb 11:8). Isaiah writes, "O Israel my servant, Jacob, whom I have chosen, you descendants of Abraham my friend, I took you from the ends of the earth, and called you from its remotest parts" (Isa 41:8–9). The furthest land from Israel on a spherical earth is South America. However, if the world was envisioned as an island, then understanding Ur to be at its edge is logical for ancient Near Eastern peoples. Similarly, in sharply denouncing the "wicked and adulterous generation" of His day, Jesus proclaims, "The Queen of the South will rise at the judgment with this generation and condemn it; for she came from the ends of the earth to listen to Solomon's wisdom, and now One greater than Solomon is here" (Matt 12:42; cf., 1 Kgs 10:1–13). The Lord is referring to the Queen of Sheba, whose land was in the southwest corner of the Arabian Peninsula. From an ancient geological perspective, this city is at end of the earth. Fig 4-4 identifies the ancient sites of Ur and Sheba.

The purpose of Dan 4, Isa 41, and Matt 12 is not to reveal that the earth literally has ends like a table. Rather, this ancient Near Eastern understanding of geology is an incidental vessel that transports infallible Messages of Faith. To Nebuchadnezzar, the revelation was a command to repent of sin. For Israel, it was a comforting message that God had personally chosen them to be His people. And to the corrupt generation in Jesus' day, it was a warning that there will be a judgment day. But at the same time, "One greater than Solomon" had descended to earth to reveal divine wisdom so we could live in fullness and joy.

The Underworld and Underside of the Earth

Ancient geology held that the earth had an underside and an underworld. Such notions are reasonable. We all experience the phenomena of places that are above and below us. The Old Testament refers to the underworld as sh^e'ōl, and English translations render this Hebrew word as the "grave," "pit," and "hell." In 40 of the 65 times that it appears, the context and associated terminology (going down to, depths of) indicates that sh^e'ōl is below the surface of the earth (Num 16:31–33; Prov 5:5; Isa 14:15). Similarly, the New Testament calls this region hādes or geenna and it is often translated as "hell." In half of the 20 times these Greek words appear, the context presupposes a place below the earth's surface (Matt 11:23; Luke 10:15; Rev 20:14).

The New Testament also refers to a region "under the earth." The apostle John praises, "I heard every creature in heaven and on earth and under the earth and on the sea, and all that is in them, singing, 'To Him who sits on the throne and to the Lamb be praise and honor and power for ever and ever!'" (Rev 5:13; cf., Rev 5:3; Eph 4:9–10). As noted earlier, Paul writes that "at the name of Jesus every knee should bow, in heaven and on earth and under the earth" (Phil 2:10). However, English Bibles fail to render fully the meaning of the last phrase in the original Greek. Translated more precisely, *katachthoniōn* refers to "the beings down (*kata*) in the chthonic (*chthovios*) or subterranean world." Ancient Near Eastern literature reveals that this 3-tier structure of the entire universe was the science-of-the-day.[12] For the biblical writers, "the underworld" and "the underside of the earth" were every bit as real as the heaven, earth, and sea. These terms were not poetic figures of speech, nor were they only "an appearance" or "phenomenological" as some understand today.

By applying the Message-Incident Principle to Phil 2:10 and Rev 5:13, it is evident that the purpose of these verses is not to reveal that the universe has three physical tiers. Rather, the Holy Spirit employs ancient scientific categories that refer to the totality and immensity of the cosmos. In so doing, the divine revelation is that Jesus is Lord over every region of the entire creation.

The Flat Earth

The Bible never specifically states that the earth is flat. Rather, scriptural evidence from terms and contexts indicates that this ancient geological notion was assumed to be a fact by the inspired writers and their readers. In the same way that when we see the word "earth" and automatically visualize a spherical planet, they immediately pictured a flat surface. Combining the previous six geological features, the ancients believed that the earth was like a round table with edges, an underside, and stable legs. As noted earlier, if it was the Holy Spirit's intention to disclose modern scientific facts in the Bible, then surely He would have revealed that our home is a sphere. But nowhere in Scripture is the earth referred to as a globe, nor is it ever compared to an object like a ball or an orange. This silence speaks volumes against the popular Christian belief that scientific concordism is an inerrant and infallible feature of the Bible.

The idea that the earth was flat is perfectly logical from an ancient phenomenological perspective. Anyone looking out from an elevated position perceives the world to be a level plain bordered by the horizon. This ancient geology is reflected in the well-known passage on the temptation of Jesus. Matthew 4:8 states, "Again the devil took Jesus to a very high mountain and showed Him all the kingdoms of the world and their splendor." The Greek word in this verse translated into English as "world," is *kosmos*, which literally means "the entire universe or sum total of everything that exists." Yet everyone knows that there were great civilizations in China and South America at this time, and no matter how tall this mountain might have been, it was not possible for Jesus to see "all the kingdoms of the world." Without a doubt, understanding Scripture in this way is not only challenging, but also quite counterintuitive.

Application of the Message-Incident Principle avoids a needless "conflict" or "contradiction" between the Bible and modern geology in Matt 4:8. The Holy Spirit's intention was not to reveal earth science in this verse. Rather, God used the geology-of-the-day as a vessel to deliver the inerrant revelation that in taking on our very humanity, Jesus was tempted by the devil in every way as we are. But instead of falling into sin, our Lord and Savior was victorious!

ANCIENT ASTRONOMY

Ancient peoples were enthralled by the grandeur and majesty of the heavens. The biblical writers in particular made numerous references to astronomical bodies and structures. One of the most beloved is Ps 19:1, "The heavens declare the glory of God; the skies proclaim the work of His hands."[13] Indeed they do! The Creator has inscribed a non-verbal revelation deeply into the celestial world to show us His eternal strength and divine character.

This section examines biblical passages that refer to the heavens. It will become clear that God's Word offers an ancient understanding of astronomy. Because of their ancient phenomenological perspective, the inspired writers of Scripture believed: (1) the sun actually moved across the sky every day, (2) a solid dome-like structure, called the "firmament," enclosed the circumferential sea and circular earth, (3) a body of water was held up by the firmament, (4) the heavens had foundations and ends, (5) the sun, moon, and stars were embedded in the firmament, (6) the stars will fall to the earth and heaven will be rolled up at the final judgment, and (7) the heavens were divided into two regions: the lower heavens, including the atmosphere and the firmament; and the highest heavens, the realm of God and angels.

The Daily Movement of the Sun across the Sky

Ancient peoples believed that the sun literally crossed the sky each day. Experiencing the phenomenon of the sun traveling from east-to-west led inspired writers without hesitation to incorporate this idea into Scripture.

As the psalmist proclaims, "The sun rises at one end of the heavens and makes its circuit to the other" (Ps 19:6). Similarly, King Solomon writes, "The sun rises and the sun sets, and hurries back to where it rises" (Eccl 1:5; cf., Ps 50:1). Most Christians are familiar with Joshua's request that God stop the sun from setting in order to have more daylight to fight a battle. In answering his prayer, "The sun stopped in the middle of the sky and delayed going down about a full day" (Josh 10:13). And Jesus accommodated to His listeners by saying that our Father in heaven "causes His sun to rise on evil and good" (Matt 5:45). In total, the Bible makes over 60 references to the sun's daily movement across the sky.

Of course, no one today believes that the sun actually rises and sets. Though it certainly looks like it does, our modern phenomenological perspective recognizes that this is only an appearance when in actual fact the earth is rotating on its axis to produce this visual effect. Similarly, our use of the phrases "the setting sun" and "the rising sun" are poetic and figurative expressions that are informed by modern astronomy. But in ancient times the physical world was understood through an *ancient phenomenological perspective*. What ancient peoples saw with their eyes, they believed to be literally true. For them, the sun actually moved across the sky and the phrases "the setting sun" and "the rising sun" were concrete facts of nature.

History shows that belief in the daily movement of the sun remained as late as the seventeenth century. The Galileo affair focused on this very issue (and not on whether or not the earth was flat, as many misunderstand).[14] For that matter, in the previous century, protestant reformer Martin Luther used the Bible to claim that the sun literally moved. He was aware of Copernicus' new theory that the earth and planets circled around the sun (heliocentricity), but wrote-off the famed scientist because "the fool will turn the whole science of astronomy upside down."[15] Luther employed a strict literal interpretation of the Bible in order to defend an earth-centered view of the universe (geocentricity). By appealing to the miracle in Josh 10, he argued, "Holy Writ declares it was the sun and not the earth which Joshua commanded to stand still."[16] The depiction of creation in Luther's 1534 translation of the Bible presents further evidence of his geocentric understanding of the universe (Fig 4-6).[17]

Clearly, Luther was a scientific concordist. But Christians today reject geocentric astronomy and the literal interpretation of verses stating

Fig 4-6. The Geocentric Universe of Martin Luther. Redrawn by Andrea Dmytrash.

that the sun moves across the sky. Instead, they view Ps 19, Eccl 1, Josh 10, and Matt 5 in light of modern astronomy. That is, believers employ science to interpret Scripture. They also know that the purpose of these passages is to reveal God's Creatorship and Lordship over the sun, and not its position and operation in the heavens. In a subtle way, Christians already embrace the Message-Incident Principle, and they have a precedent in place for moving beyond scientific concordism.

The Firmament

Ancient astronomers believed that the circular earth and circumferential sea were enclosed by a firm dome overhead. From an ancient phenomenological point of view, the "vault" of the sky certainly appeared to be a solid immovable structure, similar to an inverted bowl. Early English translations of the Bible, like the King James Version, refer to it as the "firmament." For example, on the second day of creation God said, "'Let there be a firmament in the midst of the waters, and let it divide the waters from the waters.' And God made the firmament, and divided the waters which were under the firmament from the waters which were above the firmament: and it was so. And God called the firmament 'Heaven'" (Gen 1:6–8). Likewise, the King James Version renders Ps 19:1 as "The heavens declare the glory of God and the firmament sheweth His handywork."

Everyone knows there is no solid structure above the earth. Some modern translations of the Bible attempt to resolve this conflict between Scripture and science by using the word "expanse" instead of "firmament."[18] In doing so, they give the impression that on the second creation day God creates a vast empty region, alluding to outer space and the earth's atmosphere. However, this betrays the meaning of the Hebrew word *rāqîa*ʿ. The root of this noun is the verb *rāqaʿ* which means "to flatten," "stamp down," "spread out," and "hammer out." That is, this Hebrew verb carries a nuance of flattening something solid rather than opening a broad empty space. Exodus 39:3 and Isa 40:19 use *rāqaʿ* for pounding metals into thin plates, and Num 16:38 employs *riqqûaʿ* (broad plate) in a similar context. The verb *rāqaʿ* is even found in a passage referring to the creation of the sky, which is understood to be a firm surface like a metal. Job 37:18 asks, "Can you join God in spreading out the skies, hard as a mirror of cast bronze?" (cf, Exod 24:10; Job 22:14; Ezek 1:22).

In addition, early translations of Scripture conserve the original sense of *rāqîa'*. The Greek translation of the Old Testament, called the "Septuagint" and dated about 250 BC, renders this Hebrew word as *stereōma*, which means the "vault of heaven."[19] This noun is related to the adjective *stereos*, a common term for "firm," "hard," and "solid." The importance of the Septuagint cannot be overstated since New Testament writers often used it in quoting Old Testament passages. Similarly, the Latin translation of the Bible, the Vulgate, translates *rāqîa'* as *firmamentum*. This word is also associated with an adjective (*firmus*), from which derives the English word "firm." The Latin Bible was written during the fifth century AD and served the Church for over one thousand years. Its impact upon early English translations like the King James Version is clear in that it renders *rāqîa'* as firmament. Thus, the traditional and conservative understanding of this Hebrew term, as reflected in the early translations of the Bible, indicates that God created a solid structure over the earth on the second day of creation.

The presence of the term firmament in the Bible provides valuable insights for understanding the science in Scripture. By revealing that "the firmament proclaims the work of God's hands" in Ps 19, the Holy Spirit employs an ancient astronomical notion as a vessel to reveal the theological truth that the cosmos reflects intelligent design and points to the Creator. Moreover, the fact that God in Gen 1 creates a firmament to separate the waters above from the waters below is evidence that Scripture uses an ancient understanding of the origin of the heavens. Stated precisely, *divine creative action is filtered through ancient astronomical categories.*[20] The Holy Spirit descended to the intellectual level of the Hebrew writers and used their understanding of *how* the heavens were assembled. But in light of the Message-Incident Principle, this ancient view of astronomical origins is incidental to the divine revelation *that* God created the heavens.

The Waters Above in the Heavens

Ancient Near Eastern astronomy asserts that a body of water is held up by the firmament. As unusual as this is to our twenty-first century scientific categories, such a notion is very logical from an ancient phenomenological perspective. The color of the sky's dome is a changing blue similar to a lake or sea. As well, rain falls to the ground from above. These ancient peoples had no way of knowing that the blue of the heavens was a visual effect due to the scattering of short wave light in the upper atmosphere.

The Bible affirms the existence of a heavenly sea. As noted previously, Gen 1:6–8 states that the Creator made a firmament to separate the "waters above" from the "waters below." In Ps 104:2–3, "God stretches out the heavens like a tent and lays the beams of His upper chambers on their waters." Calling forth praise from the sun, moon, and stars, Ps 148:4 appeals to this heavenly sea, "Praise the Lord you highest heavens and you waters above the skies." And Jer 10:12–13 records, "God stretches out the heavens by His understanding. When He thunders, the waters in the heavens roar." Some Christians attempt to argue that the water referred to in these passages is water vapor. However, biblical Hebrew has words (*'ēd, nāśî', 'ānān*) that mean "vapor," "mist," "or cloud," and the inspired writers did not used them in these passages.[21]

The waters above do not correspond to any physical reality known to modern astronomy. This fact directly challenges scientific concordism. Put more bluntly, the Bible refers to a structure in the heavens that does not exist. Martin Luther recognized this problem and argued,

> We Christians must be different from the philosophers [i.e., natural philosophers or scientists] in the way we think about the causes of things. And if some are beyond our comprehension like those before us concerning the waters above the heavens, we must believe them rather than wickedly deny them or presumptuously interpret them in conformity with our understanding.[22]

Of course, Christians today certainly do not consider themselves "wicked" or "presumptuous" for rejecting the idea of a heavenly sea. This problem vanishes in light of the Message-Incident Principle. The Holy Spirit accommodated to the ancient astronomy of the Hebrews in order to reveal that God created the visually dominant blue "structure" overhead. This infallible divine disclosure remains steadfast for us—the Creator made the phenomenon of the blue sky.

The Foundations and Ends of the Heavens

Ancient astronomers believed that the firmament rested on foundations or pillars. This is a logical conclusion because this heavenly structure appeared to be solid and immovable. Moreover, the visual impact of the horizon led to the reasonable conclusion that the dome of heaven had "ends" (See Fig 4-5). The Bible reflects these ancient astronomical concepts in the phrases "the foundations/pillars of the heavens" (Job 26:11; 2 Sam 22:8) and "the ends of the heavens" (Deut 4:32; Isa 13:5; Ps 19:6; Matt 24:31).

These ancient astronomical ideas offer clues into the interpretation of a few puzzling biblical passages. For example, 2 Sam 22:8 states, "The earth trembled and quaked, the foundations of the heavens shook; they trembled because God was angry" (cf., Job 26:11; Isa 13:13; Joel 2:10). Psalm 68:7–8 is even more baffling, "O God, when You marched through the wasteland, the earth shook, the heavens poured down rain" (cf., Judg 5:4). The King James Version translates the final clause of this verse as "the heavens dropped." The Hebrew language allows for both translations. According to twenty-first century scientific categories, these Scriptures make no sense. If the physical heavens in the Bible refer to outer space, how is it possible to shake the foundations of empty space? Why would the heaven and earth tremble at the same time? And why would heaven drip or drop if the earth is shaken?

The logic of these unusual biblical passages emerges if the ancient science is respected. The immobility of heaven and earth led ancient peoples to believe that these structures were set on foundations. The stability of the horizon where the ends of heaven (i.e., the ends of the firmament) met the flat world also contributed to the notion that they were connected. Thus, shaking the pillars of either of these structures was transmitted to the foundations of the other. In addition, the Hebrews at times saw slight changes in terrain after earthquakes as well as water seepage from cisterns. It is understandable then, that they envisioned the waters above either dripping through the heavenly vault or the firmament dropping a bit during such geological events.[23]

However, the purpose of these unusual passages is not to reveal the structure and operation of the universe. Instead, the Holy Spirit employs this incidental ancient science to reveal the inerrant Message of Faith that God is in total control of the heavens and the earth.

The Sun, Moon, and Stars in the Firmament

Ancient peoples concluded that the sun, moon, and stars were set in the firmament. From an ancient phenomenological perspective, this idea is reasonable. These astronomical bodies are in front of the blue heavenly sea and appear to be positioned in the surface of a structure upholding it. The Bible affirms this ancient astronomy. On the fourth day of creation, God said,

> Let there be lights in the firmament of heaven to separate the day from the night, and let them serve as signs to mark seasons and days and years, and let them be lights in the firmament of heaven to give light on the earth.' And it was so. God made two great lights—the greater light to govern the day and the lesser light to govern the night. He also made the stars. God set them in the firmament of heaven to give light on the earth, to govern the day and the night, and to separate light from darkness. And God saw it was good. And there was evening, and there was morning—the fourth day. (Gen 1:14–19)

Some Christians attempt to harmonize this passage with modern astronomy. They suggest that the Hebrew word traditionally translated as "firmament" actually refers to the "expanse" of outer space. But as noted previously, this betrays the meaning of *rāqîaʿ*.

The purpose of the fourth creation day is to reveal a radical theological message to the ancient world. More specifically, it is a polemic (a cutting critique) against pagan astral religion. Most people at that time believed the sun, moon, and stars were gods. But the biblical author, through the Holy Spirit, stripped these astronomical bodies of their divine status and made them mere creations of the Hebrew God. Even more radically, the Scripture threw these "gods" into servitude! Instead of men and women serving the heavenly bodies as demanded by astrological religions, the inspired writer states that the sun, moon, and stars were made to serve humanity. In other words, the Bible puts the heavenly bodies in their proper place. They have value because they are God's "good" creations, but they are definitely not gods worthy of worship.

Martin Luther's interpretation of the heavenly bodies in Gen 1 reveals once more the problem with scientific concordism. He claims, "Scripture . . . simply says that the moon, the sun, and the stars were placed in the firmament of the heaven, below and above which are the waters . . . The bodies of the stars, like that of the sun, are round, and they are fastened to the firmament like globes of fire" (see Fig 4-6).[24] Of course, no Christian today believes that the heavens are arranged in this way. Luther's astronomy serves as a caution against the use of the Bible in understanding the structure of the physical world. The ancient science in Scripture simply does not correspond to physical reality.

Falling Stars and Rolling Up of the Heavens

Ancient astronomy assumed that stars are quite small and that they sometimes dislodge from the firmament and fall to the earth. Undoubtedly, their appearance as luminous specks against the night sky, as well as the intermittent sighting of a streaking meteor, led to this very reasonable notion. It even appears in Scripture. Stars both "fall" to the earth (Isa 34:4; Matt 24:29; Rev 6:13) and can be "thrown down" to it (Dan 8:10; Rev 12:4). Scripture also employs ancient astronomy to describe the disassembling of the heavens at the end of the world on judgment day. God will shake the firmament, causing the stars to fall to earth, and then He will roll up this heavenly structure.

The prophet Isaiah envisions the end time period in this way: "All the stars of the heavens will be dissolved and the sky rolled up like a scroll; all the starry host will fall like withered leaves from the vine, like shriveled figs from the fig tree" (Isa 34:4). Similarly, Jesus prophesies that at "the coming of the Son of Man . . . the stars will fall from the sky, and the heavenly bodies will be shaken" (Matt 24:27, 29). John in the book of Revelation also pictures the end of the world: "The stars in the sky fell to earth, as late figs drop from a fig tree when shaken by a strong wind. The sky receded like a scroll, rolling up" (Rev 6:13–14). These Scriptures all make perfect sense from an ancient phenomenological point of view. Stars were small enough to fall to the earth, and the firmament, which was depicted as a tent canopy being spread out in the beginning of the world, would be rolled up at the end of time.

Certainly, caution is required when interpreting passages about the end times because they feature poetic language. However, this is not to say that everything referred to in prophecies has no correspondence to the real world, and consequently can be written off as "merely figurative." For example, Isa 34, Matt 24, and Rev 6 mention astronomical realities: heaven, earth, stars, and other heavenly bodies. No one denies their existence. In modern science, the use of familiar objects and processes to describe the structure and operation of the physical world is a well-established practice. Similarly, the inspired writers of these three passages use well-known objects (strong wind, withered leaves, vines, fig trees, late/shriveled figs) and processes (falling of withered leaves, dropping of late figs, rolling of scrolls) to describe the structure of the heavens and how they will be dismantled at the end of time. In the same way that the biblical writers literally believed in the ancient astronomy describing the assembly of the heavens, they also accepted the literal disassembly of these celestial structures.

End times passages describing the stars falling to earth and the heavens rolling up provide important insights for understanding the science in the Bible. Scripture clearly uses an ancient astronomy as a vessel to reveal the theological truth that the Creator will disassemble the world at the final judgment. The Holy Spirit accommodated to the intellectual level of the biblical authors and used their understanding of the structure of the heavens. Stated more precisely, *divine judgmental action is filtered through ancient astronomical categories.*[25] But in light of the Message-Incident Principle, this ancient astronomy is incidental to the infallible revelation that God will end the creation and that He will judge men and women.

The Lower Heavens and the Upper Heavens

Ancient Near Eastern peoples believed that the heavens had two basic regions—the lower heavens and the upper heavens. The former includes the atmosphere, the firmament with its luminary bodies, and the sea of waters above. The latter is the celestial realm where God/s and other celestial beings reside. It is important to emphasize that according to these ancients, both regions are real *physical* locations, with the upper heavens resting upon the lower heavens. The Bible features this ancient astronomy.

The Hebrew word for "heavens" is *shāmayim*. It carries many meanings and the context of the passage in which it appears normally determines its interpretation. This term can refer to the dome of heaven as seen on the second day of creation when "God called the firmament 'heavens'" (Gen 1:7). It can also mean "atmosphere" or "air" as found in the phrases "the birds of the heavens" (Gen 2:19–20; Ezek 31:6) and "the clouds of heavens" (Dan 7:13). *Shāmayim* includes the waters above the firmament. As the psalmist writes, "God stretches out the heavens like a tent and lays the beams of His upper chambers on their waters" (Ps 104:2–3; cf., Ps 148:4). This verse also identifies the location of the Creator's celestial dwelling place: it rests upon the heavenly sea. From an ancient perspective, the prayers of the Hebrews to God make sense: "Look down from heaven, your holy dwelling place, and bless your people Israel" (Deut 26:15; cf., Ps 33:13–14; Isa 40:22). Occasionally in the Old Testament, the upper heavens are differentiated as *shāmayim shāmayim* (literally, heavens of heavens) and translated "highest heavens." For example, "God made the heavens, the highest heavens with all their host, and the earth and all that is on it" (Neh 9:6; cf., 1 Kgs 8:27; Ps 148:4).

In the New Testament, the distinct heavenly structures of ancient astronomy are collapsed into one Greek word, making it difficult at times to understand and translate. *Ouranos* is rendered in modern English Bibles as "heaven" and "sky." In the lower heavens, this term can refer to the atmosphere or air as seen in the phrases "the birds of the heaven" (Matt 6:26; Luke 9:58) and "the clouds of heaven" (Matt 26:64; Mark 14:62). *Ouranos* also means the firmament since it is "opened" (John 1:51; Acts 7:56), "shaken" (Matt 24:29; Heb 12:26) and "rolled up" (Heb 1:12; Rev 6:14). Intimations exist for the waters above since the "sky" can be "shut" from rainfall (Luke 4:25; Rev 11:6). Regarding the upper heavens, *ouranos* refers to where God and His angels dwell in scores of New Testament passages. For example, "As Jesus was coming up out of the water, He saw heaven being torn open and the Spirit descending on Him like a dove. And a voice came from heaven: 'You are my Son, whom I love; with you I am well pleased'" (Mark 1:10–11).

Ancient astronomy casts light on a number of unusual biblical passages referring to the heavens. The opening of "the windows or floodgates of the heavens" in Noah's flood account (Gen 7:11) means that the waters above were being released through passageways in the firmament. The idea that the divine dwelling place was set on the waters above (Ps 104:3) brings meaning to Jeremiah's assertion, "When God thunders, the waters in the heavens roar" (Jer 10:13). In fact, the Hebrew word for "thunder" (*qōl*) means "voice." Together, these ancient notions clarify Ps 29:3 and 10, "The voice of the Lord is over the waters; the God of glory thunders, the Lord thunders over the mighty waters. . . . The Lord sits enthroned over the flood; the Lord is enthroned as King forever." In other words, thunder is the voice of God and He is seated on a throne above the heavenly sea, from which came the water for Noah's flood.

In the tower of Babel account, men thought they could build a structure to "reach to the heavens" (Gen 11:4) because according to ancient astronomy the divine heavenly realm was a physical place just above the earth. This ancient science is also seen in Jacob's dream (Gen 28:12–17). Scripture records, "Jacob saw a stairway resting on the earth, with its top reaching to heaven, and angels of God were ascending and descending on it. There above the ladder stood the Lord . . . Jacob was afraid and said, 'How awesome is this place! This is none other than the house of God; this is the gate of heaven.'" Thus, like the divinely inspired dream of King Nebuchadnezzar in which the great tree at the center of the earth grows to touch heaven (Dan 4:10–11), Jacob's vision from the Lord was delivered through an ancient understanding of astronomy. In other words, the Holy Spirit accommodated and descended to the human level in the revelatory process.

To summarize, the Bible definitely presents a 3-tiered universe as illustrated in Fig 4-1. This view of the cosmos was the best science-of-the-day thousands of years ago in the ancient Near East, and it was embraced by the inspired writers of God's Word and their readers.[26] References in Scripture to the earth set on immovable foundations, the heavens similar to a tent canopy, and the rising and setting sun are not fanciful poetic statements. These verses were intended to describe the literal structure and actual operation of the world. The use of common objects, like tents and building foundations, were models meant to convey the genuine arrangement of the heavens and the earth. But it is clear that the biblical understanding of geology and astronomy does not correspond to physical reality. Scientific concordism fails.

However, Messages of Faith are efficiently delivered through the incidental ancient geology and ancient astronomy in Scripture. Christians from every generation have understood that God is the sovereign Creator and Sustainer of the heavens and earth. Of course, recognizing the ancient science in the Bible is at first challenging. And reading beyond this ancient phenomenological perspective of nature is quite counterintuitive. Yet with time and practice this is possible, and it is particularly important in the origins debate. An implication of the ancient geology and ancient astronomy in the Bible is that the biology in Scripture should also be ancient. But before examining this crucial notion, well-known concordist interpretations often heard in Churches can now be re-evaluated.

EXCURSUS: EXAMPLES OF SCIENTIFIC
CONCORDISM RECONSIDERED

Circle of the Earth and Suspension of the Earth over Nothing

The two most popular verses used to "prove" that modern science is found in the Bible are Isa 40:22 and Job 26:7.[27] The former is simply presented as, "God sits enthroned above the circle of the earth," and the latter, "God spreads out the northern skies over empty space, and suspends the earth over nothing." Read through twenty-first century scientific categories, Isa 40 could be seen as depicting the outline of planet earth from outer space, and Job 26 as referring to it being suspended by gravitational forces. If these are correct interpretations, then modern science was placed in Scripture well before these discoveries. Scientific concordists argue that only a God who transcends time could have revealed these facts of nature, and consequently, this proves that the Bible is divinely inspired.

But these two examples are classic *biblical proof texts*. That is, they are taken out of their context and then manipulated by reading into them notions never intended by the human author or the Holy Spirit. In its entirety, Isa 40:22 reads, "God sits enthroned above the circle of the earth, and its people are like grasshoppers. He stretches out the heavens like a canopy, and spreads them out like a tent to live in." Clearly, this verse presents a universe with three tiers. The cosmos is compared to a tent with canopy above and a flat floor below. This is a familiar metaphor/model that is used in Scripture to describe the structure of the world (Pss 19:4–5, 104:2–3). Moreover, the ancient science in Isa 40:22 is consistent with other passages in this biblical book. Isaiah asserts that at the judgment "the sky will be rolled up like a scroll" and "all the starry host will fall" to earth (Isa 34:4). He also claims that God is "the Creator of the ends of the earth" (40:28) and that He took Abraham "from the ends of the earth, from its farthest corners" (41:9). Thus, Isa 40:22 must be interpreted in its context and in the light of ancient science. The "circle of the earth" refers to the circumferential shore of a flat earth (Fig 4-5).

The scientific concordist interpretation of Job 26:7 also tears this verse out of its chapter and book. The ancient astronomy is clearly seen a few verses later, "The pillars of the heavens quake, aghast at God's rebuke" (26:11). Belief that the heavens had foundations makes sense because the inspired author accepted the reality of the firmament as seen in the rhetorical question, "Can you join God in spreading out the skies, hard as a mirror of cast bronze?" (37:18). The location of the divine dwelling in the 3-tier universe is reflected in another query, "Who can understand how He thunders from His pavilion?" (36:29). In other words, the Lord lives just overhead in an area where the rumble of thunder arises. The book of Job also features an ancient geology: "God unleashes His lightning beneath the whole heaven and sends it to the ends of the earth" (37:3), "He shakes the earth from its place and makes its pillars tremble" (9:6), and "Where were you when [God] laid the earth's foundation?" (38:4). In addition, the Hebrew word *tālāh*, which is translated "suspends" in Job 26:7, appears in contexts of hanging up an object like a utensil on a peg (Isa 22:24), weapons on a wall (Ezek 27:10), or a lyre on a tree (Ps 137:2). It does not refer to hovering in empty space, but to hanging from some perch. Job 26:7 simply states that the earth is not hung from anything in the 3-tier universe.

The scientific concordist interpretations of Isa 40:22 and Job 26:7 are proof texts. They rip these verses out of Scripture and their ancient scientific context. The popular concordist understandings of the "circle" of the earth and the "suspension" of the earth over nothing are un-biblical.

Water Canopy and Water Vapor Theories

Scientific concordists offer two theories for the waters above made on the second day of creation. Young earth creationists assert that this term refers to a canopy of water that enveloped the earth before the flood in Gen 6–9. Progressive creationists claim that the waters above are water vapor in the atmosphere. But a closer examination of these concordist interpretations reveals numerous difficulties.

In the classic defense of young earth creation, *The Genesis Flood: The Biblical Record and Its Scientific Implications* (1961), Henry Morris and John Whitcomb claim:

> On the second day of creation, the waters covering the earth's surface were divided into two great reservoirs—one below the firmament and one above; the firmament being the "expanse" above the earth now corresponding to the troposphere. . . . With the Biblical testimony concerning a pre-flood canopy of waters, we have an adequate source for the waters of a universal flood.[28]

Fig 4-7 (B) depicts Morris and Whitcomb's water canopy theory. They contend there was a unique environment on earth before Noah's flood

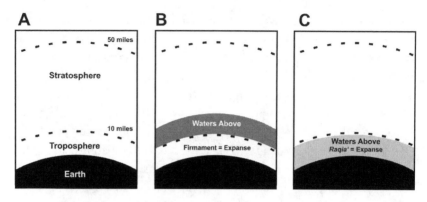

Fig 4-7. Scientific Concordist Interpretations of the Waters Above. Structure of Lower Atmosphere (A), Water Canopy Theory (B), Water Vapour Theory (C). Note that both concordist models read the modern notion of a spherical earth into the Bible.

that allowed people to live over 900 years as recorded in the Gen 5 genealogy. With the collapse of these protective waters during the deluge, temperature and humidity dropped, and damaging radiation began to fall upon earth. As a result, lifespan reduced progressively, from 600 years to 148 as stated in Gen 11, and then to ages seen today.

However, problems abound with the water canopy theory. First, note that Morris and Whitcomb have an erroneous understanding of the word "firmament." They believe that it is an atmospheric "expanse" that corresponds to the troposphere. But the Hebrew word *rāqîaʿ* is an ancient astronomical notion that refers to a solid structure in the heavens. Second, on the fourth creation day God places the sun, moon, and stars *in* the firmament, which obviously cannot be the troposphere. Third, Pss 104 and 148 were written during King David's reign in the tenth century BC, and these passages refer to a heavenly sea. In other words, the purported water canopy was still intact well after Noah's flood. Finally, it must be pointed out that Morris and Whitcomb have departed from the *conservative* Christian interpretation of the waters above. As the writings of Martin Luther reveal, the Church for over 1500 years believed there was a body of water just overhead in heaven.

Leading progressive creationist Hugh Ross defends the water vapor theory of the waters above. In dealing with the second day of creation, this scientific concordist asserts, "God's 'separation' of the water accurately describes the formation of the troposphere, the atmospheric layer just above the ocean where clouds form and humidity resides, as distinct from the stratosphere, mesosphere, and ionosphere lying above." Consequently, he defines the Hebrew word *rāqîaʿ* as "the atmosphere immediately above the surface of the earth."[29] Fig 4-7 (C) illustrates Ross's interpretation of the waters above. However, a mistaken understanding of *rāqîaʿ* repeats the erroneous conclusion that it refers to an atmospheric expanse, specifically the troposphere. Once more the problem appears with the placement of the sun, moon, and stars in this region. Finally, if the inspired author had intended the waters above to mean vapor, there were Hebrew terms (*'ēd*, *nāsî'*, *'ānān*) that were available to him. But he did not use them.

The canopy and water vapor theories force into Scripture modern scientific categories that are alien to the Word of God. Both models are based on the earth being spherical and enveloped by the troposphere. But as noted earlier in this chapter, this is an eisegetical reading of the term "earth." As a result, young earth creationist and progressive creationist views of the waters above are un-biblical.

ANCIENT BIOLOGY

The Bible also features an ancient understanding of biology. Passages referring to the structure and operation of living organisms are fewer than those that deal with the heavens and the earth, but similar to geology and astronomy in Scripture, biology is viewed through ancient phenomenological categories. The Word of God offers an ancient conception of: (1) taxonomy, (2) botany, (3) human reproduction, and (4) suffering, disabilities, and diseases.

Taxonomy

The human impulse to categorize plants and animals appears throughout history. King Solomon became famous not only for his godly wisdom, but also his taxonomical knowledge. 1 Kings 4:33 states that he "described plant life, from the cedar of Lebanon to the hyssop that grows out of walls. He also taught about animals and birds, reptiles and fish." The classification of life in Scripture is from an ancient perspective and often overlooks anatomical and physiological differences that are foundational to modern taxonomy.

For example, the bat is categorized as a bird. According to Lev 11:13–19, "These are the birds you are to detest and are not eat because they are detestable: the eagle, the vulture, the black vulture, the red kite, any kind of black kite, any kind of raven, the horned owl, the screech owl, the gull, any kind of hawk, the little owl, the cormorant, the great owl, the white owl, the desert owl, the osprey, the stork, any kind of heron, the hoopoe and *the bat*" (italics added). Of course, such a classification is reasonable because bats fly. However, these creatures are not birds but mammals with distinguishing non-avian features such as body hair, mammary glands, and a placental attachment. Similarly, the coney (also known as the rock badger or hyrax) and the rabbit are classified as ruminants. Leviticus 11:5–6 states, "The coney, though it chews the cud, does not have a split hoof; it is unclean for you. The rabbit, though it chews the cud, does not have a split hoof; it is unclean for you." The repetitive and side-to-side jaw actions of both of these animals give the visual impression of chewing the cud, but neither are ruminants with multiple-chambered stomachs.

The purpose of these passages in the book of Leviticus is not to reveal taxonomy. Rather, the practice of dietary laws was part of God's plan in separating the Hebrews from the pagan cultures around them. That is, the Message of Faith throughout Leviticus is that God was personally creating a holy nation to serve His purposes.

Taxonomical categories based on an ancient phenomenological perspective of living organisms also appear in Gen 1. On the third day of creation, vegetation is classified with regard to the production of seeds, including "seed-bearing plants" and "trees that bear fruit with seeds." The creation of animals on days five and six reflects their ecological niche—air, sea, or land. The taxonomy of land animals is based on both their type of locomotion and level of domestication—livestock, crawlers, or wild. Of particular significance to the origins debate, Gen 1 indicates that living creatures do not change. The phrase "according to its/their kind/s" appears ten times and reflects static or immutable taxonomical categories. Such a classification makes perfect sense thousands of years ago. In the eyes of ancient peoples, hens laid eggs that always produced chicks, ewes only gave birth to lambs, and women were invariably the mothers of infants. Therefore, the divine acts that created living organisms in Gen 1 are shaped by an ancient biology. Stated more precisely, *God's creative action in the origin of life is filtered through ancient taxonomical categories.*[30] This biblical fact has far-reaching implications and these are explained in subsequent chapters.

But again, the intention of Scripture is not to present categories for biological classification. The purpose of Gen 1 is to reveal that God made plants and animals, including men and women. In order to do so, the Holy Spirit knelt down to the intellectual level of the ancient Hebrews and employed their taxonomy as an incidental vessel in proclaiming the Message of Faith that He is the Creator of each and every living creature.

Botany

The beginning of agriculture in the ancient world played a major role in the advancement of civilization. The importance of harvesting for the Hebrews is seen in their Feast of Weeks (Harvest) and Feast of Ingathering (Tabernacles). The former celebrated the first fruits in late spring (Lev 23:15–21), and the latter crops in autumn (v. 33–43). Knowledge of plants, their seeds, and the land in which they were sown was essential information for the survival of ancient peoples. The Bible presents a number of ancient botanical concepts.

Many Christians are familiar with Jesus' parable of the mustard seed and the problem concerning His assertion about the size of this seed. The Lord asks, "With what can we compare the kingdom of God, or what parable will we use for it? It is like a mustard seed, which, when sown upon the ground, is the smallest of all the seeds on the earth; yet it grows up and becomes the greatest of all shrubs, and puts forth large branches, so that the birds of the air can make nests in its shade" (Mark 4:30–32).[31] However, the mustard seed is not "the smallest of all seeds on the earth." Orchid seeds are much smaller, to cite one example. But perceived through the eyes of ancient individuals, mustard seeds were the smallest seeds. The Lord's purpose in this parable is not to teach botany. Rather, He uses the science-of-the-day in order to reveal an inerrant prophecy about the kingdom of God.

Similarly, Jesus employed an ancient understanding of seed germination. He asserts, "The hour has come for the Son of Man to be glorified. I tell you the truth, unless a kernel of wheat falls to the ground and *dies*, it remains only a single seed. But if it dies, it produces many seeds" (John 12:24–25). The apostle Paul also uses this botanical concept, "But someone may ask, 'How are the dead raised? With what kind of body will they come?' How foolish! What you sow does not come to life unless it *dies*" (1 Cor 15:35–37). Everyone today knows that if a seed dies, it decomposes and will not germinate. Yet from an ancient phenomenological perspective this idea is reasonable. Just prior to germination, the covering of a seed breaks down, giving the appearance that the seed rots and dies. But Jesus and Paul are not offering the science of how plants sprout. More importantly, a Message of Faith is being revealed. The Lord is prophesying His resurrection and the growth of the Church, and the apostle is affirming that Christians in the future will be raised from the dead to enjoy eternal life.

Ancient individuals also observed a causal connection between crop production and soil quality. The parable of the sower employs this ancient agricultural knowledge (Matt 13:3–9). Accordingly, seeds fail to germinate on hard paths, some are choked by competition, and those in deep soil fully take root. However, ancient botany had no idea about plant genetics and the critical part that DNA played in growth. Consequently, it appeared that seeds were passive and that the soil completely dictated plant development. Jesus uses this ancient scientific notion in the parable of the growing seed. He states, "This is what the Kingdom of God is like. A man scatters seed on the ground. Night and day, whether he sleeps or gets up, the seed sprouts, though he does not know how. *All by itself* the soil produces grain—first the stalk, then the head, then the full kernel in the head. As soon as the grain is ripe, he puts the sickle to it, because the harvest is come" (Mark 4:26–29; italics added). Once more, the Lord descends to the knowledge level of His audience by using first-century botany in order to reveal an infallible truth regarding the growth of God's Kingdom and the end of the age.

Human Reproduction

The birth of children was a central and celebrated aspect in ancient cultures, including the nation of Israel. Large families were esteemed and a mark of God's blessing. As the psalmist states, "Sons are a heritage from the Lord, children a reward from Him. . . . Blessed is the man whose quiver is full of them" (Ps 127:3, 5). Consequently, infertility was deemed a "disgrace" and assumed to be a problem limited to the wombs of women. This idea is expressed by Rachel upon realizing she was pregnant. After an answer to prayer had "opened her womb," she gratefully announced, "God has take away my disgrace" (Gen 30:22–23).

It is not surprising that ancient peoples understood human reproduction through botanical categories since agriculture was a major part of their life. They conceptualized that "seeds" were "planted" by a man during sexual intercourse, and "fruit of the womb" developed within a woman. This "1-seed" model of reproduction, also known as "preformatism," makes sense from an ancient phenomenological perspective.[32] Males ejaculate during sex, giving the impression that they are the only direct contributors in the creation of life, while females appear to be involved indirectly as receptacles. This ancient view of human reproduction is

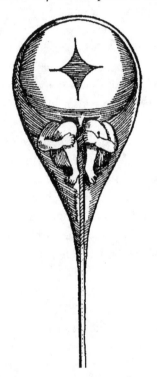

evident in a passage from the Greek poet Aeschylus during the fifth century BC: "The mother is no parent of that which is called her child, but only the nurse of the new-planted seed that grows. The parent is he who mounts. She preserves a stranger's seed, if no god interferes."[33] The ancients believed that an entire miniature human being was tightly packed within a man's "seed." Historically, this notion persisted as late as the seventeenth century even after the invention of the first microscopes (Fig 4-8).[34]

The Bible also features the 1-seed model of human reproduction. Hebrews 11:11 records, "By faith Abraham even though he was past age—and Sarah herself was barren—was enabled to become a father because he considered Him faithful who had made the promise." This English rendition fails to give the full meaning of

Fig 4-8. Seventeenth-Century Depiction of the 1-Seed Theory. An entire miniature human is packed tightly into a male "seed."

the original Greek. Literally translated, the clause "was enabled to become a father" is actually "was enabled to throw down seed." The Greek expression "*kattaballō* (to throw down) *sperma* (seed)" is a technical term found only in association with males and refers to ejaculation. The agricultural analogy to seeding a field is obvious. Of course, the modern English word "sperm" comes from *sperma*, but originally this Greek word had three meanings: (1) the seed planted in fields, (2) the seed men release during intercourse, and (3) the descendants in a family. In Hebrew, the noun *zera'* also carries these same denotations and the related verb *zāra'* refers to sowing, scattering seed, and being made pregnant. In other words, an expectant woman is understood as one who has been seeded by a man. Nowhere in Scripture is there mention of women contributing seed during sex, or having seed in their reproductive organs. Without the advantage of microscopes, this was a perfectly logical notion from an ancient point of view.

Hebrews 7:9–10 further illustrates the 1-seed model of reproduction. The author writes, "One might even say that Levi, who collects the tenth, paid the tenth through Abraham, because when Melchizedek met Abraham, Levi was still in the body of his ancestor." A more precise translation of the Greek in the final clause is: "in the reproductive organs of his ancestor."[35] Of course, this makes no sense in light of twenty-first century biology. But it is very reasonable if an entire person is within the seed of a man, and within this tiny individual another even smaller being in the reproductive organs, and so on. In other words, the ancient understanding of reproduction is like a set of Russians dolls with one doll inside another. The book of Genesis records that Abraham fathered Isaac, who then was the father of Jacob, who finally fathered Levi. From an ancient phenomenological perspective, Levi was literally "in the reproductive organs" of Abraham at the time the tenth was paid to Melchizedek.

Biblical references to human infertility also reflect an ancient reproductive biology. Only women are stated as "barren" in Scripture, never men. Examples include Sarah (Gen 11:30; Heb 11:11), Rebekah (Gen 25:21), Rachel (Gen 29:31), and Elizabeth (Luke 1:7, 36).[36] The Hebrew word for barren ('āqār) clearly shows the connection ancient peoples envisioned between reproduction and agriculture. It comes from the verb 'āqar which means "to uproot, pluck up" as seen in the phrase "a time to plant and a time to uproot" (Eccl 3:2). Similarly, Greek words for barren (steiros, steriphos) are related to the adjective stereos, which as noted previously with the word stereōma (firmament), means "firm," "hard," and "solid." In particular, steriphos is used to describe both firm ground and infertile women. Why would a female be considered "uprooted" and "hard" should she not be able to bear children? It is because ancient science understood wombs to be like fields. Barrenness was due to seeds being plucked up after they had been "planted" by a man during intercourse. Undoubtedly, seeing miscarriages contributed to this idea. As well, the womb of a barren woman was like hard ground in which seeds do not take root.

It must be emphasized that the Bible's attribution of barrenness to only females is in no way intended to disrespect women. Modern medicine has discovered that infertility is caused 30–40% of the time by males, 30–40% by females, and the remainder by both or is unknown.[37] But from an ancient phenomenological perspective, it makes sense to believe that male seed never fails. Wheat and barley were common crops in the ancient Near East, and it is estimated that the germination rate of their seeds was more than 80%.[38] Thus, in the eyes of ancient farmers sowing a field, it would appear that seeds are always successful and productive. They also saw that scanty crops resulted if the field was poor. This ancient agricultural notion is found in Jesus' parable of the sower. Hard ground, shallow soil filled with rocks, and land infested by competing weeds inhibit the development of seed. Only in a "good" field does seed grow into a full crop. In the same way, only a "fertile" womb "produces" the "fruit" of children.

The purpose of passages in Scripture referring to infertility is not to reveal the facts of reproductive biology. No Christian doctor today studies the Word of God in order to understand the physical processes behind this problem. Rather, these biblical passages are examples of God answering prayer and fulfilling His promises. This is the Message of Faith. The exact cause behind each incident of infertility in Scripture cannot be known because the problem is cast in an incidental ancient science—the 1-seed model of reproduction. Of course, it is within the Holy Spirit's power to reveal the actual cause of barrenness. When applicable, He could have stated that flagella motility in sperm cells was poor. But would any ancient person have understood this? No. Instead, God reveals at the comprehension level of His people in order not to confuse or distract them. The miraculous birth of children to barren women in Scripture testifies to His sovereign power over nature and fulfills His promise of creating a holy nation. And most importantly, with the knowledge that male "seed" is absolutely necessary in procreation, ancient peoples in first-century Israel would have completely understood that a dramatic divine event had occurred when a virgin girl became pregnant (Matt 1:18).

It must be noted that ancient reproductive biology is implied in Gen 1. On the sixth day of creation God said, "Let the *land* produce living creatures according to their kinds: livestock, creatures that move along the ground, and wild animals" (Gen 1:24). Of course, this idea makes no sense to twenty-first century biology. But it is reasonable in light of the

1-seed model of reproduction and the perceived similarities between plant and animal development. The creation of new organisms in both cases involves the sowing and growth of seeds in a fertile field. Moreover, the parallel panels in Gen 1 suggest similar creative mechanisms in the earth on the third and sixth creation days (see Fig 6-3). In the former God commands, "Let the land produce vegetation" (v. 11), and in the latter, "Let the land produce living creatures" (v. 24). Even the Hebrew verb translated "produce" (*yāsā'*) in verse 24 is the same one used in verse 12, "And the land produced vegetation."

Some might argue that the creation of land animals on the sixth day of creation echoes the ancient pagan notion of mother earth.[39] However, the radical divine revelation in Gen 1 is that there is only one Creator God. In the same way that the creation of the sun, moon, and stars on the fourth day of creation strips away any hint of divinity from these heavenly bodies, so too the sixth day rejects completely the belief that the earth is a god or a mother. Though the ancient origins notion of the earth producing animals appears in Gen 1, the inspired writer puts the God of the Hebrews in complete control of the process. The Message of Faith is clear: not only does God command all creatures to come forth from the earth, but He is also Creator of the earth.

Suffering, Disabilities and Diseases

From the dawn of civilization, humans have attempted to treat various physical afflictions. In ancient medicine, supernatural explanations played a prominent role in understanding suffering, disabilities, and diseases. A central cause for pain, handicaps, and pathology was an evil spirit invading the body of an individual. Justification for these attacks included fate, sorcery, carelessness, and sin. As a result, medical treatment in the ancient world was directed at eliminating the evil presence, and it integrated physical protocols and religious rituals. Pharmacological remedies (emetics, laxatives, diuretics), water purification (bathing, enemas), and surgery (bloodletting, skull puncturing) were used alongside incantations, exorcisms, and sacrifices.[40]

The Bible presents the ancient medical notion of a causal connection between evil spirits and physical afflictions. In passages dealing with Jesus' healing ministry, the gospel writers understood common disabilities and diseases to be caused by demonic possession. For example, Luke, who was a doctor, records, "Jesus was driving out a demon that was mute. When the demon left, the man who had been mute spoke" (Luke 11:14). Likewise Matthew writes, "Then they brought Him a demon-possessed man who was blind and mute, and Jesus healed him, so that he could both talk and see" (Matt 12:22). The Gospels also include an account of a father who approaches the Lord in hope that his son would be healed of an evil spirit. The man reports that the boy is "an epileptic" and that "a spirit seizes him and he suddenly screams; it throws him into convulsions so that he foams at the mouth." After calling the boy to Him, "Jesus rebuked the demon, and it came out of the boy, and he was healed from that moment" (Matt 17:14–18, cf., Mark 9:17–27; Luke 9:38–43).

It is quite significant that the Lord Himself employs the notion of demonic spirits as the cause of well-known physical afflictions. In the case of the epileptic boy, Jesus directly ordered, "You deaf and mute spirit, I command you, come out of him and never enter him again" (Mark 9:25). In another episode, Doctor Luke recounts,

> On a Sabbath Jesus was teaching in one of the synagogues, and a woman was there who had been crippled by a spirit for eighteen years. She was bent over and could not straighten up at all. When Jesus saw her, he called her forward and said to her, "Woman, you are set free from your infirmity." Then he put his hands on her, and immediately she straightened up and praised God. . . . Jesus said, "Should not this woman, a daughter of Abraham, whom Satan has kept bound for eighteen long years, be set free on the Sabbath day from what bound her?" (Luke 13:10–13, 16)

Clearly, these passages present an ancient understanding of suffering, handicaps, and pathology characteristic of the medicine-of-the-day. The Lord used the common idea of a causal connection between demonic activities and being deaf, mute, or crippled.

Of course, no Christian doctor, nurse, or other healthcare professional believes that evil spirits are the cause of epileptic seizures, the loss of sight or hearing, and the inability to talk or stand upright. For the most part, medical science has proven that these disabilities and diseases have physical mechanisms that can be treated by physical means. Spiritual causes, such as demonic activity within a person, are not considered in medical diagnosis and treatment, and Christian medical staff in no way

feel they are compromising their faith.* However, associating these afflictions with an evil cause is quite logical from an ancient phenomenological
perspective. For example, consider an epileptic seizure. It is a very disturbing scene. Who in the ancient world would not think that a demonic force
had entered the stricken individual? Even today, some people who have
not enjoyed a modern education might be led to the same conclusion.

Biblical passages attributing physical afflictions to evil spirits and
Jesus' healing of these conditions offer a number of valuable insights.
First, the Lord comes down to the level of ancient peoples by employing
their view of medicine. In other words, He accommodates. His purpose in
these passages is not to reveal the mechanisms of suffering and pathology,
but to present the Message of Faith that He is Lord over the entire world,
including every ailment that afflicts humans. By performing miraculous
healings throughout Israel, even on the day of rest, He confirms both His
Divinity and His claim that "the Son of Man is Lord even of the Sabbath"
(Mark 2:28).

Second, the actual curing of disabilities and diseases by Jesus was
discernible from an ancient phenomenological perspective. Though
ancient peoples did not understand the physical causes for these medical conditions, it was well within their intellectual ability to know with
complete certitude whether a miracle had in fact happened. For example,
in John 9:1–41 the Lord healed a man who was blind from birth. On
that same day, this individual appeared before an inquisition by skeptical
Pharisees. He was not able to tell them much about Jesus, but he stated
quite clearly, "One thing I do know. I was blind but now I see" (v. 25).
Undoubtedly, this man never understood the pathological mechanisms
of his childhood affliction, but he knew with absolute certainty that the
Lord had healed him. Indeed, a miraculous intervention had occurred.

Finally, passages in which Jesus heals physical afflictions attributed
to demons reveal an ancient understanding of causality, or etiology
(Greek *aitia* means "cause" and "reason for this"). For ancient people,
supernatural causes in the physical world were as real as natural causes.
The belief that demonic activity was the reason for common medical
conditions is logical from an ancient phenomenological perspective. But

---

* This is not to say that Christian healthcare workers do not pray for their patients,
nor to say that God cannot heal interventionistically. However, this is to underline that
medical practice is based on understanding the physical mechanisms of disabilities and
diseases, and treating these conditions with physical protocols.

the clinical sciences today do not recognize this etiological factor. For example, dental disease is the most common affliction suffered by humans. In the twenty-five years that I practiced dentistry, I never once diagnosed a demon causing tooth decay or gum infections. Nor have any of my colleagues, many of whom are devout conservative Christians. These dental problems are due to inadequate oral hygiene and poor diet. In fact, I have yet to see a prayer group in any church asking the Lord to heal a decaying tooth. Instead, Christians visit their dentist. To my mind, this only confirms my belief that evil spirits do not cause dental disease.* Therefore, much caution is required when reading passages in Scripture about causal connections between supernatural activity and physical afflictions, since these most likely reflect an ancient notion of causality.

In light of this last point, there are some intriguing considerations with regard to Gen 3 and God's judgment of Eve in the garden of Eden. For her sinful act, the Lord states, "I will greatly increase your pains in childbearing; with pain you will give birth to children" (v. 16).[41] But questions arise: Did the Creator really change and/or introduce pain receptors in Eve's reproductive organ after she had sinned? Have all women inherited these from her? From a practical perspective, is the use of anaesthetics and pain relievers to manage suffering in labor subversion of God's judgment and against His will? Or is this verse reflecting an ancient understanding of the etiology and original cause of the extreme pain women experience during childbirth?

From an ancient phenomenological perspective, making a causal connection between evil and this suffering is quite logical. In the same way that evil spirits were understood to cause epilepsy, so too a supernatural etiology is a reasonable explanation for severe labor pangs. Genesis 3:16 clearly presents a causal connection between the sin of Eve and the pain of childbirth, and this suffering was inflicted through a supernatural act of judgment by God. However, few today believe that epileptics have demons, and a parallel situation emerges: the possibility exists that the suffering experienced in giving birth is not the result of a divine judgment that extends to all women. Consideration must be given to the notion that

---

* I want to make it very clear that I am not dismissing the existence of demonic activity. On a few occasions, I have personally experienced this terrifying reality. My point is simply to underline that ancient peoples commonly believed evil spirits were often the cause of physical afflictions. However, as science has advanced, natural mechanisms of pathology have been discovered.

Gen 3 uses an ancient understanding of the causal origin of labor pain as an incidental vessel to deliver an infallible Message of Faith: God judges human sin. Stated concisely, *divine judgmental action for the sin of Eve might be filtered through ancient medical categories.* This provocative idea is further examined in the next chapters.

CHAPTER SUMMARY

The Bible presents an ancient science of the structure and operation of the universe and life. Hundreds of statements in Scripture regarding the earth, heavens, and living organisms paint a coherent picture of the world that is consistent with science a few thousand years ago. This view of nature is perfectly logical for generations that did not enjoy the privilege of looking through telescopes or microscopes. More specifically, the writers of Scripture understood the physical world from an ancient phenomenological perspective. This is not to be confused with our modern phenomenological point of view, which is informed by twenty-first century science. What the biblical peoples saw with their naked eyes, they believed actually existed and occurred in front of them—the sun literally rose and set every day, the world definitely had three immovable tiers, and living organisms were truly unchanging and reproduced only "according to their kinds." These phenomena were not merely appearances as they are for most of us today. Nor were the inspired writers using poetic language in describing nature as we sometimes do. The science in the Bible was the best science-of-the-day.

The Message-Incident Principle is foundational for understanding statements in Scripture that refer to nature. In disclosing spiritual truths, the Holy Spirit descended to the level of the writers and employed their geology, astronomy, and biology as a vessel. In other words, He accommodated. For example, through use of the 3-tier universe, the Bible reveals God's creatorship, lordship, sovereignty, ordinance, sustenance, omniscience, omnipresence, and omnipotence. This ancient understanding of the structure and operation of the cosmos also transports the theological facts that nature declares the Creator's glory, He will bring the present world to an end, and humanity will be judged for their sins. Therefore, it is necessary for modern readers of God's Word to *separate* the Message of Faith from the incidental ancient science, and not to *conflate* these together. According to the Message-Incident Principle, inerrancy and infallibility rest in the spiritual truths of Scripture instead of its views on the structure and operation of the physical world.

This chapter demonstrates the need for developing principles of biblical interpretation for passages dealing with the natural world. The thought experiment picturing the scene in Gen 1:2, which most of us at first envision as a spherical earth surrounded by water, reveals how easy it is to read twenty-first century scientific categories into an ancient text. This eisegetical tendency is natural, and learning to respect the ancient science in Scripture is certainly counterintuitive. Yet with time and practice, recognizing that the Bible refers to a flat circular earth is within the conceptual reach of everyone. However, it is much more difficult to believe that the divine judgment of severe birth pain upon Eve for her sin is the reflection of ancient medicine and an ancient notion of causality and etiology. This is not only disturbing, but it raises the question of whether or not Christians can trust what they read in Scripture. Despite these challenges, believers are still faced with the command to drink deeply from the Word of God. Better questions exist: Are Christians aware of their interpretive method? Can they justify it? Does it lead to an exegetical reading of Scripture? Are their principles of interpretation ultimately rooted in the Bible? We all interpret the Word, and it only makes sense that we do it well.

Evolutionary creation recognizes and respects the ancient geology, ancient astronomy, and ancient biology in the Bible. This origins position contends that the science-of-the-day a few thousand years ago has far-reaching implications for the modern origins debate, the interpretation of Scripture, and the notion of biblical inerrancy and infallibility. The next chapter begins to explore these important issues.

5

The Bible and Science:
Beyond Conflict and Concordism

THE ANCIENT SCIENCE IN the Bible has significant implications. It immediately calls into question the belief held by many Christians that God revealed basic scientific principles in Scripture thousands of years prior to their discovery by modern science. Evidence from the Bible itself calls believers to reconsider the truthfulness of scientific concordism. In particular, it challenges anti-evolutionists and their use of the first chapters of the book of Genesis to explain the origin of the universe and life. The ancient view of nature in God's Word also raises questions about biblical inerrancy and infallibility. Why is there a conflict instead of an accord between science and Scripture? Did the Holy Spirit make a mistake in the revelatory process? Or asked more bluntly, does God lie in the Bible?

In order to answer these questions, this chapter embraces the following assumption: As the Word of God judges our thoughts and remodels our mind (Heb 4:12; Rom 12:1–2), features like the ancient science in Scripture assist us in evaluating and reshaping our view of how the Holy Spirit revealed through the inspired writers. In other words, this chapter employs an inductive Bible study method and appeals directly to evidence from Scripture. Grasping the consequences of the ancient understanding of nature in the Word is at first unsettling for Christians. Readers must be warned that I make many pointed and sometimes disturbing statements about the meaning of several biblical passages. However, it is necessary to underline that these challenges are not directed at Scripture itself, but at *popular interpretations* offered by believers. The Bible is the foundation of our faith, and the conclusions of this chapter are in complete submission to the Word of God.

The first section presents important implications regarding the ancient science in Scripture. Using evidence from the last chapter, it focuses on the issue of origins and proposes a role for God's Word in this debate. Next, principles of biblical interpretation are developed for passages that deal with nature. The necessity of embracing the Message-Incident Principle becomes even more evident for those reading Scripture today. This chapter closes by exploring an Incarnational approach to biblical inerrancy and infallibility. It looks to the greatest act of divine revelation—God revealing Himself in the person of Jesus—and then identifies instructive parallels between the Lord and statements in Scripture referring to the physical world.

IMPLICATIONS OF ANCIENT SCIENCE

The Bible plays a critical role in the origins debate for many Christians. Both young earth creationists and progressive creationists assert that the opening chapters of Genesis reveal an outline of how God actually created the universe and life. These anti-evolutionists claim that the Creator intervened dramatically in the origin of living organisms. In particular, they hold tenaciously to the belief that the Lord made Adam and Eve as stated in Gen 2, and they reject outright the notion of human evolution. Clearly, scientific concordism is the foundational interpretive principle behind these popular Christian views of origins.

Fig 5-1 summarizes evidence from the last chapter and compares the Bible's view of the structure and operation of the world to physical reality as understood by most people today. It is obvious that scientific concordism fails. There is no correspondence between the conceptualization of nature in the Book of God's Words and our common knowledge of the Book of God's Works. Certainly, this fact will trouble many Christians. But this is evidence from the Bible itself. Christian faith demands that we shape our beliefs according to the inspired Word. Consequently, the ancient science in Scripture has serious implications for: (1) the historicity of the events recorded in Gen 1, (2) divine creative action at the beginning of the world, (3) divine judgmental action at the end of the world, and (4) the ancient understanding of causality in nature.

EARTH & HEAVENS

Structures	Reality
Flat circular earth with ends, foundations & underside	No
Flat circumferential sea around earth & bordered by horizon	No
Firmament overhead in heaven & set on foundations	No
Sun, moon & stars set in firmament	No
Sea of waters above in heaven held up by firmament	No
Beams of Divine dwelling set in waters above	No

Operations	
Earth is immovable	No
Sun moves daily across sky & under horizon	No
Sun, moon & stars move through firmament	No
Stars occasionally fall to earth	No

PLANTS, ANIMALS & HUMANS

Structures	
Mustard seed is the smallest of all seeds	No
Bats are birds	No
Rabbits & rock badgers are ruminants	No
Male reproductive seed contains a miniature person	No
Female reproductive organs are seedless	No
Female womb is a field for male reproductive seed	No

Operations	
Seeds die before germination	No
Earth is the only cause of seed growth	No
Females are the only cause of infertility	No
Demons cause epilepsy, blindness, deafness, etc.	No

Fig 5-1. The Failure of Scientific Concordism

The Historicity of Events in Genesis 1

Fig 5-1 offers a subtle and crucial point regarding the creative events stated in Gen 1. According to this account, the firmament was created on the second creation day and it was used to raise the body of waters above. This chapter also claims that the sun, moon, and stars were set in the firmament on the fourth day of creation. However, there is no firmament overhead. There is no heavenly sea of water above the earth. And there are no astronomical bodies set in a firmament. Therefore, *since the heavens are not structured in this way, Gen 1 cannot be a historical account of the actual events that created the heavens.*

It follows that if creation days two and four are not a revelation of astronomical origins, then neither are the third, fifth, and sixth days of creation a historical record of the origin of living organisms. To suggest otherwise is inconsistent. This would rip apart the interwoven creative acts of inanimate structures and living creatures that make up the fabric of Gen 1. The view of origins in this creation account is rooted ultimately in an ancient phenomenological perspective of the physical world. To the eyes of ancient people, the universe was a static 3-tier structure and living organisms were also static, since they never changed into other life forms. In attempting to understand the origin of the world, they conceived that it was created quickly and completely. Considering the limited physical evidence held by the ancients, this conceptualization was perfectly logical.

Even though Gen 1 features an ancient phenomenological viewpoint with no correspondence to physical reality, Christians throughout the ages have always grasped its central Message of Faith: God is the Creator of the world. This is the power of the Bible. It is a *sufficient* divine revelation and human ability is *proficient* in discerning its eternal truths. Yet this ancient origins science has a profound implication. The Gen 1 creation account is not a historical record of actual events in the origin of the universe and life.

Divine Creative Action in Assembling the World

Fig 5-1 also challenges the popular Christian understanding of the Creator's activity in origins. As just noted, Gen 1 records events about the assembly of the heavens that never happened. It attributes to God the creation of the firmament, the lifting of the waters above, and the placement of the sun, moon, and stars in the heavenly dome. Psalm 104 adds that He sets the beams of His celestial dwelling in this sea overhead. However, *since this is not the structure of the heavens, God did not create the astronomical world as stated in the Bible.* The upper half of Fig 5-2 summarizes this divine creative action in the assembly of the heavens. Again, consistency argues that if Gen 1 does not reveal the actual divine action in the origin of astronomical bodies as recorded on the second and fourth days of creation, then neither are the third, fifth, and sixth creation days revelations of how God created plants, sea and flying creatures, and land animals and humans, respectively.

CREATIVE
Assembly of Heavens
Firmament lifted up & supports waters above
Sun, moon & stars placed in firmament
Beams of Divine dwelling set in waters above

DIVINE
ACTION

JUDGMENTAL
Disassembly of Heavens
Heavenly bodies in firmament shaken
Stars in firmament fall to earth
Firmament rolled up

Fig 5-2. Divine Action in the Heavens

To be sure, the Creator made the universe and life. But the biblical writers deliver this Message of Faith using the science-of-the-day. More specifically, divine creative action is filtered through ancient categories on origins. This is also the case with statements in Scripture regarding the Creator's activity in the daily operations of the world. The psalmist states that God holds the earth stationary on its foundations (Ps 75:3), and Jesus asserts that the Father causes the sun to rise (Matt 5:45). But everyone knows that the earth moves through space and that the "movement" of the sun every day is only a visual effect. Since these operations do not actually occur in nature, God does not enact them as stated in Scripture. Instead, the Bible uses the ancient scientific notions of the immovability of the earth and the movement of the sun across the sky to reveal the Creator's providentialistic action in daily operations. In the same way, the attribution of divine creative action is adapted to the level of ancient people by using their understanding of how the world was assembled.

More precisely, "*de novo* creation" is the ancient conception of origins found in the Bible. This category employs the Latin terms *de* meaning "from" and *novus* referring to "new." In other words, it is a view of creation that results in things and beings that are brand new.[1] This type of creative activity is *quick* and *complete*. It appears in nearly all ancient creation accounts and involves a Divine Being/s acting rapidly through a series of decisive events, resulting in cosmological structures and living creatures that are fully formed. Grasping this ancient notion of creation is a key to understanding Gen 1–11 and the modern origins debate.

De novo creation appears throughout Scripture, and this fact has a number of significant implications. First, divine creative action is filtered through this ancient understanding of origins. Consequently, the biblical creation accounts do not reveal how God actually created the world. Second, the popular Christian belief that the Creator intervened dramatically in the creation of plants and animals is without foundation. Young earth creationists and progressive creationists argue that Gen 1 reveals God created separate groups of life "according to its/their kind/s." However, the *de novo* creation of living organisms is an ancient understanding of origins. Finally, since Gen 1 and 2 use an ancient phenomenological perspective of the origin of life, the possibility must be entertained that Gen 3 offers an ancient view of the origin of physical suffering and death.

Divine Judgmental Action in Disassembling the World

Fig 5-1 also offers insights into God's activity prior to the final judgment. According to the Bible, the Creator will disassemble the heavens at the end of the world. He begins by shaking the heavenly bodies in the firmament, all the stars then fall to earth, and lastly the firmament is rolled up.[2] However, *since this is not the structure of the heavens, God will never dismantle the astronomical world as stated in Scripture.* The lower half of Fig 5-2 summarizes divine judgmental action in the disassembly of the heavens. The parallel to divine creative action in the assembly of the heavens is evident. In both cases, the Holy Spirit employs the same ancient astronomy in the revelatory process.

The purpose of end times passages that describe the disassembly of the heavens is not to reveal that the universe has three tiers. Instead, an ancient astronomy, which made perfect phenomenological sense to the biblical writers and their readers, is used as a vessel to deliver a Divine Theology regarding the final judgment. The inerrant messages in these passages include: God is in total control of the cosmos, humans are sinners and are accountable for their sins, God will judge humanity for their actions on judgment day, and the Creator will bring the present physical universe to an end. Thus, in the same way that creation accounts do not reveal how God made the world, neither do end times passages disclose how He will end it. But a more important parallel emerges. The Divine Theology at both the beginning and end of the Bible reveals a central and unifying theme—humanity's sinfulness and God's judgment of sin.

The fact that Scripture is not a revelation of actual events in nature at the coming judgment has intriguing implications for origins. Genesis 3 records that God launched suffering and death into the world as judgment for the sins committed by Adam and Eve. Since divine judgmental action in the disassembly of the heavens at the end of time will never be enacted as stated in the Bible, then it is possible that the acts of judgment by the Creator at the beginning of the world did not literally happen either. In other words, as Scripture employs an ancient astronomy to reveal that God will judge the world in the future, then it is feasible that an ancient science of the origin of pain and mortality is being used in Gen 3 to reveal *only* the fact that He judges sin. Stated directly, the garden of Eden account might not reveal how physical suffering and death actually entered the world.

The Ancient Understanding of Causality in Nature

Using a wide definition, the notion of causality refers to all cause-effect relationships. It is a basic intellectual category that everyone experiences and needs in order to understand and live in the world. Repeated patterns of events lead to predictability that then contributes to psychological stability. In fact, the recognition of cause-and-effect is so deeply ingrained in the brain that it operates instinctively even in animals (e.g., Pavlov's dog). The concept of causality is also a pillar of modern science. Narrowing the definition, it is the belief that physical events are the result of natural causes that operate in a regular and repeatable manner. This concept is the foundation of the scientific method and it has led to the amazing technological advances that we enjoy every day.

Ancient peoples experienced and embraced the notion of causality. Their science is evidence of this fact. However, their understanding of cause-effect relationships in nature differs markedly from that of today. Ancient causation is often agentic and interventionistic. That is, willful agents or personal beings are causal factors that act dramatically in the origin and operation of the world. In the ancient mindset, the notions of "supernatural" and "natural" are intertwined and not demarcated sharply. To illustrate, ancient individuals believed that thunder and lightning were acts of divine aggression from heaven. The Bible also features this notion: "The Lord thundered from heaven; the voice of the Most High resounded. He shot arrows and scattered the enemies, bolts of lightning and routed them" (2 Sam 22:14–15). Notably, nearly all the occurrences of the word lightning in Scripture are associated with God's direct activity. With regard to origins, many ancient peoples believed that gods created the heavens and the earth through rapid decisive acts and then swiftly fashioned mature humans from earth.[3] Similarly, *de novo* events by the God of the Hebrews quickly created the universe and life, including a completely formed man and woman fashioned in His hands (Gen 2). And like the ancient cultures around them, Israel and the early Church believed that demons and evil spirits caused suffering, disabilities, and diseases.

In contrast, the modern scientific notion of causality is based on and limited to law-like natural processes in the physical world. The causes are impersonal and without any hint of agency. They are repeatable, predictable, and usually gradual. Causality in nature is not the result of the changing will of an agent who acts in a dramatic and interventionistic way. In particular, the categories of "natural" and "supernatural" are well defined today. The history of science features the shift from an ancient to modern understanding of causality. In astronomy, God and angels are no longer thought to intervene in the retrograde motion of planets because the movement of the earth alone explains this visual phenomenon. Gradual geological processes, instead of a global flood launched because of divine judgment, now explain stratification in the earth's crust. And in medicine, conditions like epilepsy are not cured by exorcising demons, but controlled with medication. It is important to point out that an anti-God movement did not lead this historical trend. In fact, a majority of those involved in defining the modern notion of causality were devout Christians.[4]

Yet obvious concerns arise in light of the historical shift from ancient to modern causality. Are all statements of divine action in Scripture, including the miraculous healings of Jesus, merely ancient causation that never happened? Could it be that God's activity in the lives of Christians in the past and today are misunderstandings of natural causes, like the supernatural activity once believed to be involved in epilepsy, lightning, and retrograde motion? Is claiming that the Creator acts providentially in the laws of nature merely a remnant of the past and a psychological crutch for believers today? Stated incisively, is divine action "nothing but" ancient causality with no basis whatsoever in reality?

No doubt about it, these concerns are reasonable, but they are answerable. First, the biblical authors and their readers may not have understood that the rising and setting sun were visual effects caused by the rotation of the earth, but divine interventionistic acts like those of Jesus were well within their range of comprehension. An ancient individual at a wedding would have known that barrels of water had actually been turned into wine (John 2:9). First-century Jews were capable of determining if a paralytic carried into a house on a pallet later walked out on his own (Matt 9:5–7). And most certainly, a man born blind was well aware that he was healed from blindness and could now see (John 9:25).

Second, the history of science features another trend. As scientists probe deeper into the world, they have discovered greater and more magnificent manifestations of beauty and levels of complexity and functionality. Who has not felt the impacting force of nature as they look through a microscope or telescope? Though not a proof for God's existence or activity, anthropic coincidences and fine-tuning in nature certainly provide compelling physical evidence for an argument of intelligent design. That is, instead of pointing away from divine action, the advance of science offers a growing body of data with more astonishing revelations of intelligence and providentialistic activity in the laws of nature.

Finally, the fact that 40% of leading American scientists today believe that God answers prayer is significant evidence for the reality of divine action, since these individuals are some of the most objective and critical thinkers in the world. They are scholars who are not easily convinced, nor led by whimsical flights of fantasy. Undoubtedly, they have experienced powerful events in order for them to claim a belief in divine action. If skeptics want to use a psychological theory of delusion or hysteria to explain away the personal experiences of these scientists, then they should also entertain personal rebellion and the reality of sin as a cause of their own unbelief.

Regrettably, many Christians view the impact of science on religion in a negative light. Scientific discoveries have led to a "reduction" in divine action. However, it is vital to emphasize that this "loss" involves only *our understanding* of God's activity, not His actual involvement in the world. Instead, science contributes positively to religion. It improves biblical interpretation by showing that the science in Scripture is ancient. In particular, it assists in determining the historicity of events in Gen 1 by recognizing that divine creative action is filtered through the ancient category of *de novo* creation. Science also contributes to the development of categories of divine activity. Beginning modestly with a demarcation between "natural" and "supernatural" established by early Greek science, seventeenth-century scientists popularized the category of providentialism and emphasized God's sustaining activity in the operation of the world.[5] And today the differentiation between "personal" and "cosmo-logical" divine action is implied in the views of the 40% of American theist-scientists. They experience the former in their private life and the latter in the professional practice of science. In sum, scientific advance has contributed both to understanding how the Holy Spirit revealed through the Scriptures and how He actually created the world and continues to be active in it.

The *de novo* creative acts in Gen 1 and 2 typify an ancient under-standing of causality in nature. The significance of this assertion for the Christian anti-evolutionary positions is profound. It argues that the in-terventionism in origins defended by young earth creationists and pro-gressive creationists is an ancient view of causality, and it has no basis in reality. God-of-the-gaps models of divine activity in nature also fail for the same reason. With this being the case, an intriguing implication emerges. It is possible that ancient causation undergirds the acts of divine judg-ment in Gen 3—snakes losing their legs, birth pain increasing in women, fields growing weeds and thorns, and humans suffering and dying. In this way, the purpose of the garden of Eden account is not to reveal actual and literal acts by God, but to disclose His holy character, abhorrence of sin, and the fact that He judges us for our sinful actions. Reading Gen 3, then, would require Christians to distinguish the divine acts in nature from the nature of the Divine Being.

To conclude, the ancient science in the Bible has far-reaching con-sequences for the origins debate. The failure of scientific concordism indicates that Scripture must not be used as a source of information to determine how God created the universe and life. The intention of God's Word is to reveal Messages of Faith. In order to deliver inerrant spiri-tual truths as effectively as possible, the Holy Spirit employed the origins science-of-the-day held by the biblical writers thousands of years ago. Consequently, readers of Scripture today must not *conflate* this incidental ancient science with the Divine Theology it transports. Instead, we need to *separate* the infallible messages from their ancient vessel so that they can be applied to our life today.

Indeed, acknowledging the ancient science in God's Word leads to a rejection of popular literal interpretations of the biblical creation ac-counts. For some Christians this is quite a challenge. Yet recognition of the ancient understanding of origins moves the relationship between the Bible and science beyond conflict and concordism. First, Scripture cannot clash with the evolutionary sciences because it does not reveal how God actually created the world. Christians then have no biblical reason to reject evolution. Likewise, neither can skeptics argue against Christianity by pointing to conflicts between Gen 1 and science. Second, Scripture does not feature scientific concordism because the Holy Spirit used ancient science in the revelatory process. Thus, there is no justification for young earth creationists and progressive creationists to align modern scientific data with the biblical origins accounts. All attempts are destined to fail.

PRINCIPLES OF BIBLICAL INTERPRETATION

The ancient science in Scripture contributes valuable evidence to developing interpretive principles for passages that refer to the physical world. Simply defined, "hermeneutics" are rules of interpretation. Whether people are aware of it or not, everyone holds and uses hermeneutical categories. Since reading the Bible is an essential aspect of our faith journey, it behooves us to comprehend these rules and to apply them properly. This section presents nine interpretive principles for a richer understanding of passages that deal with nature, especially the creation accounts.

Biblical Sufficiency and Human Proficiency

The Bible is a sufficient divine revelation. It offers the knowledge necessary for salvation, righteous living, and a personal relationship with the Creator of the world. As the apostle Paul states, Scripture is "God-breathed" and "thoroughly equips" Christians "for every good work" (2 Tim 3:16–17). However, the fact that the Bible features an ancient science is significant. It subtly indicates that scientific information about nature is not essential for a holy life. In particular, the ancient origins science in the creation accounts indirectly reveals that how God made the world is not foundational to the doctrine of creation. Stated bluntly, understanding origins is ultimately irrelevant to one's walk with the Lord.

Humans are proficient in understanding the central message of Scripture. Despite historical, cultural, and individual differences, those yearning for God have always met Him through the Gospel. Evidence for this efficiency is found in every generation by the transformed lives of men and women who have faithfully read the Bible. This ability also extends to the creation accounts. The Message of Faith rises above the incidental ancient origins science that transports it. Though Christians have held a wide variety of contradictory views on origins, in the end they have come to embrace the historic doctrine of creation. Even today, young earth creationists, progressive creationists, and evolutionary creationists all agree that the essence of Gen 1–11 reveals: God created the world, the creation is very good, humans are created in the Image of God, He intended us to be in personal relationships and especially with Him, all men and women have fallen into sin, God judges humanity for their sins, and He created a chosen people to serve His purposes.

By God's grace, the faith messages in Scripture transcend the hermeneutical skills of those in search of the Lord. For example, most Christians today are unaware of the actual meaning of the word "firmament." Yet they have come to affirm God's Creatorship on the second day of creation (Gen 1:7) and the reflection of His workmanship in the heavens (Ps 19:1). Understanding the Bible is not simply an intellectual exercise confined to professional theologians. Hermeneutics includes a spiritual requirement. As Jesus points out, it necessitates ears that "hear" and eyes that "see" (Matt 13:11–17). Grasping God's Word begins on our knees in reverent submission before Him. This is not to dismiss the work of theologians on principles of interpretation, since these are needed to understand challenging issues like the origins debate. Rather, it is to encourage everyone to read Scripture, no matter what their level of hermeneutics, because the sufficiency of the Word and the proficiency of human ability assure access to the living Creator.

Literalism and Historicity

Literalism is a feature that has marked biblical hermeneutics throughout Church history, and it continues in many Christian circles today, especially with regards to origins. A number of factors contribute to this reading approach. First, it is the most common and natural way to communicate. Everyone begins with a literalist hermeneutic while learning to read on the knee of their parents. As well, it is the "default mode" of most people who have not had the privilege of professional studies in literature and theology. Second, there is a powerful connection between the literal reading of the Bible and a holy lifestyle. This approach to Scripture has consistently been affirmed in the lives of Christians following the Lord's commands verbatim. Finally, statements in Scripture regarding nature were, for the most part, intended to be read literally. The inspired authors viewed the world through an ancient phenomenological perspective. What they saw with their eyes, they believed was literally real, and their intention was to communicate this physical reality to their readers.

The tendency to read Scripture literally confers historicity. That is, it predisposes the Bible to being seen as a historical document throughout. As a result, a majority of Christians believe that Gen 1–11 is a record of actual events outlining the origins of the universe, life, and first human communities. Other factors support the assumed historicity of these chapters. The biblical authors and Jesus often refer to people and events in Gen 1–11, implying their historical reality. The Church throughout time has also held this view. And the acceptance of scientific concordism and historical concordism today by young earth creationists and progressive creationists continues to promote literalist interpretations of the origins accounts. As a result, many Christians assume that God's preferred method of revelation involves the use of literal and historical statements.

However, there are biblical reasons to re-evaluate this common interpretive trend. The fact that Jesus often used parables—stories that are neither literally nor historically true—is evidence that divine revelation is not confined to literal and historical statements. The ancient science in Scripture is also proof that it is impossible to believe that every verse in the Bible is literally true. And the fact that Gen 1 features an ancient origins science indicates that not every event recorded in Scripture is historically accurate (e.g., the *de novo* creation of the firmament). Clearly, the Holy Spirit does not reveal exclusively through literal and historical statements in the Bible. Of course, a great number of passages are literally and historically true. The bodily resurrection of Jesus is a literal and historical event. Consequently, Christians are forced to make hermeneutical decisions in reading Scripture. The question arises: Will modern science contribute to deciding if a passage is to be interpreted literally and historically?

Hermeneutical Primacy of Science

Whether Christians are aware of it or not, modern scientific knowledge plays a significant role in their interpretation of biblical passages about the natural world. For example, those who attempt to explain away the rising/setting of the sun in Scripture with the "poetic" and "phenomenological language" arguments unwittingly affirm this notion. It is their acceptance of modern astronomy that directs them (albeit eisegetically) to assert that these passages are similar to the use of the terms "sunrise" and "sunset" today.[6] In fact, the identification of the ancient science in Scripture requires modern scientific information. One needs to know the earth spins on its axis daily before recognizing that references to the sun's mobility are an ancient astronomy. Thus, knowledge of nature is indispensable in biblical interpretation. Stated more explicitly, science has hermeneutical primacy over Scripture in passages dealing with the structure, operation, and origin of the physical world.

Galileo defended this approach to the relationship between the Bible and science. He wrote, "In disputes about natural phenomena one must begin not with the authority of scriptural passages but with sensory experience and necessary demonstrations . . . Indeed, after becoming certain of some physical conclusions, we should use these as very appropriate aids to the correct interpretation of Scripture."[7] The famed astronomer concluded that "when one is in possession of this [scientific information] it is a gift from God."[8] For Galileo, the Book of God's Works informs the interpretation of the Book of God's Words in passages referring to nature.

Evolutionary creation asserts that cosmology, geology, and evolutionary biology are also "gifts from God." These sciences not only reveal how the Creator made the world, but they are also "very appropriate aids" in understanding Gen 1–11. Like the astronomy in Galileo's time, the evolutionary sciences today have hermeneutical primacy over the biblical statements about the physical origin of the universe and life, including humanity. However, evolutionary creationists are quick to point out the limits of science in biblical interpretation. Scientific discoveries have no impact whatsoever on the Messages of Faith. For example, the reality that humans bear God's Image and the fact that they are sinful are theological statements that are not part of science. No scientific instrument can detect these spiritual realities. In this way, the evolutionary sciences separate the chaff of ancient origins science in Gen 1–11 from the kernels of eternal spiritual truth.

Scope of Cognitive Competence

Biblical authors saw the physical world and thought about it differently than people do today. Men and women in every generation have looked at nature through a cognitive "scope" and understood it within their intellectual capacity. History reveals that the competence to know the cosmos has increased over time. Stated another way, this visual metaphor indicates that scientific knowledge has boundaries. It is limited to an intellectual field of vision provided by the instruments and techniques of science, and it is conditioned by the intelligence, imagination, and education of those from various cultures and points in history. Thanks to telescopes and microscopes, and "standing on the shoulders of scientific giants" before us, we enjoy a wider scope of cognitive competence than biblical peoples.[9] They were not competent to know the structure of the heavens, the size of a mustard seed compared to other seeds, or the anatomy and physiology of human reproduction. It must be underscored, though, that this fact in no way disrespects earlier generations, because we would have held the very same scientific notions had we lived in their day.

But some Christians fear that if they concede the Bible has an ancient science, then this places them on the proverbial "slippery slope" to liberal theology, and maybe even a loss of faith. Roughly stated, the argument is as follows: if statements in Scripture about nature are not scientifically, historically, and literally accurate, then neither are the miracles and resurrection of Jesus. This is a reasonable concern. However, the scope of cognitive competence acts like a set of "hermeneutical brakes" on this dreaded slope. As noted in the last section, first-century individuals were certainly capable of knowing whether or not water had been turned into wine, a paralytic had walked away, and a man born blind could now see. And for a generation that saw many crucifixions, it was well within the scope of cognitive competence of witnesses to the death and resurrection of Jesus to know these events had actually happened. Undoubtedly, being competent to grasp this literal and historical fact is more significant to Christian faith than scientific facts on the structure, operation, and origin of the world.

The interpretation of biblical passages referring to nature requires reconstructing the ancient mindset. That is, Christians today must read Scripture as if microscopes and telescopes did not exist. This leads to an appreciation for the logic of the ancient phenomenological perspective. In particular, viewing the biblical creation accounts through the narrow scope of cognitive competence of the inspired writers makes sense of seemingly bizarre passages. For example, in Gen 1 the separation of the waters above by the firmament or the appearance of land animals out of the earth are perfectly rational applications of *de novo* creative action to a 3-tier understanding of the universe and a 1-seed theory of reproduction, respectively. But more significantly, recognition that the biblical creation accounts reflect an ancient scope of cognitive competence indicates that their purpose is not to reveal how God made the world or how humankind arose on earth.

Implicit Scientific Concepts

Men and women live in a physical world and have no choice but to have some sort of understanding of nature. Psychological health demands that people know their surroundings. History reveals that knowledge of the universe and life has been an indispensable component in the religious and philosophical beliefs of every generation.[10] For many individuals, some ideas about nature are embedded deeply in the mind and are rarely questioned. In other words, they hold scientific concepts that are implicit. These notions are simply absorbed from the culture with little thought, yet function powerfully in shaping an understanding of the physical world.

Biblical interpretation requires an awareness of the "implicit scientific concepts" of both the ancient writers and the subsequent readers.[11] Too often the assumptions about nature held by the former are unwittingly substituted for those embraced by the latter. For example, a spherical universe embraced by many in the sixteenth century appears in Martin Luther's translation of the Bible (Fig 4-6). This eisegetical approach is also found in the canopy theory of young earth creation and the vapor theory of progressive creation. Both anti-evolutionary positions assume the *rāqîaʿ* (firmament) to be the troposphere that envelops our planet (Chapter 4 Excursus). And as noted at the beginning of the last chapter, most Christians today, with little to no thought, read the word "earth" in Gen 1:2 and picture a sphere. But in all these cases, interpreters fail to recognize that Scripture features a 3-tiered universe, and they automatically read their science into the passage.

The tendency for modern readers to introduce their implicit scientific concepts into Scripture is aggravated by the fact that words evolve conceptually over time. For instance, Gregg Easterbrook writes, "Suppose you accept the Big Bang theory of the origin of the universe. Here's what you believe: Once upon a time, all the potential of the cosmos—all the potential for a *firmament* of 40 billion galaxies at last count—was packed into a point smaller than a proton."[12] Clearly, the meaning of firmament today is not the same as that of the author of Gen 1. It is critical, then, that biblical interpretation be informed by historical studies on the scientific categories of the ancient Near East (e.g., circular earth of the Babylonian world map, 1-seed reproduction with Aeschylus's writings, *de novo* creative action in other ancient creation stories). In this way, Scripture can be read exegetically, respecting the inspired ancient author's implicit concepts of nature.

Attribution of Divine Action in Nature

The Bible attributes to God activity in the past origin, present operation, and future end of the physical world. This divine action is cast in the science-of-the-day thousands of years ago. That is, in the same way that the inspired writers picture the structure of the universe through a 3-tier model, they envision the Creator's involvement in its assembly, function, and disassembly using ancient scientific categories. Scripture presents three basic types of cosmological activity by God: (1) attribution of divine creative action, (2) attribution of divine operational action, and (3) attribution of divine judgmental action.[13]

Recognizing and respecting the ancient science in actions attributed to God clarifies biblical interpretation and assists in formulating Christian doctrine. Examples of these three types of divine cosmological activity explain this notion. First, the placement of the sun, moon, and stars in the firmament on the fourth creation day is not a revelation of how the heavens were actually made. Rather, this attribution of divine creative action is to proclaim that God created the heavenly bodies and ordained them to serve humanity. Second, Matt 5:45 states, "God causes His sun to rise on the evil and the good." The purpose of this verse is not to affirm the daily movement of the sun across the sky, but the Lord's sovereignty over and sustenance of this astronomical operation. And third, attributing to the Creator the rolling up the heavens at the end of the world employs an ancient astronomy to deliver faith messages on the reality that the present creation will cease to exist and that the Lord will judge men and women for their sins.

The filtering of God's activity in the natural world through ancient scientific categories has a crucial implication for the origins debate. Stated precisely, *the biblical creation accounts attribute to the Creator acts which in fact never literally happened.* Appreciating the attribution of divine creative action in Gen 1 and 2 indicates that the creation of the world in six days and the fashioning of Adam from the earth are not actual historical events. Similarly, identifying the attribution of divine judgmental action in Gen 3 suggests that God's launching of pain and mortality into the world never actually occurred as stated. In other words, the cosmic fall is rooted in ancient scientific categories that do not correspond with nature. Consequently, Christians must open the Book of God's Works in order to discover the physical origins of human life, suffering, and death.

Authorial Intentionality

The author of a written work aims to communicate ideas and beliefs through his or her words. The correct interpretation of any literary piece requires readers to discover and respect these intended notions, because everyone agrees that reading personal assumptions, opinions, or agendas into a text is unacceptable. The Bible is unique in that it features a dual authorial intentionality. Scripture is authored by the Holy Spirit and by the ancient writers. Consequently, biblical interpretation involves identifying both the divine and human purposes of a passage.

Dual authorial intentionality appears especially in Scriptures referring to the physical world. Consider Jesus' healing of the epileptic boy (Matt 17:14–18; Mark 9:14–29; Luke 9:38–43). The human authors, who included Dr. Luke, could only conceptualize the convulsions and foaming at the mouth through ancient medical categories. They intended to communicate that a demon had in fact seized the child. But more importantly, the Gospel writers wanted to tell their readers that Jesus had healed him. In doing so, they purposefully revealed the theological message that Jesus is Lord over everything, including human afflictions. Similarly, the primary intention of the Divine Author in this account was to offer this revelation. The Holy Spirit also intended the human authors to use their understanding of epilepsy. Instead of confusing them with the modern facts about this medical condition, which God could have done, He accommodated to their level of science. In this way, the inspired writers and the readers were not distracted from the Message of Faith by an incomprehensible explanation of brain anatomy, physiology, and pathology.

The aphorism on the relationship between Scripture and science popularized by Galileo underscores divine authorial intentionality: "The intention of the Holy Spirit is to teach us how one goes to heaven and not how heaven goes." The famed astronomer also recognized that "the primary purpose of Holy Writ is the worship of God and salvation of souls."[14] These hermeneutical insights are applicable to the origins debate today. The intention of the Holy Spirit in the creation accounts is to teach us *that* God made the world, and not *how* He actually did it. In particular, the primary purpose of Gen 1–11 is to direct worship away from the creation toward the Creator, and to underline that humans are sinners, implying their need of a Savior.

Accommodation

A critical question immediately arises the moment Christians recognize that statements about nature in Scripture do not correspond with physical reality: Does God lie in the Bible? According to the Word itself, God "does not lie" because "it is impossible for God to lie" (Titus 1:2; Heb 6:18). Yet, the Holy Spirit inspired Scriptures make numerous statements about the structure, operation, and origin of the natural world that are scientifically incorrect.

Let me answer this question very directly: God does NOT lie in the Bible. Rather, He accommodates to the level of the ancient writers and their readers when referring to nature in order to reveal as effectively as possible Messages of Faith. Four arguments support the principle of biblical accommodation. First, it is a corollary of divine revelation. That is, built into the notion that God reveals to humans is the reality and fact that the Infinite Creator has to descend to the level of finite creatures in order to communicate. Second, the notion of accommodation is inherent in the mystery of the Incarnation. In becoming a man, God "humbled Himself" in order to be the ultimate act of divine revelation (Phil 2:8). Third, Jesus accommodated in His teaching ministry. He often used parables or earthly stories, which included ancient scientific notions, in delivering heavenly messages. Finally, accommodation is experienced and even used by Christians today. In prayer, God speaks to us employing our language and intellectual categories. And when a four-year-old asks "the question" about where babies come from, parents answer by descending to the level of the child. They communicate the central message—a baby is a gift from God when a mom and dad love each other—without presenting the anatomical and physiological details of sex.

The principle of accommodation is also used in modern translations of the Bible. It is most prominent in Eugene Peterson's *The Message*, which attempts to present the Scripture's "tone, rhythm, events, and ideas in everyday language."[15] For example, he renders the mustard seed parable in Matt 13:31–32 as: "God's kingdom is like a pine nut that a farmer plants. It is quite small as seeds go, but in the course of years it grows into a huge pine tree, and eagles build nests in it."[16] Petersen definitely delivers the Message of Faith that Jesus intended, but substitutes the ancient botany regarding mustard seeds with that of a tree known to most people in America today. In this translation the power of the inerrant and infallible Word of God transcends the incidental use of a pine nut and tree.

Accommodation to modern readers is possible with the biblical creation accounts. Genesis 1:1–5 could be re-written with categories from contemporary science:

> [1] During billions of years God created the heavens and the earth through evolution.
>
> [2] Now the world did not exist before the creation of space, time and matter.
>
> [3] And God said, 'Let there be an explosion.' And there was an explosion.
>
> [4] God saw it was good, and He separated the explosion from nothingness.
>
> [5] God called the explosion 'The Big Bang.' This was the First Cosmological Epoch.

Again, eternal Messages of Faith are preserved—the fundamental beliefs that God created the world and that the creation is good.[17] This Divine Theology is delivered employing an incidental modern science that is familiar to many today. And should a better scientific theory than evolution be discovered in the future, the inerrant and infallible messages of Gen 1:1–5 will be easily accommodated to a new understanding of origins.

Literary Genre

Literary genre refers to the type, kind, or form of a written work. The Bible features a wide variety of literature, including poetry, narrative, chronicles, proverbs, letters, and prophecy, to mention a few. Determining the genre of any literary piece is the most important hermeneutical decision. Stated incisively, literary genre *dictates* interpretation.

To illustrate, take Jesus' teaching: "I tell you that anyone who looks at a woman lustfully has already committed adultery with her in his heart. If your right eye causes you to sin, gouge it out and throw it away" (Matt 5:28–29). Of course, no Christian today takes this command literally. These verses appear in a unique section of the Lord's Sermon on the Mount (Matt 5:21–48), which is characterized by the extensive use of hyperbole. In fact, if these admonitions were intended as verbatim, Jesus would be in violation of His own teaching. He states in Matt 5:22, "I tell you that anyone who is angry with his brother will be subject to judgment," but Mark 3:5 records that He looked at the Pharisees "in anger." Similarly, the Lord asserts that "anyone who says, 'You fool!' will be in danger of the fire of hell" (Matt 5:22), yet later He called these religious leaders "blind fools" (Matt 23:17).[18] Thus, it is absolutely necessary to recognize that a part of the Sermon on the Mount features deliberate overstatements that are not intended to be taken literally. By respecting this genre, the Bible is not commanding Christians to pluck out their body parts, nor is Scripture presenting a conflict between Jesus' words and actions. Yet questions arise: What is the literary genre of Matt 5:21–48? Does anyone today employ hyperbole in such an unusual way? Is this passage possibly an ancient genre?

Similar questions emerge with regard to Gen 1–11. What type of literature seamlessly integrates a Divine Theology with an ancient origins science and gives the distinct impression of being a historical record of the creation of the universe, life, and humanity? Who today writes using parallel panels (Fig 6-3), genealogies with mystical numbers (Fig 6-5), or chiastic structures (Fig 6-6)? And what is to be made of accounts that include a tree that imparts eternal life through consumption of its fruit, a fast-talking snake tempting a woman to sin, or the survival of life from a worldwide flood in an ark? The possibility must be entertained that the opening chapters of Scripture feature an ancient literary genre. In this way, the Holy Spirit accommodated by using the *literature-of-the-day* in order to facilitate the communication of faith messages. Determining the literary genre of Gen 1–11 dictates its correct interpretation. The next two chapters focus upon this critical issue.

In sum, the hermeneutical principles outlined in this section open the way to a relationship between the Bible and science that moves beyond conflict and concordism. Passages referring to nature neither clash with nor correspond to modern scientific knowledge because the Holy Spirit intentionally accommodated Scripture to the cognitive level of ancient peoples. An appreciation of biblical hermeneutics leads Christians to make informed interpretive decisions in order to draw out "pure spiritual milk" from its incidental ancient vessel (1 Pet 2:2).

AN INCARNATIONAL APPROACH TO BIBLICAL INERRANCY AND INFALLIBILITY

The Bible states that "all Scripture is God-breathed" and that the "words of the Lord are flawless" and "true" (2 Tim 3:16; 2 Sam 22:31; Ps 12:6). Indeed, Christians reading the Word encounter the living Creator of the world and acknowledge the flawlessness and truthfulness of its inspired life-changing messages. Over the centuries the Church has fully embraced this "high" view of Scripture, and today biblical revelation is often qualified with the terms "inerrant" and "infallible."[19]

Many Christians assume that since the Bible is "God-breathed," "flawless," and "true," this includes statements about the physical world. For these believers, scientific concordism is a feature of biblical inerrancy and infallibility.[20] However, Scripture definitely presents an ancient science. References to nature in the Book of God's Word do not correspond to physical reality in the Book of God's Works. Scientific concordism fails. Therefore, a reassessment is necessary with regard to the meaning of the flawlessness, truthfulness, and inspiration of Scripture as it pertains to statements about the structure, operation, and origin of the universe and life.

This section examines biblical inerrancy and infallibility in light of the ultimate act of divine revelation—the Incarnation (Latin: *in* "in" *carnis* "flesh"). God taking on human flesh in the person of Jesus provides instructive parallels in order to appreciate how the Holy Spirit inspired the words of humans in passages that refer to the physical world. Similarities appear between the Bible and: (1) the dual nature of the Lord, (2) His entering the world as a man at a certain point in history, and (3) His teaching style in proclaiming the Good News.

Ontological Parallel

A central belief of Christianity is that Jesus is both fully divine and fully human. Using a philosophical term that refers to the ultimate nature of being or existence, the Lord has a dual ontology (Greek *ontos* is the participle of the verb "to be," which is translated "being"). Of course, this is a profound mystery. How can the infinite Creator of the universe also be a finite creature in the world? How could divine spiritual essence have at the same time a human physical body? Yet the Bible clearly states that God accommodated by becoming a man in order to reveal His love for us.

Being thoroughly human, Jesus undoubtedly experienced the limits and problems of a physical body—the need for food and sleep, the common aches and pains, and even the embarrassment of body odor and bad breath. In other words, God's ultimate act of revelation came through a fallible and imperfect human vessel. In addition, most Christians would agree that whether the Lord was six feet tall or five foot two, His actual height was not essential to the gospel He proclaimed. Whether His eyes were brown or blue is also incidental to His saving Message of Faith. Of course, this is not to say that God taking on human flesh was not important, because this act was utterly necessary for His sacrificial death on the Cross. The point being made is that Jesus' specific human characteristics are incidental to the Good News. His proclamation of salvation could have been delivered as effectively had He been thin or heavy, with dark hair or blond, etc. Consequently, inerrancy and infallibility rest in the gospel the Lord preached, not the clay vessel through which He delivered this message.

Similar to Jesus' dual ontology, the Bible features both divine and human characteristics. For example, the New Testament is written in Koine Greek (*koine* means "common"). This ancient dialect is an unrefined form of Greek that was spoken by the average person in the streets. It is today a dead language because no community uses it. Yet despite its roughness and death, Koine Greek transports divinely inspired Messages of Faith. Our knowledge of Jesus comes through an undignified language. This fact might disturb some Christians who assume that the Holy Spirit would have employed the most sophisticated form of Greek at that time. But this is not the case. The Gospel is written in Koine—an ancient, dead, and vernacular human dialect. Therefore, it is possible for a less than impeccable vessel, like an incidental ancient street language, to transport God's inerrant and infallible Word.

Temporal Parallel

Christian faith asserts that Jesus both transcends time and has entered into human history. The Lord's temporality is also a mystery. Stated precisely, time is a characteristic of the creation and not the Creator. How is it possible for the eternal God to be bound within the period of first-century Palestine? How can He dwell both in and out of time? Yet the Message of Faith reveals that God accommodated by leaving eternity to enter into the creaturely boundaries of history.

As a consequence of being in time, Jesus' life and ministry were adapted to an ancient Palestinian era. He worked a typical job as a carpenter, traveled by foot and donkey, and ate the foods and drank the drinks of the day. The Lord spoke Aramaic, the vernacular language of the region, and He taught with parables using the common ideas held by people at that time. It is conceivable that the Incarnation could have occurred at another point in history with the revelation of the identical inerrant and infallible salvation message. For example, if Jesus had come to America today, He might be in a computer-related occupation, would certainly travel to speaking engagements by car or plane, and probably eat Big Macs and drink Coke. The Lord would speak English and proclaim the Good News using analogies that twenty-first century people could understand. Undoubtedly, He would employ modern science in some parables. His sacrificial death to reveal His love for us would not have been on a cross, but some other form of torture and execution. In other words, the actual point in history when Jesus came into the world is incidental. To be sure, God's entering time is absolutely vital for salvation. But in doing so, the eternal Creator submitted Himself to being adapted into history.

Like Jesus' temporality, the Bible both transcends time and is bound within history. Scripture offers timeless truth written during various ancient historical eras. The actual periods when the Holy Spirit inspired the sacred writers are incidental to the inerrant and infallible Message of Faith. That is, there is nothing inherently special about any specific point in the past. In the same way that the Lord's timeless nature rises above His historicity, the eternal truths in Scripture transcend the ancient historical conditions during which they were revealed. Evidence for this fact is seen in the lives of men and women changed by the Gospel in every generation. The Message of Faith is not only relevant for people in the past, but also for us today, and for those in the future.

Pedagogical Parallel

Jesus taught the Word of God using the words of humans. This pedagogical (Greek: *paidos* "child" *agō* "to lead") feature is a mystery that is often overlooked. How can any notion in the infinite mind of the Creator be communicated and then understood by the finite mind of creaturely men and women? Yet Scripture declares that God "has spoken to us by His Son" (Heb 1:2). In order to teach, the Lord accommodated to the intellectual level of humanity. Notably, His ministry is characterized by the use of parables (Matt 13:34; Mark 4:2). Instead of focusing on literal historical accounts, Jesus often employed stories to reveal the kingdom of heaven.

Parables are earthly stories with heavenly meanings. They are illustrations comparing everyday life to the spiritual realm. For example, the parable of the Good Samaritan appeals to the danger of travel in ancient Palestine and well-known groups of individuals—priests, Levites, and Samaritans. The message of this story does not depend on whether the events on the road between Jerusalem and Jericho actually happened. The inerrant and infallible spiritual truth is found in the lesson on mercy. For that matter, the power of this story is proven by the fact that Good Samaritan Laws exist today against those who fail to help others in need. Moreover, the divine and timeless essence of this parable is evident in that its message can be retold today. It could be adapted as a story about different motorists on a freeway passing a person injured in an accident. A limousine and sports car drive by, but an old second-hand sedan stops and its driver offers assistance. The Lord's use of parables is powerful evidence that God frequently reveals through non-literal and non-historical literary genres.

Jesus also employs ancient science to teach the Good News. He often appeals to the agricultural knowledge of His listeners as seen in the parables of the Good Sower (Mark 4:1–9), the seed growing secretly (Mark 4:26–29), and the mustard seed (Matt 13:31–32). Teaching in this manner in no way undermines the inerrancy and infallibility of His lessons. Rather, this pedagogical technique makes the Gospel more accessible to the ancient audience. Undoubtedly, had Jesus lived today He would teach employing the marvelous discoveries of science. Thanks to the microscope, the mustard seed parable might be re-accommodated as: The kingdom of heaven is like a moss spore that falls to the ground; it is the smallest of all "seeds," but when grown it is the widest of plants, extending across the forest floor, so that tiny creatures come and make their home in it.[21]

Similar to the pedagogy of Jesus, the Bible is the Word of God taught through the words of humans. The Lord employed well-known teaching techniques and common ideas, including the science-of-the-day, to proclaim the Gospel. These were vital in delivering the inerrant and infallible Message of Faith. Yet they are also incidental, because other instructional methods and popular notions could have been used. The example of Jesus opens the door to the possibility that the Holy Spirit employed non-literal and non-historical methods in other parts of Scripture, such as the creation accounts, to facilitate the communication of spiritual truths. By accommodating to the pedagogy and intellectual categories of the ancient world, the Lord taught about the will and love of God in a fashion understood by everyone at that time.

In sum, features of the Incarnation assist in understanding the nature of biblical revelation. Jesus' ontology, temporality, and pedagogy have inerrant and infallible divine elements as well as incidental human aspects. This is a consequence of God emptying Himself and taking on flesh to become a man. Despite having a fragile human body bound in time and using imperfect ancient words, the Lord taught in a way that men and women could proficiently grasp the salvation message sufficiently revealed in the Good News. He employed a now disproved ancient science that was based on the ancient phenomenological perspective of fallible and errant humans to reveal the kingdom of God. Similarly, rough dead languages, past cultural practices, and ancient teaching techniques in the Bible provide necessary, but incidental, vessels for delivering Messages of Faith. The parallels between the ultimate act of divine revelation and Scripture are evident. As "the Word became flesh" (John 1:14), so too divine thoughts became "fleshy" words.

Fig 5-3 depicts an Incarnational approach to biblical inerrancy and infallibility. The correspondence to the Message-Incident Principle is obvious. The Message of Faith is the inerrant and infallible timeless Word of God, while the incidental ancient science features less than perfect historically conditioned words of humans. This approach has a significant implication for the origins debate. Biblical inerrancy and infallibility do not extend to the statements in Scripture about *how* God created the world, but *that* He created. The failure of scientific concordism indicates that knowledge of the divine creative method is not ultimately relevant

Fig 5-3. An Incarnational Approach to Biblical Inerrancy and Infallibility

to Christian faith. Instead, Scripture itself demonstrates that errant and fallible ancient science can reveal Holy Spirit inspired truths regarding creation, sin, and judgment. In light of Jesus, *the Bible is the inerrant and infallible eternal Word of God transcending time and incarnated in the incidental imperfect words of humans within history.*[22]

CHAPTER SUMMARY

The relationship between the Bible and science is today often marked by the perception of conflict and the practice of concordism. These popular approaches are rooted in the assumption held by many Christians and non-Christians alike that Scripture reveals modern scientific facts. Moving beyond this misperception and misinterpretation of God's Word begins in the inspired Text itself with the identification of the ancient science, and ends with the conclusion that scientific concordism fails. Stated simply, the Bible is not a book of science. In this way, an Incarnational approach to Scripture as embraced by evolutionary creation asserts that the Word of God will never determine the age of the rocks, but will always lead men and women to the Rock of Ages.

This chapter opened with three incisive questions: Why is there a conflict instead of an accord between science and Scripture? Did the Holy Spirit make a mistake in the revelatory process? Does God lie in the Bible? These can now be answered. First, the science in Scripture is the science-of-the-day thousands of years ago. It was the best understanding of nature at that time, and readers of the Word today must respect this fact. Thus, the so-called conflict or lack of accord between the Bible and science do not in essence exist. Both problems are based on a false interpretive assumption—the belief in scientific concordism. Second, the

Holy Spirit did not make a mistake during the inspiration of Scripture. In order to reveal spiritual messages as effectively as possible, He intentionally descended to the level of the ancient writers and allowed them to use their science. Finally, God does not lie in the Bible. He accommodates Incarnationally. In the same way that He took on fallible human flesh in the person of Jesus to reveal His love for us, the Creator employed imperfect human ideas about nature to disclose in Scripture that He ordained and sustains the world, including our very existence.

De novo creation is a key concept in understanding the modern origins debate. This ancient origins science integrates an ancient notion of causality with an ancient phenomenological perspective of nature. Regrettably, young earth creationists and progressive creationists fail to recognize that divine interventionistic acts in the biblical creation accounts are an ancient conception of the assembly of the universe and life. But more troubling, these anti-evolutionists conflate the Message of Faith with this incidental ancient origins science, claiming it as a feature of biblical inerrancy and infallibility. In contrast, evolutionary creationists assert that the attribution of divine creative action in Scripture is an accommodation to the level of ancient peoples. *De novo* creation in Gen 1 and 2 is an incidental, but necessary, vessel to reveal the simple theological fact that God created the entire world. Consequently, evolutionary creationists enjoy freedom from both the frustration of attempting to align Scripture with science and the fear that scientific progress will undermine the Bible and their faith.

To the surprise of many, modern science plays a critical role in biblical interpretation. It identifies the ancient science in Scripture and contributes to separating this incidental feature from the Message of Faith. In other words, science assists in refining and purifying the Word. Yet the hermeneutical primacy of science certainly leads to a counterintuitive reading of the Bible. It calls into question the traditional interpretation of many passages that Christians throughout the ages have believed to be literal and historical accounts. Particularly challenging is the attribution of divine creative and judgmental actions in Gen 1–11. According to this hermeneutical approach, God never created a starry firmament as stated in Gen 1. Consistency argues that this is also the case with the origin of humanity on the sixth creation day, and the fashioning of Adam and Eve as presented in Gen 2. And if the description of divine judgment in Gen 3 is accommodated through an ancient science, as it is with end times passages on the dismantling of the heavens, then suffering and death did not enter the world as commonly believed.

Of course, these last notions are rarely if ever heard in churches and most Christians will undoubtedly find them distressing. However, the type of literature found in the opening accounts of Scripture—the creation, the fall, the flood, and the formation of the Hebrew people—dictates their interpretation. The next two chapters attempt to identify the literary genre of Gen 1–11, and in doing so, reconsider the traditional literal reading of these passages as a historical record of actual events.

6

The Ancient History in Genesis 1–11

THE FIRST ELEVEN CHAPTERS of the Bible are foundational to Christian faith. They include well-known accounts of the creation of the world in six days, the fall of Adam and Eve into sin, and the destruction of life by a flood except those saved in the ark with Noah. Today more than half of American adults believe that the central events recorded in Gen 1–11 are "literally true, meaning it happened that way word-for-word."[1] According to many Christians, the Holy Spirit dictated to secretary-like biblical writers facts concerning the creation of humans and their earliest activities. For these believers, historical concordism in Gen 1–11 is fundamental to their faith and origins position.

It has long been acknowledged that Scripture describes actual historical events. The scientific discipline of biblical archaeology explores the history of ancient Palestine and the surrounding regions. Evidence collected from sites in the Middle East confirms the existence of many customs, places, and peoples referred to in the Bible. To mention a few examples, the Old Testament record is consistent with archaeological data regarding religious practices (stone altars, blood sacrifices, holy mounts), nomadic life (tenting, herding, hospitality), cities (Rameses, Babylon, Jerusalem), nations (Egyptians, Assyrians, Canaanites), and kings (Sennacherib, Nebuchadnezzar, David). The New Testament also presents accurate history of first-century Palestine in regards to the Jewish religion (Pharisees, temples, sacrifices) and the Roman occupation (Pontius Pilate, centurions, crucifixion). And solid evidence supports the historical reality of a man named "Jesus of Nazareth" and the beginning of the Church.

However, some Christians do not accept the historicity of Gen 1–11. In other words, they reject historical concordism in the opening chapters of Scripture. This minority of believers, including evolutionary creation-ists, claim that actual history begins roughly around Gen 12 and God's calling of Abraham to the promised land.[2] They argue that similar to the way the Bible features an ancient science, Gen 1–11 presents an ancient understanding of history. As a result, no correspondence exists between actual human events in the past and those recorded in the first chapters of Scripture. Notably, these born-again believers do not accept the historical reality of Adam and Eve.

Christians who reject historical concordism in Gen 1–11 are quick to point out that the authorial intention of the Holy Spirit was not to offer an outline of real events at the beginning of human history. Rather, the Bible opens with a Divine Theology that focuses on the spiritual char-acteristics of men and women. It reveals that humans have been created by God, they are the only creatures bearing His Image, they were meant to be relational with themselves and the Creator, all have damaged their relationship with Him, He judges them for their sins, and Israel is His chosen instrument to bless the entire world. These believers employ the Message-Incident Principle to interpret statements about human origins and their activities in the opening chapters of Scripture. Stated precisely, Gen 1–11 features an *incidental ancient history* that delivers inerrant and infallible Messages of Faith about the human spiritual condition.

An important qualification is necessary regarding the term "ancient history." Of course, it is often used to describe an account of human events that actually happened during ancient times. But in this book, an-cient history refers to the historical views held by ancient peoples. It is the ancient *understanding* of history, the history-of-the-day a few thousand years ago. In the same way that "ancient science" is an understanding of the physical world held by ancient individuals, ancient history is their conceptualization of human events that preceded them. In particular, Gen 1–11 features an account of the origin of humanity and its earliest activities as conceived by the ancient Hebrews. Similar to their science, this view of history is based on an ancient phenomenological perspective of events, places, and peoples. Fig 6-1 presents Gen 1–11 in light of the Message-Incident Principle.

This chapter offers biblical evidence that challenges the historicity of Gen 1–11. No doubt, many Christians will find this troubling at first. Yet like the previous two chapters, an inductive Bible study method is used. The hermeneutical assumption previously embraced is recast: As

Fig 6-1. Genesis 1-11 and the Message-Incident Principle

the Word of God judges the thoughts of our heart and remodels our mind (Heb 4:12; Rom 12:1–2), so too features in Gen 1–11 must evaluate and reshape our view of how the Holy Spirit revealed Himself through the inspired writers in these opening chapters. Stated another way, if Scripture itself indicates that events like the creation of Adam and Eve never happened, then biblical interpretation and Christian theology must submit to the evidence in God's Word. But before examining Gen 1–11 directly, the introduction of categories is required in order to appreciate the complexity of these chapters.

INTRODUCTORY CATEGORIES

To most people, Gen 1–11 reads like a historical record of past events. Even though spectacular supernatural episodes are found in these chapters, they appear to be a straightforward account intended to be understood literally as history. To suggest otherwise is counterintuitive. For example, the main passages are introduced by the title "These are the generations of . . . " which can also be translated as "This is the family history of . . ." (Adam 5:1, Noah 6:9, sons of Noah 10:1, Shem 11:10, Terah 11:27).[3] The historicity of Gen 1–11 also seems to be supported by numerous references to well-known places, practices, and peoples.

Geographical referents appear, like the Euphrates and Tigris Rivers (2:14), the Ararat Mountains (8:4) and the plain of Shinar (11:2). Ancient cultural advances such as bronze and iron tools (4:22), instruments like the harp and flute (4:21), and towers built with baked bricks and tar (11:3) are also mentioned. Religious practices include the establishment of a divine covenant (9:8–17), separating clean and unclean animals (7:2, 8), crop and animal offerings (4:3–4), and burnt sacrifices on an altar (8:20). Dozens of ancient Near Eastern peoples are referred to, such as the Assyrians (10:11–12), Philistines (10:13), and Canaanites (10:18). Some of the most important cities in the ancient world are mentioned, including Babylon, Nineveh, and Calah (10:10–11). Finally, the opening chapters of Scripture state that the earliest ancestors of the Hebrews left from Ur of the Chaldeans (11:28), stayed in Haran for a time (11:31), and eventually came to the land of Canaan (12:5). Though it is nearly impossible to find archaeological evidence confirming this small tribe, such migrations occurred in ancient times, and the places referred to definitely existed.

It is reasonable then to believe that Gen 1–11 is an actual record of sequential events in human history. In fact, the literal interpretation of these chapters has been upheld by Christians throughout the ages and continues to be accepted by the majority of believers today. But a closer examination reveals deeper conceptual realities. This section presents four introductory categories, and it will become evident that Gen 1–11 is much more complicated than most Christians assume.

Oral Traditions

Oral traditions are accounts of a preliterate people used to explain its origins and place in the world. Also known as "oral histories," these are ultimately etiological and they answer questions that every society has asked: Who created the heavens and the earth? Where do we come from? How did our community and the nations around us arise? And why are there hardships in the world?

The primary function of oral traditions is to present and reinforce the foundational beliefs and values that bind a community together. They act like a social contract or charter. Oral histories usually include an explanation of origins that features: a 3-tiered universe, *de novo* creation of the world, community formation with genealogies, and adversities people experience. In other words, they are both scientific and historical in character. Oral traditions are also brief and story-like, facilitating their word-of-mouth transmission down through the generations. Held in memory, numerous versions of the basic account emerge with differing details. But the core notions that define and cement the people together remain preserved. Otherwise, the community would never function as a society.[4]

The question arises: Did the ancient Hebrews ever have oral traditions? Biblical evidence for Israel's literacy first appears in the book of
Exodus after she had left Egypt. There are passages that refer to reading
(24:7), writing (17:14; 24:4, 7, 12; 32:16, 32; 34:1, 27), and written records
(scroll: 17:24; book: 24:7; 32:32–33; stone tablets: 24:12; 31:18; 32:15–16,
19; 34:1, 4, 28–29). Notably, the Lord orders Moses, " 'Write down these
words, for in accordance with these words I have made a covenant with
you and Israel.' And he wrote on the tablets the words of the covenant—
the Ten Commandments" (Exod 34:27–28). In contrast, God did not
command Abraham to write down the covenant that He established with
him and his descendants. Instead, male circumcision was "the sign of the
covenant" (Gen 17:11). The significance of this subtle scriptural evidence
cannot be overstated.

The fact that God uses a sign instead of written words in the covenant
with Abraham suggests that although writing had been invented, he and
his family were preliterate people. The lack of any references to writing
during the patriarchal period (Abraham, Isaac, and Jacob) described in
Gen 12–50 also supports this contention. And if the traditional dates for
Abraham (2000 BC) and Moses (1250 BC) are employed, it argues that
the Holy Spirit began the revelatory process as an oral tradition that was
later written down after the Hebrews had left Egypt.[5] This aligns well with
the archaeological evidence—literacy in Israel begins roughly around
1200 BC.[6] Therefore, if the events in Gen 12–50 concerning Abraham and
his descendants arose from word-of-mouth accounts, then it follows that
this should also be the case with Gen 1–11. The early Hebrews must have
had oral traditions to bind their community together into a functional society. And like every other oral history, these inspired accounts certainly
included explanations for the origin and first activities of humanity.

Oral traditions lie behind Gen 1–11. Characteristics pointing back to
a preliterate past clearly appear: a 3-tier universe (Gen 1), *de novo* creation
of the world (Gen 1, 2), community formation with genealogies (Gen 4, 5,
10, 11), and the origin of adversities like surrounding enemies (Gen 10)
and suffering and death (Gen 3). But more important than these incidental features, the divinely inspired beliefs and values in these oral accounts
acted as a social charter that united God's chosen people and separated
them from the neighboring pagan nations. The earliest oral traditions of
the Hebrews undoubtedly focused on a covenant relationship involving

obedience to a single Holy Creator. This inerrant and infallible Message of Faith became the foundational belief undergirding Gen 1–11.

Ancient Epistemology

Oral traditions are characterized by an ancient epistemology. Sometimes termed "primitive thinking" or "pre-logical mentality," this is not to disrespect the intellectual ability of preliterate peoples, but to point out that they never enjoyed the intensely critical mindset of today.[7] The fact that a modern individual can for the most part understand oral traditions (and the ancient literature that later rose from these) indicates that ancient epistemology is not completely irrational or illogical. However, important differences exist between the intellectual categories of past and present peoples, and this produces a challenge for reading Gen 1–11 today.

The ancient epistemology in oral traditions is marked by a lack of concern for strict internal coherence. In contrast to contemporary thinking, there is no compulsion to eliminate all inconsistent statements. Consequently, contradictions and incoherence not only appear within the individual accounts, but also between the variant versions circulating through the preliterate community.[8] In addition, oral cultures do not enjoy the wide spectrum of complex intellectual categories found in literate societies today. Epistemological notions are fewer and simpler. To illustrate, none of these accounts include the abstract idea that the entire world was created out of nothing (*creatio ex nihilo*).[9] Instead, oral histories present much of the cosmos as being made from pre-existent material. And as noted in the previous chapter, the notion of causality in nature for ancient people was characteristically agentic and interventionistic. Agents like gods, angels, and demons were accepted without question as causal factors in the origin and operation of the world. The ancient mindset had no clear demarcation between the categories of natural and supernatural, leaving these intertwined.

Logical problems are expected in Gen 1–11, since these chapters originate ultimately from oral traditions shaped by an ancient epistemology. For example, the classic problem in Gen 4 of where Cain's wife came from never troubled the inspired author and his readers. Despite less critical intellectual categories, the Divine Theology in Gen 1–11 was sufficiently revealed using an ancient epistemology in such a way that men and women could proficiently understand it. With this being the case, there is a significant implication for twenty-first century Christians. Failing to respect the mindset reflected in these chapters and forcing the extreme rational standards of today upon them is a subtle and destructive form of eisegesis. The correct reading of the biblical origins account, then, requires believers to think like preliterate ancient Hebrews. To use a colloquialism, cut Gen 1–11 some epistemological slack.

Ancient Motifs

A motif is a reappearing image, symbol, character, word, phrase, theme, or situation. Many of these are found in the art, literature, and oral traditions of both ancient and modern peoples. The importance of motifs to a society cannot be overemphasized. They are frameworks upon which the worldview of a community is displayed. To offer an example of a common motif, consider the use of evergreens in late December. Christians proclaim their belief in the Incarnation by decorating Christmas trees with the star of Bethlehem, the angel Gabriel, and the holy family. But the secular value of political correctness has renamed this period "the holiday season," and many strip this seasonal symbol of its religious images to desecrate it with pagan materialistic themes. Motifs are vessels that frequently transport the most cherished beliefs and values of a people.

Ancient origins accounts throughout the world often feature four basic motifs.[10] It is necessary to qualify that all four motifs are not always explicit or present, the details between them vary dramatically, and they may appear in different oral traditions and/or written accounts within a community or civilization. Yet general outlines of the main events in origins are commonly found. Termed "major motifs," these include: (1) *de novo* creation—the quick and complete fashioning of the universe and life, including many times a first man and woman, (2) lost idyllic age—the disruption of an original harmony in the world and the continuing effects of this event into the present, (3) great flood—the destruction of life and the survival of a few humans and some animals, often in a boat, and (4) tribal formation—the origin of a people from a single founding male individual. Ancient origins accounts also feature "minor motifs" which add detail to major motifs and are specific to a time and region. To mention a few that appear in ancient Mesopotamia: origin of the world from a watery pre-creative state, extraordinary longevity before a great deluge, birds released by the flood hero afterward, and mystical creatures like the cherubim. The presence of these major and minor motifs in Gen 1–11 is obvious.

It must be underlined that though the ancient motifs in origins accounts are often seen today as symbolic, figurative, or allegorical, they were not simply flights of fantasy and literary license.[11] The major motifs, in particular, were the central scientific and historical paradigms-of-the-day. In attempting to understand the beginning of the world and their community, ancient peoples not only looked back (retrospection), but they also cast back (retrojection. Latin: *retro* "backward" *jecere* "to throw") their present categories and experiences into the past. For example, they noticed that through animal and plant reproduction life arose relatively quick and structurally complete. As well, the ancients fashioned objects with their own hands. Thus, in order to understand origins, they retrojected these everyday phenomena and conceptualized a *de novo* view of creation. Some envisioned gods mating and giving birth to different parts of the world, others believed that living organisms arose from a mother earth, and several thought that humans were fashioned from dirt in the hands of a God/s. Considering when these notions were conceived, they were very logical reconstructions of the past.

It is also important to note that the motifs in ancient Near Eastern origins accounts were established well before the Hebrews became a people. The earliest archaeological evidence for Israel is a reference to her around 1200 BC.[12] But literate nations had been in existence in Mesopotamia and Egypt since about 3000 BC, and written records from these regions reveal many of the motifs found in Gen 1–11. Israel had undoubtedly been exposed to these scientific and historical paradigms, since her origins were in Mesopotamia (Abraham from Ur, Gen 15:7) and she had once lived in Egypt (Jacob and his descendants, Gen 46:26; Moses raised in the Pharaoh's court, Exod 2:10). As well, travel and trade between these two cradles of civilization certainly spread their motifs throughout Palestine both in oral and written forms.[13]

Therefore, God's chosen people arose in a world in which *de novo* creation, the lost idyllic age, the great flood, etc., were the fundamental facts of science and history. Since these major motifs predate Israel by many centuries, their presence in Gen 1–11 indicates that she inherited them from the surrounding nations. However, under the inspiration of the Holy Spirit, these paradigms were cleansed of their pagan theology, and replaced with spiritual truths. In other words, God accommodated to the level of the ancient Hebrews by using the motifs-of-the-day as incidental scientific and historical frameworks to reveal inerrant Messages of Faith.

Written Sources and Redaction

As the ancient Hebrews became literate, they began to write down their oral traditions, producing a record of the beliefs and values that defined and united their community. A variety of documents undoubtedly emerged at first since variant oral accounts are common in preliterate societies. But under the guidance of the Holy Spirit, these written sources were selected, organized, and edited into what eventually has become Gen 1–11. This process is known as "redaction."

Biblical scholars recognize that Gen 1–11 features two basic sources. Passages with differences in style, terminology, and content point to distinct authors, usually labeled as Priestly (P) and Jahwist (J).* For example, P is characterized by elaborate poetic structures, the divine name "God" (*'Ĕlōhîm*), and a transcendent picture of the Creator as seen in Gen 1. In contrast, J is a free-flowing narrative with the "Lord" (*Yahweh*) on earth relating intimately to men and women, as found in Gen 2–4. Scholarly consensus dates J with the emergence of a stable society that would include scribes, such as that during King David's reign about 1000 BC. This is consistent with archaeological evidence that reveals increasing Hebrew literacy at that time.[14] The P source is often dated about 500 BC, after the Jews returned from the exile in Babylon (597–538 BC), but some contend it was written around the same time as J.[15]

Whether the redaction of J and P occurred early (1000 BC) or late (500 BC), Gen 1–11 is a composite work. More evidence for the two sources is presented in the next section, and its significance will become clear. Briefly stated, so-called "contradictions" in Gen 1–11 often pointed out by skeptics, or the "smoothing out" of these by Christians, only reflect differences in J and P. These purported conflicts are ultimately incidental to the Divine Theology that is revealed in both sources. Thus, the biblical

---

* It is necessary to underline that my use of the terms "J" and "P" is not an endorsement of Julius Wellhausen's Documentary (JEPD) Hypothesis. In recent years, this theory regarding the origin of the first five books of the Bible has come under much scholarly criticism. However, this is not to say that there were no written accounts employed in the inspiration of Scripture. The labeling of these sources as "J" and "P" is deeply embedded in commentaries on Gen 1–11, and I use this categorization merely for conventional reasons.

revelatory process was not a simple dictation by the Holy Spirit to passive secretary-like scribes, a view held by many Christians. Instead, the first chapters of Scripture evolved over time through an ordained and sustained ancient literary process featuring written sources and their redaction.[16]

In sum, Gen 1–11 is much richer and more complex than most assume. Behind these chapters lie oral traditions, ancient epistemology, ancient motifs, and redacted written sources. The exact process that produced Gen 1–11 is not known. In fact, it is doubtful that it will ever be known with complete certainty. There are no passages in Scripture that specifically cite the author/s of these opening chapters, the date/s when they were written, or the sources that were used in redaction.[17] Even more problematic, the Hebrews began as a preliterate people with an oral tradition, and obviously it is not possible to recover the spoken words of the original and developing social charter that united them in a covenantal relationship with God. However, considering biblical and archaeological evidence, it is possible to construct a rough sketch of likely contributing factors that eventually led to Gen 1–11. Fig 6-2 offers an outline of this Holy Spirit inspired revelatory process.

Recognizing the many ancient features behind Gen 1–11 has a significant implication—Christians must learn to respect these when reading Scripture. To be sure, this is counterintuitive. Yet we already do this with natural revelation. For example, are there any Christians who have not experienced the divine revelatory power of a sunset? Of course, it is natural for them to see the sun "dropping" below the "horizon." But when they stop and think about it, they know that there is a deeper physical reality that is incidental to this non-verbal revelation in nature. The "movement" of the sun is really the result of the earth's rotation, and the "flatness" of the horizon is due to their narrow visual field since they cannot see the curvature of the planet. However, as believers watch a sunset and experience a mystical moment of divine disclosure, do many ever think of the astronomical reality actually occurring? Does knowledge of the scientific facts behind this phenomenon undermine the revelation that a sunset declares the glory of God? No.

Similarly, it is natural to read Gen 1–11 literally as a historical record. Most Christians throughout the ages have done so, and it has consistently revealed their spiritual character and their relationship to God. But there are deeper conceptual realities (oral traditions, ancient epistemology, ancient motifs, redacted written sources) in these opening chapters that

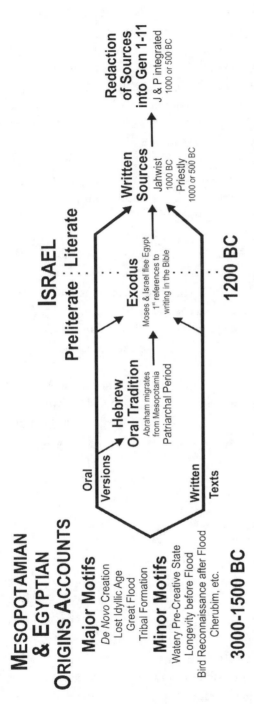

Fig 6-2. The Origin of Genesis 1-11. Mesopotamian and Egyptian accounts of origins predate Gen 1-11 by hundreds of years. It is not possible to determine exactly when the motifs in these pagan renditions were conceived. Some undoubtedly arose in early oral traditions that were later inscribed after the invention of writing in Mesopotamia and Egypt around 3000 BC. Written records from these two civilizations reveal that origins motifs were well-established throughout the ancient Near East by 1500 BC. In other words, concepts like de novo creation, lost idyllic age, great flood, etc., were the historical paradigms-of-the-day. The striking similarities between Mesopotamian and Egyptian origins motifs and those in Gen 1-11 indicate that Israel inherited them from her neighbours. There are a number of probable explanations for how these motifs entered the Hebrew community, but determining the precise process is impossible. Israel began as a preliterate people and the oral environment facilitated the modification and shaping of the motifs she acquired. Abraham came from Ur and most likely used Mesopotamian origins motifs in an early Hebrew oral tradition that featured a covenant with a Holy Creator. Moses was raised in Egyptian royalty and would have been exposed to many ancient Near Eastern origins accounts and their motifs. Being literate, he might have written one of the earliest sources of Gen 1-11. And since Israel was geographically positioned between Mesopotamia and Egypt, she was certainly exposed to motifs from these two great civilizations since travel and trade between them was common. Thus, the motifs in origins accounts were intellectual categories throughout the ancient Near East when, under the guidance of the Holy Spirit, the oral tradition behind Gen 1-11 was conceived, later written down, and these sources eventually redacted together.

187

point away from the historicity of the events. Like modern astronomical knowledge, recognizing these ancient categories in Gen 1–11 does not in any way change the Message of Faith. Instead, a greater appreciation of the divine revelatory process emerges that is analogous to understanding the finely tuned mechanisms in a sunset. Introducing modern Christians to these ancient conceptual realities will be similar to when believers first learned of Galileo's astronomy. At that time it was quite counterintuitive to accept that the earth moved, and equally so today to believe that Gen 1–11 is not like a "DVD" of human origins. Yet the seventeenth-century Church came to terms with Galileo's science, and twenty-first century Christians will eventually grasp the incidental nature of the ancient history in the opening accounts of Scripture.

This chapter now turns to examining directly the historicity of Gen 1–11. Each section begins with biblical evidence to demonstrate that the events described cannot be a literal and actual historical record of the origins and first activities of humans. Parallels to pagan creation accounts from the ancient Near East are also presented to show that common motifs were part of the intellectual context in the region, and that the Hebrews, under the inspiration of the Holy Spirit, employed and sanctified these in their understanding of the beginning of the world. Next, some very basic scientific evidence is used to complement the scriptural data. It is not the intention of this book to deal extensively with science. However, well-accepted physical facts (e.g., the order of fossils in the geological record) can be employed to test a few scientific predictions based on the different Christian origins positions. Finally, every section closes by underlining the most important feature of Gen 1–11—the revelation of inerrant and infallible Messages of Faith.

THE HISTORICITY OF GENESIS 1–11

The Historicity of the Pre-Creative State (Gen 1:1–2)

The doctrine of creation out of nothing underlines God's power, freedom, and unicity. Yet few Christians are aware that the opening scene in the Bible presents a dark, watery earth in a chaotic state with no mention of when it was created or who/what created it, if indeed it was created. Genesis 1:2 simply states that matter is in existence (earth and water) and that time is underway (Spirit of God hovering over the waters). Not only does this raise questions about the traditional doctrine of *creatio ex nihilo*, it challenges directly the historicity of the events described in this verse. And to complicate the issue, there are problems with translation of the first verse of the Hebrew Bible and questions about how it is grammatically related to Gen 1:2–3.

No one absolutely knows the correct translation of Gen 1:1. In English Bibles, this verse is rendered either "In the beginning God created the heavens and the earth" or "When God began to create the heavens and the earth." Many modern versions include both translations and place one in a footnote (Appendix 1). Old Testament scholars agree that the Hebrew language allows for both renditions, and as a result there are two basic ways to arrange Gen 1:1–3.

The *parenthetic* approach to the grammatical structure of the first three verses in Scripture proposes that Gen 1:2 is a parenthesis which describes the opening scene in the Bible. To identify this break, English translations place verse 2 either in dashes or begin this verse with the disjunctive word "now."[18] Thus, Gen 1:1 and 1:3 make up one sentence: "In the beginning God created the heavens and the earth, and God said, 'Let there be light.'" The *titular* grammatical arrangement of Gen 1:1–3 asserts that Gen 1:1 is the title of the creation account. In this way, Gen 1:2 is also the scene setting sentence with the Spirit of God moving over the dark, watery, chaotic earth. Despite the challenges in translating and arranging the opening verses of the Bible, one conclusion is well established: Scripture opens with a pre-creative state and no mention of its creation or Creator, or whether it was in fact created.

Becoming aware that the Bible begins with a watery earth already in existence is a challenge to most Christians and to the doctrine of *creatio ex nihilo*. Yet its presence in Gen 1:2 should not be surprising, but even expected, since the Word of God employs the origins science-of-the-day. Other creation accounts in the ancient Near East open with this motif, often called "the chaos." Mesopotamians, Egyptians, and Greeks believed in an uncreated disorganized state out of which arose the world and even the gods.[19] The Babylonian origins account *Enuma Elish* is particularly instructive. It begins:

> When on high the heaven had not been mentioned,
> Firm ground below had not been called by name,
> Naught but primeval Apsu [fresh water], their begetter,
> And Mummu-Tiamat [sea water], she bore them all,
> Their waters commingling as a single body [chaos waters];

No reed hut had been matted, no marsh land had appeared,
When no gods whatever had been brought into being,
Uncalled by name, their destinies undetermined,
Then it was that the gods were formed within them
[chaos waters].[20]

The similarity to Gen 1:2 is obvious. The scene of this pagan creation account opens with water already in existence. The use of the word "when" at the beginning of the passage also indicates that time was underway.

However, the theology in Gen 1 is radically different from that in the *Enuma Elish*. Genesis 1:2 places the Spirit of God in total and complete control over the pre-creative state. As well, the primeval water in Scripture is not personalized and given a name like in this Babylonian creation account. It is simply called "the deep" and "the waters." And most importantly, there is no hint of other gods. In the same way that the inspired author strips away divinity from the sun, moon, and stars on the fourth creation day, he also de-deifies the chaos and places it under the command of the God of the Hebrews.

Indeed, there is a serious theological problem if the pre-creative state in Gen 1:2 actually existed. It questions directly the doctrine of creation out of nothing because this verse implies that the dark watery earth was never created. In other words, it is eternal, and a dualistic worldview emerges with two central timeless realities—the pre-creative state and God. But this difficulty vanishes if the writer of Gen 1 was using an ancient motif and thinking through ancient epistemological categories. It is unlikely that he even sensed the theological issue regarding dualism. In fact, the first evidence for the notion of *creatio ex nihilo* appears well after the composition of Gen 1 (See Appendix 2: Creation Out of Nothing).[21] Consequently, modern readers must be careful not to force their abstract concepts and tight twenty-first century logic upon Gen 1:2. They must learn to identify the ancient motifs and think through the ancient epistemological categories of the Hebrews when reading God's Word.

The existence of the pre-creative state has significant implications for the origins debate. Both young earth creationists and progressive creationists assume that Gen 1:1–3 reveals scientific facts about the creation of space, time, and matter. More specifically, creation scientists assert that the earth was created *ex nihilo* during the creation week, and by adding the genealogies in the Bible they conclude that the planet is about 6000 years old. But this method fails, because Gen 1:2 does not state when the earth was created—it was simply there at the beginning of God's creative action. In other words, Scripture does not offer a temporal marker from which to date the earth.*

Progressive creationists also interpret Gen 1:1–3 under the assumption that it is scientifically concordant. They claim that Gen 1:1 refers to the Big Bang and that this explosive event is God's initial creative act and the beginning of the space-time-matter continuum. Old earth creationists also assert that Gen 1:2 follows this verse chronologically and reveals the condition of the early earth.[22] But as noted, the opening scene of the Gen 1 creation account is Gen 1:2, not Gen 1:1. The Bible begins with the earth, water, and time already in existence and no mention of when they were created. Thus, it is not possible to align Gen 1:1 with the Big Bang. To the surprise of many Christians, young earth creation and progressive creation are un-biblical. Once again, scientific concordism fails.

The opening verses of Scripture offer valuable insights. No one absolutely knows how to translate Gen 1:1 in the Hebrew Bible or how to arrange grammatically Gen 1:1–3. Considering the importance of an introduction to a literary work, one might reasonably assume that the Holy Spirit would have made these verses foolproof in the revelatory process. But He did not. Thus, the possibility must be entertained that in a very subtle way the Lord is indicating that the purpose of Gen 1:1–2 is not to reveal scientific facts about origins. In particular, disclosing abstract and complex notions like creation out of nothing and the beginning of time were never the divine authorial intention. Instead, the Bible opens with the simple infallible revelation that the God of the Hebrews is the only Creator.

The pre-creative state in Gen 1:2 points away from the historicity of the first chapter of Scripture. The chaos is an origins motif that prefaces a number of ancient Near Eastern creation accounts. The inspired biblical writer uses it in the same way that he employs the *de novo* creation of a 3-tier universe. He strips away pagan religious beliefs and employs the pre-creative state as an incidental vessel to reveal the Message of Faith that the Hebrew God was Lord from the very beginning of creation.

---

* Learning this biblical fact was critical in my shift away from young earth creation. See my personal story, pp. 349–51.

The Historicity of the Creation Week (Gen 1:3 to 2:3)

Throughout the ages most Christians have believed that Gen 1 is a basic historical outline of the origin of the universe and life. The traditional translation of the opening phrase (In the beginning), the orderly sequence of creative events over six days, the concluding sentence of each creation day (There was evening and there was morning), and the blessing of the seventh day as a day of rest have understandably led to this belief. However, ancient scientific notions, poetic features, and numerous motifs within this creation account, along with simple scientific predictions based on information drawn from it, argue against the historicity of this chapter.

The creation of the heavens in Gen 1 provides indisputable evidence that this account is not a historical record. As stated previously numerous times, the origin of the firmament and the raising of the waters above on the second day of creation never actually happened. These astronomical structures do not exist, and thus could not have been made. Similarly, the placement of the sun, moon, and stars in the firmament on the fourth day never occurred either because there is no solid heavenly dome overhead in which to set these astronomical bodies. Therefore, Gen 1 is not a record of the history of the creation of the heavens, and consistency demands that this chapter is not a history of the origin of life, including humanity.

Ancient poetic features in Gen 1 also point away from its historicity. Most importantly, this chapter is structured on the Hebrew work week and Sabbath. By placing God's creative acts in the first six days and His rest on the seventh day, the inspired author achieves a theological purpose. The framework becomes a model or typology affirming the Fourth Commandment. More specifically, there is no mention of the Sabbath in Scripture until Moses receives this divine ordinance in Exod 20. In other words, the Priestly author, who lived (1000/500 BC) after Moses (1250), retrojected this commandment in shaping the poetic structure of Gen 1.

It is important to note that young earth creationists often use the Fourth Commandment to defend their view of origins. However, the use of Exod 20:11 needs to be reconsidered in light of ancient science: "For in six days the Lord made the heavens and the earth, the sea, and all that is in them, but He rested on the seventh day. Therefore the Lord blessed the Sabbath day and made it holy." It must be remembered that the words "heavens" and "earth" in the Bible do not have the twenty-first century meanings of outer space and a globe, respectively. Exodus 20 subtly refers

FORMLESS	EMPTY
tōhû	*bōhû*
Day 1	**Day 4**
Separate	Decorate
Day	Sun
Night	Moon & Stars
Day 2	**Day 5**
Separate	Decorate
Waters Above	Flying Creatures
Waters Below	Sea Creatures
Day 3	**Day 6**
Separate	Decorate
Water	Land Animals
Land	Humans
(Plants)	(Plants for Food)

Day 7
Sabbath

Fig 6-3. Genesis 1: Creation Account Parallel Panels

to the creation of a 3-tiered universe. Therefore, this ancient origins science needs to be separated from the message to honor the Sabbath.

Parallel panels are another poetic feature in Gen 1. Fig 6-3 illustrates that Gen 1:2 sets up this ancient literary structure by describing the pre-creative state with the rhyming Hebrew words *tōhû* (formless) and *bōhû* (empty). During the first three days, God deals with the problem of formlessness by defining the boundaries of the universe. In the last three days, He fills and decorates the world with celestial bodies and living creatures to resolve the emptiness. Parallels emerge between the two panels. On the first day of creation, God creates light in alignment to the fourth day's placement of the sun, moon, and stars in the firmament. The separation of the waters above from the waters below on the second creation day provides an air space for birds and a sea for marine creatures, which are both made on the fifth day. And during the third creation day, God commands dry land to appear followed by plants and fruit-bearing trees in anticipation of the sixth day and the origin of land animals and humans and their need for food. Recognizing the parallel panels in Gen 1 resolves the well-known contradictions of light existing three days before the creation of the sun, and there being evenings and mornings prior to the fourth day. These problems disappear if modern readers respect this ancient poetic framework.

The inspired author of Gen 1 retrojected the Sabbath commandment into this creation account, because it dictates the number of days during which God creates. The parallel panels also control the order of divine creative events. But as everyone knows, actual history does not unfold in such a patterned and artificial fashion. For as long as people have been recording events about the inanimate world, living organisms, and themselves, these accounts have never corresponded with the Hebrew work week and Sabbath, or with parallel panels. The theological agenda and ancient poetic framework in Gen 1 indicate that this account is not a historical record of actual divine acts in the creation of the universe and life.

Genesis 1 typifies the major motif of *de novo* creation that appears throughout the ancient world. Origins are quick and complete. This conceptualization is rooted in an ancient phenomenological perspective of nature—the 3-tiered universe, the mating and birth of animals and humans, and the seeding and growth of plants. *De novo* creation also features an ancient notion of causality—the decisive and interventionistic acts of divine beings. As a result, ancient peoples retrojected commonly observed astronomical, reproductive, and agricultural categories back into the creative events of God/s.

For example, in *Enuma Elish*, after the first divine beings arise out of the watery chaos, they mate together to give birth to different gods, and then battle amongst themselves, resulting in the creation of the earth and heavens. The champion god Marduk cuts the goddess Tiamat's body into two parts, forming dry land and the firmament. Another Mesopotamian creation account, *Enki and Ninhursag*, describes the god of water impregnating the earth goddess, who gives birth to the goddess of plants. Ancient peoples often referred to the earth as "mother earth" since vegetation in their eyes mysteriously appeared before them, and they retrojected this power of fertility to the creation of animals, humans, and other gods from the earth. Similarly, the Egyptians understood origins through ancient reproductive categories. In one version of *Creation by Atum*, the god Atum masturbates and his seed gives rise to the gods of air and moisture. They in turn mate to produce the earth, the sky, and all the creatures (cosmic, divine, and human). Another rendition has the air god appear once Atum lifts the firmament from the earth.[23]

The parallels between Gen 1 and these ancient Near Eastern origins accounts are striking. The world is created *de novo*, heaven (firmament) and earth are separated by a decisive divine act, and echoes of the notion of mother earth even appear with God's command on the fifth creation day, "Let the land produce living creatures" (Gen 1:24). However, the theology in Genesis is radically different from that in the Mesopotamian and Egyptian creation stories. In Gen 1 the heavens, earth, plants, and animals are completely stripped of divinity and personhood. There is only one God and no mention whatsoever of any other gods. He creates the world with utter ease through verbal commands. For that matter, His ordering the earth to produce animals on the fifth day of creation sends a revolutionary theological message to the surrounding nations. Genesis 1 uses their ancient phenomenological notion that the earth produces life, but strips away its motherhood and submits the earth to the control of the Hebrew God. In other words, the biblical author through the Holy Spirit cleanses this ancient origins motif of its pagan earth worship.

Modern science also assists in determining the historicity of Gen 1. The geological record features a fossil pattern that has been known for more than 150 years (Appendix 7 Fig 4). In fact, the basic outline was established about 1850 by a majority of conservative Christians, and it pre-dates Darwin's famed book on biological evolution, *On the Origin of Species* (1859). In other words, it was formulated by anti-evolutionists.[24] Christian leaders in the origins debate today rarely question the integrity of the geological record because it is there in front of their eyes, plain to see. Therefore, the fossil pattern in the crust of the earth can be compared to patterns predicted by the anti-evolutionary origins positions. The significance of this scientific evidence is that it is well within the reach of lay people and does not require specialized knowledge.

Appendix 7 Fig 1 presents the fossil pattern prediction of young earth creation. This view of origins asserts that the universe and life were created as described literally in Gen 1. Soon afterwards, sin entered the world and so too the physical death of humans and living organisms. Thus, at the bottom of the geological record there should be the remains of every creature that God made during the creation week, including all extinct animals. Notably, one would expect to find dinosaurs (which are reptiles) and humans together at the base of the fossil record. Therefore, scientific creationism predicts a "creation basal layer." Even assuming the young earth creationist belief in Noah's global flood, this evidence would remain in the bottom geological strata because of one simple fact: bones and teeth do not float. However, it is obvious that the fossil pattern predicted by young earth creation does not even come close to the actual geological facts (Fig 4).

Appendix 7 Fig 2 outlines the fossil pattern prediction of progressive creation. This position claims that Gen 1 offers a historical outline of God's creative acts over eons of time and that the creation "days" represent geological epochs of hundreds of millions of years. However, conspicuous inversions exist in the fossil order between the progressive creationist prediction and the scientific facts. Geology indicates that fish appeared more than 400 million years before fruit trees while Scripture states these life forms were created on the fifth and third creation day/age, respectively. Genesis 1 places the origin of land animals after the appearance of birds and marine creatures. But the fossil record indicates terrestrial animals like reptiles arose nearly 200 million years before the first birds and about 300 million years before whales, one of the "great creatures of the sea" (v. 21). And according to Gen 1, plants and trees were created one "day" before the sun. Yet without sunlight, botanical life would not have been able to bear seed and fruit over millions of years during the third epoch.

Another obvious problem for progressive creation arises with the divine provision of food for animals on the sixth day/age. After God declares to the humans, "I give you every seed-bearing plant on the face of the whole earth and every tree that has fruit with seed in it. They will be food for you" (Gen 1:29), He then states, "And to all the beasts of the earth and all the birds of the air and all the creatures that move on the ground— everything that has the breath of life in it—I give every green plant for food" (v. 30). Therefore, progressive creation predicts that the fossil record up to the creation of humanity should feature animals that are vegetarians. However, science reveals that flesh-slaughtering teeth abound throughout geological strata for hundreds of millions of years before humans (see carnivorous dentitions of the shark, T-Rex dinosaur, and saber-toothed tiger in Appendix 7 Figs 5 and 4 and Fig 9-2, respectively). The first reference in Scripture to the eating of flesh by humans and animals only appears after Noah had left the ark (Gen 9:3–5). Notably, vegetarianism is an ancient motif and it ends with the loss of the idyllic age.

A comment also needs to be made with regard to the interpretation of the word "day" in Gen 1 by progressive creationists. In order to defend their position, they often appeal to 2 Pet 3:8, "With the Lord a day is like a thousand years, and a thousand years are like a day." Following this approach, it is assumed that the six days represent six extensive periods of time, and that these are in alignment with the time scales offered by the modern sciences of geology and cosmology. However, there are two difficulties with this understanding of Scripture. First, every time the Hebrew term day (*yōm*) appears in the Old Testament with a number, it refers to a regular 24-hour day. Second, Gen 1 defines each day with the concluding statement: "There was evening and there was morning—the first [second, third, etc.] day." Thus, the creation days are 24-hour periods and not geological or cosmological epochs. The progressive creationist interpretation of the days in Gen 1 is un-biblical.

A personal commitment to scientific concordism forces young earth creationists and progressive creationists to reject biological evolution. Their primary biblical argument rests in the phrase "according to their/its kind/s." It appears 10 times in Gen 1 and refers to the reproduction of living organisms. Anti-evolutionists contend this category reveals that there are basic groups or types of life, and that these are essentially fixed and unchanging, though some modification can occur within a "kind."[25] Consequently, macro-evolution (e.g., fish to amphibians) is rejected while micro-evolution (e.g., varieties of dogs) in a grouping is accepted. However, young earth creationists and progressive creationists fail to recognize the ancient science in Gen 1. The category of "according to their/its kind/s" reflects an ancient taxonomy that is based on an ancient phenomenological perspective of living organisms. As noted before, ancient peoples always saw hens producing chicks, ewes birthing lambs, and women bearing infants. In conceiving the origin of life, they logically retrojected this observation and concluded that each type of reproductive group (roosters/hens, rams/ewes, male/female humans) must have been created *de novo*. Therefore, the failure to identify this incidental ancient taxonomy in Gen 1 is the basis for the rejection of biological evolution by young earth creation and progressive creation.

In contrast, evolutionary creation rejects scientific concordism. This conservative Christian origins position makes no fossil pattern prediction based on the Bible (Appendix 7 Fig 3). In fact, it asserts that biological evolution is one of the easiest theories to falsify. If only one fossil is out of order in the geological record, then this scientific paradigm collapses. For example, the discovery of a human tooth in the strata of the dinosaurs would destroy this theory completely. To date, there has never been a fossil out of place. And considering the incalculable number of fossils that have been discovered, it is doubtful any will ever be found.

The major motif of *de novo* creation, emphasis on the Sabbath, ancient poetic frameworks and the geological record all indicate that Gen 1 is not a record of actual events in the origin of the world. Interpretations of this chapter based on the assumption of scientific concordism by young earth creationists and progressive creationists fail. This biblical and scientific evidence calls into question the historicity of human origins on the sixth day of creation. Yet despite the challenge to the traditional literal interpretation, Christians throughout the ages have come to recognize that the primary purpose of Gen 1 is to reveal the Message of Faith that God is the Creator. Men and women also understand the unique position they enjoy in the world. As Gen 1:27 states, "God created man in His own image, in the image of God He created him; male and female He created them."

The Historicity of the Creation of Adam and Eve (Gen 2:4–25)

Generations of Christians have firmly believed that the creation of Adam and Eve in Gen 2 is an elaboration of the account of human origins briefly presented on the sixth creation day in Gen 1. This traditional literal interpretation asserts that human history begins with the events in the garden of Eden. However, conflicts in the order of God's creative acts exist between these first two biblical chapters, bringing into question the historicity of at least one if not both accounts. As well, ancient Near Eastern motifs and scientific problems in Gen 2 indicate further that this account is not historical.

The conflicting order of creation events between Gen 1 and 2 is closely connected to human origins:

Genesis 1		Genesis 2	
vegetation (fruit)	3rd Day	man	v. 7
birds	5th Day	vegetation (fruit)	v. 8–9
land animals	6th Day	land animals and birds	v. 19
man and woman	6th Day	woman	v. 22

The most glaring difficulty with the view that Gen 2 offers details on the events of the sixth creation day involves the origin of birds. Genesis 1 states that God created "*every* winged bird according to its kind" (v. 21) on the fifth day, but Gen 2 claims the Lord God formed "*all* the birds of the air" (v. 19) after the man was made (v. 7). Significantly, both verses use the same Hebrew adjective (*cōl* "all, every").[26] Regarding vegetation, fruit trees for consumption were made three days before the man according to the first chapter of Genesis, but after his creation in the second chapter (v. 9). A conflict in creative order also appears with land animals and humans. Genesis 1 places the origin of "livestock, creatures that move along the ground, and wild animals" (v. 24) before the creation of male and female humans, while Gen 2 puts the forming of "*all* [*cōl*] the beasts of the field" (v. 19) in between the fashioning of Adam from dust (v. 7) and Eve from his side (v. 22).[27]

However, these event conflicts between Gen 1 and 2 evaporate if the Holy Spirit used two different, yet complementary, creation accounts in the revelatory process. Note that each has an introductory statement/title: "In the beginning God created the heavens and the earth" (Gen 1:1) and "This is the account of the heavens and the earth when they were created" (Gen 2:4). If Gen 2 was elaboration of the sixth creation day and in particular human origins, then one would expect titles like "This is the account of the sixth day of creation" or "This is the account of the creation of humanity." Moreover, distinct characteristics in these chapters indicate that they are independent versions of origins, conventionally categorized as the Priestly and Jahwist:

	Genesis 1 (P)	**Genesis 2 (J)**[28]
Literary Style	Poetic Structured and Repetitive	Narrative Free-Flowing
Scene Setting	Cosmic	Pastoral
Divine Name Hebrew	God *'Ĕlōhîm*	Lord God *Yahweh 'Ĕlōhîm*
Creative Action	Verbal Commands	Hands-On
Divine Being	Transcendent and Heavenly	Immanent and Earthly
Relationship to Humans	Regal	Personal
Food Commands	Without a Prohibition Focus on Sustenance	With a Prohibition Focus on Obedience

By juxtaposing two creation accounts, the Bible opens with a revelation that God is both the transcendent Creator of a vast cosmos and the immanent Maker of each and every person. In this way, the divine editorial intention in redacting Gen 1 and 2 is to reveal the fullness of the Lord's character, and not the details of how He actually created the world.

Gen 2 features the major motif of *de novo* creation and focuses on the origin of humanity. The use of earth to fashion a man quickly and completely often appears in Mesopotamian creation accounts. For example, *Atrahasis* presents a goddess who mixes clay with the blood of a slain god to fashion 7 males and 7 females.[29] In *Enki and Ninmah*, a drunken goddess uses earth and makes imperfect human beings. And the *Hymn to the Mattock* reflects the 1-seed theory of reproduction when a god strikes the ground with a hoe-like axe "so that the seed from which people grew could sprout from the field."[30] The gods in many of these pagan accounts create humanity in order to free themselves of work. In effect, men and women are slaves. But in sharp contrast, Gen 2 features a faith message that the Lord cares for humanity and meets their physical (food) and psychological (companionship) needs. Intimations of the God of Love are being revealed at this early stage in biblical revelation.

The motif of *de novo* creation often includes the notion that the world was originally harmonious or even perfect.[31] This is clearly seen in both Gen 1 and 2. But the latter chapter offers more details and reflects a number of ancient Near Eastern minor motifs. Belief in a primeval paradise or idyllic age is found in the Mesopotamian account of *Enki and Ninhursag*. It describes the land of Dilmun, a place that is "pure," "clean," and "bright" where "the lion does not kill, the wolf does not plunder the lamb" and "old men do not say, 'I am an old man.'" The motif of gaining eternal life through the consumption of a mystical food appears in the *Story of Adapa* and the *Epic of Gilgamesh*. In both accounts the opportunity is lost. Significantly, the latter has a serpent that steals the "plant of life" from the hero. And sacred trees are a reappearing theme and symbol in the literature and art of not only the ancient Near East, but throughout the world. In these accounts, trees are placed prominently in the center of the scene, and are often flanked by animals, people, and supernatural beings.[32]

The parallels between these motifs and Gen 2 are obvious. Scripture describes the garden of Eden as an ideal setting with two trees bearing mystical fruit in the middle of it, animals in harmony with Adam, and the Lord God in direct contact with him. The implication of *de novo* creation and its associated minor motifs in the opening chapters of Scripture is quite significant. The common Christian belief that the world was originally perfect is ultimately rooted in incidental ancient motifs. Stated more precisely, there never was an idyllic paradise at the beginning of time.

Though Gen 2 includes a number of ancient Near Eastern motifs, it delivers Messages of Faith that are radically different from pagan beliefs. The Lord is in a personal relationship with humankind. In fact, He cares about the man and woman. This relationship features obedience to a Holy God and accountability before Him. Humans have the freedom not to observe His commands, but there are serious consequences if they disregard them. Thus, the motifs in Gen 2 are intellectual categories-of-the-day upon which is placed a Holy Spirit inspired revelation defining the basic relationship between God and us. Like the ancient science in Scripture, the *de novo* creation of humanity, an idyllic age in the distant past, mystical foods with the power to endow knowledge and eternal life, etc., are ancient ideas and incidental vessels that transport Divine Theology.

Modern science also helps uncover whether or not Gen 2 is a record of actual events. Viewed as a historical account, a fossil pattern prediction can be made. It would be similar to that of young earth creation (Appendix 7 Fig 1) without the bars representing fish, amphibians, and whales, since these organisms are not mentioned. But like the previous scientific concordist predictions, this fossil pattern does not match the actual geological evidence (Fig 4). In addition, Gen 2:10–14 defines the location of the garden of Eden—somewhere near the Tigris and Euphrates Rivers. Thus, Gen 2 predicts that human fossils should first appear in Mesopotamia. But the geological record reveals that anatomically modern humans lived in East-Central Africa for about 100,000 years before entering the Middle East (Appendix 10 Fig 11. For the dating of fossils and archaeological artifacts, see Appendices 8 and 9). Clearly, scientific and historical concordism in Gen 2 fail.

The conflicts in creation events between the first two chapters of Scripture, the numerous ancient Near Eastern motifs, and the modern scientific evidence all indicate that Gen 2 is not a historical account of human origins. Many Christians might be threatened by such facts. But these features contribute to a better understanding of the revelatory process used by the Holy Spirit. In a subtle way, the Bible itself is revealing that its purpose is not to disclose how God made the universe and life, including humanity. As well, the conflicts and motifs provide an invaluable service. They focus believers on the Message of Faith instead of the incidental ancient history of human origins.

Genesis 2 complements the Divine Theology in Gen 1 and asserts that humanity is a special and unique creation. We are the only creatures in a personal relationship with the Creator. This chapter also reveals that men and women were made to enjoy the mystery of marriage. So beautifully stated, "A man will leave his father and mother and be united to his wife, and they will become one flesh" (v. 24). And most importantly, Gen 2 reveals that God sets limits on human freedom, and failure to respect these boundaries has serious consequences.

The Historicity of the Fall of Humanity in the Garden of Eden (Gen 3)

Throughout the ages the Church has tenaciously held that the fall of Adam and Eve in the garden of Eden is a historical fact. As punishment for his sin, God condemns Adam to suffer through life and then to die. The New Testament supports the traditional literal reading of events in Gen 3. The apostle Paul states directly, "Death came through a man" (1 Cor 15:20) and "Sin entered the world through one man, and death through sin" (Rom 5:12). However, the ancient motifs in Gen 3, the ancient understanding of causality, and the fossil record all point away from the historicity of this chapter and the causal connection between sin and death.

Genesis 3 is richly adorned with numerous ancient motifs. It is framed on the belief embraced by many early cultures that a primeval idyllic age was lost, resulting in the present world with its hardships and afflictions.[33] Significantly, this major motif sometimes includes the first humans falling from grace and being punished by God/s. Minor motifs also appear in Gen 3. It opens with a fast-talking snake tempting Eve. The symbolization of evil by serpents appears in ancient literature, as does the personification of animals by having them speak. This chapter repeats the Gen 2 motifs of the sacred trees and presents more explicitly the notion that eternal life can be acquired through the consumption of a special food. Genesis 3 closes with the tree of life being guarded by a flaming sword and cherubim. The latter are found throughout ancient Near Eastern religious art, including the sacred objects of the Hebrews (Exod 25:18–22, 26:31; 2 Chr 3:7). To the surprise of many Christians, cherubim are not angels, but composite beings made up of the body of a lion/bull, the wings of a bird, and the head of a man (cf. Ps 18:10). Such hybrid creatures protecting the gods and holy places are another motif in the ancient Near East (e.g., Egyptian sphinx).[34]

The implication of so many ancient motifs in Gen 3 is clear: they point away from the historicity of this chapter. But it makes perfect sense that the Holy Spirit used the motifs-of-the-day in the same way that He accommodated to the level of the ancient Hebrews by employing the science-of-the-day. These frameworks and categories were foundations of the ancient mindset and utilizing them facilitated biblical revelation. Thus, the Message of Faith in Gen 3 is not dependent upon the historical reality of a lost idyllic age, a talking snake, mystical fruit, or cherubim. Instead, these ancient motifs are incidental to a Divine Theology that was radically different from the pagan beliefs surrounding the Hebrews.

Genesis 3 reveals the reality of human sin. Even though Adam and Eve were tempted by evil, they freely and deliberately disobeyed God. This chapter is also a revelation of reactions and responses to being caught in sin. After eating the forbidden fruit, the first couple are ashamed and afraid, and try hiding from the Lord. When confronted by Him, they rationalize their sinfulness. The man not only blames his wife, but in a subtle fashion he places the ultimate responsibility for his transgression upon the Creator! Adam complains that it was "the woman *You* put here with me" that led him into sin (v. 12; italics added). Eve then blames the snake. However, Gen 3 reveals that humans are responsible for their actions and are accountable before God. The consequences of disobedience are significant because the Creator judges men and women for their sins.

Genesis 3 engages another foundational human experience—the reality of suffering and death, and the attempt to justify the existence of these harsh realities in a world created by a Holy God. Categorized as "theodicy" (Greek: *theos* "God" *dikē* "justice"), coming to terms with pain and mortality has been a consuming topic throughout history. Genesis 3 causally connects suffering and death to the sins committed by Adam and Eve. The apostle Paul repeats this notion in the New Testament (Rom 5–8; 1 Cor 15). It must be noted that Gen 3 is not referring to spiritual death as progressive creation claims. Verse 19 definitely refers to physical death because in judging Adam the Lord states, "For dust you are and to dust you will return." Often termed the cosmic fall, divine judgment includes other physical changes in nature.[35] Birth pain for the woman increases (v. 16), thorns and thistles infest fields (v. 18), and this passage implies that snakes lose their legs (v. 14). Paul also recognizes that sinful events in the garden of Eden caused physical transformations in the world. He asserts that "the whole creation has been groaning" because it "was subjected to frustration" and placed "in bondage to decay" (Rom 8:20–22).

Since Gen 3 refers to changes in nature, modern science can assist in determining the historicity of the causal connection between human sin and physical pain, decomposition, and mortality. The geological record reveals without any doubt whatsoever that suffering and death have existed in the world for hundreds of millions of years before the appearance of humans on earth (Appendix 7 Fig 4). As well, legless snakes, thorns, and thistles predated people by 100, 50, and 25 million years, respectively.[36] Therefore, human sin is not causally connected to the origin of biological pain, decay, and mortality. If there was a causal connection between the sin of Adam and physical death as stated in Gen 3, then the fossil pattern predicted by young earth creation would be found (Appendix 7 Fig 1). Human remains should appear at the lowest level of geological stratification along with the bones of every life form ever created.

As an actual record of history, the traditional literal interpretation of Gen 3 conflicts irreconcilably with modern science. Once more, scientific and historical concordism fail. A solution to this problem exists, but it requires knowledge of how ancient peoples thought and a reading of the garden of Eden account in a way that is utterly counterintuitive. As noted in previous chapters, Christians must first identify the ancient intellectual categories in Scripture, and then separate these incidental features from the Messages of Faith.

Genesis 3 is structured upon the ancient motif of a lost idyllic age. This major motif was not simply a literary device as often understood today, but rather refers to a primeval period believed to have once existed. It was a part of the history-of-the-day. Such an idea was logical to ancient peoples. They experienced numerous afflictions and struggles, and they rationally concluded that there was a cause for these phenomena. Attempting to find an etiology for suffering was no different than explaining the origin of the firmament, which they conceived had entered the world abruptly through a supernatural cause. So too was the entrance of troubles and hardships at one point in the past. The corollary or logical implication of this ancient reasoning is that prior to the introduction of adversities, the world was in a happier and more harmonious state. For the inspired author of Gen 3, the harsh realities of birth pangs, sweaty and painful work, thistles and thorns, and ultimately death, all pointed back to the loss of an original utopian creation.

The fall in Gen 3 also features ancient notions of causality. But the etiology for the lost idyllic age is unique to the Hebrews. It integrates three facets: the temptation of evil, the sinfulness of humanity, and the divine judgment of sin. Stated precisely, the *instigating cause* for the fall is the snake and its seducing challenges to God's command, the *precipitating cause* leading to physical adversities in the world is the sin of Adam and Eve, and the *enacting* or *enforcing cause* that introduces suffering and death into the creation is God's punishment for human sin.

Explained more fully, Gen 3 employs ancient motifs and ancient notions of causality in order to deliver a Divine Theology on sin. The snake is the incarnation of evil and intimates the notion held throughout the ancient world of a causal connection between physical disorders and demonic spirits. Similarly, the rebellion of Adam and Eve and the suffering and death they came to experience reflects the causal connection between sin and affliction that was also assumed by ancient peoples. And the attribution of divine judgmental action in Gen 3 is an accommodation to the common motif that the world actually fell from an original idyllic age. In this way, the Holy Spirit uses the intellectual categories of the ancient Hebrews and neighboring nations to reveal the reality, manifestation, and consequence of human sin.

Reading Gen 3 today requires looking beyond the major motif of a lost idyllic age, the minor ancient Near East motifs, and the ancient notions of causality connecting the origins of physical afflictions to demonic activity, human sin, and divine judgment. In other words, *twenty-first century Christians must recognize that all events described in Gen 3 never actually happened as stated*. No woman was ever tempted in an idyllic garden by a sinister talking snake; two rebellious people did not eat mystical fruit that imparted knowledge of good and evil; and God never launched suffering and death into the world in judgment for their sinfulness. Therefore, the fall of humanity into sin did not occur as stated in the Bible, and the cosmic fall never happened.

Without a doubt, this reading approach is completely counterintuitive, and even threatening. Yet with an awareness of the ancient intellectual categories in Gen 3, and practice in looking beyond these to what the Holy Spirit intended to reveal, it becomes more comfortable. This situation is similar to when Christians learn the actual meaning of the term firmament in Gen 1. At first many are troubled that the Bible makes statements about God creating the heavens that are not true. This is also the case with the final judgment. Scripture states that the Lord will roll up the heavens like a scroll, which obviously cannot happen. But equipped with a knowledge of ancient astronomy and an appreciation that the attribution of divine creative and judgmental action is intentionally accommodated in the revelatory process, believers eventually recognize two facts: The second day of creation is not a literal account of past events in the history of the heavens, and biblical passages about the end of the world are not a record of how the heavens will actually be dismantled. By employing a similar approach, Christians can come to terms with the fact that the events described in Gen 3 never happened either.

Numerous ancient motifs, ancient concepts of causality, and the geological record indicate that Gen 3 is not a historical account. The implications of this conclusion are far reaching. They directly call into question traditional belief in the historicity of the fall of Adam and Eve. Concerns are also raised about the apostle Paul's literal reading of this chapter as seen in Rom 5–8 and 1 Cor 15. And the traditional doctrine of original sin, which is based on the assumption that the garden of Eden account is historical, appears suspect. More will be said on these issues in the next two chapters.

Despite the traditional literal reading of Gen 3 as actual history, the revelatory power of this divinely inspired account has been affirmed over and over again throughout the ages. It has consistently convicted men and women of their sins, and has left them knowing that God judges them accordingly. Genesis 3 is one of the most penetrating pictures of human nature. Who has not experienced the spiritual-intellectual dynamic of the garden of Eden? Is anyone not tempted to disobey their Maker? And who has not tried to rationalize their sin before the Holy Spirit? Clearly, the inerrant and infallible Messages of Faith in Gen 3 transcend the incidental ancient motifs and ancient categories of causality through which they are revealed.

The Historicity of the First Family and Adam-Cain Genealogy (Gen 4)

The fall of humans in the garden of Eden is soon followed by sinful events within the first family mentioned in Scripture. Adam and Eve give birth to Cain and Abel, and the older brother murders the younger. In other words, Gen 3 and the first sin against God is immediately followed by the first sin against another human being. Genesis 4 also includes the first genealogy in Scripture and the beginnings of civilization—agriculture, city building, music, and metallurgy. It seems reasonable that the incidents in this chapter actually occurred in the past since most are within normal experience. But problems with the events, ancient poetic features, and conflicts with modern science indicate that this chapter is not a record of early human history.

One of the best known difficulties in the Bible deals with the origin of Cain's wife. After murdering Abel, God banishes him to the land of Nod, and there "Cain lay with his wife, and she became pregnant" (Gen 4:17). But where did this woman come from, since only he and his parents were alive? The same problem arises with Cain's immediate response to his punishment. He complains that "whoever finds me will kill me" (v. 14). But God responds, "Not so; if anyone kills Cain, he will suffer vengeance seven times over" (v. 15a). The context of Gen 4 again indicates that people were living in Nod at that time. Otherwise, why would Cain be worried for his life? And why would God comfort him? Finally, the Lord condemns him to "be a restless wanderer on the earth" (v. 12), yet he had to remain in one place if he built a city (v. 17). So, is Cain a restless wanderer or a city dweller? Reading Gen 4 as literal history is obviously problematic.

These difficulties quickly disappear if modern readers do not force their tight twenty-first century logic upon this chapter. Like the origin of the pre-creative state in Gen 1:2, questions about the origin of Cain's wife or his potential killers probably never crossed the mind of the ancient writer or readers. Similarly, most would not have recognized Cain being presented as both a wanderer of the earth and a resident of a city. This inconsistency, like the conflicting order of creative events between Gen 1 and 2, was not noted then, and Christians are rarely aware of it now. The problems with events connected to Cain in Gen 4 evaporate if the ancient mindset of the inspired writer is respected. It is only reasonable to cut Gen 1–11 some epistemological slack.

Ancient poetic features in the Adam-Cain genealogy also point away from the historicity of this chapter. Fig 6-4 reveals that this lineage is highly structured and repeatedly uses the mystical number 7. In the ancient Near East, 7 was permeated with meaning and used symbolically.[37] The Bible often employs it and its multiples to convey the notions of completion,

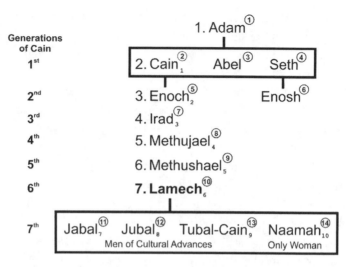

Fig 6-4. Genesis 4: Adam-Cain Genealogy. Naamah is the only woman in the lineage and she does not contribute a cultural advance like her brothers. Her inclusion is conspicuous and appears to be for stylistic reasons. The placement of Naamah produces a genealogy with 14 individuals, which is a doubling of the mystical number 7. The line from Cain to her is a symmetrical total of 10. Notably, the Hebrew mystical number 12 is not found in any significant arrangement, contrasting this genealogy to those of God's chosen people in Gen 5 and 11.

perfection and fulfillment. For example, 7s shape the genealogies of Jesus in Matthew and Luke (Appendix 3). The Gen 4 genealogy has a total of 14 (7 x 2) individuals. Cain's line has 7 generations, drawing attention to the last one and the origin of cultural advances. The boastful and vengeful murderer Lamech is the 7th generation from Adam in order to depict fully the results of human sin begun in the garden of Eden. He is a prototype of evil. The symmetrical number 10 also appears in this genealogy. There are 10 individuals from Adam to Lamech, and Cain's line has a total of 10 people. These poetic features point away from Gen 4 being a strict literal and historical record, since actual genealogies do not unfold in such an artificial and patterned fashion with 7s and 10s.

The purpose of Gen 4 is both etiological and theological. It explains the spread of sin throughout the world. In particular, the inspired author uses the major motif of tribal formation. This ancient conceptualization of origins assumes that communities and nations arise from one male individual and descend through one paternal genealogical line (e.g., Rome was founded by Romulus). This motif also echoes *de novo* creation and the ancient notion of causality in that humans and sin entered the world abruptly at one specific point. Genesis 4 establishes the rebellious Adam-Cain genealogy and it stands in contrast to the chosen Adam-Seth lineage about to be given in Gen 5. In this way, the Bible establishes very early two basic categories of human beings—those not walking with the Lord and those who follow Him.

Modern science also assists in ascertaining the historicity of Gen 4. Similar to stratification and fossils in the geological record, archaeological sites consist of layers of earth containing human artifacts. Many settlements have been inhabited for thousands of years and relics like pottery and tools from different periods appear progressively through the strata of soil and debris. Radiometric dating complements the evidence found in these sites by demonstrating that the age of archaeological layers increases steadily from the upper to lower regions (Appendices 8 and 9). Consequently, it is possible to compare this scientific evidence with archaeological predictions based on Gen 4 and the origin of civilization.

Archaeologically significant artifacts in Gen 4 include: flocks and crops (v. 3), a city (v. 17), tents and herds (v. 20), harps and flutes (v. 21), and tools made of bronze and iron (v. 22). Notably, these cultural advances arose in only eight generations, and the latter three with the sons of Lamech. Therefore, these artifacts should appear together near the lowest levels of archaeological stratification if Gen 4 is an actual historical record of the origins of human civilization. However, this prediction does not align with the scientific facts. The first evidence for plant and animal domestication in the ancient Near East appears about 9000 BC and permanent settlements 7000 BC. The earliest flutes are dated 30,000 BC and the harp (lyre) 3000 BC. Bronze is utilized in implements by 3200 BC, and widespread use of iron is found only after 1200 BC.[38]

This conflict between Scripture and science is easily resolved if Gen 4 presents an incidental ancient understanding of the beginning of civilization. In fact, the origin of cultural advances is a common ancient motif. The Greeks believed that literature, music, dance, etc., came from goddesses known as "the Muses." Babylonian texts report that Seven Sages taught humans the arts of civilization *before* a worldwide flood. The Mesopotamian account *Enki and Ordering of the World* states that gods are responsible for instituting agriculture, animal domestication, field implements, weaving, and house building.[39] In the same way that ancient people reasoned that everything in the world was created *de novo*, they also envisioned the origin of cultural advances to be quick and complete. Often they attributed an innovation to a single individual. This ancient conceptualization is evident in Gen 4. But instead of gods or semi-gods imparting cultural knowledge, the inspired author strips away pagan beliefs from this motif to assert that humans are responsible for the origin of civilization.

Though Gen 4 fails to align with the archaeological record, it offers subtle historical referents to the time about when this chapter was first conceived. Verse 22 states that Tubal-Cain "forged all kinds of tools out of bronze and iron." In other words, the inspired author lived after the widespread use of iron around 1200 BC. (This would be similar to finding an undated letter with a reference to a laptop computer. Everyone would conclude that it was written after the mid-1980s.) From his ancient phenomenological perspective, it was reasonable to assume that bronze and iron implements were invented simultaneously. But more subtly, there is no mention in Gen 4 of the origin of writing as seen in a number of other cultural origins motifs. Thus, the basic ideas in this chapter were likely conceived in a preliterate community, and circulated in an oral form prior to being written down at a later time. Together, this societal type and mention of iron provide historical referents that are consistent with the archaeology of the early Hebrew peoples—they were a preliterate people living in the ancient Near East roughly around 1200 BC.[40]

Problems with the events, ancient poetic features, and conflicts with archaeology indicate that Gen 4 is not a literal historical account. However, the Message of Faith is obvious. Sinfulness includes evil acts against other humans, and God judges us for these. This chapter also presents the word "sin" for the first time in the Bible. The Lord warns Cain, "Sin is crouching at your door; it desires to have you, but you must master it" (v. 7). However, he fails to obey and murders his brother. God banishes Cain to a life of wandering. Despite sin and alienation, the Lord protects him from being murdered; the very sin he committed! This providential act of sustenance is undeserved. Genesis 4 foreshadows the grace found in Jesus. For God sustains us even while we are wandering sinners alienated from Him. And by sending His Son to be murdered for us on the Cross, sin is not only mastered, but conquered.

	Age at Son's Birth	Period Lived after Birth	'60 Times X' Formula	
	A	**B**	**A X 12 =**	**B X 12 =**
1. Adam	**130**	**800**	60 X 26	60 X 160
2. Seth	**105**	807	60 X 21	60 X 160*
3. Enosh	**90**	815	60 X 18	60 X 163
4. Kenan	**70**	840	60 X 14	60 X 168
5. Mahalalel	**65**	830	60 X 13	60 X 166
6. Jared	162	**800**	60 X 31*	60 X 160
7. Enoch	**65**	300	60 X 13	60 X 60
8. Methuselah	187	782	60 X 36*	60 X 155*
9. Lamech	182	**595**	60 X 35*	60 X 119
10. Noah	**500**	[450]	60 X 100	60 X 90

Fig 6-5. **Genesis 5: Adam-Seth Genealogy and Ancient Stylistic Numbers.** Bold numbers are multiples of five (0 or 5). * Mystical number 7 is subtracted from non-multiple of five and then multiplied by 12 in order to fit '60 Times X' formula. [450] derives from Gen 9:29.

The Historicity of the Adam-Seth Genealogy (Gen 5)

Genesis 5 is a striking genealogy listing men who lived an average age of 912 years. For each individual, three temporal references are given: the age when he fathers a son, the number of years he lives after this birth, and his total lifespan. Such a detailed chronology has reasonably led most Christians to believe that Gen 5 is an actual record of human origins beginning with Adam. But a closer examination leads away from the traditional literal interpretation of this ancestral lineage.

Fig 6-5 reveals that the numbers in Gen 5 feature patterns that are not seen in real genealogies. The most obvious are the age when a man has a son and the period of years he lives after the birth. Fifteen of these 20 temporal referents are multiples of 5 (i.e., numbers ending in 0 or 5). A random set of 20 should only have about 4 numbers divisible by 5. Using just this single feature, the statistical probability that Gen 5 is a natural genealogy is about 1 in 6 million.[41] Moreover, the five non-multiples of 5 (162, 187, 182, 807, 782) are multiples of 5 with the addition of the stylistic number 7. Adding 7 to an age reflecting stylistic numbers is found in Genesis. For example, Abraham lived 175 years (12 x 14) + 7 and Sarah 127 years (12 x 10) + 7; Gen 25:7 and 23:1, respectively. Finally, 7 of the 10 men father a son at an age that is a multiple of 5. Does this mean that sexual activity and/or fertility in 70% of marriages only occurred every five years in the life of the husband? It is obvious that the time references in Gen 5 are contrived and artificial.

An appreciation of a minor motif and literary techniques used in ancient Mesopotamia sheds light on Gen 5. Extraordinary longevity before the flood was part of the history-of-the-day. Sumerian king lists (Sumer was the southern region of Babylonia) show that prior to the deluge, rulers governed for tens of thousands of years (Appendix 4). Moreover, these reigns were in multiples of one hundred years, and nearly all of them could be converted into a "60^2 times X" formula. It is not surprising that 60 is prominent in this calculation because not only was Babylonian mathematics based on this number, but it also carried a mystical status similar to 7. Thus, the duration of reigns in the king lists are stylized. This ancient literary technique is used to emphasize the importance of these rulers, whom the ancient Mesopotamians believed had descended from heaven.

The motif of longevity prior to the deluge appears in Scripture with the inspired writer placing Gen 5 in front of Noah's flood account (Gen 6–9). Stylistic numbers are also employed in this genealogy. The individuals total a symmetrical 10, and the 7th person is the unique Enoch, who "walked with God" and did not die like the others because he was "taken away by God" (v. 24). Mathematical formulas *might* be behind the numbers in Gen 5.[42] Multiplying the ages/periods by 12 can be fitted into a "60 times X" formula as shown in Fig 6-5. For the non-multiples of five, subtracting 7 and then multiplying by 12 also fits this calculation. The significance of the number 12 to the Hebrews is well known, especially in the book of Genesis. Canaan and his descendants total 12 (10:15–18), Nahor had 12 sons (22:20–24), Ishmael fathered 12 tribal rulers (25:12–15), the wives of Esau birthed 12 chiefs (36:15–18), and the sons of Jacob became the 12 tribes of Israel (49:1–28). Though Gen 5 still embraces the notion of longevity prior to the flood, its reduction of lifespan as compared to the reigns of Babylonian kings could be a statement by the inspired author against wildly unrealistic ages of tens of thousands of years. In this way, his intention to write history is reflected by lowering the ages to values nearer those that he experienced.

Most people today see a genealogy as a simple list of ancestors. But in the ancient world the purpose of the tribal formation motif was to explain and justify the existence of the community. Like the stylized genealogies of Jesus, Gen 5 is primarily theological. Stripping away the pagan belief that pre-diluvian kings shared in divinity, the inspired writer underlines that everyone in the Adam-Seth line is human and dies (except Enoch). This genealogy of God's chosen people also contrasts against the rebellious Adam-Cain lineage of Gen 4. The seventh individual in each genealogy (godly Enoch and wicked Lamech, respectively) magnifies the difference between these two spiritual heritages. The lack of stylistic numbers in Gen 4 further indicates this ancestral line is not favored like that which follows in the next chapter. The Message of Faith in Gen 5 transcends its motifs and mystical ages. These incidental features deliver the divine revelation that the Hebrews are a selected people who have a unique relationship with the Holy Creator.

The stylistic numbers in Gen 5 are very problematic for young earth creation. This position asserts that the age of the universe is 6000 years old, and calculates this figure by adding up the genealogies in Scripture. The literal interpretation of the time references in Gen 5 is absolutely necessary for creation science, providing a period of 1656 years between the creation of Adam and the flood of Noah. However, the ages and time periods in this genealogy are contrived, not actual. Like the pre-creative state in Gen 1:2, young earth creationists lose another temporal marker from which to date the age of the earth. By failing to identify and respect ancient literary techniques, they eisegetically impose their twenty-first century understanding of genealogies upon Gen 5.

Further difficulties with a strict literal interpretation of the Adam-Seth genealogy arise with the explanation creation scientists offer for the longevity of individuals before the flood and the reduction of lifespan afterward. They argue that the formation of the waters above on the second day of creation provided a unique environment that allowed humans to live for more than 900 years prior to Noah's flood. This protective water canopy collapsed during the global deluge, leading to dramatic climatic change and the entrance of damaging radiation. The lifespan of living organisms then reduced to that seen today. However, young earth creationists fail to realize that longevity prior to the flood is an ancient Near Eastern motif. And as noted earlier, Scripture indicates that the heavenly sea never fell since it was believed to be overhead well after the Noahic deluge (Ps 104:3, 148:4). Once again, young earth creation is un-biblical.

Progressive creation attempts to harmonize modern science with the Gen 5 genealogy. It recognizes the overwhelming physical evidence that the earth is not 6000 years old (Appendix 8). This position also acknowledges fossil evidence that indicates anatomically modern humans appeared on earth about 200,000 years ago, and that for the last 50,000 years, they have lived on every continent except the Americas and Antarctica (Appendix 10 Fig 11). In order to squeeze this scientific evidence into Gen 5, old earth creationists claim that the Adam-Seth genealogy has immense gaps in it. Consequently, they push the origin of Adam back to tens of thousands of years ago.[43] However, there is no evidence of gaps or discontinuities in this lineage—Scripture clearly states that fathers beget a son, who then beget their son, etc. The progressive creationist interpretation of Gen 5 eisegetically forces twenty-first century science into an ancient understanding of human origins. It too is un-biblical.

The use of stylistic numbers and the ancient motifs of longevity before the flood and tribal formation indicate that the genealogy in Gen 5 is not a literal record of actual people at the beginning of human history. The purpose of this chapter is to reveal the divine providentialistic origin of the Hebrew community. Similar to the way that Gen 1 and 2 use an ancient origins science to reveal that God created the universe and life, Gen 5 employs an ancient genealogy and the history-of-the-day as incidental vessels to declare that He ordained and sustained a holy nation. In both cases, Scripture does not disclose the Lord's actual creative events. But the Message of Faith is evident: God is the Creator of both the world and the Hebrew people.

The Historicity of the Sons of God Episode (Gen 6:1–4)

Genesis 6:1–4 is one of the most intriguing passages in the Bible.* The earliest interpreters understood the "sons of God" to be heavenly beings, like angels, who mated with human women. The children born of these unions were giants and heroic men. But troubled by the notion that celestial and terrestrial creatures procreated, later biblical commentators claimed that the sons of God were human beings, either the sons of Seth or earthly rulers and judges. Despite these interpretive differences, Gen 6:1–4 offers invaluable insights into the divine revelatory process and the historicity of the opening chapters of the Bible.

The expression "sons of God" appears only a few times in the Old Testament and the context of these passages is always a celestial scene. In

---

* Gen 6:1–4 was the topic of my masters thesis in theology. I outline its impact on my hermeneutics in my personal story, pages 348.

the book of Job, Satan and the sons of God present themselves before the Lord. The place of this meeting is heaven, because Satan has just arrived "from roaming through the earth and going back and forth in it" (1:7, 2:2). Similarly, Job 38:7 states that the sons of God are joyously shouting at the beginning of creation when the foundations of the earth were set in place. A heavenly scene is apparent in Ps 89:6–7: "Who in heaven is comparable to the Lord? Who among the sons of God is like the Lord, a God greatly feared in the council of the holy ones, and awesome above all those who are around him?" The two other appearances of this expression also allude to a celestial context (Ps 29:1, 89:6). Clearly, "sons of God" in the Old Testament refers to heavenly beings. Thus, Gen 6:1–4 records that celestial creatures and human women mated and procreated.

The belief that gods and humans had sex and then gave birth to extraordinary beings was a widespread motif in the ancient Near East. For example, an Egyptian account describes a god mating with the queen mother who later gives birth to the Pharaoh. The Babylonian epic hero Gilgamesh is partly divine and partly human, and he was born to the goddess Ninsun and the human king Lugalbanda.[44] As noted previously, ancient reproductive biology viewed women basically as fields for the seed of men. The belief that gods had reproductive seed was also commonly accepted at that time (e.g., the masturbating Egyptian god Atum). Therefore, male celestial beings sowing their seed in the womb of female human beings, as suggested in Gen 6:1–4, made perfect sense to ancient peoples like the Hebrews.

The sons of God episode assists in understanding the biblical revelatory process. First, the writer under the inspiration of the Holy Spirit uses a common notion held in his generation. In the same way that Gen 1–11 employs ancient science, this short passage also includes the well-known reproductive concept that heavenly creatures and humans could procreate. Second, like the other ancient motifs in these opening chapters of Scripture, the author of Gen 6:1–4 understood this episode to be historical. It was part of the history-of-the-day. Finally, the biblical writer uses this motif primarily for theological purposes. It is a polemic against the pagan approval of sexual unions between gods and people, and it subtly refutes any belief that humans can gain eternal life through these mixed couplings—God limits lifespan to 120 years (v. 3). Strategically placed before Noah's flood account, this passage is also justification for God to destroy the world because the boundaries He established between heaven and earth were being broken by the celestial-human matings. In other words, sin was bursting throughout the entire cosmos.

Genesis 6:1–4 features a motif that was part of the intellectual make-up of the ancient Near East. Dare I use the word "myth" to describe the literary genre of this passage?* Did the Holy Spirit use a common ancient myth as an incidental vessel in the revelatory process? If indeed these four verses are a myth, then they are definitely not an account of historical events. Despite this possibility, the Message of Faith is obvious. Genesis 6:1–4 underlines the reality of sin. It complements Gen 6:5–8, which focuses upon "how great man's wickedness on the earth had become" (v. 5). Together these eight verses introduce the biblical flood account and anticipate another foundational theological fact: God judges sin.

The Historicity of Noah's Flood (Gen 6:5 to 9:19)

Christians in every generation have accepted that Noah's flood was a historical event. As a matter of fact, a worldwide deluge was the central principle in geology at the turn of the eighteenth century.[45] A recent poll of American adults shows that 60% believe literally in "Noah and the ark, in which it rained for 40 days and nights; the entire world was flooded; and only Noah, his family, and the animals on the ark survived."[46] Interpreting Gen 6–9 as history is reasonable because it features a chronology with numerous temporal referents. In addition, there are over 300 flood accounts scattered throughout the world, suggesting the reality of a catastrophic deluge in the distant past. However, scriptural and scientific evidence indicate that a flood never happened as stated in the Bible.

Serious problems with the traditional literal interpretation of Gen 6–9 appear in its chronology—the dates and days do not align. This difficulty is clearly seen in the period between the start of the flood and the landing of the ark in the Ararat Mountains. The events and times are as follows:

---

* Readers will note that this is the first time that I have used the term "myth" in this book. It is an explosive word in conservative Christian circles. Further discussion on the various definitions of myth appear in the next chapter, pages 259–61.

- 600th year, **2nd** month and 17th day of Noah's life. Flood begins. Springs of the deep burst and floodgates of heaven open (7:11)
- **40 days** rain falls (7:12, 17)
- Waters rise and cover the highest mountains (7:18–20)
- All life outside the ark perishes (7:21–23)
- **150 days** flood prevails over the earth (7:24)
- God remembers Noah (8:1a)
- God sends a wind and the waters recede (8:1b)
- Springs of the deep and floodgates of heaven close (8:2a)
- Rain stops (8:2b)
- Waters recede (8:3a)
- **150 days** waters decrease (8:3b)
- 600th year, **7th** month and 17th day of Noah's life. Ark lands in Ararat Mountains (8:4)

Adding the number of days (40 + 150 + 150) that are mentioned between the two Noahic dates totals 340. If the 40 days of rain are included in the 150-day period that the flood prevails over the earth, then the sum is 300. However, according to the dates of Noah's age there are exactly 5 months between the start of the flood and the landing of the ark. Using either a lunar (29½ days) or 30-day month provides only 147½ and 150 days, respectively. In order to correct this glaring discrepancy, many historical concordists collapse all the events between Gen 7:11 and 8:4 into a 150-day period. But this approach betrays the sequential order of consecutive events plainly stated in Scripture.

Conflicts between the events in Gen 6–9 also raise doubts concerning the historicity of the flood account. To mention three obvious examples:

Two different divine orders are given to load the animals in the ark. In Gen 6:19, God (*'Ĕlōhîm*) commands Noah to bring "*two* of every kind of bird, of every kind of animal and of every kind of creature that moves along the ground." But in Gen 7:2–3, the Lord (*Yahweh*) commands him to take "*seven* of every kind of bird," "*seven* of every kind of clean animal" and "*two* of every kind of unclean animal."

Two conflicting accounts of entering the ark exist. Genesis 7:7–8 states that Noah, his family, and the animals went into the ark, and "after seven days the floodwaters came" (v. 10). However, Gen 7:13–15 asserts that every person and every animal entered the ark "on the very day" that "all the springs of the great deep burst forth, and the floodgates of the heavens were opened" (v. 11).

Two different versions are presented of when the rain ceased. According to Gen 7:12, it rained for 40 days and 40 nights, implying that the rain ended after 40 days. But Gen 8:2 states that "the rain stopped" after the 150–day period during which the flood prevailed on earth (7:24).

Problems with chronology in the biblical flood account and conflicts between its events are resolvable if two separate, yet complementary, versions of the deluge lie within Gen 6–9. Like the creation accounts, there is evidence for Jahwist and Priestly sources. But in contrast to the simple juxtaposition of Gen 1 and 2, the original flood renditions are woven together into a single narrative, making their identification more difficult. Appendix 5 Figs 1-7 present the standard verse distribution of the two sources, the reassembling of these verses into their respective J and P versions, and the linguistic and stylistic features in each account. Three lines of biblical evidence indicate that Gen 6–9 is a composite of two distinct sources:

First, the reassembled Jahwist and Priestly flood accounts stand on their own as coherent narratives (Figs 2 and 5). Both include an introduction describing the sinful state of the world before the flood and the divine justification to destroy it. In each version, Noah is warned of the coming flood and ordered to preserve life in the ark. The two versions emphasize his obedience. P states that "Noah did all that *God* commanded him" (6:22), and J records, "Noah did exactly all that the *Lord* commanded him" (7:5). Each rendition describes the launching of the floodwaters and their retreat. And both accounts conclude with events after the deluge and a divine promise never to destroy the world again with water.

Second, terms and phrases in the J and P flood narratives are characteristic of Gen 2–4 (J) and Gen 1 (P), respectively (Figs 3 and 6). To cite a few examples, the Jahwist creation and deluge versions feature the divine name "Lord" (*Yahweh*) and terms "man" (*'ish*), "woman" (*'ishshâ*), "evil," "offering," "curse/d," and "rain." In contrast, the Priestly origins and flood renditions are distinguished by the use of the word "God" (*'Ĕlōhîm*), the command to "be fruitful and increase on the earth," the assertion that "man is made in the Image of God," and the categorization of life "according to its/their kind/s."

A Noah & his sons Shem, Ham & Japheth (6:9-10)
B   Promise to flood & to establish Covenant (12-18)
C   Preservation of life & food for sustenance (19-22)
D   Command to enter ark (7:1-3)
E   **7 days** waiting for earth to flood (4-10)
F   **40 days** waters increase & ark floating (11-17)
G   **150 days** waters prevail (18-24)
CENTER   **GOD REMEMBERS NOAH** (8:1)
G'   **150 days** (end of) waters abate (2-5)
F'   **40 days** (end of) waters decrease & ark resting (4-6)
E'   **7 days** (periods of) waiting for earth to dry (7-14)
D'   Command to leave ark (15-22)
C'   Multiplication of life & food for sustenance (9:1-7)
B'   Promise not to flood again & to remember Covenant (8-17)
A' Noah & his sons Shem, Ham & Japheth (18-19)

Fig 6-6. Genesis 6–9: Flood Account Chiasm

Finally, the J and P deluge accounts have their own distinct linguistic and stylistic characteristics, indicating that two different authors wrote them (Figs 4 and 7). Only the Jahwist version uses the terms "face" (9X), "heart" (4X), "wipe out" (4X), and the phrase "never again will I repeat to . . ." (2X). While "all flesh" (13 X), "covenant" (9X), "waters triumphed over the earth" (4X), and "two from all, two by two from all" (3X) appear exclusively in the Priestly account. In addition, the J flood uses 7s in its chronology (4X) and counting of clean animals (2X), and 40s (4X) to number the days and nights rain fell on earth. In contrast, P is marked by multiples of the stylistic number 60 in Noah's age at the start of the flood (600 years), the length of the ark (300 cubits), and duration of the deluge (300 days).

The Holy Spirit inspired redactor of the biblical flood account not only integrated the J and P versions, but he used a poetic framework to do so. Fig 6-6 reveals a chiasm in Gen 6–9.[47] This ancient literary technique often appears in the Old Testament. It is made up of two parts: the first half is a mirror image of the second, producing a reversed sequence of ideas or words. Especially striking in the flood chiasm is the use of stylistic numbers and the corresponding days of 7s, 40s, and 150s. The purpose of a chiastic structure is to focus attention on its center and the main point of the account. In the biblical flood chiasm, Gen 8:1 emphasises the

Message of Faith that "God remembered Noah" in the midst of His wrath judging human sin.

To summarize, scriptural evidence for two distinct sources and a poetic framework in Gen 6–9 argues against the traditional interpretation of Noah's flood as literal history. Accurate reports of human activities do not have chronological problems and are not in conflict with each other. Nor does real history unfold in a chiastic pattern. The biblical flood account itself demonstrates the failure of strict historical concordism.

The discovery of Mesopotamian flood stories casts further doubt on Gen 6–9 being a literal record of actual events in history. These include the Sumerian Flood (2000–1700 BC), the Epic of Atrahasis (1700 BC), and the Epic of Gilgamesh (1600 BC). Fig 6-7 compares these pagan renditions with the biblical deluge. The similarities are striking and indicate a relationship between the earlier Mesopotamian versions and the later inspired Hebrew composition of the J and P accounts and their redaction into Gen 6–9.

Notably, the biblical flood account and the preserved Mesopotamian renditions feature: divine justification to destroy the world by a flood; divine warning to build a boat and its construction by the flood hero; a deluge that destroys all life on earth; preservation of the hero, his family, and animals in the boat; the hero's sacrifice to God/s who smell/s the offering; divine reward to the hero; and the use of stylistic numbers 7 and 60. In particular, the parallels between Gen 6–9 and the Epic of Gilgamesh are extraordinary (Appendix 6). Both accounts tell about the boat landing on a mountain after the flood, the hero opening a hatch, a dove and raven used in determining whether or not the earth is dry, and stylistic 7-day periods for the bird reconnaissance. However, most of the similarities between the scriptural and pagan flood renditions are theologically inconsequential and ultimately incidental. For example, the release of birds in 7-day intervals does not reveal anything about the nature of God.

More significantly, radical differences in theology exist between the biblical and Mesopotamian flood accounts. In a word, the gods of the pagan stories are pathetic. Human noise and overpopulation is their justification to destroy the world with a flood. These divine beings are frightened by the deluge and cower up into the heavens. During the flood they get hungry because there are no humans to feed them sacrifices, and after it they "crowded around like flies about the sacrificer" (Appendix 6 v. 161). Finally, the gods offer the hero eternal life in order that he share

	Sumerian Flood 2000-1700 BC	Epic of Atrahasis 1700 BC	Epic of Gilgamesh 1600 BC	Biblical Flood 1000-500 BC
God/s	*37 lines missing*			
Number	many gods	many gods	many gods	one Holy God
Reason to destroy humans		noise	overpopulation	sin
Warn/s hero of flood	✔	✔	✔	✔
Flood Hero				
Name	Ziusudra	Atrahasis	Utnapishtim	Noah
Builds ark	✔	✔	✔	✔
Age given	(36,000 years)*	(600+ years)**		600 yrs
Construction of Ark	*40 lines missing*			
Materials used (e.g., pitch)		✔	✔	✔
Multiple decks		✔	✔	✔
Roof		✔	✔	✔
Dimensions (cubits)			120 X 120 X 120	300 X 50 X 30
Duration		7 days	7 days	
Preservation of Life in Ark	*40 lines missing*			
Family of hero		✔	✔	✔
Animals		✔	✔	✔
Birds		✔	✔	✔
Wild & domestic		✔	✔	✔
Clean & unclean		✔		✔
Flood				
Ark door closed		✔	✔	✔
Destruction of all life	✔	✔	✔	✔
Duration	7 days	7 days	7 days	40/150 days
God/s frightened by flood		✔	✔	
Retreat of Flood	*58 lines missing*			
Ark rests on mountain			Mt Nisir	Ararat Mts
Hero opens hatch	✔		✔	✔
Bird reconnaissance			✔	✔
Dove & raven			✔	✔
Duration			7 days	7/7 days
Water removed & earth dried			✔	✔
Duration			7 days	150/40/7/7 days
After Flood	*39 lines missing*			
Hero sacrifices to God/s	✔	✔	✔	✔
God/s smell/s sacrifice		✔	✔	✔
God/s regret/s flood & quarrel		✔		
God/s offer/s hero	Eternal life	Eternal life?	Eternal life	Covenant

Fig 6-7. Comparison of Mesopotamian and Biblical Flood Accounts. Regrettably some passages in the Sumerian and Atrahasis accounts have not been preserved, suggesting that more parallels to the Biblical flood probably exist. *Age from the Sumerian King list. **No specific age is given, but temporal periods are marked 4 times by the phrase "600 years, less than 600, passed."

in their divinity. In sharp contrast, the God of Noah's flood is a Holy God in total control of the universe. Rampant sin is the justification for the flood. This Divine Being offers Noah a covenant with Him, not eternal life or divinity. And Gen 6–9 features a central faith message: God judges sin and saves the righteous from His judgment.

The discovery of more than 300 flood stories dispersed throughout the world offers insights into the ultimate origins of the biblical flood account. Fig 6-8 shows where some of these are found.[48] It is important to note that many appear on major river systems that repeatedly break their

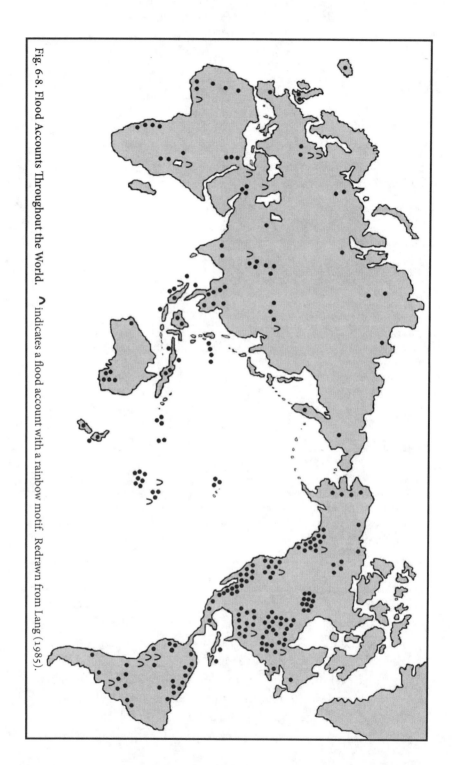

Fig. 6-8. Flood Accounts Throughout the World. ∧ indicates a flood account with a rainbow motif. Redrawn from Lang (1985).

banks (e.g., Tigris, Euphrates, Mississippi), in regions susceptible to flash flooding (mountainous west coasts of North and South America), and areas often devastated by tsunamis (Southeast Asia and Pacific Islands). Understood from an ancient phenomenological perspective, it is not surprising that such traumatic episodes led to accounts of a destructive flood in these places. In the same way that many ancient cultures believed that an angered God/s was pounding in heaven overhead and throwing bolts of lightening during storms, so too catastrophic inundations were connected causally to divine wrath. Thus, the major motif of a great flood arose *independently* throughout the ancient world in a rational attempt to understand these natural phenomena.

Viewed in this light, the psychological impact of the Tigris and Euphrates Rivers flooding and destroying nearby towns and villages undoubtedly lies behind the Mesopotamian flood accounts. The archaeological record reveals major deposits of silt between strata of human occupation, indicating the complete disruption of communities at different points in history. To mention a few, sedimentary layers are found in the ancient cities of Ur (12 feet thick), Nineveh (6), Uruk (5), Shurrupak (2), Kish (1), and Lagash (1).[49] The dates of these deposits range from 3500–2600 BC. It is not a coincidence that the setting of the Mesopotamian flood stories is at the southern end of the Tigris and Euphrates since this region is particularly susceptible to flooding. The hero in the Sumerian, Atrahasis, and Gilgamesh accounts comes from Shurrupak, a city in between these two rivers. Thus, the motif of a great flood has actual historical incidents behind it. There likely was an individual/s who saved his/their family and some animals on a boat or barge, and over time his/their story was included in the Mesopotamians' understanding of history.

It must be emphasized that Mesopotamian flood stories were established well before the Hebrews appeared in the ancient Near East. In other words, Israel inherited this major motif along with its associated minor motifs (e.g., bird reconnaissance), whether through oral versions and/or written texts (see Fig 6-2). Consequently, the biblical flood account at best includes distant echoes of actual past events in Mesopotamia, but this is not to be confused with the detailed historical concordism of Gen 6–9 defended by many Christians today.

Modern science also demonstrates the failure of the anti-evolutionist interpretations of the biblical deluge. Young earth creation claims that a recent global flood destroyed the world except for life preserved in Noah's ark. This position assumes that the ages in the Gen 5 genealogy are literal, and calculates the flood at about 2344 BC, 1656 years after the creation week in Gen 1 (4000 BC). It also asserts that a primary source of the floodwaters came from the collapse of a water canopy that once enveloped the earth ("waters above" in Gen 1:7). Creation science accepts the geological record and the countless number of fossils in the crust of the earth. However, instead of being laid down over hundreds of millions of years, this position argues that most stratification was produced in one year during Noah's worldwide deluge and that fossils in these layers are evidence of living organisms that died during this catastrophic event.

On the surface, the young earth creationist interpretation of Noah's flood and the geological record is persuasive. It is a scientific fact that most of the strata and fossils in the earth's crust were laid down in water. The parallel geological layers indicate this is the case. But a closer examination of the fossil pattern prediction based on a worldwide deluge reveals an insurmountable problem (Appendix 7 Fig 1). Noah's flood would have produced a "global flood layer" with strata featuring the mixing of bones and teeth of every animal ever created. In fact, depending on the turbulence of the deluge, specific gravity should have placed heavier bones (e.g., dinosaurs, elephants) near the bottom of the flood layer and lighter ones at the top. But no such fossil pattern exists in the crust of the earth (Fig 4). Instead, a very consistent geological record is found with the sequential appearance of fish first, amphibians next, then reptiles, and mammals last.

The size of the ark is also a serious problem for creation science. Genesis 6:15 states its dimensions in feet as 450 x 75 x 45. This is a little longer than a football field, fifteen feet above the goal posts, and well inside the yardage numbers. Modern taxonomy identifies over 6 million species of living animals today, and the fossil record reveals that these are far less than 1% of all the species that have ever lived on earth. Limiting the number of animals to those described in Gen 6–7 (mammals, reptiles, birds), a rough calculation suggests that nearly 15 million of them entered the ark.[50] To put perspective on this number, the average professional football stadium only holds 75,000 people, which is about 200 times fewer than the number of creatures saved by Noah. It is hard to see how they could all be packed into a structure that fits well within a football field. In addition, large creatures like dinosaurs are particularly problematic. For example, there are 30 known species of brachiosaurs that average 150,000 pounds in weight, 100 feet in length, and 30 feet high at the shoulder. And space for food to sustain life through the year-long flood was also required (Gen 6:21). Obviously, there would not have been enough room for all the animals and their various foods to fit in the ark.

Extinction is another acute difficulty for young earth creation. Since well over 99% of all species are now extinct, the question arises: If every type of air breathing organism was on the ark, then why bother saving them in the first place? Creation scientists contend that the collapse of the water canopy led to mass extinctions because of dramatic climate change and direct radiation. But again, the Bible reveals that the heavenly sea was intact after the flood. Moreover, there is not a hint in Scripture that nearly all the animals went extinct after the deluge. Instead, God commands Noah, "Bring out every kind of living creature that is with you—the birds, the animals, and all the creatures that move along the ground—so that they can multiply on the earth and be fruitful and increase in number upon it" (Gen 8:17). In fact, His covenant extended to *all* the animals leaving the ark: "I now establish My covenant with you and with your descendants after you and with *every* living creature that was with you—the birds, the livestock and *all* the wild animals, *all* that came out of the ark with you—*every* living creature on earth" (9:10, italics added; Hebrew adjective *cōl* appears 4x). God's stated intention for animals after the flood was that they repopulate the earth, not for nearly all of them to become extinct.

Progressive creation also defends historical concordism in regards to the flood, but argues that it was local and not global. This position notes that the reference to the floodwaters covering "all the high mountains" in Gen 7:19 can be interpreted as rising over "all the high hills" because the Hebrew word *har* can be translated either way. According to this approach, the flood inundated only the hills in the Mesopotamian plain. As well, old earth creation contends that the 18 references to "all" living creatures in Gen 6–9 refer to just the animals in the region. Thus, this view of origins does not expect the earth's crust to show the effects of a worldwide flood. And the problem with animal extinction evaporates because the only organisms drowned in the flood were those in a local area.

At a superficial level, the local flood theory is compelling. As noted, sedimentary layers indicative that human life was disrupted are found near the Tigris and Euphrates Rivers. But the progressive creationist interpretation of the flood has a fatal problem. The Bible identifies the hills/mountains (*har*). Gen 8:4–5 states, "The ark came to rest on the Mountains of Ararat" and then waters receded until "the tops of the mountains became visible." Similar in height to the Rockies in North America, this range has peaks over 16,000 feet high. The biblical flood account also asserts that "all the high mountains" were covered by water "to a depth of more than twenty feet" (Gen 7:19–20). Therefore, most of the planet would have been inundated, and nearly all the animals on earth drowned. If this event happened, there should be a flood layer throughout the world with the remains of all modern creatures along with human cultural artifacts, just like in a tsunami. However, no such deposit exists.

The young earth and progressive creationist interpretations of the flood are un-biblical. The former depends on the collapse of a purported water canopy; the latter is based on the notion that the Noahic deluge was only local. Scientific predictions based on Gen 6–9 also fail. There is no evidence for a global flood layer in the crust of the earth. Historical concordists are unaware of the ancient science in the biblical flood account. This destructive event is the *de-creation* of a 3-tier universe. The opening of the "windows of the heavens" (Gen 7:11) releases the waters above, undoing the separation of the pre-creative waters by the firmament on the second day of creation. The bursting of "springs of the deep" (v. 11) reverses the divine command on the third creation day for the earth to rise out of the waters of the deep which covered it. In other words, Noah's flood is a return to the watery pre-creative state in Gen 1:2. God is undoing the world He created. By respecting the ancient intellectual categories in Gen 6–9, Christians today will recognize that scientific and historical concordism in this account is not only impossible, but unnecessary.

Scripture and science reveal that the biblical flood account is not a literal historical record. Of course, like all other ancient peoples, the Hebrews believed in the reality of a great deluge. It was part of the history-of-the-day. The late arrival of Israel in the ancient Near East indicates that they inherited the flood motif from surrounding nations, most likely the Mesopotamians. And similar to all historical accounts, many interpretations for the reason behind the events existed. The Hebrews viewed this catastrophe in light of a Holy God. Actual local incidents certainly lie behind the Mesopotamian flood stories, and a Noah-like individual/s survived to tell his/their story. However, the details of these events will probably never be recovered, and focusing upon them fails to grasp the purpose of the Noahic deluge in the Bible.

The flood motif in Gen 6–9 is an incidental vessel that delivers Messages of Faith. This account underlines the fact that judgment and destruction await those who disobey God. But it also offers encouragement for those who follow Him because they are saved from His wrath. In particular, the flood account presents the Lord's initiating grace. Even after He judges the world, He recognizes that "the inclination of the human heart is evil from youth" (Gen 8:21). Yet God still establishes a covenant with humanity. This divine act of reaching out to men and women foreshadows the New Testament covenant. As the apostle Paul writes, "God demonstrates His own love for us in this: While we were sinners, Christ died for us" (Rom 5:8).

The Historicity of the Origin of Nations (Gen 9:20 to 10:32)

The Bible states that after the flood the descendants of Noah's three sons repopulated the entire world: "from them came the people who were scattered over all of the earth" (Gen 9:19; also 10:32). Genesis 10 presents the "table of nations" which outlines this dispersion along the familial lines of Shem, Ham, and Japheth. Well-known ancient kingdoms (Egypt, Assyria), cities (Babylon, Nineveh), and peoples (Canaanites, Philistines) are listed. As a result, many Christians accept the historicity of this account as the ultimate origin of societies and civilizations. But a close examination of Scripture supplemented with scientific evidence leads away from this traditional and literal interpretation.

Fig 6-9 reveals that Gen 10 is structured along geographical, political, and theological lines. The sons of Japheth were peoples north and west of Israel. Ham's descendants lived in Palestine and bordered this region to the east and south. Many of them interacted with the chosen line of Shem and often they were her enemies. Genesis 10 also uses stylistic numbers. The total number of nations and individuals that descended from Noah's sons is 70.[51] Japheth has 7 sons and 7 grandsons. Egypt fathers 7 peoples. The Shemites feature a striking series of increasing multiples of 7. In addition, the symmetrical number 10 appears in the lines of Ham to Caphtorim, Cush to Dedan, and Shem to Mash. Significantly, Canaan and his descendants total the Hebrew mystical number 12. The contrived character of the table of nations casts doubt on it being a literal and historical account for the simple fact that societies do not arise in such a stylized fashion.

The structure and stylistic numbers in Gen 10 accentuate two basic Messages of Faith: the unity of all humanity and the unicity of the descendants of Shem. The 7s and 10s underline the importance of the entire human family, and in particular, the reality that God has a chosen people.

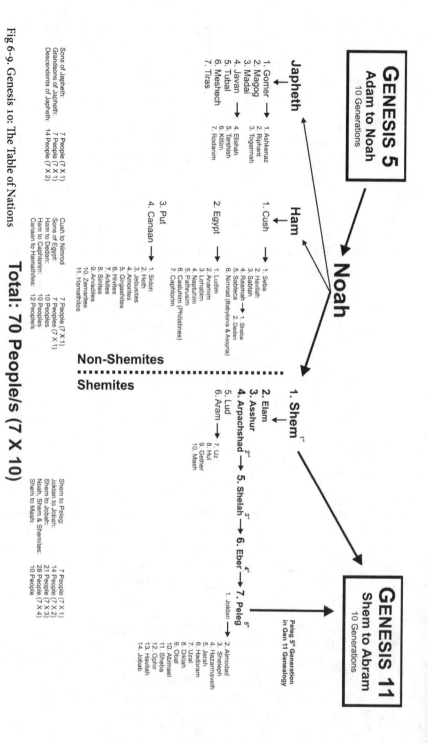

Fig 6-9. Genesis 10: The Table of Nations

GENESIS 5
Adam to Noah
10 Generations

Noah

Japheth

1. Gomer
2. Magog
3. Madai
4. Javan
5. Tubal
6. Meshech
7. Tiras

1. Ashkenaz
2. Riphant
3. Togarmah

4. Elishah
5. Tarshish
6. Kittim
7. Rodanim

Sons of Japheth: 7 People (7 X 1)
Grandsons of Japheth: 7 People (7 X 1)
Descendents of Japheth: 14 People (7 X 2)

Ham

1. Cush
2. Egypt
3. Put
4. Canaan

1. Seba
2. Havilah
3. Sabtah
4. Raamah — 1. Sheba
5. Sabteca   2. Dedan
6. Nimrod (Babylonia & Assyria)

1. Ludim
2. Ananim
3. Lehabim
4. Naphuhim
5. Pathrusim
6. Casluhim (Philistines)
7. Caphtorim

1. Sidon
2. Heth
3. Jebusites
4. Amorites
5. Girgashites
6. Hivites
7. Arkites
8. Sinites
9. Arvadites
10. Zemarites
11. Hamathites

Cush to Nimrod   7 People (7 X 1)
Sons of Egypt: 7 Peoples (7 X 1)
Ham to Dedan: 10 Peoples
Ham to Caphtorim: 10 Peoples
Canaan to Hamathites: 12 People/s

Non-Shemites
••
Shemites

1. Shem 1ˢᵗ
2. Elam
3. Asshur
4. Arpachshad 2ⁿᵈ
5. Shelah 3ʳᵈ
6. Eber 4ᵗʰ
7. Peleg 5ᵗʰ

5. Lud
6. Aram — 7. Uz
8. Hul
9. Gether
10. Mash

Peleg 5ᵗʰ Generation
in Gen 11 Genealogy

1. Joktan
2. Almodad
3. Sheleph
4. Hazarmaveth
5. Jerah
6. Hadoram
7. Uzal
8. Diklah
9. Obal
10. Abimael
11. Sheba
12. Ophir
13. Havilah
14. Jobab

Shem to Peleg: 7 People (7 X 1)
Joktan to Jobab: 14 People (7 X 2)
Shem to Jobab: 21 People (7 X 3)
Noah, Shem & Shemites: 28 People (7 X 4)
Shem to Mash: 10 People

GENESIS 11
Shem to Abram
10 Generations

Total: 70 People/s (7 X 10)

228

Stylistic features also emphasize a polemic against the Canaanites. The table of nations is prefaced by the sin of Ham seeing Noah naked (Gen 9:20–27). The inspired author identifies this son as "the father of Canaan," and three times an angered Noah states that Canaan will be a slave to his brothers. This three-time repetition is an ancient literary device employed for emphasis and it strikes hard against the people who became a chronic enemy of the Hebrews. As well, placing 12 people/s in the Canaanite line stylistically foreshadows the conquest of the Promised Land by the 12 tribes of Israel.

Many of the nations, cities, and peoples listed in Gen 10 are well known to ancient Near Eastern archaeology and history.[52] However, these modern academic disciplines, along with other historical sciences, reveal that the spread of humanity throughout the world and the establishment of these societies do not support the historicity of the table of nations. There is no evidence that: (1) human occupation on earth was completely disrupted by Noah's flood in 2344 BC, (2) the world was then repopulated starting in the Middle East, and (3) ancient Near Eastern nations and cities were founded within a few generations after the flood. Several lines of evidence support this position.

Geology. The traditional literal interpretation of Gen 10 necessitates a global flood to destroy all of humanity in order for the entire world to be repopulated by Noah's descendants. But there is no geological evidence whatsoever of a global flood layer to indicate that a worldwide deluge wiped out human life on earth.

Anthropology. Anatomically modern humans first appeared in Africa about 200,000 years ago (ya). They spread throughout the world entering the Middle East (100,000 ya), Southeast Asia (65,000), Europe (45,000), Australia (45,000), and the Americas (15,000). Appendix 10 Fig 10 outlines this origin and dispersion. Obviously, these times and places do not align with Gen 10 and the notion that everyone today descends from one ancient Near Eastern family in 2344 BC.

Archaeology. Scientific predictions based on the table of nations do not align with the archaeological evidence. Communities and nations have continuously inhabited regions of the ancient Near East since their inception. The earliest permanent villages were built about 7000 BC in Jericho, Catalhoyuk (Turkey), and Umm Dabaghiyah (Iraq). By 3500 BC, complex societies emerged in Mesopotamia and Egypt. At that time, the former featured the first city (Uruk) with a population of more than

10,000 people. Between 2500–2400 BC, Egypt had tens of thousands of workers construct the great pyramids. There is no evidence at all in the archaeological record that human occupation on earth was completely disrupted by a global flood in 2344 BC and that the entire world was subsequently re-peopled from one family.

History. The invention of writing in the ancient Near East around 3300 BC led to records chronicling kingdoms and dynasties in Mesopotamia and Egypt. This evidence, coupled with archaeological data, is particularly relevant to the origin of some cities and peoples mentioned in Gen 10. In Assyria (northern Mesopotamia), the city of Nineveh was founded about 4500 BC and Calah 3000. The land of Shinar (southern Mesopotamia) saw Uruk (Erech) established approximately 4000 BC and Babylon 2500. In Palestine, the Canaanites appeared around 2000 BC and the Philistines in 1200. And the first evidence for the existence of the Hebrews is 1200 BC. This data demonstrates that Gen 10 is inaccurate. These Mesopotamian cities and Palestinian peoples did not arise within a few generations after a global flood, but at different times over a period of more than 3000 years.

Archaeological and historical discoveries do not support the historicity of the events in the table of nations, but these facts make a vital contribution in its dating and interpretation. The temporal referents that are the latest in Gen 10 indicate this chapter was conceived roughly around 1000 BC. The Hebrew community (v. 22–25) became literate and large enough to be noticed by other nations by 1200 BC. The Philistines (v. 14) appear in Palestine about the same time. Calah only becomes a "great city" (v. 12) near 1000 BC. And other identifiable peoples and the estimated dates of their origin include: Madai 1300 BC, Meshech 1100, Tiras 1200, Sheba 1000, and Dedan 1000 (v. 2, 7).

This dating of Gen 10 is consistent with other time referents in the book of Genesis. The use of bronze and iron in Gen 4:22 reflects a period following the transition between the Bronze and Iron Ages in 1200 BC. The phrase "Ur of the Chaldeans" (11:28, 31; 15:7) appears only after the Chaldeans entered Mesopotamia around 1000 BC. Reference to the territory of Dan (14:14) indicates that this Hebrew tribe was already established in Palestine and points to a time later than the Period of Judges (1200–1020). Genesis 36:31 alludes to the first king over Israel and Saul's reign from 1020 to 1000. Finally, the "district of Rameses" (47:11) most likely refers to a region constructed by Rameses II, the pharaoh of Egypt between 1279–1213 BC.[53]

These temporal markers argue that the table of nations presents an ancient phenomenological perspective of the origin of societies as conceived by the Hebrews roughly about 1000 BC. In the same way that ancient individuals logically reasoned that everything in the world was created *de novo*, the writer of Gen 10 envisioned the beginnings of the nations around him to be quick and complete within a few generations after the flood. More precisely, this chapter features the ancient major motif of tribal formation. The history-of-the-day assumed that peoples and kingdoms descended through a genealogical line from one male individual, and the founder's name sometimes became an "eponym" (Greek: *epi* "upon" *onoma* "name"). In Gen 10, for example, Canaan is the father of the "Canaanite clans" (v. 15–18). And though his name was not an eponym, Nimrod established nine cities in Mesopotamia (v. 9–12). In other words, the table of nations is a retrojection of countries, cities, and peoples surrounding Israel approximately 1000 BC and conceptualized through the ancient motif that communities formed along simple genealogical lineages.

Genesis 10 is not an accurate historical record of the origin of nations. Rather, it is an ancient understanding of the beginning of peoples and kingdoms in the ancient Near East, reflecting the geographical, political, and theological beliefs of an inspired Hebrew author living about 1000 BC. But more importantly, this incidental ancient history of the rise of nations delivers essential Messages of Faith—the unity of all humans and the unicity of Israel. In particular, Gen 10 foreshadows God's promise to Abraham and all of humanity: "I will make you into a great nation and I will bless you . . . and all the peoples on earth will be blessed through you" (Gen 12:2, 3).

The Historicity of Language Confusion at the Tower of Babel (Gen 11:1–9)

Christians throughout the ages have interpreted the tower of Babel and the confusion of language as a historical account. Today, archaeology and history identify places and practices mentioned in Gen 11:1–9. The plain of Shinar (southern Mesopotamia) and the city of Babel (Babylon) were well known in the ancient Near East. Physical evidence also confirms the building of towers (ziggurats) with baked brick and bitumen (asphalt) in this region.[54] But Scripture and science argue against the traditional literal reading of this passage.

Conflicts exist between Gen 10 and 11 with regard to the dispersion of humanity and the origin of languages, pointing away from the historicity of these events. The former chapter states that nations and peoples arose in an orderly fashion along the lines of Noah's family and that each had its own language (10:5, 20, 31). This account presupposes that humans spread out into the world from the landing site of the ark in the mountains of Ararat (10:1; 8:4). Of note, Shinar is mentioned as just one of many regions populated after the flood. Ham's grandson Nimrod begins his kingdom there and establishes four cities, including Babel (10:10).[55] Once they were completed, he then moves northward to Assyria to build four more. There is no hint in Gen 10 of any rebellion against God, language confusion, or humans refusing to disperse throughout the earth.

In contrast, Gen 11 claims that the "whole world had one language" and that men had settled in Shinar. They blatantly sin against the Lord by not spreading throughout the world. In order to keep themselves in one place, they begin to build a city named "Babel." Significantly, Gen 11:9 states that it is "*there* the Lord then confused the language of the *whole* world." In other words, all of humanity was in Shinar at that time. Not being able to understand one another, "they stopped building the city" (v. 8) and Babel was never completed. Humans were then forced to scatter from Shinar "over the face of the whole earth" (v. 9).

As noted before, conflicts between events in Gen 1–11 are easily resolved if readers respect the fact that a Holy Spirit inspired redactor employed two basic sources. Genesis 10 displays stylistic features of the Priestly writer. It is highly structured with repetitive formulaic phrases similar to the days of creation in Gen 1 and the genealogies in Gen 5 and 11. The names of Noah's three sons—Shem, Ham, and Japheth—only appear in P passages (Gen 5:32; 6:10; 7:13; 9:18, 22–23, 26–27; 11:10, 11). The picture of God implied in Gen 10 is a transcendent heavenly being distant from humanity. On the other hand, the tower of Babel episode in Gen 11 is a free-flowing narrative typical of the Jahwist author. The divine name "Lord" is used five times (v. 5, 6, 8, 9a, 9b) and the common J expression "the face of . . ." three times (v. 4, 8, 9) in only eleven verses.[56] And God in this chapter is near humans and comes to earth to see their activities. Thus, instead of being troubled by conflicts between Gen 10 and 11, Christians should recognize that each chapter has an incidental ancient history that delivers an inerrant Divine Theology.

In conceiving a 3-tier universe, ancient peoples believed that God/s was literally just overhead in heaven. Their construction of towers, ziggurats, and pyramids reflects a deep yearning to be connected to Him/them and to attain eternal life, and even divinity. It is in this context that the tower of Babel account must be understood. Thus, the building of "a tower that reaches to the heavens" in Gen 11:4 makes perfect sense from an ancient phenomenological perspective. However, the inspired Hebrew author quickly rejects the pagan belief that humans, on their own, can transcend their mortal condition and become like God (cf. Gen 3:3, also a J passage). The Lord judges their sin and arrogance by confusing language, and the entire project to enter heaven ends abruptly. A mocking polemic against Babylonian religion also appears in this account. The term "Babel" to these pagans refers to "the gate of god," but to the Hebrews it means "mixed up, confused." The Message of Faith in Gen 11 is obvious: human attempts to become God are babbling nonsense that will always fail.

The ancient phenomenological point of view also sheds light on the confusion of language in Gen 11. The existence of numerous tongues in the ancient Near East naturally led to the question of how and why these arose. The frustration people experience with others who speak a different language could easily be retrojected to a time in the past when the world had gone awry. And it was reasonable to conceive that the confusion of an original language spoken in the idyllic age was because of divine judgment. A similar motif of a god changing languages appears in the Mesopotamian account of *Enmerka and the Lord Aratta*.[57] In addition, the category of *de novo* creation predisposed ancient peoples to assume that languages originated quickly and completely, like everything else—the inanimate world, living organisms, nations, etc. There was no reason for them to believe that any of these evolved over extensive periods of time. Thus, the inspired author of Gen 11 encountered many languages around him, and quite logically conceived that these had originated suddenly as God's judgment for human sin in the same way that other frustrating realities had entered the world (e.g., suffering and death in Gen 3).

Science also dismisses the historicity of the confusion of language at the tower of Babel. The traditional literal interpretation of this passage makes numerous assertions that are open to scientific investigation: (1) the destruction of life on earth by a global flood about 2344 BC, (2) the

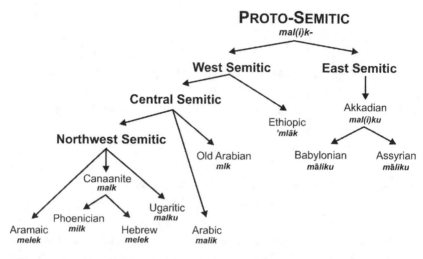

Fig 6-10. **Linguistic Evolution of the Ancient Semitic Languages.** The noun 'king' offers an example of how these languages have changed over time. The three basic consonants (m-l-k) remain constant while shifts occur in vocalization.

settlement of all humanity in Shinar after the deluge, (3) the speaking of only one language there at that time, and (4) the dispersion of humans throughout the world from Shinar. But as noted before, there is not a hint of geological evidence for a global flood at anytime during earth history, nor is there any archaeological proof indicating that human life was extinguished and then rekindled in the Middle East. In fact, at the time traditionally assigned for the flood, people were living throughout the world and speaking a variety of different languages, some already having been written down for nearly 1000 years in Mesopotamia and Egypt.

Linguistic analysis of ancient Near Eastern languages indicates that they evolved over time like all other languages. Written records reveal that words and grammar change slowly through history. Related terms, known as "cognates," assist to classify languages into families indicative of their origins. For example, similarities in Germanic (German, Dutch, English) and Romance (French, Spanish, Portuguese) language groups provide data to construct their respective linguistic evolutionary trees. Fig 6-10 offers an outline of the ancient Semitic family of languages with an example of a cognate for each.[58] In light of this diagram, a question arises: if it was God's intention to confuse human language at the tower of Babel, then why would He have used cognate languages, giving the impression that they evolved over time?

The account of the confusion of language at the tower of Babel is not historical. It presents an ancient phenomenological perspective of the origin of languages. More importantly, this ancient motif is an incidental vessel that delivers a central Message of Faith that appears repeatedly throughout Gen 1–11: God judges sin. In particular, Gen 11:1–9 reveals the nauseating arrogance of human pride and the raw stupidity of men and women attempting to become divine through their own means. We are not gods, and God will not stand such hubris.

The Historicity of the Shemite Genealogy (Gen 11:10–29)

Genesis 11 features a genealogy of individuals who lived an average age of 333 years. A trend appears with human lifespan reducing progressively from Shem's 600 years to Nahor's 148. Notably, 7 of 10 ages when a man fathers a son are within familiar ranges (29–35 years). The shifting of these time referents toward values of today has led many Christians to believe that Gen 11 is an actual record of ancestors from the flood survivor Shem to the patriarch Abram (who is later renamed "Abraham" in Gen 17:5). However, a careful inspection of this genealogy undermines the traditional literal interpretation.

Fig 6-11 reveals that the ages and periods in Gen 11 have statistically significant patterns similar to Gen 5. Twelve of the 20 are multiples of 5. The probability of such a feature appearing in a natural genealogy this size

	Age at Son's Birth	Period Lived after Birth	Age at Death	'60 Times X' Formula	
	A	B	A + B	A X 12 =	B X 12 =
1. Shem	100	500	[600]	60 X 20	60 X 100
2. Arphaxad	35	403	[438]	60 X 7	—
3. Shelah	30	403	[433]	60 X 6	—
4. Eber	34	430	[464]	—	60 X 86
5. Peleg	30	209	[239]	60 X 6	—
6. Reu	32	207	[239]	60 X 5*	60 X 40*
7. Serug	30	200	[230]	60 X 6	60 X 40
8. Nahor	29	119	[148]	—	—
9. Terah	70	[135]	[205]	60 X 14	60 X 27
10. Abram	[100]	[75]	[175]	60 X 20	60 X 15

Fig 6-11. Genesis 11: Shemite Genealogy and Ancient Stylistic Numbers. Bold numbers are multiples of five (0 or 5). * Mystical number 7 is subtracted from non-multiple of five and then multiplied by 12 in order to fit '60 Times X' formula. — Numbers that do not conform to mathematical formula. [ ] derive from Gen 11:32 (Terah), Gen 21:5, 25:7 (Abram).

is about 1 in 12,000. In addition, 7 of the 10 ages when a man has a son is a multiple of 5, again raising the question of whether sexual activity and/or fertility only happened every 5 years in 70% of marriages. Obviously, the temporal referents in Gen 11 are contrived and artificial. Mathematical formulae using the ancient stylistic numbers *might* explain the patterns in this genealogy (cf. Fig 6-5). The ages/periods that are multiples of 5, if multiplied by 12, can be fitted into a "60 times X" calculation. But most of the non-multiples of 5 do not conform, even with the subtraction of 7 prior to their being multiplied by 12. This breaking down in symmetry of the stylistic formulas along with the reduction in age as the genealogy progresses suggests the emergence of a new epoch.

Significantly, the reigns of Sumerian kings immediately after the flood decrease in length and deteriorate symmetrically in a manner somewhat similar to Gen 11. Appendix 4 Fig 2 shows that there are roughly three transitional periods. The first features an average governance of 942 years and all of these fit into the "60 times X" formula. Reigns in the middle period lower to a mean of nearly 627 years and only about half conform to the calculation. The third series moves closer to times commonly experienced in real history with an average of almost 29 years, and none of these can be placed into "60 times X." However, 8 of the 11 in this grouping are whole fractions of 60. It is evident that the Babylonian ruling periods after the flood are stylized and not an actual historical record.

The Gen 5 and 11 genealogies and the Sumerian king lists feature the ancient motif of a transition from the idyllic age to present time. This notion makes perfect sense from an ancient phenomenological perspective. The history-of-the-day accepted the existence of an earlier utopian epoch in which people lived extraordinarily long periods. It was only logical that human lifespan would have reduced to intervals experienced by those composing oral traditions and/or written accounts of origins. More than likely, the names appearing near the end of the Gen 11 genealogy are dim memories of some actual people who were significant in the early Hebrew community. Confirming which individuals are historical in this genealogy is impossible since most would have lived during a preliterate period, and oral evidence can never be recovered.

Stylistic features shared with Gen 5 indicate that the Priestly writer composed the Gen 11 genealogy. The latter is highly structured and includes a repetitive formula: X lived A years and fathered Z, and X lived B

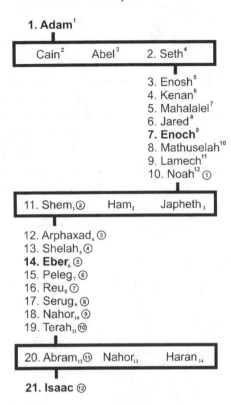

Fig 6-12. Origin of the Hebrews Genealogical Framework. Only the individuals in the line from Adam to Isaac have their ages given in Gen 1-11. These numbers are also stylised. Both features indicate the uniqueness and importance of God's chosen people.

more years and had other sons and daughters. Both genealogies feature numerous ages/periods that are multiples of 5 and seem to use stylistic numbers 12 and 60 in mathematical formulas. In fact, combining Gen 5 and 11 and including Isaac's birth from Gen 21 produces a strikingly symmetrical poetic framework. Fig 6-12 presents the lineage of God's chosen people, the Hebrews. It begins and ends with a theologically significant individual, Adam and Isaac, respectively. Multiples of 7 are employed to identify important people. Enoch is the man who "walked with God" (7th position), Eber is viewed as the traditional father of the Hebrews (14th), and Isaac is the promised child (21st). The Hebrew mystical number 12 is the total in the direct ancestral lines of Adam to Noah and Noah to Isaac. The symmetrical number 10 positions Noah (10th) and Abram (20th). Finally, 3 sets of 3 sons border and split the Gen 5 and 11 genealogies.

Obviously, the origin of the chosen line in Scripture is contrived and not literally or historically accurate. But the Message of Faith is evident: In the beginning God created the Hebrews to be His holy people.

The poetic framework uniting the Gen 5 and 11 genealogies and their stylistic use of numbers are problematic for young earth creation. This position is dependent on these time references being literal and historical. In calculating the universe to be 6000 years old, these anti-evolutionists derive one third (1946 years) of this age from Gen 5 (1656) and Gen 11 (290). But the obvious poetic structures, mystical numbers, and statistically significant patterns in these genealogies demonstrate that they are artificial, not real. Like the pre-creative state in Gen 1:2, creation scientists lose another temporal marker from which to date the age of the earth.

Difficulties also arise with the young earth creationist explanation for the reduction in lifespan through the Gen 11 genealogy. This position asserts that the collapse of the protective water canopy during the flood caused a decrease in ages to that experienced today. But as noted many times, the Bible reveals that the waters above and the firmament remained in the heavens after the flood. By failing to recognize and respect the ancient motif of lifespan reduction after the idyllic age, creation scientists eisegetically impose their twenty-first century understanding of genealogies upon Scripture. The strict literal interpretation of the ages in Gen 5 and 11 by young earth creation is un-biblical.

Many lines of evidence within the Gen 11 genealogy indicate that it is not a literal historical record. Of course, the inspired author intended to write an account of the origins of Israel. Using both the ancient historical notion that lifespan reduced after the flood and the techniques for constructing genealogies at that time, he interprets the creation of the Hebrew community in light of the Faith Message that God was personally active in choosing her to be His people. In particular, the Shemite lineage strategically connects the primeval past, as understood by ancient peoples, to Abraham and the patriarchs, where historicity really begins. Through incidental ancient genealogies, the early chapters of Genesis underline that the God of the Hebrews is the Lord of history.

CHAPTER SUMMARY

Genesis 1–11 presents an ancient history of human origins. Biblical evidence indicates that these chapters are not a literal record of actual events in the past. Conflicts between the accounts point to independent sources that were redacted together. Ancient poetic literary devices like the parallel panels in Gen 1, the flood chiasm in Gen 6–9, and stylistic numbers in many passages undermine further the historicity of Gen 1–11, since real historical events do not unfold in such symmetrical ways. Ancient motifs are also obvious in these opening chapters. *De novo* creation, lost idyllic age, great flood, and tribal formation are central paradigms making up the history-of-the-day held by ancient Near Eastern peoples. Scientific evidence complements the facts of Scripture. Geology, anthropology, archaeology, history, and linguistics offer a tightly integrated account of human origins which conflicts irreconcilably with the traditional and strict literal reading of the opening chapters of the Bible. Clearly, historical concordism in Gen 1–11 fails.

The Message-Incident Principle is essential in understanding biblical statements about the beginning of human history. Similar to the ancient science in Scripture, Gen 1–11 features an ancient phenomenological perspective of the origins of humanity. It is necessary then to separate, and not conflate, this incidental ancient history from the many inerrant and infallible Messages of Faith. To mention but a few: the Creatorship and Lordship of the Hebrew God over a very good world, the unity of all men and women through bearing the Image of God, the privilege of having relationships with other people and in particular with the Creator, the reality of human sin and divine judgment of sinners, and the unicity of the Hebrew community as the Lord's chosen people. The power of this Divine Theology in Gen 1–11 has been proven time and again by changed lives throughout history, affirming the sufficiency of these inspired chapters and the proficiency of human ability to understand their messages. And the confirmation of Israel as God's instrument of grace is evident in her blessing all the nations through His Words and the Word Incarnate.

Recognizing and respecting the ancient intellectual categories in Gen 1–11 has significant implications for the origins debate. Young earth creation and progressive creation are based upon the assumption that these chapters feature historical and scientific concordism. But the central paradigms of history in opening passages of Scripture are ancient Near Eastern motifs, which the Hebrews inherited from their surrounding neighbors and then sanctified under the guidance of the Holy Spirit. Science also rejects the Christian anti-evolutionary positions. The geological evidence falsifies fossil pattern predictions based on creation science and day-age creation. The failure of these popular views of origins frees Christians from conflict and concordism, and it calls us to open the Book of God's Works in order to understand the physical origins of humanity.

Without a doubt, this chapter presents a counterintuitive reading of Gen 1–11. Some Christians will certainly find this approach uncomfortable. It raises a serious concern: Can we trust what we read in Scripture? But the reality is that every believer interprets the Bible, and the better question is: Do we do it well? The importance of hermeneutics is again obvious. Using the biblical evidence from this chapter, we turn now to explore further the subtleties and challenges in understanding Gen 1–11.

7

Genesis 1–11 and History:
Beyond Conflict and Concordism

THE ANCIENT HISTORY IN Gen 1–11 has significant implications. It raises serious questions about the truthfulness of the Bible and Christianity. The Church throughout the ages has read these opening chapters as literal historical accounts—the creation of Adam and Eve in the garden of Eden, the entrance of suffering and death into the world as judgment for sin, and the destruction of living organisms by a flood except those saved in the ark with Noah. Today, a majority of Christians are quick to argue that rejecting the historicity of these events undermines the New Testament. Jesus explicitly refers to Adam, Eve, and Noah. And the apostle Paul clearly states that Adam's sin led to the origin of physical death. If Gen 1–11 is not historically accurate, then why should anyone believe that Scripture is inerrant and infallible?

Fig 7-1 summarizes biblical evidence from previous chapters to show that scientific concordism and historical concordism in Gen 1–11 fail. Notably, statements dealing with early human activities do not correspond to reality in the past. This table also presents an important overlapping area between origins (natural history) and human history. According to Gen 3, the appearances of snakes without legs, thorns and thistles, and suffering and death are connected causally to the sin of Adam and Eve. As well, Gen 1 indicates that prior to the fall animals were vegetarians, and the eating of flesh only appears after they disembark the ark in Gen 9. Consequently, these assertions are scientifically testable and their historicity determinable. However, the fossil record without any doubt whatsoever demonstrates that the physical changes mentioned in Gen 3 originated millions of years before the appearance of the first humans.

ORIGINS (Natural History)

	Reality
Firmament raised waters above	No
Sun, moon & stars set in firmament	No
Divine dwelling set in waters above	No
De novo creation of life	No
Fruit plants created before fish	No
Birds created before land animals	No

ORIGINS & HUMAN HISTORY

Origin of snakes without legs after humans	No
Origin of thistles & thorns after humans	No
Origin of suffering & death after humans	No
Humans & animals vegetarians before flood	No
Origin of flesh eating after flood	No

HUMAN HISTORY

De novo creation of humans	No
Origin of cultural advances in a few generations	No
Human lifespan 900+ years before flood	No
Pairs of all air-breathing animals fitted into ark	No
Flood rose above Ararat Mountains	No
Destruction of all humans on earth by flood	No
Repopulation of earth from ANE after flood	No
Origin of ANE nations/cities in a few generations	No
Origin of languages in ANE in one generation	No
Human lifespan reduced from 600+ years after flood	No

Fig 7-1. The Failure of Scientific and Historical Concordism in Genesis 1–11

Similarly, the incalculable number of flesh-slaughtering teeth through-out geological strata proves that carnivorous animals existed for eons prior to humanity. This evidence calls into question the trustworthiness of Scripture and traditional Christian beliefs. In particular, there are no causal connections as literally stated in Gen 3. If death existed for hundreds of millions of years before humans (Appendix 7 Fig 4), then how can anyone accept Paul's assertion that "sin entered the world through one man, and death through sin" (Rom 5:12)?

Regrettably, this evidence leads a number of people to assume that there is an irreconcilable conflict between Gen 1–11 and the modern understanding of history. On the one hand, many Christians dismiss academic research on the origin and earliest activities of humans. They argue that all statements dealing with history in Scripture are true and accurate because the Holy Spirit inspired them. On the other hand, non-Christians reject the historicity of Gen 1–11, and as a result, so too the Bible and Christianity. Interestingly, these believers and unbelievers share two basic assumptions. First, both presuppose that Gen 1–11 features historical concordism. This popular belief is rooted in a simplistic literal reading of Scripture and it is fueled by the evolution vs. creation dichotomy entrenched in the mind of most individuals. Second, these two groups of concordists conflate Christian faith with their understanding of the first chapters of Scripture. They unwittingly fuse the strict literal interpretation of the creation and fall of humanity with the incarnation and resurrection of Jesus. However, is there a way to move beyond this conflict and concordism in Gen 1–11?

The present chapter attempts to answer this question. It opens by examining processes involved in the writing of history. This section argues that common ancient motifs like *de novo* creation and the lost idyllic age were the best historical paradigms-of-the-day, and that the authors of Gen 1–11 under divine inspiration used these. Next, the most important principle in biblical interpretation is approached—the identification of the literary genre. Genesis 1–11 is a complex and unique type of literature. Determining the genre not only sheds light on the historical statements in these chapters, but it also contributes to resolving the origins debate. This chapter closes by asking directly whether Adam and Noah were real people in history. The answer will be one of the most challenging conclusions in this book.

HISTORIOGRAPHY, ANCIENT MOTIFS AND DIVINE INSPIRATION

Every culture and nation has an understanding of its origin and heritage. Historical accounts contribute significantly in defining who a people are, how they live, and where their future is headed. In other words, embedded in the history of a society are its values, beliefs, and worldview. For Christians, the Bible is foundational to the faith of their community, and it is profoundly historical in character. Scripture presents an account of the origins of Israel and the Church, and of God working through these chosen people. In particular, the New Testament is a record of the most critical event in history—the Incarnation.

The process of writing about past human events is not simply the listing of as-it-happened facts. Known as historiography (Greek: *historia* "history," *graphō* "to write"), it recognizes that every historical account is historically conditioned. That is, each is composed at a specific point in time and reflects metaphysical assumptions, available sources of knowledge, and literary practices of the period. Thus, all histories have a bias. This is not to say that there are no actual facts of the past in these written records. But it is to acknowledge that historical accounts are reconstructions that are filtered through the intellectual categories of their authors.

Histories are not only retrospective (to look back), but they are also retrojective (to cast back). Historians extrapolate their intellectual categories backward into the past in order to explain earlier events. For example, the writers of Gen 1–11 retrojected the experience of seeing living organisms created quickly and completely into their conceptualization of human origins. Considering when these chapters were written, this was a very reasonable reconstruction of events. In fact, creation accounts throughout the ancient world feature the *de novo* origins of humanity, and often with the fashioning of a first man and woman. Yet over time, scientific and historical data have increased (anthropological fossils, archaeological artifacts, ancient Near Eastern written records), widening the scope of cognitive competence of historians and producing a more accurate history of human beginnings. Therefore, it is vital to identify the beliefs and assumptions of historians, the historical data available to them, and the time period during which their account was written.

It must be emphasized that the metaphysical notions embraced by any historian are determinative, and even dictatorial, factors in reconstructing the past. These retrojected beliefs control historiography. They not only select and reject available historical sources and materials, but they also stand in judgment of whether earlier events occurred or not. For example, the academic discipline of history in secular universities is steeped in positivist and dysteleological categories. Often called "the scientific study" of history, this perspective asserts that human history is driven by "nothing but" social, political, and economic forces. The notion that God is behind history or involved in it is not even a consideration. It is clear that these historians retroject a *personal commitment* to religious unbelief into their writing of history. However, should there exist a Divine Being who interacts with humanity throughout history, it becomes obvious that the historiographical method of positivists and dysteleologists is hopelessly flawed at its foundations. This secular approach will never offer a complete account of human history.

The historiographical assumptions of many Christians today also dictate their understanding of the origin and first activities of humanity.

Believers presuppose that Gen 1–11 presents historical accounts that are similar to DVDs, journal reports, television newscasts, etc. Just open the first chapters of Scripture, and the as-it-happened facts of history are before our eyes to be read literally. However, this is a forcing of twenty-first century standards of recording history into accounts of the past that were composed thousands of years ago. To correct this eisegetical tendency, believers must respect the ancient history in Gen 1–11 in a way similar to when dealing with the ancient science found throughout Scripture. As well, we need to appreciate the implicit historical concepts and literary techniques used by the inspired authors. Therefore, Christians must embrace an Incarnational approach to the historiography of the opening chapters of the Bible. Stated precisely, *Gen 1–11 is the Word of God written in the words of ancient human historians.*

Simplistic black-and-white understandings of Gen 1–11, such as "every verse is historically true" or "Scripture is false because there are no historical facts in its first chapters" fall short. These one-size-fits-all interpretive approaches fail to appreciate ancient historiography and the process of divine inspiration. Instead, the key to moving beyond conflict and concordism with the historical statements in Gen 1–11 is recognition of the ancient motifs.

Ancient Motifs and the Conceptualization of Ancient History

Today, the term "motif" is most often associated with literature. In novels, plays, and poetry, motifs are common typological themes, characters, and symbols. They are usually literary devices with no intention of being literal history. But this was not the case in the ancient world. For the most part, ancient motifs were conceptualizations of reality.[1] Often etiological, they explained the causes behind the origin of nature, peoples, and situations. Thus, many ancient motifs are reconstructions of the past that functioned as historical paradigms. Considering the scope of cognitive competence at that time, the conception of motifs was a very logical process. It involved ancient peoples retrojecting their experiences of: (1) general revelation—both natural and moral, (2) personal divine action, and (3) a phenomenological perspective of the physical world.

Common spiritual and physical phenomena often led the ancients to similar major motifs in their accounts of origins. These encompassing paradigms are not always present in every version, nor are they explicit in each. And the details vary extensively between societies. For example, there is a wide range of views on how God/s made the world: procreation of components of the cosmos through the mating of divine beings, use of the cut up body parts of gods, or simple verbal commands. Yet basic events reappear in many creation accounts. It is possible to speculate on the rationality behind the conceptualization of the four major motifs and to see that these are logical reconstructions of the past.

De Novo Creation. The natural revelation of intelligent design impacted ancient peoples and led them to believe a Creator/s formed the world. They also perceived that they lived in a 3-tier universe. Thunder and lightning were reasonable evidence to conclude that a powerful Divine Being/s lived just overhead in heaven, and that these dramatic meteorological phenomena were His/their interventionistic acts. Thus, in conceptualizing origins, the ancients retrojected and integrated in various combinations their: (1) notion of causality that a God/s acts in nature interventionistically, (2) phenomenological perception that the inanimate cosmos is a static structure and that living organisms are immutable, (3) observation of creative acts through plant and animal reproduction, (4) own activity in fashioning different objects with their hands, (5) perception that living organisms after death decompose to become dust and earth, (6) implicit understanding that the age of the world was limited to the genealogies of the community, and (7) personal experience of the real and living God in their lives. As a result, ancient peoples logically concluded that only a few tens of generations ago, the creation of the universe and life was quick and produced complete inanimate structures and life forms, and that a Divine Being/s had created these through interventionistic acts cast in familiar embryological and manual processes, including the use of earth as material for making living organisms.

Lost Idyllic Age. Ancient creation stories often feature a world that was at first peaceful, pleasurable, and in some cases, seemingly perfect.[2] The retrojection of intelligent design and the yearning for comfort from hardships undoubtedly contributed to this notion. But many origins accounts also include a great calamity that led to the loss of the idyllic age. Something went drastically wrong, and the effects of this event continue to impact people and the world negatively in the present. Harsh realities and the struggle to survive demanded an explanation. The general revelation of right and wrong inscribed on the human heart led many ancient peoples to conceptualize that a God/s, angered by their misbehavior, had launched His/their fury upon the world in the distant past. Such an idea made sense by retrojecting the terror and destruction produced by meteorological phenomena (thunder and lightning, flash floods, violent wind, etc.) along with the belief that these were judgmental interventionistic acts of a Heavenly Being/s living just above the earth in heaven. In a number of creation accounts, the sins and failings of the first humans are the cause for divine wrath, but it can also be attributed to a trickster or negative/evil force. Understood in this way, the lost idyllic age motif is one of the earliest theodicies conceived by humans.

Great Flood. As noted in the last chapter, over 300 flood accounts have been discovered around the globe. This motif is in many ways a variant of the lost idyllic age, as a destructive deluge is unleashed on the world by a Divine Being/s in judgment for misbehavior. Yet the great flood is different in that it is not merely a retrojection of present physical and spiritual phenomena to reconstruct the past. Deluge accounts have actual historical events behind them. Arising primarily in preliterate societies, oral traditions undoubtedly developed after people had survived a catastrophic river flood or ocean tsunami, whether by boarding a boat or barge, or simply floating on debris.[3] Similar to their conceptualization of thunder and lightning during storms, ancient people were quite logical in making a causal connection between a destructive deluge and divine judgmental intervention for their failings or sins, of which moral revelation convicted them. As well, many flood accounts include a rainbow motif (see Fig 6-8). The beautiful spectrum of colors, the peacefulness after a storm, and the breaking of sunlight through the darkness were reasonably understood as a sign that divine anger had subsided. The Heavenly Being/s was appeased and life could move forward afresh, meeting a human desire for new spiritual beginnings.

Tribal Formation. Creation accounts often present the origin of the community as descending from a founding individual, in most cases a male. The tribal formation motif is a logical retrojection of numerous notions and experiences: (1) A corollary of the *de novo* creation of humans is that the first generation descended from the originally created person or pair of people—the ancestral head of the tribe.[4] (2) Ancient reproductive biology focuses on male seed and leads to the conclusion that the community originated from a first father. (3) The wonder and marvel of childbirth is a powerful natural revelatory event that is causally connected to divine action. The retrojection of this experience of intelligent

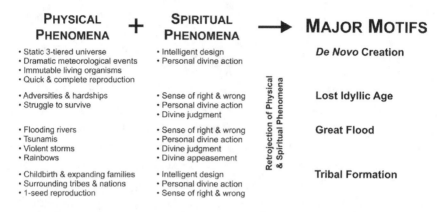

PHYSICAL PHENOMENA	+	SPIRITUAL PHENOMENA	→	MAJOR MOTIFS
• Static 3-tiered universe • Dramatic meteorological events • Immutable living organisms • Quick & complete reproduction		• Intelligent design • Personal divine action		*De Novo* Creation
• Adversities & hardships • Struggle to survive		• Sense of right & wrong • Personal divine action • Divine judgment		Lost Idyllic Age
• Flooding rivers • Tsunamis • Violent storms • Rainbows		• Sense of right & wrong • Personal divine action • Divine judgment • Divine appeasement		Great Flood
• Childbirth & expanding families • Surrounding tribes & nations • 1-seed reproduction		• Intelligent design • Personal divine action • Sense of right & wrong		Tribal Formation

(Vertical label between columns: Retrojection of Physical & Spiritual Phenomena)

Fig 7-2. **Origin of Major Motifs.** Ancient motifs are logical reconstructions of the past that retroject a phenomenological perspective of the physical world with experiences of spiritual reality. General revelation is a significant factor in the conceptualization of these ancient historical paradigms. The impact of intelligent design in nature and the convicting power of the law written on human hearts led to origins accounts that feature a Creator/s and numerous moral themes. In particular, the countless sacrifices and offerings made throughout the ancient world to appease God/s for failings and sins testify to the reality of moral revelation.

design logically results in the belief that God/s was behind the formation of the society. (4) The experience of expanding families and the limits of memory, extrapolated back in time, returns to an original ancestor who lived only a few tens of generations ago. This being the case, real people who were known or remembered by the community would be included in its ancestral lineages. (5) Most genealogies begin with a founding person whose name sometimes becomes the eponym for the society. (6) The presence of surrounding peoples and nations required an explanation. In particular, a need arose to understand the origin of enemies and their wrongful actions, which moral revelation identified. A reason commonly given was that the founding father of the foes had committed an offensive act in the past. In other words, origins accounts include political polemic at the time of composition, and it is often retrojected back against an enemy tribal head. Therefore, similar to the accounts of a great flood, there exist some actual people, events, and situations behind the tribal formation motif. Fig 7-2 summarizes physical and spiritual phenomena that contributed to the origin of the four major motifs.

The conceptualization of minor motifs in ancient origins accounts also reflects a logical process. In contrast to the broad scope of major motifs, these are narrower reconstructions of the past that often reflect regional characteristics (e.g., geography, climate, animals, foods, etc.). Minor motifs are components within a major motif that customize and add detail to the encompassing historical paradigm. They are like individual actors, props, and subplots used in a play to deliver its central theme. A few examples of minor motifs in Gen 1–11 and other ancient Near Eastern origins accounts include:

Pre-Creative Watery State. Mesopotamian, Egyptian, and Hebrew origins accounts often begin with a watery pre-creative state, and no mention of when it appeared or who created it. From an ancient phenomenological perspective, the ever-present blue skies over the Middle East, suggesting a heavenly sea, and the notion that water surrounded this region at the horizon, reasonably led to the belief that these two bodies of water were at one time united before being separated by a Divine Being/s.[5]

Longevity, Vegetarianism and Mystical Nourishment. The psychological trauma of physical death has led men and women in every generation to yearn desperately for longevity and eternal life. Ancient Near Eastern peoples often retrojected this primal desire back to an idyllic age characterized by incredibly long lifespan and potential freedom from death.[6] This period also saw a harmony between humans and animals. A corollary of such a world is vegetarianism. The natural empathy people sense toward animals when they are slaughtered certainly contributed to this notion. In addition, the quenching and recuperative power of fresh water, especially in a hot and arid region like the Middle East, reasonably led to the belief that there were water sources that could restore youth, extend life, and even overcome death. Similarly, the sustenance offered by fruit and its delightful taste provided natural phenomena behind the notion of mystical nourishment. Thus, it is not surprising that trees and plants with supernatural powers often became motifs and part of the intellectual framework of the ancient world.[7]

Mystical Creatures. Ancient people believed that the world was filled with a variety of supernatural beings. The intellectual fluidity of oral cultures and the less critical standards of the ancient mindset provided a conceptual environment ideally suited for the birth of mystical creatures. Certainly, some of these find their origin in human imagination and dreams, but experience with the natural world was also a contributing factor to this motif. For example, the fear of snakes and their venomous bites powerfully struck the ancient psyche and logically connected this creature to evil. The impressive characteristics of certain animals, such as the ferocity of lions and the flying ability of birds, saw these amalgamated into hybrid beings like the powerful cherubim. And the 1-seed understanding of reproduction, along with the assumed proximity of heavenly beings to humans on earth, made their mating and giving birth to giants, heroes, monsters, etc., quite reasonable.

Origin of Cultural Advances. The struggle to survive was eased over time by a variety of human innovations. To cite but a few: controlling fire, construction of shelters, planting and harvesting crops, domestication of animals, smelting metals, fabrication of tools, making musical instruments, and the invention of writing. These all contributed to the rise of human culture, and modern science reveals that they evolved over time. However, ancient peoples conceived the origin of cultural advances through their historiographical categories. The major motifs of *de novo* creation and tribal formation provided an intellectual matrix leading them to envision innovations appearing quickly and completely, each the creation of one individual in the past.

To summarize, the ancient motifs in origins accounts are not whimsical flights of fantasy or merely literary devices in fictitious stories. Most are logical conceptualizations of the past rooted in spiritual and physical phenomena. Some even have actual historical events and people behind them, such as local floods and community ancestors. Thus, creation account motifs were the historical paradigms of ancient peoples. And like all accounts of history, they were open to varying metaphysical interpretations. For the Hebrews, ancient Near Eastern motifs were shaped in the inspired revelatory light of the Creatorship and Lordship of a Holy God.

Ancient Motifs and the Development of Genesis 1–11

Obvious parallels exist between Gen 1–11 and the motifs in origins accounts throughout the ancient world. The similarities are even more striking when comparing these chapters to other ancient Near Eastern versions. Yet this should not surprise anyone. The Hebrews were a people living and interacting with the tribes and nations around them. It is only reasonable to expect that they shared some customs, languages, and ideas, including creation account motifs. Of course, the Divine Theology in Gen 1–11 is radically different from the pagan beliefs in these other renditions. Consequently, under the inspiration of the Holy Spirit, the

Hebrews must have freed the motifs-of-the-day from their religious ideology and replaced it with infallible Messages of Faith.

It is not known exactly how ancient Near Eastern motifs became part of Gen 1–11. As noted previously, it is unlikely that the development of these chapters will ever be understood with complete certainty (see Fig 6-2). Yet evidence from Scripture, archaeology, and history provide data points to construct a rough outline of this revelatory process. Four basic phases likely occurred:

First, the Hebrews inherited most of the motifs in Gen 1–11 from their surrounding neighbors. The Mesopotamians and Egyptians were established civilizations for well over 2000 years prior to the appearance of Israel in the ancient Near East. Written records from these two cultures reveal that the basic motifs found in Gen 1–11 were already part of the intellectual framework throughout the region. In other words, the Hebrews arose in a world in which *de novo* creation, the lost idyllic age, the great flood, etc., were the facts-of-history.

Second, Israel began modifying and sanctifying ancient Near Eastern motifs while she was a preliterate tribe. An oral society provides an intellectual environment that is quite fluid, and this facilitates the shaping and development of its oral tradition.[8] That is, in contrast to literate cultures where written texts set ideas "in stone," preliterate peoples are able to adjust their views as they engage new ideas and challenges. Thus, Israel could easily change and rearrange the motifs she inherited from the surrounding nations as her oral tradition developed under the guidance of the Holy Spirit. And typical of historiography, the accepted historical facts were interpreted in light of her inspired metaphysical beliefs. The Hebrews placed their God as Creator of a world that was made *de novo*, human sin and divine judgment as the causes for a lost idyllic age and a great flood, and the ancestral tribe of Israel at the center of human history.

A modern analogy explains further the intellectual plasticity associated with oral traditions. Consider the view that most people have today of Darwin's famed *On the Origin of Species* (1859). Regrettably, few have ever read the book, yet with confidence they assert that it is about how evolution rejects intelligent design and the existence of God. In other words, this common assumption is rooted in an oral tradition that circulates throughout popular culture and the church. Of course, these individuals correctly identify the central motif in the *Origin*—the theory of biological evolution. But since most are trapped in the origins dichotomy, they automatically interpret oral accounts of the evolutionary paradigm through a dysteleological metaphysics and make Darwin one of the founding fathers of modern atheism.[9] In a similar way, preliterate Israel grasped the motifs of the ancient Near East, but into these basic historical paradigms she integrated a Divine Theology.[10]

Third, the introduction of writing within the Hebrew community began to solidify her Holy Spirit inspired oral tradition into documents. Archaeological evidence for literacy in ancient Israel first appears after 1200 BC, and this date aligns well with the temporal markers in both Gen 1–11 and the rest of the book of Genesis.[11] In committing the oral tradition to writing, the inspired authors also stylized it with ancient poetic features. This "dressing up" of the motifs with chiasms, parallel panels, and stylistic numbers even shaped the record of events. Of course, such a historiographical method would never be accepted today. But the intellectual fluidity, ancient epistemology, and literary conventions of that time allowed it, and twenty-first century Christians have to respect these features.

Finally, written sources were redacted into what has become Gen 1–11. No matter how or when these documents were assembled, the intention of the redactor was to reconstruct the past. In particular, the use of the *tôlēdôt* formula in the titles dividing the book of Genesis into ten sections indicates that his purpose was definitely historiographical. This Hebrew phrase can be translated as "These are the generations of . . . ," "This is the family history of . . . ," or "This is the history of . . . ." Significantly, six *tôlēdôt* titles appear in Gen 1–11 (heaven and earth, 2:4; Adam, 5:1; Noah, 6:9; sons of Noah, 10:1; Shem, 11:10; Terah, 11:27). In other words, the redactor pieced together an encompassing history of the origins of the world, its disruption from an idyllic state, a destructive worldwide flood, and the beginning of the Hebrews and other nations. Through the *tôlēdôt* formula he also connected these opening chapters to the rest of Genesis and the Patriarchs (Ishmael, 25:12; Isaac, 25:19; Esau, 36:1; Jacob, 37:2). In this way, the redactor placed the God of the Hebrews as Lord over all of history. Fig 7-3 presents an outline of the origin of the major motifs in Gen 1–11.

The popular and simplistic understanding of the biblical revelatory process as dictation by the Holy Spirit to passive, secretary-like scribes fails to appreciate evidence from Scripture, archaeology, and history. Divine inspiration is a much more dynamic and interactive process between God and human authors, as seen with the use of ancient Near Eastern motifs in

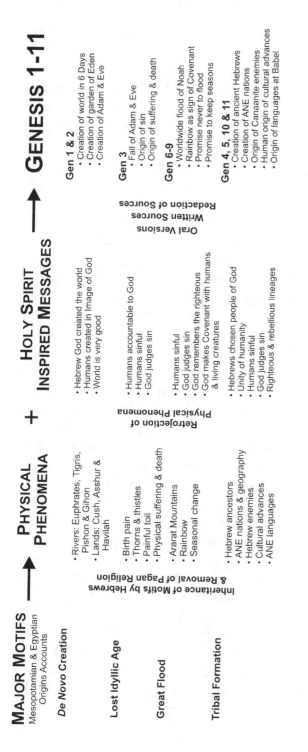

Fig 7-3. Origin of Major Motifs in Genesis 1-11. The Hebrews were an ancient people who understood the logic behind the motifs they inherited from surrounding neighbours. These paradigms integrated common physical and spiritual phenomena into a logical reconstruction of the past. Special revelation through the Holy Spirit sanctified these historical frameworks with Messages of Faith. The Hebrews also retrojected their local knowledge and specific issues into the major motifs. For example, explanations were included for the origins of their Canaanite enemies and for suffering and death in a world made by a Holy Creator. ANE: ancient Near East.

253

the development of Gen 1–11. This process can be pictured as the inheritance of antique intellectual furniture by the fledgling preliterate Hebrew tribe. Inspired by the Holy Spirit, Israel stripped away pagan cloth from the historical frameworks and then re-upholstered them with the fabric of holiness, featuring a covenant with a single righteous Creator. And in the same way that furniture is arranged in a room to serve a purpose, the Hebrews placed their God on the throne in heaven as Lord over the footstool of the creation, and their community as the lamp shedding light upon human history.

Implications of Ancient Motifs

The ancient motifs in Gen 1–11 have significant consequences for the interpretation of these chapters. Modern readers must identify and respect these commonly held notions because they are the implicit historical concepts and paradigms of the ancient Hebrews. The recognition of these motifs has profound implications for the divine and human acts stated in the biblical origins accounts, and in particular for understanding the Christian anti-evolutionary positions.

The record of God's activity with people in Gen 1–11 is filtered through ancient motifs. More specifically, the *attribution of divine creative action* in the origins of humanity, the Hebrew community, and all other nations is cast in the motifs of *de novo* creation and tribal formation. As well, the *attribution of divine judgmental activity* is delivered through the lost idyllic age and the great flood. These ancient motifs do not correspond to reality in the past, and consequently, none of the divine events involving humans actually occurred as stated in Gen 1–11. This situation is identical to statements regarding God's creative and judgmental actions in the assembly and disassembly of the heavens in the Bible. The incidental ancient astronomy has no impact whatsoever on the Messages of Faith that it transports, and so too the incidental ancient motifs offering inerrant revelations about the Lord's relationship with humanity. In addition, the *attribution of human action* in these chapters is also framed on common motifs-of-the-day in the ancient Near East. For example, eating from a mystical tree or building an ark are recycled ancient motifs delivering eternal truths on human disobedience and obedience, respectively. Thus, *Gen 1–11 attributes to God and humans acts that in fact never literally happened in the past.*

With this being the case, it is now obvious that the foundations of the Christian anti-evolutionary positions are rooted in the major and minor motifs of Gen 1–11. These motifs are also the basis for the assumption that the opening chapters of Scripture feature historical concordism. However, young earth creationists and progressive creationists fail to recognize that statements dealing with humanity are founded upon ancient reconstructions of the past. These ancient paradigms were inherited by the Hebrews and then sanctified with a Divine Theology inspired by the Holy Spirit. In other words, anti-evolutionism and Gen 1–11 historical concordism are not set in reality of the past, but in an ancient understanding of history.

Moreover, the fierce opposition to human evolution by anti-evolutionists is ultimately based on an ancient major motif—the *de novo* creation of humanity. The dramatic intervention of God in making a fully formed man and woman in Gen 1 and 2 never happened because this is an ancient conception of origins. Similarly, Gen 3 is structured on the lost idyllic age motif. This chapter is not a historical record of a cosmic fall in which an originally perfect world was disrupted at a point in time by the introduction of suffering and death. As well, there never was a worldwide flood as described in Gen 6–9, since this is only a motif that arose in ancient societies susceptible to flooding. And the tribal formation of peoples and nations in Gen 4, 5, 10, and 11 is not historical, but an ancient understanding of community origins. Instead of offering the facts-of-history, the Holy Spirit through these ancient historical paradigms reveals simply that God created men and women in His Image, they have all sinned, He judges them for sin, and Israel is His chosen instrument for blessing humankind. Therefore, *Gen 1–11 does not reveal actual past events in the creation of humanity, the entrance of sin into the world, the judgment of the first sinners, or the origin of the Hebrews and all other nations.*

Minor motifs in Gen 1–11 are also behind a number of popular anti-evolutionary notions and practices. For example, the vegetarianism in Gen 1 and 2 appears in other accounts of an idyllic age. This dietary practice certainly has health benefits, but Christians including it as part of their faith are enforcing a requirement based on a characteristic of an incidental ancient motif. Longevity in Gen 5 is another feature of the idyllic period. Attempts to determine the age of the world or to explain extraordinarily long lifespan with clever physiological arguments are wrongheaded because the ages in these genealogies reflect an ancient understanding of a distant epoch that never existed. Finally, the belief that the rainbow in Noah's flood account was the first manifestation of this meteorological phenomenon fails to recognize that it is a minor motif found in many flood stories throughout the world (Fig 6-8).

To conclude, the divine and human events stated in Gen 1–11 are based ultimately on ancient Near Eastern motifs inherited by the Hebrews. These motifs were the best historical paradigms-of-the-day. Like all other accounts of history, Israel retrojected her metaphysical notions and current situations into these understandings of the distant past; but in contrast to surrounding neighbors, her beliefs and values were a special revelation inspired by the Holy Spirit. Regrettably, failure to recognize the motifs in Gen 1–11 has led many Christians to embrace historical concordism, and to conflate this ancient history with the Divine Theology. As a result, they often perceive conflict between the biblical origins accounts and the modern view of the beginning of human history. This is a common misreading of Scripture. In order to correct this situation and move beyond conflict and concordism in Gen 1–11, we must separate, and not conflate, the incidental ancient motifs from their inerrant Messages of Faith.

TOWARD THE LITERARY GENRE OF GENESIS 1–11

The key to interpreting any written work begins with the identification of the literary genre. It is obvious why Gen 1–11 is the most counterintuitive part of Scripture to understand. These chapters have deeply embedded motifs that were first conceived as oral traditions through an ancient mindset. They then passed through a complex developmental process, involving the sanctification and modification of these ancient historical paradigms, as well as the redaction of later written sources. This has led modern theologians to coin a variety of categories describing the type of literature in Gen 1–11. These include: pre-history, proto-history, suprahistory, primeval prologue, cosmic epic, ancestral epic, national legend, creation story, primeval story, cosmology, cosmogony, myth, mythopoeic, mythopoetic, creation myth, primeval myth, historicized myth, etc.

This section attempts to define the literary genre of Gen 1–11. Using well-known categories, it presents these in the format of a question, and then answers in varying degrees both affirmatively and negatively, pointing to similarities with current types of literature, yet at the same time significant differences from them. In this way, the counterintuitive character of Gen 1–11 and the challenge of understanding these chapters will become more evident.

Is Genesis 1–11 a Fable, Fairy Tale, or Make-Believe Story?

The common thread that runs through these modern categories of literature is that authors employ pure imagination and fanciful literary license. The situations described are outlandish and unrealistic. The theme is often "good vs. evil" with the former prevailing in the end. They happen "once upon a time" in "a land faraway" and virtuous characters always "live happily ever after." Fables, fairy tales, and make-believe stories also have the purpose of entertaining their readers. There is not a stitch of literal historical truth in these types of literature.

Genesis 1–11 certainly strikes many today as amusing stories that were made-up. It includes a fast-talking snake, mystical trees in an idyllic garden, cherubim and a flashing sword protecting paradise, humans who live over 900 years, and people and animals saved in an ark from a world-wide flood. The names of some individuals and places are word plays and fable-like.[12] For example, the Hebrew words "Adam" (*ādām*) and "earth" (*ădāmâ*) accentuate that man was an "earthling" and made from the dust of the ground. "Eve" (*hawwāh*) sounds similar to the verb "to live" (*hāyâ*) and the adjective "living" (*hay*) since she is the mother of life. The name "Noah" is related to the noun *nahat* (rest, quietness) since he brought comfort and relief. The root of the word "Eden" refers to "luxury" and "delight." *Nōd* means "wandering," an appropriate name for the land to which Cain was banished. And the good vs. evil theme unfolds between righteous (Seth and Shem) and rebellious (Cain and Canaan) ancestral lines.

However, Gen 1–11 is not a fantasy produced by unbridled imagination. Using the best scientific and historical paradigms-of-the-day, the inspired authors and especially the final redactor composed an account of the origins of the universe, living organisms, and human communities, in particular that of the Hebrews. Real places and peoples are mentioned in these chapters. Geographical referents include the Tigris and Euphrates Rivers, the Ararat Mountains, and the plain of Shinar. The table of nations features numerous identifiable ancient Near Eastern countries. Figurative language certainly appears in Gen 1–11, but the human authorial intention of these chapters was to reconstruct actual events in the past, and *not* to tell an entertaining fable, fairy tale, or make-believe story.

Is Genesis 1–11 a Parable or Allegory?

Parables and allegories are alike in that their purpose is to offer a truth or lesson about life. In contrast to the literary genres just mentioned, the situations described are more realistic and based on common everyday experience. Concisely defined, a parable is an earthly story with a heavenly meaning. An allegory tends to be a longer account that also uses concrete individuals and circumstances to deliver abstract or spiritual concepts. Like fables, fairy tales and make-believe stories, the intention of parables and allegories is not to present literal "DVD" history.

The Lord used parables throughout His teaching ministry. The Gospels often identify this literary genre with the introduction "Jesus told them a parable . . ." (Matt 13:24), and at times its interpretation is prefaced by "This is the meaning of the parable: . . ." (Luke 8:11). The term "allegory" appears in Scripture on few occasions (Ezek 17:2; Gal 4:24). It is certainly possible that the events in parables and allegories could have happened. For example, the parable of the Good Samaritan (Luke 10:30–36) features people, a dangerous route, and political/religious situations that were real in first century Palestine. But Jesus' listeners were aware of this literary genre and the fact that its purpose is to reveal spiritual truth through a non-literal and non-historical story.

Some people today consider Gen 1–11 an extended parable or allegory. They view the accounts of the creation, garden of Eden, worldwide flood, etc., as earthly stories revealing heavenly messages. To be sure, spiritual truths are the core of these opening chapters, but there is no evidence that the inspired authors were employing these literary genres. (In fact, if this were the case, then it would mean that the writers had an understanding of origins other than that being presented in Genesis. But written records throughout the ancient Near East do not offer even a hint of support for this contention.) No passage in Gen 1–11 begins by identifying it as a parable or allegory, and none are followed by an interpretation. Instead, the *tôlēdôt* formula, "These/this are/is the generations/family history/history of . . . ," is used 6 times in these 11 chapters, indicating clearly that they are historiographical in character. The human authorial intention in Gen 1–11 was to write a historical account of actual people, places, and situations, and *not* a parable or an allegory.

Is Genesis 1–11 a Legend, Epic, or Folklore?

These literary genres feature dim historical elements from the distant past. In other words, they possess a nucleus of factual history. They are also heroic in character and magnify the exploits of individuals, tribes, and nations. These stories often present the formation of the community, conquests of her enemies, and strong nationalistic interests. They begin as oral traditions and over time evolve with the achievements of the hero or the nation becoming more embellished and even unrealistic. As a result, many today view legends, epics, and folklore as largely unhistorical.

Genesis 1–11 is similar to these genres in that it has remnants of actual history. A local flood/s and even a flood hero/s are undoubtedly behind the numerous flood accounts in the ancient Near East, including the J and P versions later redacted into Gen 6–9. The genealogies in Gen 4, 5, 10, and 11 most likely include some real people. The table of nations in Gen 10 lists numerous identifiable cities, regions, and countries. Making the Canaanites slaves because their purported forefather Ham looked upon Noah's nakedness is clearly a nationalistic statement against this chronic enemy of Israel. And in an unrealistic way, these first chapters of Scripture magnify and embellish the Hebrew peoples. Genesis 10 presents them as the center of human history with all peoples and nations descending from the three sons of Noah.

At the same time, Gen 1–11 is quite different from legends, epics, and folklore in that it is not an unbridled glorification of a hero/s, a nation, or their achievements. In fact, the central theme throughout these chapters is that sin thrived among the ancestors of the Hebrews. The first man and woman are sinners. The first family is dysfunctional because of sin. Sinfulness marks the lives of important figures (Cain, Lamech, Ham). Even with the few godly individuals in Gen 1–11, there is no excessive magnification of their holiness. In fact, their frailty is revealed. Abel made a pleasing offering to the Lord, and then he was murdered. Noah was a righteous man, but became drunk and exposed. In this way, Scripture differs significantly from legends, epics, and folklore by focusing on a central factor that shapes human history—the reality of sin.

Is Genesis 1–11 a Myth?

For most people, the term "myth" means something that is completely untrue. It refers to fictitious events and imaginary supernatural beings, and is often associated with the ancient Greek gods and their wild adventures. Christians are particularly opposed to myths because they are denounced in the Bible. The apostle Paul warns:

> For a time will come when men will not put up with sound doctrine. Instead, to suit their own desires, they will gather around them a great number of teachers to say what their itching ears want to hear. They will turn their ears away from the truth and turn aside to myths. 2 Tim 4:3–4

The falsity of myths also appears in 1 Tim 1:4, 4:7, Titus 1:14, and 2 Pet 1:16. Consequently, this word is usually depicted in a very negative light. However, myth is also a professional literary category that refers to an account that conveys the beliefs and values of a community. Defined in this way, the central myth of Christianity is that God became flesh in the person of Jesus who died on the Cross for our sins. Similarly, the myth of dysteleological evolution is that the universe and life are products of blind chance and irrational necessity.[13] Therefore, myths are not necessarily limited to being fanciful non-historical accounts, but can be rooted in real people and actual events.

The many motifs in Gen 1–11 certainly give these chapters a mythical flavor, as this term is popularly understood. The major motifs of *de novo* creation, the lost idyllic age and the great flood are surreal, and they appear repeatedly in creation myths throughout the ancient world. The minor motifs of a sinister snake, mystical fruit that imparts eternal life, and hybrid creatures like cherubim are imaginative, and these have parallels in the mythologies of the Greeks, Egyptians, and Mesopotamians. In particular, the account in Gen 6:1–4 of celestial beings mating with human women, who then give birth to giants and heroes, strikes everyone today as a Greek myth. This notion was also a common belief in the ancient Near East. To be sure, recognizing these features in both Scripture and the literature of cultures surrounding the ancient Hebrews is disturbing to Christians who assume that Gen 1–11 is literal "DVD" history. The question immediately arises as to whether or not these chapters are nothing but a myth.

However, it must be remembered that motifs are logical conceptualizations of past and present realities conceived through an ancient mindset. In fact, the word "myth" was coined after most ancient Near Eastern origins accounts had become established in their respective cultures.[14] That is, the original formulators of motifs never thought of themselves as myth-makers. Instead, they were attempting to reconstruct the past and to understand the present. But more importantly, the divine beings depicted in the pagan creation myths are radically different from the Creator in Gen 1–11. These gods are pitiful. They constantly battle among themselves, require sacrifices to overcome their hunger, and destroy humans for frivolous reasons. Some accounts tell of the body parts of murdered gods being used to make the world. In striking contrast, the biblical God is Holy. There is not a hint that other gods exist to oppose Him. He creates the world with complete ease. And His sustaining grace extends to undeserving sinful human beings.

Regrettably, the negative baggage conflated with the term "myth" makes it a misleading, if not useless, literary category today. Should the word be employed, then qualification is necessary. A myth can be defined as follows:

MYTH = MOTIFS + METAPHYSICS

Motifs are the framework of a myth and feature the science and history-of-the-day, whether ancient or modern. Upon these basic paradigms of conceived reality rest the metaphysical beliefs of a community or society, ranging widely from pagan to Hebrew, dysteleological to Christian, etc. In this sense, Gen 1–11 can be seen as the Holy Spirit inspired origins myth of the ancient Hebrews.

Is Genesis 1–11 a Narrative?

Narratives are accounts or reports of events that can be either factual or fictional. They usually present incidents and circumstances in a logical and sequential order, such as sentence-by-sentence and paragraph-by-paragraph. This broad literary genre can include direct quotations from an individual and/or dialogue between people, giving to the account a realistic element of actual personal relationships. Today the term "narrative" in popular Christian circles often refers to a straightforward factual and historical record of past events.[15]

Many passages in Gen 1–11 can be categorized as narrative, particularly the free flowing accounts of the Jahwist writer. The intention of the inspired authors, and especially that of the redactor, was to provide an orderly record of the origin of the world and the formation of the Hebrew

community. However, the Bible itself reveals various internal conflicts between the events reported in Gen 1–11, pointing away from the historicity
of the narratives (e.g., order of the creative acts, chronology of the flood).
Scientific and historical evidence also demonstrates that the main incidents
never happened (e.g., *de novo* creation of life, introduction of death after
human origins). At best, the narratives in these opening chapters include
only a few dim recollections of events (e.g., local floods) and people (e.g.,
possibly a flood hero, some ancestors in genealogies) from the distant past,
arising out of oral traditions. Thus, the narrative characteristics of Gen
1–11 do not by necessity confer historicity to these passages.

The numerous dialogues in Gen 1–11 also give the impression that
these chapters are historical. Not only do people talk to one another,
but they also speak with God. Most Christians assume that, since these
conversations are placed in quotation marks, Scripture is offering a word-
for-word transcript of actual conversations. Yet a closer examination suggests otherwise. Once more, the creation of the firmament is instructive.
Genesis 1:6 and 8 state, "And God said, 'Let there be a firmament between
the waters to separate water from water.' . . . And God called the firmament
'heaven.'" But a solid dome supporting a body of water overhead has never
existed. Did the Creator actually state this command? Obviously, no. Did
the inspired writer *put words in the mouth* of God? Clearly, yes. But never
forget, this occurred under the accommodating guidance of the Holy
Spirit. Note that this is also the case with other divine statements—the
setting of heavenly bodies in the firmament, the entrance of suffering and
death, the destruction of life by the flood, etc. Therefore, the many commands and conversations quoted in Gen 1–11 do not necessarily make
these chapters records of actual history.

Most Christians will be troubled by the fact that events in the opening narratives of Scripture, and in particular the very words of God quoted
in these passages, are not consistent with scientific and historical reality.
However, it is essential to note that this biblical evidence challenges only
a popular understanding of divine inspiration. It calls into question the
assumption that the Holy Spirit dictated to secretary-like Hebrew authors
word-for-word the origins accounts, and since God only tells the truth
He would be bound to reveal only true science and history. This approach
overlooks the Lord's willingness to accommodate His revelation to the
level of ancient peoples by using the ideas-of-the-day as incidental vessels. The conflicting events and purported dialogues do not undermine

the fact that Gen 1–11 is literally the Word of God; they merely point away from the narratives being literal transcripts of actual conversations and records of real incidents in the past.

Creation accounts throughout the world assist in appreciating the nature of Gen 1–11, and ultimately the Holy Spirit inspired revelatory process. Similar to Scripture, the majority of these accounts are narratives of events and include conversations between a variety of characters— animals, mystical creatures, humans, and a divine being/s.[16] Two conclusions emerge. First, none of these narratives are scientifically or historically accurate; in fact they conflict irreconcilably with one another. Their significance rests in the power of the metaphysics that united the community and gave it meaning. Second, in composing origins accounts, ancient authors had no difficulty conceptualizing events between people and god/s, and even putting words into their mouths. Of course, by today's standards such a practice is completely unacceptable. Yet this is the way it was in ancient cultures, including the Hebrews. In this light, the Holy Spirit accommodated to this ancient literary practice during the revelatory process that led to the creation of Gen 1–11.

Is Genesis 1–11 Poetry?

The term "poetry" is a wide literary category that refers to a structured writing style in contrast to free flowing narrative. It is often characterized by the use of figurative language, fanciful images, and meaningful symbols. Actual events may lie behind poetic literature, but this medium best lends itself to the communication of less tangible ideas that are emotive, abstract, and spiritual. In popular circles today, especially among many Christians, poetry often refers to literature that is non-literal and non-historical.

Genesis 1–11 abounds with ancient poetic features, particularly the structured passages composed by the Priestly author. Literary frameworks are obvious in the parallel panels of the first creation account, the repetitive formulas in the Sethite and Shemite genealogies, and the chiasm of Noah's flood. These chapters are also decorated with rich symbolism. Mystical numbers shape the dates and chronologies of events and the lifespan of individuals. The imagery of a speaking snake who tempts a woman, a paradisal garden with trees imparting eternal life and ethical knowledge, and a first man named "earthling" with his wife called "mother of life" strike many individuals as a figurative story with spiritual meaning. These literary characteristics argue that Gen 1–11 is poetic and it was never intended to be literal or historical.

But the structured and stylistic elements in the opening chapters of Scripture are surface features of a deeper understanding of reality held by the Hebrews and other ancient peoples. To them, the motifs in Gen 1–11 were facts of science and history, and not merely literary symbols or images.[17] The inspired authors not only cleansed these of pagan beliefs, but they also dressed them up using the poetic techniques-of-the-day. Undoubtedly, the literary liberties taken by these writers shock twenty-first century readers (e.g., manipulation of the number of people and their ages in genealogies). In particular, the freedom to integrate and modify motifs into the Gen 2–3 account of human origins clashes with the modern notion of history (e.g., putting words in the mouth of a tempting snake, making mystical fruit impart ethical knowledge, having sin lead to the loss of the idyllic age). Yet from the perspective of an ancient epistemology, this literary license was perfectly acceptable when writing about the past.

It must be pointed out that a subtle form of eisegesis with Gen 1–11 manifests among many of those immersed in modern literary categories. They are quick to write-off the historicity of these chapters as poetry, allegory, story, etc. But again, the major and minor motifs were conceptualizations of reality for ancient peoples. These motifs only became *figurative* over time with the growth of scientific and historical knowledge. As they were slowly *de-historicized*, Gen 1–11 began to be interpreted as a poetic account.[18] The fact that English literature is profoundly shaped by biblical categories aggravates this situation. These motifs became literary devices and powerful symbols in some of the greatest works of literature (e.g., Milton's *Paradise Lost*). In other words, modern individuals have been conditioned to read into Gen 1–11 de-historicized motifs. To be sure, the imagery in the garden of Eden strikes many people *today* as only a story, but this was not the case *yesterday* in the ancient world.

The poetic interpretation of Gen 1–11 is similar to the use of the "poetic language argument" for the Kenotic Hymn in Phil 2.[19] Both are easy and simple "quick-fix" solutions that attempt to write-off scientific and historical problems in Scripture. But as noted with Phil 2:10, there is no evidence to indicate that Paul wanted to describe the structure of the cosmos in poetic terms because this would necessitate that he knew the world was not made up of three tiers. So too, if the inspired authors of the opening chapters of the Bible had intended to write a figurative account of origins, it implies they had a knowledge of origins different to that stated in these chapters. However, there is no evidence that this is the case. Genesis 1–11 certainly features a "poetic dressing up" of the scientific and historical facts understood by the ancient Hebrews, but these features do not undermine the human authorial intention to compose an account of how the world and humanity actually originated.

Is Genesis 1–11 Science?

Using the most basic definition, science deals with knowledge about the physical world. It is an attempt by men and women to understand the structure, operation, and origin of the universe and life, including themselves. Defined in this way, science has existed since the dawn of humanity. For ancient peoples, dramatic interventions by supernatural beings were part of their knowledge of how the physical world worked and came into being. Today, the scientific method and its instruments limit the investigation of the cosmos and living organisms to only natural causes and processes.

Genesis 1–11 includes knowledge regarding nature. Therefore, science appears in these chapters. The redactor of the book of Genesis clearly intended to present a record of how the universe and life originated. He begins the second creation account with the *tôlēdôt* formula: "This is the *tôlēdôt* of the heavens and earth when they were created" (Gen 2:4). As noted, this Hebrew term is used nine other times in Genesis to introduce the history of a family. In other words, the redactor thought that the creation events in Gen 2 were as real and as historical as the activities in the early Hebrew community. Genesis 2:4 could be translated, "This is the history of the heavens and earth." Similarly, if Gen 1:1 ("In the beginning God created the heavens and the earth") is a title that a redactor added to the first creation account, then it suggests he intended Gen 1 to be understood as a natural history.[20]

However, the science in Gen 1–11 is an ancient science. It features an ancient origins science based on an ancient phenomenological perspective of nature and conceptualized through ancient notions of causality. Modern science without any doubt has proven: the universe and life were not created *de novo* in six days six thousand years ago; suffering and death never entered the world after the appearance of humans; and a worldwide flood did not at one time envelope the earth. Scientific concordism fails. Scientific predictions based on literal interpretations of Gen 1–11 also fail. God's *de novo* creative acts and the creation of life "after their kinds" are accommodations by the Holy Spirit to the level of the ancient Hebrews in order to reveal as efficiently as possible that He is the Creator. Thus, God-of-the-gaps models and anti-evolutionary arguments based on the science in Gen 1 and 2 are a misguided use of Scripture.

Is Genesis 1–11 History?

Employing a wide definition, history refers simply to an orderly account of events in the past. Understood this way, it includes both "natural history" and "human history." However the most common meaning of this term deals with the activities of men and women. This definition consists of "pre-history," the period from the appearance of the first humans to the birth of writing; and it also includes "written history" as recorded in inscriptions and documents from past generations.

Genesis 1–11 was intended to be an encompassing account of events at the beginning of the world. It is both a history of nature and a history of humanity, with emphasis on the Hebrews. The redactor of these chapters collected written sources on origins and organized them into an orderly sequence. His addition of the *tôlēdôt* formula throughout the book of Genesis is clear evidence that his purpose was historiographical. The major motifs in his sources were the historical paradigms-of-the-day. Ancient peoples did not view these as fanciful and imaginary stories. And like all historians, the redactor selected, interpreted, and even shaped the historical facts in light of his worldview. He believed that the God of the Hebrews is Lord over history, and he made Him the Creator of the world, the Judge of humanity for their sin, and the Maker of a special community that would bless all the nations.

But the history in Gen 1–11 is an ancient history. Intimately connected to ancient science, it is an ancient phenomenological perspective of human origins first conceived in oral societies and filtered through ancient notions of causality. The implicit scientific concepts of that time led to *implicit historical concepts* that undergird the motifs in ancient creation accounts. In particular, the notion of *de novo* creation lies behind the origin of Adam and Eve, the tribal beginning of the Hebrews and surrounding nations, and the appearance of languages and cultural advances. All of these originate quickly and completely. In addition, the history in Gen 1–11 is shaped by ancient literary conventions. The sequences of many events are set in poetic frameworks, and temporal referents are stylized with mystical numbers. And the redaction of different sources produces contradictions between passages. Clearly, actual historical accounts are not built on recycled and dressed up ancient origins motifs whose events conflict with one another.

Modern anthropology, archaeology, and history assist in revealing that Gen 1–11 contains few to no as-it-happened historical facts. There was never a pain and death-free vegetarian age, a time when people lived more than 900 years and all spoke the same language, or a repopulation of the earth from three married couples after a worldwide flood. Historical concordism in Gen 1–11 fails. At best, foggy shadows exist in these chapters of a local flood/s and its survivor/s as well as some genealogical individuals arising from the collective memory of the preliterate Hebrew community.

Is Genesis 1–11 Theology?

Simply defined, theology deals with words (*logos*) about God (*theos*). Genesis 1–11 includes numerous statements revealing His character, laws, acts, and the world He made. But this Divine Theology is not presented in an organized and systematic way, similar to a creed or modern theological textbook. There is no well-defined doctrine of God, creation, humanity, sin, etc. Theological principles are set tightly within ancient motifs. Consequently, it is necessary first to separate the inerrant revelation from the incidental frameworks, and then to formulate doctrinal and creedal statements. Three features of the theology in Gen 1–11 must be noted.

First, though these chapters are foundational to the Bible, they are the *beginning* of the revelatory process and subtly anticipate a later fulfillment. Stated more precisely, theology develops through Scripture. For example, consider offerings and sacrifices to God. These religious rituals are mentioned in Gen 1–11 with Cain, Abel, and Noah, but none of these passages directly associates this practice with atonement for human sin, even though the notion of sin is a central theme. Later in the Old Testament, Moses explicitly defines the connection between sin and sacrifice. And even later, Jesus fulfilled the sacrifice for sin on the Cross. In fact, the New

Testament abolishes the Mosaic revelation of atonement through animal sacrifice. Hebrews 10:4 states, "Those sacrifices are an annual reminder of sins, because it is impossible for the blood of bulls and goats to take away sin." Thus, the opening chapters of Scripture must be understood in light of the overall theological development that occurs through the Bible.

Second, Gen 1–11 introduces a theodicy. It offers an explanation for one of the greatest questions asked by men and women in every generation: Why do we suffer and die? The answer given is that Adam sinned and God sentenced him to suffering and death. This theodicy is cast within the major motif of the lost idyllic age, and it reflects a corollary of *de novo* creation (i.e., death can only occur after living organisms have been made quickly and completely).[21] Moreover, because theology develops through Scripture, consideration must be given to the possibility that the theodicy in Gen 1–11 is the *beginning* of the revelatory process on this issue. In other words, the final word on theodicy, like offerings and sacrifices, is not found in the opening chapters of the Bible, but rather in the fulfilling light of Jesus' suffering and death.

Finally, Gen 1–11 is typological (Greek *tupos* means "type, example, model, symbol"). One of the most obvious theological patterns is the six days of creation followed by a day of rest, which models the Hebrew work week and Sabbath. The inspired author clearly manipulated the number of creation days to serve his theological intention. Other typologies include: Adam as the representative of all humans and their sinfulness; the genealogies of Cain and Seth depicting, respectively, peoples alienated from and chosen by God; Noah as a model of righteousness protected from divine judgment; and the Hebrews as the prototypical instrument of God's grace for a fallen world. Again, later theological developments in the New Testament fulfill these typologies and shed further light on the Sabbath, human sinfulness and righteousness, and the New Israel revealing the Lord's unfathomable love for humanity.

Is Genesis 1–11 Literal?

For the most part, the opening chapters of the Bible were intended to be a literal account of the origin of the world and the formation of the Hebrew community. The original writers used some poetic license and stylistic dressing up of the ancient scientific and historical facts. But these inspired individuals, and especially the redactor, believed they were reporting events that had actually occurred in the past. Later biblical authors understood Gen 1–11 as literal history. In fact, Jesus Himself appealed to passages in these accounts verbatim. And the Church throughout most of time up until today has held that the main events in these chapters literally happened.

However, modern science and history reveal that there is incontestable evidence that falsifies a literal reading of Gen 1–11. Scientific and historical concordism fail. As well, numerous conflicts between the events in these chapters indicate that they could not have occurred as stated. Many Christians assume that literalism is God's preferred method of communication in Scripture. But they fail to appreciate the implications of the Holy Spirit entering the world to reveal Himself and His will to the ancient Hebrews. Divine revelation had to be accommodated to their ancient intellectual categories. Everyone at that time believed that the world was literally created *de novo*, that an idyllic age had once literally existed and ended, and that a flood literally destroyed the entire world. If it were the Holy Spirit's intention to reveal modern scientific and historical facts about the past, and it was well within His power to do so, would anyone have accepted these, let alone have understood them? For example, if God dictated to biblical authors that He created the universe and life through an evolutionary process beginning with the Big Bang, would ancient preliterate people have grasped and believed this notion?

Regrettably, it is a popular assumption both inside and outside the Church that if Gen 1–11 is not a literal account of origins, then it is not the Word of God. Stated another way, if a literal reading of these chapters conflicts with modern scientific and historical facts, then the Bible is errant and fallible, and not trustworthy. But the problem is not with Scripture, it is with later generations who fail to appreciate the Incarnational character of the revelatory process. To modify the aphorism of the fifth chapter, *Gen 1–11 is the inerrant and infallible Word of God communicated through incidental literal statements about origins made by humans within history.* Today, we must read beyond the vessel of literal scientific and historical assertions into which the Holy Spirit poured Messages of Faith.[22]

Is Genesis 1–11 True?

The question of whether Gen 1–11 is true is a return to the question asked earlier, "Does God lie in the Bible?" The answer given was an absolute

NO! God does not lie, He accommodates. Lying requires *the intention* to deceive. In contrast, accommodation recognizes *the need* to communicate truth in a way that is understandable to an intended audience. All parents do this with their children, and the Father has also done this with us, His children. In fact, God has to accommodate in order to reveal Himself to men and women. He is the Creator; we are the creatures. It is logically impossible for finite minds to understand an infinite Divine Being unless He descends to our human level. It is by grace that the Holy Spirit began the biblical revelatory process, using intentionally the categories of the ancient Hebrews.

The science and history in Gen 1–11 were considered true at the time these chapters were being conceived, orally transmitted, written down, and eventually redacted. Statements about the origin of the physical world, the beginning of humanity, and the formation of a chosen people were truths-of-the-day, the best knowledge of that period from a Hebrew perspective. Of course, modern science and history demonstrate that these statements do not correspond to reality. But instead of viewing this as an unanswerable conflict, these academic disciplines assist Christians to focus attention on the purpose of the opening chapters of Scripture—the revelation of a Divine Theology. The central feature of Gen 1–11 is theological concordism. Today, believers must read beyond the accommodation made by the Holy Spirit in order to embrace the inerrant and infallible Messages of Faith.

Human history testifies to the reality that Gen 1–11 is utterly true. The power of the eternal Truths in these chapters is proven by the countless lives that have been impacted and changed in every generation. As a matter of fact, God's promise to Abraham that "all the peoples on earth will be blessed through you" has been fulfilled (Gen 12:3). There is no other community whose theology has blessed the world as much as his descendants—Israel and the Church. In my humble opinion, you can bet your eternal life on the Truths in Gen 1–11.

Toward the Literary Genre

In light of the discussion above, it is now possible to propose a genre for Gen 1–11. Simply stated, it is an ancient origins account. More precisely, the Bible opens with *the ancient origins account of the Hebrews inspired by the Holy Spirit*. A closer examination of each component in this proposal explains further this complex and unique literary genre.

Ancient. Genesis 1–11 is ancient. It originated in the ancient Near East thousands of years ago. These chapters feature ancient science and ancient history. They are built on recycled ancient motifs and reflect oral traditions of an ancient pre-literate society. The scientific and historical notions in Gen 1–11 were conceived through an ancient epistemology that featured an ancient notion of causality and an ancient phenomenological perspective. Eventually written down using ancient poetry and literary techniques, the original sources were put together through ancient methods of redaction to become the first chapters of the Word of God.

Origins. Genesis 1–11 deals with origins. It outlines the beginning of the universe and life, including humans. Special attention is directed to the formation of the Hebrew community. These chapters also present the origin of harsh realities in the world. They focus on the entrance of human sin and deal with the introduction of suffering and death. As well, the roots of political tensions between the Hebrews and surrounding nations are offered, especially the chronic problem of the Canaanites. In this way, Gen 1–11 is both a science of the origin of the cosmos and a history of the origins of humanity and the Hebrews.

Account. Genesis 1–11 is an orderly account. Its purpose is to inform, explain, and justify. These chapters are descriptive in that they report events, people, and circumstances. They were intended by the inspired authors and the later redactor to be, for the most part, a literal record of origins. Genesis 1–11 is also etiological. It gives causes and reasons for the origin of the physical world, nations, and their languages, and the reality that plagues humanity—sin against the Creator and other human beings. Finally, these chapters are a justification for the existence of brutal realities in the world. Suffering and death were divine judgments for the sins of Adam and Eve, and the enemies surrounding the Hebrews were a consequence of Ham's sin against his father. Like other accounts of origins, Gen 1–11 looks back into the past in order to understand the present and to offer hope for the future.

Of the Hebrews. Genesis 1–11 is distinctly Hebrew. It strips away pagan religious beliefs and values from ancient Near Eastern motifs and replaces these with a radical theology: The Hebrew God is a Holy Creator in complete control of the world. In particular, He created the Hebrew community to be His chosen instrument through which all the nations on earth are blessed. Accommodating to a tribal understanding of community formation, the Holy Spirit discloses that the Creator actually enters into history for the benefit of humankind. In this way, Gen 1–11 is typological and foreshadows the Incarnation and the Lord's blessing of the world through the Church.

Inspired by the Holy Spirit. Genesis 1–11 is the Word of God. It features the foundations of a Divine Theology that is authoritative for every man and woman. These chapters are the *beginning* of the revelatory process inspired by the Holy Spirit, and they anticipate further development and fulfillment. Intentionally accommodated by God to the level of the ancient Hebrews, Gen 1–11 is a sufficient divine revelation and each generation has been proficient in grasping its life-changing Messages of Faith. In the light of Christ, these chapters are Incarnational. The Holy Spirit entered the world to deliver the inerrant and infallible Word of God in the words of ancient Hebrews in history.

To conclude, Gen 1–11 is a rich, complicated, and special literary genre. In order to understand these chapters fully, they must be read in a counterintuitive fashion. Christians today must look beyond the intended literal statements of the human authors and the intended accommodation of the Holy Spirit. Viewed in this way, there is no conflict between history and the first chapters of Scripture because historical concordism is not a feature of this inspired ancient Hebrew origins account. By respecting the literary genre of Gen 1–11, believers will discover the Lord's Eternal Truths in their purity and full glory.

WERE ADAM AND NOAH HISTORICAL?

The historicity of Adam and Noah fuels intense discussion in the modern origins debate. Young earth creationists and progressive creationists cling tenaciously to the belief that both men did in fact exist. The position of the Church throughout the ages has affirmed that Adam was the first man to live, and the first to sin. Similarly, Christian tradition accepts that Noah survived a destructive flood. Based on concordist interpretations of Gen 1–11, these views also draw compelling support from the New Testament. Jesus and Paul both refer explicitly to Adam and Noah, leading many to believe that this conclusively establishes their reality. Before any Christian moves away from the historicity of two central biblical figures, these passages must be dealt with directly.

This section focuses on the most important New Testament references to Adam and Noah in order to determine whether these Scriptures confirm their historicity. It also revisits evidence from Gen 1–11 presented in the last chapter, and summarizes features relevant to this issue. Finally, a brief review of some basic scientific data sheds light on whether or not Adam and Noah were historical.

The Historicity of Adam

Powerful biblical evidence used to defend the traditional literal interpretation that Adam was the first man who ever lived comes from Jesus. In appealing to Gen 1:27 and Gen 2:24, the Lord admonishes:

> Haven't you read that at the beginning the Creator 'made them male and female,' and said, 'For this reason a man will leave his father and mother and be united to his wife, and the two will become one flesh.' So they are no longer two, but one. Therefore what God has joined together, let man not separate. (Matt 19:4–6 [cf. Mark 10:2–9])

First, it must be noted that the context and authorial intention of this passage are not a debate over the historicity of Adam. Rather, Jesus is responding to a question about divorce. The Pharisees had asked Him, "Is it lawful for a man to divorce his wife for any and every reason" (v. 3)? Second, it must be remembered that the Lord uses ancient science throughout His teaching ministry—geology (Sheba at the ends of the earth), astronomy (falling of all the stars to earth and rolling up of the heavens), botany (mustard seed the smallest of all seeds), and medicine (demons a cause of diseases and disabilities).[23] It is only consistent that He would also employ an ancient understanding of human origins—the *de novo* creation of man and woman. Finally, Jesus' use of Gen 1:27 and Gen 2:24 is typological. The relationship between Adam and Eve is an archetype or model of what God intended marriage to be. Indeed, this is a faith message in dire need of being heard by today's generation.

The apostle Paul also provides persuasive scriptural evidence for the traditional belief that Adam was historical. In sketching the history of salvation, he places Adam's sin and death alongside references to the days of Moses and the sacrificial gift of Jesus. Paul writes:

> Therefore, just as sin entered the world through one man, and death through sin, and in this way death came to all men, because

all sinned—for before the law was given, sin was in the world. But sin is not taken into account when there is no law. Nevertheless, death reigned from the time of Adam to the time of Moses, even over those who did not sin by breaking a command, as did Adam, who was *a pattern* of the One to come. But the gift is not like the trespass. For if the many died by the trespass of the one man, how much more did God's grace and gift that came by the grace of the one Man, Jesus Christ, overflow to the many! (Rom 5:12–15; italics added)

Similarly, Paul writes to the Corinthians, "For since death came through a man, the resurrection of the dead comes also through a Man. For as in Adam all die, so in Christ all will be made alive. . . . So it is written: 'The first man Adam became a living being;' the last Adam, a life-giving spirit" (1 Cor 15:21, 45). But again, the context and intention of these passages are not debating the historicity of Adam. They focus on the reality of sin and the fact that Jesus frees men and women from their sinfulness and offers them resurrection from death and eternal life. Moreover, it must be remembered that Paul employs the science-of-the-day in his inspired letters. He uses the 3-tier universe in one of the most significant passages in the New Testament—the kenosis of Jesus (Phil 2:5–11). Consistency demands that since this apostle holds an ancient understanding of the structure of the universe, then he undoubtedly accepted an ancient view of human origins—*de novo* creation. Finally, Paul presents Adam as an archetype. In fact, he even employs the Greek word *tupos* ("type, pattern, model, example") in Rom 5:14 and states explicitly that Adam "was a pattern of the One to come."

References to Adam by Jesus and Paul do not confirm that he was historical. Nor does his being mentioned in the New Testament confer historicity to him in Gen 1–11 (this is the so-called "conferment or bestowment argument"). The existence of Adam as the first man was an unchallenged assumption held by the Lord's listeners, the apostle and his readers. It was the history-of-the-day for the Jews. In the same way that references to a 3-tiered world by Jesus and Paul do not establish or bestow reality to this understanding of the structure of the universe in Gen 1, the mention of Adam in the New Testament does not make him a real person in history.[24]

Many features in Gen 1–11 also point away from the historicity of Adam. These include:

Literary Genre. As noted several times, determining the genre of any written work is the key to its interpretation. Genesis 1–11 is an ancient origins account. It is built on recycled ancient Near Eastern motifs which are neither scientifically nor historically accurate. Consistency demands that this is also the case with human origins in these chapters.

Ancient Science. Genesis 1 and 2 feature an ancient understanding of the creation of the world. Like all other ancient origins accounts, divine creative action is *de novo*. But the quick and complete creation of the heavens, earth, and life is rooted in an ancient notion of causality and an ancient phenomenological perspective of nature. Thus, the historicity of the *de novo* creation of Adam in Scripture is based on ancient science.

Contradictory Order of Creation Events. The sequence of divine creative acts in Gen 1 and Gen 2 do not align. In particular, the events surrounding the origins of humanity are contradictory. Birds and animals are created before man in Gen 1, while in Gen 2 they are made after him. These two different and irreconcilable accounts indicate that the Bible is not a record of actual events at the beginning of human history.

Tribal Formation. The descent of all humanity from Adam is an ancient understanding of community origins. His name in Hebrew (*ʾādām*) means "man" and functions as an eponym for the human family. In fact, tribal formation from a single individual is ultimately rooted in an ancient scientific notion—the *de novo* creation of humanity. Recognizing these two major ancient motifs argues against the historicity of Adam as the forefather of every man and woman.

Ancient Genealogies. The ancestral lists in Gen 1–11 are clearly manipulated. The ages and number of individuals in real genealogies are not stylized in this way. The brevity of the Gen 4, 5, 10, and 11 lineages reflects their preliterate past and the limits of human memory. Any attempt to establish the historicity of Adam through these ancient genealogies falls short.

Traditional Literal Interpretation. The Church in every generation has assumed that Adam literally lived a few thousand years ago. This is not surprising since science up to the nineteenth century accepted *de novo* human origins. As a result, the historicity of Adam was never debated, nor was it ever an issue defined in any creed. This fact can be viewed as providentialistic. The historical reality of Adam, whether one accepts it or not, is not essential to Christian faith.

Modern science also rejects the traditional and literal belief in the historicity of Adam. To summarize some of the most basic evidence:

Geology. The fossil record proves without any doubt that scientific predictions based on concordist interpretations of Gen 1–11 fail (Appendix 7). The traditional belief that Adam preceded suffering and death in the world is falsified by overwhelming geological evidence. In particular, fossil evidence for carnivores abounds, featuring fish, amphibians, reptiles, and mammals with vicious flesh-slaughtering dentitions. Physical pain and death existed hundreds of millions of years before humans appeared on earth.

Anthropology. Fossils of various pre-human species are found in Africa across a 5-million-year period (Appendix 10 Figs 8 and 9). The first anatomically modern humans emerged in central east Africa about 200,000 years ago. They did not arrive in the Middle East until 100,000 years later (Appendix 10 Fig 10). The literal interpretation of Gen 1 and 2 claiming that humans were created *de novo* around 4000 BC in Mesopotamia is disproved by the anthropological data.

Archaeology. About 50,000 years ago, behaviorally-modern humans and their artifacts began to appear in Europe, Asia, and Australia (Appendix 9 Fig 2, Appendix 10 Fig 10). Similar evidence is found in North and South America 15,000 years ago. In the Middle East, well-established communities were in existence by 7000 BC. Again, the traditional view that Adam is the first human on earth around 4000 BC does not come close to the archaeological data.

History. Written records appear in Mesopotamia and Egypt roughly after 3000 BC. This body of ancient literature has creation accounts featuring the *de novo* origin of humans. Historical evidence for the Hebrews in the Middle East only appears around 1200 BC. It is clear that God's chosen people inherited the motifs-of-the-day to compose their origins accounts, including the quick and complete origin of humanity. In other words, belief in the existence of Adam is rooted in the ancient motif of *de novo* creation, and this notion originates ultimately from the nations surrounding the early Hebrews.

The biblical and scientific evidence does not support the historicity of Adam. Undoubtedly, all the inspired authors of Scripture believed that he had literally once existed. But this was the science and history-of-the-day. Nevertheless, Adam plays a vital role in the Bible. He is an incidental ancient vessel used by the Holy Spirit to reveal the Messages of Faith that

God created humans in His Image, they wilfully sin against Him, and He judges men and women for their sinfulness. To be sure, the conclusion that Adam never existed has significant implications for the events in Gen 3 and the origins of sin, suffering, and death. These are dealt with in the next chapter.

The Historicity of Noah

Compelling scriptural evidence for the traditional literal interpretation of Noah and the flood comes from Jesus Himself. The Lord warns:

> No one knows about that day or hour, not even the angels in heaven, nor the Son, but only the Father. As it was in the days of Noah, so it will be at the coming of the Son of Man. For in the days before the flood people were eating and drinking, marrying and giving in marriage, up to the day Noah entered the ark; and they knew nothing about what would happen until the flood came and took them all away. That is how it will be at the coming of the Son of Man. (Matt 24:36–39 [cf. Luke 17:26–27])

First, it must be noted that the authorial intention and context of this passage is not dealing with whether or not Noah and the flood were historical. Instead, Jesus is teaching about the end of the age and His return. Second, the Lord uses ancient categories in this revelation. He asserts earlier in the passage that in the last days "the stars will fall from the sky, and the heavenly bodies will be shaken" (v. 29) and that angels "will gather the elect from the four winds, from one end of the heavens to the other" (v. 31). Of course, this future event in history will not happen as stated literally because the universe does not have three tiers. In the same way, Jesus employs the ancient historical notion of a worldwide flood, which never literally occurred, to deliver His Message of Faith. Lastly, the Lord uses Noah's flood account typologically. Pointing back to the prologue of the deluge (Gen 6:1–8), He reveals that sin will be rampant in the world prior to the Second Coming, and humanity will be oblivious to the pending divine judgment.[25] Christians can be comforted because Noah is an archetype of God's saving grace to those who are righteous and obedient. Believers will be spared from the coming wrath at the final judgment.

The apostle Peter also offers persuasive biblical evidence for the traditional view that Noah was historical. In his first letter, he places the flood account alongside the historical reality of Christ's sacrificial death and resurrection. He writes:

> For Christ died for sins once for all, the righteous for the unrigh-teous, to bring you to God. He was put to death in the body but made alive by the Spirit, through whom also he went and preached to the spirits in prison who disobeyed long ago when God waited patiently in the days of Noah while the ark was being built. In it only a few people, eight in all, were saved through water, and this water *symbolizes* [Greek: *antitupos*] baptism that now saves you also—not the removal of dirt from the body but the pledge of a good conscience toward God. It saves you by the resurrection of Jesus Christ, who has gone into heaven and is at God's right hand—with angels, authorities and powers in submission to Him. (1 Pet 3:18–22; italics added)

Again, the context of this passage and the authorial intention show that it is not a debate about the historicity of Noah. The focus is upon Jesus' death on the Cross in order to conquer sin and death. In a subtle way, Peter employs the 3-tier universe to conceptualize events before and after Christ's resurrection. From his ancient category set, he envisions that the Lord descended into the underworld to preach and then ascended into heaven to sit at the side of God. Finally, Peter uses the flood account typo-logically. In fact, he states that the water of baptism is the "antitype" (i.e., the figurative fulfillment) of the floodwaters. Symbolically, it represents the judgment from which Christians are saved.

References to Noah and the flood by Jesus and Peter do not prove the historicity of this man or destructive event. Nor does their mention in the New Testament make Gen 6–9 historical. The existence of Noah and the reality of a worldwide deluge were facts of history for the Jews and early Christians. But these notions were part of an ancient understanding of history. The appearance of Noah and the flood in the New Testament does not confirm their reality or confer historicity to them any more than references to a 3-tier universe by Jesus and Peter establish this as the structure of the cosmos.[26]

A number of features in Gen 1–11 also point away from the his-toricity of Noah in the biblical flood account. To cite a few of the most significant:

Literary Genre. Literary genre dictates interpretation. Genesis 6–9 is centered in an ancient origins account. Bordered by recycled ancient Near

Eastern motifs that are neither scientifically nor historically accurate, consistency argues that this is also the case with Noah's worldwide flood.

Ancient History. The deluge is a central historical paradigm that appears throughout the ancient world. Real flooding events in susceptible regions and survivors of these undoubtedly lie behind many accounts. However, the Hebrews inherited the flood motif from their neighbors. Consequently, Noah at best represents an unknown individual/s who lived through a local flood/s, most likely in the Mesopotamian flood plain.

Contradictory Order of Flood Events. The events in Gen 6–9 conflict internally. In particular, the length of the flood in days and the Noahic dates cannot be arranged into a coherent chronology. This inconsistency is understandable because two different versions (J and P) lie behind the biblical flood account. With this being the case, it is clear that these chapters are not a record of actual events about Noah and a worldwide deluge.

Tribal Formation. Genesis 10 states that after the flood all of humanity descended from a single individual through his three sons. Placing Noah as the tribal head of everyone living today points away from his historicity because it is based on an ancient understanding of community origins.

Ancient Genealogies. Though the ancestral lineages in Gen 1–11 are manipulated and stylized, they likely include memories of some actual individuals from the distant pre-literate past. This is probably the case in regard to a real local flood survivor/s who is behind the biblical Noah. However, ancient genealogical features cast doubt on the historicity of events involving Noah: his position in Gen 5 as the tenth generation from Adam, his symbolic age of 600 years at the beginning of the deluge, and his fathering three sons in a way similar to Adam and Terah (Fig 6-12).

Traditional Literal Interpretation. The reading of Gen 6–9 as a literal historical record of Noah and the flood appears throughout Church history. Yet this is not surprising, since believers in all generations accepted the historicity of Gen 1–11. In fact, prior to the birth of modern geology in the eighteenth century, marine fossils on the tops of mountains and layers of stratification everywhere in the earth's crust offered reasonable evidence for a global flood.[27] But more importantly, the historicity of Noah never led to the formulation of doctrine or creed. This fact subtly points to the Holy Spirit's providentialistic guidance of the Church over time. Stated another way, the historical reality of Noah is not foundational to Christian faith.

Modern science also rejects the traditional and literal belief in the historicity of Noah as recorded in Gen 6–9. Some basic evidence includes:

Geology. Stratification in the earth's crust provides indisputable proof that a global flood obliterating all living organisms never occurred. Such a catastrophic event would have produced a fossil pattern similar to the prediction of young earth creation (Appendix 7 Fig 1). But no global flood layer exists. Thus, the account in Gen 6–9 of Noah surviving a worldwide deluge is not historical.

Anthropology. In the 200,000-year fossil record of anatomically modern humans, there is no evidence of the disruption of the entire world by a flood. As well, no proof exists that people living today arose from the Middle East in 2400 BC.[28] The anthropological data shows continuous human occupation on every continent for more than 50,000 years with the exception of Antarctica and the Americas (Appendix 10 Fig 11). Clearly, the idea that Noah repopulated the world through his three sons after a global flood is inaccurate.

Archaeology. Significant sedimentary layers near the Tigris and Euphrates Rivers indicate that human occupation has been disrupted at different times by local inundations. These deposits date from 3500–2600 BC. It is almost certain such a destructive event/s and an actual survivor/s led to various Mesopotamian flood accounts. Since the Hebrews inherited and sanctified the flood motif from her surrounding neighbors, Noah and the biblical deluge likely represent a vaguely remembered individual/s from the distant past who lived through a local flood/s on the Tigris and/or Euphrates Rivers.

History. Written Mesopotamian flood accounts predate the first historical record of the Hebrews by many centuries. The Sumerian Flood, Epic of Atrahasis, and Epic of Gilgamesh were composed between 2000–1600 BC, while mention of Israel in the ancient Near East does not appear until 1200 BC. As well, evidence for Hebrew literacy is only found after the latter date. The numerous parallels between the Mesopotamian versions and Gen 6–9 indicate that God's chosen people inherited the notion of a worldwide flood. In other words, the person of Noah is rooted in an ancient motif that originates from the nations neighboring the early Hebrews.

To conclude, Scripture and science do not support the historicity of Noah as described in Gen 6–9. Of course, every biblical author believed that he existed and survived a world-destroying flood on an ark. But this was the history-of-the-day for the Jews and early Christians. At best, Noah points back to an obscure individual/s who lived through a local deluge/s, most likely in the Mesopotamian flood plain. But more importantly, the biblical flood is an incidental vessel that reveals the inspired message that God judges human sin and saves righteous individuals from His wrath.

CHAPTER SUMMARY

Recognizing and respecting the ancient Near Eastern motifs in the first chapters of Scripture moves the relationship between Gen 1–11 and history beyond conflict and concordism. *De novo* creation, the lost idyllic age, the great flood, and tribal formation were the best historical paradigms-of-the-day a few thousand years ago. These reconstructions of the past are quite logical. They retroject an ancient phenomenological perspective of the world, an ancient notion of causality, and the experience of spiritual phenomena (natural/moral revelation, personal divine action). The Hebrews inherited this ancient history from surrounding nations, and like all historiography, interpreted it in the light of their metaphysical beliefs and values. Consequently, the opening chapters of the Bible are not a factual account of the origin of humans and their first activities. Evidence from modern science and history complements this conclusion by demonstrating that historical concordism fails. Instead, the purpose of Gen 1–11 is to reveal the ultimate nature of men and women, and their relationship with the Creator.

For the most part, the inspired human authors and redactor of Gen 1–11 intended to write a literal and historical record of the origin of the world and the Hebrew community. The New Testament writers and the Church throughout the ages also understood this to be the case. But evidence within the Bible itself and data from science and history demonstrate that the literal reading of Gen 1–11 as a historical account produces internal contradictions and does not align with external reality. Today, Christians must read beyond the human authorial intention and literal historiography. The literary genre of the opening chapters of Scripture is complex. It is an ancient origins account built on recycled ancient motifs under the guidance of the Holy Spirit. In particular, believers need to understand that the attribution of divine and human acts in Gen 1–11 is cast in and shaped by the motifs. Stated incisively: most of the people mentioned never existed in history, and most of the events never literally happened. To be sure, this is a very counterintuitive and even threatening way to approach Scripture.

The revelatory power of Gen 1–11 is not dependent upon these chapters being literal and historical, but on the inerrant and infallible Messages of Faith. Rejecting the historicity of Adam does not in any way undermine the facts that God created humanity in His Image and that humans are sinful. Similarly, acknowledging that there is no evidence for a literal Noah and worldwide flood does not negate the divine revelation that the Creator judges sinners and protects the righteous from His judgment. Adam and Noah are typological. These two central biblical figures are Holy Spirit inspired pictures defining the foundations of human spirituality. Undoubtedly, debate over the historicity of Adam and Noah will continue for many years. Yet Christians must never lose perspective on this issue. We are first and foremost Christ-ians, and not Adam-ites or Noah-ites. Adam never died on the Cross for our sins; Noah never rose from the dead to give us hope of eternal life. But Jesus did in history during the first century.

Evolutionary creation embraces an Incarnational approach to Gen 1–11. These chapters are the inerrant and infallible Word of God accommodated to an incidental historiography that was conceived by ancient humans. The use of this ancient understanding of history in the revelatory process sets a significant precedent. It opens the door for Christians to employ the modern conception of human origins as an incidental vessel in delivering the Divine Theology of Gen 1–11 to our generation. In this way, the creation of humankind in the Image of God and the entrance of sin into the world can be viewed in light of geology, anthropology, and evolutionary biology. The next chapter explores this new and refreshing approach.

8

A Christian Approach to Human Evolution

THE CREATION OF HUMANITY is an explosive and divisive topic in the origins debate today. Most Christians tenaciously defend that God created Adam and Eve as stated in Scripture.[1] The thought that we have evolved from ape-like creatures is usually perceived as a threat to our dignity. For many, this idea reduces us to "nothing but" animals controlled by physical impulses. In some Christian institutions, simply questioning whether or not we descend from Adam and Eve can lead to disciplinary action against a pastor, teacher, or professor. In fact, individuals like me have been barred from teaching in denominational colleges and seminaries because we accept human evolution.[2]

Despite the volatility of the issue of human origins, four theological principles unite all Christians. First and foremost, God created humanity. We are not an accident and merely the result of blind chance. It was the Lord's plan and purpose to make people. Second, humans have been created in the Image of God. We are the only creatures that enjoy such a privileged status. This principle stands in sharp contrast to the atheistic belief that we are nothing but animals, and it commands us to respect both others and ourselves. Third, men and women are sinners. We have all rebelled against our Creator, sinned against other human beings, and even violated the creation. Everyone is responsible for their actions, and each is in control over their physical instincts and desires. On the day of judgment, God will call on us to give an account for our conduct. Finally, only Jesus offers redemption from sin. As Acts 4:12 states, "Salvation is found in no one else, for there is no other name under heaven given to men by which we must be saved."

DYSTELEOLOGICAL EVOLUTION	EVOLUTIONARY CREATION
Atheistic	Christian
Driven by Blind Chance	Ordained & Sustained by God
"Nothing but" animals controlled by physical instincts	Created in the Image of God & fallen into sin

HUMAN EVOLUTION

Fig 8-1. Human Evolution: Two Interpretive Approaches. The popular assumption both inside and outside the Church is that human evolution is dysteleological, and that men and women are ultimately a meaningless fluke of nature. In contrast, evolutionary creationists assert that God ordained and sustained a teleological process of evolution that led ultimately to the creation of humanity, who bear His Image and have all fallen into sin. This diagram reflects the Metaphysics-Physics Principle. The science of human evolution is based on observations and experiments from a wide range of disciplines, including geology, palaeontology, genetics, evolutionary biology, etc. The ultimate belief in whether this natural process is teleological or dysteleological requires an intellectual-spiritual "jump" from this physical evidence to its metaphysical assessment.

Regrettably, the origins dichotomy has entrenched in the mind of most people the belief that God would never have created humans through evolution. This popular either/or approach also prevents many from entertaining the possibility that the Image of God and human sin could have been manifested during an evolutionary process leading to the emergence of men and women. However, the origins dichotomy is a false dichotomy. It blinds Christians from seeing the scientific evidence for human evolution, and it puts a stumbling block between non-Christians familiar with this data and an understanding of their true spiritual nature. As a corrective, evolutionary creation offers a fresh approach to human origins. It asserts that physical evidence for human evolution is convincing, powerful, and indeed overwhelming. Appendix 10 introduces some of this data. Evolutionary creation also claims that God created humanity through a teleological natural process, which He ordained and sustained, resulting in creatures bearing His Image but fallen into sin. Fig 8-1 contrasts this Christian view of human evolution against the atheistic interpretation assumed by many today.[3]

Another common misconception fuels the controversy over human origins. Most people assume that the theory of evolution claims we

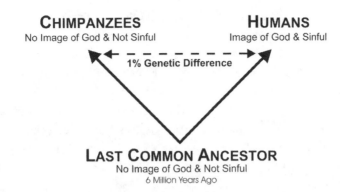

CHIMPANZEES
No Image of God & Not Sinful

HUMANS
Image of God & Sinful

1% Genetic Difference

LAST COMMON ANCESTOR
No Image of God & Not Sinful
6 Million Years Ago

Fig 8-2. Evolution of Chimpanzees and Humans: Physical Features and Spiritual Realities. The Image of God and sinfulness are manifested only along the line leading to humans from the last common ancestor leading to humans. Note that in actuality this line represents numerous branches like a tree and includes many pre-humans found in the fossil record (see Appendix 10 Figs 7 and 8).

evolved from monkeys. Not true. Humans and monkeys emerged on separate evolutionary lines that split about 30 million years ago (Appendix 10, Fig 5). However, it is true that they are our distant relatives. Actually, chimpanzees are our closest evolutionary "cousins" (about 250,000th cousin) with which we share a common ancestor that lived around 6 million years ago. Of course, this fact often provokes a gut reaction. To put it in popular language, the idea that we are related to chimps "creeps out" a lot of people. Yet there is another way to view this situation. Fig 8-2 outlines physical and spiritual relationships between humans, chimpanzees, and their last common ancestor as understood by evolutionary creation. Instead of threatening Christian faith, evolution complements theological principles in regard to the ultimate nature of men and women.

Science reveals that humans and chimpanzees share about 99% of the same genes. In fact, we have some matching genetic errors, termed "pseudogenes," indicating that these were inherited from our common ancestor (Appendix 10). Thus, the Lord has evolved a creature that *in the flesh* is nearly identical to us. But is there any doubt that we are radically different from chimps? For example, has anyone ever read a chimp poem or enjoyed a chimp love song? Where are the chimpanzee food banks, hospitals, and universities? Are chimps sending spacecrafts to distant planets? Have they ever started a world war? Do chimps create environmental crises because of flagrant greed? Have these primates developed moral systems denouncing hatred? Or how about chimp religion? Is there chimpanzee praise and worship music? Do chimps have prophets through whom God revealed His will? Did a chimp messiah die for their sins? Are all these behavioral differences between humans and chimpanzees simply accounted for in a 1% difference in genes? Hardly.

Obviously a radical shift occurred along the human evolutionary line that led eventually to us and our extraordinary achievements and disgraceful failures. There is no archaeological evidence to indicate that this happened with the last common ancestor, and none on the chimpanzee branch of evolution. According to evolutionary creation, God created only humans "in His own image" and "likeness" (Gen 1:26–27). Men and women reflect aspects of the Creator's character such as spirituality, morality, rationality, and personality. In particular, we enjoy the gift of boundless creative potential.[4] In addition, humans are radically different from chimps and our common ancestor because we are the only sinful creatures in the world. As the apostle Paul states, "All have sinned and fall short of the glory of God" (Rom 3:23). We are capable of the most heinous transgressions imaginable. Therefore, instead of being a threat to Christianity, human evolutionary science complements the Bible in revealing that WE ARE SO MUCH MORE THAN MERE FLESH!!!

This chapter presents a Christian approach to human evolution. It opens by examining the manifestation of God's Image and humanity's sinfulness during the evolutionary process. Appealing to the use of ancient motifs in Gen 1–11 as a precedent, inerrant and infallible Messages of Faith are recast within a modern motif—the evolution of life. Next, an attempt is made to justify why the all-loving and all-powerful God of the Bible would have created humanity through a process marked by violent competition, natural selection, and survival of the fittest. Of course, making sense of suffering and pain never comes to a completely satisfying conclusion. Mystery is a significant factor. Nevertheless, insights drawn from Scripture bring some perspective on the character of biological evolution. The chapter closes with the sin-death problem. Genesis 3 clearly states that Adam's sin led to the beginning of physical death, and Paul restates this notion in Rom 5–8 and 1 Cor 15. But science demonstrates that death was in the world hundreds of millions of years prior to the appearance of humans. Without a doubt, this is the most challenging problem faced by evolutionary creation, and providing a reasonable solution is critical.

THE MANIFESTATION OF THE IMAGE
OF GOD AND HUMAN SIN

A majority of Christians claim that human evolution cannot be reconciled with the foundational beliefs that we bear the Image of God and that we are sinners. Historical concordism undergirds this assumption. These believers conflate Messages of Faith concerning the spiritual nature of humanity with their unbending acceptance of the historicity of Adam. But they fail to recognize and respect the ancient history in Gen 1–11. In contrast, evolutionary creation rejects the popular literal interpretation of the biblical creation accounts and separates the Divine Theology from the incidental ancient understanding of human origins. This Christian approach contends that an appreciation of the metaphysical essence of God's Image and humanity's sinfulness, coupled with an awareness of our epistemological limits in fully comprehending these spiritual characteristics, opens a way to consider their manifestation during human evolution.[5]

The Image of God and human sin are metaphysical realities. Stated more precisely, they are spiritual realities. Even though they are very real, they are not like physical entities or objects. Neither can be placed in a test tube to have its weight or volume measured, nor are they located in any particular organ or part of the human body. God's Image and human sinfulness are not like a virus that can be passed through a cough, a blood transfusion, or touching of hands. Nor are they found in genes that are inherited from generation to generation. As metaphysical realities, the Image of God and human sin are beyond and behind our physical reality, yet at the same time they are intimately related to our material being since it is through our bodies that we both reflect the Creator's likeness and break His commandments. Therefore, it is by definition impossible to detect directly the Image of God and human sinfulness through the methods of science.

Human embryological development offers insights into the metaphysical nature of God's Image and human sin. Illuminating questions can be asked: While in our mother's womb, when do we begin to bear the Image of God? Do we get one-half an Image from her egg cell and the other half from our father's sperm cell? Or does our Maker inject divine likeness in a *punctiliar* (i.e., one precise point) manner in development, such as at fertilization, two-cell stage, first heartbeat, or beginning of brain activity? Or does God's Image originate in a gradual fashion across many embryological stages? Similarly, when do we become sinners? Do we get one-half a sin from the egg and the other half from sperm? Or do humans become sinners at one specific moment in time like fertilization, two-cell stage, etc.? Or do we slowly become morally accountable and then sinful? Fig 8-3A summarizes this range of possibilities for the manifestation of human spiritual characteristics during embryological development.[6]

Many Christians recognize that there are no clear and definitive answers to these questions. No biblical passage reveals when, where, or how each of us begins to bear the Image of God during embryological development, or when, where, or how we first fall into sin. As noted in the fourth chapter, Scripture's view of reproductive biology is an ancient understanding (1-seed theory), and therefore it cannot address these questions because they are informed by modern science.[7] In addition, notice how these questions are cast in categories that are typical of scientific investigation—when? where? and how? They attempt to treat the non-physical realities of God's Image and human sin almost like physical entities or objects. This is not to say that these questions should not be asked, since all honest questions are good questions. To be sure, there is manifestation of the Image of God and sin as humans develop. But trying to use precise scientific categories to understand metaphysical realities is categorically inappropriate.

Nevertheless, these unanswerable questions are informative. They thrust us to the edge of our human ability to know, and they force us to deal with the category of mystery. We have a creaturely epistemology, and consequently our knowledge is limited. As Paul recognizes, "We know in part . . . we see but a poor reflection" (1 Cor 13:9, 12). Scripture affirms the reality of mysteries and employs this term over 30 times (e.g., Job 11:7; Dan 2:28; 1 Cor 13:2). This is not to say that human knowledge has no value; God created us with the ability to know Him and His world both truly and sufficiently. Rather, it is to underline that our knowledge cannot penetrate all aspects of reality during this earthly existence. We will never grasp every facet of God's "ways and thoughts" (Isa 55:8–9). Embracing the category of mystery is not an "easy way out" or a surrendering to incompetence and ignorance in order to account for something we could understand. Instead, it reflects God's ordained limits on human knowledge. The problems that arise in understanding the manifestation of the Image of God and sin during human development leads to the conclusion that it is ultimately mysterious.

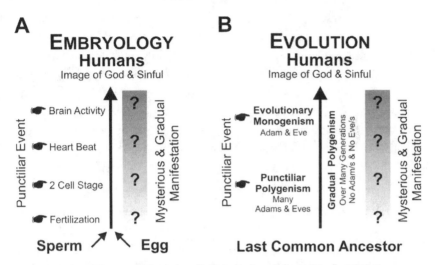

Fig 8-3. Origin of Human Spiritual Realities in Embryology and Evolution. Many possibilities exist for conceptualizing the manifestation of the Image of God and human sin. The embryological stages presented in (A) are arbitrary and any other points/periods in development could be used. This is also the case with the evolutionary line (B) from the last common ancestor that humans share with chimpanzees. There is no attempt in this latter diagram to define actual times/epochs for the manifestation of spiritual realities during human evolution.

This epistemological limitation sheds light on the appearance of spiritual realities during human evolution. Instructive questions can also be asked: When exactly did the ancestors of humans begin to bear God's Image? Five million years ago? Three million years ago? When they began to develop stone tools? At the hunter-gatherer stage? How was divine likeness given to the precursors of humans? Was it implanted in one punctiliar act in one single pre-human couple? Or did it come about through a gradual manifestation across numerous generations? Similarly, when did non-human ancestors become morally responsible and then fall into sin? Five million years ago, three million years ago, etc.? Did sin enter the world at one precise point because of one single act of rebellion against God? Or did humanity slowly become accountable and sinful as a group across many generations?

Note again that these questions subtly feature the assumption that God's Image and human sinfulness are like physical entities or objects that can be understood using science-like categories—when? where? and how? But as with embryological development, spiritual realities are not open to this type of precise analysis. In addition, the Bible does not shed any light on these modern questions because human origins are cast in ancient science and ancient history. Yet this is not to say that the questions above are not good and fair questions. In fact, they must be asked because they offer insights. These questions bring us once more to the edge of our creaturely ability to know, and they place before us another mystery. In the same way that we cannot fully conceive the manifestation of the Image of God and sin during embryological development, the appearance of these spiritual realities through human evolution is as mysterious.

Models on Spiritual Origins in Human Evolution

In order to examine further the emergence of human spirituality during the evolutionary process, Fig 8-3B outlines three basic models. The parallels to development in the womb are evident. It is important to note that the line between the last common ancestor and modern humans represents a significant number of pre-human transitional creatures (see Appendix 10 Figs 7 and 8). These models include:

Evolutionary Monogenism (Greek: *monos* "one" *genesis* "beginning"). This position suggests that God at one point in time selected a single pair of individuals from a population of evolving pre-humans.[8] He then intervened dramatically to implant His Image and in an instant made them morally accountable. Soon afterwards, these two humans sinned through a specific rebellious act. The remaining pre-humans became extinct, and everyone today descends from this first couple who are identified as Adam and Eve.[9]

Punctiliar Polygenism (Greek: *polus* "many" *genesis* "beginning").[10] According to this view, the Creator at one point in time interventionistically embedded His Image into all evolving pre-humans or a select group of these individuals. At that precise moment these beings were made morally responsible, but everyone soon sinned. This understanding of human origins suggests that there was one generation of many "Adams" and "Eves."

Gradual Polygenism. This approach asserts that the Image of God and human sinfulness were gradually and mysteriously manifested through many generations of evolving ancestors. The origin of spiritual characteristics that define and distinguish humanity is not marked by a single punctiliar event in history. Rather, these metaphysical realities arose slowly and in a way that cannot be fully comprehended. Their manifestation during human evolution is similar to that in embryological development. Consequently, there never was an Adam/s or Eve/s.

Evolutionary creation embraces gradual polygenism. This approach is free from the assumption that the first chapters of the Bible feature scientific and historical concordism. In contrast, evolutionary monogenism and punctiliar polygenism are concordist models, in varying degrees. Both appeal to punctiliar events in Gen 1–3: the quick and complete origin of humans bearing God's Image and the fall of Adam and Eve into sin. However, the creation of humanity at one precise point in time as recorded in Gen 1 and 2 is an ancient understanding of origins—*de novo* creation. And since the existence of Adam and Eve is ultimately dependent on this ancient science, then obviously their punctiliar fall into sin has no historical basis because they never existed in the first place. Evolutionary monogenism and punctiliar polygenism are proof text uses of Scripture that tear these punctiliar events out of their ancient intellectual context and conflate them with the current theory of human evolution. These models mix together ancient science and modern science. The problem with this interpretive method is the same as any attempt to conflate the *de novo* creation of the firmament in Gen 1 with Big Bang cosmology. It is hermeneutically inappropriate.

Original Sin and Other Issues

An evolutionary creationist approach to human spiritual origins raises a number of issues. In particular, gradual polygenism views the traditional Christian doctrine of original sin in a new light. It must be underlined that theological formulations have a human element, and that they should always be open to revision as the knowledge of Scripture and science advances. Significantly, the category "original sin" is not in the Bible. This doctrine was formulated by St. Augustine (354–430 AD) at a time when *de novo* creation was the science-of-the-day.[11] Throughout most of history, the Church has firmly upheld his understanding of original sin, but so too this ancient science of human origins. Consequently, a reconsideration of Augustine's doctrine can occur only after science presents a better understanding of the origin of humanity. This situation is similar to the reinterpretation of biblical passages referring to an immovable earth. It happened following the rejection of geocentricity by seventeenth century astronomy.

In light of the discovery of human evolution, evolutionary creation proposes a reformulation of the notion of original sin. First, this position separates the Message of Faith in Gen 3—all humans are sinners—from its underlying ancient motifs of *de novo* creation and the lost idyllic age. Clearly, Augustine's view of original sin was intimately connected, if not conflated, to these ancient scientific and historical paradigms. Second, evolutionary creation places the inerrant spiritual truth of human sinfulness within an incidental modern scientific vessel—the gradual evolution of humankind. Viewed in this way, the entrance of sin into the world was not a punctiliar event committed by two individuals. Instead, original sin was manifested mysteriously and gradually over countless many generations during the evolutionary processes leading to men and women.

To be sure, gradual polygenism is a challenging notion to most Christians. Three other issues are often raised regarding this understanding of human origins. These concerns are reasonable, but evolutionary creationists propose a solution for each:

If Adam did not exist, then he did not sin and there is no need for Jesus' dying on the Cross. Evolutionary creation argues that the central purpose of Gen 3 and the garden of Eden account is to reveal that all men and women are sinners. Therefore, everyone needs to be redeemed by the Blood of the Lamb. Gradual polygenism affirms the reality of sin, and that sin did indeed enter the world during human evolution. However, this entrance was not due to one punctiliar, rebellious event committed by one man.

If we do not know exactly when the Image of God and human sin entered the world, then these spiritual characteristics do not exist. This complaint can be recast in the context of human embryological development: If we do not know exactly when each of us starts to bear God's Image and becomes a sinner, then these spiritual characteristics do not exist. Of course, no Christian would accept such a proposition. The fact that Scripture does not reveal when each of us begins to manifest these metaphysical features does not undermine their reality. Gradual polygenism asserts that the Image of God and human sin are non-negotiable principles of the Christian faith.

If human spiritual characteristics emerged gradually over countless many generations, then the eternal destiny of extinct "transitional" creatures is problematic. Determining the eternal destiny of anyone rests with God alone, not humans. Development in the womb again provides an insight. Roughly 50% of fertilized eggs eventually result in miscarriages.[12] What is their status in eternity? This is another good question, but clearly in the realm of mystery. Similarly, the eternal destiny of extinct beings, some of whom appear to have expressed modest religious behavior, is beyond human comprehension and ultimately not a problem for gradual polygenism.[13]

By respecting the purpose and limits of both Scripture and science, evolutionary creation offers an integrated approach to the origin of human spiritual uniqueness. Free from scientific and historical concordism in the biblical creation accounts, it is not forced to envision the manifestation of the Image of God and human sin as punctiliar events in history. Instead, this Christian view of origins asserts that spiritual characteristics arose mysteriously and gradually during human evolution. Despite our intellectual limitation in understanding fully their entrance into the world, two foundational beliefs exist: we are the only creatures who have been created in God's Image, and we are the only creatures who have sinned and are in need of a Savior.

SUFFERING AND DEATH IN EVOLUTION

A serious challenge faced by evolutionary creation is to justify why the all-loving and all-powerful God of the Bible would have created life, including humans, through a violent, wasteful, and senselessly competitive process like evolution. The inordinate amount of time needed for living organisms to evolve magnifies this problem. For a large number of non-Christians, the present suffering in the world is the main stumbling block to faith, and this aspect of biological evolution leads them further away from their Creator. Equally troubled, many Christians reject evolution on moral grounds and argue that a Holy God would never use such a wicked and merciless method to create a "very good" world and humans bearing His Image (Gen 1:27, 31). This is certainly an acute concern for evolutionary creation.

The opening section draws insights from Scripture and science in order to show that there are parallel issues that assist believers in coming to terms with the notion that the Lord created life through a process that includes suffering and death. Next, biblical passages that deal directly with the purpose of pain and mortality are examined. The closing section proposes an evolutionary creationist approach to understanding suffering and death in evolution.

Biblical Insights

Most Christians are repulsed by the evolutionary concepts of natural selection and the survival of the fittest, and quickly dismiss the thought that God would use such cruel mechanisms in creating life and humans. However, the ultimate purpose of the Christian faith must be considered in this discussion. Does the gospel message not include notions that could be termed "spiritual selection" and "the survival of the spiritually fittest"? At the final judgment, are sheep not going to be separated from goats (Matt 25:31–46)? Will wheat not be brought into the barn whilst weeds are bundled and burned (Matt 13:24–30)? And people, whose names are not in the "book of life," are they not going to be thrown into the lake of fire (Rev 20:15)? Few Christians relish the thought of eternal damnation. But it is a harsh reality ordained by God to serve His purpose in creating a body of individuals to enjoy eternity with Him. As believers come to terms with the reality that many will be lost forever, their justification for this harsh future reality can be applied to the evolutionary process, putting some divine perspective on natural selection and the survival of the fittest.

Christians must also consider the suffering and death associated with the sacrificial system that God commanded in the Old Testament. To mention only a few examples: Every morning and evening the Jews burned an innocent lamb in order to offer "an aroma pleasing to the Lord" (Num 28:8). The seven day feasts of Passover and Tabernacles witnessed the slaughter of 8 goats, 15 rams, 71 bullocks, and 105 lambs (Num 28–29).[14] And for poor people like Joseph and Mary, a pair of blameless doves or pigeons were destroyed following the birth of a child, one as a burnt offering and the other as a sin offering (Lev 12:8). However, the New Testament reveals the inadequacy of animal sacrifice. As Heb 10:11 states, "Day after day every priest stands and performs his religious duties; again and again he offers the same sacrifices, *which can never take away sins*" (italics added). In other words, countless creatures have been wasted in a sacrificial system that has never atoned for one single sin. And since God does not permit one single sparrow to fall to the ground against His will (Matt 10:29), it is clear that He was fully aware of the suffering and death of sacrificial animals, including the two doves or pigeons required for purification after the birth of Jesus (Luke 2:22–24). Yet the Lord allowed it because these sacrifices had a purpose—they were a "reminder of sins" (Heb 10:3). Similarly, pain and mortality in evolution might fulfill another divine purpose.

God's creative methods today offer further insights into evolutionary suffering and death. Science reveals that the processes of reproduction and development include wastage, competition, pain, and mortality. Every menstrual cycle destroys an egg, blood, and womb tissue. Millions of sperm cells are wasted in ejaculation, and after a competitive race to the egg only one is necessary for fertilization. As noted previously, 50% of fertilized eggs die in the womb. Pregnancy and birth are agonizing and excruciating physical processes. Most significantly, the death of cells is programmed into genes, and it is an indispensable creative mechanism (termed "apoptosis") during embryological development. For example, if the tissue between finger bones did not die, then our hands would only be paddles. In other words, cell death is an ordained and sustained process used by God in "knitting us together in our mother's womb" to become "fearfully and wonderfully made" (Ps 139:13–14).

Ecological science also reveals insight into suffering and death. Predation is necessary in sustaining life on earth, and Scripture affirms it as part of God's good plan. In fact, the psalmist sees the Creator involved in feeding all creatures, including those that prey on others.

> You [God] bring darkness, it becomes night,
>   and all the beasts of the forest prowl.
> The lions roar for their prey
>   and seek their food from God. . . .
> There is the sea, vast and spacious,
>   teeming with creatures beyond number—
>   living things both large and small. . . .
> These all look to You to give them
>   their food at the proper time.
> When You give it to them, they gather it up;
>   when You open Your hand,
>   they are satisfied with good things. (Ps 104:20–21, 25, 27–28)

> The eyes of all look to You [God],
>   and You give them their food at the proper time.
> You open Your hand and satisfy the desires
>   of every living thing.
> The Lord is righteous in all His ways and loving
>   to all He has made. (Ps 145:15–17)

Many will find it difficult to believe that predatory attacks are "righteous," "loving," and "good things." In particular, biblical writers knew of the violent nature of lions. These animals "devour prey" (Num 23:24), "break bones" (Isa 38:13), and "rip and tear to pieces" (Ps 7:2) other living organisms. But Scripture indicates that predation is part of God's ordained and sustained plan. Thus, Christians need to re-evaluate their assumptions about the notion of "goodness" as it relates to the biological world. In this way, the suffering and death associated with evolution can be viewed in a new light, and even be seen as a good aspect of the Lord's method of creation.

Coming to terms with the moral implications of evolution is certainly a challenge, but Christians must never forget the Bible reveals that God's creative activities in making a holy people included suffering and death. The creation of a territory for Israel to inhabit involved obeying the divine commandment to wipe out completely the nations in the land of Canaan: "You must destroy them totally. Make no treaty with them and show them no mercy" (Deut 7:2). The violent and vicious character of the Israelite invasion is typified by the fall of Jericho. Scripture records, "They devoted the city to the Lord and destroyed with the sword every living thing in it—men and women, young and old, cattle, sheep and donkeys" (Josh 7:21). And the Bible acknowledges God's part in the ruthless destruction of this city. In setting up the attack, the Lord states to Joshua, "See, I have delivered Jericho into your hands" (Josh 6:2). Most would agree that the agony and terror launched upon this city was not only excessive, but even senseless. Why waste animals and innocent children?

The creation of the Church is also linked to suffering and death. It begins with the birth of Jesus prophesied hundreds of years earlier by Isaiah (Isa 7:14). But King Herod's ruthless slaughter of children in an attempt to murder the Lord is also foretold through Jeremiah. As Matthew writes:

> When Herod realized that he had been outwitted by the Magi, he was furious, and he gave orders to kill all the boys in Bethlehem and its vicinity who were two years and under, in accordance with the time he had learned from the Magi. Then what was said through the prophet Jeremiah was fulfilled:
>
> > A voice is heard in Ramah, weeping and great mourning,
> > Rachel weeping for her children and refusing to be comforted
> > because they are no more [Jer 31:15]. (Matt 2:16–18)

Again, senseless and excessive suffering and death are associated with God's creative activity, and even prophesied. Why did He stand aside and allow innocent children to be murdered and their mothers overwhelmed with heartache? Just so that the Scripture could be fulfilled?

Finally, God's creation of the New Testament covenant is founded on the suffering and death of an innocent Man. The most vile and violent act in the Bible is the crucifixion of Jesus. Also prophesied by Isaiah, "It was the Lord's will to crush Him and cause Him to suffer" even "though He had done no violence, nor was any deceit in His mouth" (Isa 53:9–10). That is, the Father ordained ahead of time the torture and execution of His Son. The creation of the new covenant, that Christians enjoy today, is a covenant based on the shedding of innocent Blood.

To summarize, if believers are distressed by the unmerciful nature of biological evolution, they should also be deeply troubled by the suffering and death connected to God's creative and sustaining action in the natural world today and the formation of a holy people in the past. In particular, if the ruthless character of the evolution of life, most of which falls upon animals, is really a good reason to reject evolution as historically true, then how do Christians come to terms with the historicity of the cruel Old Testament sacrificial system and the violent eradication of men, women, and children in the conquest of Canaan, especially since both were willed by the Lord? And most importantly, how can believers justify in clinging to the historical reality of the Cross and its supreme brutality to the Father's own dear Son, a critical event that also was His will? Making peace with these scriptural facts offers insights into dealing with disturbing evolutionary notions like natural selection and the survival of the fittest. In doing so, Christians will come to realize that concerns about biological evolution simply pale and gradually dissipate.

Theodicy: Coming To Terms with Suffering and Death

Christians have wrestled with the problem of suffering and death since well before the discovery of biological evolution and the challenges to faith that this scientific theory presents. This dilemma can be stated as follows:

- If God is completely good, then He must want to eliminate suffering and death.

- If God is unlimitedly powerful, then He must be able to eliminate suffering and death.

      ☞ However, suffering and death exist.

            Therefore, God is not completely good and/or He is not unlimitedly powerful.

In acknowledging the weight of this problem, theologians throughout history have attempted to justify their belief in a personal God by offering rational explanations termed "theodicies" (Greek: *theos* "God" *dikē* "justice"). These defenses often begin by distinguishing between human evil (murder, greed, rape, etc.) and natural evil (earthquakes, hurricanes, birth defects, etc.), and then they usually provide different reasons for the origin and purpose of suffering and death.

Augustine proposed the most influential theodicy in the history of Christianity. He asserted that God created a world that was *originally perfect*, but Adam's sin in the garden of Eden led to the entrance of suffering and death. Commonly termed the cosmic fall, human evil is causally connected to natural evil and the disruption of the entire creation. Clearly, Augustine's theodicy is dependent on a strict literal interpretation of Gen 3. But scientific and historical concordism are not features of Gen 1–11, leaving this traditional theodicy without a foundation in reality. In addition, there is a serious moral problem with Augustine's approach. Does a just and righteous God condemn the whole creation, including every subsequent generation of humans, to suffering and death because one man committed one sin at one point in the distant past? Is it reasonable and equitable that the excruciating pain experienced by women in childbirth is due to Eve's rebellion? Does the sin of Adam cause an innocent baby in the womb to be stricken by cancer and die before birth?

The Bible does not deal with theodicy in an explicit and systematic fashion. Instead, Scripture presents a developing approach to understanding suffering and death that finds its ultimate fulfillment in the teaching and life of Jesus. The notion that biblical revelation is progressive is central to Christian faith. The fact that Scripture is made up of the Old and New Testaments is proof that God reveals in stages. Theological development appears with the strict Levitical laws observed by Israel ("unclean" foods of Lev 11) later giving way to the freeing spirit of the law enjoyed by the Church ("Jesus declared all foods 'clean'" Mark 7:19; see also Rom 14:14). The simple offerings in the early chapters of Genesis (4:3–5, 8:20) progress to the complex sacrificial system instituted by Moses, including the slaughter of bulls and goats to atone for sin (Lev 4). These practices are subsequently replaced by the once for all sacrifice on the Cross. In fact, the New Testament reveals the ineffectiveness of the Mosaic system because "it was impossible for the blood of bulls to take away sin" (Heb 10:4). Even ethical practices evolve in Scripture. Adulterers and adulteresses were to be stoned to death according to the Old Covenant (Deut 22:22), while Jesus commands a woman caught in adultery simply to "leave her life of sin" (John 8:11).

Similarly, theodicy develops through the Bible. There are *roughly* three basic stages that can be identified: (1) the fall of Adam and Eve, (2) the trials of Job, and (3) the teaching and life of Jesus.[15]

The first theodicy in Scripture appears in Gen 3 with the rebellion and judgment of Adam and Eve. The central purpose of this account is to reveal the reality that we are all sinners and that God judges our sin. But in an implicit way, it also deals with the two most challenging questions that people have wrestled with throughout history. First, why do we suffer? In particular, why do mothers experience pain in giving birth? Why are fields infested with thorns and thistles? And why is work necessary and painful? Second, why do we die? Humans are the only creatures who recognize their inevitable death, and history reveals countless ways in which they have attempted to overcome their mortality. The answer Gen 3 offers for these fundamental questions of existence is that God introduced suffering and death into the world because Adam and Eve sinned. It is ultimately a divine judgment. Consequently, and without any apology whatsoever, the Gen 3 theodicy features a causal connection between sins committed in the garden of Eden and our daily suffering and inescapable death.

The second stage of theodicy in Scripture appears in the book of Job.[16] Well-known for its treatment of the problem of human suffering, God gives Satan permission to test Job's faithfulness through a series of horrific afflictions. These include the destruction and theft of his possessions, the death of his children, and his own debilitating disease. Though an evil being is still associated with the harsh realities of life, the Bible is now intimating that there is purpose behind suffering and death. These circumstances are used to test faith. In attempting to understand and justify Job's dreadful situation, his friends repeatedly echo the theodicy of Gen 3—sin causes suffering and death.[17] However, the inspired author clearly indicates that this view is inadequate. In the final chapters of the book (38–41), God addresses Job. Most significantly, the Creator never appeals to Gen 3 and the sin of Adam as a cause or justification for the destruction, death, and suffering that engulfed Job.

Instead, God offers a non-verbal theodicy. He simply points to the physical world and asks Job about its origins and operations. Stated another way, the Creator employs intelligent design in nature to reveal His sovereignty over the entire creation, and by implication, suffering and death as well. Humbled by this line of divine interrogation, Job recognizes the mysterious aspect of theodicy. He confesses, "Surely I spoke of things I did not understand, things too wonderful for me to know" (Job 42:3). Yet despite this limitation, design in nature offers Job comfort and a way of coming to terms with his afflictions and pain. The book of Job is evidence that theodicy in Scripture advances beyond Gen 3 and the causal connection between sin and the brutal realities of suffering and death.

Biblical theodicy comes to fulfillment in Jesus. Common belief in the first century continued to intimate notions gleaned from Gen 3. But as Luke records, the Lord moved beyond the notion that sin causes suffering and death:

> Now there were some present at the time who told Jesus about the Galileans whose blood Pilate had mixed with their sacrifices. Jesus answered, "Do you think that these Galileans were worse sinners than all the other Galileans because they suffered this way? I tell you, no! But unless you repent, you too will all perish. Or those eighteen who died when the tower in Siloam fell on them—do you think they were more guilty than all the others living in Jerusalem? I tell you, no! But unless you repent, you too will all perish." (Luke 13:1–5)

Jesus disconnects sin from suffering and death in these examples. The sins of the mutilated Galileans were not the cause of Pilate's moral evil against them. Nor were the sins of those killed in Siloam connected to the natural evil of gravity toppling the tower. The Lord uses these two situations to advance a relationship between sin and *eternal* death—everyone must repent of their sins lest they perish forever. Most importantly, this is a progressive shift in biblical revelation as human sin is now causally connected to *spiritual* death.[18]

Jesus advances the understanding of theodicy even further. His radical approach asserts that there is divine purpose in suffering and death. John writes:

> As Jesus went along, He saw a man blind from birth. His disciples asked him, "Rabbi, who sinned, this man or his parents, that he was born blind?" "Neither this man nor his parents sinned," said Jesus, "but this happened so that the work of God might be displayed in his life." (John 9:1–3)

Once more, Jesus moves beyond echoes of the Gen 3 theodicy and disconnects suffering from sin. Suffering is meant to glorify God. This is not a heartless disregard for the pain caused by natural evil like a birth defect, because the Lord certainly identifies with human agony. For example, after Lazarus's death due to an illness, He was "deeply moved in spirit and troubled," and He "wept" (John 11:33, 35). Yet earlier Jesus had proclaimed that his "sickness will not end in death. No, it is for God's glory so that God's Son may be glorified through it" (11:4). Indeed, the raising of Lazarus, like the healing of the man born blind, glorified God because it showed His sovereign reign over suffering and death.

Jesus' teaching on theodicy comes to fulfillment in His submission to suffer and die on the Cross. There is eternal purpose in the crucifixion—believing men and women are graciously offered salvation. As the author of Hebrews concisely states, "Christ was sacrificed once to take away the sins of many people . . . and we have been made holy through the sacrifice of the body of Christ Jesus once for all" (Heb 9:28, 10:10). Jesus also saw His suffering and death as ordained by God with the intention to glorify them both. Just prior to the crucifixion He prayed, "Father, the time has come. Glorify your Son, that your Son may glorify you. . . . I have brought you glory on earth by completing the work you gave me to do. And now, Father, glorify me in your presence with the glory I had with you before the world began" (John 17:1, 4–5). Because of Jesus, suffering and death have God-glorifying and eternal meaning.

The New Testament writers follow the theodicy that the Lord taught and lived. John understands that Peter's death "would glorify God" (John 21:19). James recognizes that suffering tests faith and leads to spiritual growth. He asserts, "Consider it pure joy, my brothers, whenever you face trials of many kinds, because you know that testing of your faith develops perseverance" (Jas 1:2–3). So too Paul, who claims, "We rejoice in our sufferings, because suffering produces perseverance; perseverance, character; and character, hope" (Rom 5:3). This apostle also views suffering from an eternal perspective. He writes, "I consider that our present sufferings are not worth comparing to the glory that will be revealed in us . . . For our light and momentary troubles are achieving for us an eternal glory that far outweighs them all" (Rom 8:18; 2 Cor 4:16–17). And Paul concludes, "All things work together for good for those who love God" (Rom 8:28). Indeed, God reigns sovereignly over everything, including our pain and pending mortality.

The developing theodicy in Scripture has a very significant implication. The formulation today of any view on the meaning of suffering and death must be rooted in Jesus' fulfillment of theodicy. In particular, the Lord disconnects sin from pain and mortality. Thus, the causal connection between human sin and these harsh realities stated in Gen 3 is only an early phase in the divine revelatory process. Like the animal sacrificial system, the garden of Eden account serves the purpose to remind us that we are sinners. And in the same way that Christians today do not sacrifice animals to atone for their sins, so too we are not required to include in our understanding of theodicy the Gen 3 causal connection between human sin and the origins of suffering and death in nature. The door opens for an evolutionary view of origins in which God is sovereign over "all things," including natural selection and the survival of the fittest.

Toward an Evolutionary Creationist Theodicy

In light of these scriptural passages on suffering and death, it is possible to outline an evolutionary theodicy from a Christian perspective. Similar to the way in which the biblical principles of creation, intelligent design, and divine ordinance and sustenance are applicable to evolution, evolutionary creation proposes the following features:

Suffering and Death in Evolution Are Part of the Divine Creative Method

The Bible, with no apology whatsoever, reveals that God commanded, prophesied, and permitted many human beings to suffer and die in the creation of Israel and the Church. In other words, suffering and death are part of God's creative method. Evolutionary creation argues that as Christians develop a theodicy to justify this divine activity, they should then apply it to the evolution of life. Undoubtedly, coming to terms with the extermination of innocent children in the creation of a holy people to serve the Lord will prove to be much more difficult than accounting for the extinction of a species of fish millions of years ago.

Scripture also asserts that God is providentially active in animal predation and human embryological development. Yet science reveals that these biological processes feature wastage, competition, pain, and mortality. By analogy, evolutionary creation contends that suffering and death in the evolution of life are creative mechanisms that were also ordained and sustained by the Creator.

Suffering and Death in Evolution Are Purposeful

The Word of God clearly reveals that suffering and death have purpose in both this life and the hereafter. The Lord's ultimate plan for the present world is to provide an environment for the selection of spiritually fit men and women to enjoy eternal life with Him. However, the unfit will not survive the judgment, since "weeping and gnashing of teeth" (Matt 8:12) and the "second death in the lake of fire" (Rev 20:14) await them. To be sure, coming to terms with the reality of eternal damnation is gut-wrenching. But as Christians do so, it makes the challenge of accepting the natural selection and the survival of a fitter species of frog over those that become extinct seem quite trivial.

The Bible also states that suffering and death come to fulfillment in Jesus. That is, they have a divine purpose. Both are indispensable in the creation and development of spiritual life, and both glorify God. Similarly, evolutionary pain and mortality have creative purpose in the origin of physical life. Suffering drives the fittest to survive, resulting in the selection of advantageous genes. The death of weak creatures serves to eliminate less desirable traits from species. As a matter of fact, evolution needs organisms to die in order to free up resources on earth; otherwise life would be trapped as simple forms. Evolutionary suffering and death also glorify God. In the same way that pain and cell death are processes in human reproduction and development leading to "fearfully and wonderfully made" creatures, both contribute to the evolution of a world that "declares the glory of God." In particular, suffering and death have purpose in fulfilling God's primary evolutionary goal—the creation of men and women.

Suffering and Death in Evolution Are Very Good

The continuing impact of Augustine's literalism and theodicy leads most Christians to believe that the "very good" creation proclaimed in Gen 1:31 refers to a world that was originally perfect. To aggravate this situation, many believers today conflate secular and pagan notions of "good" with this verse. This is similar to the concoction of the nauseating "health and wealth" gospel embraced by too many believers in affluent countries. As a result, few see evolution in a positive light.

Understandably, the *de novo* creation of the world and the notion of a primeval idyllic age imply an original perfection. But the fact remains—this is an ancient understanding of origins without foundation in physical reality. More precisely, these are ancient motifs recycled by the inspired Hebrew authors who composed the biblical creation accounts. In addition, it must be underlined that the only one who defines the concept of "good" is the Author of Good. If God created through an evolutionary process, and since Gen 1:31 reveals the Divine Theology that He created a "very good" world (see also 1 Tim 4:4), then it follows that goodness also extends to suffering and death in evolution.[19] In other words, the Message of Faith regarding the goodness of the creation must be separated from the ancient motifs of *de novo* creation and the idyllic age found in Gen 1 and 2.

The Bible affirms God's sovereignty over the workings of all things in the creation. Some natural mechanisms are certainly repugnant and distasteful, such as suffering and death. Yet, human emotional reactions to these do not negate their goodness. As Scripture reveals, predatory attacks are ordained and sustained by the Creator and claimed to be "righteous," "loving," and "good things." In fact, predation is absolutely necessary for maintaining a healthy ecological balance in nature. By analogy, the violence, waste, and merciless competition in the evolution of life over eons of time, though troubling and even repulsive, are good aspects in the creative method of the Holy God. Indeed, this is a "very good" world, and it includes the suffering and death necessary for living organisms to evolve.

Suffering and Death in Evolution Are Not Causally Connected to Sin

Theodicy develops through the Bible and comes to fulfillment in the teaching and sacrificial death of Jesus. Gen 3 definitely presents a causal relationship between sin and physical suffering and death. However, the book of Job begins a disconnection between these that is completed in the New Testament by the Lord. In light of this theological development, evolutionary creation contends that the connection between Adam's sin and the origin of physical suffering and death is neither a reality nor a necessity of Christian faith. More must be said on this topic, and the next section focuses entirely on the sin-death problem.

To conclude, coming to terms with suffering and death is never an easy or comfortable process. It is usually a heart-wrenching, humbling experience that leaves many of us intellectually and emotionally drained and unsatisfied. Yet in the fulfilling light of Jesus, pain and mortality ultimately have an eternal purpose rooted in the will of our sovereign and holy God. This is also the case with biological evolution. As difficult as it may be at first for Christians to appreciate, suffering and death are part of the Creator's glorifying activity in making a world that is perfectly suited for us to develop a genuine loving relationship with Him. Indeed, the evolved creation is very good.

THE SIN-DEATH PROBLEM

The greatest challenge for evolutionary creation is to explain biblical passages that refer to a causal connection between the sin of Adam and the origin of physical death.[20] Genesis 3 presents death entering the world because God condemned Adam to die in judgment for his sin, Paul in Rom 5 and 1 Cor 15 understood the fall of the first man to be literal history, and the Church throughout time has firmly upheld the historicity of this event in the garden of Eden. However, evolutionary science reveals overwhelming evidence that death existed for hundreds of millions of years before the appearance of humans. Any Christian approach to evolution must deal with this problem directly.

Genesis 3:17 and 19 presents the causal connection between sin and death. God had earlier warned Adam, "You must not eat from the tree of knowledge of good and evil, for when you eat of it you will surely die" (2:17). But Eve gave Adam fruit from this tree, and "he ate it" (3:6). God then said to Adam, "Because you listened to your wife and ate from the tree about which I commanded you, 'You must not eat of it,' . . . by the sweat of your brow you will eat your food until you return to the ground, since from it you were taken; for dust you are and to dust you will return" (3:17, 19). This condemnation came to pass and "Adam lived 930 years, and then he died" (5:5). It is necessary to underline that these passages deal with physical death and not spiritual death, as progressive creation attempts to argue. The statement "for dust you are and to dust you will return" can only refer to bodily death.

The sin-death problem becomes particularly acute in the New Testament. Romans 5:12–19 and 1 Cor 15:20–49 place Adam's sin and death alongside God's gift of salvation and resurrection from the dead through Jesus. Paul asserts that "sin entered the world through one man, and death through sin, and in this way death came to all men, because all sinned. . . . For if the many died by the trespass of the one man, how much more did God's grace and gift that came by the grace of the One Man, Jesus Christ, overflow to the many!" (Rom 5:12, 15). Similarly, "For since death came through a man, the resurrection of the dead comes also through a Man. For as in Adam all die, so in Christ all will be made alive" (1 Cor 15:21). The context of the latter chapter is quite significant. The apostle deals with the question of Christians who have physically died, or "fallen asleep" (v. 6, 18, 20). He assures believers that "Christ has indeed been raised from the dead" (v. 20; also see 12–16, 35, 42, 52–53), and that God will also bring them back to life at the end of time (v. 23–24, 54–55). Clearly, 1 Cor 15 pertains to bodily death, and not spiritual death.

Most Christians assert that Gen 3, Rom 5, and 1 Cor 15 are so clear and definitive that any scientific evidence indicating that physical death precedes human existence has to be false. In fact, some go as far as to claim that the causal connection between sin and death is foundational to Christian faith. For example, young earth creationist Henry Morris, in his article "The Vital Importance of Believing in Recent Creation," argues that if Adam's sin did not lead to physical death, then:

> death is not really the wages of sin, as the Bible says [Rom 6:23], for violence, pain, and death reigned in the world long before sin came in. God is directly responsible for this cruel regime, not Adam. . . . If physical human death was not really an important part of the penalty for sin, then the agonizingly cruel physical death of Christ on the cross was not necessary to pay that penalty, and thus would be a gross miscarriage of justice on God's part. This would lead us to conclude further that we have no real Savior. . . . If suffering and death in the world—especially the suffering death of Christ—are not the result of God's judgment on sin in the world, then the most reasonable inference is that the God of the Bible does not exist.[21]

Interestingly, some dysteleological evolutionists also assume that Christianity is dependent on a strict literal interpretation of the sin-death passages. But instead of undermining evolution, this approach is used to reject the Faith. In a paper entitled "The Meaning of Evolution," atheist G. Richard Bozarth asserts:

> Christianity has fought, still fights, and will fight science to the desperate end over evolution, because evolution destroys utterly and finally the very reason Jesus' earthly life was supposedly made necessary. Destroy Adam and Eve and the original sin, and in the rubble you will find the sorry remains of the Son of God. It takes away the meaning of his death. If Jesus was not the redeemer that died for our sins, and this is what evolution means, then Christianity is nothing.[22]

There is a certain logic running through the arguments offered by Morris and Bozarth. But it is dependent on a literalist hermeneutic of the first chapters of Genesis. Both men hastily assume that these passages are scientifically and historically concordant, and as a result, they disrespect the complex literary genre. No consideration whatsoever is given to the possibility that the Holy Spirit accommodated to the level of the ancient Hebrew authors by using their science, history, epistemology, poetry, and motifs. But worse, Morris and Bozarth conflate their sin-death interpretation with the Cross. This strict literal reading of Scripture forces young earth creationists to reject biological evolution, and dysteleological evolutionists to spurn Jesus' gift of salvation.

In order to propose a solution for the sin-death problem, it is necessary to deal with a number of issues. First, the central problem is identified along with related difficulties. Next, biblical precedents based on scriptural evidence from previous chapters are presented and their implications for the causal connection between sin and death offered. The development of theological concepts through Scripture also contributes precedents and insights to view sin-death passages in a new light. Finally, the integration of the biblical and theological precedents provides a scriptural basis for moving beyond the traditional and strict literal reading of the origins of human sin and physical death in Gen 3, Rom 5, and 1 Cor 15. This section concludes that the sin-death problem is rooted ultimately in an inadequate interpretive method. I must forewarn readers that the proposed solution is quite complex and brings together many arguments and lines of biblical evidence.[23] In particular, it is dependent on a very counterintuitive reading of Scripture.

Central Problem and Related Difficulties

There certainly appears to be an irreconcilable conflict between Scripture and science regarding the origin of physical death. The Bible presents a causal connection between the sin of Adam and the beginning of mortality. Not only does God introduce death into the world in judgment of human sin, but also other physical changes, including suffering. He causes the snake to lose its legs, the woman to labor in childbearing, work to be painful, and fields to produce thorns and thistles (Gen 3:14–18). However, the fossil record demonstrates conclusively that physical death and suffering have been on earth for hundreds of millions of years before the appearance of humans. Notably, flesh-eating teeth abound throughout geological strata for nearly the last half-billion years. Snakes, thorns, and thistles have also existed well before people. In other words, there is no physical evidence to support the traditional belief in the cosmic fall. Does this mean that Christians and non-Christians are forced into a dichotomy and a choice between Scripture and science?

Related difficulties arise with the traditional literal interpretation of the sin-death passages. It asserts that God launched suffering and death upon the entire creation in judgment for one sin by one man at one point in the distant past, and that this divine punishment has extended to every generation in history up until today. Yet what are Christians to make of the morality of this excessively heavy-handed penalty for only one man's sin? Has the entire creation been "groaning," "subjected to frustration," and in "bondage to decay" (Rom 8:20–22) because of one rebellious act in the garden of Eden? Do women experience excruciating pain during childbirth today because of one sin by Eve? Is our inevitable death due to Adam at one time biting into the fruit of a forbidden tree? Does this reflect the justice of a Holy God?

In addition, the Bible states that Jesus "has freed us from our sins by His Blood" (Rev 1:5). Scripture also declares to Christians that "you were washed, you were sanctified, you were justified in the name of the Lord Jesus Christ and by the Spirit of our God" (1 Cor 6:11). And the book of Hebrews claims that believers "have been made holy through the sacrifice of the body of Jesus Christ once for all" (Heb 10:10). However, there is a painfully obvious fact of life: Christians still die. If believers have been washed clean of all their sins by the Blood of Jesus, then why do they continue to die? And why is their death no different than that of non-believers? Christians do not live any longer than non-Christians, nor are they exempt from fatal diseases, such as cancer. Surely, Jesus' taking away of our sins should also be able to redeem us from the punishment of physical death that God delivered in judgment for Adam's original sin. The Blood of the Lamb is sufficient and proficient, is it not?

Biblical Precedents and Implications

As challenging as the sin-death problem and its related difficulties appear to be, history reveals that conflicts between Scripture and science are usually resolved by re-examining traditional literal interpretations of the Bible. A solution begins with the Word of God in order to establish biblical precedents. These scriptural facts have been presented in previous chapters, and drawing out their implications in this subsection may shock Christians at first.[24] However, the Message-Incident Principle cushions the impact and provides a way to reconsider the traditional belief in an actual causal connection between sin and death.

Ancient Phenomenological Perspective of the Physical World

The Bible makes statements about the physical world that are false.* The mustard seed is not the smallest of all seeds. The earth is not stationary. And there is no firmament holding up a body of water overhead. In particular, modern astronomy disproves the 3-tier universe found in passages by the authors of Gen 1–11, the apostle Paul, and the Lord Jesus. But recognizing that Scripture understands the physical world and its creation from an incidental ancient phenomenological perspective easily solves this problem. It is only consistent that biblical statements regarding

---

* I fully expect this first sentence, like those introducing the next four biblical precedents, to be torn out of context by critics and manipulated to serve their purposes. Please note: I do not say that God lies in the Bible. Lying requires deceptive and malicious intent. The Lord is not a God of deception and malevolence. Instead, the Holy Spirit accommodates in Scripture. To soften this sentence, I could have written: The Bible makes statements about the physical world that are *not literally true*. Or, the Bible makes statements about the physical world that *do not correspond to reality*. Of course, by employing the word "false" I am being polemical. At this point in the book, I feel that it is the time to make very precise and unapologetic statements regarding the scientific and historical assertions in the creation accounts, and for Christians to deal directly with their implications.

the origin of death are also a product of this ancient way of conceiving physical reality. In other words, the entrance of mortality into the world, as stated in Gen 3 and then repeated in Rom 5 and 1 Cor 15, derives from an incidental ancient science. The implication is clear: the origin of physical death presented in Scripture cannot be true.

Attribution of Divine Creative Action

The Bible makes statements about how God created the world that are false. This is a troubling fact because Christians expect Scripture to be accurate when it deals directly with the Creator. But the creation of the heavens never happened as stated in Gen 1. There is no firmament or sea of water above the earth; and the sun, moon and stars are not embedded in this solid dome. God did not create these heavenly structures as described on the second and fourth creation days. However, the Message-Incident Principle quickly resolves this difficulty. The Holy Spirit accommodated by using an ancient understanding of the assembly of the heavens (*de novo* creation) as a vessel to reveal that He created the astronomical world. Consistency demands that biblical statements regarding how God created humanity are also cast in this ancient origins science. The *de novo* creation of Adam, and thus his very existence, is rooted in an ancient understanding of human origins. The consequence of this scriptural fact is profound: the traditional Christian belief that Adam actually existed cannot be true.

Attribution of Divine Judgmental Action

The Bible makes statements about how God will end the physical world in judgment of sin that are false. Scripture asserts that on judgment day, the Lord will launch His wrath and dismantle the heavens. The firmament will be shaken to dislodge the stars, these then fall to the earth, and lastly the heavenly dome will be rolled up. But there is no firmament to shake or roll up, stars are not embedded in it, and these astronomical bodies are much too large for them to fall to earth. God will never dismantle the heavens at the final judgment as stated in the Bible. In these passages the Holy Spirit employs an incidental ancient science to deliver the message that He will certainly judge sin at the end of the world. Similarly, Gen 3 employs an ancient understanding of the origin of death in order to reveal that God has judged sin from the beginning of humanity. The implication is clear: the traditional literal interpretation of Gen 3, Rom 5, and 1 Cor 15, which claims that physical death entered the world because of divine judgmental action, cannot be true.

Attribution of Supernatural Action in Suffering

The Bible makes statements about the cause of physical suffering that are false. Notably, Jesus denounces demons for causing epilepsy, blindness, deafness, muteness, and crippled backs. But science demonstrates that these afflictions have physical mechanisms.[25] In the ancient world, natural processes were often attributed to supernatural causes. The origin of diseases, disabilities, and calamities was commonly associated with evil spirits, human sin, and divine judgment. This ancient concept of causation was used by Jesus to reveal the message that He can indeed miraculously heal our physical ailments and that He is Lord over the world. Likewise, statements dealing with the origin of suffering in Gen 3 reflect ancient causality. Considering the centrality of sin for the Hebrews, it is not at all surprising that they interpreted the lost idyllic age as being caused by human transgression and divine judgment. The pain of childbirth, the agony of physical work, and the anguish of inevitable death are attributed to a supernatural cause—God judging human sin. The attribution of divine action also appears with punishment being launching upon the creation—the snake lost its legs and fields were infested with thorns and thistles. This notion of the cosmic fall reappears in Rom 8. In looking back to Gen 3, Paul states that the world "was subjected to frustration" and since then "has been groaning as in the pains of childbirth" and continues to be in "bondage to decay" (v. 20–22). The consequence of recognizing an ancient view of causality in these biblical passages is significant: the traditional belief that divine judgmental acts in the garden of Eden are literally the cause behind physical suffering in the world cannot be true.

Attribution of Divine and Human Action in Gen 1–11

Genesis 1–11 makes statements about the activities of God and humans that are false. The Creator never made the universe and life in six days, He did not destroy the entire world with a flood, nor did He confuse an original language once spoken by everyone. Noah never built an ark to preserve life on earth, ancient Near Eastern nations did not form along the tribal lines of his three sons, and all of humanity was never located in

Shinar where they attempted to build a tower to heaven. The attribution of divine (creative and judgmental) and human (sinful and righteous) acts in Gen 1–11 are cast in ancient motifs, which were inherited by the Hebrews. These ancient historical paradigms are incidental vessels employed by the Holy Spirit to deliver Messages of Faith. Consistency demands that the origin of suffering and death in Gen 3 is also framed on an ancient understanding of history—the lost idyllic age motif. This ancient conception of the distant past is a vehicle that transports the inspired revelation that the Creator judges humans for their sins. Yet the implication of this motif in Scripture is clear: the traditional belief that God literally introduced death into an idyllic primeval world cannot be true.

These five biblical precedents provide a foundation from which to reconsider the truthfulness of the causal connection between sin and death. Scripture makes numerous statements about the physical world, divine creative and judgmental action, human sinful and righteous acts, and the cause of suffering, that are false. In particular, most of the events in Gen 1–11 never literally happened. But this is not a problem whatsoever to Christian faith if believers recognize that the attribution of divine and human action is accommodated through ancient categories in order to reveal, as effectively as possible, Holy Spirit inspired Messages of Faith. Most importantly, Gen 3 is structured on the lost idyllic age motif. This common belief in the disruption of the creation at the beginning of time is based on ancient science and ancient history. Therefore, physical death did not actually enter into the world because of divine judgment for human sin. No cosmic fall ever occurred in the distant past. The causal connection that exists in Scripture between sin and death cannot be true.

Theological Precedents and Insights

A number of theological concepts develop through the Bible. As noted earlier in this chapter, the very existence of the Old and New Testaments indicates that the Holy Spirit revealed in a progressive manner. Some well-known theological developments offer precedents and insights toward a solution for the sin-death problem. Again, these at first might challenge Christians. But each theological precedent is based firmly on the Word of God.

Theological Development and the Atonement of Sin

Jesus established the principle that Divine Theology develops across Scripture. He declares, "Do not think that I have come to abolish the Law or the Prophets; I have not come to abolish them but to fulfill them" (Matt 5:17). Yet in fulfilling the Old Testament, the Lord did cancel commands that God had previously ordered the Hebrews to observe. No longer were food laws in effect since all foods were now declared clean (Mark 7:19; Lev 11). Adulteresses were to be forgiven instead of stoned to death (John 8:11; Lev 20:10). And Jesus' "once for all" sacrifice on the Cross abolished the Jewish sacrificial system (Heb 7:27, 8:13). This last theological development has profound consequences.

The book of Leviticus describes in detail numerous sacrifices that the Hebrews were to practice for the atonement of their sins. In particular, God commanded the slaughter of animals and the sprinkling of blood in order to be forgiven. However, the New Testament bluntly states that these sacrifices "can never take away sin" (Heb 10:11) because "it is impossible for the blood of bulls and goats to take away sin" (v. 4). Clearly, a problem exists. Every Christian would expect the Bible to be perfectly consistent on the critical issue of human sinfulness and reconciliation with God. But the Old Testament makes statements about how to atone for sin that are false.[26]

The principle of theological development through Scripture resolves this conflict between the Old and New Testaments on sin atonement. Indeed, the Levitical sacrificial system had an ultimate purpose that was ordained by God. As the author of the book of Hebrews explains, "Those sacrifices are an annual reminder of sin" (Heb 10:3). Though the Old Testament sacrifices never actually removed sin, because *only* the Blood of the Lamb can remove sin, they were absolutely necessary in revealing to men and women their sinfulness. This theological precedent can be applied to the sin-death problem. Assertions in Gen 3 about how sin originated with Adam serve ultimately to *remind* humans that they are sinful and that God judges their sin. And just as sin was never literally taken away through animal sacrifice, one could argue that sin never literally entered into the world through the first man mentioned in Scripture. In other words, the Old Testament sacrifices and the sin of Adam are vital incidental vessels reminding us that we are sinners. Yet analogous to sin atonement in the book of Leviticus, Gen 3 makes statements regarding the origin of sin that are false.

Theological Development and Theodicy

Jesus is the fulfillment of theodicy in the Bible. He rejected the popular belief-of-the-day that physical suffering was caused by sin. With the man born blind, the Lord stated that neither his sin nor that of his parents was the reason for his affliction (John 9:3). In fact, if Adam's sin in Gen 3 was at the root of this man's suffering, then Jesus had the perfect opportunity to say so. But He never did. This is also the case with the death of Lazarus. No mention was made that his sickness and passing were ultimately due to sin in the garden of Eden. Instead, the Lord moved the biblical view of theodicy forward to declare that suffering and death exist to display the work of God so that He and the Father may be glorified (John 11:4, 40).

As noted previously, theodicy develops in roughly three stages through the Bible. The book of Job challenges the causal connection between human sin and physical suffering and death in Gen 3. God reveals to Job that this issue is not simple. Mystery is a factor and nature's non-verbal revelation is sufficient to comfort him. Jesus and the New Testament writers then complete the revelation of theodicy. Suffering and death are redeemed and declared purposeful. Both glorify God. They also test and refine faith, are considered pure joy, and lead to the hope of eternal life. On the surface, the biblical passages on theodicy conflict. However, the principle of theological development across Scripture solves this apparent difficulty in the same way that it does for differing statements on the atonement of sin between the Old and New Testaments.

It is important to note that the Bible never explicitly abolishes the causal connection in Gen 3 between sin and suffering/death in the way that it cancels animal sacrifice.[27] Instead, the fulfillment of theodicy in the New Testament is presented as a *shift in focus inward and forward*. By glorifying God, human suffering and death direct attention to personal spiritual growth and the future hope of eternal life. The developing theodicy through Scripture offers a precedent and insights toward a solution for the sin-death problem. The Gen 3 theodicy is only the first revelatory stage. Jesus fulfills this issue later in the Bible. The traditional justification that pain and mortality in the world are actual divine judgments for human sin is akin to the Jewish sacrificial system, another initial phase in revelation. Both are incidental vessels reminding men and women of their sinfulness and that God judges sin. Consequently, Christians today must focus inward and forward to Jesus and not backward to Adam in coming to terms with suffering and death.

Theological Development Regarding Spiritual Death and Eternal Life

The notions of spiritual death and eternal life are crucial in the teachings of both Jesus and Paul. The Old Testament introduces these ideas (Isa 25:8, 26:19; Dan 12:2; Ezek 37:1–14), but they come to fulfillment in the New Testament. The term "eternal life" appears 40 times, and only in the latter (John 6:54, 10:28; Rom 5:21, 6:22–23). Though the words "spiritual death" are not found in the New Testament, this notion is clearly present (John 5:25, 8:51; Rom 7:9–13, 8:6). As Jesus states, "Whoever hears My words and believes Him who sent Me has eternal life and will not be condemned; he has crossed over from [spiritual] death to life" (John 5:24). Similarly, Paul admonishes, "Do not offer the parts of your body to sin, as instruments of wickedness, but rather offer yourselves to God, as those who have been brought from [spiritual] death to life" (Rom 6:13). In both verses, the context clearly refers to individuals who are physically alive and who move away from spiritual death.

The development of the concepts of spiritual death and eternal life in the New Testament is part of the theological shift in focus to an inward and personal spirituality. Jesus proclaims, "The kingdom of God does not come visibly, nor will people say, 'Here it is,' or 'There it is,' because the kingdom of God is within you" (Luke 17:20–21). He advances that true worship is not defined by an outward physical place like Mount Gerizim or Jerusalem, but rather by the spiritual state inside an individual. In this way the Lord admonishes, "God is spirit, and His worshippers must worship Him in spirit and truth" (John 4:24). Paul also develops this shift in focus to an inner spirituality. "Israel" is now a nation of people who by faith personally embrace God's promise to Abraham (Rom 9:6–8), "Jews" are those with "circumcised hearts" (Rom 2:28–29), and "believers" are the "temple" of the Holy Spirit (1 Cor 6:19).

Significantly, many of Paul's references to spiritual death and eternal life appear in Rom 5–8. To cite a few examples:

> Just as sin reigned in death, so also grace might reign through righteousness to bring *eternal life*. (Rom 5:21)

> For the wages of sin is death, but the gift of God is *eternal life* in Christ Jesus the Lord. (Rom 6:23)

> I found that the very commandment that was intended to bring life actually brought [*spiritual*] *death*. For sin, seizing the opportunity afforded by the commandment, deceived me, and through the commandment put me to [*spiritual*] *death*. (Rom 7:10–11)

> The mind of sinful man is [*spiritual*] *death*, but the mind controlled by the Spirit is *life* and peace. (Rom 8:6; italics added)

Of course, the interpretive challenge with these verses is to distinguish between physical and spiritual death. The context in Rom 7:10–11 and 8:6 clearly points to the latter since it refers to people who were physically alive. However, the word "death" in Rom 5:21 and 6:23 could be understood either way. This ambiguity has led to one of the most critical issues in the origins debate. Are Paul's statements about death entering the world because of the sin of Adam in Rom 5:12–19 referring to physical or spiritual death? And if they do refer to the latter, is the causal connection between sin and death in Gen 3 merely spiritual?

Progressive creationists "spiritualize" the sin-death passages in an attempt to resolve the conflict between Scripture stating that humans precede physical death and science revealing the exact opposite.[28] However, this interpretive approach falls short. The context of Gen 3 deals clearly with physical death. As noted before, God's condemnation of Adam, "For dust you are and to dust you will return" (v. 19), can only mean bodily death. Similarly, in a passage that parallels Rom 5:12–19, Paul in 1 Cor 15:20–49 is also focusing on physical death and physical resurrection. In particular, he writes, "For since death came through a man, the resurrection of the dead comes also through a man. For as in Adam all die, so in Christ all will be made alive (v. 21). Finally, Rom 8:19–23 definitely presents the cosmic fall. Reference to the creation being "subjected to frustration," in "bondage to decay" and "groaning as in the pains of childbirth right up to the present time" alongside mention of Christians waiting for the "redemption of [their] bodies" can only be understood in a physical context. In other words, Paul acknowledges that nature was changed after the entrance of sin into the world. Therefore, forcing the idea of spiritual death into Gen 3 and Rom 5:12–19 and claiming that the death introduced by Adam was only spiritual is eisegetical.

It is clear that the apostle Paul accepted two causal relationships with regard to human sinfulness: (1) sin causes spiritual death, and (2) sin is causally connected to the entrance of physical death into the world. The context of a passage usually determines which notion he employs. Yet at times both are seamlessly interwoven, leaving the interpretation uncertain. Nevertheless, his most important message is evident: those not personally committed to Jesus are spiritually dead, but through Christ they can gain eternal life. Paul uses Gen 3 and Adam as reminders that everyone is a sinner and that God judges sin. As noted in the last chapter, the intention of Rom 5 and 1 Cor 15 is not to defend the historicity of Adam and his sin and death. The events in the garden of Eden were the historical facts-of-the-day for this apostle and his generation, just like the *de novo* creation of a 3-tiered universe. The New Testament shift in focus to a personal spirituality offers an insight into Paul's sin-death passages. Instead of looking backward to the traditional literal understanding of the origin of sin and death, Christians today must direct attention inward on their spiritual state and forward to the hope of eternal life.

Typological Use of Old Testament in New Testament

The New Testament often uses the Old Testament typologically in order to explain or illustrate a theological concept. In particular, the former takes people, events, and objects from the latter to reveal that Jesus is the fulfillment of the Law and the Prophets. For example, the book of Hebrews states that the "man-made sanctuary was *only a copy* of the true one Jesus entered in heaven" (9:24) and "the Law is *only a shadow* of the good things that are coming—*not the realities themselves*" (10:1; italics added).[29] This author also points to individuals in Gen 1–11 as models of faith. "By faith Abel offered God a better sacrifice than Cain . . . By faith Enoch was taken from this life so that he did not experience death . . . By faith Noah when warned of things not yet seen in holy fear built an ark to save his family" (Heb 11:4, 5, 7; cf. Gen 4:4, 5:24, 6:22). Many Old Testament symbols, patterns, and examples point ultimately to Jesus, and others are archetypes portraying Messages of Faith.

As noted in the last chapter, the New Testament uses Adam typologically. Jesus appeals to the creation accounts, specifically Gen 1:27 and 2:24, in order to present Adam and Eve as the model for marriage that God had intended (Matt 19:3–9). As well, Paul states that Adam "was *a pattern* [Greek: *tupos*] of the One to come" (Rom 5:14). The apostle further develops this typology in describing Jesus as "the Last Adam" or "Second Man." In other words, "first man Adam" is an illustration of the prototypical sinner, while Jesus is the reality and archetypical Redeemer. The authorial intention of both Jesus and Paul in these passages is not to defend the historicity of Adam. The events in Gen 1–3 were the historical facts-of-the-day in first century Palestine. Instead, the Lord uses the picture of Adam and Eve "becoming one flesh" to admonish that marriage is a sacred institution. The Holy Spirit's ultimate purpose for presenting Adam in Rom 5 and 1 Cor 15 is similar to the Jewish sacrificial system—he is a powerful image that reminds us we are sinful and that God judges us.

The apostle Paul viewed Adam as both historical and typological. It is important not to conflate these two characteristics. Moreover, the use of typology does not confer historicity to Adam or the events in Gen 3. In fact, one might argue that the garden of Eden account is analogous to the "man-made sanctuary" and "the Law" interpreted typologically in Heb 9:24 and 10:1, respectively. That is, the events in the garden are "only a copy," "only a shadow," and "not the realities themselves." In this way, Gen 3 becomes a picture pointing forward to "the good things that are coming" and which are later fulfilled by Jesus. Considering the explicit reference to typology in Rom 5:14, the garden of Eden could be seen as a *pattern* of Calvary and the Cross "to come."

These four theological precedents offer insights into the causal connection between sin and death. Biblical revelation develops progressively and ends with a shift in focus inward to a personal spirituality and forward to the hope of eternity. The New Testament fulfills the challenging issue of theodicy, completes the notions of spiritual death and eternal life, and reminds humans of their sin by the typological use of Adam. Most importantly, the sin-death passages must be viewed through the fulfillment of Scripture by Jesus. Instead of focusing back on the causal connection between Adam's rebellion and death in Gen 3, Christians need to look ahead to the main message in Rom 5–8 and 1 Cor 15—the hope of eternal life with the Lord.

Toward a Solution for the Sin-Death Problem

The biblical and theological precedents outlined above along with their implications and insights provide a set of categories through which to view the sin-death problem in a new light. In offering a solution, this subsection argues that there never was a causal connection between the sin of Adam and the origin of physical death. Once more, Christians might find this troubling at first. But the proposed solution is deeply rooted in Scripture. In order to assist readers with this subsection, I suggest that they examine Figs 8-5 and 8-6 before commencing.

The Historicity of Adam

The Bible presents overwhelming evidence that the inspired writers understood the physical world from an ancient phenomenological perspective. In fact, there is not one verse that reveals a scientific truth prior to its discovery by modern science. Scripture features an ancient science of the structure, operation, and origin of nature. In particular, the *de novo* creation of humanity has profound implications for the traditional Christian belief in the historicity of Adam.

First, Adam never actually existed. Genesis 1 and 2 present the *de novo* creation of the heavens, earth, plants, and animals. This is an ancient origins science with no correspondence to physical reality. Consistency within these first biblical chapters demands that this is also the case with the origin of humans. The quick and complete creation of Adam is identical to the *de novo* creation of the firmament—neither happened in history. Second, Adam never actually sinned. In fact, it is impossible for him to have sinned because he never existed. Consequently, sin did not enter the world on account of Adam. Third, Adam was never actually judged by God to suffer and die. Again, he lacks existence, and as a result the ability to sin, so he was never condemned for his transgression. Thus, suffering and death are not divine judgments upon Adam, every other human after him, and the entire creation. There never was a cosmic fall.

The historicity of Adam is built on an ancient conception of origins. The traditional belief in an actual causal connection between his sin and the origin of physical death is false. Adam is an incidental vessel that delivers inerrant foundations of the Christian faith to remind us: we are created in the Image of God, we are sinful, and God judges us for our sins. Though Adam never existed, he is the prototype of the human spiritual condition. In order to understand our existence, we must see ourselves in him—Adam is you and me.

The Origin of Physical Death

Genesis 1–11 features numerous ancient motifs that Israel inherited from her neighbors. These historical paradigms were logical reconstructions of the past conceived from an ancient phenomenological mindset. In particular, the retrojection of life's adversities and harsh realities, causally connected in a variety of ways to evil spirits, human sin, and/or divine judgment, led to the major motif of a lost idyllic age. Genesis 3 is structured on this ancient historical notion of an original creation that was disrupted, and this chapter attributes the origin of physical death to God's judgment of Adam. However, the lost idyllic age is an ancient understanding of history with no correspondence to the natural world or human events in the past. Belief in the cosmic fall and consequent entrance of death are rooted ultimately in an ancient motif.

Grasping fully the implications of *de novo* creation offers further arguments against the traditional Christian view of the origin of death. First, the historicity of Adam is based on this ancient science, and as just noted, *de novo* origins does not align with physical reality. Thus, death never entered the world with Adam because he never existed. Second, consistency demands that since the origin of life in Scripture is an ancient science, then this must also be the case with the origin of death. Similarly, creative action attributed to God in Gen 1 and 2 is filtered through ancient categories. It is only consistent that the attribution of divine judgmental action in Gen 3 is an ancient understanding of the origin of death. Third, a corollary of *de novo* creation is that death can only occur *after* life has been quickly created into completely mature forms. That is, built into the very definition of *de novo* origins is the concept that death happens only *after* animals and humans have been made in their present physical states. Fig 8-4 depicts the consistency and corollary arguments.

The origin of physical death in Gen 3 is rooted in ancient history and ancient science. This chapter is framed on the major motif of a lost idyllic age and depends ultimately upon the notion of *de novo* creation. This being the case, the traditional Christian belief in an actual causal connection between sin and death is false. The Bible does not reveal how physical death actually entered the world. Genesis 3 employs an ancient

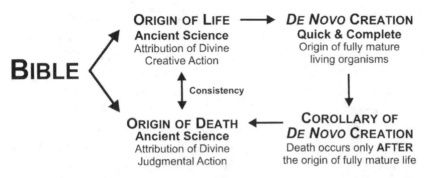

Fig 8-4. *De Novo* Creation and the Origin of Physical Death. Consistency argues that the origin of life and the origin of death in Scripture are understood from an ancient phenomenological perspective. A corollary of *de novo* creation complements this argument: the death of living organisms can only happen after their quick creation into fully mature forms. In attributing to God the origin of death, the Bible accommodates to the level of ancient peoples by using incidental ancient scientific, historical and causal categories into order to reveal the Message of Faith that He judges human sin.

understanding of the origin of death as an incidental vessel to remind us of the infallible message that God judges our sins.

The Genesis 3 Theodicy

In an implicit manner, Gen 3 engages one of humanity's greatest challenges—making sense of suffering and death. The traditional Christian theodicy (Augustinian) justifies the existence of these harsh realities by appealing to a literal reading of this chapter. Accordingly, God launched suffering and death upon the creation in judgment for the sin of Adam. But as noted earlier, this theodicy leads to an irreconcilable conflict between Scripture and science as well as other related difficulties.[30]

In order to propose a solution, it is necessary to identify three features in Gen 3: The primary purpose of the garden of Eden account is to reveal the foundation of a Divine Theology regarding the reality of sin—humans are sinners and God judges their sin. Notably, human rebellion originates with the arrogance of men and women rejecting the Word of their Creator.[31] The secondary intention of this chapter is to begin the inspired revelatory process on the issue of theodicy. Scripture later moves forward from this initial stage and comes to fulfillment in the teaching and life of Jesus. Lastly, Gen 3 uses an ancient understanding of the origin of suffering and death as a vessel to deliver both the Divine Theology on sin and the first stage of theodicy. In particular, the events in the garden of Eden are rooted in the lost idyllic age motif, the *de novo* creation of humanity and an ancient conception of the cause of suffering.

Failure to recognize these three features in Gen 3 leads to their conflation and the problems previously mentioned. A conflict between Scripture and science arises if the ancient understanding of the origin of suffering and death is not separated from the Divine Theology on sin and/or the first stage of theodicy. This error in biblical interpretation is identical to making the *de novo* creation of the firmament a part of the doctrine of creation. A more subtle and serious mistake in reading Gen 3 occurs when the theology on sin and the theodicy are conflated. The former is an infallible and foundational revelation on the reality of human sin and divine judgment of sin, while the latter is only the initial stage in understanding the reason for suffering and death. Failing to separate these two issues is like reading the book of Leviticus today and not separating the fact that atonement for sin is absolutely necessary from the first revelatory stage in the practice of atoning for sins through animal sacrifice.

Undoubtedly, it would be quite helpful if the New Testament made explicit statements abolishing the causal connection between sin and death in a fashion similar to the cancellation of the Old Testament sacrificial system. As noted previously, the book of Hebrews states clearly that animal sacrifices "can never take away sin" (Heb 10:11) because "it is impossible for the blood of bulls and goats to take away sin" (Heb 10:4). In this way, some Christians today might want the New Testament to reveal:

> It is impossible for sin to be causally connected to suffering and death because sin did not enter the world with Adam—he never existed. God created life through an ordained and sustained evolutionary process that employed suffering and death over hundreds of millions of years. During human evolution, sin was manifested gradually and mysteriously.

As much as our modern generation would value such a passage to understand origins, there are two reasons why the Holy Spirit did not inspire a biblical author to do so.

First, Christians in the early Church would never have understood this updated passage. Such a revelation would be like modernizing Phil 2:10–11 in the Kenotic Hymn:

> At the name of Jesus every knee should bow—in God's celestial realm, on every planet of every galaxy, and within the boundaries of the space-time continuum billions of light years wide—and every tongue confess that Christ is Lord.

Would Paul and his readers have any idea what was being revealed? Never. Just think of the Galileo affair less than four hundred years ago. The issue was simply whether or not the earth moved, and Christians were quite troubled by that notion. In fact, consider the confusion and division that biological evolution produces in the Church today. A divine revelation abolishing the causal connection between sin and death would have been a disruptive stumbling block to faith.

Second, the modernized passage on the origin of sin and death breaks away from the overwhelming biblical evidence that historical concordism in Gen 1–11 and scientific concordism throughout Scripture are not features of the Word of God. Over and over again, the Holy Spirit accommodates to the intellectual level of ancient people by using their categories in order to reveal inerrant Messages of Faith. The purpose of Scripture is not to disclose incidental facts about the beginning of human history or modern science well before their discovery. Revealing exactly how physical suffering and death entered the world would be blatantly inconsistent with the process of divine inspiration. Bluntly stated, the updated passage is un-biblical.

Genesis 3 employs an ancient understanding of the origin of suffering and death in the revelation of the first stage of theodicy. The events in this chapter never literally happened. There never was a cosmic fall. The traditional Christian belief in a causal connection between sin and physical death is false. Consequently, there is no conflict between Gen 3 and the fossil record. Biological pain and mortality were not injudiciously launched upon the entire creation in divine judgment for one sin of one man at one point in the past. And Jesus never died to remove all suffering and death from the present physical world. The Lord gave His life to wash away our sins so that we could enjoy life in the Spirit today and eternal life in the future. Though Gen 3 is neither historically nor scientifically concordant, it provides an indispensable service similar to the animal sacrificial system of the Hebrews. The garden of Eden account is a reminder that we are sinners and that God judges our sin. And in a subtle way, it anticipates redemption later offered through the Cross.

Paul on the Sin and Death of Adam

Passages by the apostle Paul on the sin and death of Adam are some of the most challenging in Scripture for evolutionary creation to explain. Many Christians claim that Rom 5–8 and 1 Cor 15 are unanswerable biblical proof against evolution. But the primary difficulty in understanding these chapters is that they seamlessly interweave Messages of Faith with numerous incidental ancient concepts, lending easily to their conflation. Consequently, identification of categories and resistance to collapsing these together opens the way toward a solution. Five features in Paul's sin-death passages that require recognition and respect include:

- *Genesis 3 and Ancient Origins.* Paul was a first century man steeped in the historical and scientific categories of his generation. Like everyone else, he assumed the 3-tiered universe, the *de novo* creation of the world, the lost idyllic age, and the origin of suffering and death after humans were created. The last three ancient concepts are particularly significant. Paul had no choice but to believe in the historicity of Gen 3 and the causal connection between the sin of Adam and the entrance of pain and mortality into the world. Romans 5:12–19 and 1 Cor 15:20–49 are evidence of this fact. However, the historicity of Adam, the attribution of divine judgmental action for his sin, and the origin of physical suffering and death as a consequence are notions conceived from an ancient phenomenological perspective. These events in Gen 3 never happened because they are based on ancient history and ancient science, and Paul had no way of knowing this, anymore than he could have known that the universe does not have three tiers.

- *Genesis 3 and Divine Theology on Sin.* The apostle Paul was a devout Jew who fully embraced the Divine Theology regarding sin in Gen 3. The belief that humans are sinful and that God judges their sin permeates his letters, including the sin-death passages. His writings also proclaim that atonement for human sin comes only through the sacrificial death of Jesus. The Gospel message is clearly present in Rom 5–8 (5:8–9, 6:10, 7:4, 8:3, 32–34) and 1 Cor 15 (v. 1–7). However, in accepting the Divine Theology on sin in Gen 3, Paul also assumed the ancient history and ancient science that deliver these eternal truths. This situation is similar to Phil 2:10 in which he employed 3-tier astronomy to declare the infallible message that Jesus is Lord over the entire universe. Therefore, references in Rom 5 and 1 Cor 15 to Adam, the judgment of his sin, and the consequent entrance of death are incidental ancient vessels originating from Gen 3 that Paul had to use in writing about human sin. These were the only intellectual categories available to him and his readers.

- *Genesis 3 Theodicy and New Testament Theodicy.* A key to interpreting Paul's sin-death passages is found in his theodicy. Stated precisely, he seamlessly interweaves the first revelatory stage of theodicy in Gen 3 with the New Testament fulfillment of theodicy by Jesus. To justify suffering and death in the world, he *looks backward* into the past to the sin of Adam. He has no choice but to accept the historicity of the events in Gen 3 since these were the historical facts-of-the-day for first century Jews. But more importantly, Paul *focuses forward* and views the harsh realities of life in the fulfilling light of Jesus. He introduces an eternal perspective on theodicy and justifies that "we share in His [Christ's] sufferings in order that we may also share in His glory" (Rom 8:17; cf. 8:18; 2 Cor 4:16–17), and adds that "we rejoice in our sufferings, because suffering produces perseverance; perseverance, character; and character, *hope*" (Rom 5:3, italics added; cf. 8:24–25; see next subsection). Despite our struggles and pain, Paul concludes: "we know that in all things God works for the good of those who love Him, who have been called according to His purpose" (Rom 8:28). In other words, his view of theodicy is a combination of (1) the ancient history in Gen 3 and (2) the radical theological development in the New Testament that our afflictions have eternal meaning. To put this diagrammatically:

In my experience, distinguishing these two features in Paul's theodicy is one of the most critical issues in the origins debate. Clearly, there is an intellectual tension in his position. The origin of suffering and death is cast in an ancient understanding of history with *no correspondence to reality*, while the fulfillment of these afflictions *occurs in real history*. Since this ancient history and theological development are tightly woven, it is quite natural for modern readers to link them and to view *both* as actual historical events. However, this conflates the ancient motif of a lost idyllic age with the most important event in history—the Incarnation. Christians today must separate the fulfillment of the biblical revelation on theodicy through Jesus from Paul's ancient understanding of the origin of suffering and death through Adam. Failure to do so collapses incidental ancient categories with revealed eternal truths.

- *The Hope of Eternal Life.* A central message that Paul proclaims in Rom 5–8 and 1 Cor 15 is the hope of eternal life offered through Christ's sacrificial death and testified by His bodily resurrection. In particular, Rom 8:19–25 depicts the seamless weaving of this major New Testament theme with the ancient view of origins found in Gen 3.

> The creation awaits in eager expectation for the sons of God to be revealed. For the creation was subjected to frustration, and not of its own choice, but by the will of the One who subjected it, in *hope* that the creation itself will be liberated from its bondage to decay and brought into the glorious freedom of the children of God. We know that the whole creation has been groaning as in the pains of childbirth right up to the present time. Not only so, but we ourselves who have been the firstfruits of the Spirit, groan inwardly as we wait eagerly for our adoption as sons, the redemption of our bodies. For in this *hope* we were saved. But *hope* that is seen is no *hope* at all. Who *hopes* for what he already has? But if we *hope* for what do not yet have, we wait for it patiently. (Rom 8:19–25; italics added)

In stating that the creation "was subjected to frustration," "has been groaning," and continues to be in "bondage to decay," Paul is *looking backward* to Gen 3 and God's judgment upon the entire physical world. Clearly, his position continues to reflect the first stage of theodicy, which is ultimately framed on the lost idyllic age motif and an ancient understanding of the origin of suffering and death. This passage also affirms the reality of decomposition and harsh afflictions in nature. The apostle definitely believed in the cosmic fall since he saw decay and death around him. But more significantly, he admonishes Christians to *focus forward* upon the hope of the "redemption of their bodies" and their "adoption as children of God." Thus, believers today must separate Paul's incidental ancient history and ancient science from the inerrant divine promise that the Lord will end the present world and usher in for them a glorious eternal existence. This message is our hope.

- *Typological Use of Adam.* Paul employs Adam as an archetype in his sin-death passages. In fact, he even states in Rom 5 that Adam "was a *pattern* [Greek: *tupos*] of the One to come." Similarly, 1 Cor 15 asserts that the sin of the First Adam brought divine judgment and death; and the death of the Second Adam offers justification before God and the removal of sin. Many Christians attempt to argue that Paul's mention of Adam alongside that of Jesus in these passages confirms his historicity.[32] Of course, the apostle accepted that the first man mentioned in Scripture was a real person, but that was the history and science-of-the-day. The typological use of Adam does not impart historicity to him. Moreover, this archetypal employment of an unhistorical sinful being in no way undermines the historical reality of Jesus and His taking away sin, as some contend. For example, the actual removal of sin by animal sacrifice is not historically true either, but this Hebrew practice was an invaluable symbol. It was a reminder of the reality of human sin and the need for divine atonement. Similarly, the typological use of Adam by Paul reminds Christians today of their sinfulness and the necessity of the atoning sacrifice on the Cross.

A few more comments regarding Paul's sin-death passages are necessary. First, the context of Rom 5–8 and 1 Cor 15 is not a defense of, or a debate over, the historicity of Adam and how death actually entered the world. Instead, it focuses on the reality of sin, Jesus' sacrifice for sin, and His resurrection from the dead. The literal interpretation of Gen 3 was a given for Paul as was the 3-tier universe. In other words, the human authorial intention of these passages assumed an ancient view of origins, and the divine authorial intention accommodated to this incidental understanding. Christians appealing to Paul's sin-death passages in order to establish the reality of Adam and to determine the actual origin of death fail to recognize and respect the ancient intellectual categories that shaped the scientific and historical views of the apostle.

Second, the ancient understanding of origins in Rom 5–8 and 1 Cor 15 is consistent with the statements regarding the physical world throughout the rest of Scripture. As noted previously, God could have revealed the evolutionary origins of humanity, suffering, and death. It was within His power to inspire Paul and cancel the causal connection between sin and death in the way the New Testament abolishes the Hebrew sacrificial system. But such revelations would introduce blatant inconsistencies in Scripture. Overwhelming biblical evidence indicates that the Holy Spirit did not reveal modern science ahead of its time. Casting the Message of Faith within an incidental evolutionary vessel during the first century would have been confusing, terribly disruptive, and a stumbling block to Paul, the ancient readers of his letters, and ultimately the preaching of the Gospel.

Finally, the historicity of Adam and his sin is not necessary for Christianity. Knowing how sin actually entered the world is no more essential to faith than is the knowledge of when each of us became a sinner. Despite being cast in ancient historical and scientific categories, Rom 5–8 and 1 Cor 15 have sufficiently revealed the essence of the Gospel, and every generation of believers has proficiently grasped it: the reality of human sin, the absolute necessity of the forgiveness of sins through the Cross, and the wonderful hope of eternal life with the Lord Jesus.

Paul's passages on the sin and death of Adam are quite challenging to interpret because they include five distinct features that are seamlessly interwoven—Gen 3 ancient origins, Gen 3 Divine Theology on sin, Gen 3 theodicy and the New Testament's fulfillment of theodicy, the hope of eternal life, and the typological use of Adam. The identification of these characteristics is difficult, and their conflation is easy. Therefore, categorical differentiation is necessary to separate the Divine Theology from the incidental ancient history and ancient science in Rom 5–8 and 1 Cor 15. Fig 8-5 outlines Paul's sin-death passages in the light of the Message-Incident Principle.

The biblical and theological precedents outlined in this section provide a framework through which to view the sin-death problem and offer a solution. Scripture presents many statements about the physical world that are false. This in no way undermines the authority of the Bible. Instead, it indicates that the Holy Spirit accommodated to the level of ancient peoples. The origin of suffering and death in Gen 3 is an ancient understanding with no correspondence to physical reality in the past. Scripture also shows definite theological development. Particularly challenging to the sin-death problem are the facts that theodicy develops through the Bible and that it is seamlessly interwoven with an ancient

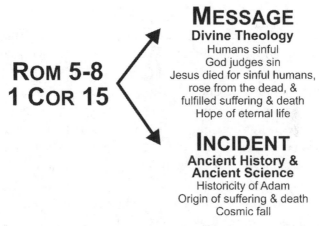

MESSAGE
Divine Theology
Humans sinful
God judges sin
Jesus died for sinful humans,
rose from the dead, &
fulfilled suffering & death
Hope of eternal life

ROM 5-8
1 COR 15

INCIDENT
Ancient History &
Ancient Science
Historicity of Adam
Origin of suffering & death
Cosmic fall

Fig 8-5. **Sin-Death Passages of Paul and the Message-Incident Principle.** Rom 5–8 and 1 Cor 15 seamlessly weave the Gospel of Jesus with the Divine Theology and ancient origins of Gen 3. Instead of looking back on the causal connection between Adam's sin and death, Christians today must move beyond the ancient history and ancient science to focus forward upon the inspired Message—the hope of eternal life.

understanding of the origin of suffering and death. Identifying these categories and reading beyond them is quite counterintuitive. Yet history offers an encouraging example that this will eventually happen and become more comfortable. After the sixteenth century, believers used Copernicus' astronomy and moved past biblical verses stating the earth is stationary and the sun crosses the sky daily. So too, twenty-first century Christians informed by evolutionary biology will read beyond the ancient origins and first stage of theodicy in Gen 3.

To conclude, there is no sin-death problem. Adam never existed, and therefore suffering and death did not enter the world in divine judgment for his transgression. The origin of physical death presented in Gen 3 is rooted in ancient history and ancient science. Consequently, sin is not causally connected to death, and no conflict exists between Gen 3 and the fossil record. To be sure, the solution proposed in this section is quite complex. But the divine revelation in Gen 3, Rom 5–8, and 1 Cor 15 is very simple: humans are sinners, God judges sin, and Jesus died for sinful men and women. The sin-death problem is ultimately the product of a conceptual distance in the categories between inspired writers of Scripture and its modern readers. Christians today must identify the incidental ancient view of origins and separate it from the inerrant Messages of Faith. Indeed, sin entered the world, but not with Adam.

CHAPTER SUMMARY

Evolutionary creation offers a Christian approach to human evolution that embraces a healthy relationship between Scripture and science. This view of origins recognizes and respects the limits of both the Book of God's Words and the Book of God's Works. The former states that we alone are created by God in His Image, that everyone has fallen into sin, and that He judges us for our sins. The latter demonstrates that humankind evolved from primitive forms of life. In light of the Metaphysics-Physics Principle, it is impossible for these theological and scientific facts to conflict. The purpose of evolutionary science is to reveal that through common descent we share flesh with other living organisms, while the divine authorial intention of the Bible is to proclaim that we are so much more than mere flesh. Evolutionary creationists conclude that human spiritual characteristics manifested gradually and mysteriously during the physical process of evolution that eventually created men and women.

The controversy over human origins in the Church is primarily the result of a literal and concordist reading of the origins accounts in Scripture. Most believers conflate the inerrant and infallible divine revelations with the incidental ancient conceptualizations of the beginning of the world. Evolutionary creation rejects the traditional assumption that these passages feature scientific concordism and historical concordism. By employing the Message-Incident Principle, this Christian position separates the Divine Theology concerning the spiritual nature of humans from the ancient understanding of their physical origins. In particular, the *de novo* creation of Adam and Eve is based on ancient science, and consequently the first man and woman in Scripture never existed. The entrance into the world of suffering and death reflects ancient history and the notion of a lost idyllic age, indicating that the events in the garden of Eden never happened. Without a doubt, recognizing and respecting this incidental ancient view of origins is quite counterintuitive, and even threatening. Yet Church history reveals the power of the biblical accounts on the creation and fall of humanity—the Messages of Faith have always been understood by those who read the Word of God on their knees. Fig 8-6 summarizes an evolutionary creationist approach to interpreting passages dealing with human origins in the Bible.

Coming to terms with suffering and death has been one of the greatest challenges faced by men and women in every generation. There is no

MESSAGE OF FAITH

God created humans
Humans bear Image of God
Humans sinful
God judges sin

INCIDENTAL ANCIENT ORIGINS

Creation of Adam & Eve
De novo creation motif
Entrance of suffering & death
Lost idyllic age motif

Fig 8-6. Human Origins in the Bible. The creation of Adam and Eve and their fall in the garden of Eden are incidental ancient vessels that remind men and women that God created us in His Image and that He will judge us for our sins.

simple solution. The discovery of biological evolution with its violently competitive processes leading to the survival of the fittest only magnifies this problem. Yet the life and teaching of Jesus fulfills the biblical revelation on theodicy. Suffering and death have divine purpose and ultimately glorify God. As Christians mature and incarnate this scripturally-based theodicy into their personal lives, they come to recognize that the challenge of evolution's vicious nature eventually fades. To be sure, evolutionary science calls for a reformulation of the traditional Christian understanding of the origin of suffering and death. The reinterpretation of Gen 3, Rom 5–8, and 1 Cor 15 in light of the evolutionary Works of God frees the inspired messages from their incidental ancient vessels. Instead of focusing backward on the causal connection between Adam's sin and his condemnation to suffer and die, we must look forward to the central revelation in the Words of God—the hope of eternal life with the Lord Jesus.

Finally, perspective is always needed when dealing with human origins. The Church is built upon no one other than Jesus Christ. Adam never died for our sins, but the Lord did. Believers are Christ-ians and not Adam-ites. The Cross should never be conflated with the historicity of Adam, his sin, and judgment. I am confident that Christians will eventually come to terms with human evolution. In doing so, we shall recast the aphorism made famous by Galileo: *The Bible does not teach us how God made humans or how suffering and death entered the world, but that we were created in the Image of the Father, Son, and Holy Spirit, that He judges our sins, and that Jesus died on the Cross in order to forgive us.*

9

Coming to Terms with Evolution: A Personal Story

MY STORY IS NOT unique. Everyone wrestles at some point with the meaning of life, and for a scientific generation like ours, this process of personal discovery is often connected to the issue of origins. It is both natural and logical. Understanding how humans came into being will affect our beliefs as to who we are, how we live, and what we hope for. Like many people, I lost my childhood faith as a university student after studying evolutionary biology. In returning to the Lord years later, I rejected evolution, as most Bible-believing Christians do. These are common experiences for people raised in a culture entrenched in the evolution vs. creation dichotomy.

At the same time, my story is rather unusual in that I completed a PhD in theology and a PhD in biology in order to make sense of origins. As well, the view of creation that I finally embraced is rarely, if ever, heard in churches. Becoming an evolutionary creationist during graduate school involved many trying moments. Yet I have come to the conclusion that struggle is a vital part of the human voyage and our relationship with the Creator. In fact, the word "Israel" is made up of the Hebrew words *śārâ* (to struggle, persist, exert) and *'ēl* (God). It first appears in the Bible after Jacob wrestled with God. Following this encounter, the Lord declared, "Your name will no longer be Jacob, but Israel, because you have struggled with God and with men and have overcome" (Gen 32:28). Since Christians are the New Israel, we can expect that our spiritual journey will include some difficult and challenging periods. Dealing with origins will be one of those times.

Before beginning my personal story I would like to make one cautionary comment. My conversion to Christianity as a young adult is one of those born-again stories. Regrettably, there is a gossipy tabloid interest in some church circles to publicize these dramatic sinner-to-saint conversions, and too often the sins of the past get glorified instead of the Blood that paid for sin. As I share a few stories about where my sinfulness led me, I pray that they not be interpreted as boasting about sin or spiritual pride. Being in rebellion toward God is nothing to be proud of. I simply want to show the intimate connection that existed between my view of origins and my behavior. The point in sharing some of this personal history is to underline that the topic of origins is indeed a very important issue. It shapes our worldview and how we act. Here now is my spiritual and intellectual journey in coming to terms with evolution.

RAISED IN THE ORIGINS DICHOTOMY

I was born into a good French-Canadian Roman Catholic home and I enjoyed a fine education provided by the Catholic school system in Edmonton, Alberta, Canada. There was unconditional love and healthy discipline in our family. My mother was a stay-at-home mom and a deeply committed Christian. Her central "commandment" to her five children was simply "be good to each other." I suspect that I will never fully appreciate the spiritual impact of her love, prayers, and godly example on our family. Dad owned a car alignment business and worked six days a week. One of his favorite "proverbs" was "When you're eighteen get the *%@# out of my fridge!" Indeed, he ingrained in his children a sense of accountability. We understood that it was our responsibility to take care of ourselves and become contributing members of society.

My faith was typical of any child in that it was dependent on those around me—family, school, and church. I distinctly remember intimate moments in prayer before the Lord that were as real as any that I experience today. I understood the difference between right and wrong at an early age, and confessing my sins brought a wonderful peace to my soul. In particular, I recall the sense of being clean following the Catholic practice of confession. I also remember the power of music at church, especially the song *Holy, Holy, Holy* which always moved me. Those early years were rather uneventful. I loved to play hockey and golf, never got into any real trouble, and even enjoyed school and got good grades when I tried. I was just an average Catholic kid growing up during the 1960s in Canada.[1]

These early childhood influences eventually gave way to the forces of a growing secular culture as I was leaving high school in 1972. I was the eldest in our family and the first among my relatives to go to a university. It was an intimidating experience to say the least. I entered Collège St. Jean, an affiliate college of the University of Alberta. The college was the intellectual and cultural center of the French-Canadian community where students could take many of their undergraduate courses in French. Sadly, the college was by and large secularized despite its Roman Catholic roots. It was steeped in the political and philosophical thinking of twentieth century French culture. Many viewed atheists Albert Camus and Jean Sartre as intellectual heroes.

I understood the message of these French philosophers to be that life was ultimately absurd and meaningless, and that our best response to this bleak reality was to take charge of our situation and live for the moment. It takes little imagination to speculate on how such a worldview is implemented by a healthy eighteen-year-old male in the process of losing his religious moorings. There were a few priests at the college, but I do not remember them ever standing up to defend God or Christianity. They were kind and everybody liked them, yet we saw them as irrelevant "nice guys." As well, I cannot recall one student who was openly Christian. There was an intellectual smugness amongst those who claimed to be agnostics and atheists, and I interpreted this attitude to mean that the best thinkers had long ago rejected the existence of God. Like any first-year university student, I was impressionable and wanted to fit in. Not recognizing the indoctrinating secular pressures upon me, it was not long before I was being swayed by the ideas and attitudes of professors and senior students.

The most powerful force shaping the development of my worldview during the early university years was science, in particular the theory of biological evolution. Scientific evidence was more convincing to my mind than the arguments of philosophers because it was tangible. Being a biology major, I quickly succumbed to a second smug attitude, which was that science is the only credible form of thinking. The so-called "artsies" in the humanities dealt only with shifting "opinions" and "subjective" knowledge, while scientists were engaged with the hard "facts" and "objective" Truth.[2] We in the science departments were the university's "pure" thinkers. The success of science in the world needed no defense because everyone enjoyed its fruits daily. It was natural then for me, like so many others, to believe that only science explained reality and would even offer solutions to all our problems. Indeed, there wasn't a better boy positivist than me!

My first course in biology was on evolutionary theory. The instructor began the introductory lecture by stating that evolution did not necessarily undermine religion. But most of us interpreted this as a politically correct statement, since after all, the college had Catholic roots. During the course we were exposed to an incredible amount of biological beauty, complexity, and functionality. Yet not once was the notion of intelligent design ever mentioned. This is regrettable, because the concept of natural revelation is a time-honored principle in Roman Catholic theology. The silence was deafening. And the message was clear: the origin of life through only natural processes fitted nicely into the secular worldview that was appearing in all my other classes. It also seemed that every aspect of our existence was marked by Darwin's mechanism of evolution, the famed concept of "survival of the fittest." I was seeing that only the strong survived in sports, academics, and of course, dating and mating. All around me a ruthless competitiveness was being subtly endorsed, and a cutthroat aggressiveness was slowly developing in me.

I then made what I thought was a logical deduction: if evolution is true, then the Bible must be wrong and Christianity is false. Scripture states that the world was created in six days, but science proves otherwise. Arriving at this conclusion was painless and involved little to no struggle. Even though I had had some real spiritual experiences, my Christian faith to that point in life was at best inherited, poorly nurtured, and never really examined. It lacked personal commitment and a mature love for God. This religious belief was typical of most of my friends in that it was dependent on our families and Catholic school education. However, my surroundings had changed. I was now in the secular university world. For the first time in my life I was consciously developing a worldview. But I started this process of self-discovery trapped in the origins dichotomy.

The decision to reject the Bible's view of origins soon came to the attention of my parents. I remember the discussion like it was yesterday. It was a classic confrontation. Mom and dad challenged my dwindling church attendance, and I defended my lack of interest in Christianity with my newly acquired scientific worldview and the theory of evolution. My parents were handcuffed and could not respond to the evidence and arguments I offered. They had never had the privilege of attending a university or studying science and biological evolution. I distinctly remember pounding on the kitchen table numerous times and stating that Noah's flood never occurred because there was no scientific evidence whatsoever for a worldwide flood. Instead, the fossil record proved that life on earth came about through evolution. I am sure that this episode was very difficult for my parents. They experienced the success of scientific advances daily, yet their first-born child was arguing that science disproves the Bible and their religious beliefs.

The break from Christianity during my first year of college did not result in immediately becoming an atheist with a view of life having no ultimate purpose or meaning. At the end of my freshman year, I recorded in my diary:

> It seems that whenever someone does something it can be explained away by examining the individual's background. The more I study this the more it seems that man is nothing but mere chemical reactions programmed by DNA. . . . But there's more, I'm sure. (28 April 1973)

Science was the most influential factor informing my worldview. I accepted that biology explained our physical origins, and this was quickly followed with the belief that psychology accounted for our behavior. DNA was not only the basic component that connected all of life through evolution, but genetics explained our mental capacities, daily behavior, and even religious tendencies, as I learned in a course on evolutionary psychology. During the early 1970s, positivism and scientism reigned in universities and students were being thoroughly indoctrinated with this secular bias. It asserted that if a statement cannot be proven scientifically, then it is meaningless, and therefore not true and of no consequence. According to this skewed view of science, religion is only an illusion and an accidental by-product of human evolution.

I was certainly going down the path to atheism. Yet as my diary entry reveals, something deep inside my soul told me that despite our biological basis and psychological conditioning, "there's more, I'm sure." I understood where the logic of my science was leading me, but intuitively I sensed some sort of ultimate purpose or meaning in the universe. Today, I realize that this "voice within" is common to all of us thanks to God's grace and the way in which He has created us. Natural revelation is a powerful declaration that the world is teleological. It also provides us with a basic sense of right and wrong referred to in Scripture as the "law written on our hearts" (Rom 2:15). But even this last ray of light was being darkened by my secular education. Psychology classes wrote off any sense of guilt or traditional morality I experienced as mere behavioral conditioning from my Roman Catholic upbringing. To have an authentic life, I was told that I had to transcend my religious baggage. And before long, my own sinfulness and the hardening of my heart saw me swept away by the values of a time that has come to be known as "the drugs, sex, and rock n' roll generation."

My soul yearned for purpose and meaning, but I had no idea where these were to be found. Entrenched in the origins dichotomy, the Bible and organized religion were not even considered in my developing worldview. I did not reject the existence of God outright, yet I lived as if He did not exist. Except, of course, when I desperately needed Him, like when it looked as if I might become a teenaged father—I sure prayed a lot then. In other words, I was basically a deist with a god-of-the-emergencies to save me from the consequences of my foolishness and immorality.

I entered the faculty of dentistry at the University of Alberta in the fall of 1974. I also joined the Canadian Armed Forces at that time in order to pay for my education. Dental school was the first time I had ever encountered people my own age who were completely committed to their religious beliefs and concerned about witnessing the Gospel. I was impressed with their many arguments for the existence of God and the belief that He had inspired the Bible. But more importantly, the greatest witness to faith was the consistent and godly lifestyle these students led. That spoke volumes to me more than any rational defense for Christianity, and I never forgot it. In many ways, I wanted what they had. Though that small voice in my soul was becoming more silent as my heart hardened, it nevertheless revealed to me that godly living was right, and deep inside my spirit I yearned for it.

Yet I was entrenched in a lifestyle marked by godlessness and lustful excesses. The details are not important, other than to confess that life centered all on my desires and me. The deism in my early university years slipped into and out of agnostic periods until finally I embraced atheism. In a revealing entry in my diary, I came to the conclusion:

> Love is a protective response characteristic of all animals, except expressed to greater levels in man because of his superior intelligence. (20 June 1977)

I remember well the period during which I wrote this entry. I was wickedly cynical at the time. One of my favorite aphorisms was "love is a herd response." In other words, humans are just a herd of procreating animals. It does not take much imagination to picture how I treated women. Even marriage didn't really mean anything because it was "nothing but" a convention invented by men to control society. There wasn't anything sacred about it, after all the Sacred did not exist. Though my heart was hardening and getting darker, there was still a small voice telling me that what I was doing was wrong. Yet this sense of guilt was rationalized away with a dysteleological interpretation of psychology and evolution. I wrote off the voice inside me as simply conditioning from my Roman Catholic upbringing, and I often repeated a mantra I had concocted:

> Psychological baggage of Catholicism, you're nothing but an animal. Psychological baggage of Catholicism, you're nothing but an animal. Psychological baggage of Catholicism, you're nothing but an animal.

In the last year of dental school, some Christians in the class invited me to a debate that eventually had a huge impact upon my life. The two participants were a leading young earth creationist from the United States and a dysteleological evolutionist from the biology department. My first thought was that this was a joke. Who could be so ridiculous as to challenge evolution at a major university? Yet, I was intrigued. Still trapped in the origins dichotomy, I reasoned that if there was a God and the Bible was true, then the issue that derailed my childhood faith—biological evolution—would have to be dealt with. So I went. The anti-evolutionist was Dr. Duane Gish from the Institute of Creation Research, the most important creation science organization in the world. He had a PhD in biochemistry from the University of California at Berkeley. This certainly caught my attention because I had never imagined that there were real scientists who were anti-evolutionists. But more shockingly, Gish took the biology professor to task.[3] I cannot remember details of the debate, but a powerful impression had been made on me. It might be possible to defend the existence of God scientifically. At a deep foundational level, my dysteleological worldview was shaken. And as my story will reveal, I never forgot the name "Gish."

A PEACEKEEPER MEETS THE PRINCE OF PEACE

I graduated from dental school in 1978 and began serving a four-year contract with the Canadian Armed Forces. It was wonderful to be out of school for the first time in my life. Secular culture had indoctrinated me into thinking that happiness was found in a self-serving lifestyle. For me, this meant fast cars, lots of parties, and playing as much golf as possible. I had the toys that most of the boys wanted. From a distance, people would say I was having the time of my life. However, I had an uneasy feeling deep inside of me. To use an aphorism of that day, I knew that "there was something wrong with this picture."

The military environment certainly provided many opportunities for wantonness. One of the most sought after postings was a six-month tour of duty on the island of Cyprus as a United Nations peacekeeper. The political situation had settled down and there was no real danger. The tour was unaccompanied, meaning that families stayed behind in Canada. We worked mornings, enjoyed the sun and sports in the afternoons, and three to four evenings a week there was some sort of social engagement with lots of alcohol. I had starting applying for Cyprus when I was still in dental school. This is the only part of my story where I'll share a few sordid details because I think they are important in understanding my conversion to Christ.

I left for Cyprus in October 1979. The night before leaving I "reasoned" that since this was the last time I would be in Canada during the 1970s, I had to celebrate. I found a party with some gentlemen from Newfoundland. They are well known for their hard drinking and in particular a moonshine called "screech." Of course, being from Western Canada, my cowboy logic led me to conclude that I had to give these east coast boys a few lessons in how to drink. I had never had screech before, and all I remember are flashes of being carried out of the party, flying across the ocean on a plane, and landing in Lahr, Germany. I was never so sick in all my life. I stayed in bed for three days and I was enraged with myself for wasting my first time in Europe. I had drunk excessively before, but never to this extent. The experience scared me. For the first time in my life, I wondered if I had a problem and whether I was losing control. Let me be clear: I am certainly not endorsing alcohol intoxication. But, if there ever was a "good" drunk, that was it. The episode shook me to the core of my being. And I've never been drunk since.

After those three pathetic bedridden days in Germany, I arrived in Cyprus to serve as the dentist to a regiment of more than five hundred soldiers. Of course, the first night started with a welcoming party. A couple of officers thought it would be a good idea to break-in the new "tooth mechanic," as I was called. Health professionals are not seen as real military personnel, but hard partying was a way to be one of the boys. I was really in no mood to drink that night; the very thought of alcohol turned my stomach. Yet there was another way to be initiated. Someone had hired a woman. I remember the chuckling in the background when she was introduced to me. I knew exactly what the boys meant when they said that it was time for me to be "a good soldier and serve my country." After offering some lame excuse to go back to the officer's quarters, I promised to return. While standing alone in my room it hit me hard that this was so very, very wrong. My stomach churned. And I didn't return. In fact, I've never returned to sexual immorality.

Looking back now, that first night on the island was critical. Not being aware of it, my actions made a loud statement—the dentist didn't drink and run around. Those decisions separated and freed me from a hard-partying crowd of guys who before would have been my best pals. Quite unintentionally, my behavior also released me from my past and opened an opportunity to re-evaluate life. Here I was, twenty-five years of age, and I started asking myself whether all that life had to offer was drinking and women. I felt empty and I felt unclean.

All the stories I had heard about Cyprus were true. It was six months of debauchery. There was excessive drinking everywhere. But what troubled me the most was seeing men with a wife (some pregnant) and children back in Canada taking advantage of Cypriot women. Canadian soldiers were viewed as a windfall to a comfortable life back in North America. The men knew it, and they used it. I was especially disturbed watching some who were the age of my father involved with women younger than me. That troubled me to no end. The evil was palpable. Yet amidst the infidelities, a light shone that I will never forget. There was an officer who would stand in line for hours almost every night at the door to the ham radio in order to speak with his wife for only five minutes, the limit of time we were allotted. He was a quiet guy. I am not sure if he was religious. But I knew two things: what he was doing was right, and I wanted to be like him. Living righteously was once again beckoning me.

I became a Christian during the Cyprus tour through reading the gospel of John. I cannot remember putting an old King James Version of the Bible in my pack when leaving Canada, nor do I recall exactly when or why I started reading Scripture. I just did. The grace of God and the mystery of a mother's prayers were undoubtedly factors. At the beginning of the tour I distinctly remember feeling dirty, but as I embraced the message of Jesus in John's gospel, I started to have a sense of cleansing. There were no visions, angels, or major crises in my life. I simply yearned for holiness. And as I read my Bible, I experienced filth being washed away from inside of me. If a conversion moment has to be chosen, it was Good Friday. Only about half a dozen soldiers showed up for the chapel service. It was there that the meaning of the Crucifixion fully gripped me—Jesus died for my sins. I began to weep during the Scripture reading and continued for the rest of the service. Distressed by my tears, a chaplain walked me back to the quarters in the hope of comforting me. He asked if there were problems with work or back at home with a girlfriend or my family. I said "no" to all of his questions and kept repeating, "Jesus died for my sins." The padre had no idea what had just occurred in his chapel . . . the power of the Gospel message had transcended its incidental messenger.

I soon sent a postcard to my mother sharing the good news. On the front of it was written: "The people living in darkness have seen a great light; on those living in the land of the shadow of death a light has dawned" (Matt 4:16). On the back was a request to send me a Bible in *normal English*! My conversion was quickly followed by an intense desire to know more about Christianity. Mom sent a modern translation of Scripture along with a number of introductory books on faith. But the most significant Christian book in my growing collection was one that I found while on holiday in Israel. I walked into a dingy little bookstore in Tel Aviv, and near the back in a dark and dusty corner was Duane Gish's famed *Evolution: The Fossils Say NO!* (1972). I remembered exactly who Gish was, and how could I interpret finding his book in such an unusual place other than God putting it in my hands? Filled with excitement, I went directly to the beach and read it in one afternoon. Gish convinced me that a massive conspiracy was happening in the scientific community. There was no evidence for evolution, and this fact was being held from the public. Still trapped in the origins dichotomy, I flipped sides once more.

The Cyprus tour changed my life forever. How do I sum up my conversion to Christianity? When I left Canada to serve as a peacekeeper,

I was spiritually empty and so intoxicated with alcoholic spirits that I hardly remember crossing the Atlantic; but six months later I returned home filled by the Holy Spirit and the peace of Jesus. Indeed, I had been born again, a new creation in Christ.

THE MAKING AND CALLING
OF A YOUNG EARTH CREATIONIST

After Cyprus, I was posted to the Canadian Armed Forces Base in Calgary, Alberta. Spiritual life up to that point had been for the most part in my room with a Bible. As a new Christian I did not understand the importance of fellowship with other believers. Then one morning in the officers club, I met a medical student who invited me to a Sunday service. It was at a large Christian Missionary Alliance Church. Being raised as a Roman Catholic, the experience of meeting evangelical Protestants was quite a "culture" shock. But that soon passed and I was blessed by the preaching of a wonderful senior pastor. His love for the Word of God impacted me deeply, and today it continues to shape both my personal life and professional practice as a theologian. This church also provided a large community of young adults. It was so refreshing to be around people my own age who were not interested in the pagan lifestyle I had previously been part of. In fact, I even discovered women for the first time in my life (ain't that amazing!?!). And they have become some of my very best friends.

I had found a spiritual home that focused on Jesus, the Bible, and living for God. Of course, being an evangelical church, the view of origins espoused by most of the members was young earth creation. This aligned well with my growing interest in Duane Gish and creation science. But more importantly, this view of origins was consistent with my reading and experience of Scripture. During the Cyprus tour, I had read the events in the gospel of John literally and this led to my conversion to Christianity. And now I was enjoying the fruits of a holy lifestyle, which was also built on the plain meaning of Scripture. Moreover, I was educated as a dentist and had never taken a university-level English course. I had little to no understanding of literature, let alone ancient literary works. And I was oblivious to the possibility that the Bible featured an ancient origins account inspired by the Holy Spirit. Therefore, it is no surprise that I was a strict literalist and a young earth creationist.

My conversion to Christianity was not only a spiritual rebirth but also an intellectual revolution. I became a voracious reader after Cyprus. Still entrenched in the origins dichotomy, I reasoned that young earth creation was the key to building a Christian worldview. I read and nearly memorized the standard books, including John Whitcomb and Henry Morris' *The Genesis Flood* (1961) and the latter's *Scientific Creationism* (1974). In the summer of 1981, I attended a week-long workshop offered by the Institute for Creation Research. It was there that I met Canada's leading young earth creationist, Margaret Helder, who has a PhD in botany. She had a remarkable impact on me and continued to encourage me well after the conference. The following winter I attended an origins debate between Gish and a scientist at the University of Calgary. The latter splattered a series of sarcastic and insulting remarks, while the former, in a professional manner, focused on scientific problems with evolution. Seeing Gish stand up in a major university and win a debate left me completely convinced of the truthfulness of creation science. A fire to defend young earth creation was beginning to burn in my soul.

I took my first public step into the origins debate in late 1981. Margaret Helder was the co-editor of *Creation Science Dialogue* and she encouraged me to contribute a brief article defending my views. Entitled "Philosophy vs. Science," I wrote:

> Whether we care to concede it or not we are born into a society that upholds a philosophical or worldview. I was the tragic end product of the current secular humanism that permeates the western hemisphere.
>
> Formally educated in the health sciences, I firmly understood that I was indeed a marvelous biomolecular machine, morally free, in an eternal expanding and contracting cosmos. Neo-Darwinian and Skinnerian theories explained physically and psychologically what I was. J.P. Sartre and Albert Camus told me not to worry about such weighty matters; after all, everything is absurd. Rather, one should live for the moment. Fluctuating between atheism and agnosticism my normal deportment was definitely marked by materialism and hedonism.
>
> In quest for comic relief in 1977 I decided to attend an evolution vs. creation debate on campus. I walked away laughing at the Bible thumper, but deep inside I realized that my foundation was under attack; not my theology, but with my own armamentarium: science. After intensive personal research, the facts clearly showed the creation model to be superior in light of the data concerning

origins. A review of the development of theology and philosophy in this past century also provided conclusive evidence of the powerful impact of this apparently innocuous doctrine.

I challenge anyone who takes pride in their objectivity to entertain seriously scientific creationism. It may very well be the most important study of your life.

Clearly, I was trapped in the origins dichotomy. But more subtly, the tangibility of science was psychologically vital for me, as it was in my first years of the university. Secular science had previously been the foundation of my atheism and immorality, now creation science undergirded my religious worldview. No doubt about it, I was reacting to my godless past, but I was still assuming that the scientific method was a central route to the Truth. Looking back now, I was in many ways a Christian "positivist."

Despite an increasing focus on the issue of origins, I knew that Jesus was the center of my belief. I sensed His presence everyday. As a maturing Christian, I could feel His hand reshaping attitudes and behaviors. It was not long before I began to wrestle with the notion of God's will. Did He really call people to do certain tasks? This issue was important because I was nearing the end of my military contract. The Canadian Armed Forces offered some fabulous opportunities. I was being allowed to assist a maxillofacial surgeon in the hospital in order to see if this dental specialty interested me. As well, there was a possibility of studying medicine at the University of Toronto while being paid my full dentist's salary. I loved the military. It was familiar and it was secure.

I suspect every Christian at some point grapples with God's will for his or her life. For me this issue became an all out war in my soul. I was completely convinced that evolution was the root of unbelief in our secular culture. Having seen Duane Gish dismantle atheists in debates at two universities made it obvious to me that this was critical work for our generation. I began to sense a calling to become a creation scientist. But it was a terrifying thought. To leave the comfort of my life and a very enjoyable career was completely against my character. I had always done things that were safe. Just about every day for two years I fluctuated violently between staying in the military and leaving in order to attack evolution. I became chronically depressed. Yet I can remember a woman in my church telling me with regard to God's will, "You just know when you are on your knees." Indeed, I knew what it was. But when I got up from my knees, did I follow His calling? No.

In September 1983 I entered medical school in Toronto. On my first Sunday before classes I went to the university to get a feel for my new surroundings. At the doors of the school a man wearing a psychedelic t-shirt and platform shoes was preaching the Gospel. He was a bit of a frightening sight. There was no one else around him, but he kept proclaiming the Good News. As I passed, he challenged me, "Do you know Jesus?" A bit insulted, I wanted to say, "Hey buddy, I've read over 400 theology books." And again he asked, "Do you know Jesus?" This time I felt convicted, and I also realized how silly my response would have been. He questioned me a third time as I walked away. I didn't respond. Then I came to a wall at the front of the medical school that had been spray painted with huge black letters spelling the words "Conditioned Response." This is a term used in psychology for the training of rats in experiments. The preaching and the vandalism converged in my mind. I was running away from Jesus like a rat conditioned to follow the most secure path in the maze of life. Somebody was trying to get through to me. And I knew Who it was.

On the first day of school, at the welcoming lecture, I sat by myself in a corner of a large auditorium. A woman came and seated herself next me. It was a bit uncomfortable because I did not know her and there were rows of free seats around me. She noticed a military crest on my briefcase, and in a foreign accent asked if I was in the armed forces. I replied, "Yes." She then said that she and her country were so grateful to the Canadian military for the peace that was brought into their lives. I immediately got an uneasy inkling. "Where is your home?" I asked. She answered, "Cyprus." This coincidence was just too much. It shook me. Jesus was reminding me of His peace that I had first tasted on that faraway island. But now there was no peace in my life despite the fact I was going to church and enjoying a fabulous career. I knew what I had to do. In fact, I had known for a long time but didn't have the guts to do it.

After the third day of school, I went home and sat in my recliner. And I sat there hardly moving well into the wee hours of the next morning. I was in wicked turmoil. I looked at all the theology books I had read; and I also saw an emergency medicine text, in which I had lost interest at page 173. From a purely logical perspective, it was obvious what my passion was. But the deeper issue was whether or not I was going to follow the sense of being called by God. Would I leave the comfort and security of my "Ur of the Chaldeans" (Gen 12:1; Heb 11:8) not knowing exactly where I was going? Weeping and depressed out of my mind, my stomach churned and churned until I rushed to the bathroom to throw up. I had hardly eaten anything the last couple of days and all I vomited were stomach fluids. Right there, with my head in a toilet bowl, I made one of the biggest decisions of my life. Three days after entering medical school, I quit. I also handed in a request to be released from the military.

OPENING THE BOOK OF GOD'S WORDS: HERMENEUTICS IS A CONTACT SPORT

In order to become a good creation scientist, I reasoned that I needed training in both theology and science. I decided to begin graduate school at Regent College in Vancouver, British Columbia, where I would focus on the early chapters of Genesis. This would be followed by studies at the Institute of Creation Research in El Cajon, California. I wrote Henry Morris and Duane Gish informing them of my plan. Gish replied and cautioned me to beware of some liberal theology on origins at Regent. But he looked forward to seeing me in the future and my joining him in the battle against evolution and secular humanism.

Regent College is one of the best evangelical graduate schools of theology in the world. Its professors include some of the most renowned Christian thinkers of the day, like the great J. I. Packer. The college achieves an amazing balance between committed spirituality and high-level academics. There was an ever-present sense of holiness among both the students and staff. I often remember professors beginning a class in prayer and wanting to open my eyes to write it down because it was so wonderful. At the same time, the school pushed me harder academically than any university I have ever attended. Students called to an academic career were more than prepared for the best PhD programs. Indeed, Regent offered an education that taught me to do scholarship not for the sake of scholarship, but for God's glory.

Of course, I had an agenda. On registration day, 30 August 1984, I outlined a battle plan in my diary and it concluded with the promise "to declare absolute and pure hell on the 'theory' of evolution." It was only a few weeks into the program when evidence for Gish's concerns about Regent surfaced. In a lecture to about one hundred students, Packer stated that the first chapters of the Bible "were obviously written in picture language." I wanted to confront him after class, but about half the students stormed the lectern ahead of me. Most were young earth creationists. I had been aware of liberal theology and had quickly developed distaste for liberal Christians. In my mind, they didn't take the Bible seriously because they didn't think it was literally true. Liberals were "theistic evolutionists" and I saw this view of origins as a compromise for people with a weak faith who didn't really trust Jesus. But hearing Packer's position on Genesis shook me. His best-selling book *Knowing God* (1973) had brought so many people to Christ. And here he was openly claiming that Genesis began with "picture language." His words seeded an unsettling tension in my mind that would take the next couple of years to come to terms with.

The pounding on my literalist hermeneutic continued in January with a three-week course on science and theology. It was a classic confrontation that has occurred in seminaries everywhere between "conservative students who took God at His Word" and "liberal professors who did not believe in the literal Word of God." A universe millions of years old was presented as an uncontested fact and evolution as the likely process for the origin of life. Students countered with literal readings of Scripture and young earth creationist arguments. It only took about thirty minutes into the course for Loren Wilkinson, an interdisciplinary scholar and the professor who lead the class, to call for a "prayer time-out" in order to cool things off. And there were a lot of these over the next three weeks. I'll confess my behavior was the worst of everyone in the room. I repeatedly used the Bible as a battle-axe.

To Wilkinson's credit, he absorbed my cheap shots. But this is not to say that he wasn't committed to his beliefs or that he wouldn't be assertive. He could be tough, yet he was always respectful. Near the end of the course I cornered him in a narrow hallway and asked him directly what he thought about young earth creation. Tersely he stated, "It is error." I can still remember how the word "error" rattled my soul. At that point in my Regent education, I had taken a philosophy course from him and had a great respect for his knowledge and integrity (In fact, he's my intellectual hero today). That moment in the hallway was powerful. And in his closing remarks to the class, he looked at me directly and said, "I must confess that I do have a serious concern, Denis. If you should ever give up your belief in creation science, would you then also give up your faith in Christ?" Ouch! That wasn't Wilkinson talking. The Holy Spirit was flowing through his words and casting a light on the foundations of my Christianity. I stammered, stumbled, and really didn't answer. Deep in my heart I knew that my relationship with Jesus was more important than any position on origins.

I walked out of this science and theology course still a young earth creationist. But it certainly opened my mind to the possibility that my reading of the Bible was in error. I began to focus more on Gen 1–11, and in my final year at Regent I wrote a masters thesis on Gen 6:1–4, the sons of God and daughters of men episode. Looking back now, there isn't a better passage in these opening chapters of Scripture to introduce a strict literalist to hermeneutics. I cannot help but suspect some divine providentialism. After writing 214 pages on these 4 verses, I didn't know what to make of this passage. Yet it was a valuable experience. I began to learn how to live with ambiguity. This was quite novel for someone like me who was trained in the sciences and saw everything in black-and-white. My positivistic tendencies were being challenged by biblical hermeneutics.

Genesis 6:1–4 also provided some specific lessons. I was amazed to discover the wide range of interpretive approaches that Christians throughout time had used to deal with this passage. Simple logic indicated that they could not all be correct. For that matter, the majority would be wrong and it would mean that some of the most important theologians in history had misinterpreted these verses. This brought perspective. I realized that Christian faith was not dependent on the interpretation of one four-verse passage in Gen 1–11. But the greatest lesson from the thesis was in understanding that biblical interpretation begins with a commitment to the actual words of Scripture. That is, the meaning of words is critical to the meaning of a passage. It was clear that the "sons of God" were celestial beings and the "daughters of men" were human beings. It didn't make any biological sense to me how they could have procreated. But this was *my* problem, not the Bible's. Scripture stated that heavenly creatures and women gave birth to giants and heroes, and my task as a theologian was to submit to the Words of God. Of course, at that time I was missing a vital category—the 1-seed theory—and this is why I didn't fully understand the passage. Yet, I was completely committed and in submission to the inspired words describing a very surreal episode. This naturally led to the thought: could it be that the Holy Spirit had used a myth in the revelatory process? A shudder reverberated through my soul. But there was more to come.

Occasionally, we experience a defining moment that changes the course of our life. One occurred when I was writing my last paper at Regent

College. I had learned in an earlier class that there were grammatical problems in translating Gen 1:1–3.[4] Being interested in the origins debate, it was obvious that I needed to have some idea of the issues. I had read these verses dozens of times before, and like everyone else, assumed that they referred to the creation of space, time, and matter. I had actually scribbled these terms in the margins of my Bible. But as my research progressed, a biblical fact began to emerge. Despite the grammatical difficulties, Gen 1:2 was definitely the opening scene of the Gen 1 creation account. A dark watery earth was already in place with no mention of when it was created. The implication was devastating for my young earth creationist position. I lost the temporal marker from which to date the earth. Shockingly, the Bible itself did not reveal when the earth came into existence.

I remember the day like it was yesterday. It was a beautiful and fresh spring morning in Vancouver with the sun flooding into the library. I was sitting at my favorite desk where I had labored daily for three years. Genesis 1:2 exploded and shattered my calling to be a creation scientist. For a brief moment, I felt deeply alienated, even betrayed. I had left an amazing military career to come to Regent and arm myself with Scripture in order to defend the inerrant and infallible biblical record of how God had created the world in six literal days. My first thought was "to hell with this. I'll get up from my desk, leave my books and everything I have in Vancouver, jump in my car, and drive home to Edmonton." I was only this paper and two exams away from finishing both Master of Divinity and Master of Christian Studies degrees. But what was the point? The vision had died.

However, this intensely dark and terrifying moment lasted no more than twenty to thirty seconds. The peace and love of the Holy Spirit quickly welled up inside of me and assured me that He had indeed called me to Regent College. My duty was to follow Him and to be the best student I could be. And yes, He had called me to focus on origins, but He was in control of my education. In calling me, the Lord had accommodated to my intellectual categories—a young earth creationist trapped in the origins dichotomy. This is where my mindset was at the time; and by grace He came down to my level. Through graduate education and particularly this paper, God freed me and made me fully aware that *how* He created His universe is ultimately incidental to the belief *that* He is the Creator. I was a creationist because I believed in a Creator. I could see it daily in the splendor of the world declaring His glory, like in that sparkling morning in Vancouver. And I could sense His presence in the love I felt in my heart at that critical moment in my walk with Him. The issue of God's creative process simply paled compared to these powerful mystical experiences.

In no time, I returned to my calling as a student and I finished what became the best paper I ever wrote at Regent. I even added a post-script that summarized my shift in understanding origins.

> I entered Regent College in September 1984 as a fire-breathing, dragon-slaying, card-carrying young earth creationist. It seems appropriate, nay, maybe even ordained that my last paper after three years at this college is this one. How I have fallen from grace!
>
> My parting thoughts on this issue of origins are now in a suspended state. I do not regress to my earlier atheism where, "In the beginning hydrogen . . . ." The idea of molecules into people defies all known biochemical laws. The sociobiological implications of the naked ape makes me wonder how man could be the apple of God's eye if humanity came about through evolution. Yet now, as a student of the Old Testament, I am beginning to question the "narrative-ness" of the opening chapters of the Bible. There seem to exist masterfully constructed, almost poetic, literary structures in this section of God's Word. It may well be that, through the creation, the fall, the sons of God episode, the flood, and the tower of Babel, God has given us stories which bear significant truths. In other words, the first part of Genesis may well be mythopoetry.
>
> It's funny, you know. I once met a theological hockey "expert" who told me that examining evolution in light of the Bible was "an irrelevant abstraction." He may be right.

When I read this post-script today there are a number of features that strike me. By the spring of 1987 I no longer accepted the "narrative-ness" or strict literal interpretation of Gen 1–11, but this did not in any way undermine my belief in the Messages of Faith in these chapters. My love for Jesus and the Bible had not changed one bit. This is the power of God's Word—it transcends our hermeneutical abilities or lack thereof.

At this time I also "suspended" my views on origins. I realized that it is perfectly acceptable for Christians not to understand how God created the world. Knowing Jesus does not require knowledge of the details of origins, but instead it involves confessing one's sinfulness and experiencing the forgiveness of sins offered through the Cross. Yet despite this claim of a suspension, I was still in the grip of evangelical anti-evolutionary arguments as evident by the comment that "the idea of molecules into people defies all known biochemical laws." Of course, I was in no position to make such a statement. Goodness gracious, I was a dentist, not a biochemist! My anti-evolutionism was also supported by the problem of justifying how a loving God could create humanity through a wasteful and vicious evolutionary process. Remarkably, I never took a class on theodicy at Regent. But this is understandable. I had only stepped away from young earth creation in the last months of the program. Up to that point, explaining the existence of pain and death was simple—Adam bit into the apple, and suffering and death were then launched upon the world. Looking back now, I did have a view of origins at that time. I held a hazy and undefined form of progressive creation. I was not aware of this origins category, and I was oblivious to the possibility that there was a conservative Christian approach to evolution.

Finally, the reference to a "theological hockey 'expert' " in the postscript was to my thesis supervisor and reader of this last paper at Regent. Dr. William Dumbrell was an Old Testament scholar from Australia and while in Canada he followed ice hockey. Knowing well my passion for my national sport, he rarely missed the opportunity to announce any loss by my beloved Edmonton Oilers. But more importantly, Dumbrell always frustrated me because he would not engage me on the origins debate, calling the issue an "irrelevant abstraction." And today, I know he's right.

Regent College was the most formative academic and spiritual experience of my life. Ironically, the evidence in Scripture undermined my vision of becoming a creation scientist. After three years of focusing on Gen 1–11, I concluded that young earth creation is un-biblical.

The sense of calling to continue my studies after Regent was clear, and this time there was no running away from God. No fluctuating, no depression, and no doubt. When on my knees, I knew exactly where I had to be. I also realized that it was time to leave the safety of an academic "cocoon of faith." In the fall of 1987, I entered a PhD program in theology specializing in science and religion at the Toronto School of Theology in the University of Toronto. The school is a consortium of seven colleges from different Christian denominations and it offers a rich and wide exposure to modern theological thought. I studied under professors who were evangelical Protestants, Roman Catholics, liberal Christians, deists, agnostics, and even atheists. Though I certainly could appreciate the arguments that skeptics of religious belief offered, there was never a moment in which I doubted my Christian faith. Actually, being exposed to unbelief and liberal theology only made my faith stronger because I saw in these belief systems anger, irrationality, and nauseating self-sufficiency. In many ways, this experience was similar to my training in the health sciences. Once I had learned the mechanisms of disease and pathology, I gained a greater appreciation for healthy anatomy and physiology.

I recognized that if I wanted to deal with the origins debate then there were issues other than Gen 1–11 that had to be explored. I headed toward historical studies in order to investigate the reactions of the first generation of evangelical scholars who encountered Darwin's theory of evolution. The research was quite a revelation. Many of these conservative Protestants embraced biological evolution and argued that it was a teleological process ordained and sustained by God.[5] Not only this, but there was little evidence that any of the leading evangelical academics at that time were young earth creationists. By the mid-1800s, they had realized that the age of the earth was millions of years old. For that matter, the spearhead document of the modern Christian fundamentalist movement, *The Fundamentals* (1910–1915), included two contributions by evangelical scholars who not only accepted an old earth, but also evolutionary change under the guidance of God.[6]

In studying these conservative Christians who first came to terms with evolution, I noted one common assumption and two arguments that often appeared in their writings. First, they adopted a Two Divine Books model. They lived the spiritual messages in the Book of God's Words and they practiced the scientific method in the Book of God's Works. Warfare did not mark their understanding of the relationship between science and religion. Second, these evangelical scholars acknowledged intelligent design in nature and extended it to include evolutionary processes. They saw the reflection of God's mind not only in the details of the world but at an overarching level across the eons of time. Finally, this first generation of evangelical evolutionists often compared the process of evolution to the mechanisms of embryology that fashion every person in their mother's womb. They argued that in both cases, humans were created by natural laws that were ordained and sustained by God.

I also researched Darwin's religious beliefs for my PhD thesis. It was another eye-opening experience that burst popular myths. In reading his diaries, notebooks, personal letters, and professional publications I gained a respect for his honesty and, in particular, his theological struggles. An unrelenting issue throughout his life was his experience with design in nature. As a scientist, Darwin read the Divine Book of Works and was impacted by the non-verbal revelation pouring forth from the creation. Even in the last year of his life, he confessed that design in nature "often comes over me with overwhelming force."[7] I was amazed by this aspect of Darwin's story. If evolution undermined the belief in intelligent design, as most Christians assume today, then one would expect the father of evolutionary theory to dismiss it completely. But he didn't. In my mind, Darwin is solid evidence that the heavens do indeed declare the glory of God!

Graduate school in Toronto offered valuable lessons from history that further opened the door to the possibility of a Christian approach to evolution. However, I was still a committed anti-evolutionist. It was now evident to me that the battle over origins would have to be fought in the scientific arena. I had a background in biology and dentistry, and I knew that teeth and jaws were critical in defending evolution. What better way would there be to attack this theory than to use some of the best-purported evidence against it? While on my knees, the calling to continue my education was clear.

OPENING THE BOOK OF GOD'S WORKS: FLYING UNDER THE RADAR AND SHOCKED AGAIN

I defended my PhD in theology on a Monday in early September 1991. The next day I flew home to Edmonton and on Wednesday began a PhD program studying biology, specializing in dental development and evolution, at the University of Alberta. No doubt about it, that's a little obsessive (and I wonder why I'm not married!). Though my training in theology had freed me from most of my scientific concordism and had introduced me to categories for a Christian perspective on evolution, I still embraced the young earth creationist vision of destroying evolutionary biology. I was now going undercover and once my doctoral program was completed, I would then declare war on evolution and the scientific establishment.

Of course, the PhD would be done with integrity. It was a matter of finding a project that suited both my supervisor and me. I had the experience in Toronto of working with a director who was an atheist, and there were topics we could agree on. My personal agenda was no one's business but mine. Hardly anyone knew why I was pursuing a second doctoral degree. If anyone asked, I just said that I was interested in teeth; after all, I was a dentist. I saw myself as a spy behind enemy lines collecting intelligence for an impending battle. In the margins of scientific papers and textbooks, I had a cryptic code to indicate problems with evolution. Anyone reading the marginalia would have no idea what it meant, or what I was planning in the future.

Safely hidden away in my apartment, I also had a notebook outlining the specific problems with dental evolution. Inspired by Charles Darwin's "Notebooks on Transmutation" in the late 1830s, it was entitled "Notebook on Immutability." As the first entry reveals, I knew that this was a rather grandiose title and I mocked myself with regard to it.

> A humble title, eh? There may be a teleological evolution, but the fact remains species do *not* transmutate on their own (i.e., without God's direct intervention); therefore, they are indeed immutable in this sense.[8]

The anti-evolutionary bravado of my young earth creationist days remained well intact. Here I was at the *beginning* of my research and I had already concluded "the *fact* remains" that life could not evolve on its own! But more interestingly, it is evident in this passage that I had yet to grasp fully the notion of teleological evolution. My idea of such a process involved God intervening and tinkering with living organisms through the eons of time, however slightly. In other words, I still embraced the God-of-the-gaps and held a modified form of progressive creation.

Of course, I could not stop thinking about theology. Near the beginning of my PhD in biology I also began a notebook on hermeneutical issues related to origins. Entitled "Notes on Genesis," the opening entry set the foundation of my interpretive approach.

> Genesis 1 is poetic and reflects ancient science. This science is the key. It's relative and it takes the rap. Ancient categories shape the science.

Reference to taking "the rap" meant that conflicts between Scripture and science were resolvable by acknowledging that the Bible featured an ancient science. My claim that this science is "relative" was another way of saying that it was incidental. But I still wrestled with concordist tendencies. Even though I had completely rejected the strict literal concordism of young earth creation, I briefly considered a progressive creationist approach to Gen 1. I asked myself in this notebook:

> Is immutability to be gleaned from Gen 1? Is creation punctiliar or
> continuous? Does Gen 1 allow for different creative periods? Can
> we glean a temporal element from Gen 1? Again, how far??? Or
> can I even ask the question?!?!

I answered the last question with "probably not." In a later entry, I also
suspected the implied immutability in Gen 1 was a reflection of an "ancient Near Eastern taxonomy." My coming to terms with evolution also
included dealing with concordist remnants still echoing in my hermeneutics. This was not a quick process.

To be sure, I was on a crusade at the beginning of my biology PhD.
Yet I was not so obsessed with attacking evolution that I was blinded from
the possibility that it could be God's creative method. In the last year of
my training in Toronto, I had seen the dentition of a chimpanzee for the
first time (Appendix 10 Fig 4A). It was a gripping moment. At that point
I had practiced dentistry for thirteen years. In restoring decayed and broken teeth, dentists shape fillings to the original anatomy of the tooth. As
I looked at the premolars and molars of a chimp, it hit me like a ton of
bricks that I had been carving these very grooves and cusps (the pointed
projections) in the teeth of my patients for years. I was aware that these
primates had about 99% of the same genes as us, but this experience of
examining their dentition was firsthand and personal. Chimp teeth were
nearly identical to human teeth. The implication was painfully obvious
. . . these creatures could easily be seen as our evolutionary cousins.

The course work for my biology PhD program began with an extensive study of the dentitions of animals that are alive today. It was an
incredible exercise. Teeth are beautiful! (I know, only a dentist would say
this.) This study led to my writing a 97-page survey on the dentitions of
mammals. It became quite clear that there was a relationship between the
form of teeth and their *function*. Fig 9-1 offers a few examples that struck
me. The gopher has huge incisors that are used for gnawing and digging.
As the cutting edge wears down, more tooth erupts from the jaw in order
to maintain the level of the bite. The back teeth of the fruit bat have flattened areas that are ideally suited for crushing ripe fruit. In contrast, the
number and size of these teeth are severely reduced in the vampire bat,
which basically has a liquid diet—blood. Its upper jaw features massive
front teeth with very sharp cutting edges that are used to lacerate unsuspecting animals.

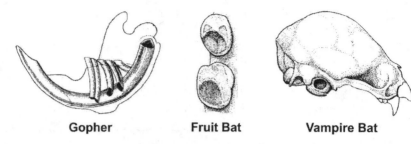

Gopher **Fruit Bat** **Vampire Bat**

Fig 9-1. Dental Form and Function. The gopher dwells mostly underground and its dentition is worn down by burrowing and eating an abrasive diet. The root tips are open-ended and allow for tooth eruption throughout life. The crushing regions on the upper molar teeth of a fruit bat appear as darken areas. The molars in a vampire bat are rudimentary and basically non-functional.

These scientific facts quickly led to thoughts about their theological implications. In my "Notebook on Immutability" I wrote:

> There seems to be little doubt that there is dental specialization. There are certain teeth for certain tasks. But the issue is this:
>
> (1) Did one type of dentition evolve into another dentition?
>
> (2) Or is it that animals have been created *de novo* and placed in their proper ecological niche with the proper dentition?

The second option was clearly a progressive creationist view of the origins of dentitions. Yet I was open to the idea that evolution accounted for amazing anatomical and functional variation in teeth as evident in the first option. At the time I didn't know how this could have occurred, but in my mind it was a reasonable possibility.

A more challenging issue arose with the origin of flesh-slashing teeth like those of tigers, sharks, and vampire bats.[9] In my "Notebook on Genesis" I pondered:

> If there was no death in early Genesis, then all the amazing killer teeth would have had to come in with sin. That is, they would have been created after the fall. Maybe this is what the fig leaf symbolizes. You're such a fundie!!!

In other words, if living organisms before the fall were sustained by consuming only plants and fruits as stated in Gen 1 and 2, then there was no reason for God to have originally created animals with teeth intended to cut and puncture flesh, since these are hardly useful for vegetarians.

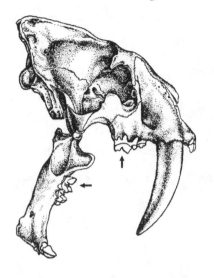

Fig 9-2. Saber-Toothed Tiger. The canines of the upper jaw (saber-teeth) are ideally suited for puncturing and slashing prey to death. The carnassials are specialized molars that are blade-like teeth used for slicing flesh of victims (arrows). Saber-toothed tigers appeared 1.6 million years ago, well before the origin of humans.

Thus, the vicious 5-inch canines in sabre-tooth tigers (Fig 9-2) would have been created after Adam and Eve had sinned. I even proposed a concordist interpretation of Gen 3 suggesting that the fig leaf coverings made by the first couple were symbolic of the new physical conditions in the world after sin had entered. That is, after the cosmic fall, God graciously equipped certain animals with a carnivorous dentition; similar to the way He took care of the first humans and clothed them. Yet I quickly mocked myself realizing that my concordism smacked of a literalist fundamentalist hermeneutic. I was starting to think about the sin-death problem from an evolutionary perspective, and I didn't have a clue how to solve it. But more importantly, I sensed no panic whatsoever for not having an explanation. There was a peace in my heart and mind. God was in control of my education and I trusted that the answer to this issue would arrive in its proper time.

Fossils answered my questions about the origin of different dentitions. This was the next major study in my course work. Robert C. Carroll's magnificently illustrated *Vertebrate Paleontology and Evolution* (1988) proved to be an invaluable resource. I began to see a definite pattern across the geological record: (1) the basic materials for teeth first arose as body armor on jawless fish, (2) the jaws of fish then became functional and simple teeth appeared, and (3) with the arrival of land animals, dentitions became specialized and passed through numerous transitional stages.

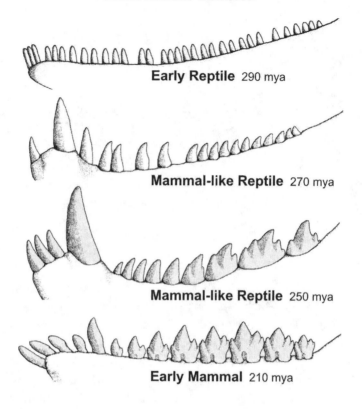

Fig 9-3. Reptile-to-Mammal Dental Evolution. Transitional stages and a pattern from simple-to-complex dentitions are evident in lower jaws. mya: million years ago. Redrawn by Braden Barr.

Fig 9-3 offers some examples. Most reptiles have simple, cone-shaped, single-rooted teeth that are all about the same size. These function well for grasping and killing prey. As reptiles evolved into mammals, teeth began to lengthen at the corner of the mouth, creating a specialized puncturing weapon (the canine) and making these organisms more proficient killers. Later mammal-like reptiles featured transitional dentitions with a reduction in the number of cheek teeth and the beginning of pointed cusps. Finally, mammals arose with distinct incisors, canines, premolars, and molars. The back teeth were now multi-rooted, wider from front-to-back, and had cusps which interlocked with those of the opposing jaw. This last dental feature increased the proficiency of chewing and allowed the animal to draw more nutrients from prey.

It was this type of scientific evidence that led me in a notebook entry to ask myself directly:

> Am I headed in an evolutionary direction? I must admit I don't feel so intimidated with evolution as when I was a young earth creationist.

Indeed, seeing the data firsthand in the Book of God's Works was a freeing experience. I recognized that this was the Lord's world and I did not need to fear the amazing discoveries that science offered. My theological speculations also continued during this period. In another entry, I wrote:

> Such a *subtleness* about God. He used an ancient text and a carpenter's Son to reveal Himself. Same goes for His informing us that He created the world. He used mythopoetry.

Clearly, an Incarnational approach to the first chapters of Genesis was beginning to crystalize in my mind. I was seeing parallels between Jesus who came as a humble human servant and Scripture that featured humble human literary categories. Yet in both cases, the powerful Messages of Faith transcended the vessels that delivered them.

In the summer of 1994 I attended my first science-religion conferences. The C. S. Lewis Institute was at Cambridge University in England and the theme focused on theological and scientific issues related to creation. It was a who's who of the modern origins debate. There were anti-evolutionists of the newly emerging Intelligent Design Theory (Phillip Johnson, Michael Behe, William Dembski, Stephen Meyer, Paul Nelson), liberal Christians (John Polkinghorne, Arthur Peacocke) and evolutionary creationists (Howard Van Till, Keith Miller). I resonated very much with the ID theorists. They were terrific guys, and I even prayed with a few of them that evolution would be overturned. Two weeks later, I traveled to Minneapolis and attended the annual conference of the American Scientific Affiliation, a science-religion organization made up of mostly evangelical Christians trained in various scientific disciplines. It was there I saw biochemist Terry Gray of Calvin College debate Michael Behe on molecular evolution. These summer conferences were eye-openers. Though I was still an anti-evolutionist at the time, there was something that was starting to nag me.

Fruit Fly

Lancet

Human

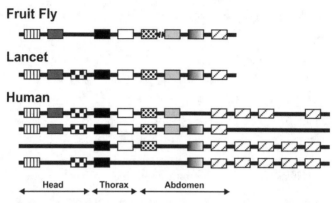

Head ◄───► Thorax ◄───► Abdomen ►

Fig 9-4. **Body Plan Genes.** Animals share a series of genes that instruct the embryological development of a basic head-to-tail pattern. Termed "*Hox* genes," these appear as "clusters" on a chromosome/s in an order that reflects essentially an anterior-to-posterior body plan. Simple organisms like insects (fruit fly) have only 1 cluster. This is also the case with the lancelet (amphioxus), a primitive fish-like creature with no brain and only a nerve cord. It would be similar to the common ancestor of vertebrates (backboned animals). During vertebrate evolution, the number of *Hox* clusters increased. Copies arose through the duplication of genes and chromosomes, which is a common occurrence in organisms (see Appendix 10 Fig 5). Humans have 4 *Hox* clusters. Genes that are missing between clusters are due to the deletion of genes, which is another well-known genetic process. Amphibians, reptiles, birds and other mammals have similar *Hox* clusters, indicating that land vertebrates descended from a common ancestor with 4 copies of the original body plan gene series.

The popular Christian argument that living organisms were too complex to have evolved gave me an uneasy feeling and left me cold. Behe had recently coined the term "irreducible complexity" to describe components of the cell, and he claimed that these could never have emerged through a gradual evolutionary process. Of course, the anti-evolutionary community quickly embraced his concept. But to say that we don't know how cells evolved and therefore God had to create them "in one fell swoop" wasn't cutting it for me anymore.[10] I knew this was a God-of-the-gaps argument. I had used this line of reasoning too many times in the past and now my training in biology was closing many of those gaps in knowledge. Along with my work on tooth anatomy in living and extinct organisms, I was also studying dental embryology. Since about 1985, biological research began focusing on the molecular makeup of cells. An amazing aspect of this work was discovering the incredible concert of finely coordinated biochemical reactions in development from fertilization to birth. As the reflection of intelligent design in embryology filled my soul with awe, this scientific evidence became the final piece of the evolutionary puzzle for me.

Briefly stated, living organisms go through embryological development using the same basic set of genetic and molecular processes. Striking evidence that animals and humans are evolutionarily related is found in corresponding genes that determine their underlying body plan (Fig 9-4).[11] In other words, as organisms evolved, they passed down the genetic instructions for the general head-body-tail pattern commonly seen today. This is just like in a family in which genes and physical characteristics descend from one generation to the next. Even more interesting, experimental studies reveal that manipulating a single developmental gene or molecule can result in dramatic changes in the anatomy of an organism. This was the key notion that led me to accept evolution. I had certainly seen a *pattern* in teeth and jaws indicative of evolution. Embryology was now offering a *process* to account for these changes. Let me give an example.

The limbs of fish, amphibians, reptiles, birds, and mammals begin as buds at the side of the body. As these grow, similar developmental genes and molecular processes sequentially appear, but they are expressed in differing combinations between animals. Simple experiments placing these molecules in a bud can alter the final number of bones in a limb and change their shapes dramatically (Fig 9-5).[12] Thus, a minor genetic modification in the release of a developmental molecule can result in a major anatomical change. With this mechanism in mind, and considering the fossil record of extinct fish and reptiles, it was easy for me to see how fins evolved into limbs (Fig 9-6).* This developmental evidence also refuted a popular Christian argument against evolution. Since the early 1970s, scientists were acknowledging that the fossil record was not revealing a gradual change in organisms as Darwin had predicted. Of course, anti-evolutionists were quick to use this evidence, as I had once done. We argued that too many genetic changes, all occurring at the same time, would be required to account for the non-gradualistic pattern in the fossils.

---

* It is important to qualify that in 1994 so-called "fish with fingers" (Fig 9-6B) had yet to be discovered. However, at that time I could envision how the fin of a lobe-finned fish, after minor changes in its developmental mechanisms, could easily evolve into the limb of early amphibians. Since 1994 two species of fish have been found, *Sauripterus* (B) and *Tiktaalik*, filling a gap in the fossil record. They appeared in the geological strata predicted by evolutionary theory. In my mind, this is the most amazing and powerful aspect of evolution. As new evidence is discovered, it always fits the basic theory.

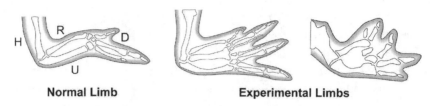

Normal Limb   **Experimental Limbs**

Fig 9-5. Experimental Limbs. The manipulation of genes and molecular processes in the developing upper limb of the chick can produce striking changes in bone anatomy. The normal limb has a humerus (H), an ulna (U), a radius (R), and 3 digits (D). In one experiment, a limb (middle) appeared with 7 chick-like digits and a new bone between the humerus and radius. Another experimental limb (right) developed 5 digits similar in number to most land animals today. Redrawn by Kenneth Kully.

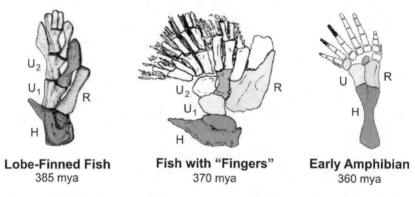

Lobe-Finned Fish   **Fish with "Fingers"**   **Early Amphibian**
385 mya   370 mya   360 mya

Fig 9-6. Fin-to-Limb Evolution. The fossil record presents a pattern from fish fins to land animal limbs as seen in a lobe-finned fish with limb-like bones, a fish with 8 finger-like bones, and an early amphibian with 8 digits. Notably, these two fish had two ulnar bones which later fused into one as seen in the amphibian. The first land animals often had 7–8 digits, reflecting their origin from "fingered" fish. These were reduced after 300 mya to the 5 digits commonly found today. Humerus (H), radius (R), ulna (U), digits (D), millions of years ago (mya).

The chance of this happening through natural processes was highly unlikely, if not impossible. However, our argument assumed a pre-1950s understanding of genetics where *one gene* was responsible for *one trait*. Modern embryological science began to demonstrate that *concentrations* and *combinations* of gene products in the developing limb provide a wide spectrum of anatomical possibilities. In particular, a small change in a gene, which commonly occurs, could shift the amount of a developmental molecule and/or its relationship to other molecules, resulting in a large change as seen in the fossil record.

This new research on the relationship between evolution and embryology emerged in the early 1990s and was termed "evolutionary developmental biology," or "evo-devo" for short. At first scattered through the professional literature in technical papers, this evidence for evolution began to converge in my mind in the fall of 1994 while I was preparing for the most challenging of all academic examinations—the PhD comprehensive. (This is an oral exam in front of 7 or 8 professors, and it is "open season" on the student. Any question is fair game, and most who have gone through the grilling process rarely have their self-image stroked!) Just a month before the exam, I was in Northern Alberta teaching dental students in a satellite clinic of the university. It was there that the pieces of evo-devo evidence came together and made complete sense. It was also during that two-week period that I read my first paper on theodicy and evolution. As noted earlier, I'm a bit embarrassed to admit that I went through graduate school in theology and never did a course on the problem of suffering and evil. However, with evolution becoming a reality for me, a timely and providential paper cleared away any theological stumbling blocks with regard to theodicy.

Gary Emberger's "Theological and Scientific Explanations for the Origin and Purpose of Natural Evil" was published by the *Journal of the American Scientific Affiliation* in September 1994. This paper underlined that Christianity for the most part had been shaped by the theodicy of St. Augustine. Accordingly, it was assumed that God had originally created a *perfect world* that was later corrupted by human sin. But Emberger also introduced me to the theodicy of Irenaeus, the Bishop of Lyons (130–202 AD). This Church father argued that the Creator had initially made an *innocent world*, and natural evils were part of His plan for the spiritual development of humans. In other words, Irenaeus proposed a pedagogical theodicy. This made a lot of sense at a personal level. I had come through trying experiences, and despite the pain and suffering, I could see these as being good for my growth as a Christian. Of course, I was far from formulating a detailed evolutionary theodicy. But reading Emberger's short, nine-page paper a number of times during the five-hour bus ride from Northern Alberta back to Edmonton opened a door to reconsidering the causal connection between sin and death.

Needless to say, my plate was more than full. The scientific evidence for evolution was jumping out at me with evo-devo, I was thinking seriously about theodicy for the first time in my life, and I had a PhD comprehensive to pass in the first week of December. The night before the exam, I was invited to a study group formed by Christian professors. I justified that if I didn't know the information for the exam by now, then I'd never know it for the next morning. Best to take a night off and relax. The professors were from different evangelical colleges in town: Baptist, Lutheran, and Christian Reform. The topic for the evening was a review of Mark A. Noll's recently published book *The Scandal of the Evangelical Mind* (1994). At that time, Noll was teaching history at one of the most important evangelical colleges in the United States, Wheaton College in Illinois. Notably, this school requires that its professors sign a statement of faith indicating that they accept the historicity of Adam.[13] The book opens with a thunderous indictment: "The scandal of the evangelical mind is that there is not much of an evangelical mind."[14] Ouch! Noll's intention was not to be insulting. He is a very committed and wonderful evangelical Christian. His purpose was to capture the attention of his fellow brothers and sisters, and to correct a serious problem in their religious tradition. For me the evening was a freeing experience. And yes, even providentialistic. I was realizing more than ever that the anti-evolutionism that had gripped me in my evangelical church, and that had directed critical decisions in my life, did not meet credible academic standards.

By God's grace, I survived the comprehensive exam with minimal bruising to my psyche! To complete the PhD program, I spent the next two years doing experimental work on tooth development. A few weeks after the "comp," following a typical 16-hour day in the lab, I sat down at my computer and decided to send an e-mail to Terry Gray, the Christian evolutionist I had seen debate Michael Behe during the past summer. I hadn't planned on contacting Gray that day. In fact, I hardly knew him. But something deep inside my soul led me to write a "confession."

> Date: Sat, 31 Dec 1994 23:49:26 (MST)
> From: Denis Lamoureux <dlamoure@ualberta.ca>
> To: grayt@calvin.edu
> Subject: Falling From Grace
>
> Dear Terry,
> Well it's 1995 in your part of the continent—Happy New Year! I spent this last day of 1994 examining the fin/limb structure of the extinct lobe-finned fish Eusthenopteron. Considering the latest

work on limb development, and following Howard Van Till in debate with others on the reflector (he's so gracious), I end the last moments of 1994 as an apostate.

Blessings,

Denis

P.S. But you're dead wrong with regard to concordism in Gen 2. Heck, we can't agree on everything!

Some background is needed to understand the particulars in this message. The "reflector" was an e-mail discussion group on origins organized by Philip Johnson, the leader of the Intelligent Design Movement. Howard Van Till was a main critic of ID theory at that time and he offered many insights into a Christian approach to evolution through his debates with others in this forum. He introduced me to the term "evolutionary creation." "The fin/limb structure of the extinct lobe-finned fish" appears in Fig 9-6 and "the latest work on limb development" in Fig 9-5. And reference to "concordism in Gen 2" was my way of saying that I did not accept the historicity of Adam and Eve. I knew that tacking them on at the end of the evolutionary process was a "proof text" use of Scripture that was categorically inappropriate.

This e-mail "confession" to Terry Gray was the second "Falling From Grace" moment in my graduate school education. The first was admitting that I was no longer a young earth creationist in the post-script of the last paper at Regent College in the spring of 1987. And eight years later, the intellectual evolutionary process was completed. I was no longer an anti-evolutionist. The transition was painless and without a hint of guilt or remorse. Of course, I was mocking myself with the comments about "falling from grace" and being an "apostate." I knew that in the eyes of many Christians I would be seen as a heretic who had lost his faith by studying evolution at a secular university. And it is true that some have walked away from Christianity after studying this subject. But I also knew that Jesus was right at my side throughout this entire experience in opening the Book of God's Works.

The day after my e-mail confession was Sunday the 1st of January 1995. I went to my Baptist Church. To celebrate the occasion, the senior pastor opened the service to the congregation and asked us for items praising God that had happened during the last year. Slowly and cautiously, people began to stand and share their stories. This was a fellowship of believers who had much to be thankful for because the Lord's blessings had been bountiful. Then, a rather mischievous little thought crossed my mind. Should I get up and say, "I want to thank Jesus for showing me the truth that He created the world through evolution?" Needless to say, the Holy Spirit convicted me right at that moment that being an evolutionary creationist would require much pastoral sensitivity. This was the first personal revelation I had experienced as a born-again Christian evolutionist. And looking back now, it continues to be the greatest lesson that Jesus has taught me in the origins debate.

So that's my story. In many ways, it is everyone's story. We are spiritual beings who live in a physical world and we were made to have a personal relationship with God. On the journey toward our Holy and Infinite Creator, there are numerous struggles since we are sinful, finite creatures. Making sense of the Two Divine Books that He has set before us is one of those challenges. Indeed, attempting to understand the relationship between Scripture and science has consumed me throughout most of my adult life. Yet as the word "Israel" indicates, wrestling with the Lord is part of being human. Having made peace with origins as an evolutionary creationist, I can now look back and make a few observations about my beliefs and life that some Christians and non-Christians might find surprising.

My love for Jesus and the Word hasn't changed one little bit since the time I was a young earth creationist. I feel His presence daily, especially when reading Scripture for my spiritual nourishment. My prayer life is the same and the sense of calling to defend Christianity continues to burn in my soul. And my ethical positions and yearning for holiness remain intact. If anything has changed, I have a much greater appreciation for the reflection of intelligent design in nature after having studied evolutionary biology. As well, my charismatic experiences with signs and wonders have increased. It was God's grace through faith that saved me from my sinfulness on an island faraway a quarter-century ago, and it is the Lord's love that continues to infuse my life every day with meaning and comfort a dozen years after coming to terms with evolution.

10

Final Thoughts and Reflections

M Y CENTRAL CONCLUSION IN this book is clear: Adam never existed, and this fact has no impact whatsoever on the foundational beliefs of Christianity. Of course, I am certainly aware of how shocking this assertion is not only to most Christians, but also to those outside the household of faith. Once this book is published, I fully expect to receive more than my fair share of criticism. Some will proof-text statements I have made, ripping them completely out of context and presenting them to the Church in the most negative light possible. However, twenty-five years ago I would have been the first in line to launch a scathing attack against anyone holding my view of origins. So, do I get upset with critics who might be less than charitable? No, not at all. Actually, I very much respect and commend their passion for the faith. Yet I must point out to my brothers and sisters in Christ that the Jesus I knew and loved as a young earth creationist is the very same Jesus I know and love today as an evolutionary creationist. We serve the same Lord.

Over the last ten years, my research has focused on attempting to develop an approach to evolution that is faithful to the foundational beliefs of Christianity. During this period, I have presented evolutionary creation in a wide variety of secular and religious settings: universities, colleges, and seminaries; professional conferences for teachers, theologians, and scientists; the general public through lectures, debates, radio, and television programs; and some Roman Catholic and evangelical Protestant Churches. In almost every case, the dialogue has been remarkably respectful and I have valued the questions and challenges that people have offered. Indeed, they have profoundly shaped my thinking. But to state the obvious, not everyone agrees with my view of origins, and I certainly do not expect them to. My primary goal is to stimulate discussion on the possibility that the God of the Bible created through an ordained and sustained evolutionary process, and for us to consider the implications. I do not for one moment believe that this book is *the* Christian position on evolution. It is only a first step that outlines *an* approach to this topic.

There has been one response to my work that has impacted me over the years and led me to believe that I am heading in the right direction. It comes from evangelical Christians who have studied science, and in particular, evolutionary biology. Once introduced to the basic tenets of evolutionary creation, they tell me that they have intuitively held this position in a loose and undefined way. Now equipped with this category, these believers can enjoy firm ownership of their view of origins. I have seen a similar response in my Science-Religion courses, especially with many of the pre-med students who are evangelicals. In preparing for medical school, they see evolutionary evidence almost every day in their biology classes. But on Sunday at church, they are told to beware of evolution. A number of them have said to me that they entered my introductory course with their faith and science in disconnected compartments of their mind. They admit that this was the only way to make sense of the world and to have some sort of peace regarding origins. I'll never forget the best student in one of my first classes. She attended a Christian Mission Alliance Church and was about to leave for medical school at the University of Toronto. Her parting words to me were, "I am now free." Yes, indeed. Free to enjoy the Book of God's Words and the Book of God's Works, and free to use these divine revelations in building a fully integrated Christian worldview.

Let me close now with a few thoughts and reflections on the origins debate, and then I will try to answer the challenging question many people have asked me: Why would the all-loving and all-powerful God of the Bible have created the world and us through an evolutionary process?

NECESSITY OF CATEGORIES

I hope that this book has convinced everyone that intellectual categories are absolutely critical in understanding the origins controversy. Nearly all of us begin our spiritual-intellectual voyage with black-and-white concepts that trap our mind in crude conflations and simple dichotomies. Learning the professional categories used by theologians and scientists frees people to make informed decisions, allowing them to move beyond the popular positions of six-day creation and atheistic evolution. In many ways, my story of coming to terms with evolution is about opening God's Two Books and grasping the conceptual foundations in each. The categories did not all come at once, nor did I completely understand them at first. For example, my view of teleological evolution at the start of my PhD program in biology was in effect a variant form of progressive creation. The writing of this book was two years longer than expected because I struggled with hermeneutical categories in Gen 1–11. It took me a while to appreciate the relationship between motifs and historiography in these early chapters. Consequently, I have no illusions that I will spend the rest of my life learning new categories and using them as intellectual tools in the construction of my worldview. I'll always be a work in progress, and you will be too.

It is significant to note that when I became a Christian, the Lord accommodated to my black-and-white category set in order to reveal the fundamental truth that He was the Creator of the world. For me, this was a thunderous revelation that changed my life dramatically. God used young earth creation as an incidental vessel to deliver this Message of Faith. In other words, He graciously meets us wherever we happen to be, including entrenched in a false dichotomy, as in my case. Moreover, I certainly believe in my heart of hearts that He did call me some twenty-five years ago to a career focusing on the origins debate. Of course, it's quite a shock that I ended up as an evolutionary creationist, considering that I had originally intended to be a creation scientist. But that's where I was at that time, and that's where the Lord started the process of renewing my mind and remodelling my life in accordance with His will (Rom 12:2). Our duty as Christians is to follow Him faithfully and fearlessly wherever that may lead (Heb 11:8).

I certainly haven't enacted this admonition to perfection. Yet struggling along in my voyage, I have come to a practical suggestion for Christians. I think that it is important for believers who are not familiar with the hermeneutics of Gen 1–11 and/or the scientific evidence for evolution to be at peace with the origins debate. It's okay not to know how God made the universe and life. At the end of my studies at Regent College I wrote that my views on origins were in a "suspended state." I was completely comfortable with this position and did not in any way feel that my faith was being compromised. My graduate school education in both theology and science made me realize that though the categories are complex, the foundational message in the Two Divine Books is simple and accessible to everyone—God created the world and us. It takes time to grasp and sort the categories on origins, and some people may never come to a well-defined position. But again, that's okay.

APOLOGETICS, POSITIVISM, AND INTELLECTUAL TENSIONS

The origins debate provides a splendid opportunity for Christian apologetics. As Peter admonishes, "Always be prepared to give an answer to everyone who asks you to give the reason for the hope you have" (1 Pet 3:15).[1] Young earth creationists and progressive creationists are driven by the admirable desire to defend the Bible and lead people to Christ. This was my reason for wanting to become a creation scientist. Anti-evolutionary apologetics assume that if we could demonstrate that evolution is false and that Scripture corresponds with *true* science, then we could *prove* that creation in six days/epochs and the God of the Bible are *scientific facts*, and religious conversion would only be a step away. However, coming to the Lord is not that simple. It is not like filling in a bubble in a multiple-choice exam. Conversion involves confessing our sins and experiencing God's love and forgiveness. Christianity is about falling in love with the God of Love.

The problem with anti-evolutionary apologetics comes back to categories. In many ways, young earth creationists and progressive creationists are like positivists. Looking back now, my desire to be a creation scientist was marked by this mechanical approach to thinking. We are socialized in a scientific culture and it is not surprising that an emphasis on science would appear in defenses for Christian faith. But apologetics that focus mostly on logical reasoning, mathematical formulas, and scientific evidence are categorically deficient and, to a certain extent, inappropriate. What ultimately matters is God's love, and the reality of that experience cannot be put in a test tube. Nor can we force anyone to love God using a simple argument, anymore than we can coerce someone to fall in love with another person. Life is much more complicated and personal. So too is religious conversion.

This is not to say that there is no place for scientific arguments in Christian apologetics. My views on intelligent design outlined in this book are clear. The beauty, complexity, and functionality in nature discovered by science are powerful divine revelations for which we are accountable. I will go so far as to speculate that anyone at the final judgment claiming that there was no evidence for the existence of a Creator will be reminded of the countless occasions when "the heavens declared the glory of God" in his or her life . . . and then he or she will be told that "they are without excuse." However, these non-verbal disclosures inscribed into the fabric of the world are limited. Intelligent design in nature does not give us the name of the Designer, nor does it reveal our ultimate problem— our sinfulness.

A category that took a while for me to appreciate during my theological training was the concept of "intellectual tension," where seemingly conflicting ideas actually complement each other. As a black-and-white thinker, these very much troubled me. Yet I have come to recognize that life does not follow simple straight lines or fit into neat little boxes. Ambiguities and paradoxes are part of this wonderful existence that are ordained and sustained by God.[2] For example, most Christians appreciate and accept the tension associated with the notion of "tough love." As well, many people claim to make "sense" of pain and suffering in the world. Some go so far as to say that afflictions and adversities have been "good" for them. It is as if life experiences have a supra-rationality or meta-logic. This is not irrational or illogical. The majority of us can look back at a painful situation and claim that we are grateful that we went through it. Recently, I have been wrestling with the paradox that genetic mutations can lead to cancer and death, yet they are also essential in biological evolution and the creation of life. I would not wish cancer on anyone, but I have met people with this condition who have told me that it was their "greatest blessing" because it brought them to the Lord. From the perspective of eternity, such a claim makes sense.

Let me offer a few intellectual tensions I have experienced with the origins controversy. I have debated both young earth creationists and leaders of the Intelligent Design Movement, and I am adamantly opposed to their views being taught in schools as an alternate theory to evolution.[3] But where would I be today had I not heard Duane Gish in 1977 at the University of Alberta? He seeded a life-changing Message of Faith in my mind—God created the universe and life. In 2000, I personally thanked Dr. Gish for standing up at my university and I even asked him to sign my copy of *Evolution: The Fossils Say No!*[4] Similarly, I reject the claim made by Intelligent Design theorists that design in nature is "scientifically detectable." This is the method of positivism being applied to faith, and it is categorically inappropriate. Nevertheless, the ID Movement has raised public awareness to the notion of intelligent design, and I consider this a valuable contribution. With regard to those holding evolutionary creation, we have an abysmal record of defending our position in public. Rarely are these Christian evolutionists seen standing up in universities to challenge dysteleological evolution. So, I live with a tension today. I disagree with the anti-evolutionists, but thoroughly appreciate their proclamation that the world is created and reflects intelligent design. I agree with evolutionary creationists, yet I am embarrassed by how little we've contributed to the Church and modern culture.

HERMENEUTICAL CONSIDERATIONS AND CONCERNS

The counterintuitive approach to biblical interpretation presented in this book is another intellectual tension. I have argued that the inspired human authors intended Gen 1–11 for the most part to be read literally, but at the same time that these chapters are not a literal account of actual events in the past. Similarly, the purpose of the redactor was to present a history of the origins of the world and the Hebrews, yet I have defended that at best there are only a few historical echoes (local floods and their survivor/s; some genealogical ancestors) in the opening chapters of Scripture. In other words, as one who embraces a complementary, yet non-concordist, relationship between the Two Divine Books, I am a non-literal literalist. Many Christians conclude that my hermeneutical position is contradictory. How can I say that the Bible is truly the Word of God and at the same time assert that nearly all of the incidents described in Gen 1–11 are false?

To begin, it must be underlined that I am in complete and utter submission to the words of Scripture. It was a shock for me as a young earth creationist to recognize that Gen 1:2 refers to an earth and no mention of when it was created or by whom. I lost my temporal marker from which to date our planet. Similarly, realizing that the sons of God in Gen 6:1–4 were celestial beings that mated with human women made no biological sense to me. Yet I understood that my calling as a theologian was to accept and submit to whatever the words in this passage meant, despite my reservations. And discovering that the Hebrew word *rāqîaʿ* refers to the firmament, and working out the implications of this fact, crushed any belief I had in scientific concordism. But instead of losing my Christian faith or viewing this situation as a defect in Scripture, the Holy Spirit convinced me that this biblical evidence was an opportunity to understand His revelatory process. Eventually, I came to recognize and respect the incidental ancient motifs in Gen 1–11, and then I saw the stumbling block of concordism removed from the path toward a Christian understanding of evolution. The Hebrews used the science and history-of-the-day in delivering Messages of Faith. This biblical precedent invites our generation to take these very same eternal truths and to place them within the evolutionary motif of our time.

There is another tension that arises with regard to hermeneutics. If my approach to Gen 1–11 is correct, then it means that nearly all Christians throughout history, including modern young earth creationists and progressive creationists today, have misinterpreted the opening chapters of Scripture. One might assume that the Holy Spirit would have enlightened believers about the science and history in Gen 1–11. But He never did. Again, this subtle evidence is for our edification. It indicates that God's purpose is not to reveal facts about physical origins. It also calls us to correct theological formulations that have been unwittingly conflated with incidental ancient elements from Scripture. There are intriguing issues to be considered by those holding a non-concordist hermeneutic. For example, what are the implications of our physical evolutionary past for the spiritual reality of temptation? Even though Christians in every generation have overlooked the ancient science and ancient history in Gen 1–11, what never ceases to amaze me about these chapters is that believers have consistently identified the Messages of Faith. The history of interpretation reveals that those with "ears to hear" and "eyes to see" have always discerned life-changing eternal truths, despite their hermeneutical skill level. Indeed, as the Lord states with regard to His Word, "It will not return to Me empty, but will accomplish what I desire and achieve the purpose for which I sent it" (Isa 55:11).

A question that Christians always raise about my hermeneutical approach to Gen 1–11 is where do I draw the line? Or asked more directly, if Adam is not historical, then is this also the case with Jesus and His crucifixion and resurrection? The answer lies in the foundational interpretive principle of literary genre. The early chapters of Scripture and the Gospels are completely different types of literature. So, no, the interpretive method I present in this book is *not* applicable to the New Testament and the record of the Lord's ministry. Genesis 1–11 is built on recycled ancient Near Eastern motifs that are ultimately a retrojection into the distant past of an ancient phenomenological perspective of the world. In sharp contrast, the New Testament is based on the testimony of people who actually encountered Jesus. Some eyewitnesses wrote down their experiences, like the apostle John in the opening of his first letter.

> That which was from the beginning, which we have heard, which we have seen with our eyes, which we have looked at and our hands have touched—this we proclaim concerning the Word of Life. The life appeared; we have seen it and testify to it, and we proclaim to you the eternal life, which was with the Father and has appeared to us. We proclaim to you what we have seen and heard, so that you also may have fellowship with us. And our fellowship is with the Father and with his Son, Jesus Christ. (1 John 1:1–3)

In fact, there is a modern historiographical tone at the beginning of the gospel of Luke, as the inspired doctor outlines his method.

> Many have undertaken to draw up an account of the things that have been fulfilled among us, just as they were handed down to us by those who were eyewitnesses and servants of the Word. Therefore, since I myself have carefully investigated everything from the beginning, it seemed good also to me to write an orderly account for you, most excellent Theophilus, so that you may know with certainty of the things you have been taught. (Luke 1:1–4)

Luke's authorial intention is clearly historiographical. His purpose is "to write an orderly account" of the events surrounding the ministry of Jesus in order that it "may be known with certainty." Luke is not composing a fable, an allegory, or some fictitious story. His method is a "careful investigation" of "handed down" sources, which include those of "eyewitnesses."[5] And most importantly, Luke interprets history as being "fulfilled" in his day by the Incarnation.

I am mindful that most Christians have not had the privilege of a theological education. As a new believer I remember a graduate student using his Greek New Testament to correct me. It was frustrating because I couldn't respond. I simply wasn't equipped. The interpretation of Gen 1–11 that I am proposing could be experienced in a similar way. It's not comfortable. And it is perfectly acceptable to ask, "Can Lamoureux be trusted?" So how does the average person sitting in the pew evaluate the work of theologians with years of university and seminary training?

First, it must be noted that God has equipped the Church with the ministry of teachers (1 Cor 12:28; Eph 4:11). Christians need to identify individuals who are properly trained to deal with challenging issues like origins and place them in positions of leadership. Second, the Lord has also gifted every believer with spiritual discernment (1 Cor 2:12–16; Phil 1:9–10). This being the case, my suggestion to Christians is this: Are you hearing the precious name of Jesus on the lips of a theologian? Is this the Spirit of the Lord that you know and walk with every day? Most believers are aware that suspicious theologies and false doctrines have come out of universities and seminaries. The faith disemboweling beliefs of the so-called "Jesus Seminar" is an example. It dismisses the Lord's divinity and rejects His bodily resurrection from the grave. But I am confident that men and women in a personal relationship with Jesus can discern whether or not the voice of God exists in the writings of any theologian. As the apostle Paul states, "No one can say, 'Jesus is Lord,' except by the Holy Spirit" (1 Cor 12:3).

PASTORAL AND PEDAGOGICAL IMPLICATIONS

One of the most important and challenging aspects of the origins debate deals with practical issues that arise from this controversy. Recognizing the emphasis that many Christians place on this topic, how are we to deal with the diversity of views found in the Church? What position on origins are we to preach from our pulpits and teach in our Sunday schools and Christian educational institutions? Outside the Church, is it the duty of believers to force publicly funded school boards and privately owned publishing houses to include their view of origins in curricula and textbooks? And when witnessing to non-Christians, should we impose our understanding of God's creative method and include it as part of the Gospel? Of course, these questions could become the subject of a number of books. I certainly do not have all the answers. But here are a few preliminary thoughts.

The origins debate is a potentially divisive issue in the Church. To keep harmony within a fellowship, some Christian leaders refuse to discuss this topic. Though such an approach has practical advantages, history reveals that believers have always raised questions about the creation of the world. It is a subject that is too important to ignore, and the apostle Paul offers helpful insights. A significant theme in his letters was admonition against divisions in the body of Christ (Rom 16:17; 1 Cor 1:10, 11:18, 12:25; Titus 3:10). In applying this principle today, we should never be divided because of our views on how God created the universe and life. Let this issue become a difference among us. Proverbs 27:17 states, "As iron sharpens iron, so one man sharpens another." Instead of dividing us, the origins debate offers an opportunity to learn from one another and to develop a better understanding of the revelations in God's Two Books. And most importantly, perspective is always needed with this subject. We must never conflate any origins position with the Cross of Christ. Nothing other than our sin should be nailed to the Cross.

Another important pastoral theme in the inspired letters of Paul deals with the problem of stumbling blocks. He calls on mature Christians not to let the eating of food sacrificed to idols become an issue since this was an obstacle for some believers (Rom 14:1–3, 13–17; 1 Cor 11:31–33). Similarly, I do not think that origins should be a central topic in any church. Focusing on God's creative method in Sunday morning preaching would distract people from the messages in Scripture and invite unnecessary controversy. However, I do believe that at some point, Sunday schools and Christian schools must introduce students to the various categories on origins, including evolutionary creation. In this way, if young men and women are ever convinced of evolution, possibly during their college education, they will have a category that protects them from stumbling and losing their faith, as I did. Those who have a grasp of the spectrum of origins positions are also equipped to dismiss the popular myth held by many non-Christians that belief in Jesus requires the rejection of evolution. Regrettably, too many Christian anti-evolutionists have set this stumbling block between the Lord and those in need of Him. As the apostle Paul writes, "Now is the time of God's favor, now is the day of salvation. We put no stumbling block in anyone's path, so that our ministry will not be discredited" (2 Cor 6:2–3).

The next few comments might seem a bit edgy. I have concerns with regard to public education. For example, consider the 1995 "Statement on Teaching Evolution" prepared by the National Association of Biology Teachers. The first point in this declaration states:

> The diversity of life on earth is the outcome of evolution: an unsu-
> pervised, impersonal, unpredictable and natural process of temporal
> descent with genetic modification that is affected by natural selec-
> tion, chance, historical contingencies and changing environments.[6]

This statement conflates evolutionary science with a dysteleological world-view, and in the eyes of unsuspecting teachers and students, it "baptizes" this belief system with scientific authority. Young earth creationists and progressive creationists have been absolutely correct in objecting to the misuse of public funds for such an insidious indoctrination of children with this distinctly anti-Christian ideology. In a democratic society, public education must reflect the views and intentions of the American people, and not the dysteleological and humanist beliefs of a skewed dictatorial minority.

In fact, the founding document of the United States, the *Declaration of Independence*, not only affirms the existence of a Creator, but accepts that He acts providentialistically in the world and that He is the basis for human rights and morality.[7] Moreover, 96% of Americans are united in affirming that there is a God or Universal Spirit. Thus, any government-funded institution that aggressively undermines belief in the Creator outlined in the *Declaration* betrays the nation. The promotion in public education of dysteleological evolution and secular humanism is an attack on the metaphysical foundations of America. Stated precisely without regard to political correctness, those indoctrinating children with a pur-poseless worldview are enemies of the union. This situation is consonant with Paul's understanding of an ongoing spiritual warfare.

> For though we live in this world, we do not wage war as the world
> does. The weapons we fight with are not the weapons of the world.
> On the contrary, they have divine power to demolish strongholds.
> We demolish arguments and every pretension that sets itself up
> against the knowledge of God. (2 Cor 10:3–5)

A modern day "stronghold" set up against the knowledge of God is a public school system dedicated to brainwashing children with atheistic evolution and godless humanism. American Christians have every right to destroy and eradicate this spiritual darkness from public education.

As a balance, a few pointed remarks need to be directed at Christians. Telling the truth is a biblical principle particularly important to the ori-gins debate. The Ninth Commandment states, "You shall not give false testimony against your neighbor" (Exod 20:16; Deut 5:20). A corollary of this commandment is that believers must evaluate whether or not they are in a position to make a truth claim. Too many times, leading Christian anti-evolutionists have broken this commandment by stepping beyond their expertise and guiding the Church to reject biological evolution. It should be obvious that individuals trained in law, engineering, mathematics, astronomy, philosophy, history, or education have a limited knowledge of evolutionary theory. Consequently, they are not in a position to criticize it. Many prominent anti-evolutionists are professional academics with excellent credentials in their disciplines. But as individuals who have mastered a complex body of knowledge, they should know better than to step outside their field and make authoritative statements in public. Being an authority in one area does not make one an expert in an unrelated field. This misappropriation of academic authority breaks the Ninth Commandment, inviting discord within the body of Christ and introducing potential stumbling blocks to faith throughout the culture.

I opened this subsection acknowledging that I definitely do not have all the answers to the many pastoral and pedagogical issues that arise from the origins debate. This is an opportunity for a lot of creative thinking to be done by pastors and teachers. After having taught this controversy for over ten years at a publicly funded university, I have come to the conclusion that good education exposes students to all positions and categories. I believe that this is a good pastoral principle as well. My teaching experience has also shown me that the origins debate provides an excellent subject to develop critical thinking skills and to begin the construction of an integrated worldview. In this way, young men and women are liberated from the prison of the origins false dichotomy into which most of us have been socially conditioned. And now they are free to enjoy the God-glorifying evidence in science and the life-changing truths in Scripture.

WHY WOULD GOD CREATE THROUGH EVOLUTION?

I am often asked this question. It is usually followed by a related one: If God created the world through an evolutionary process, then why did the Holy Spirit not reveal this fact in the Bible? These are good and fair questions, but how can I possibly respond when most people are entrenched in the origins dichotomy and are not familiar with the basic categories in this book? By this point readers will recognize that there are no quick and easy answers to these questions. A serious information problem exists both inside and outside the Church regarding the relationship between Scripture and science, and before any attempt is made to respond, people need to be introduced to the categories and spectrum of possibilities. And that takes time. However, if I had to answer the question in the title of this section in one sentence, it would be in this way: *God created through evolution because it provided the perfect world in which we could develop a personal and loving relationship with Him.* Let me explain.

First, it must be underlined that God can do whatever He wants. This may seem blunt, but after all, He is God. He could have created the universe and life only a few moments ago and given us memories to make us believe that we have lived for many years; or He could have made the world as claimed by either young earth creation or progressive creation. Ultimately, it is the Creator's decision, and obviously not that of the creatures, no matter what our expectations and assumptions. If He created us through evolution, who are we to question His creative method? The prophet Isaiah captures this thought when he compares God to a potter and humans to clay pots.

> As if the potter were thought to be like the clay!
> Shall what is formed say to him who formed it,
>   "He did not make me"?
> Can the pot say of the potter,
>   "He knows nothing"? (Isa 29:16 [see also 45:9, 64:8])

The apostle Paul extends Isaiah's analogy, "Does not the potter have the right to make out of the same lump of clay some pottery for noble purposes and some for common use?" (Rom 9:21). Applying this idea to an evolutionary context, is it not God's prerogative to create life through evolution using similar genes, cells, and tissues, and then to take one organism to bear His Image? Of course it is. Again, He is God. And using this line of argument with regard to the Word of God, can the Bible say to the Holy Spirit, "Why did you compose and inspire me in this way?" The Lord can reveal Himself in Scripture in any fashion He so chooses, including the use of ancient science and ancient history as incidental vessels. One last time, He is God.

As an evolutionary creationist, I reject young earth creation and progressive creation for both biblical and scientific reasons. Scientific and historical concordism in Gen 1–11 fail (Figs 5-1 and 7-1), and the fossil pattern predictions of these anti-evolutionary positions do not align with the geological record (Appendix 7 Figs 1, 2 and 4). But more importantly, I believe that if God created the world through either of these interventionistic ways, and then revealed this fact in Scripture, it would undermine the very character of this world and its ultimate purpose. Such a provocative claim requires more explanation.

The Bible clearly states that faith is fundamental to human experience (Matt 17:20; Eph 2:8; Heb 11:1–39). In order for us to develop a truly loving relationship with the Lord, we need to have genuine freedom to accept or reject Him. Thus, He has placed Himself at a certain distance from us so that we are not coerced or forced into relating to Him. The problem with the Christian anti-evolutionary positions is that they in effect attempt to put the God of the Bible into a test tube to *prove* His existence. If the geological record aligned with the scientific predictions of either young earth creation or progressive creation, then there would be no debate. This would be incontestable proof that God exists and that the Bible is His Word. Only a Being who transcends time could have revealed scientific and historical facts on origins to ancient authors well before modern scientists and historians discovered this information. If this were the case, faith would not be required in understanding the ultimate character of the world. And reading the Two Divine Books would be restricted to simple logic and mathematics, nothing more.

In contrast to the crypto-positivism of the anti-evolutionists, I view science and Scripture in a complementary relationship that emphasizes the necessity of faith. God created the world and inspired the Bible, featuring in each Divine Book both His noticeability (*Deus Revelatus*; Latin for "God who reveals") and His hiddenness (*Deus Absconditus*; "God who hides"). In this way, He made the perfect setting for our ultimate beliefs to develop in freedom. The Creator has gifted us with reason and intuition in order to take a step of faith toward a relationship with Him. This is not so-called "blind faith." Rather, it is belief that is informed by His Works and Words. Notably, this approach does not embrace the positivist epistemology that ultimate beliefs are proven only through logical analysis and scientific investigation. Mysteries, intellectual tensions, and life experiences contribute to the development of our worldview and our relationship with the Creator. In particular, love is the most powerful and formative factor in shaping our deepest beliefs. The Two Divine

Books offer sufficient revelations of God, and human ability is proficient in grasping their ultimate meaning and implications. Consequently, men and women are accountable before their Maker and Judge with regard to these disclosures. I am convinced that Divine noticeability overwhelms Divine hiddenness. Yet at the same time, *Deus Absconditus* tempers *Deus Revelatus* in order for faith to be an essential aspect of our life.

The Book of God's Works reveals an evolutionary world. No doubt about it, the evolution of living organisms is a vicious process characterized by waste, suffering, and death. Natural selection, survival of the fittest, and countless extinctions mark the violent history of life on earth. Evolutionary science also paints a picture of a world dominated exclusively by physical processes with no gaps in nature for purported divine interventions. God has given humans the freedom to focus on these ruthless features in the formation of their ultimate beliefs, which in many cases have led to deism, agnosticism, and atheism. However, I contend that the amazing reflection of intelligent design in the world overrides the merciless character of evolutionary mechanisms. Moreover, the apparent fine tuning in the closed continuum of natural laws points to these being ordained and sustained by an unfathomable Mind. And what I find astonishing is that the deeper science probes into nature, greater are the manifestations of beauty, complexity, and functionality. From my perspective, it takes more insight and power to create the universe and life through an evolutionary process than it does to tinker and adjust an incomplete creation at different points in time. Yet as the Metaphysics-Physics Principle indicates, skeptics and believers alike make a faith jump from their science to their ultimate beliefs.

The Book of God's Words features accounts of origins that are built on recycled ancient motifs that the Hebrews inherited from surrounding pagan nations. Numerous contradictions and conflicts between the events appear in Gen 1–11. The opening chapters of Scripture do not align with the facts of modern science and history. Again, the Lord has given men and women the freedom to focus on these characteristics and to use them in rejecting biblical revelation. Of course, I consider such criticism of the Word of God by skeptics to be simplistic, and academically shallow. It completely fails to recognize and respect the ancient intellectual context within which Scripture was first conceived and later written down. The Bible had to be accommodated in order to be understood by ancient peoples. Ironically, most skeptics embrace the literalist hermeneutic of fundamentalism. But more importantly, the history of biblical interpretation reveals that eternal messages in the creation accounts overpower the incidental ancient vessels that deliver them. By God's grace, believers in every generation have grasped the life-changing truths revealed by the Holy Spirit in Gen 1–11. A feature of Scripture that I find truly amazing is that despite the hermeneutical skill level, anyone sincerely searching for God can discover Him in the Bible. As a new Christian with little to no appreciation of the literary genre of the origins accounts, I was able to grasp that God was the Creator, humans were created in His Image, and we are all sinners. Today, I recognize that the Message-Incident Principle assists in separating the Divine Theology from ancient science and ancient history in Gen 1–11; but whether or not one believes that the message is divinely inspired requires faith.

So, why would God create through evolution and not reveal this fact in the Bible? A design-reflecting evolutionary world and an inspired ancient origins account provide a context that is perfectly suited for humans to love their Creator and be loved by Him. In claiming that creation is perfect, I am not affirming the traditional belief that He first made a world that was a paradise. The idyllic age is an ancient motif with no correspondence to reality. Instead, this "very good" (Gen 1:31) cosmos features the *ideal* manifestation of divine noticeability and divine hiddenness that allows for a real loving relationship to emerge between God and us.* It is a world in which men and women are free to see only natural processes and to assume that no Creator exists. At the same time, this is a place where we can view His presence everywhere and experience His providentialistic activity every day, including on occasion, dramatic intervention. Pain in the world can be used to point away from His existence; or through suffering and death we may meet Him and even learn to grow in His grace. People are also free to interpret the Bible as "nothing but" another ancient religious text steeped in pre-scientific ideas that are now discredited. And Scripture can be read by those who look beyond its ancient vessel with "eyes that see" the Creator who died on a Cross

---

* In this way, the concept of intelligent design could be extended beyond the traditional belief that beauty, complexity, and functionality reflect an Intelligent Designer. That is, design in the world includes even the unsavory aspects of pain, suffering, and death since these features play an essential role in developing an authentic relationship with the Lord. From this expanded understanding of intelligent design, light is shed on Paul's claim, "We know that in *all things* God works for the good of those who love Him, who have been called according to His purpose" (Rom 8:28; my italics).

for us—the ultimate act of love. The God of Love does not force Himself upon us, because that is not the nature of love. In the same way that you cannot coerce anyone to love you, it is impossible for the Lord to make you love Him.

To complete the series of "why would God . . ." questions, an answer needs to be given to justify the causal connection between the sin of Adam and the entrance of physical death clearly stated in Scripture. As noted in the last chapter, I contend that the sin-death problem is the greatest challenge to evolutionary creation. Hopefully, I have offered a reasonable and persuasive solution. But here is a speculation on why I think the Holy Spirit allowed this causal connection in Scripture and for it to become prominent in Christian faith.

A central theme throughout the Bible is remembrance. The Fourth Commandment states, "Remember the Sabbath by keeping it holy" (Exod 20:8). The elaborate sacrificial system of Hebrews was "an annual reminder of sins" (Heb 10:4). And Jesus at the Last Supper called Christians to participate in communion and to do it in "remembrance" of Him (Luke 22:19; 1 Cor 11:24–25). As finite sinful beings we often forget our place in the world—we are creatures made by God and we are accountable before Him. Too many times, we also take Him for granted. In light of these passages and experiences, the causal connection between sin and death as stated in Scripture offers a perfect reminder. Every death we see thrusts us to the reality that we are sinners. Nearly every funeral we attend repeats the divine judgment in the garden of Eden, "For dust you are, and to dust you shall return" (Gen 3:17). Death reminds men and women that they will stand before their Maker on judgment day. But the Good News is that Jesus died for our sins, and the symbol of the Cross is a reminder that He has conquered death.

Let me close with three biblical passages that have come to shape my evolutionary creationist understanding of a complementary relationship between science and Scripture. The eleventh chapter of the book of Hebrews is the great passage on faith. It begins,

> Now faith is being sure of what we hope for and certain of what we do not see. This is what the ancients were commended for. By faith we understand that the universe was formed at God's command, so that what is seen was not made out of what was visible. (Heb 11:1–3)

These verses reveal the ontological status of the world. Its ultimate character is that of a creation in which men and women express faith. This passage is also a divine disclosure on the epistemological status of humanity. We might be "sure" and "certain" of our beliefs, but ultimately, this assuredness is rooted in faith. Science has conclusively demonstrated that evolution is the mechanism through which the world was formed, but faith leads to the understanding that it is God's creative method. Therefore, I am expressing my faith when I confidently state that I believe the Father, Son, and Holy Spirit created the universe and life through an ordained, sustained, and design-reflecting evolutionary process.

The thirteenth chapter in the First Book to the Corinthians is best known for the wonderful passage on love, but it also offers further insights into our creaturely ability to know. The apostle Paul writes:

> Now we see but a poor reflection; then we shall see face to face. Now I know in part; then I shall know fully, even as I am fully known. And now these three remain: faith, hope and love. But the greatest of these is love. (1 Cor 13:12–13)

We are to expect mysteries and intellectual tensions in life. My worldview will not explain completely every aspect of this existence. Here are a few examples of issues that I wrestle with: I'll never fully grasp the meaning of the Trinity. However, if there is a Creator, then His manifestation in a "logical conundrum" such as "One God in Three Persons" would be consistent with a Divine Being so utterly different from creatures like us. An evolutionary theodicy has given me some comfort with the problem of suffering, but this is an issue I doubt anyone entirely comes to terms with. Yet looking back on painful personal experiences, they now in an unusual way "make sense" and I'm even grateful for them. And though divine noticeability through intelligent design plays a significant role in my worldview, God's hiddenness and seeming absence grips me on occasions. I'll confess, I have deistic, agnostic, and even atheistic thoughts. But these quickly dissipate as I contemplate the revelations in nature and the experience of love. In contrast to my belief thirty years ago, I have come to the conclusion that it takes more faith to believe that love is "nothing but" a herd response, than it does to believe that it is a gift from God. *Love* only makes sense in the fulfilling light of the Incarnation and the *hope* the Lord Jesus offers men and women through *faith*. In these three I remain anchored.

Jesus' teaching on the Commandments fulfills my understanding of the complementary relationship between His Works and Words. The Lord commands:

> Love the Lord your God with all your heart and with all your soul and with all your mind. This is the first and greatest Commandment. (Matt 22:37–38)

In applying this foundational principle of faith to my life, loving God with my mind requires me to open and read His Two Books with faithfulness and fearlessness. As the dedication at the beginning of this book reveals, my students have taught me this valuable lesson. Christians often cite an aphorism for the practice of science attributed to Kepler, "O God, I am thinking Thy thoughts after Thee." His words can be recast to describe the theological discipline of hermeneutics, "O Holy Spirit, I am studying Your revelatory process after You." To be sure, reading the Two Divine Books in graduate school was initially quite a shock to me. It is so counterintuitive. But loving God means trusting Him. The Potter knew exactly what He was doing when He created life through evolutionary mechanisms and inspired Gen 1–11 by using an ancient literary process. Intelligent design in nature and Messages of Faith in Scripture thrust us to the feet of our Creator. In my mind, the First Commandment boils down to saying "thank You." Thank You for creating the spectacular works of nature; and thank You for the inspired words of the Bible and the unfathomable gift of the Incarnate Word.

So this is where the journey has led me to this point in my life. I have learned to accept mysteries, to live with spiritual and intellectual tensions, and to appreciate the importance of personal experience in the construction of my worldview. As a son of the God of Israel, struggle is an ordained feature of my sustained creaturely existence. On one hand, I see my lifework as relevant. Christians and non-Christians ask questions about origins, and I believe that answering these is part of defending the faith and loving God with my mind. Contributing to this discussion has significant pastoral and pedagogical implications. Yet on the other hand, what I do is so irrelevant. Knowing how God created the world is not essential to being a Christian. I have committed a large part of my career to obsessing over obscure details in Scripture and science that are of little to no consequence to the faith of most people. I often wonder, what's the point in understanding the evolution of a tooth from an extinct reptile, when there are so many children in the world needing their teeth freed from decay and pain? I'm a dentist; I could help them. This troubles me and humbles me.

Yet despite these ambiguities, I am so thankful to the Lord for my calling. It has been an amazing adventure to spend most of my adult life pondering mysteries and realities with the Two Divine Books opened before me. I am particularly grateful for the privilege to teach and research in the newly formed academic discipline of Science and Religion. Rarely does a day pass without an exciting revelation in God's Works and Words. And yes, my voyage has led me to one very surprising conclusion. I love Jesus, and I don't believe Adam ever existed. But more importantly, as the children's Sunday school song has taught me, my hope rests in that "Jesus loves me, this I know, for the Bible tells me so."

Credits and Permissions

The author and publisher wish to thank the following for the illustrations included in this edition.

Fig 3-10. Cosmological Evolution of the Four Basic Forces in Nature. Based on Andrew Fraknoi, David Morrison and Sidney Wolff, *Voyages Through the Universe*, vol. 2, *Stars, Galaxies and Cosmology* (Fort Worth: Saunders College Publishing, 1997), 578.

Fig 4-5. Babylonian World Map. Redrawn by Kenneth Kully. Based on Jeremy Black and Anthony Green, *Gods, Demons and Symbols of Ancient Mesopotamia: An Illustrated Dictionary* (Austin: University of Texas, 1992), 53; Lloyd R. Bailey, *Genesis, Creation and Creationism* (New York: Paulist Press, 1993), 174.

Fig 4-6. The Geocentric Universe of Martin Luther. Redrawn by Andrea Dmytrash. Based on Martin Luther, *Luther Bible of 1534, Complete Facsimile* (Köln: Taschen, 2003), no page number.

Fig 4-8. Seventeenth-Century Depiction of the 1-Seed Theory. Image taken from Google Images. Nicolas Hartsoeker (1656–1725) from his *Essai de Dioptrique* (1694).

Fig 9-1. Dental Form and Function. Gopher: Max Weber, *Die Säugetiere* (Jena: Von Gustav Fischer, 1904), 481. Fruit Bat and Vampire Bat: Terry A. Vaughan, *Mammalogy*. 3rd edition (New York: Saunders College Publishing, 1986), 111, 128. Reprinted with permission of Brooks/Cole, a division of Thomson Learning: www.thomsonrights.com. Fax 800–730–2215.

Fig 9-2. Saber-Toothed Tiger. A. S. Romer, *Vertebrate Paleontology*, 3rd edition (Chicago: University of Chicago Press, 1966), 234. Reprinted with permission of University of Chicago Press.

Fig 9-3. Reptile-to-Mammal Dental Evolution. Redrawn by Braden Barr. Based on Robert L. Carroll, *Vertebrate Paleontology and Evolution* (New York: W. H. Freeman and Company, 1988), 196, 365, 386, 406, 408.

Fig 9-5. Experimental Limbs. Drawn by Kenneth Kully. Based on A. Hornbruch and L. Wolpert, "Positional Signalling by Henson's Node when Grafted to the Chick Limb," *Journal of Experimental Morphology* 94 (1986), 261.

Fig 9-6. Fin-to-Limb Evolution. M. I. Coates, J. E. Jeffrey and M. Rut, "Fins to Limbs: What the Fossils Say," *Evolution and Development* 4 (2002), 392; Fig 3a and 3b; 394 Fig 5a. Reprinted with permission of Basil Blackwell Publishers.

Appendix 7

Fig 5. Shark Jaw and Dentition. Lower Jaw of Shark: Charles S. Tomes, *A Manual of Dental Anatomy* (London: A. & J. Churchill, 1898), 240. Single Shark Teeth: Redrawn by Braden Barr. Based on Robert L. Carroll, *Vertebrate Paleontology and Evolution* (New York: W. H. Freeman and Company, 1988), 68.

Fig 6. Tyrannosaurus Rex Skull and Dentition. T-Rex Skull and Jaws: Courtesy of Tracy Ford. T-Rex Single Tooth: Drawn by Braden Barr.

Appendix 10

Fig 1. Similarities in Skeletons. Monkey Skeleton: Daris R. Swindler, *Introduction to the Primates* (Seattle: University of Washington Press, 1998), 143. Reprinted with permission of University of Washington Press. Gorilla and Human Skeletons: Roger Lewin, *Human Evolution: An Illustrated Introduction*, 2nd ed. (Cambridge, MA: Blackwell Scientific Publications, 1989), 65. Reprinted with permission of Blackwell Scientific Publications.

Fig 2. Similarities in Rib Cages and Hip Bones. Chimpanzee, *A. afarensis* and Human Ribs and Hips: William A. Haviland, Dana Walrath, Harald E. L. Prins and Bunny McBride, *Evolution and Prehistory: The Human Challenge*, (with info Trac®) 7th ed. (Toronto: Wadsworth/Thompson Learning, 2005), 154; Fig 6.7. Reprinted with permission of Wadsworth, a division of Thompson Learning: www.thomsonrights.com. Fax 800–730–2215.

Fig 3. Similarities in Dentitions. Chimpanzee, *A. afarensis* and Human Dentitions: Roger Lewin, *Human Evolution: An Illustrated Introduction*, 2nd ed. (Cambridge, MA: Blackwell Scientific Publications, 1989), 70. Reprinted with permission of Blackwell Scientific Publications.

Fig 9. Evolution of Skulls in Pre-Humans and Humans. Artwork © Copyright D. J. Maizels, 1994.

Appendix 1
Translations of Genesis 1:1–3

King James Version (1611)

[1] In the beginning God created the heaven and the earth.
[2] And the earth was without form, and void;
    and darkness was upon the face of the deep.
  And the Spirit of God moved upon the face of the waters.
[3] And God said, Let there be light: and there was light.

Footnote: none

American Standard Version (1901)

[1] In the beginning God created the heavens and the earth.
[2] And the earth was waste and void;
    and darkness was upon the face of the deep:
    and the Spirit of God moved upon the face of the waters.
[3] And God said, Let there be light: and there was light.

Footnote: none

Revised Standard Version (1952)

[1] In the beginning God created the heavens and the earth.
[2] The earth was without form and void,
    and darkness was upon the face of the deep;
    and the Spirit of God was moving over the face of the waters.
[3] And God said, "Let there be light," and there was light.

Footnote: or When God began to create

New American Standard Bible (1960)

[1] In the beginning God created the heavens and the earth.
[2] And the earth was formless and void,
    and darkness was over the surface of the deep;
    and the Spirit of God was moving over the surface of the waters.
[3] Then God said, "Let there be light"; and there was light.

Footnote: none

New International Version (1978)

[1] In the beginning God created the heavens and the earth.
[2] Now the earth was formless and empty,
    darkness was over the surface of the deep,
    and the Spirit of God was hovering over the waters.
[3] And God said, "Let there be light," and there was light.

Footnote: none

Jewish Publication Society (1982)

[1] When God began to create the heaven and the earth
[2] —the earth being unformed and void, with darkness over the surface
    of the deep, and a wind from God sweeping over the water—
[3] God said, "Let there be light," and there was light.

Footnote: or In the beginning God created

New Jerusalem Bible (1985)

[1] In the beginning God created heaven and earth.
[2] Now the earth was a formless void,
    there was darkness over the deep,
    with a divine wind sweeping over the waters.
[3] And God said, "Let there be light," and there was light

Footnote: or When God began creating

New Revised Standard Version (1991)

[1] In the beginning when God created the heavens and the earth,
[2] the earth was a formless void
    and darkness covered the face of the deep,
    while a wind from God swept over the face of the waters.
[3] Then God said, "Let there be light"; and there was light.

Footnote: or When God began to create or In the beginning God created

Appendix 2
Creation Out of Nothing (Creatio Ex Nihilo)

THE CHRISTIAN DOCTRINE OF creation includes the belief that God created the world out of nothing. That is, He did not use eternal pre-existing material. The Creator precedes all things and everything that exists is dependent upon Him. He not only created matter, but also space and time. However, Christians are surprised to discover that God's creative activity in Gen 1 is not exclusively *creatio ex nihilo*. This notion seems to appear with regard to the origin of light, the firmament, the heavenly bodies, and the first humans. But the opening scene of the creation account is Gen 1:2, which describes a dark, watery, chaotic earth already in existence and gives no mention of who created it or when it was created, if indeed it was created.

In the Old Testament, the Hebrew word *bārā'* (to create) lends itself to the notion of *creatio ex nihilo*. God is almost always the subject of this verb. Notable exceptions include Josh 17:15, "go up into the forest and clear [*bārā'*, i.e., cut down the forest] land for yourselves" (also v. 18) and Ezek 23:47, "the mob will stone them and cut [*bārā'*] them down with their swords." As well, *bārā'* invariably involves the appearance of something brand new. For example, God creates "a new thing" (Jer 31:22) and "a new heavens and a new earth" (Isa 65:17). And whenever this verb is found, rarely is there mention of what is used, if anything, in the creative process. Understandably, most Christians assume that *bārā'* means to create out of nothing. However, a closer examination indicates that it does not carry this notion exclusively.

Bārā' appears about 50 times in the Old Testament with meanings to create, make, shape, form, and cut down. Ancient Near Eastern languages related to Biblical Hebrew have words (termed "cognates") that come from the same root as *bārā'* and mean to create, form, shape out, found, build, separate, divide, split, pare, and fashion by cutting.[1] Significantly, a large part of God's creative action in Gen 1 involves acts of separation, in particular the shaping of pre-existent matter. He begins by cutting through the darkness with light in order to divide night from day. The Creator then splits the primeval waters in two with the firmament, forming the heavenly waters above and the seas below. Next, this lower body of water is gathered into one place to separate the sea from dry ground. Thus, Gen 1 includes divine creative activity that is *creatio ex aliquo* (creation out of something). In this light, the word *bārā'* in the first verse of the Bible could be translated, "In the beginning God *cut, separated*, and *created* the heavens and the earth."[2]

Moreover, *bārā'* is employed interchangeably in the Old Testament with the common everyday word *'āśâ* (to make, to do). That is, inspired writers used *bārā'* synonymously with a verb that most often refers to the making of things out of pre-existent material. In the opening chapters of Genesis, Adam and Eve "made" coverings with fig leaves (3:7), God "made" garments for them from animal skins (3:21), and Noah "made" the ark with cypress wood and pitch (6:14). The interchangeability of these two verbs appears in a number of passages. For example, God promises both to "create" (Isa 65:17) and "make" (66:22) a new heavens and new earth. He also declares to Israel, "I will do ['āśâ] wonders never before done [bārā'] in any nation in all the world" (Exod 34:10). It is important to note that the biblical creation accounts reveal that the Creator both "created" and "made" the heavens, the earth and humans.

> This is the account of the heavens and the earth when they were created [*bārā'*]. When the Lord God made ['*āśâ*] the earth and heavens, . . . (Gen 2:4)

> Then God said, 'Let us make ['*āśâ*] a man in our image,' . . . So God created [*bārā'*] man in his own image. (Gen 1:26–27)

This interchangeability with *'āśâ* indicates that the ancient Hebrews did not restrict the meaning of *bārā'* to creation out of nothing. In other words, "to create" is not a technical term in Scripture referring exclusively to *creatio ex nihilo*.

The context of the creation accounts in Scripture also offer insights into the meaning of *bārā'*. In Gen 1:27 God creates (*bārā'*) humanity with no mention of whether He uses pre-existent material, alluding to *creatio ex nihilo*. But in Gen 2:7 He "formed man from the dust of the ground" and in Gen 2:22 He "made a woman from the rib He had taken out of the man." Similarly, birds were created (*bārā'*) on the fifth day of creation (Gen 1:21) seemingly out of nothing, yet Gen 2:19 states that the Lord "formed out of the ground all the birds of the air." Though an apparent conflict exists between Gen 1 and 2, it obviously was not problematic for the redactor because he juxtaposed the Priestly and Jahwist creation accounts to each other. In fact, he likely did not notice the difficulty in the same way that he never perceived the conflicting order of creative events between the first two chapters of Scripture. A fully developed understanding of the notion of *creatio ex nihilo* was beyond the redactor's ancient epistemological categories, since history reveals that this idea appears well after the J and P creation accounts were placed together. To summarize, *bārā'* is not limited to creation out of nothing. This verb for the ancient Hebrews included the idea that God created out of something.

Historically, the concept of *creatio ex nihilo* first appears about 250 BC.[3] The apocryphal book 2 Maccabees states, "I beg you, my child, to look at the heaven and the earth and see everything that is in them, and recognize that God did not make them out of things that existed" (7:28, NRSV). Though not as explicit, this notion is definitely implied in the New Testament.

> God gives life to the dead and calls into being that which does not exist. (Rom 4:17 [NASB])

> There is but one God, the Father, from whom all things came and for whom we live; and there is but one Lord, Jesus Christ, through whom all things came and through whom we live. (1 Cor 8:6 [NIV])

> He [Jesus] is the image of the invisible God, the firstborn of all creation; for in Him all things in heaven and on earth were created, things visible and invisible, whether thrones or dominions or rules or powers—all things have been created through Him and for Him. He Himself is before all things, and in Him all things hold together. (Col 1:15–17 [NIV])

> By faith we understand that the universe was formed at God's command, so that what is seen was not made out of what was visible. (Heb 11:3 [NIV])

Thus, there is a critical difference between the concept of creation in the New Testament and that found in the first chapters of the Old Testament. In Gen 1, God creates by shaping a dark, watery earth already in existence, while Heb 11:3 states that the universe "was not made out of what was visible." Some Christians might be troubled by such a contradiction in the Bible.

The solution to this problem is threefold. First, it is important to appreciate that biblical revelation is progressive. The definitive example of theological development in God's Word is Jesus. The Lord claimed that He "fulfilled" the Scriptures (Matt 5:17; Mark 14:49; Luke 22:37). The New Testament writers also understood His ministry in this way and refer to it over 50 times (Matt 8:17; John 13:18; Acts 13:33). The consequence of divine revelation coming to fulfillment progressively in stages is that there is an incomplete element in earlier revelations. This is the case with the notion of creation in the Bible. Genesis 1 and 2 begin the inspired revelatory process, definitely embracing *creatio ex aliquo*, and possibly including *creatio ex nihilo* for some things and beings. But Jesus fulfilled the Divine Theology on creation in the New Testament. As Col 1:15–17 states, He is the Creator who existed before all things. Thus, revelatory fulfillment discloses that the Lord created the entire world out of nothing.

Second, biblical revelation is accommodated to a certain audience at a certain time in history. Again, Jesus is the perfect example. In God taking on human flesh, He also embraced the language and intellectual categories of first century Palestine in order to communicate as effectively as possible. Similarly, the biblical creation accounts are a revelation of the Creator and His creation adapted to the level of the ancient Near Eastern peoples. The Holy Spirit employed the ancient motifs of *de novo* creation and the pre-creative state as vessels to deliver a Divine Theology in the opening chapters of Scripture.[4] In particular, the notion that the universe was created out of a pre-existent dark watery chaos was the science-of-the-day. Moreover, there is no evidence to indicate that the early Hebrews engaged complex and abstract ideas such as the origin of space, time, and matter. In fact, biblical Hebrew does not have a word for "matter." It is doubtful that the writer of Gen 1 and his readers asked, "When did the pre-creative state appear? Who created it? Was it eternal?" These questions were simply not part of their ancient epistemological context.

Finally, biblical revelation is Incarnational in that it features a human authorial intention. Recognizing and respecting this characteristic is a challenge to modern readers of Scripture because it is counterintuitive. For example, the creative process in Gen 1 features the verbal command "And God said, . . ." ten times. Many Christians today assume that this reflects the notion of *creatio ex nihilo*. But to ancient peoples, a verbal command, including the giving of names, was quite significant. It indicated superiority and control. Therefore, creation through God's words and His naming of the light "day," the darkness "night," the firmament "heavens," the dry ground "earth," and the waters below "sea" (v. 5, 8, 10) were striking statements to the ancients declaring that He ruled over the world. In particular, these creative events are acts to conquer the dark watery earth of Gen 1:2. Viewed in this way, it is doubtful that the human author intended to communicate the notion of creation out of nothing in the divine verbal commands of Gen 1.

A paraphrase displays more clearly the ancient intellectual categories in the opening verses of Scripture:

> When God began to make the heavens and the earth, there was a dark watery earth already in existence. The Spirit of God ruled completely over this formless and empty situation. Then by verbal commands, God cut and separated the pre-creative state to fashion and name "the heavens" and "the earth."[5]

The Message of Faith is obvious—the God of the Hebrews formed the world. *Creatio ex nihilo* was not fundamental to ancient Israel's inspired theology when her creation accounts were composed. Yet this is unsurprising since the concept was not part of the ancient Near Eastern mindset at that time. Regrettably, though understandably, many Christians eisegetically impose modern scientific categories upon the word "create" in Scripture. Today, the term "creation" is often conflated with abstract categories from physics like the "space-time-matter continuum." However, these believers fail to identify and separate the incidental ancient science of a pre-creative state from the inerrant and infallible theology. Since modern conceptual baggage is fused to the word "create," terms with less technological clutter, like "make" and "rule" serve best to capture the authorial intention of the inspired writers. From this perspective, the Bible opens with a simple revelation of the divine makership and rulership of the world.

The belief that God created the world out of nothing is foundational to the Christian doctrine of creation. However, the Holy Spirit only revealed this notion at a time when it was within the epistemological grasp of the writers and their readers. Consequently, modern Christians must draw upon biblical passages that intentionally deal with *creatio ex nihilo* when dealing with this issue. None of us today would appeal to the sacrificial system outlined in the Old Testament in formulating a Christian doctrine of atonement. Rather, we turn to the New Testament and the sacrifice of Jesus as the only and once-for-all payment of our sins (Heb 10:2, 10, 12). So too with the concept of creation out of nothing. Instead of using the Gen 1 and 2 creation accounts, we must employ relevant passages to discover that the fulfillment of the doctrine of creation is found in Jesus. As John 1:3 reveals, "Through Him all things were made; without Him nothing was made that has been made."

Appendix 3
Genealogies of Jesus

I N THE ANCIENT NEAR East, the number seven was saturated with meaning and used symbolically.[1] The Bible often employs 7 and its multiples to convey the notions of completion, perfection and fulfillment. For example, God takes 7 days in Gen 1 to complete the creation of the world and institute a day of rest. The Sabbath is the seventh day, the Day of Atonement in the seventh month, and the Year of Jubilee (rest) after 49 years (7 x 7). Monthly offerings were to include 7 male lambs without defect (Num 28:11), and a young bull's blood was to be sprinkled 7 times for unintentional sin (Lev 4:6). In the New Testament, the book of Revelation is steeped in symbolic 7's. There are seven: churches (1:4), lamp stands (1:12), stars (1:16), spirits (3:1), lamps (4:5), seals (5:1), horns (5:6), eyes (5:6), angels (8:2), thunders (10:7), heads (12:3), plagues (15:8), bowls (17:1), hills (17:9), and kings (17:10). And Jesus uses stylistic 7's. He commands Peter to forgive sinners "not seven times, but seventy-seven times [(7 x 11) or seven times seventy (7 x 70)]" (Matt 18:22). In other words, forgiveness is to be complete and perfect.

Symbolic 7's and multiples of 7 appear in the two genealogies of Jesus. Matthew's rendition (Fig 1) is divided symmetrically into three sections of 14 (7 x 2). As verse 17 states, "Thus there were 14 generations in all from Abraham to David, 14 from David to the exile to Babylon, and 14 from the exile to the Christ." The number 14 is significant because it is the symbolic number (termed "gematria") of David. The Hebrews gave a numerical value for each letter in their consonants-only alphabet (vowels were simply understood). The word for "David" is made up of two d's (daleth) and one w (waw), the fourth and sixth letters in the Hebrew alphabet, respectively. Thus, the gematric formula for Dwd is $4 + 6 + 4 = 14$.[2] In this way, Matthew subtly emphasizes that Jesus is the fulfillment of

1st 14 Generations	1 Chr 1:34, 2:1-15	2nd 14 Generations	1 Chr 3:4-5, 3:10-16	3rd 14 Generations	1 Chr 3:17-24
1. Abraham	✔	1. Solomon	✔	1. Shealtiel	Pedaiah
2. Isaac	✔	2. Rehoboam	✔	2. Zerubbabel	✔
3. Jacob	✔	3. Abijah	✔	3. Abiud	Hananiah
4. Judah	✔	4. Asa	✔	4. Eliakim	Shecaniah
5. Perez	✔	5. Jehoshaphat	✔	5. Azor	Neariah
6. Hezron	✔	6. Joram	✔	6. Zadok	Elioenia
7. Ram	✔		Ahaziah	7. Akim	End of Genealogy
8. Amminadab	✔		Joash	8. Eliud	
9. Hahshon	✔		Amazriah	9. Eleazar	
10. Salmon	✔	7. Uzziah	✔	10. Matthan	
11. Boaz	✔	8. Jotham	✔	11. Jacob	
12. Obed	✔	9. Ahaz	✔	12. Joseph	
13. Jesse	✔	10. Hezekiah	✔	13. Jesus	
14. David	✔	11. Manasseh	✔	14. Christ	
		12. Amon	✔		
		13. Josiah	✔	**Total: 42**	
			Jehoiahkim		
		14. Jeconiah	✔		

Fig 1. Matthew's Genealogy of Jesus (1:1-16). ✔ indicates agreement between Matt 1 and the genealogies found in 1 Chr 1-3.

the promise that the Messiah would come through the royal Davidic line (2 Sam 7:11-16; Ps 89:19-37). His focus on this theme is evident by the fact that he uses the phrase "Son of David" 9 times while it appears only 3 times in each of the gospels of Mark and Luke. Moreover, the stylistic intention of Matthew's genealogy clearly appears in the second group of generations. It omits four individuals from the lineage in 1 Chr 3 in order to maintain the symmetry of 14. Similarly, the third grouping assigns two places to the Lord. Finally, the total number of generations is 42, which could be viewed as a multiple of seven (7 x 6) and/or David's gematria (14) multiplied by 3, since repeating something three times was used for emphasis in the ancient Near East.

In Luke's genealogy of Jesus (Fig 2), there are 77 people from God to the Lord. The inspired author is making a statement with this doubly perfect number that ancient readers would understand—Jesus is the perfect divine fulfillment. Notably, Luke 3 does not align with Matthew's genealogy, sharing only 17 individuals in the line from Abraham to Jesus. Moreover, the former has 42 (7 x 6 and/or 14 x 3) generations from David to Jesus while the latter has 28 (7 x 4). In fact, 36 people in Luke's rendition (numbers 4 to 20 and 23 to 41) are unknown and not found in the Old Testament. And remarkably, Luke and Matthew do not agree on who is the father of Joseph—Heli and Jacob, respectively. Attempts to solve the conflicts between these genealogies by suggesting one list is

Generations of Sons	Matt 1:1-16		Matt 1:1-16		Gen 5:1-32, 11:10-26
1. Jesus		29. Joshua		57. Terah	✓
2. Joseph	✔	30. Eliezar		58. Nahor	✓
3. Heli		31. Jorim		59. Serug	✓
4. Matthat		32. Matthat		60. Reu	✓
5. Levi		33. Levi		61. Peleg	✓
6. Melki		34. Simeon		62. Eber	✓
7. Jannai		35. Judah		63. Shelah	✓
8. Joseph		36. Joseph		64. Cainan	
9. Mattahias		37. Jonam		65. Arphaxad	✓
10. Amos		38. Eliakim		66. Shem	✓
11. Nahum		39. Melea		67. Noah	✓
12. Esli		40. Menna		68. Lamech	✓
13. Naggi		41. Mattatha		69. Methuselah	✓
14. Maath		42. Nathan		70. Enoch	✓
15. Mattahias		43. David	✔	71. Jared	✓
16. Semein		44. Jesse	✔	72. Mahalaleel	✓
17. Josech		45. Obed	✔	73. Cainan	✓
18. Joda		46. Boaz	✔	74. Enos	✓
19. Joanan		47. Salmon	✔	75. Seth	✓
20. Rhesa		48. Nahshon	✔	76. Adam	✓
21. Zerubbabel	✔	49. Amminadab	✔	77. God	
22. Shealtiel	✔	50. Ram	✔		
23. Neri		51. Hezron	✔	**Total: 77**	
24. Melki		52. Perez	✔		
25. Addi		53. Judah	✔		
26. Cosam		54. Jacob	✔		
27. Elamadam		55. Isaac	✔		
28. Er		56. Abraham	✔		

Fig 2. Luke's Genealogy of Jesus (3:23–38). ✔ indicates agreement between Lk 3 and the genealogy of Jesus in Matt 1. ✓ between Lk 3 and Gen 5:1–32 and 11:10–26.

Jesus' maternal heritage fails to recognize the ancient 1-seed theory of reproduction and that family "seed" comes from men only.

Undoubtedly, there are real historical individuals included in the two versions of the Lord's genealogy (e.g., Abraham, Isaac, Jacob, David, Joseph). Luke and Matthew are definitely emphasizing Jesus' humanity. But the obvious stylistic use of mystical 7's to shape these genealogies indicates that their primary purpose is theological, and not historical in the sense of offering a strict literal record of His ancestors. Otherwise, the lineages in Matt 1 and Luke 3 would conflict irreconcilably. Instead of viewing this situation as a contradiction in the Bible, it subtly reveals an important interpretive insight—the central purpose of genealogies in Scripture is to deliver Messages of Faith. The ancestries in Gen 4, 5, and 11 need to be seen in this light. In other words, twenty-first century readers must not impose their modern understanding of family trees on an ancient genealogy. To do so is eisegetical.

Appendix 4
Sumerian King Lists

Ancient Mesopotamian literature includes lists of Sumerian kings who reigned before and after a great flood. One rendition (W-B 444) opens, "When kingship was lowered from heaven, kingship was first in Eridu. In Eridu, Alulim became king and ruled 28,800 years."[1] Fig 1 presents the other pre-diluvian kings and the length of their reigns. Notably, versions of this list (W-B 62, Berossos) feature differences in the periods of governance, indicating the freedom ancient authors had to manipulate numbers for stylistic purposes. Near the middle of W-B 444, it is recorded that "Eight kings ruled them [i.e., five cities] for 241,000 years. Then the flood swept over the earth. After the flood had swept over the earth and when kingship was lowered again from heaven, kingship was first in Kish. In Kish, Ga . . . ur became king and ruled 1200 years." Fig 2 lists the other post-diluvian kings.

King	Ancient Document			'60^2 Times X' Formula		
	W-B 444	W-B 62	Berossos	W-B 444	W-B 62	Berossos
Alulim	28,800	67,200*	36,000	60^2 X 8	*	60^2 X 10
Alalgar	36,000	72,000	10,800	60^2 X 10	60^2 X 20	60^2 X 3
Enmenluanna	43,200	21,600	46,800	60^2 X 12	60^2 X 6	60^2 X 13
Enmengalanna	28,800	not listed	46,800	60^2 X 8	–	60^2 X 13
...kidunnu	–	72,000	–	–	60^2 X 20	–
...alimma	–	21,600	–	–	60^2 X 6	–
Evedoragxos	–	–	64,800	–	–	60^2 X 18
Ammemon	–	–	43,200	–	–	60^2 X 12
Dumuzi	36,000	28,800	36,000	60^2 X 10	60^2 X 8	60^2 X 10
Ensipazianna	28,800	36,000	36,000	60^2 X 8	60^2 X 10	60^2 X 10
Enmenduranna	21,000*	72,000	-	*	60^2 X 20	–
Ubartutu	18,600*	28,000	28,800	*	60^2 X 8	60^2 X 8
Ziusudra	–	36,000	64,800	–	60^2 X 10	60^2 X 18
Average:	30,150	45,560	41,320			

Fig 1. Reigns of Sumerian Kings *Before* the Flood and Ancient Stylistic Numbers. All reigns are in years. * indicates that a number does not fit into a "60^2 times X" formula, but it is divisible by 60.

King

King	Reign (Years)	'60 Times X' Formula
Ga . . . ur	1200	60 X 20
Nidaba	960	60 X 16
Bu.an . . .	840	60 X 14
Kalibum	960	60 X 16
Qalumum	840	60 X 14
Zuqapiq	900	60 X 15
Atab	600	60 X 10
Masha	840	60 X 14
Arwi'um	720	60 X 12
Etana	1560	60 X 15

Average: 942

King	Reign	Formula
Balih	400	–
En-me-nunna	660	60 X 11
Melam-Kishi	900	60 X 15
Bar-sal-nunna	1200	60 X 20
Samug	140	–
Tizkar	305	–
Ilku'	900	60 X 15
Ilta-sadum	1200	60 X 20
En-men-barage-si	900	60 X 15
Aka	629	–
Mes-kiag-gasher	324	–
En-me-kar	420	60 X 7
Lugalbanda	1200	60 X 20
Dumunzi	100	–
Gilgamesh	126	–

Average: 626.9

King	Reign	Formula	
Ur-Nungal	30	–	*
Utul-kalamma	15	–	*
Labah . . .	9	–	*
En-nun-dara-Anna	8	–	
Mes . . . he	36	–	*
Melam-Anna	6	–	*
Lugal-ki-tun	36	–	*
Mes-Anne-pada	80	–	
Mes-kiag-Nanna	36	–	*
Elulu	25	–	
Balulu	36	–	*

Average: 28.8

Fig 2. Reigns of Sumerian Kings *After* the Flood and Ancient Stylistic Numbers. All reigns are from the W-B 444 document. The arrangement in three columns is not in the text, but is used to show a pattern in the reduction of reign length and a breakdown in the symmetry of numbers. — does not fit in "60 times X" formula with a whole number. * divisible by 60 into a fraction of one.

Appendix 5
Jahwist and Priestly Sources of the
Biblical Flood Account (Gen 6–9)

THE TRANSLATIONS PRESENTED IN this appendix follow the original Hebrew as literally as possible in order to accentuate linguistic similarities and differences. At times the grammatical constructions will be clumsy to English-speaking readers. For example, the divine promise in the Jahwist flood account begins with the clause "never again will I repeat to . . ." (Gen 8:21 [2x]) while in the Priestly rendition the phrase is "never again will . . ." (Gen 9:11, 15).

Fig 1. Verse Distribution of Jahwist and Priestly Sources

Jahwist (J)	Priestly (P)	Jahwist (J)	Priestly (P)
6:5-8		7:22-23	
	6:9-22		7:24-8:2a
7:1-5		8:2b-3a	
	7:6		8:3b-5
7:7-8		8:6	
	7:9		8:7
7:10		8:8-12	
	7:11		8:13a
7:12		8:13b	
	7:13-16a		8:14-19
7:16b-17		8:20-22	
	7:18-21		9:1-19

Fig 2. Jahwist Flood Account

Introduction. Sinful State of the World before the Flood and Divine Justification for Destruction

6 ⁵The LORD saw that the evil of man on the earth was great, and that every imagination of the thoughts of his heart was only evil all of the day. ⁶The LORD was sorry that He had made man on the earth, and it hurt His heart. ⁷The LORD said, "I will wipe out man, whom I have created, from the face of the ground—from man, to animal, to crawler, and to bird of the heavens—for I am sorry that I made them." ⁸But Noah found favor in the eyes of the LORD.

Divine Warning of the Flood and Preparation for Preservation of Life in the Ark

7 ¹The LORD said to Noah, "Go into the ark, you and all your household, because I found you righteous before my face in this generation. ²Take with you 7 pairs [literally: seven seven, or seven by seven] from every clean animal, a man and his woman, and two from every animal that is not clean, a man and his woman, ³also 7 pairs from every bird of the heavens, male and female, to keep alive seed on the face of all the earth. ⁴For in 7 days from now I will send rain on the earth, 40 days and 40 nights; and I will wipe out from the face of the earth all the standing which I made." ⁵Noah did exactly all that the LORD commanded him. ⁷Noah entered, and his sons, and his wife, and his sons' wives into the ark from the face of waters of the flood—⁸from clean animal and from animal that is not clean, and from bird, and all that crawls on the ground.

The Launch of the Flood

¹⁰ It was after the 7 days the waters of the flood came on the earth ¹²and the rain fell on the earth 40 days and 40 nights. ¹⁶ᵇThe LORD shut him in. ¹⁷The flood was 40 days on the earth, the waters increased, they lifted the ark, and it rose from on the earth. ²²All that had the breath of life in its nostrils, from all that was on the dry land, they died. ²³It wiped out all the standing that was on the face of the ground—from man, to animal, to crawler, and to bird of the heavens. They were wiped out from the earth. Only Noah was left and that with him in the ark.

The Retreat of the Flood

8 [2b]The rain from the heavens was stopped. [3a]The waters receded from the earth and they continued to recede. [6]It was at the end of 40 days and Noah opened the window of the ark that he had made. [8]He sent out a dove from him to see if the waters had subsided from the face of the ground. [9]But the dove found no place to set her foot and she returned to him to the ark because the waters were on the face of all the earth. He put out his hand and took her and brought her with him into the ark. [10]He waited yet another 7 days and he repeated to send out the dove from the ark. [11]The dove returned to him in the time of evening. And behold a freshly plucked olive leaf was in her mouth! Noah knew that the waters had subsided from on the earth. [12]He waited yet another 7 days and he sent out the dove out. But she did not repeat to return to him again. [13b]Noah removed the covering from the ark and looked. And behold the faces of the ground were dry!

Conclusion. After the Flood and Divine Promise Never to Flood the World Again

[20]Noah built an altar to the LORD. He took from every clean animal and from every clean bird, and he offered burnt offerings on the altar. [21]The LORD smelled the pleasant smell. The LORD said in His heart, "Never again will I repeat to curse the ground because of man though the imagination of the heart of man is evil from his youth. Never again will I repeat to strike all living as I have done. [22]While all the days of the earth—seedtime and harvest, cold and heat, summer and winter, day and night will not rest."

Fig 3. Terms and Phrases in Gen 2–4 (J) and the Jahwist Flood Account

	Gen 2–4 (J)	J Flood Account
LORD (*Yahweh*)	29x. 2:4, 5, 7, 8, 9, 15, 16, 18, 19, 21, 22; 3:1, 8 (2x), 9, 13, 14, 21, 22, 23; 4:1, 3, 4, 6, 9, 13, 15 (2x), 26	10x. 6:5, 6, 7, 8; 7:1, 5, 16b; 8:20, 21 (2x),
ground (*ădāmâ*)	14x. 2:5, 6, 7, 9, 19,; 3:17, 19, 23; 4:2, 3, 10, 11, 12, 14	6x. 6:7; 7:8, 23; 8:8, 13b, 21
Evil	2:9, 17; 3:5, 22	6:5 (2x), 8:21

	Gen 2–4 (J)	J Flood Account
curse/d	3:14, 17; 4:11	8:21
Offering	4:3, 4, 5	8:20
Rain	2:5	7:4, 10; 8:2b
man (*'îsh*) woman (*'ishshâ*)	2:23, 24	7:2 (2x)
breath of life "in nostrils"	2:7	7:22
repeat/ed to (a verb)	4:2, 12	8:10, 21 (2x)
face of the ground	2:6; 4:14	6:7, 8:8, 13b
ratio of appearance of terms 'earth' (*'ereṣ*) and 'ground' (*ǎdāmâ*)*	9/14	15/6

*Gen 1 ratio is 16/1 and P flood 31/2.

Fig 4. Terms, Phrases and Literary Style Characteristics in Jahwist Flood Account

Face	9x. 6:7; 7:1, 3, 4, 7, 23; 8:8, 9, 13b
Heart	6:5, 6; 7:21 (2x)
wipe out	6:7; 7:4, 23 (2x)
imagination	6:5; 8:21
clean animal and animal that is not clean	7:2,8; also see 8:20 (2x)
from man, to animal, to crawler, and to bird of the heavens	6:7; 7:23
never again will I repeat to . . .	8:21 (2x)
(also: she did not repeat to . . .)	8:12
The Lord given anthropomorphic characteristics:	
He is sorry He made humanity	6:6
His heart is hurt	6:6
He smells an offering	8:21
He talks in His heart	8:21
Stylistic 7 and 40:	
7 pairs	7:2, 3
7 days	7:4, 10; 8:10, 12
40 days and nights	7:4, 12
40 days	7:17; 8:6

Fig 5. Priestly Flood Account

Introduction. Sinful State of the World before the Flood and Divine Justification for Destruction

6 ⁹These are the generations of Noah. Noah was a righteous man. He was blameless among his contemporaries. Noah walked with GOD. ¹⁰Noah fathered three sons: Shem, Ham and Japheth. ¹¹The earth was corrupt in GOD's sight and was filled with violence. ¹²GOD saw the earth. And behold, it was corrupt, for all flesh on earth had corrupted its ways.

Divine Warning of the Flood and Preparation for Preservation of Life in the Ark

¹³GOD said to Noah, "I have determined to put an end to all flesh, for the earth is filled with violence because of them. So I am going to destroy them with the earth. ¹⁴Make yourself an ark of cypress wood; make rooms in the ark, and coat it inside and out with pitch. ¹⁵This is how you are to make it: The length of the ark 300 cubits, its width 50 cubits, its height 30 cubits. ¹⁶Make a roof for the ark, and finish it to 1 cubit above. Put a door in the side of the ark. Make lower, second and third decks. ¹⁷Now behold, I am going to bring the flood of waters on the earth to destroy all flesh that has in it the breath of life from under the heavens; all that is on the earth will die. ¹⁸But I will establish my covenant with you, and you will enter the ark—you, and your sons, and your wife, and your sons' wives with you. ¹⁹From all the living, from all flesh, two from all you will bring into the ark to keep alive with you; they will be male and female. ²⁰From the bird according to its kind, and from the animal according to its kind, from the crawler of the ground according to its kind; two from all will come to you to be kept alive. ²¹But you: Take every food that is eaten, and store it. It is food for you and for them." ²²Noah did all that GOD commanded him; so he did.

The Launch of the Flood Waters

7 ⁶Now Noah was 600 years old when the flood waters came on the earth. ⁹Pairs [literally: two two or two by two] came to Noah to the ark, male and female, as GOD commanded Noah. ¹¹In the 600th year of Noah's life, in the 2nd month in the 17th day to the month, on that day all the springs of the great deep burst forth, and the windows of the heavens were opened. ¹³On that very same day, Noah, and Shem, Ham and Japheth, the sons of Noah, and Noah's wife, and the three wives of

his sons with them entered the ark; [14]they and every wild animal according to its kind, and every domesticated animal according to its kind, and every crawler on the earth according to its kind, and every bird, and every wing. [15]They came to Noah into the ark two by two from all flesh that has in it the breath of life. [16a]Those that came, male and female from all flesh, they entered just as GOD had commanded him. [18]The waters triumphed and increased greatly over the earth, and the ark floated on the surface of the waters. [19]The waters triumphed greatly greatly over the earth, and all the high mountains were covered that were under all the heavens. [20]To a depth of 15 cubits the waters triumphed and the mountains were covered. [21]All flesh that crawls on the earth died—consisting of every bird, and consisting of every domesticated animal, and consisting of every wild animal, and consisting of every swarmer swarming on the earth, and all man. [24]The waters triumphed over the earth 150 days.

The Retreat of the Flood Waters

8 [1]GOD remembered Noah and every wild animal and every domesticated animal that were with him in the ark. GOD sent wind over the earth, and the waters subsided. [2a]The springs of the deep and the windows of the heavens were closed. [3b]The waters decreased at the end of 150 days. [4]The ark rested in the 7th month in the 17th day to the month on the mountains of Ararat. [5]The waters continued to decrease until the 10th month; in the 10th in the 1st to the month the tops of the mountains were seen. [7]He sent out a raven, and it went back and forth until the waters were dried up from on the earth. [13a]And it was in the 601st year in the 1st to the 1st month, the waters were dried from on the earth. [14]In the 2nd month in the 27th day to the month, the earth was completely dry.

Conclusion. After the Flood and Divine Promise Never to Flood the World Again

[15]GOD spoke to Noah, saying, [16]"Come out of the ark, you, and your wife, and your sons, and the wives of your sons with you, [17]all the living that is with you from all flesh—consisting of every bird, and consisting of every animal, and consisting of every crawler crawling on the earth. Bring them out with you so that they can swarm on the earth and be fruitful and increase on the earth." [18]Noah came out, and his sons, and his wife, and his sons' wives with him; [19]all the living, every crawler, and every bird,

every crawler on the earth, according to their clans, they came out from the ark.

9 ¹GOD blessed Noah and his sons. He said to them, "Be fruitful and increase and fill the earth. ²The fear and dread of you will be on all the life of the earth, and on every bird of the heavens, on all that crawls the ground, and on all the fishes of the sea; into your hands they are given. ³Every crawler that lives will be food for you, as I gave you the green plants, to you everything. ⁴But flesh with its life, its blood, you must not eat. ⁵But surely, I will demand your blood for breaths of you, from the hand of all life I will demand, and from the hand of man, from the hand of a man his brother I will demand the breath of the man. ⁶Whoever sheds the blood of man, by man his blood will be shed; because in the Image of GOD He made man. ⁷But as for you, be fruitful and increase; swarm on the earth and increase on it."

⁸GOD said to Noah and to his sons with him, saying, ⁹"Behold, I establish my covenant with you and with your descendants after you ¹⁰and with all breath of life that was with you—with every bird, with every domesticated animal, and with every wild animal, of all those that came out of the ark, with all life of the earth. ¹¹I establish my covenant with you. Never again will all flesh be cut off by waters of the flood. Never again will there be a flood to destroy the earth." ¹²GOD said, "This is the sign of the covenant I am making between me and you and every living breath that is with you, a covenant for generations to come: ¹³I have set my bow in the cloud, and it will be the sign of the covenant between me and the earth. ¹⁴When I bring clouds over the earth and the bow is seen in the clouds, ¹⁵I will remember my covenant that is between me and you, and between every living breath, and with all flesh. Never again will the waters become a flood to destroy all flesh. ¹⁶When the bow is in the clouds, I will see it and remember the everlasting covenant between GOD and every living breath and with all flesh that is on the earth." ¹⁷GOD said to Noah, "This is the sign of the covenant that I have established between me and all flesh that is on the earth." ¹⁸The sons of Noah who came out of the ark were Shem, Ham and Japheth. Ham was the father of Canaan. ¹⁹These were the three sons of Noah, and from these all the earth was populated.

Fig 6. Terms and Phrases in Gen 1 (P) and the Priestly Flood Account

	Gen 1 (P)*	P Flood Account
GOD ('Ĕlōhîm)	35X 1:1, 2, 3, 4 (2x), 5, 6, 7, 8, 9, 10 (2x), 11, 12, 14, 16, 17, 18, 20, 21 (2x), 22, 24, 25 (2x), 26, 27 (2x), 28 (2x), 29, 31; 2:2, 3 (2x).	16x. 6:9b, 12, 13, 22; 7:9, 16a; 8:1 (2x), 15; 9:1, 6, 8, 12, 16, 17
God said to . . . , "Be fruitful and increase (and fill) on the earth"	1:28	8:17, 9:2, 9:7
God blessed (humanity and creatures)	1:22, 28; 2:3; 5:2	9:1
make/made man in the Image of God	1:26–27; 5:1–3	9:6
according to its/their kind(s)	1:11, 1:12 (2x), 1:21 (2x), 1:24 (2x), 1:25 (3x)	6:20 (3x), 7:14 (3x)
male and female	1:27	6:19; 7:9, 16
wild animal and domesticated animal	1:24, 1:25	7:14, 7:21, 8:1, 9:10
crawler of the ground/earth	1:25	6:20, 8:19
crawler crawling on the earth	1:26	7:14, 8:17
birds referred to as 'wing'	1:21	7:14
I [God] give/gave to you green plants for food	1:29–30	9:3
it will be food for you	1:29	9:3
fish/es of the sea	1:28	9:2
deep	1:2	7:11, 8:2
swarm	1:20, 1:21	8:17, 9:7
ratio of appearance of terms 'earth' ('ereṣ) and 'ground' (ădāmâ)	16/2	31/2

*Note: Verse divisions in the Bible are artificial and not part of the original manuscripts. Gen 1 creation account extends to Gen 2:3.

Fig 7. Terms, Phrases and Literary Style Characteristics in Priestly Flood Account

all flesh	13X. 6:12, 13, 17, 19; 7:15, 21, 15 (x2); 9:11,15 (2x), 16, 17
Covenant	9X. 6:18; 9:9, 11, 12 (x2), 13, 15, 16, 17

Fig 7. Terms, Phrases and Literary Style Characteristics in Priestly Flood Account (continued)

Food	6:21 (2x), 9:3
Mountains	7:19, 20; 8:4, 5
Remember	8:1; 9:15, 16
two from all, two by two from all	6:19, 20; 7:15
springs of the great deep and windows of the heavens	7:11, 8:2
waters triumphed over the earth	7:18, 19, 24; also see 7:20
bow in the clouds	9:13, 14, 16
never again will . . .	9:11 (2x), 15
Stylistic 60:	6:15; 7:6, 20, 24; 8:3
length of ark	300 cubits = 60 x 5
height of ark	30 cubits = 60/2
volume of ark (calculated)	450, 000 = 60² x 125
age of Noah[1]	600 years = 60 x 10
depth of waters over mountains	15 cubits = 60/4
duration of Flood	300 (150 + 150) days = 60 x 5

Appendix 6
Epic of Gilgamesh Flood Account

THE EPIC OF GILGAMESH is a Mesopotamian poem made up of twelve tablets. The eleventh includes an account of a great flood that destroys the world. This poem was first composed around 2000 BC, but the deluge story was probably not added until 1600 BC.[1] The story is about Gilgamesh, the king of the city of Uruk in Southern Mesopotamia, and his quest to gain eternal life. In his pursuit, he meets Utnapishtim, the flood hero who was given immortality. In the first part of the eleventh tablet, Utnapishtim recounts events of the deluge. He also reveals that there is a magical plant that can restore youth. Gilgamesh then obtains the plant, but it is stolen by a snake.

This epic features a number of motifs from Sumerian poems of an earlier period. Yet the central story of Gilgamesh is an original work. In other words, the author/s borrowed and re-cycled motifs to develop their new theme. The many parallels between the Epic of Gilgamesh and the later composed biblical flood account (1000/500 BC) suggests that the Hebrews practiced a similar literary process. Guided by the Holy Spirit, the writers of Noah's deluge used common ancient Near Eastern motifs to reveal the innovative theme that a single Holy God judges human sin.

Introduction[2]

8   Utnapishtim said to him, to Gilgamesh:
"I will reveal to thee, Gilgamesh, a hidden matter
    and a secret of the gods will I tell thee:
Shuruppak[a]—a city which thou knowest,

---

a. Shuruppak was an ancient city in Southern Mesopotamia between the Tigris and Euphrates rivers. It was in an area susceptible to flooding.

and which on the Euphrates' banks is situated—
that city was ancient, as were the gods within it,

14 when their heart led the great gods to produce the flood.

∼

The Gods Warn Hero of the Flood

[The gods said to Utnapishtim:]

23 Man of Shuruppak, son of Ubar-Tutu,
    tear down this house, build a ship!
Give up possessions, seek thou life.
Forswear worldly goods and keep the soul alive!
Aboard the ship take thou the seed of all living things.[b]
The ship that thou shall build,
    her dimensions shall be to measure.
Equal shall be her width and her length.
Like the Aspu[c] thou shall ceil[d] her.
I understood, and I said to Ea[e], my lord:
'Behold, my lord, what thou has ordered,

34 I will be honoured to carry out.'

∼

Building of the Ship

54 The little ones carried bitumen,
    while the grown ones brought all else that was needful.
On the 5th day I laid her framework.
One whole acre was her floor space,
    120 cubits the height of each her walls,
    120 cubits each edge of the square deck.
I laid out the contours and joined her together.
I provided her 6 decks, dividing her thus into 7 parts.

b. Note the 1-seed theory.

c. Body of fresh water below the earth. In the context of the verse, the earth seals it over.

d. That is, to place a ceiling.

e. A god who lived in Aspu. See also footnote c.

Her floor plan I divided into 9 parts.
I hammered water plugs into her.
I saw to the punting-poles and laid in supplies.
6 sar[f] measures of bitumen I poured into the furnace,
   3 sar of asphalt I also poured inside.
3 sar of oil the basket-bearers carried,
   aside from the 1 sar of oil which the calking consumed,
69 and the 2 sar of oil which the boatman stowed away.

Loading and Launching of the Ship

76 On the 7th day the ship was completed.
   The launching was very difficult,
     so that they had to shift the floor planks above and
     below, until two-thirds of the structure had gone into the water.
   Whatever I had I laded upon her:
   Whatever I had of silver I laded upon her.
   Whatever I had of gold I laded upon her.
   Whatever I had of all the living beings I laded upon her.
   All my family and kin I made go aboard the ship.
   The beasts of the field, the wild creatures of the field,
     all the craftsmen I made go aboard.
   Shamash[g] had set for me a stated time:
   'When he who orders unease at night,
     will shower down a rain of blight,
88 Board the ship and batten up the entrance!'

The Flood

89 That stated time had arrived:
   'He who orders unease at night, showers down a rain of blight.'
   I watched the appearance of the weather.
   The weather was awesome to behold.
   I boarded the ship and battened up the entrance.
   To batten down the ship, to Puzur-Amurri, the boatman,

---

f. A "sar" is the number 3600 (or 60²). It represents about 8000 gallons.

g. The sun god.

I handed over the structure together with its contents.
With the first glow of dawn, a black cloud rose up from the horizon.
Inside it Adad[h] thunders, while Shullat and Hanish go in front,
    moving as heralds over hill and plain.
Erragal[i] tears out the posts.
Forth comes Ninurta[j] and causes the dikes to follow.
The Anunnaki[k] lift up the torches, setting the land ablaze with
    their glare.
Consternation over Adad reaches to the heavens,
    who turned to blackness all that had been light.
The wide land was shattered like a pot!
For one day the south-storm blew, gathering speed as it blew,
    overtaking the people like a battle.
114 No one can see his fellow, nor can the people recognize heaven.

The Gods Terrified by the Flood

113 The gods were frightened by the deluge,
    and, shrinking back, they ascended to the heaven of Anu.[l]
The gods cowered like dogs crouched against the outer wall.

≈

125 The gods, all humbled, sit and weep, their lips drawn tight,
    one and all.
6 days and 6 nights
Blows the flood wind, as south-storm sweeps the land.

End of the Flood and Landing of the Ship on Mt. Nisir

129 When the 7th day arrived,
    the flood-carrying south-storm subsided in the battle,
    which it had fought like an army.
The sea grew quiet, the tempest was still, the flood ceased.

h. The storm god.
i. The underworld god.
j. A god associated with war.
k. A term for the gods of the earth.
l. According to Mesopotamian astronomy, the heaven of Anu is the highest heaven of many heavens.

I looked at the weather: stillness had set in,
   and all of mankind had returned to clay.
The landscape was level as a flat roof.
I opened the hatch, and light fell upon my face.
Bowing low, I sat and wept, tears running down on my face.
I looked about for coastlines in the expanse of the sea:
In each of 14 regions there emerged a region-mountain.
On Mount Nisir^m the ship came to a halt.
Mount Nisir held the ship fast, allowing no motion.
One day, a 2nd day, Mount Nisir held the ship fast,
   allowing no motion.
A 3rd day, a 4th day, Mount Nisir held the ship fast,
   allowing no motion.
144 A 5th day, a 6th day, Mount Nisir held the ship fast,
   allowing no motion.

Bird Reconnaissance after the Flood

145 When the 7th day arrived, I sent forth and set free a dove.
   The dove went forth, but came back;
      since no resting-place for it was visible, she turned around.
   Then I sent forth and set free a swallow.
   The swallow went forth, but came back;
      since no resting-place for it was visible, she turned around.
   Then I sent forth and set free a raven.
   The raven went forth and, seeing that the waters had diminished.
154 He eats, circles, caws, and turns not around.

Disembarkment of the Ship and Sacrifice to the gods

155 Then I let out all [the creatures] to the four winds and offered
      a sacrifice.
   I poured out a libation on the top of the mountain.
   7 and 7 cult-vessels I set up,
   Upon their pot-stands I heaped cane, cedarwood, and myrtle.
   The gods smelled the savour, the gods smelled the sweet savour,
161 The gods crowded around like flies about the sacrificer.

---

m. Mount Nisir is likely Pir Omar Gudrum (or Pira Magrun) in Iraq and it is south of
the Lower Zab River.

Argument Among the Gods

162 When at length the great goddess[n] arrived,
    she lifted up the great jewels which Anu had fashioned
    to her liking:
'Ye gods here, as surely as this lapis upon my neck I
    shall not forget,
I shall be mindful of these days, forgetting them never.
Let the gods come to the offering;
But let not Enlil[o] come to the offering,
    for he, unreasoning, brought on the deluge
    and my people consigned to destruction.'
When at length as Enlil arrived,
    and saw the ship, Enlil was wroth.
He was filled with wrath over the Igigi gods:[p]
'Has some living soul escaped?
No man was to survive the destruction!'
Ninurta opened his mouth to speak, saying to Enlil:
'Who, other than Ea,[q] can devise plans?
It is Ea alone who knows every matter.'
Ea opened his mouth to speak, saying to Enlil:
'Thou wisest of gods, thou hero,
    how couldst thou, unreasoning, bring on the deluge?
On the sinner impose his sin.
On the transgressor impose his transgression!
Yet be lenient, lest he be cut off.
Be patient, lest he be dislodged!
Instead of thy bringing on the deluge,
    would that a lion had risen up to diminish mankind!
Instead of thy bringing on the deluge,
    would that a wolf had risen up to diminish mankind!
Instead of thy bringing on the deluge,
    would that a famine had risen up to lay low mankind!

---

n. Ishtar the fertility or mother goddess.
o. The god of air, wind, and storms who brought about the flood.
p. The heavenly gods.
q. The god of waters on earth who revealed to Utnapishtim of the coming flood.

Instead of thy bringing on the deluge,
  would that a pestilence had risen up to smite down mankind!
It was not I who disclosed the secret of the great gods.
I let exceedingly wise [Utnapishtim] see a dream,
  and he perceived the secret of the gods.
188 Now then take counsel in regard to him!'

Conclusion—Reward of Eternal Life

189 Thereupon Enlil went aboard the ship.
  Holding me [Utnapishtim] by the hand, he took me aboard.
  He took my wife aboard and made her kneel by my side.
  Standing between us, he touched our foreheads to bless us:
  'Hitherto Utnapishtim has been but human.
  Henceforth Utnapishtim and his wife shall be like unto us gods.
  Utnapishtim shall reside far away, at the mouth of the rivers!'
196 Thus they took me and made me reside far away, at the
    mouth of the rivers."[3]

Appendix 7
Fossil Pattern Predictions of the Christian Origins Positions

THE BASIC PATTERN FOR the appearance of fossils in the crust of the earth was established by the mid-1800s. Significantly, most geologists at that time were anti-evolutionists. Limiting the organisms to those mentioned in Gen 1 and setting aside consideration for the age of the earth, it is obvious that the fossil pattern predictions of young earth creation (Fig 1) and progressive creation (Fig 2) fail to align with the scientific facts (Fig 4). Evolutionary creation argues that no prediction is possible because Gen 1 features an ancient origins science (Fig 3).

There are other serious problems not presented in these diagrams. The first fish were jawless. About 100 million years after their appearance, fish with jaws and teeth are found in the fossil record (See Appendix 9 Fig 2). In particular, sharks have multiple rows of teeth that are shed throughout their lifetime (Fig 5). Young earth creation predicts that shark teeth should be scattered across the original ocean floor; in other words, at the very lowest levels of the marine fossil record. But incalculable numbers of these teeth only appear after 400 million years ago (mya). Similarly, dinosaurs like the famed T-Rex continuously replace teeth during their lifetime (Fig 6). However, this reptile and its countless shed teeth are confined to a narrow region that is relatively high in the geological strata, between 85 and 65 mya. A world created *de novo* 6000 years ago should have the remains of T-Rex along with every other plant and animal ever made, including humans, at the base of the fossil record ("creation basal layer"). But this prediction does not align with the scientific facts.

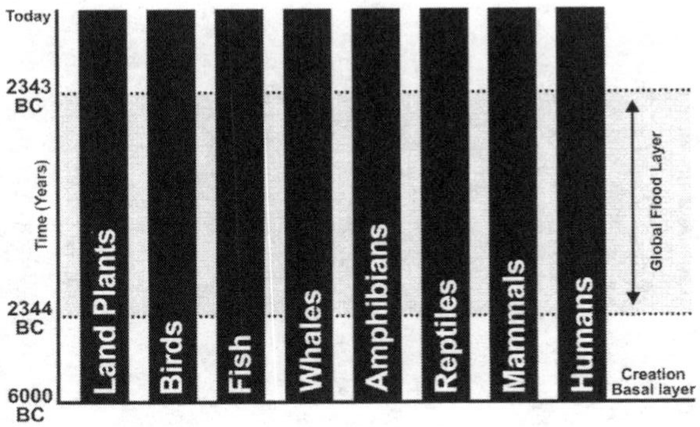

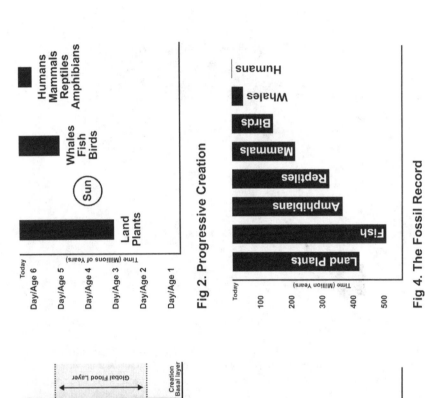

Fig 1. Young Earth Creation

Fig 2. Progressive Creation

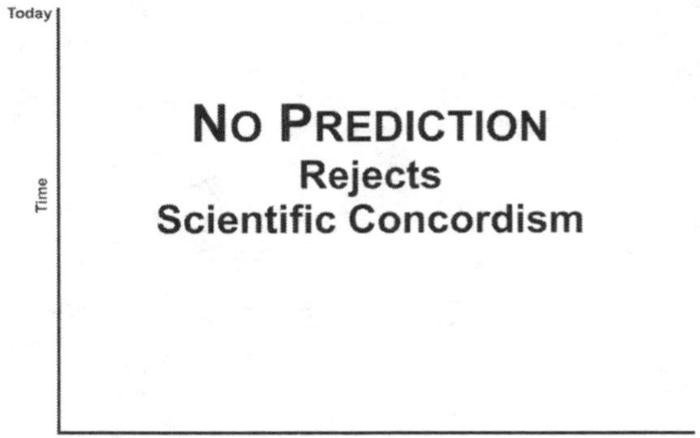

Fig 3. Evolutionary Creation

Fig 4. The Fossil Record

419

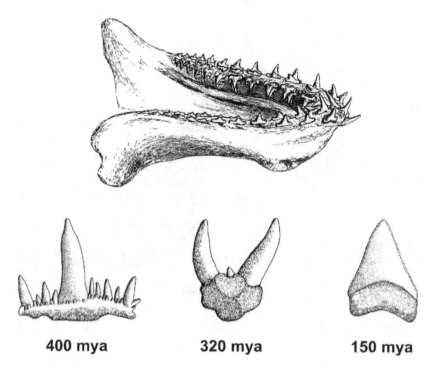

400 mya   **320 mya**   **150 mya**

Fig 5. Shark Jaw and Dentition. Rows of teeth develop inside of the mouth and move to the outside of the jaw where they are shed continually (top). Like a fingerprint, species of shark have a distinct tooth anatomy. The fossil record presents layers of strata marked by distinct teeth indicative of the evolution of sharks (bottom). The tooth on the far right is that a Great White Shark. mya: million years ago. Single teeth redrawn by Braden Barr.

Finally, land plants appear about 420 mya. Many of these release millions of microscopic pollen grains during their reproductive cycle (they are a common cause of allergies today). In a young earth creationist world, every geological layer should have pollens. But they do not. Fruit-bearing (flowering) plants should also appear throughout the fossil record. However, they are only found near the top of geological strata (after 130 mya). According to progressive creation, flowering plants were created during the third day/age before fish, birds, amphibians, reptiles, and mammals. Yet once more, an anti-evolutionary prediction fails to match the scientific evidence. And of course, how these plants survived for millions of years without sunlight introduces another irresolvable problem (Fig 2).

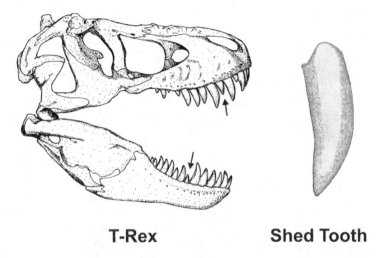

T-Rex   Shed Tooth

Fig 6. Tyrannosaurus Rex Skull and Dentition. Spaces in the dental row are sites of where a tooth was lost. Replacement teeth later erupt into the gaps (arrows). The shed teeth of T-Rex (right) are over 6 inches long and do not have a root because it was broken down by the developing replacement tooth under it. Notably, teeth this size only appear in the fossil record between 85–65 million years ago. This flesh-puncturing and slashing dentition is clear evidence that death was in the world well before humans appeared. See also Appendix 8 Fig 1. Skull courtesy of Tracy Ford; tooth redrawn by Braden Barr.

Appendix 8
Age of the Earth

THE AGE OF THE earth continues to be a controversial issue in a number of churches. Young earth creationists contend that belief in a 6000 year-old world is biblical, and even essential to Christian faith. They calculate this age by adding up the genealogies in Scripture. They also claim that most of the layers of stratification in the crust of the earth were laid down in 1 year during Noah's flood. However, geologists rejected these ideas more than 250 years ago. This appendix offers a few basic facts on why young earth creationist views are not even considered within the scientific community.[1]

A way to understand the age of the earth and geological stratification is to consider that it functions similar to an in-basket. "Layers" of paper at the bottom were the first to be deposited in the basket and are "older" than the "younger" ones near the top, which were put in later. Sometimes a piece of paper has a time reference, such as the postmark on an envelope or the date on a bill. These temporal markers are independent of each other and function like different "clocks" to reveal when paper "strata" in the basket were laid down. Consequently, it is possible to reconstruct the history of papers as they were put in an in-basket and even offer dates for when some were placed. A top-to-bottom pattern results with the "ages" of papers progressively increasing. The crust of the earth features similar layering and time markers.

LAYERS DEPOSITED ON EARTH

Three simple examples demonstrate that the earth is exceedingly older than 6000 years. This evidence focuses on layers that are deposited progressively over time.

First, the seasonal accumulations at the bottom of lakes that once existed number in the tens to hundreds of thousands. Known as "varves," these layers appear as light and dark bands distinguishing sediments deposited during the spring/summer and fall/winter periods, respectively. The Green River Formation in the Western United States averages 2000 feet in thickness and in some places features more than 1 million annual varves.

Second, coral reefs are made up of limestone that is laid down by the coral animals. These deposits also have layers with yearly banding. The rate of accumulation is known (5 to 8 millimeters per year) and measuring the thickness of a reef can determine its age. In the Pacific, the Eniwetok reef is more than 4500 feet thick and estimated to be at least 200,000 years old.

Third, polar ice sheets feature tens of thousands of annual snow layers. Winter in this region does not have sunlight, and consequently no daily evaporation occurs on the surface layer of snow. This produces dense and fine-grained snow crystals that appear as a dark band. In summer, snow is warmed during the day and cooled at night, resulting in a light-colored layer with low density, coarse-grained crystals. The Greenland ice sheet is over 2 miles thick in areas and has yearly bands revealing that it is more than 100,000 years old.

The power of these three examples of naturally occurring layers is that they are independent of each other. The first involves seasonal runoff in freshwater lakes, the second excretions from tropical saltwater organisms, and the third snowfall in polar regions. In other words, this scientific evidence acts as three completely different clocks (e.g., hour glass, spring wound, and digital), and they all indicate that the age of the earth is much, much older than 6000 years.

TIME MARKERS AND RADIOMETRIC DATING

The crust of the earth features numerous time markers that are used to calculate the age of its layers of stratification. These "clocks" are unstable atoms that change into other atoms at a constant rate. Known as "radiometric dating," this is another issue that regrettably creates controversy in some churches.

A simple analogy introduces the basic principle of this dating method. Imagine that three new and different types of candles are lit simultaneously and placed in a room. After a while they are extinguished at the same time, and the wax drippings collected from each. The candles are then relit and the time needed to produce the same amount of dripping on each is determined. Even though the candles may burn at different rates, the length of time that they were burning in the room can be calculated. In this case, three independent "clocks" will offer the identical period of time.

Radioactive atoms are unstable and naturally change into other atoms. The rate of change is measurable and found to be constant. It is expressed as a "half-life," which is defined as the amount of time it takes for half of the radioactive atoms in a sample to become another type of atom. For example, a certain form of potassium turns into the gas argon and has a half-life of 1,300,000,000 years. That is, it takes 1.3 billion years for half of the former to become the latter; this same amount of time for half of the remaining potassium to change into more argon; and another 1.3 billion years for another reduction in half of the diminishing potassium sample, etc. In other words, the number of potassium atoms in the original sample is being reduced by 1/2, 1/4, 1/8, etc. Therefore, knowing the ratio of potassium to argon in rock can determine its age. High amounts of the former indicate a young age, while low amounts an old age (or vice versa using argon).

Volcanoes spew mineral ash that contains potassium. The extreme temperatures expel the argon gas, and when minerals in the ash cool and solidify, only the potassium is incorporated. In this way, the potassium-argon clock is set back to "o." As stratification in the earth's crust accumulates over time, volcanic ash layers are also laid down, and their ages are determinable. Other radioactive materials are also found in geological strata. Different forms of uranium change into certain types of lead at rates similar to potassium and argon. These often appear in deposits made from molten rock (e.g., lava flows). As the rock cools and hardens, certain minerals crystalize and incorporate only uranium. Thus, the radiometric clock is reset at "o" for lead, allowing the rock to be dated. The power of these two methods is that they are independent of each other and provide ages that are both consistent and progressive in the geological record. It must be noted that there are several other radiometric atoms that are used for dating the earth, and they provide similar results. Fig 1 illustrates radiometric dating of strata.

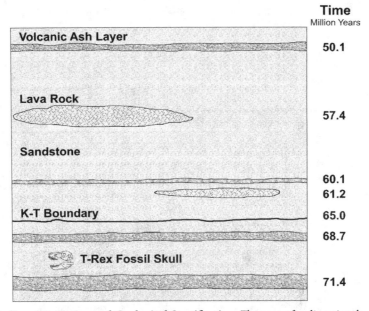

Fig 1. Radiometric Dating and Geological Stratification. The ages of radioactive deposits increase progressively in deeper layers of the earth's crust. Different radiometric "clocks" provide similar dates in strata near the same level such as the ash layer (61.0 million years ago) and lava rock (61.2) in the middle of the diagram. Objects that cannot be dated directly are assigned an age within a range like the T-Rex skull (68.7 to 71.4 mya). A distinct geological layer, termed the "K-T Boundary," is found throughout the world and marks a mass extinction of plants and animals, including the dinosaurs. See Fig 2. Drawn by Braden Barr.

GEOLOGICAL TIME TABLE

The crust of the earth features innumerable layers. These are easily seen in the walls of the Grand Canyon and the sides of the Rocky Mountains. Strata are distinguished by their contents. In particular, different plant and animal fossils appear in the geological record in a progressive pattern from simple life forms near the bottom to more complex ones at the top. Independent time markers are also found in these layers. The ages of stratification decrease from bottom-to-top and reflect the sequential depositing of radiometric materials. Fig 2 outlines the basic geological timetable.

Young earth creationists claim that most of the layers in the earth's crust were laid down in 1 year during Noah's flood, which they contend was global. However, three simple features in the geological record reveal the problems with this anti-evolutionary belief.

Era	Period	Age Million Years	1st Fossil Evidence
CENOZOIC	Quaternary		Humans
		2	Archeological Artifacts Pre-Humans
	Tertiary		Whales, Primates
MESOZOIC		65	Dinosaurs Extinct
	Cretaceous		Flowering Plants
		144	Birds
	Jurassic		
		208	
	Triassic		Mammals, Dinosaurs
PALEOZOIC		**245**	
	Permian		
		286	
	Carboniferous		Reptiles, Seed Bearing Plants
		360	
	Devonian		Amphibians
		408	Jawed Fishes
	Silurian		Land Plants
		438	
	Ordovician		
		505	Jawless Fishes
	Cambrian		Marine Animals with Skeletons
PRECAMBRIAN		**570**	
	Proterozoic		Soft-Bodied Marine Animals Marine Plants
		2500	
	Archean		Single Cell Life
		4600	Origin of Earth

Fig 2. The Geological Time Table. Periods are sometimes defined by dramatic differences in the fossil record such as between the Cretaceous and Tertiary. Two-thirds of plants and animals, including the dinosaurs, disappeared 65 million years ago. These two periods are separated by the K-T Boundary which features 20 to 30 times the normal level of iridium (See Fig 1). This rare element is common in asteroids. Evidence of a 125 mile-wide impact site below the Yucatan Peninsula in Mexico indicates an asteroid impact caused this mass extinction.

First, a worldwide flood would produce strata with a mixing of all living organisms. But the scientific facts reveal an orderly progression in the appearance of life forms indicative of evolution. The pattern for fossil plants shows: single cells→marine plants→land plants→seed bearing plants→flowering plants. Similarly, for animals: single cells→soft-bodied marine animals→marine animals with skeletons→jawless fishes→jawed fishes→amphibians→reptiles→mammals→primates→pre-humans→humans. To date, not *one* fossil plant or animal has been found outside of this pattern.

Second, a year-long global deluge would form layers in the earth's crust with radiometrically datable materials mixed together. As a result, strata would never feature a progressive sequence of ages in the hundreds of millions of years. However, the geological record presents a consistent temporal pattern that decreases from 4.6 billion years at its lowest levels up to the highest strata today with zero age. Significantly, there is not *one* layer in the crust of the earth with radioactive deposits that is outside the geological timetable.

Third, a biblical flood would not produce geological features pointing to normal animal behavior. According to Gen 7:17–20, rain fell for 40 days and covered the highest mountains, which are identified as the Ararat Mountains (8:4). Since the height of this range is about 16,000 feet, it means that water rose 400 feet each day, or about 16 feet each hour (the rate doubles if Mount Everest is used). But geological strata present innumerable complex animal tunnels and dens, some even with stored food. Reptile and bird nests are also found, and sometimes with eggs. It is doubtful that animals being threatened by 16 feet of rushing water every hour would be involved in such burrowing and building activities.

The evidence for an exceedingly old earth is overwhelming. The scientific facts presented in this appendix hardly scratch the surface. Many other dating methods exist, and like different "clocks" they date geological strata as well over 6000 years. Of course, some Christians argue that God created the world with the appearance of age. But this strikes hard against the character of the Creator, implying deception. This argument also questions our divinely given ability to discover His world. Galileo faced a similar complaint with regard to astronomy, and his response is quite applicable today:

> I do not think one has to believe that the same God who has given us senses, language and intellect would want us to set aside the use of these . . . so that we would deny our senses and reason even in the case of those physical conclusions which are placed before our eyes and intellect . . . . Indeed, who wants the human mind put to death?[2]

Appendix 9
Carbon-14 Dating and the Archaeological Record

MANY CHRISTIANS ASSUME THAT the carbon-14 dating method is used to determine the age of the earth. Not true. Carbon-14 is a radioactive atom and its half-life is only 5700 years. After 10 half-lives, just a small fraction ($1/1024^{th}$) of these atoms in an original sample would remain, making accurate calculations nearly impossible. The upper limit of this method is around 50,000 years. In contrast, potassium/argon and uranium/lead have half-lives that are over 1,000,000,000 years and these radioactive materials are more suitable for dating the age of the earth (see Appendix 8). However, C-14 is an excellent tool in determining younger ages, like those of artifacts found at archaeological sites.

Carbon-14 forms in the upper atmosphere as cosmic radiation collides with nitrogen. It then combines with oxygen to form carbon dioxide (CO_2). The most common form of CO_2 uses carbon-12, which is stable and non-radioactive. These two types of carbon dioxide are found in a relatively constant ratio. Through photosynthesis, plants incorporate both forms of CO_2, and animals in turn consume these. In particular, carbon is used in the formation of their bones. Once an organism dies, there is no new carbon-14 being assimilated and this carbon returns to nitrogen because it is radioactively unstable. Therefore, the C-14 in a piece of wood or bone decreases over time. Since carbon-12 is stable, the amount of carbon-14 that has been lost can be determined by comparing the C-14/C-12 ratio in a sample to that in living organisms. The rate that carbon-14 decays into nitrogen is constant (5700 year half-life), and consequently the age of organic material can be calculated. The reliability of this dating method has been repeatedly confirmed. It provides similar ages for bones in graves marked with a date, and for wooden structures (buildings, chairs, boats, etc.) that are dated by historical documents.

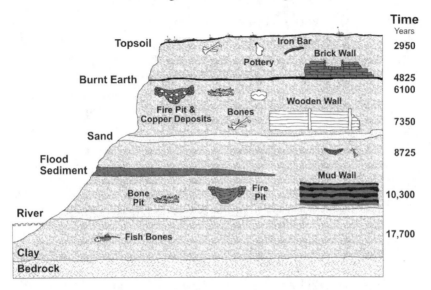

Fig 1. **Carbon-14 Dating and Archaeological Stratification.** The dates of carbon materials (bone, wood, charcoal) increase progressively in deeper layers of earth. Like independent "clocks," different carbon artifacts give the similar C-14 dates at the same stratum level. Drawn by Braden Barr.

The archaeological record is similar to the geological record. It features many layers of earth with independent time markers.[1] And like the fossils in the earth's crust, the complexity of human artifacts increases over time.

Fig 1 presents an example of an archaeological site near a river. The C-14 dating of different organic (carbon-based) materials provides a sequential series of ages throughout the strata. Note that the lowest layers are the oldest. The bones of slaughtered animals in collection pits and charcoal from fire pits are particularly useful since they are found at most sites. Notably, bones and charcoal are independent of each other and provide consistent dates when they appear in the same level as shown at three places in the diagram (6100, 8725, and 10,300 years). A sedimentary layer indicates that a major flood occurred between 10,300 and 8725 years ago. Evidence for such events is common in riverbanks, but their extent is limited and shows that flooding is always local. Fish bones at the lowest levels demonstrate that this river once meandered from its present position about 17,700 years ago. Technological progression also appears through the strata as seen with building materials which are at first mud, then wood, and finally brick. Different styles of pottery and its decoration are particularly important in marking archaeological periods. Similar development occurs with metals, and their appearance is used to define major stages such as the Copper and Iron Ages.

Fig 2 outlines the archaeological timetable and the appearance of some significant artifacts.[2] The first sites are about 2.5 million years old and feature simple stone tools near bones that were cut for meat and crushed for marrow. Through the upper and middle Paleolithic periods, tools slowly become more complex, fire is eventually controlled, and the butchered remains of a variety of large ancient animals (e.g., hippos, horses, wild cattle), indicative of group hunting, begin to appear. After 50,000 years ago, there is a dramatic increase in the number and sophistication of archaeological materials. These include specialized tools (hunting, fishing), the use of new materials (antler, ivory, ceramic), and art (figurines, jewelry, cave paintings). Notably, the first indisputable archaeological evidence for religious behavior appears with intentional burials and several sites have items assumed to be necessary in the next life. Some scientists have termed this spectacular shift in the quality of artifacts as the "creative explosion" or "human revolution" and attribute it to the arrival of "behaviorally modern humans" (see Appendix 10).

It is important to point out that the archaeological record does not align with young earth creation. There is no evidence whatsoever for a global flood in strata where human artifacts appear. Numerous flood deposits appear, but always near rivers and the extent is never far from their banks. An archaeological chronology based on strict literal readings of Gen 1–11 also falls short. Plant and animal domestication appeared 11,000 years ago and not after 4000 BC with Cain and Abel. Scripture indicates that the former built a city around that time, but permanent settlements were present 9000 years ago, and Mesopotamia had a city (Uruk) with a population of over 10,000 by 3500 BC. Reference to iron tools in Gen 4 is also problematic. The events in this chapter are prior to the flood, which creation scientists date at 2456 BC. But iron only appears in the archaeological record after 1200 BC. Finally, the young creationist belief that humans were created *de novo* 6000 years ago completely ignores the scientific evidence for people behaviorally similar to us having lived on earth for 50,000 years.

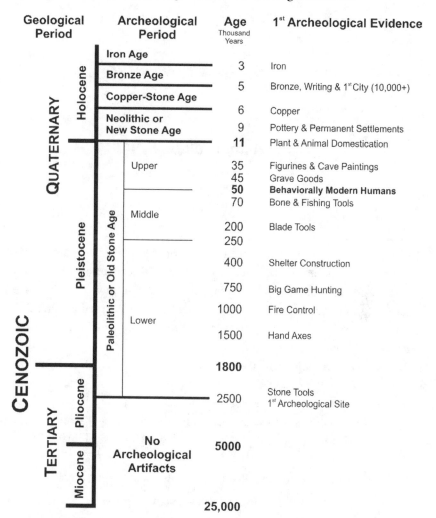

Fig 2. The Archaeological Timetable. Artifacts are not produced through natural processes. They reflect conscious thought and are found only in the very upper layers of the earth's crust. Compare this timetable with Appendix 8 Fig 2 in order to see the relationship between the geological and archeological records.

The similarity and complementarity of the archaeological and geological records are obvious. Layers of stratification can be dated and their contents progressively increase in complexity over time. The former points to a biological evolution leading to humans, and the latter to an intellectual and cultural evolution culminating in people with religious inclinations.

Appendix 10
Human Evolution

M ANY CHRISTIANS ARE TROUBLED with the notion of human evolution and contend that there is no supporting scientific evidence. They argue that at best the physical data is misinterpreted; at worst, some believe that it is fabricated and part of a secular conspiracy. However, nearly all biologists today claim that the facts for human evolution are powerful, convincing, and even overwhelming. This appendix presents some introductory evidence in order to encourage readers to examine further the scientific literature.[1]

One way to view human evolution is to compare it to a family. In both cases, similarities appear between living relatives, as well as between individuals today and those who are no longer alive. Akin to family members in a genealogy, evolutionary trees leading to humans present different pre-human species that descended along ancestral lines.

Living Evolutionary Relatives: Anatomical Similarities

At every family reunion, physical resemblances between relatives are evident. Similar noses, jaws, eyes, etc. often appear with grandfathers/mothers, uncles/aunts and cousins, and even those who are distantly related. Similarities increase between closer relatives, as seen between siblings and their parents. The nearest living evolutionary relatives of humans are the higher primates—monkeys, lesser apes (like gibbons), and great apes (orangutans, gorillas, chimpanzees). Their basic anatomy clearly resembles ours as seen in Figs 1-3.

Monkey   **Gorilla**   **Human**

Fig 1. **Similarities in Skeletons.** Monkeys, gorillas and humans share similar bones with differences in shapes and proportions. Skeletal anatomy reflects the type of locomotion on the ground. Monkeys are quadruped (walking on four equal-sized limbs), gorillas semi-quadruped (long-armed knuckle-walkers) and humans biped (using only long-legged hind limbs). The big toe in monkeys and apes is angled away from the foot (arrow), providing the ability to grasp and facilitating life in trees.

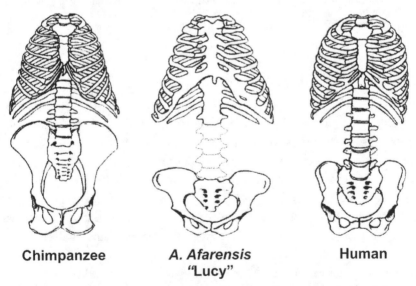

Chimpanzee   *A. Afarensis*   **Human**
              "Lucy"

Fig 2. **Similarities in Rib Cages and Hip Bones.** Chimpanzees have a pyramid-shaped rib cage and massive hip bones characteristic of monkeys and apes. In humans, the former is more barrel-shaped and the latter shorten for bipedal locomotion. The pre-human *Australopithecus afarensis* combines some of these anatomical features. Commonly known as "Lucy," it had an ape rib cage and human-like hip bones indicative of bipedalism.

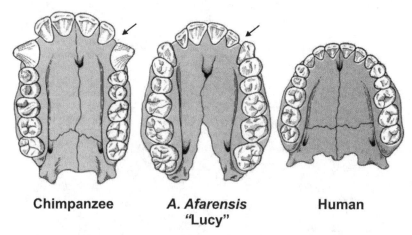

Chimpanzee   **A. Afarensis**   **Human**
                         "Lucy"

Fig 3. Similarities in Dentitions. Dental features shared between chimpanzees and humans include: 6 square-shaped molars with 4 cusps (points on the tooth surface) at the back of the jaw, 4 pre-molars or bicuspids (2 cusps), 2 canine (eye-tooth) at the corner of the jaw, and 4 incisors in the front. Chimpanzees differ from humans in that the jaws and tooth rows at the back of the mouth are parallel to each other. Their canines are also very large and a space, termed a "diastema" (arrow), appears between it and the incisors. The posterior jaws and dental rows of humans curve gently and are angled toward the anterior, the canine is not prominent, and there is no space in front of it. The dentition of *Australopithecus afarensis* (Lucy) features the human characteristic of small canine and the diastema found in monkeys and apes. The shape of this pre-human's jaws and tooth rows is slightly curved and between that of chimpanzees and humans.

Living Evolutionary Relatives: Genetic Similarities

Genetic evidence powerfully demonstrates that humans are related to other higher primates. As the genes of immediate family members are more similar than those of distant relatives, science has discovered genetic similarities between our living evolutionary relatives and us. Fig 4 reveals that monkeys are distantly related (93% similar genes), while chimpanzees are our closest "cousins" (99%). It is necessary to emphasize that we did not descend from either of these primates. Regrettably, many Christians assume that the theory of evolution states that humans evolved from monkeys. Not true. We share common ancestors that are now extinct. About 30 million years ago, the evolutionary line to monkeys separated from that leading to lesser apes, great apes, and humans. Around 6 million years ago, two distinct lineages descended from an extinct primate known as "the last common ancestor," and millions of years later chimpanzees and human beings evolved separately.

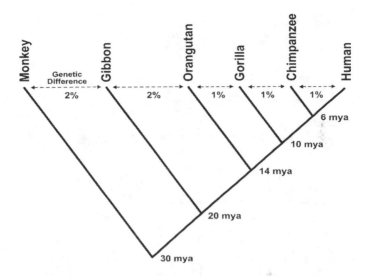

Fig 4. Humans and Higher Primates: Genetic and Evolutionary Relationships. Genes change very slowly over time at a relatively constant rate. This natural process is known as "genetic drift" and is caused mostly by random mutations in DNA. It functions like a "genetic clock" and estimates can be calculated for when evolutionary lines separated in the past. Notably, this genetic family tree aligns closely to the fossil evidence. mya: million years ago.

Evolutionary relationships between monkeys, apes, and people are also supported by the fact they have similar defective genes called "pseudogenes."[2] Just like a bad trait that is passed down through a family, genetic errors have descended along related evolutionary lines. For example, a gene required to produce Vitamin C does not function in monkeys, chimpanzees, and humans, and a diet including this essential nutrient is needed for survival (e.g., by eating fruits). But it is functional in nearly all other animals. The existence of this same genetic error in chimps and people indicates that it was passed down from their last common ancestor about 6 million years ago (Fig 4).

Humans also have numerous olfactory (sense of smell) pseudogenes. About 600 of our 1000 genes for the production of scent receptors are defective. In contrast, a greater portion of these are functional in lesser and great apes, providing them with a keener sense to smell foods, enemies, etc. Humans have the potential for a greater olfactory ability, if the errors in these genes were corrected. But as our brains evolved, we created new strategies for gathering food and protecting ourselves from enemies, reducing the need for an acute olfactory sense. In other words, there was no

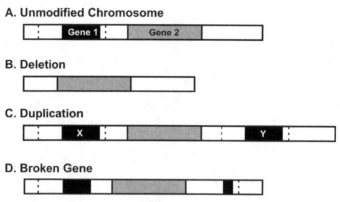

A. Unmodified Chromosome

B. Deletion

C. Duplication

D. Broken Gene

Fig 5. Chromosome Aberrations. A significant source of new genetic material during evolution arises through duplications. The original Gene 1 (X) continues to function while the duplicate Gene 1 (Y) is free to change through genetic drift until a new gene emerges with a different function. Notably, the fracture site in a number of broken genes occurs at exactly the same place on DNA in both humans and chimpanzees. This indicates the aberration was present in their last common ancestor and was passed down. Dashed lines in chromosomes appear to orient readers.

selective pressure to maintain this ability and it was lost as genes naturally changed over time. The fact that we have so many olfactory pseudogenes reflects our evolutionary history and relatedness to modern apes.

Humans and other higher primates share other chromosomal aberrations. It is well known that segments of DNA on a chromosome can be deleted and lost (Fig 5B). As well, duplications of parts of chromosomes commonly occur, and these can then be inserted at another position (C). In fact, deletion and "copy-and-paste" events are ongoing today in humans. Between any two people, there is a genetic difference of up to 10 large deletions and/or duplications. These have an average length of at least 400,000 DNA base pairs (human chromosomes have a total of 3 billion base pairs). Other chromosomal anomalies include genes that have been "cut-and-pasted" to a different position. At times, only a segment of a gene is excised and then placed at another site, resulting in a truncated or "broken gene" (D). A comparison between human and higher primate genes reveals that we share many of these genetic aberrations at identical positions on chromosomes. This evidence indicates that deletion, copy-and-paste, and cut-and-paste events occurred in our common ancestors, and that this genetic history was then passed down along related evolutionary lines.

Finally, striking evidence for human evolution is found in our chromosome 2. A prominent genetic difference between the great apes and us

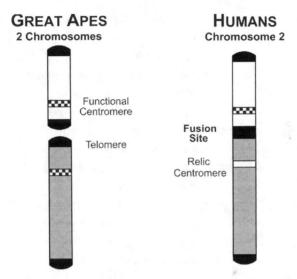

GREAT APES
2 Chromosomes

HUMANS
Chromosome 2

Functional
Centromere

Telomere

Fusion
Site

Relic
Centromere

Fig 6. Human Chromosome 2. Telomeres are present at the ends of every chromosome. A centromere is a region on a chromosome that connects chromosome pairs together during cell division. Human Chromosome 2 features a telomeric region near the centre and a non-functional centromere, indicating that it was originally two separate chromosomes similar to those found in chimpanzees, gorillas and orangutans.

is that they have 48 chromosomes (24 pairs) and we 46 (23 pairs). As Fig 6 illustrates, human chromosome 2 is made up of two previously independent chromosomes. A comparison of this chromosome with chimpanzee chromosomes 12 and 13 reveals that they contain essentially the same genes, and arranged in a similar sequence along the chromosomes. In other words, after the separation of the human and chimp evolutionary lineages from the last common ancestor about 6 million years ago (Fig 4), two chromosomes fused into one sometime along the branch leading to our creation.

Dead Evolutionary Relatives: Fossil Record Similarities

The pre-human fossil record offers some of the most tangible evidence for human evolution. It can be compared to the pictures in a family album. Anatomical similarities (shape of heads, jaws, teeth, etc.) appear between dead relatives and living descendants. Family albums do not have photographs of every relative or each moment in the life of an individual. Yet no one doubts that generations of individuals have lived in the past and are related to each other. The fossil record is similar in that it offers "snap shots" of the descent from pre-humans to humans.

Fig 7 presents the facts for human evolution: the fossils and their dates.[3] Anatomical features between adjacent pre-human fossils are quite similar, which makes classification difficult. For example, some scientists reject the genus *Paranthropus* and place the species of *aethopicus, boisei,* and *robustus* with *Australopithecus.* As a consequence, it is not possible to determine with absolute certainty all evolutionary relationships and the pathway to humans. Fig 8 outlines an evolutionary tree based on modern scientific literature.[4] Though scientists debate over the interpretation of fossils and their relationships to each other, none question the fact that humans descended from earlier pre-humans.

Evolutionary progression appears through the fossil and archaeological records leading eventually to modern men and women. A well-known pattern is seen in skull anatomy and braincase volume (Figs 9). Other developments in notable pre-humans include:

Australophithecus afarensis stood about 4 feet tall and is often described as being "ape from the waist up" and "human from the waist down." Best known from the famous fossil named "Lucy," this pre-human had a cranial capacity (400–500 cubit centimeters) a little larger than a chimpanzee (370–380 cc), yet it walked upright, and footprints from 3.5 mya indicate in a fashion similar to us. Though its hip bones are comparable to ours (Fig 2), fossil evidence suggests the feet had a long and angled first toe, indicating that Lucy could still grasp tree branches like a monkey or ape. Other transitional features appear in her jaws and teeth (Fig 3).

Homo habilis had a brain that was increasing in size and hands that were freed from locomotion. Also called "handy man," this pre-human was the first species to make stone tools. These first archaeological sites

---

Fig 7. **Pre-Human and Human Fossil Record (top).** Evolutionary relationships are not presented in this diagram, only the period when a species lived. The pre-humans make up the evolutionary line to humans arising from the last common ancestor of humans and chimpanzees. The chimpanzee is included for comparison. Since the genetic difference between us and this ape is only 1%, it indicates that the genes of pre-humans differed even less. Consequently, debates are expected in classifying these species and then determining their evolutionary relationships. Numbers in brackets indicate the number of known fossil specimens. A: *Australopithecus*, P: *Paranthropus*, H: *Homo.*

Fig 8. **Evolutionary Relationships between Pre-Humans and Humans (bottom).** This diagram presents evolutionary pathways based on one interpretation of the fossil facts. Four genera (shaded areas) are outlined with their respective species. The skulls of the species in bold are presented in Fig 9. *Ardipithecus* (*ardi* "ground" *pithekos* "ape"), *Australopithecus* (*australis* "southern" *pithekos* "ape"), *Paranthropus* (*para* "near" *anthropos* "man") *Homo* (*hominis* "man").

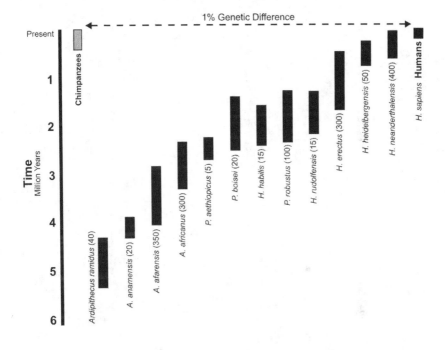

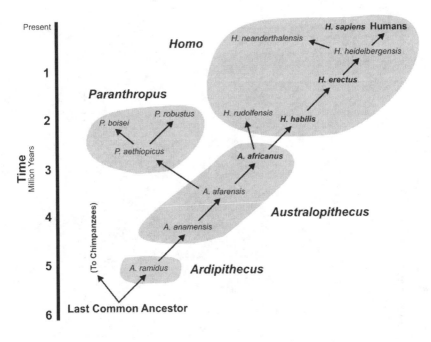

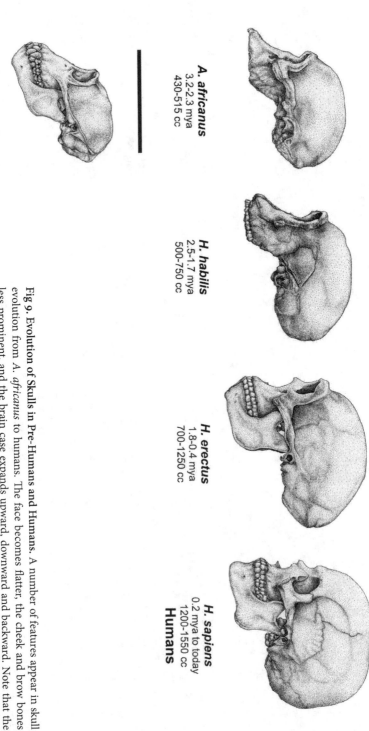

A. africanus
3.2-2.3 mya
430-515 cc

H. habilis
2.5-1.7 mya
500-750 cc

H. erectus
1.8-0.4 mya
700-1250 cc

H. sapiens
0.2 mya to today
1200-1550 cc
Humans

Chimpanzees
0.4 mya to today
370-380 cc

Fig 9. Evolution of Skulls in Pre-Humans and Humans. A number of features appear in skull evolution from *A. africanus* to humans. The face becomes flatter, the cheek and brow bones less prominent, and the brain case expands upward, downward and backward. Note that the chimpanzee is not in this evolutionary lineage and is included for comparison. Skull volume in cubit centimetres (cc). Artwork © Copyright D. J. Maizels, 1994.

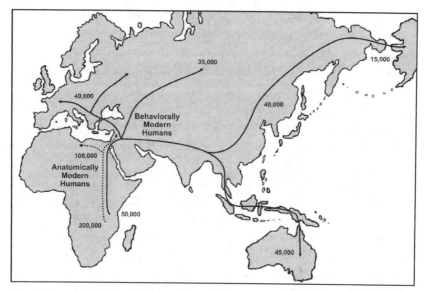

Fig 10. Spread of Modern Humans. The geological and archeological records reveal that anatomically modern humans (dashed line) appeared before behaviorally modern humans (solid line). The former had a limited dispersion and the latter spread throughout the world to become us today.

are about 2.5 million years old, and they feature tools beside extinct animal bones that were cut and crushed. The foot bones of *H. habilis* were remarkably similar to ours, suggesting it walked proficiently but grasped poorly with its feet.

Homo erectus was proportionally similar to "humans from the neck down" and had a brain volume nearing that of ours today. This was the first pre-human to leave Africa. Around 1.8 mya it spread into the Middle East, and then Europe, South East Asia, and China. Archaeological evidence reveals that *H. erectus* developed sophisticated tools like spears and hand axes, controlled fire and cooked with it, and constructed primitive shelters.

Lastly, *anatomically modern humans* appeared in South East Africa about 200,000 years ago. They moved into Mediterranean regions 100,000 years later. Their archaeological sites are not much different than those of the various pre-humans living at that time. However, 50,000 years ago *behaviorally modern humans* arose in Africa. As noted earlier in Appendix 8, archaeology reveals a dramatic change in the sophistication and innovation of artifacts at that time, often termed the "creative explosion" or "human revolution." Current genetic research complements this evidence. It demonstrates that there is remarkably little variation between humans today, and consequently all of us today descended from a small population of individuals living no more than 50,000 years ago.[5] Fig 10 outlines approximate routes and dates of the dispersal of humans into other parts of the world.

The fossil and genetic evidence for human evolution introduces a number of challenging questions to both young earth creationists and progressive creationists. What is to be made of the anatomical progression over time in the pre-human and human fossil record? It certainly looks like humans evolved, but is this only an appearance? And what about transitional creatures like *Australopithecus afarensis*? Lucy features both ape and human characteristics and she appears in the fossil record (3.5 mya) about midway between us and the last common ancestor (6 mya) that we share with chimpanzees. Did God place her there to deceive us? In addition, if the Lord created humans *de novo* as stated in Gen 1 and 2, then it is puzzling why He would recycle two ape chromosomes and fuse them together to make our chromosome 2. Is the Creator not more creative? As well, why would He put a functional gene for the production of Vitamin C in most animals, but reuse the defective one He placed in chimpanzees for humans? And what is the purpose in putting identical broken genes at the same place on chromosomes in higher primates and us? Of course, all these difficulties are easily explained if the Father, Son, and Holy Spirit created men and women through an ordained and sustained evolutionary process.

As noted in the introduction, this appendix hardly scratches the surface of the evidence for human evolution. But even with this limited data set, a pattern definitely appears. The geological and archaeological records show a progression indicative of physical and behavioral evolution: ape-like pre-humans→human-like pre-humans→anatomical humans→ humans behaving like us. The theory of human evolution is so easy to disprove. Find only one human tooth or one archaeological site made by men and women in strata with dinosaurs 100 million years ago, and it collapses completely. But no such evidence has ever been found. And I doubt any ever will. The scientific data clearly demonstrates that we evolved through a natural process and that we share flesh with other living creatures. However, it is obvious that we are more than flesh. During the evolutionary process, we mysteriously began to bear the Image of God and became aware that we are sinners.

NOTES

PREFACE

1. Billy Graham, "Doubts and Certainties: David Frost interview" BBC-2, 1964, in David Frost, *Billy Graham: Personal Thoughts of a Public Man. 30 years of Conversations with David Frost* (Colorado Springs: Chariot Victor, 1997), 73–74.

2. Pope John Paul II, "Message to Pontifical Academy of Sciences on Evolution," *Origins: CNS Documentary Service* 26 (5 Dec 1996): 415; "Scripture and Science: The Path of Scientific Discovery," *Origins: CNS Documentary Service* 11 (15 Oct 1981): 279.

CHAPTER 1

1. Henry M. Morris, "Foreword" in John D. Morris, *The Young Earth* (Colorado Springs: Creation-Life Publishers, 1994), 4–5; *Many Infallible Proofs: Practical and Useful Evidences of Christianity* (San Diego: Creation-Life Publishers, 1980), 229. Italics added.

2. Morris, "Foreword," 4.

3. Henry M. Morris, *The Troubled Waters of Evolution* (San Diego: Creation-Life Publishers, 1982), 75.

4. Julian Huxley, "The Evolutionary Vision" in Sol Tax and Charles Callender, eds., *Evolution After Darwin* (Chicago: University of Chicago Press, 1960), 252–53, 260.

5. Ibid., 252.

6. This phrase is the title in Julian Huxley's *Religion without Revelation* (London: Max Parrish, 1957 [1927]).

7. See Stanley L. Jaki, *Genesis 1 Through the Ages* (London: Thomas Moore Press, 1992).

8. For example, see my comments in Phillip E. Johnson and Denis O. Lamoureux, *Darwinism Defeated? The Johnson-Lamoureux Debate on Biological Origins* (Vancouver: Regent College Press, 1999), 32–35.

9. Note that this is not to succumb to another false dichotomy. The purpose of this chapter is to introduce categories that are further qualified later in the book. The next chapter will present two basic types of teleological evolution.

10. It is important to distinguish the biblical and traditional understanding of intelligent design from that of today's Intelligent Design Movement (or Intelligent Design Theory).

The latter proposes that design is associated with miraculous interventions in the origin of life. This book presents the former, which simply states that the creation impacts everyone, declaring God's glory and revealing His eternal power and divine nature (Ps 19:1; Rom 1:20). The issue of intelligent design is further explained on pp. 63–81.

11. Edward J. Larson and Larry Witham, "Scientists Are Still Keeping the Faith" *Nature* 386 (3 Apr 1997): 435–36.

12. Simply adding the theists (40%) and the agnostics (15%) together indicates that the scientific majority is not dysteleological. Attempts to respond to my argument by appealing to the fact that Larson and Whitham later reported that three-quarters of so-called "greater scientists" (members of the National Academy of Sciences) rejected a personal God misses the point. First, NAS scientists only make up a tiny percentage of the scientific community (less that 1%). Second, most being senior academics and undergraduates during the 1960s and 70s, it can be argued that they were socially conditioned by scientism and positivism. Edward J. Larson and Larry Witham, "Leading Scientists Still Reject God" *Nature* 394 (23 Jul 1998): 313.

13. Gregg Easterbrook, "Science and God: A Warming Trend?" *Science* 277 (15 Aug 1997): 890.

14. Ibid., 893.

15. Further discussion of this intellectual-spiritual dynamic appears on pp. 69–73.

16. Charles R. Darwin, *On the Origin of Species. A Facsimile of the First Edition.* Introduced by Ernst Mayr. (Cambridge: Harvard University Press, 1964 [1859]), 488. See also 186, 188, 189, 413 (twice), 435.

17. Charles R. Darwin, *The Life and Letters of Charles Darwin.* Edited by Francis Darwin, 3 vols. (London: John Murray, 1887), 1:304.

18. For Darwin's views on evolution and religion, see Denis O. Lamoureux, "Theological Insights from Charles Darwin" *Perspectives on Science and Christian Faith* 56 (March 2004): 2–12; "Charles Darwin and Intelligent Design" *Journal of Interdisciplinary Studies* 15 (2003): 23–42.

19. Computer search performed 8 Jan 07 employing Illumina (CSA) and BIOSIS Previews. I am grateful to Donna Meen at the St. Joseph's College Library for her assistance in this survey.

20. Philip Schaff, ed., *The Creeds of Christendom.* 3 vols. Revised by David S. Schaff (Grand Rapids: Baker Books, 1983 [1931]), 2:45. The word translated "Maker" reflects the Greek version of this creed and is derived from the common verb *poieō* meaning simply "to make." Latin versions of this creed employ *Creatorem* from which comes the noun "Creator."

21. Ibid., 58. Instead of *Creatorem*, the Latin version employs *Factorem*, meaning "doer" or "maker" and from which derives the noun "fashioner." Ibid., 60.

22. The notion of creation out of nothing does not appear in Gen 1, but it is clearly implied in the New Testament. See pp. 188–91 chapter 6 and the section entitled "The Historicity of the Pre-Creative State (Gen 1:1–2)" and Appendix 2: Creation Out of Nothing (*Creatio Ex Nihilo*) pp. 391–96.

23. I am mindful that some readers will object to the category "theological concordism." However, it is used at this time for heuristic reasons. As the argument in this book progresses, the terms "Divine Theology" and "Message of Faith" will be employed in

referring to this notion.

24. Prior to the twentieth century, the term "history" was extended to include the history of the universe as seen with the category of "natural history." If unqualified, in this book it is restricted to "human history"; that is, human activities in the past. The history of the cosmos is placed in the next category, "scientific concordism."

25. This is another popular understanding of the term "concordism." Also called the "day-age theory," it harmonizes the days of Gen 1 with periods and events discovered by modern cosmology and geology. In the next chapter, this position is categorized as "progressive creation."

26. Like many conservative theologians, I view actual history beginning roughly about Gen 12 with Abraham and his family. See also the introduction to chapter 6, pp. 180–82.

CHAPTER 2

1. No Author, "Six in 10 Take Bible Stories Literally, But Don't Blame Jews for Death of Jesus." No pages. Survey conducted 6–10 February 2004 with a random sample of 1011 adults by ICR-International Communications Research Media, Pa. Accessed July 6, 2006. Online: http://www.icrsurvey.com/studies/947a1%20Views%20of%20the%20Bible.pdf. Seven Gallup Polls between 1982 and 2006 reveal similar results in that 44–47% of American adults believe that "God created human beings pretty much in their present form at one time within the last 10,000 years or so." No Author, "Science and Nature." No pages. Accessed December 23, 2006. Online: http://www.pollingreport.com/science.htm.

2. Classic literature includes: Henry Morris and John Whitcomb, *The Genesis Flood: The Biblical Record and Its Scientific Implications* (Presbyterian & Reformed Press, 1961); Duane T. Gish, *Evolution: The Fossils Say No!* (San Diego: Creation-Life Publishers, 1972); Ken Ham, *The Lie: Evolution* (Green Forest, AR: Master Books, 1987). See also Ronald L. Numbers, *The Creationists: The Evolution of Scientific Creationism* (Berkeley and Los Angeles: University of California Press, 1992).

3. Martin Luther, *Luther's Works. Lectures on Genesis: Chapters 1–5*. Jaroslav Pelikan, ed. (Saint Louis: Concordia Publishing House, 1958), 3, 5.

4. See also Mark 10:2–9; Luke 11:51; Luke 17:26–27.

5. See Exod 31:17; 1 Chr 1:1–4; Job 31:33; Ps 33:6–9; Isa 54:9; Ezek 14:14, 20; Rom 5:12–14, 8:18–25; 1 Cor 11:7–12, 15:21–22, 38–41, 45–47; 2 Cor 11:3; 1 Tim 2:13–15; Heb 4:1–11, 11:4–7, 12:24; 1 Pet 3:20; 2 Pet 2:4–5, 3:5-6; 1 John 3:12; Jude 6, 11, 14.

6. Henry M. Morris, "Strong Delusion," *Back to Genesis* (No. 133), in *Acts and Facts* (January 2000) Institute for Creation Research, El Cajon, CA; *The Troubled Waters of Evolution* (San Diego: Creation Life Publishers, 1982), 75; Gish, *Evolution*, 10.

7. Galileo Galilei, "Letter to the Grand Duchess Christina," in Maurice A. Finocchiaro, ed. and trans., *The Galileo Affair: A Document History* (Berkeley: University of California Press, 1989), 109. I am grateful to Owen Gingerich for his assistance.

8. Ibid., 96. The aphorism actually belongs to Cardinal Baronio, but Galileo made it famous.

9. Leading works include: Hugh Ross, *Creation and Time: A Biblical and Scientific Perspective on the Creation-Date Controversy* (Colorado Springs: NavPress, 1994); *The Genesis Question: Scientific Advances & the Accuracy of Genesis* (Colorado Springs:

NavPress, 1998); Alan Hayward, *Creation and Evolution* (Minneapolis: Bethany House Publishers, 1985). A recent survey reveals that 48% of biologists in American evangelical colleges are progressive creationists. John C. Sutherland, "Evangelical Biologists and Evolution," *Science* 309 (1 July 2005): 51.

10. Also known as "baramins." This term is made up of the Hebrew verb *bārā'* (to create) and noun *min* (kinds).

11. See Appendix 1 regarding the meaning of *bārā'*.

12. Luther, *Works*, 30.

13. The term "irreducible complexity" was coined in Michael J. Behe, *Darwin's Black Box: The Biochemical Challenge to Evolution* (New York: Free Press, 1996), 39.

14. This origins position is only beginning to be defined. Currently, the best work is a collection of papers by Christian scholars from a variety of academic disciplines. Keith B. Miller, ed., *Perspectives on an Evolving Creation* (Grand Rapids: Eerdmans, 2003). See also Kenneth R. Miller, *Finding Darwin's God: A Scientist's Search for Common Ground between God and Evolution* (New York: Cliff Books, 1999); Darrel R. Falk, *Coming to Peace with Science: Bridging the Worlds Between Faith and Biology* (Downer's Grove: InterVarsity Press, 2004); Francis S. Collins, *The Language of God: A Scientist Presents Evidence for Belief* (New York: Free Press, 2006).

15. A qualification is in order regarding the category of "Divine Theology." The term "theology" often refers to the human practice, including its limitations and failings, of understanding God and His Word. In this book, I am using "Divine Theology" synonymously with the "divine revelation" in the Bible. In other words, it is the "Message of Faith." The word "theology" is made of the Greek terms *theos* (God) and *logos* (Word). Approached in this way, "Divine Theology" refers to the inspired and inerrant/infallible Word of God revealed in Scripture.

16. Regarding the term "ancient history," see the introduction to chapter 6, pp. 178–79.

17. This phrase is attributed to the astronomer Johannes Kepler (1571–1630).

18. My use of the term "complementary" is intentional. The Latin derivative, *complēre*, means to finish and to fulfill. The verb complement refers to adding something that is lacking in order to be complete. From an evolutionary creationist perspective, Scripture and science finish or fulfill each other, making our understanding of origins complete.

19. For further explanation of the categories of "general revelation" and "special revelation," see chapter 3, pp. 63–65.

20. The impact of sin on human thinking is explained in chapter 3, pp. 67–69.

21. Other terms used to describe this view of origins include: positivism, reductionism, naturalism and metaphysical naturalism.

22. The phrase "nothing but" often appears in the arguments of dysteleological evolutionists.

23. Regarding the psychological impact of the success of science, see Ian G. Barbour, *Religion in an Age of Science* (San Francisco: Harper, 1990), 3; John Polkinghorne, *One World: The Interaction of Science and Theology* (Princeton: University Press, 1986), 6.

24. Carl Sagan, *Demon Haunted World: Science as a Candle in the Dark* (New York: Ballantine Books, 1997).

25. A qualification needs to be made regarding what may appear to be a harsh judgment against dysteleological evolutionists and a betrayal of my insistence that respect character-

izes discussions on origins. I make no apology for what the Bible clearly states—atheists are fools. Of course, the term "fool" is controversial since today it carries the nuances of stupid, idiotic, etc. But the biblical notion of knowledge is holistic, integrating seamlessly the so-called "facts" and godly wisdom. A person, then, could be brilliant in determining scientific facts (which atheists do very well), but at the same time—because of sin—a complete failure in recognizing the religious implications of this data. Thus, foolishness is tied directly to sinfulness and the rejection of the greatest of all commandments: To love God with all our heart, soul, strength and *mind* (Matt 22:37; Mark 12:30; Luke 10:27).

26. No Author, "Religion Index Hits Ten-Year High," *Emerging Trends: Journal of the Princeton Religion Research Center* 18 (Mar 1996), 4.

27. Four references are made in the *Declaration* to the Creator: "Nature's God," "their [humanity's] Creator," "the Supreme Judge of the world," and "divine Providence." See also my comments in chapter 10, p. 377.

28. These two categories are often called "theistic evolution." Properly defined, theism refers to a personal God. Thus, theistic evolution best describes evolutionary creation. However, the term theism takes on several other meanings today, ranging from the god of deism to a simple reference to the mystery and beauty of the universe. I suggest that avoiding the category theistic evolution in origins reduces confusion and misunderstanding.

29. This point will be presented in much more detail through chapters 4–7.

CHAPTER 3

1. Note that a third component could be included—divine action in the future of the cosmos. Many religions like Christianity assert that the world will come to an end. Science offers two basic theories. The universe will experience either a heat death in which energy is completely spread out, or it will oscillate eternally between Big Bangs and Big Crunches. The latest scientific evidence seems to suggest the former. I have not included this third component of divine action for the sake of simplicity and the fact that it is so speculative in science. However, God's activity at the end of the world will be considered in chapter 5, pp. 153–54.

2. The Big Bang might seem like a divine cosmological intervention in origins. However, the definition of the term "interventionism" assumes that the world already exists. That is, an interventionistic act involves God "coming" (Latin: *venire* "to come") "into" (Latin: *inter* "among, between, during") the universe. But according to Big Bang theory, there was no cosmos in existence prior to this explosive event. Space, time, and matter only arose after it had occurred. Thus, the Big Bang is a unique creative event outside the categories presented in this chapter.

3. The distinction between the personal and cosmological contexts in which God acts must be emphasized. There are times when these appear to overlap. For example, the well-known miracle of the sun stopping during Joshua's battle with the Amorites (Josh 10:12–14) could be interpreted as cosmological interventionism. However, such an act was manifested within a personal context—God's relationship with the Israelites. Thus, Joshua's miracle is personal interventionism. Inversely, the Creator's action in "knitting us together in our mother's womb" might be regarded as personal providentialism (Ps 139:13). But such a categorization fails to appreciate the nature of personal relationships. It lacks intellectual and emotional communication typical of a relationship, and therefore this is an example of cosmological providentialism.

4. Michael J. Behe, *Darwin's Black Box: The Biochemical Challenge to Evolution* (New York: Free Press, 1996), 39; Stephen C. Meyer, "The Origin of Biological Information and the Higher Taxonomical Categories" *Proceedings of the Biological Society of Washington* 117 (2004): 213–39. The Biological Society of Washington has since disclaimed Meyer's paper revealing that it did not pass through a proper review process.

5. Christopher B. Kaiser, *Creation and the History of Science* (Grand Rapids: Eerdmans, 1991), 180–83; Diogenes Allen, *Christian Belief in a Postmodern World: The Full Wealth of Conviction* (Louisville: Westminster/John Knox Press, 1989), 45–49.

6. Davis A. Young, *The Biblical Flood: A Case Study of the Church's Response to Extrabiblical Evidence* (Grand Rapids: Eerdmans, 1995), 98–119.

7. For an introduction to the history of the concept of Two Divine Books, see G. Tanzella-Nitti, "The Two Books Prior to the Scientific Revolution" *Perspectives on Science and Christian Faith* 57 (Sept 2005): 235–48.

8. Other significant passages supportive of intelligent design include Proverbs 8:22–31; Job 38–41; Ps 8, 104.

9. See my earlier comments with regard to the term "fool" in chapter 2, endnote 25.

10. A regrettable consequence of the Reformation was the eventual removal of the apocrypha from protestant Bibles. Interestingly, it was included in the first edition of the King James Version (1611). My position is the traditional approach used for over one thousand years in the Church. Apocryphal books enlighten the Old and New Testaments, as Wisdom 13:1–9 demonstrates. This passage is from the NRSV.

11. This point is quite significant with regard to Intelligent Design Theory being promoted in Christian circles today. Scripture makes no reference that design is associated to irreducible complexity or dramatic interventions to account for the first cell or Cambrian phyla.

12. Note that metaphysical assumptions appear in science, and downward arrows indicative of these could have been added to Fig 3-5. For example, most scientists are realists and assume the intelligibility of nature. In other words, the relationship between science and religion is in fact reciprocal. But for the sake of simplicity and the issue at hand (intelligent design), these assumptions are not included in the diagram. For more on the metaphysical notions in science, see John F. Haught, *Science and Religion: From Conflict to Conversation* (New York: Paulist Press, 1995), 22–25; Barbour, *Religion in an Age of Science*, 17–19; Polkinghorne, *One World*, 6–15.

13. A third component exists in the ontological design parameter—an optimization gradient. For the engineered characteristic, it ranges from flawlessly ordered/functional to completely disordered/dysfunctional: and for the artistic characteristic, from perfectly beautiful to shamefully ugly. This third component opens the way to acknowledge that the engineered and artistic characteristics of design are not optimal. Yet from my perspective, nature's beauty, complexity, and functionality far outweigh its ugly, disordered, and dysfunctional aspects. For the sake of simplicity, I have not included this third component in the model.

14. The epistemological design parameter includes a third component—an epistemological impact of sin gradient. It ranges from complete submission to God to utterly rebellion against Him by a "depraved mind." To be sure, this is a provocative concept for our generation because most view knowledge as detached from spirituality. Again, for the sake of simplicity, I have not included this third component in the model.

Notes to Chapter Three

15. See Pope John Paul II, "*Fides et Ratio* [Faith and Reason]," *Origins: CNS Documentary Service* 28 (15 Oct 1998): 323–25; chapter entitled "Sin and Its Cognitive Consequences," in Alvin Plantinga, *Warrant of Christian Belief* (New York: Oxford University Press, 2000), 199–240. Plantinga is recognized as one of the most important philosophers today.

16. The Intelligent Design Movement exemplifies this interpretation of design. It asserts that design in nature is scientifically detectable. However, this approach fails to recognize the Metaphysics-Physics Principle. There is no mathematical proof to move from the scientific data to religious and philosophical beliefs. Moreover, there is no instrument in science that can detect intelligent design in nature. See William Dembski, *The Design Inference* (Cambridge: Cambridge University Press, 1998).

17. Richard Dawkins typifies this intelligent design interpretation. He writes, "The complexity of living organisms is matched by the elegant efficiency of the *apparent* design. If anyone doesn't agree that this amount of complex design *cries out* for an explanation, I give up. . . . This is probably the most powerful reason for the belief, held by the vast majority of people that have ever lived, in some kind of supernatural deity" (italics added). But in an attempt to justify unbelief, Dawkins asserts that, "it is as if the human brain were specifically designed to misunderstand Darwinism [i.e., dysteleological evolution and apparent design], and find it hard to believe." Richard Dawkins, *The Blind Watchmaker* (London: Penguin, 1986), xiii, xvi, xv. Of course, the counter argument is that our brains have been designed by God in order to understand that design is real and that atheism is false. This is the position I embrace. See page 101 in this chapter.

18. For beauty as a characteristic of design in science, see Thomas Dubay, *The Evidential Power of Beauty* (San Francisco: Ignatius, 1999), 129–226. The epigraph of this book is a quote from Hans Urs von Balthasar, "Every experience of beauty points to infinity."

19. See endnote 17 above and Dawkins' view of the impact of design through history.

20. Walter Bauer, *A Greek-English Lexicon of the New Testament and other Early Christian Literature*, William F. Arndt and F. Wilbur Gingrich, eds. (Chicago: University Press, 1958), 60. See also Wisdom 13:8.

21. Paul, M. Churchland. *The Engine of Reason, the Seat of the Soul: A Philosophical Journey into the Brain* (Cambridge: MIT Press, 1995), 4–5. I am grateful to Jason Rohick and Jeremy Bamford for their assistance.

22. The phrase is from Behe, *Darwin's Black Box*, 39. See also our exchange: Michael J. Behe, "Design vs. Randomness in Evolution: Where Do the Data Point?" *Canadian Catholic Review* 17 (1999): 63–66; Denis O. Lamoureux, "A Box or a Black Hole? A Response to Michael J. Behe" *Canadian Catholic Review* 17 (1999): 67–73.

23. John D. Barrow and Frank J. Tippler, *The Cosmological Anthropic Principle* (Oxford: Oxford University Press, 1986), xi. Italics added.

24. It must be pointed out that a subtle difference exists with the use of the term "coincidence" in personal providentialism and cosmological providentialism. Divine activity in the former is interactive and irregular. It is intended for developing a personal relationship between humans and God. The latter is mechanical and repeatable. Its purpose in origins is to create the world, making it accessible to scientific analysis. But together, both forms of providentialism affirm an indirect or hidden aspect to divine action.

25. For a popular introduction, see Hugh Ross, *The Creator and the Cosmos: How the Greatest Scientific Discoveries of the Century Reveal God* (Colorado Springs: NavPress, 1993), 105–35.

26. Stephen Hawking, *A Brief History of Time* (New York: Bantam, 1988), 121–22.

27. Paul W.C. Davies, *God and the New Physics* (London: Penguin Books, 1983), 179.

28. Alister E. McGrath, *The Foundations of Dialogue in Science and Religion* (Oxford: Blackwell, 1998), 113.

29. Ibid. McGrath suggests that anthropic evidence is "strongly consistent" with belief in a Creator. Though an evangelical Christian, he fails to grasp fully the force and implications of natural revelation as revealed in Ps 19 and Rom 1. Scripture does not state that the heavens are "strongly consistent" with the notion that they were the "work of God's hands." Rather, they "declare" and "proclaim" this is in fact the case, and that humans are "without excuse" regarding the implications of the non-verbal revelation in nature.

30. Roger Penrose, *The Emperor's New Mind: Concerning Computers, Minds, and The Laws of Physics* (Oxford: Oxford University Press, 1989), 343–44. Italics original.

31. Freeman Dyson, *Disturbing Universe* (New York: Harper and Row, 1979), 250.

32. Peter D. Ward and Donald Brownlee, *Rare Earth: Why Complex Life Is Uncommon in the Universe* (New York: Copernicus Springer-Verlag, 2000), xxi. See also Stuart Ross Taylor, *Destiny or Chance: Our Solar System and Its Place in the Cosmos* (Cambridge: Cambridge University Press, 1998).

33. Ibid., xxv.

34. Ibid., 16, 275.

35. Ibid., xxvii, xxviii.

36. Other notable works include: Noble laureate Christian de Duve, *Vital Dust* (New York: Basic Books, 1995); Simon Conway Morris, *Life's Solution: Inevitable Humans in a Lonely Universe* (Cambridge: University Press, 2003); John Barrow, Simon Conway Morris, Stephen Freeland, and Charles Harper, eds. *Fitness of the Cosmos for Life: Biochemistry and Fine-Tuning* (Cambridge: Cambridge University Press, 2007).

37. Denton's *Evolution: A Theory in Crisis* (New York: Adler and Adler, 1985) is a pillar in the anti-evolutionary community. However, Denton states that his book was "intended to be an attack" on the notion that "all evolution can be plausibly explained by the accumulation of successive small random mutations." He laments the use of his work by anti-evolutionists, but confesses, "If I had used the terms Darwinism and evolution more carefully, much confusion could have been avoided." Michael J. Denton, "Comments on Special Creation" in *Darwinism Defeated?* 142. The fact that Denton lined up on my side of the debate against Phillip Johnson in this book is evidence for his acceptance of evolution. In a personal communication with me, he writes, "I reject vigorously the gradualistic Darwinian conception of evolution via tiny incremental advantageous steps guided entirely and exclusively by natural selection (i.e., Darwin's causal theory). I still see the empirical evidence and especially the recent evidence of evolutionary developmental biology as supporting a far more saltational model of evolution. However, there is no doubt in my mind that the process of evolution has occurred as the result of natural processes and not divine intervention even though the causal factors have not yet been fully identified or characterised." 3 September 2006. Quoted with permission.

38. Michael Denton, *Nature's Destiny: How the Laws of Biology Reveal Purpose in the Universe* (New York: Free Press, 1998), 19, 101, 117.

39. Ibid., 265.

40. Ibid., 281.

41. Simon Conway Morris lists more than 400 striking examples of parallel evolution in his *Life's Solution*, 457–61. This evolutionary phenomenon is the central theme of his book. Morris argues that the "recurrent tendency of biological organization to arrive at the same 'solution' to a particular 'need'" leads to the conclusion that "the emergence of human intelligence is a near-inevitability." Ibid., xii.

42. The term "Cambrian Explosion" is regrettable. Many anti-evolutionists assume the word "explosion" is indicative of a divine interventionistic event. This was never the intention. Considering that geological time is in billions of years, a 5–10 million-year period would seem "explosive."

43. Ibid., 297. Of course, anti-evolutionists interpret this as a site of divine intervention.

44. Richard Swinburne, *The Existence of God* (Oxford: Clarendon Press, 1991), 138. I am grateful to Denise Young for calculating the statistics of this event.

45. Davies, *God and New Physics*, 189.

46. John F. Haught, *Science and Religion: From Conflict to Conversation* (New York: Paulist Press, 1995), 133–34.

47. It is important not to confuse an "ideal" cosmos with one that features "optimal" beauty, complexity, and functionality. This world is "perfect" for humans to develop a relationship with the Creator. Including features that are less optimal is part of His plan. This notion is developed further in this section.

48. See endnote 24 above regarding the use of this term with personal providentialism.

49. For an introduction to the breath-taking complexity of embryological development see Scott F. Gilbert, *Developmental Biology*, 8th ed. (Sunderland: Sinauer, 2006).

50. For an introduction to the scientific evidence for mass extinctions, see David R. Raup, *Extinction: Bad Genes or Bad Luck?* (Norton: New York, 1991).

51. For an introduction, see Daniel Howard-Snyder and Paul K. Moser, *Divine Hiddenness: New Essays* (Cambridge: Cambridge University Press, 2002).

52. See endnotes 13 and 18.

53. See Edward O. Wilson, "Hardwired for God: Is Our Search for Divinity Merely a By-product of Evolution?" *Forbes ASAP* (4 October 1999), 132–34.

CHAPTER 4

1. See Stanley Jaki, *Genesis 1 Through the Ages* (New York: Thomas More Press, 1992); Paul H. Seely, *Inerrant Wisdom: Science and Inerrancy in Biblical Perspective* (Portland: Evangelical Reformed, 1989).

2. The translations of Greek and Hebrew words in this book are common renditions from standard lexicons. These are not cited in each case and include: Walter Bauer, *A Greek-English Lexicon of the New Testament and other Early Christian Literature*, William F. Arndt and F. Wilbur Gingrich, eds. (Chicago: University of Chicago Press, 1958); Henry George Liddell, *A Greek-English Lexicon*, revised by Henry Stuart Jones (Oxford: Oxford University Press, 1996); Francis Brown, S. R. Driver and C.A. Briggs, *Hebrew and English Lexicon of the Old Testament* (Oxford: Clarendon Press, 1951).

3. Some readers might be quick to argue that Job 26:7 and Isa 40:22 imply that earth is spherical. These verses are dealt with later in the chapter in the Excursus on pp. 132–33.

4. The Greek word *kenoō* means "to pour out" and "to empty." The clause "made himself nothing" in Phil 2:7 refers to the self-emptying of God and His becoming a man in the person of Jesus.

5. The possibility exists that Paul might have held a geocentric (Platonic/Aristotelian) understanding of the cosmos with the "underworld" either in the core of the earth or at the antipode. Nevertheless, my point remains in that he accepted an ancient science. It is interesting to note that in the fifth century, debate existed within the Church regarding whether the structure of the world was 3-tiered or geocentric. See St. Augustine, *Literal Meaning of Genesis*, John Hammond Taylor, trans. 2 vols. (New York: Newman Press, 1982), 1:58–59.

6. I cannot overemphasize the importance of grasping this subtle point. To be sure, it is counterintuitive. But it is essential for reading biblical passages about the physical world and understanding their meaning.

7. For the sake of simplicity, I will classify biblical statements dealing with the earth under the category of geology (Greek *gē* means "earth" and "land"). Of course, some of the features listed could be classed as geography (3, 4, 5, 7) and even astronomy (1).

8. Maurice A. Finocchiaro, ed. and trans., *The Galileo Affair: A Document History* (Berkeley: University of California Press, 1989), 292.

9. Grasping the idea that contradictions in Scripture are at times the result of biblical authors having different scientific views is vital in resolving conflicts in Gen 1–11. Chapter 6 explores this idea further.

10. For a picture of this world map on a cuneiform tablet, see Edmond Sollberger, *The Babylonian Legend of the Flood* (London: Trustees of the British Museum, 1961), 45.

11. The explanation for the top of a tree that "reached to heaven" appears in the next section—Ancient Astronomy.

12. See Luis I. J. Stadelmann, *The Hebrew Conception of the World* (Rome: Biblical Institute Press, 1970); John H. Walton, *Ancient Near Eastern Thought and the Old Testament: Introducing the Conceptual World of the Hebrew Bible* (Grand Rapids: Baker Academic, 2006), 165–78; Lloyd R. Bailey, "The Cosmology of the Ancient Semites," in his *Genesis, Creation and Creationism* (New York: Paulist Press, 1993), 172–85; Jaki, *Genesis 1*, 275–79.

13. For the sake of familiarity, this is a popular English translation of Ps 19:1 (NIV Bible). The second ancient astronomical feature presented in this subsection will show that this rendering of the original Hebrew word as "sky" is eisegetical.

14. See Jeffery Burton Russell, *Inventing the Flat Earth: Columbus and Modern Historians* (New York: Praeger, 1991). For an introduction to the Galileo affair, see Charles Hummel, *The Galileo Connection: Resolving Conflicts between Science and the Bible* (Downers Grove: InterVarsity Press, 1986).

15. Agnus Armitage, *The World of Copernicus* (New York: Signet, 1963), 90. See also Martin Luther, *Table Talk* in *Luther's Works* vol. 54 (Philadelphia: Fortress Press, 1967), 359.

16. Ibid.

17. Martin Luther, *Luther Bible of 1534, Complete Facsimile* (Köln: Taschen, 2003), no page number. This diagram faces Gen 1.

18. Modern Bibles using "expanse" include the influential New International Version and New American Standard. However, *Today's NIV* (2002) translates *rāqîaʿ* as "vault."

19. For an excellent introduction, see Paul H. Seely, "The Firmament and the Water Above. Part I: The Meaning of *rāqîaʿ* in Gen 1:6–8" *Westminster Theological Journal* 53 (1991), 227–40.

20. The implications of this biblical fact are significant and will be elaborated in the next chapter on pp. 164–65 under the category "Attribution of Divine Creative Action." Also see endnote 25, in this chapter.

21. For *'ēd*, see Gen 2:6 ("A mist came up from the earth and watered the whole surface of the ground") and Job 36:27; for *nāsi'*, see Jer 10:13, 51:16, and Ps 135:7; for *'ānān*, see Gen 9:13 ("I have set my rainbow in the clouds, and it will be a sign of the covenant between me and the earth."), Gen 9:14, 16, and Exod 24:15. Note that there are at least three other Hebrew words for "cloud" and these were not used in Gen 1. Regarding the vapor theory of the "waters above," see excursus p. 133–35.

22. Martin Luther, *Luther's Works: Lectures on Genesis, Chapters 1–5*, J. Pelikan, ed. (St. Louis, Concordia 1958 [1536]), 30.

23. A similar notion is reflected in "God bent/bowed the heavens and came down" (2 Sam 22:10).

24. Luther, *Lectures on Genesis*, 42–43.

25. Similar to the comment in endnote 20 above, there are significant implications regarding this biblical fact. These will be elaborated in the next chapter on pages 164–65 under the category "Attribution of Divine Judgmental Action."

26. For introductions to ancient Near Eastern literature featuring these ancient sciences, see endnote 12 above.

27. See Henry M. Morris, *Many Infallible Proofs*, 232, 242; Hugh Ross, "Biblical Forecasts of Scientific Discoveries." No pages. Accessed November 13, 2006. Online: http://www.reasons.org/resources/apologetics/forecasts.shtml.

28. Henry Morris and John Whitcomb, *The Genesis Flood: The Biblical Record and Its Scientific Implications* (Presbyterian and Reformed Press, 1961), 77, 229. See also Joseph C. Dillow, *The Waters Above: Earth's Pre-Flood Vapor Canopy* (Chicago: Moody Press, 1982).

29. Hugh Ross, *The Genesis Question: Scientific Advances and the Accuracy of Genesis* (Colorado Springs: NavPress, 1998), 34, 201.

30. This is a key notion and its implications are fully explained in the next chapter. Suffice to say at this time that Gen 1 does not even hint at the evolution of life. However, this fact is not problematic for evolutionary creation because this origins position rejects scientific concordism.

31. This passage is from the NRSV. The NIV translates this verse as the mustard seed "is the smallest seed that *you plant* in the ground." However, the pronoun "you" and the verb "plant" are not in the original Greek or any variants. Kurt Aland, Matthew Black, Carlo M. Martini, Bruce M. Metzger, and Allen Wikgren, *The Greek New Testament*, third ed. (West Germany: United Bible Societies, 1983), 136; cf., 49. A similar attempt by the NIV to mitigate this scientific problem occurs with "the smallest of all *your* seeds" in Matt 13:32. But even the NIV interlinear does not support this rendition. See Alfred Marshall, *The New International Version Interlinear Greek-English New Testament* (Grand Rapids: Zondervan, 1976), 56; cf., 153.

32. For a brief introduction on the history of preformation, see Ernst Mayr, *The Growth*

of Biological Thought: Diversity, Evolution, and Inheritance (Cambridge, Massachusetts: Belknap Press, 1982), 106, 645.

33. Aeschylus, *Aeschylus I: Oresteia* Richard Lattimore, trans. and intro. (Chicago: University Press, 1953), 158; lines 658–61. Aeschylus further argues for a 1-seed view of reproduction, "I will show you proof of what I have explained. There can be a father without a mother. There she stands, the living witness, daughter of Olympian Zeus, she who was never fostered in the womb" (lines 662–65).

34. Joseph Needham, *A History of Embryology* (Cambridge: Cambridge University Press, 1934), 184. The drawing of a human sperm cell is by Nicolas Hartsoeker (1656–1725) from his *Essai de Dioptrique* (1694).

35. The Greek word translated "body" in this verse is *osphus*, which can refer to "waist, loins," and in particular to "the place of reproductive organs." Clearly, the use of "body" in most English translations is euphemistic; cf., Acts 2:30.

36. See also Judg 13:2–3; 1 Sam 2:5; Job 24:21; Ps 113:9; Isa 54:1; Luke 23:29; Gal 4:27. Note Deut 7:14 is a merism. This figure of speech is similar to that used by couples who say, "We are pregnant."

37. Susan C. Stuart, "Male Infertility." No pages. Accessed July 26, 2007. Online: http://www.thedoctorwillseeyounow.com/articles/other/malein_29/#back2.

38. I am grateful to botanists Jack Maze and René Belland for their assistance in calculating the germination rate.

39. See the chapter entitled "Mother Earth and the Cosmic Hierogamies" in Mircea Eliade, *Myths, Dreams and Mysteries* (New York: Harper and Row, 1967), 155–89. The ancient notion of mother earth is further dealt with on pp. 194–95.

40. David C. Lindberg, *The Beginnings of Western Science: The European Scientific Tradition in Philosophical, Religious, and Institutional Context, 600 BC to AD 1450* (Chicago: University Press, 1992), 18–20.

41. Note the implication of God *increasing* Eve's pain in childbirth: pain existed before the fall of humans into sin, and thus, would have been a feature of the "very good" creation. However, I doubt that this subtle reference in one single verse will undermine the longstanding Christian belief in the cosmic fall, as supported by powerful passages such as Rom 8:19–21.

CHAPTER 5

1. It is important to note that *de novo* creation is not necessarily *creatio ex nihilo* (creation out of nothing). For example, the waters in Gen 1:2 are used to make the "waters above" on the second creation day. See chapter 6, pp. 188–90 and Appendix 2: Creation Out of Nothing (*Creatio Ex Nihilo*), pp. 391–96.

2. Attempts to use the "poetic language argument" with these end time passages falls short in the same way these do with claims that the biblical authors were using the "rising/setting" of the sun metaphorically.

3. See chapter 6, pp. 194–95.

4. See Christopher B. Kaiser, *Creation and the History of Science* (Grand Rapids: Eerdmans, 1991).

5. Ian G. Barbour, *Religion and Science: Historical and Contemporary Issues* (New York:

Harper San Francisco, 1997), 3–74.

6. See chapter 4, pp. 107–9.

7. Galileo Galilei, "Letter to the Grand Duchess Christina," in Maurice A. Finocchiaro, ed. and trans., *The Galileo Affair: A Document History* (Berkeley: University of California Press, 1989), 93.

8. Ibid., 105.

9. This aphorism is first attributed to Bernard of Chartres in the twelfth century and later popularized by Isaac Newton in the seventeenth century.

10. See Frederick Ferré, *Concepts of Nature and God* (Athens, GA: Philosophy Department, 1989), vii.

11. This principle was inspired by John F. Haught's "implicit cosmological assumptions" in his *Science and Religion: From Conflict to Conversation* (New York: Paulist Press, 1995), 18.

12. Gregg Easterbrook, *Toronto Globe and Mail* (24 Oct 99). Italics added.

13. My choice of the term "attribution" is intentional and underlines the nuances of "*considered* as belonging to" and "*thought* as caused by." In this way, it allows for the possibility that an act of attributing might be mistaken. As everyone knows, considerations and thoughts are at times erroneous. Also note my use of the term "cosmological." I am distinguishing these three types of divine action from God's activity in *personal* relationships. See section on "Divine Action" in chapter 3 and endnote 3 of that chapter.

14. Galileo, "Christina," 93.

15. Eugene H. Peterson, *The Message: The New Testament in Contemporary Language* (Colorado: NavPress, 1993), title page.

16. Ibid., 36. Regrettably (understandably), Peterson does not employ his re-accommodation method in the translation of the early chapters of Genesis.

17. In fact, the notion of *creatio ex nihilo* is included in my translation. As it will be pointed out in the next chapter this concept is not in Gen 1. See pages 188–89. I am grateful to Jennifer Elliott for her assistance in this translation.

18. In addition, Jesus commands us "to turn the other cheek" (Matt 5:39), yet being struck in the face before the high priest there is no evidence He did (John 18:22–23). The Lord also admonishes, "do not judge" (Matt 7:1), yet He states that we will recognize false prophets by their fruits (7:16), implying that we have no choice but to judge their actions.

19. In his influential book on biblical inerrancy, Harold Lindsell comments, "A word needs to be said about the use of the words *infallible* and *inerrant*. There are some who try to distinguish between these words as though there is a difference. I do not know of any standard dictionary that does not use these two words interchangeably. All of them use them synonymously." In his *The Battle for the Bible* (Grand Rapids: Zondervan, 1981), 27; italics original. I will also use these two terms in this way.

20. This notion is presented in a monumental work on evangelical hermeneutics. See "The Trustworthiness of Scripture in Areas Relating to Natural Science" in Earl D. Radmacher and Robert D. Preus, eds., *Hermeneutics, Inerrancy and the Bible: Papers from the International Council on Biblical Inerrancy Summit II* (Grand Rapids: Zondervan, 1984), 283–348.

21. Of course, a spore is technically not a seed since most are haploid. But I believe the analogy makes my point.

22. I am indebted to Ladd's aphorism, "The Bible is the Word of God given in the words of men in history." George Eldon Ladd, *New Testament and Criticism* (Grand Rapids: Eerdmans, 1967), 12.

CHAPTER 6

1. A survey asked American adults whether the following statements were "literally true" or "not literally true": (1) "The creation story in which the world was created in six days," (2) "The story of Noah and the ark in which it rained for 40 days and nights; the entire world was flooded; and only Noah, his family, and the animals on their ark survived." Sixty-one percent take the former literally and 60% the latter. Eighty-seven percent of evangelical Protestants believe both accounts are literal records of events. No Author, "Six in 10 Take Bible Stories Literally, But Don't Blame Jews for Death of Jesus." No pages. Surveyed conducted 6–10 February 2004 with a random sample of 1011 adults by ICR-International Communications Research Media, Pa. Accessed July 6, 2006. Online: http://www.icrsurvey.com/studies/947a1%20Views%20of%20the%20Bible.pdf.

2. For scholarly works defending the historicity of Gen 12–50, see Kenneth A. Kitchen, *On the Reliability of the Old Testament* (Grand Rapids: Eerdmans, 2003); Iain W. Provan, V. Philips Long and Tremper Longman III, *A Biblical History of Israel* (Louisville: Westminster John Knox Press, 2003).

3. Gordon J. Wenham, *Genesis 1–15* (Waco: Word Books, 1987), xxii.

4. David C. Lindberg, *The Beginnings of Western Science* (Chicago: University of Chicago Press, 1992), 5–13; Jan Vansina, *Oral Tradition as History* (Madison: University of Wisconsin Press, 1985).

5. Concern that divine revelation in an oral form would be forgotten is unfounded. The Holy Spirit could easily maintain the collective memory of the preliterate Hebrews until it was written down. See John 14:26 and 2 Thess 2:15 with regard to New Testament teachings.

6. Richard S. Hess, "Literacy in Iron Age Israel," in V. Philips Long, David W. Baker and Gordon J. Wenham, *Windows into Old Testament History* (Grand Rapids: Eerdmans, 2002), 82–102.

7. The classic treatment of this subject is Henri Frankfort, H.A. Frankfort, John A. Wilson, Thorkild Jacobsen, and William A. Irwin, *The Intellectual Adventure of Ancient Man: An Essay on Speculative Thought in the Ancient Near East* (Chicago: University of Chicago Press 1977 [1946]).

8. The importance of this notion will be seen with the biblical creation and flood accounts.

9. See the subsection in this chapter "The Historicity of the Pre-Creative State (Gen 1:1 to 1:2)," 188–91; and Appendix 2: Creation Out of Nothing (*Creatio Ex Nihilo*), 391–96.

10. Thompson's *Motif-Index* is an invaluable resource outlining ancient motifs. Obviously, my identification of four major motifs is to focus upon the central events in Gen 1–11. However, these are clearly evident in the ancient literature. Thompson's categories include "Cosmogony and Cosmology" (heaven, earth, humanity), "Establishment of Natural Order" (golden age), "World Calamities" (including the deluge), and "Distribution and differentiation of people." Stith Thompson, *Motif-Index of Folk-Literature: A Classification of Narrative Elements in Folktales, Ballads, Myths, Fables, Mediaeval Romances, Exempla,*

Notes to Chapter Six

Fabliaux, Jest-Books, and Local Legends (Bloomington: Indiana University Press, 1955–1958), 1:126–34, 182–89, 194, 202–12.

11. Regarding myths in ancient Mesopotamia, Dina Katz notes, "The Sumerians seem to have perceived mythological reality as historically actual." *The Image of the Netherworld in Sumerian Sources* (Bethesda: CDL Press, 2003), 56. See also Walton, *Ancient Near Eastern Thought*, 43–44.

12. The first extrabiblical reference to Israel is in the Merneptah (Israel) Stele, which is dated either 1209 or 1208 BC. It records military victories by Pharaoh Merneptah and includes the statement, "Israel is laid waste, his seed is not." Provan et al., *History of Israel*, 169.

13. Fragments of Mesopotamian flood accounts appear in Palestine around 1400 BC. John Bright, *A History of Israel*, 3rd ed. (Philadelphia: Westminster Press, 1981), 89; Wenham, *Genesis 1–15*, xliv, 162.

14. See Hess, "Literacy," 87–88.

15. See Wenham, *Genesis 1–15*, xxxvii–xxxix, xlii–xlv; Richard Elliott Friedman, *The Bible with Sources Revealed* (New York: HarperSanFrancisco, 2003), 1–31; Tremper Longman III, *How to Read Genesis* (Downers Grove: InterVarsity Press, 2005), 49–55.

16. Christians troubled by this notion must remember that Luke (1:1–4) and John (1:1–3) acknowledge the use of sources in writing their respective books. In fact, the New Testament went through an editorial selection process. The number of books deemed to be inspired by God increased over time (e.g., Hebrews, James, and Revelation were late additions), and it was not until the fourth century that the Church finally established the canon.

17. The traditional belief that Moses used written sources from Adam, Noah, the patriarchs, etc., to compose Gen 1–11 is exactly that—a traditional belief. Nowhere in Scripture does it say directly that this is the case. And like all traditions, this belief is open to re-evaluation.

18. The disjunctive *waw* in Gen 1:2 of the MT complemented by the particle *de* of the LXX clearly indicates that this verse is not temporally sequential to Gen 1:1. Thus, the *consecutive* grammatical approach that the first three verses of Scripture present a successive order of events is not possible. See KJV. Wenham, *Genesis 1–15*, 11–17; Westermann, *Genesis 1–11: A Commentary*, John J. Scullion trans. (Minneapolis: Augsburg Publishing House, 1987), 78, 93–102.

19. Frankfort et al., *Intellectual Adventure*, 50–52, 170–172.

20. James B. Pritchard, ed. *Ancient Near Eastern Texts Relating to the Old Testament*, 3rd ed. (Princeton: Princeton University Press, 1969), 60–61 (hereafter cited as *ANET*).

21. In particular, see Appendix 2, endnote 3.

22. Hugh Ross, *The Genesis Question* (Colorado Springs: NavPress, 1998), 17–19. A variant progressive creationist interpretation suggests that the creation of light on the first day (Gen 1:3) refers to the Big Bang. However, this is even more problematic because the earth is already in existence (v. 2), and according to Big Bang theory, the earth evolved about 10 billion years after this explosive event.

23. *ANET*, 5–6. See also Frankfort et al., *Intellectual Adventure*, 53–54.

24. See Davis Young, *The Biblical Flood: A Case Study of the Church's Response to Extrabiblical Evidence* (Grand Rapids: Eerdmans, 1995); Peter J. Bowler, *Evolution: History of an Idea* (Berkeley: California University Press, 1984), 117.

25. Anti-evolutionists have coined the term "baramin" to define these taxonomical groupings. It derives from the Hebrew words *bārā'* (to create) and *min* (kind, type).

26. Attempts to restrict the adjective "all" creates more problems that it solves. For example, in Gen 1 it would mean "all" those creatures except the ones created in Gen 2, and in the latter chapter "all" those made in the garden of Eden. Not only does this produce two creative periods for birds, animals, vegetation, etc., but it also results in an inconsistent use of this adjective. A less tortuous approach is to suggest Gen 1 and 2 are two separate origins accounts.

27. The suggestion that Gen 2:8 and 19 are parenthetical and refer to previous creative acts (e.g., NIV's "Now the Lord God had . . .") is not supported by the Hebrew Bible. Both verses feature a consecutive *waw*.

28. These features in Gen 2 also appear in Gen 3 and 4, indicating that Gen 2:4 to 4:26 is a literary unit composed by J. It is important to note that the divine name "Lord God" occurs only in Gen 2 and 3 and nowhere else in the Pentateuch. Friedman contends that the redactor added the term "God" to "Lord" in order to smooth the transition from Gen 1 (P) to Gen 2–4 (J). Friedman, *Sources Revealed*, 35.

29. The significance of the number 7 to ancient Near Eastern peoples will be presented with Genesis 4 and 5 and in Appendix 3: Genealogies of Jesus.

30. Walter Beyerlin, ed. *Near Eastern Religious Texts Relating to the Old Testament* (Philadelphia: Westminster Press, 1978), 75. See also Stephanie Daley, *Myths from Mesopotamia* (Oxford: University Press, 1989), 4, 16–17; *ANET*, 68.

31. Mircea Eliade, one of the greatest scholars of comparative religions, states, "In more or less complex forms, the paradisiac myth occurs here and there all over the world." *Myths, Dreams and Mysteries* (New York: Harper and Row, 1967), 59. He refers to the loss of the paradisiac stage as "the fall" and "the fall of man." Ibid., 60, 63, 66. See also "The Perfection of the Beginnings" in his *Myth and Reality* (New York: Harper and Row, 1963), 50–53.

32. *ANET*, 38, 102, 96. Jeremy Black and Anthony Green, *Gods, Demons and Symbols of Ancient Mesopotamia: An Illustrated Dictionary* (Austin: University of Texas, 1992), 170–71. For artistic depictions of sacred trees, see Richard Heinberg, *Memories and Visions of Paradise: Exploring the Universal Myth of a Lost Golden Age* (Los Angeles: Jeremy P. Tarcher, Inc., 1989), 46, 60, 64, 66, 90.

33. This motif is sometimes referred to as the lost golden age. See Eliade, *Myths, Dreams and Mysteries*, 59–72; Eliade, *Myth and Reality*, 50–53; Richard Heinberg, *Paradise*, 81–111; David Adams Leeming and Margaret Adams Leeming, *Encyclopedia of Creation Myths* (Santa Barbara: ABC-CLIO, Inc., 1994), viii.

34. See "Beasts of the Gods," in Black and Green, *Gods, Demons and Symbols*, 39–40. For a Mesopotamian depiction of a cherub see "Cherubim," J.D. Douglas, ed., *The New Bible Dictionary* (Grand Rapids: Eerdmans, 1979), 208.

35. A few comments are in order with regard to the Lord cursing the ground in Gen 3:17. On the surface this verse seems to conflict with other passages in Scripture. The creation is stated to be "very good" in Gen 1:31, it is celebrated in Job 38–39 and Psalms 104 and 145, and it "declares the glory of God" in the beloved 19th Psalm. The Hebrew verb *ărar* (curse) carries nuances of "to bind" and "to snare." In particular, this involves the bondage of something with obstacles, rendering it powerless and banding it from a previous state or condition. Therefore, when God said to Adam, "Cursed in the ground because of you" (Gen 3:17), He was binding it from its original fruitfulness during the idyllic age, and condemn-

ing Adam to a life of painful and sweaty labor. Sin changed the relationship between Adam and the Lord, and the cursing of the ground is ultimately incidental to this foundational shift in how humans relate to their Creator. Notably, curses in the Old Testament are relational. They are connected with moral and ethical obligations to God and neighbor. In other words, curses are not magical, and the Lord's cursing of the ground did not change its ontological status. It remains very good. Instead, reference to the ground being "cursed" is a phenomenological statement, and indeed it reflects a fact about physical reality—the world is a challenging place to live in. It has many unsavory features, and we struggle in it to survive. The author of Gen 3 uses the phenomenological perception that nature is in bondage to decay, suffering, and death as an incidental vessel in order to reveal the Message of Faith that God judges human sin. In this way, an evolutionary creation can be believed as ontologically "very good" and "declaring God's glory," and at the same time, acknowledged phenomenologically as a world in which the fittest survive through natural selection. Victor P. Hamilton, "*ārar*" in R. Laird Harris, Gleason L. Archer, Jr. and Bruce Waltke, *Theological Wordbook of the Old Testament*, 2 vols. (Chicago: Moody Press, 1980), 1:75–76.

36. For the loss of legs in snakes see, Michael W. Caldwell and Michael S. Y. Lee, "A Snake with Legs from the Marine Cretaceous of the Middle East," *Nature* 386 (17 April 1997): 705–9. Identification of the "thorns and thistles" in Gen 3:18 is challenging, and debate exists between botanists. These broad categories open the way for numerous candidates. Thorns (Hebrew *qôs*) most likely refer to Palestinian Bramble (*Rubus sanctus*) or Elmleaf Bramble (*Rubus ulimfolius*), and the genus *Rubus* appeared about 50 million years ago. Thistles (*dardar*) are within the family Asteraceae, which appeared about 25 million years ago. Despite the difficulty of determining exactly the plants that are being referred to in Gen 3:18, thorns and thistles predate humans by many tens of millions of years. See Irene Jacob and Walter Jacob, "Flora" in David N. Freedman, editor-in-chief, *Anchor Bible Dictionary*, 6 vols. (New York: Doubleday, 1992), 2:815–16; R. K. Harrison, "Thorns," in J. D. Douglas, ed., *The New Bible Dictionary* (Grand Rapids: Eerdmans, 1962), 1273. I am grateful to botanists David Cass, Kathleen Pigg, Melanie DeVore, and Jack Maze for their assistance.

37. See "Numbers: Sacred and Symbolic Usage (and the Number Seven in Particular)" in Lloyd R. Bailey, *Genesis, Creation, and Creationism* (New York: Paulist Press, 1993), 157–60.

38. These dates are standard in archaeology. See Kenneth L. Feder, *The Past in Perspective: An Introduction to Human Prehistory* (Boston: McGraw-Hill, 2004), 329, 389.

39. Black and Green, *Gods, Demons and Symbols*, 163–64; Beyerlin, *Near Eastern Religious Texts*, 79–80.

40. It is important to note that my identification of these two features in Gen 4 is not to succumb to historical concordism. Rather, it is to acknowledge that actual historical realities at the time of the inspired writer lie behind his retrojection of these in reconstructing the past.

41. I am grateful to Don Robinson for this calculation and the one that appears with Gen 11. Carol A. Hill includes other features from this genealogy and calculates there is "a chance of probability of one in a billion!" In her "Making Sense of the Numbers of Genesis," *Perspectives on Science and Christian Faith* 55 (Dec 2003): 244.

42. I am not dogmatic about these mathematical proposals. Other approaches to the numbers have been offered. Enoch's 365-year lifespan certainly seems to reflect the days in a year. Lamech's 777 is the addition of the Jupiter and Saturn years, Jared's 962 that of

Venus and Saturn. Wenham, *Genesis 1–15*, 134. Another possibility employs the common stylistic number 40. If the ages at the time of death are sorted out and an average taken of those above (969 + 962 + 950 + 930) and below (910 + 905 + 895 + 777) the median age (912 years of Seth), then subtracting 40 from the former (952.75) and adding 40 to the latter (871.75) is 0.5 from the calculated median (912.25). See also Bailey, *Genesis*, 61–64.

43. Progressive creationist Hugh Ross accepts that the ages in Gen 5 are literal, but contends this genealogy contains gaps. He places the creation of Adam somewhere between 8000 to 24,000 years ago. Ross, *Genesis Question*, 55–57, 107–10, 117–25.

44. Westermann, *Genesis 1–11*, 379–81; Wenham, *Genesis 1–15*, 143.

45. Young, *Biblical Flood*, 66.

46. See note 1 above for citation.

47. Asymmetries are expected in the chiasm since two separate sources were redacted. For example, there is only one 7-day period in E, but E' includes two and possibly three such intervals (these passages come from the J flood account). Notably, a smaller and complementary chiasm appears in Gen 9:12–17.

A God said, "This is the sign of the covenant" (verse 12)

    B Bow in the clouds (13–14)

        Center "I Will Remember My Covenant" (15)

    B' Bow in the clouds (16)

A' God said, "This is the sign of the covenant" (17)

This passage is in the P flood account. Poetic structures characterize the Priestly author (Gen 1, 5, 11), and it seems evident that the flood chiasm in Gen 6–9 derives ultimately from his version.

48. *Redrawn. Based on Bernhard Lang, "Non-Semitic Deluge Stories and the Book of Genesis: A Bibliographic and Critical Survey" *Anthropos* 80 (1985): 605–16. The December 2004 tsunami in South East Asia certainly made me understand why so many flood accounts appear in this region.

49. Lloyd R. Bailey, *Noah: The Person and the Story in History and Tradition* (Columbia: University of South Carolina Press, 1989), 28–37. See also Jack Finegan, *Archaeological History of the Ancient Middle East* (Boulder: Westview, 1979), 25; Paul Seely, "Noah's Flood: Its Date, Extent, and Divine Accommodation," *Westminster Theological Journal* 66 (2004): 291–311.

50. This is a *very* conservative calculation. Today there are roughly 4000 species of mammals, 6000 reptiles, and 9000 birds, making a total of 19,000 species. However, well over 99% of all species have gone extinct, suggesting that God in Gen 1 had originally created at least 1,900,000 of these three classes of creatures. Not including the calculation of the clean and unclean animals for the sake of simplicity, the total number of animals in the ark would be 800,000 mammals (4000 X 2 male/female X 100), 1,200,000 reptiles (6000 X 2 male/female X 100), and 12,600,000 birds (9000 x 2 male/female x 7 x 100).

51. The total number of people/s is in fact 71, but scholarly consensus suggests that the original count was 70. Wenham, *Genesis 1–15*, 213–14. The appearance of Sheba and Dedan in verse 7 is suspicious, introducing an asymmetry into the table. Genesis 25:3 states they are the sons of Jokshan, not Raamah. If Sheba and Dedan are a later editorial addition to Gen 10, and the Philistines (a chronic Hebrew enemy) are included in the total, the number becomes 70. The importance of this symbolic number in the book of Genesis

is also seen with the 70 people in Jacob's family who entered Egypt (Gen 46:27).

52. The dates presented in this section are standard archaeological estimates and based on: Wenham, *Genesis 1–15*, 216–232; Westermann, *Genesis 1–11*, 504–528; Freedman, *Anchor Bible Dictionary*, 1:49, 490, 807, 877, 1024, 1219; 2:321, 331, 374, 473, 571, 1074; 3:81, 85, 650; 4:93, 274, 462, 471, 711, 1118; 5:326, 664, 678, 775, 861, 1064, 1169; 6:331, 594, 670.

53. Historical concordists argue that these references are anachronisms. That is, they are editorial additions/corrections made by a later writer. Of course, this is a possibility. But those offering this argument do so in order to defend the traditional and literal interpretation. At this point it should be clear that such an approach to Gen 1–11 falls short. The "anachronism argument" reminds me of the "appearance of age argument" used by young earth creationists (i.e., the universe "looks" old). Both defenses are in fact subtle affirmations of the evidence they hope to dismiss.

54. Paul H. Seely, "The Date of the Tower of Babel and Some Theological Considerations," *Westminster Theological Journal* 63 (2001): 15–38.

55. Some English Bibles like the NIV translate the Hebrew *bābel* as "Babylon" in order to mitigate the conflict of events between Gen 10 and 11.

56. See Appendix 5 Fig 3, pp. 404–5.

57. Beyerlin, *Near Eastern Religious Texts*, 86–87.

58. Patrick R. Bennett, *Comparative Semitic Linguistics: A Manual* (Winona Lake: Eisenbrauns, 1998); Ludwig Koehler and Walter Baumgartner, eds. *Hebrew and Aramaic Lexicon of the Old Testament: Study Edition* (Leiden: Brill, 2002); Ignace Gelb, eds. *The Assyrian Dictionary*. Vol. 10 (Chicago: University of Chicago, 1977). I am grateful to Old Testament scholars Brian P. Irwin, Tyler Williams, and Timothy Scott for their assistance.

CHAPTER 7

1. See Katz, *Sumerian Sources*, 56; Walton, *Ancient Near Eastern Thought*, 43–44; Tremper Longman III, *Genesis*, 61–63; John Van Seters, *Prologue to History: The Yahwist as Historian in Genesis* (Louisville: Westminister John Knox, 1992), 10–23.

2. Eliade, *Myths, Dreams and Mysteries*, 59–72; Eliade, *Myth and Reality*, 50–53; Heinberg, *Paradise*, 81–111, Leeming and Leeming, *Creation Myths*, viii.

3. For example, numerous accounts emerged following the 26 Dec 2004 tsunami in Southeast Asia.

4. In some creation accounts, a group of individuals were originally created. This view of human origins is known as "polygenism." For an example, see the Mesopotamian story of Atrahasis, p. 200.

5. Creation by the separation of opposites is a common ancient Near Eastern motif.

6. If humans died during this idyllic time, it was usually peaceful and after a long lifetime.

7. See diagrams of sacred trees in Heinberg, *Paradise*, 59–66; Black and Green, *Symbols*, 170–71.

8. For example, genealogies modify in accordance to societal structures. See Vansina, *Oral Tradition*, 178–85.

9. This misrepresents Darwin's beliefs in the *Origin of Species*. See pp. 8–9.

10. Wenham notes that "the Atrahasis Epic from the early second millennium shows that the basic plot of Gen 1–11 was already known then." Wenham, *Genesis 1–15*, xxxix.

11. See chap 6, 230–31.

12. Word play characterizes the J author. See Friedman, *Sources Revealed*, 36.

13. Midgley states, "Evolution is the creation-myth of our age. By telling us our origins it shapes our views of what we are. It influences not just our thought, but our feelings and actions too, in a way that goes far beyond its official function as a biological theory. In calling it a myth, I am not of course saying that it is a false story. I mean that it has great symbolic power, which is independent of its truth. Is the word religion appropriate to it? This will depend on the sense we give to that very elastic word." Mary Midgley, "The Religion of Evolution" in John Durant, ed., *Darwinism and Divinity* (Oxford: Basil Blackwell, 1985), 154.

14. Kirk notes that Plato (427–347 BC) was the first to use the term "myth" and at that time it "meant no more than telling stories." This term was eventually replaced by *logos* to mean "direct statement." G.S. Kirk, *Myth: Its Meaning and Functions in Ancient and Other Cultures* (Berkeley and Los Angeles: California University Press, 1973), 8, 249.

15. As young earth creationist Henry Morris states, Gen 1–11 is "clear, definite, sequential and matter-of-fact, giving every appearance of straightforward historical narrative." Henry M. Morris, *The Genesis Record: A Scientific and Devotional Commentary on the Book of Beginnings* (Grand Rapids: Baker, 1979), 84.

16. For example, see Absarkoes Indians, the Fang people and Hopi Indians in Leeming and Leeming, *Encyclopaedia of Creation Myths*, 63–64, 91–92 and 125–30, respectively.

17. I must qualify that the possibility exists the inspired authors dressed up Gen 1–11 with symbols and allegories. For example, the talking snake might be a literary device to deliver the spiritual reality of temptation. If so, then a non-historical element was embedded within an ancient historical paradigm (lost idyllic age). Of course, modern historiography rejects such an amalgamation of a figurative being with an event understood to be factual. But this would not be troublesome to individuals with an ancient epistemology, which characteristically features a blurred supernatural-natural demarcation and an agentic view of causality marked by the interventionistic activity of God/s and mystical beings. The literary sophistication to create allegories certainly existed in ancient Israel. It seems that the book of Job is not a record of historical events. I doubt that Satan can enter God's presence to debate Him. It seems unlikely that the Creator would be so frivolous as to allow Job's ten children to be murdered in order for Satan to make a point. The account of Jonah living inside a fish for three days also appears to be an allegory to reveal a theological message. However, should the original sources behind Gen 1–11 include literary symbols and allegories, they were *historicized* by the redactor and understood as historical by later biblical authors like Paul.

18. A similar process occurred with the Greeks near the end of the fifth century BC. At that time the historicity and literalness of their myths were being questioned. In order to preserve these accounts, the Greeks began to focus on their deeper meanings and coined the term "allegory." *Allēgoria* means "figurative speech" and it is composed of the adjective *allos* "other" and the verb *agoreuein* "to speak publicly." Richard N. Soulen, *Handbook of Biblical Criticism*, 2n ed. (Atlanta: John Knox Press, 1981), 15.

19. For poetic language argument, see chapter 4, p. 107–8.

20. For the titular construction of Gen 1:13, see chapter 6, p. 189.

21. This corollary is a challenging concept to grasp at first. In teaching this notion at the university level, I have found that students take a while to understand it. This concept is further developed in the next chapter. See pp. 320–21 and Fig 8-4.

22. This approach follows Stanley Jaki who argues for "an interpretation of Genesis 1 which is literal without being literalistic and eliminates thereby the specter of concordism." Jaki, *Genesis 1*, back cover.

23. See pp. 118, 128, 137, and 142–43, respectively.

24. There are only a few verses outside Gen 1–11 that refer to Adam. 1 Chronicles 1:1, Luke 3:38, and Jude 14 place him in a genealogy. He is used in order to argue for Church practices in 1 Tim 2:13–14 and 1 Cor 11:8–9.

25. The flood prologue includes the mythological account of celestial beings mating with human women (Gen 6:1–4), arguing further against the historicity of this pre-deluge period.

26. Similar references to Noah and the flood appear in 2 Pet 2:5, 3:3–7. Again the focus is not a discussion on historicity, but on the future day of judgment. Notably, Peter also uses the ancient minor motif of pre-creative waters in 3:5 ("the earth was formed out of water and with water"). Mention of Noah occurs only a few times outside of Gen 1–11. He is part of a genealogy in 1 Chr 1:1, 4. And he is used typologically in Isa 54:9, Ezek 14:14, 20, and Heb 11:7. This last verse is particularly significant since other individuals from Gen 1–11 (Abel, Cain, Enoch) are employed to exemplify the meaning of faith.

27. See Davis A. Young, *The Biblical Flood: A Case Study of the Church's Response to Extrabiblical Evidence* (Carlisle: Paternoster Press and Grand Rapids: Eerdmans), 26.

28. It is estimated that the genetic variation found in the human population today requires about 50,000 years. See Appendix 10, endnote 5.

CHAPTER 8

1. Gallup Polls (1982, 1993, 1997, 1999, 2001, 2004, 2006) reveal that between 44–47% of American adults believe "God created human beings pretty much in their present form at one time within the last 10,000 years or so." No Author, "Science and Nature." No pages. Accessed December 23, 2006. Online: http://www.pollingreport.com/science.htm.

2. For example, consider the situation that transpired with anthropologist Alex Bolyanatz at Wheaton College. See Beth McMurtrie, "Do Professors Lose Academic Freedom by Signing Statements of Faith?" *The Chronicle of Higher Education* (24 May 2002), A12–A16.

3. Note that this is not to succumb to another false dichotomy. In fact, there are a number of teleological interpretations of human evolution, such as that offered by deism. The purpose of this diagram is to contrast evolutionary creation with the common assumption that the evolution of humanity is dysteleological.

4. A detailed exposition of the notion of the Image of God is not necessary for my argument. It suffices simply to affirm that humans bear this ontological reality. For an excellent introduction, see J. Richard Middleton, *The Liberating Image: The Imago Dei in Genesis 1* (Grand Rapids: Brazos Press, 2005).

5. The term "manifestation" is specifically chosen and used figuratively. The Latin word

manifestus means "palpable," and it derives from *manus* (hand) and *festus* (seized). In the context of human evolution, the Creator's hand was involved in making the Image of God palpable. Similarly, "tangible" sin entered the world at the hands of men and women. Though the palpability of these spiritual realities is not scientifically detectable, humans are fully aware and knowledgeable of their existence.

6. For the sake of illustration, I am limiting human development to the womb. Of course, some argue that humans become sinners only after an individual becomes intellectually and spiritually cognizant. My purpose is to draw parallels between embryology and evolution in order to focus upon the mysterious nature of the manifestation of human spiritual characteristics in both.

7. Some Christians appeal to Ps 51:5 and argue that humans are sinners from conception: "Surely I have been a sinner from birth, sinful from the time my mother conceived me." However, it is methodologically precarious to build a doctrine on only one verse. Moreover, the word translated as "conceived" is the Hebrew *yāḥam*, which means "to be hot." In other words, it refers to when a woman is in heat sexually. This verse is not dealing with the modern scientific notion of fertilization because the biblical understanding of reproduction is the 1-seed theory. Finally, it must be noted that this Psalm is highly figurative. David asks God to wash him "whiter than snow" and to "let the bones You have crushed rejoice" (v. 7–8). Thus, he is employing hyperbole in order to underline his sinfulness in verse 5, and not offering a theological statement on the origin of sin for individuals.

8. This category must be contrasted with "Traditional Monogenism," which is the literal *de novo* creation of Adam from the dust of the ground and the origin of Eve from flesh of his side (Gen 2:7, 22).

9. The epigraph of this book reveals that Billy Graham is comfortable with the possibility of this view of human evolution. Evolutionary monogenism appears in Roman Catholic documents. See Pope Pius XII, "*Humani Generis* (1950)," in Claudia Carlen, ed., *The Papal Encyclicals 1939–1958* (USA: McGrath Publishers, 1981), 181–82; No Author, *Catechism of the Catholic Church* (Ottawa: Canadian Conference of Catholic Bishops, 1992), 88, 90.

10. This position is not to be confused with the evolutionary model of punctuated equilibrium. In contrast to Darwin's gradualistic view of evolution, the latter asserts that organisms remain static for long periods of time followed by rapid change during short intervals. It is an entirely physical process and does not involve divine interventions. Punctiliar polygenism involves God intervening dramatically into nature at one point along the pre-human evolutionary line to introduce the metaphysical reality of the Image of God.

11. According to Augustine, the doctrine of "original sin" has two aspects. First, it was the sin that was originally committed by Adam and Eve in the garden of Eden. Second, it was the sin nature that was passed down to each human in every generation.

12. Medline Plus Medical Encyclopedia states, "It is estimated that up to 50% of all fertilized eggs die and are lost (aborted) spontaneously, usually before the woman knows she is pregnant." No Author, "Miscarriage," No pages. Accessed July 31, 2007. Online: http://www.nlm.nih.gov/medlineplus/ency/article/001488.htm

13. For example, Neanderthals buried their dead with flowers suggesting they might have had a notion of life after death.

14. R.J. Thompson, "Sacrifice and Offering" in J. D. Douglas, ed., *The New Bible Dictionary* (Grand Rapids: Eerdmans, 1979), 1116.

15. A couple of qualifications are in order. First, note the italicization of the term

"roughly." My intention is not to offer a complete presentation on theodicy. For my argument, all I require is to demonstrate that theodicy develops through Scripture. The Gen 3 account, the book of Job, and the teachings of Jesus provide well-known data points to defend this theological development. Other biblical passages could have been used to support my case. For example, the notion that evil can be used by God to serve His purposes appears later in Genesis. After being betrayed by his brothers, Joseph told them, "You intended to harm me, but God intended it for good to accomplish what is now being done, the saving of many lives" (Gen 50:20). Second, I recognize that the *actual writing* of the book of Job might pre-date Gen 3. However, I am respecting the canonical order. Moreover, it is reasonable to speculate that Job is subsequent to the oral tradition that lies behind Gen 3 since the latter is necessary for the function of pre-literate communities like the early Hebrews. The conceptual maturity of the theodicy in Job compared to Gen 3 also points to a later time in the intellectual-spiritual development of Israel.

16. See my comment on the literary genre of this book in chapter 7, endnote 17.

17. This theodicy also appears in Proverbs. For example, "Misfortune pursues the sinner, but prosperity is the reward of the righteous" (Prov 13:21; also see 11:21, 12:21).

18. See pp. 315–17 regarding the notion of spiritual death in Scripture.

19. See chapter 6, endnote 35 with regard to the cursing of the ground in Gen 3:17.

20. To be more precise, Adam does not *directly* cause death to enter the world. He does not have the power to do so. Rather, God introduces death in judgment of his sin. Consequently, the relationship between Adam's sin and the origin of physical death is an *indirect* causal connection. See the three facets of causality in Gen 3, p. 205.

21. Henry M. Morris, "The Vital Importance of Believing in Recent Creation," *Back to Genesis 138* (June 2000), b-c.

22. G. Richard Bozarth, "The Meaning of Evolution," *The American Atheist*, 20 (February 1978), 30.

23. I certainly appreciate the principle of parsimony in the construction of theories, whether scientific or theological. The simple solution to the sin-death problem could be stated as follows: The historicity of Adam, his sin, and subsequent death are ultimately based on the recycled ancient motifs of *de novo* creation and lost idyllic age. In reality, there is no causal connection between sin and death because Adam never existed, and he could not sin and then be condemned to die. Paul accepts the sin-death connection because this was the science and history-of-his-day, and the Holy Spirit accommodated to his intellectual level by employing these incidental ancient motifs. Thus, the sin-death problem is not a problem. Or argued another way: Paul in Phil 2 uses ancient astronomy (3-tiered universe) to deliver the message that Jesus is Lord over the world; similarly, he employs ancient biology (*de novo* origins of humans and its corollary that physical death is subsequent to the creation of life) in Rom 5 and 1 Cor 15 to reveal that every person is a sinner and that God judges each of us. However, I doubt that many Bible-believing Christians would accept, let alone fully appreciate, such a solution even though it might be parsimonious and true. The fact that the exhaustive intellectual tradition of Roman Catholic scholarship continues to wrestle with this issue is evidence of the challenge of the sin-death problem. See *Catechism of Catholic Church*, 88–93, 216. Compare with criticisms offered by Michael J. Walsh, *Commentary of the Catechism of the Catholic Church* (Collegeville, MN: Liturgical Press, 1994), 97–111; Joan Acker, "Creationism and the Catechism," 183, *America* (16 Dec 2000), 6–9.

24. The scriptural evidence behind each precedent is as follows: (1) Ancient

Phenomenological Perspective of the Physical World: chapters 4 and 5, (2) Attribution of Divine Creative Action: pp. 164–65, (3) Attribution of Divine Judgmental Action: pp. 164–65, (4) Attribution of Supernatural Action in Suffering: pp. 145–46, 153–54 (5) Attribution of Divine and Human Action in Gen 1–11: pp. 254–55.

25. Again, this is not to discount the possibility of demonic action in some rare cases. See footnote, p. 145.

26. Using incisive language, Calvin comments on the role of the law and sacrificial system: "For what is more vain or absurd than for men to offer a loathsome stench from the fat of cattle in order to reconcile themselves to God? Or to have recourse to the sprinkling of water and blood to cleanse away their filth? In short, the whole cultus of the law, taken literally and not as shadows and figures corresponding to the truth, will be utterly ridiculous." John Calvin, *Institutes of the Christian Religion*, John T. McNeill, ed., Ford Lewis Battles, trans., 2 vols. (Philadelphia: Westminster Press, 1960 [1559]), 1:349 [2.7.1]. I am grateful to Randal Rauser for introducing me to this passage. It must also be added that concern for the salvation of believers in the Old Testament is unfounded since the atonement of sin through the sacrifice of Christ also extends to them. For Heb 9:15 states, Jesus "has died as a ransom to set them free from the sins committed under the first covenant."

27. The reason for this is offered in the next section, Genesis 3 Theodicy, pp. 321–23.

28. Hugh Ross claims that Rom 5 "addresses spiritual death" and that Adam "died spiritually" in the garden of Eden. Similarly, he states that 1 Cor 15 "must refer to spiritual death rather than physical death." Hugh Ross, *Creation and Time* (Colorado Springs: NavPress, 1994), 61.

29. See note 26 above and Calvin's view on the purpose of the law and sacrificial system.

30. See section "Central Problem and Related Difficulties" pp. 308–9.

31. I expect critics to argue that I am guilty of this very sin. Note: I fully embrace without any reservation whatsoever the Word of God. However, I am challenging a traditional literal *interpretation* of Scripture that continues within the Church today.

32. More specifically, this argument posits that since Jesus is a real individual in history, His mention with Adam in the same passage indicates that Adam is also an actual historical person. On the surface, this is a reasonable appeal to consistency. However, it completely disregards the ancient understanding of human origins clearly evident in Gen 1–11. Moreover, this line of argumentation could be used to defend the 3-tier universe: Jesus is a real individual in history, His being mentioned with the 3-tier universe in Phil 2:10 bestows historical reality to the 3-tier universe. I doubt anyone would defend such a position; nor should the historical reality of Jesus be used to confer historicity upon Adam.

CHAPTER 9

1. As a child I was completely unaware of the ongoing shift in French-Canadian Roman Catholicism. See Michael Gauvreau, *The Catholic Origins of Quebec's Quiet Revolution* (Montreal and Kingston: McGill-Queen's University Press, 2005).

2. There is a delicious irony here since I am today classified as an arts professor at the university.

3. University of Alberta paleontologist Michael Caldwell reviewed the audiotape of the debate and confirms this outcome. Notably, Caldwell is an atheist.

4. See chapter 6, pp. 188–91.

5. Leading works on this subject include: James R. Moore, *The Post-Darwinian Controversies: A Study of the Protestant Struggle to Come to Terms with Darwin in Great Britain and America 1870–1900* (Cambridge: University Press, 1979); David N. Livingstone, *Darwin's Forgotten Defenders: The Encounter Between Evangelical Theology and Evolutionary Thought* (Grand Rapids: Eerdmans, 1987).

6. See contributions by James Orr and George Frederick Wright in *The Fundamentals: A Testimony of Truth*, 12 vols. (Chicago: Testimony Publishing Company, 1910–15).

7. Charles R. Darwin, *The Life and Letters of Charles Darwin*. Edited by Francis Darwin, 3 vols. (London: John Murray, 1887), 1:316.

8. Regrettably, I did not date the entries in this notebook or the one I am about to mention, "Notes on Genesis."

9. For an example of shark teeth, see Appendix 7 Fig 5, p. 420.

10. Behe, *Darwin's Black Box*, p. 39.

11. See F. H. Rundle, J. L. Bartels, K. L. Bentley, C. Kappen, M. T. Murtha and J/W. Pendleton, "Evolution of *Hox* Genes," *Annual Review of Genetics* 28 (1994): 423–42; G. Panopoulou and A.J. Poustka, "Timing and Mechanism of Ancient Vertebrate Genome Duplications" *Trends in Genetics* 21 (2005): 559–67.

12. Fig 9-5 based on A. Hornbruch and L. Wolpert, "Positional Signalling by Henson's Node when Grafted to the Chick Limb," *Journal of Experimental Morphology* 94 (1986), 257–65; Scott F. Gilbert, *Developmental Biology*, 8th ed. (Sunderland: Sinauer, 2006), 518–24.

13. The faith statement includes two significant articles: "WE BELIEVE that God directly created Adam and Eve, the historical parents of the entire human race; and that they were created in His own image, distinct from all other living creatures, and in a state of original righteousness. WE BELIEVE that out first parents sinned by rebelling against God's revealed will and thereby incurred both physical and spiritual death; and that as a result all human beings are born with a sinful nature that leads them to sin in thought, word, and deed." No Author, "Wheaton College Statement of Faith." No pages. Accessed August 25, 2007. Online: http://wheaton.edu/welcome/mission/html. See also endnote 2 chapter 8, p. 463.

14. Mark A. Noll, *The Scandal of the Evangelical Mind* (Grand Rapids: Eerdmans, 1994), 3. Ten years after the publication of this book, Noll writes, "I remain largely unrepentant about the book's historical arguments, its assessment of the evangelical strengths and weaknesses, and its indictment of evangelical intellectual efforts, though I have changed my mind on a few matters." In his "'The Evangelical Mind Today" *First Things* 146 (Oct 2004), 34. I am grateful to Nabers Cabaniss Johnson for pointing out this article to me.

CHAPTER 10

1. 1 Peter 3:15 is the classic verse used to depict Christian apologetics. Though it appeals to "reason," note that Christianity ultimately rests upon "hope."

2. Grasping the category of antinomy was critical at an early point in my faith. See J. I. Packer, *Evangelism and the Sovereignty of God* (Grand Rapids: InterVarsity, 1961), 25.

3. This is not to say that students should not be informed of the anti-evolutionary positions. As I am about to argue, a complete education includes understanding the origins

debate and it should be part of teaching para-scientific issues.

4. I gave Dr. Gish a copy of my debate with Phillip Johnson, *Darwinism Defeated?* (1999), and respectfully suggested that we viewed God's methods of creating the world and inspiring the Bible somewhat differently.

5. 2 Peter 1:16–18 could also be added: "We did not follow cleverly invented stories when we told you about the power and coming of our Lord Jesus Christ, but we were eyewitnesses of his majesty. For he received honor and glory from God the Father when the voice came to him from the Majestic Glory, saying, 'This is my Son, whom I love; with him I am well pleased.' We ourselves heard this voice that came from heaven when we were with him on the sacred mountain."

6. National Association of Biology Teachers, "Statement on Teaching Biology," *American Biology Teacher* 58 (1995), 61. In fairness to the NABT, the statement was modified in 1997 (though not completely purged of dysteleological nuances) by removing the words "impersonal" and "unsupervised." Nevertheless my point remains: it is shocking that such a philosophically naive and skewed statement was even published by such an important educational organization. See Eugenie Scott, "NABT Statement on Evolution Evolves" 21. May 1998. No pages. Accessed August 27, 2007. Online: http:/www.ncseweb.org/resources/ articles/8954_nabt_statement_on_evolution_ev_5_21_1998.asp. The NABT's latest statement on evolution is found at: hppt:/nabt.org/sites/S1/index.php?p=65. I am grateful to Eugenie Scott, the executive director of the National Center for Science Education, for her assistance.

7. *The Declaration of Independence* affirms "Nature's God," humanity's "Creator," "divine Providence" and "the Supreme Judge of the World." No Author, "Action of Second Continental Congress, July 4, 1776. The Unanimous Declaration of the Thirteen United States of America." No pages. Accessed June 22, 2001. Online: http://memory.loc. gov/const/declar.html. Similarly, in Canada the Charter of Rights and Freedoms begins: "Whereas Canada is founded upon principles that recognize the supremacy of God and the rule of law." No Author, "Part I: Canadian *Charter of Rights and Freedoms*" in "Schedule B: Constitution Act, 1982." No pages. Accessed December 22, 2004. Online: http://laws. justice.gc.ca/en/charter/index.html.

APPENDIX 1

1. *King James Version* (Cleveland: World Publishing, [1611] 1954); *American Standard Version* (New York: Thomas Nelson & Sons, 1901); *Revised Standard Version* (New York: Thomas Nelson & Sons, 1952); *New American Standard Bible* (La Habra, CA: Lockman Foundation, 1960); *New International Version* (New York: New York International Bible Society, 1978); *Jewish Publication Society* (Philadelphia: Jewish Publication Society of America, 1982); *New Jerusalem Bible* (Garden City, NY: Doubleday, 1985); *New Revised Standard Version: Catholic Edition* (Nashville: Catholic Bible Press, 1991).

APPENDIX 2

1. Francis Brown, S. R. Driver and Charles Briggs, *A Hebrew and English Lexicon of the Old Testament* (Oxford: Clarendon Press, 1951), 135; R. Laird Harris, Gleason L. Archer and Bruce Waltke, *Theological Wordbook of the Old Testament*. 2 vols. (Chicago: Moody Press, 1981), 1:127.

2. See comment in endnote 5 below.

3. Gerhard May argues that *creation ex nihilo* arose in the second century AD. He contends that 2 Macc 7:28, Rom 4:17, Col 1:15–17, and Heb 11: 3 are referring to "creation out of non-being." In other words, matter existed but it was not in the form of a known "being" or "something." I am not convinced of May's thesis, but if correct it does not affect my central point. The conceptual development in the New Testament would prepare the way for later formulation in a way similar to the doctrine of the Holy Trinity. See Gerhard May, *Creatio Ex Nihilo: The Doctrine of 'Creation Out of Nothing' in Early Christian Thought*, A. S. Worrall, trans. (Edinburgh: T&T Clark, 1994), 6–7, 26–29.

4. Though not a watery chaos, a pre-creative state is alluded to in Gen 2:4b. This verse is the scene-setting sentence of the Jahwist creation account and 4a is the title.

5. Readers will note that my earlier paraphrase employs the Hebrew absolute state, while this one is in the construct. This is done in order to reflect the problem of translating Gen 1:1. See chapter 6, p. 189.

APPENDIX 3

1. See "Numbers: Sacred and Symbolic Usage (and the Number Seven in Particular)" in Lloyd R. Bailey, *Genesis, Creation, and Creationism* (New York: Paulist Press, 1993), 157–60.

2. An understanding of gematria solves a popular interpretive issue today. Rev 13:18 states, "This calls for wisdom. If anyone has insight, let him *calculate* the number of the beast, for it is man's number. His number is 666." The gematric calculation for Nero Caesar, the murderer of early Christians, is 666: N 50, R 200, W 6, N 50 and Q 100, S 60, R 200.

APPENDIX 4

1. James B. Pritchard, *Ancient Near Eastern Texts Relating to the Old Testament*, 3rd ed. (Princeton: Princeton University Press, 1967), 265–66. W-B 62 and Berossos in Lloyd Bailey, *Genesis, Creation, and Creationism* (New York: Paulist Press, 1993), 60. See also Thorkild Jacobsen, *The Sumerian King List* (Chicago: University of Chicago Press, 1939).

APPENDIX 5

1. Readers will notice a stylistic asymmetry occurs in the P flood account with the Noahic ages. Four of the five ages offering the year, month, and day are tightly clumped together (Gen 8:4, 9, 13a, 14). This chronological precision also clashes with the ages/periods found in the other P sources in Gen 1–11. The genealogies in Gen 5 and 11 are given in years only. Moreover, Noahic dates are quite striking because such detail in the Old Testament occurs solely with the prophecies of Ezekiel (e.g., 1:1; 24:1). Some speculate that these five ages reflect a later calendar (possibly the Jubilees calendar in order to assure that major flood events never fall on a Sabbath) and they were added after the redaction of the P and J flood accounts. If this is case, then Noah's age of 600 years without mention of the month and day in Gen 7:6 is original and the only Noahic age in the P account. See Wenham, *Genesis 1–15*, 179–81.

Notes to Appendices Six to Ten

APPENDIX 6

1. James B. Pritchard, *Ancient Near Eastern Texts Relating to the Old Testament*, 3rd ed. (Princeton: Princeton University Press, 1967), 72–73; Gordon J. Wenham, *Genesis 1–15* (Waco: Word Books, 1987), 159.

2. Abridged 11th Tablet from Pritchard, *ANET*, 93–95.

3. Pritchard, James; *Ancient Near Eastern Texts Relating to the Old Testament*—Third Edition with Supplement. © 1950, 1955, 1969, renewed 1978 by Princeton University Press. Reprinted by permission of Princeton University Press.

APPENDIX 8

1. The scientific information in this appendix appears in standard geological textbooks. Christians who offer accessible introductions on the age of the earth include: Davis A. Young, *Christianity and the Age of the Earth* (Grand Rapids: Zondervan, 1982), "The Discovery of Terrestrial History," in Howard Van Till, Robert E. Snow, John H. Stek and Davis A. Young, *Portraits of Creation* (Grand Rapids: Eerdmans, 1990), 26–81; Paul Seely, "The GISP2 Ice Core: Ultimate Proof that Noah's Flood Was Not Global," *Perspectives on Science and Christian Faith* (Dec 2003), 252–60; Hugh Ross, *Creation and Time* (Colorado Springs: NavPress, 1994), *A Matter of Days* (Colorado Springs: NavPress, 1994).

2. Galileo Galilei, "Letter to the Grand Duchess Christina," in Maurice A. Finocchiaro, editor and translator, *The Galileo Affair: A Document History* (Berkeley: University of California Press, 1989), 94, 96.

APPENDIX 9

1. An accessible introduction to these dating methods and others is found in Colin Renfrew and Paul Bahn, *Archaeology: Theories, Methods and Practice* 3rd ed. (London: Thames and Hudson, 2000), 118–29.

2. Based on Patricia C. Rice, *Biological Anthropology and Prehistory: Exploring Our Human Ancestry* (Boston: Pearson Education, 2005); Kenneth L. Feder, *The Past in Perspective: An Introduction to Human Prehistory* 3rd ed. (New York: McGraw-Hill, 2004); William A. Haviland, Dana Walrath, Harald E. L. Prins and Bunny McBride, *Evolution and Prehistory: The Human Challenge*, 7th ed. (Toronto: Wadsworth/Thompson Learning, 2005). I am grateful to archaeologist Darryl Bereziuk for his assistance.

APPENDIX 10

1. Two excellent introductions with striking pictures of actual pre-human fossils are Paul F. Whitehead, William K. Sacco and Susan B. Hochgraf, *A Photographic Atlas for Physical Anthropology* (Englewood, CO: Morton Publishing Company, 2005); Donald Johanson and Blake Edgar, *From Lucy to Language* (New York: Simon and Schuster, 2006).

2. Christian cell biologist Graeme Finlay provides accessible and well-documented introductions to evolutionary genetics. See his "*Homo Divinus*: The Great Ape that Bears God's Image," *Science and Christian Belief* 15 (2003): 19–24; *God's Books: Genetics and*

Genesis (Auckland: TELOS Publications, 2004). See also Christian geneticists Francis S. Collins, *The Language of God: A Scientist Presents Evidence for Belief* (New York: Free Press, 2006), 124–42; Darrel R. Falk, *Coming to Peace with Science: Bridging the Worlds between Faith and Science* (Downers Grove: InterVarsity Press, 2004), 169–98. For a more technical introduction see M.A. Jobling, Me.E. Hurles and C. Tyler-Smith, *Human Evolutionary Genetics: Origins, Peoples and Disease* (New Delhi: Garland Publishing, 2004).

3. Based on Patricia C. Rice, *Biological Anthropology and Prehistory: Exploring Our Human Ancestry* (Boston: Pearson Education, 2005); Kenneth L. Feder, *The Past in Perspective: An Introduction to Human Prehistory* 3rd ed. (New York: McGraw-Hill, 2004); William A. Haviland, *Human Evolution and Prehistory* 6th ed. (Toronto: Wadsworth/ Thompson Learning, 2003). For an excellent summary, see Pamela R. Willoughby, "Palaeoanthropology and the Evolutionary Place of Humans in Nature," *International Journal of Comparative Psychology* 18 (2005), 60–90. I am grateful to anthropologists Pamela Willoughby and Anne Holden for their assistance.

4. This diagram features an orthogenic (straight line) view of human evolution. Note that there is no x-axis, which allows me to take this liberty. Indeed, this interpretation of the fossil record reflects my belief that God intended humans to be the crown of creation. In addition, for heuristic reasons, this line from the last common ancestor to humans complements Fig 8-2.

5. Pamela R. Willoughby, *The Evolution of Modern Humans: A Comprehensive Guide* (Lanham, MD:AltaMira Press, 2007), 131, 139–45; see also her "Evolutionary Place," 76, 81–84.

Glossary

Anthropic Principle
The concept that the laws of nature are finely tuned and lead inevitably to the evolution of the universe and life, including humans in particular.

Argument from Design
An argument for the existence of God that appeals to the beauty, complexity, and functionality seen in nature. See also **Intelligent Design.**

Atheism
The belief that God does not exist.

Concordism
A popular interpretive approach to the Bible that suggests there is a correspondence or alignment between Scripture and modern science. In this book, the term is expanded in order to distinguish accord between: (1) the Bible and the spiritual realm—theological concordism, (2) the Bible and human history—historical concordism, and (3) the Bible and the physical world—scientific concordism. See also **Scientific Concordism.**

Conflation of Ideas
The collapsing of distinct ideas into one single notion. For example, the scientific theory of evolution is often blended with the secular philosophy of atheism, leading many to assume that evolution can only be a godless and purposeless natural process.

Cosmic Fall
The belief that the physical world was dramatically changed after the entrance of human sin. God launched suffering, decay, and death upon the whole creation in judgment for the sin of Adam in the garden of Eden.

Creation
The basic belief that the universe and life is the product of a Creator. The doctrine of creation, as held by professional theologians, makes no reference to the method through which God created.

Glossary

Deism
The belief in an impersonal God. He created the world, but never enters it to interact with humans.

Dichotomy of Ideas
The division of an issue into only two simple positions. A "black-and-white" or "either/or" approach to a topic. Some dichotomies are *true dichotomies*. For example, the world is either purposeful or purposeless. However, many dichotomies are *false dichotomies* because most issues are not limited to only two simple positions. The popular view of the origins debate is often confined to either "creation in six 24-hour days" or "evolution by blind chance." This book argues that this assumption is a false dichotomy.

Dysteleology
The belief that the world has no plan or purpose. Existence is ultimately meaningless and driven only by blind chance.

Eisegesis
The erroneous practice of reading notions that were not intended by the author *into* a written work. Contrast **Exegesis**.

Evolution
The scientific theory that the universe and life, including humans, arose through natural processes. Though this term usually refers to the evolution of life (biological evolution), it can also be applied to the natural mechanisms producing galaxies, stars, and planets (cosmological evolution), and the earth (geological evolution). As a scientific theory, evolution makes no reference at all as to whether its natural processes are purposeful (teleological) or purposeless (dysteleological). Therefore, qualification of this term is often necessary. See also **Teleology; Dysteleology**.

Exegesis
The correct practice of reading notions that were intended by the author *out of* a written work. Contrast **Eisegesis**.

General Revelation
Divine revelation that is manifested through the natural world and human conscience. It offers a general outline of God's character and His purposes. This type of revelation comes in two basic ways: (1) Natural Revelation—the Creator has inscribed a revelation of His power and divinity in the beauty, complexity, and functionality of the world (Ps 19:1–4; Rom 1:19–20), and (2) Moral Revelation—the Lord has written moral laws on the human heart (Rom 2:14–15). See also **Special Revelation**.

Hermeneutics
The rules for reading a written work.

Humanism (Secular Humanism)
An ethical approach that places humanity in the role traditionally held by God as the only determiner of values and morals.

Glossary

Intelligent Design
The traditional belief that the beauty, complexity, and functionality in nature reflect the rational mind of a Creator. See also **Argument from Design.**

Interventionism
Divine action in the world that is dramatic and "breaks" normal routine. See also **Providentialism.**

Positivism
The assumption that truth only comes through logical analysis and scientific investigation. This approach to knowledge considers spiritual truths to be meaningless and irrelevant.

Providentialism
Divine action in the world that is subtle and "works" through normal routine. See also **Interventionism.**

Scientific Concordism
Commonly known as "concordism," this is a popular interpretive approach to the Bible that aligns modern science with statements in Scripture about the physical world. It assumes that the Holy Spirit revealed scientific facts to the biblical writers thousands of years before their discovery by science. For example, the day-age theory matches the creation days in Gen 1 with geological periods in the history of the earth.

Scientism
A popular understanding of science that blends (conflates) modern science and a godless and purposeless worldview. See also **Conflation.**

Special Revelation
Divine revelation that is specific. It includes: (1) The Incarnation—the central Christian belief that God became a man in the person of Jesus in order to reveal Himself both through words and actions, (2) Biblical Revelation—the belief that the Holy Spirit inspired human writers to reveal God and His will through the words of Scripture, and (3) Personal Revelation—the experience that God communicates specifically to humans today through prayers, signs, and wonders. See also **General Revelation.**

Teleology
The belief that the universe has plan and purpose. For Christians, teleology is rooted in the Father, Son, and Holy Spirit.

Theism
The belief in a personal God who is in an intimate relationship with humans.

Theodicy
An argument justifying the existence of pain, suffering and death in a world created by an all-loving and all-powerful God.

Subject Index

Subject Index

Scripture Index

2 Timothy

3:8–9	74
3:16	xv, 13, 169
3:16–17	31, 158
4:3–4	260

Titus

1:12	166
1:14	260
3:10	376

Hebrews

1:2	172
1:2–3	11
1:10–12	11
1:11	92
1:12	130
2:4	64
2:10	11
4:1–11	445n5
4:12	148, 179
6:18	166
7:9–10	140
7:27	313
8:13	313
9:24	317, 318
9:28	301
10:1	317, 318
10:2	396
10:3	294–95, 313
10:4	268, 299, 313, 322, 383
10:10	301, 308, 396
10:11	294, 313, 322
10:12	396
11:1	71
11:1–3	383
11:1–39	380
11:3	11, 393, 394, 469n3
11:4	317
11:4–7	445n5
11:5	317
11:7	317, 463n26
11:8	117, 345, 369
11:11	139, 140

Hebrews (continued)

12:24	445n5
12:26	130

James

1:2–3	301

1 Peter

1:21	63
2:2	169
3:15	370, 467n1
3:18–22	278
3:20	445n5

2 Peter

1:16	260
1:16–18	468n5
2:4–5	445n5
2:5	463n26
3:3–7	463n26
3:5	463n26
3:5–6	445n5
3:7	11
3:8	196
3:12–13	11

1 John

1:1–3	374
3:12	445n5
4:8	64
4:16	64

Jude

6	445n5
11	445n5
14	445n5, 463n24

Revelation

1:4	397
1:5	308
1:8	11